STAN

The Life and Times of David Rowland Francis

MW00475727

. . . And as I look back on it I am convinced that
. . . the Czar of all the Russians . . .
had no premonition of the storm that was brewing . . .
no idea that he was standing on a volcano.

David R. Francis
RUSSIAN MEMOIR

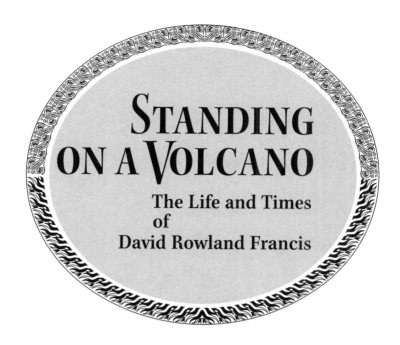

STANDING ON A VOLCANO

The Life and Times of David Rowland Francis

Harper Barnes

MISSOURI HISTORICAL SOCIETY PRESS

SAINT LOUIS

IN ASSOCIATION WITH

THE FRANCIS PRESS

To Roseann Weiss

Distributed by Southern Illinois University Press

Library of Congress Cataloging-in-Publication Data

Barnes, Harper, 1937–

    Standing on a volcano : the life and times of David Rowland Francis / Harper Barnes.

       p.   cm.

    Includes bibliographical references (p.   ) and index.

    ISBN 1-883982-13-8 (cloth : alk. paper) – ISBN 1-883982-17-0 (pbk. : alk. paper)

       1. Francis, David Rowland, 1850–1927. 2. Mayors – Missouri – Saint Louis – Biography. 3. Saint Louis (Mo.) – Politics and government. 4. Governors – Missouri – Biography. 5. Missouri – Politics and government – 1865–1950. 6. Louisiana Purchase Exposition (1904 : Saint Louis, Mo.). 7. Ambassadors – United States – Biography. 8. Ambassadors – Russia – Biography. 9. Soviet Union – History – Revolution, 1917–1921. 10. Saint Louis (Mo.) – Biography. I. Title.

F474.S253 F733 2001

977.8'03'092—dc21

[B]   2001031731

Cover photo: Ambassador Francis and Mikhail Rodzianko on the balcony of the
         U.S. Embassy in Petrograd, 1917. Photo taken by Philip Jordan, MHS.

Design by Susan Lane Piper

Photo edited by Duane Sneddeker

Index by Thelda Bertram

Printed in the United States by Sheridan Books, Inc,

∞ the paper used in this publication meets minimum requirements of the
  ANSI/NISO Z39.48-1992 (R 1997) (Permanence of Paper).

5   4   3   2   1   01   02   03   04   05

Contents

BOOK TWO

Foreword

Among the framed copies of historic photographs in the hall of the Jefferson Memorial's executive offices is a picture of David R. Francis turning over the keys to this very building to the mayor. The ceremonial portrait is quintessential David Rowland Francis; it is the perfect image of a successful American businessman and civic leader in the early part of the twentieth century, proud of his contributions to the community, pleased with his accomplishments and with himself. This is the David R. Francis I meet nearly every working day.

Others may hold a different image of Francis. The civic minded may recall either the portrait of the thirty-four-year-old "boy mayor" or a picture of him as the youngest governor of our state. History buffs, both local and worldwide, perhaps may remember one of the literally hundreds of photos taken during the course of the 1904 World's Fair or Francis's figure standing on the U.S. Embassy's balcony facing a crowd of revolutionaries in Russia. These images not only have a place in the story of David R. Francis, but also in our own stories, just as that historic photograph outside my office is part of my own story.

Francis's legacy to the city of St. Louis has tangible reminders in our landscape. Washington University students exercise and compete in the Francis Field House and on Francis Field, the primary venue for the 1904 Olympics that Francis helped bring here. Families walk off their frozen custards in southwest city's Francis Park, land that Francis donated to St. Louis. Francis's effects on the city are clear and powerful, as we see in *Standing on a Volcano,* but only half this book is concerned with his accomplishments on the homefront. In 1916, Francis was called upon to serve his country as ambassador to Russia, a position that would thrust him to the forefront of U.S. foreign affairs. Francis's deft diplomacy and strong leadership, mired in controversy and intrigue, was just one story in a country lost in wars—civil wars, world wars, the cold war—throughout most of the twentieth century. Yet Francis's story endures in diplomatic history and in a museum in Vologda, a town in northern Russia that Francis transformed into the diplomatic capital of Russia

Thus *Standing on a Volcano* is, as all good biographies must be, more than just an album of illustrations of a life. The story that Harper Barnes tells is thoroughly researched and well written, comprehensive in scope and detail, with a fascinating and important personality as its subject. But it is also a useful story, one that illustrates the effects of a distant and different time on our own present and depicts the humanity that we share with this historic personage.

We can never know the whole story, whether of an individual, an era, or a place, but through the evidence that has survived, we can preserve and develop connections with the past that are crucial to explaining our present and ensuring a future for ourselves and our descendants. We can explore the humanity that we share with the generations that have gone before us and sustain our expectations for the generations to come after us.

—Robert R. Archibald
President, Missouri Historical Society

Prologue

We are all seting on a bomb Just waiting for some one to tuch a match to it.
If the Ambassador gets out of this Mess with our life we will be awful lucky. . . .
These crazy people are Killing each other Just like we Swat flies at home.
—Philip Jordan from Russia, 1917[1]

D AVID FRANCIS stood inside the front door of the American Embassy in Petrograd, just out of the west wind that blew a chilled, late-April mist from the Gulf of Finland. The wind swirled with sounds, its own whistle and moan mixed with the flap of the large American flag above the doorway and the roar of a thousand chanting voices from a mile away on the Nevsky Prospect.

Francis held a large revolver in his right hand. He had never fired the gun, but he was prepared to shoot anyone who tried to cross the threshold of this little outpost of the United States in the capital of Russia. Beside him was the man who had brought him the gun, Philip Jordan.

Jordan, a slight, light-skinned African American, had been Francis's valet for more than twenty years. Even though neither of them would have been comfortable speaking the word that defined their relationship, they were friends, and Francis trusted Jordan more than any other man in treacherous revolutionary Petrograd.

Less than half an hour before, Jordan had interrupted the regular Sunday evening dinner party at the embassy to report that the Petrograd police had called. An anarchist mob had assembled in the vast square in front of the Kazan Cathedral and was gathering fury for a march on the American Embassy and a showdown with the ambassador.

Francis apologized for the interruption, rose from the table and headed downstairs. After he was out of earshot of his guests, he said to Jordan, "Phil, load my gun."

As they stood in the entrance to the embassy they could hear the sounds of the mob growing near. It couldn't have been more than half a mile away. The anarchists were shouting something, a steady, rolling two-syllable chant that sounded like a name, but the wind erased its meaning.

What the hell were they mad about this time? Francis wondered.

Jordan shook his head. He didn't know, either.

On another late-April evening thirteen years before, with Philip Jordan nearby, David Francis had stood at dusk with the wind in his face as a hundred thousand people shouted his name, while around them miles of lights twinkled on and illuminated the Ivory City he had created on land once known as the Wilderness. The 1904 St. Louis World's Fair was a fantasy city that, in outward appearance, was a dazzling blend of Greece and Rome, Jerusalem and Egypt, but that contained within it all the technological miracles of the new twentieth century. It lasted for seven months, during which David Francis was said to be the most photographed man in America. At the end, he stood on another dark evening surrounded by another vast crowd and wept as the lights went out for the last time. Rockets exploded above him, and his name and face were momentarily carved with fire in the sky above the magical city that he had willed into being. It was, he was certain at the time, his grandest achievement.

Twelve years later, Woodrow Wilson lured the sixty-five-year-old businessman/ politician back into public service by offering him a mission that challenged and excited him: go to Russia as ambassador and negotiate a new commercial treaty with the government of Tsar Nicholas II. But in March 1917, in the middle of the Great War that raged across Europe, hundreds of thousands of Russians, many of them displaced peasants, took to the wide streets of Peter the Great's westward-facing capital and overthrew the Tsar. It was a revolution that David Francis, alone among Western ambassadors, immediately welcomed as a long-delayed expression of the democratic will of the people.

For David Francis, March 1917 was the Russian equivalent of July 1776. "No people so circumstanced have ever made greater sacrifices for freedom than these," he enthused. "Our form of government is their model. . . . This may be a revolution, but it is the best managed revolution that has ever taken place."[2] His enthusiasm may have run ahead of his judgment, but the advice he gave his government was sound. At his urging, the United States won favor with Russia's new leaders by being the first Western nation to recognize the left-liberal Provisional Government. Francis did everything he could to help Alexander Kerensky and the other men who tenuously held the reigns of authority in this explosive city and country. He dreamed that the revolutionaries of March could turn their vast, rich country, oppressed for centuries, into a republic second only to the United States in both freedom and prosperity.

But first they had to deal with the plague of anarchists and Reds—it was hard to tell them apart, except by the color of their flags—who took to the streets every night, sometimes ten to twenty thousand strong, and who at this moment were headed for Furstatskaya Street and the American Embassy. The shouting voices came closer, like an approaching storm.

There were a dozen or more separate revolutionary organizations in Petrograd alone, some of them almost as fiercely opposed to one another as to the government of Tsar Nicholas. And adding to the chaos were the Germans, who were happy to do anything they could to further destabilize their sprawling enemy to the northeast. Barely a week before, they had shipped the charismatic revolutionary leader Vladimir Ilyich

Lenin through Germany to Petrograd in a sealed railroad car "like a plague bacillus," in the words of Winston Churchill.[3]

Lenin's return had set the masses aflame. Francis and Jordan both thought he might well be leading the mob that moved through the streets from the Nevsky Prospect to Furstatskaya Street.

That April evening, as Francis stood at the embassy door, gun in hand, with Philip Jordan, the bravest man he knew, standing next to him, he heard new sounds in the wind—shouts of warning, screams of fear, the clatter of horses' hooves on cobblestones, and gunfire. The ominous mass chanting broke apart, to be replaced by a spreading babble, more shots, screams of pain, and running feet. The approaching storm seemed to break up into dozens of squalls and slowly dissipate. The Cossacks had arrived. The Cossacks were cruel and arbitrary killers whose allegiances shifted like the wind swirling above the Neva, and Philip Jordan considered them to be thugs on horseback, but this time both Americans silently welcomed their help in stopping the mob.

The crisis over, Francis handed his gun back to Philip Jordan, and for a moment their eyes met, and they smiled. Then David Francis returned alone to his dinner party, and to the much less overt but equally dangerous battles of diplomacy. He was surrounded by enemies, some of them on his own staff.

THE STORY OF DAVID FRANCIS guarding the door of the embassy, pistol in hand, ready to face down the rabble, eventually reached the ears of Woodrow Wilson. By then, it had become much more dramatic: Lenin and his followers had tried to storm the embassy, but Francis and his six-gun had faced them down, shouting that he would shoot the first man who crossed the threshold. He had engaged in a shouted debate about freedom and democracy with Lenin himself and had emerged victorious, a gunslinger from Missouri backing down the angry Bolshevik bear.

Francis said later that he tried to correct this melodramatic fiction but was unsuccessful. He remarked: "Everyone seemed to prefer the more sensational story, so I suppose I shall have to resign myself to this heroic role. It, at any rate, truthfully represents my intentions. All I lacked was the opportunity to carry them out."[4]

David Rowland Francis was a brash, opinionated, stubborn, smart, sometimes foolish, straight-talking, quick-acting, independent-minded, proud, self-made man who represented the United States in Russia for two and a half years, during the most tumultuous era in that country's history. Much of his activity has been shrouded in myth—some of it heroic, more of it comic and tragic.

After Lenin reached into the whirlpool he had helped create and seized power, and it became clear that neither continued war with Germany nor the establishment of a liberal democracy were among his goals, politicians looked for someone to blame for "losing Russia." Although initially praised as a true American hero, David Francis later was much maligned in the public and scholarly debate in the decades following the end of World War I. More thoughtful, balanced assessments—like that of George F. Kennan in his monumental two-volume *Soviet-American Relations, 1917–1920,* published in the 1950s—have not erased the negative portrait of David R. Francis as a nice old fellow who had no experience in diplomacy and was in way over his head representing the United States in revolutionary Russia.

Only recently, after the end of the Cold War, have historians in both Russia and the United States taken a closer look at the whole record—some of which was not available before the collapse of Communism—and begun assembling a more balanced portrait of David Francis's years in Russia. An important factor has been the rise of a generation of historians, in both Russia and the West, who no longer labor under the desperately maintained illusion that Lenin was a tough-minded but essentially decent and democratically inclined man whose idealistic republic was betrayed by the madman Stalin. Francis recognized from the beginning that Lenin was a brilliant, ruthless fanatic, and he said so repeatedly and in the strongest terms, running against the main current of conventional academic wisdom.

The dominant image of Francis springs primarily from the comments of Bruce Lockhart, a British agent who met frequently with Lenin and Trotsky. Lockhart felt that Francis—after the second Russian Revolution, the one in November 1917 that brought Lenin to power—did far too little to appease the Bolsheviks and was far too suspicious of their motives. Lockhart's published memoirs were very popular and highly influential in the 1930s. He described Francis as "a charming old gentleman of nearly eighty" (Francis was in his mid-sixties) and, after a long, bibulous social evening with Francis in 1918, wrote in his diary a phrase that has been quoted by historians countless times since: "Old Francis doesn't know a Left Social Revolutionary from a potato." Lockhart also wrote that Francis was "simple and fearless as a child." The agent added, however, that "the old gentleman was no child at poker . . . he took my money." [5]

Bruce Lockhart to the contrary, David Francis was well briefed on the ever-shifting power blocs within the important Socialist (or Social) Revolutionary Party. And ultimately the United States may have been better off represented by a shrewd poker player, one with decades of experience in dealing with political turmoil and political extremists, than it would have been with a more cautious, more circumspect career diplomat.

Even Progressive Raymond Robins, a semi-official American envoy in Russia who sharply disagreed with Francis on policy and who once had urged the State Department to bring him home, said publicly after some of the dust had settled that Francis "worked harder, stayed longer [and] met the situation with more steadiness" than any of the more experienced ambassadors on the scene. [6]

Francis, speaking no Russian and very little French, arrived in Petrograd in April 1916, a year before the United States would enter World War I. He shunned the fancy dress and expensive automobiles of the Tsarist court and the other diplomats. Partly because of his lack of superficial polish, this plain-spoken Missourian was looked down upon by more traditional European and American diplomats. At one point, other Western ambassadors and his own staff felt it was necessary to work behind his back and were reluctant to speak to him of confidential matters, under the quite understandable impression that he was enmeshed in an affair with a beautiful German spy. They sometimes made fun of him and his blunt ways, and not always behind his back. At one point, key members of his staff tried to get him sent home.

Yet David Francis would outlast them all, the disgruntled American aides and the condescending Western ambassadors alike. He refused to "abandon the Russian people," as he put it, and he remained long after the representatives of the other Western powers had fled the scene.

During his tenure in Russia, Francis was a shrewd, resourceful representative of his country, although at times he was impetuous and even foolish, particularly in the ways he mixed his private and public lives. And he was not just some provincial political hack in way over his head; he had been superbly prepared by background, education, domestic and overseas travel, and political experience to represent the United States in the midst of the most tumultuous and unpredictable political upheaval of the century. By itself, Francis's life before 1916 is a compelling, archetypal tale of a poor boy striving mightily and achieving the American dream. However, it also provides the grounding for understanding the events of 1917–1919 and the considerable role Francis played in the early history of American-Soviet relations.

By the time he reached Russia, Francis was equipped with the wit, experience, courage, and core principles to deal intelligently, pragmatically, and undogmatically with a nearly overwhelming series of unforeseen crises. At one point, under attack from powerful forces both within and without the American Embassy, he stumbled badly, but he soon recovered his footing. While working himself into exhaustion and near-fatal illness representing his country's best interests, he did everything within his power, and a number of things theoretically not within his power, to help the Russian people realize the dream of a democratic revolutionary republic. Finally, a year after the Bolshevik Revolution, he became so ill he literally had to be carried out of the country on a stretcher, vowing he would return at the head of fifty thousand American doughboys to free the Russian people. To a new generation of post-Communist Russian historians, David Rowland Francis is a hero.

GROUND PLAN
OF THE
Louisiana Purchase Exposition
ST. LOUIS, MO.
1904

BOOK
ONE

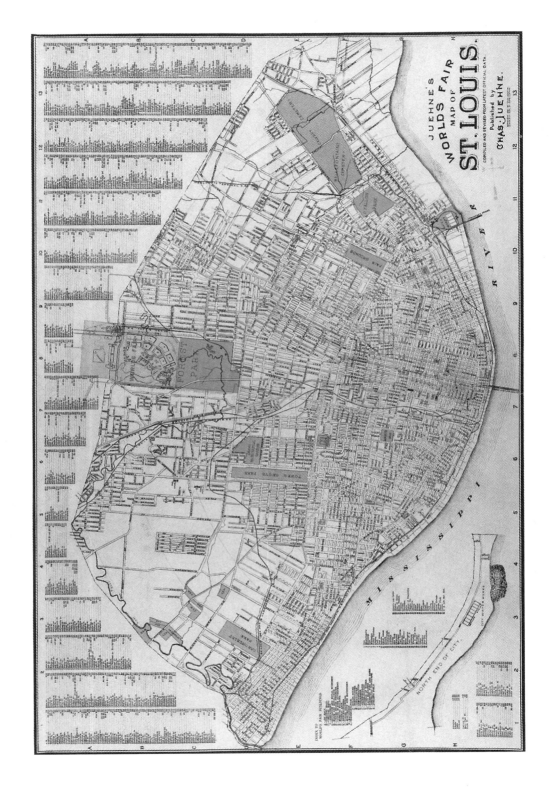

JUEHNE'S
WORLDS FAIR
MAP OF
ST. LOUIS.
COMPILED AND REVISED FROM LATEST OFFICIAL DATA.
Published by
CHAS. JUEHNE.

CHAPTER 1

The Dark and Bloody Ground

EARLY ON THE MORNING OF DECEMBER 12, 1898, after a long and exhausting battle with pneumonia, Eliza Rowland Francis finally breathed her last. She was sixty-eight years old, and for the past few months, too ill to care for herself, she had been bedridden in the home of her daughter Mollie Ellerbe. Mollie was at her mother's bedside when she died, as were other family members, including Eliza's oldest son, David Rowland Francis.

In a long obituary the next day, a St. Louis newspaper described Eliza as "a woman of remarkable strength of character" and noted, "She was descended from Scotch-Irish ancestry, possessed of all the prominent characteristics of that sturdy race, which has impressed itself so forcefully on the development of Virginia, Kentucky and Missouri."[1] The phrase "Scotch-Irish," often misunderstood, properly refers to people of Presbyterian lowland Scots ancestry, many of whom had spread into the north of Ireland by the seventeenth century. They came to this country in waves in the early and middle eighteenth century. More than any other ethnic group, they pushed white settlements westward into the Appalachians and beyond, driving back and killing the Indians, opening up the early frontier, establishing settlements, and then, often, moving on, almost obsessively continuing west to conquer new frontiers—Manifest Destiny made flesh.

As for the "prominent characteristics of that sturdy race," the Scotch-Irish were thought of as mentally and emotionally tough, physically strong, brave, stubborn, dismissive of physical pain, tight with a penny, pugnacious, unschooled (and sometimes unschoolable), impatient, quick-tempered, vengeful, suspicious of strangers, and imbued with a deep loyalty to immediate family and unquestioning obeisance to the family patriarch. These are, of course, cultural generalizations but instructive ones that have been made over the years by both outsiders and the Scotch-Irish themselves. And it makes sense that such traits would emerge in a race conditioned by centuries of physical hardship, as it battled subjugation by the English in a harsh and unforgiving land. A well-known Scotch-Irish prayer reveals acute self-awareness: "Lord, grant that I may always be right, for I am hard to turn."[2]

Eliza Francis's obituary in the *St. Louis Republic*, a paper owned in part by her eldest son, went on to say that "her father, David Irvine Rowland, was born in Botecourt county, Va., and was a member of the celebrated family of Irvines who played an important part in the history of Kentucky . . . his mother, Francis Irvine, was one of 10 sisters who left comfort and luxury in Virginia to journey on horseback to the 'Dark and Bloody Ground.'"

The progenitor of the Madison County Irvines was Christopher Irvine, who brought his young family across the Atlantic to Virginia around 1731. At least two of his sons were officers in the Colonial Army of Virginia, spending many years on the western frontier of the state fighting Indians. Irvines began moving into Kentucky in the harsh winter of 1779, barely five years after Daniel Boone had anchored a foothold for whites on the Kentucky River at Fort Boonesborough, at the northern edge of what became Madison County, Kentucky.

Irvines helped survey Madison County and were among the county's first court justices: powerful administrative/judiciary positions that led to the accumulation of land and wealth. The name Irvine still appears prominently on landmarks and roads throughout the county.[3]

Kentucky historian Thomas D. Clark observed, "If there is any one social and cultural characteristic which has been historically notable among Kentuckians generally, it has been their ready and positive identification with a specific place in the universe, their home county."[4] Madison County is a brawny land of dense hardwood forests, rolling pastures, lush fields of corn and tobacco, curling spring-fed streams, steep rounded hills called "knobs," and remote piney-woods hollows whose depths are never touched by the sun. It drapes across the western Appalachian foothills just below the Kentucky River, at the southern edge of the Bluegrass region.

Bluegrass, corn, and other crops of the region are nourished at the root by the mineral-rich water that filters through the porous limestone underpinning of much of the state. Potent with nitrates and bone-building calcium, the water is the secret of two fabled products of north-central Kentucky: bourbon corn-mash whisky and thoroughbred race horses.

You might also argue that the water, combined with sturdy genetic stock from the hardscrabble fringes of Great Britain, helps account for the tall, strong-boned frames of so many of early Kentucky's notable sons—men like Henry Clay, Abraham Lincoln, Jefferson Davis, Cassius Marcellus Clay, and David Rowland Francis.

David Francis was born on October 1, 1850, in Richmond, Kentucky, the county seat and geographical center of Madison County. Richmond is twenty-five miles south of Lexington, the state's second largest city and the commercial capital of the Bluegrass region. The region's horses and whisky-distilling methods, like much else in pre–Civil War Kentucky, from the ancestors of David Francis to the seeds of the bluegrass itself, came from Virginia. That, in part, accounts for the unmistakable Southernness of much of the state, particularly in the area around Lexington, where high-pillared, antebellum plantation houses look down on fenced green pastures and long-legged thoroughbred horses.

South of Lexington, across the Kentucky River in somewhat less elegant Madison County, David Francis was a town boy in a county of farms and pasturelands. Richmond was a rough, rural county seat, a town where political disputes were taken seriously, often leading to fistfights and brawls and sometimes to bloody knifefights and fatal, impromptu pistol duels.[5]

David was the oldest of six children of John Broaddus Francis and his second wife, Eliza Caldwell Rowland Francis. David clearly loved and honored his father, a hard-working dreamer who never quite achieved his political or vocational ambitions, but he adored his mother and was strongly influenced by her. *The Biographical Cyclopedia of the Commonwealth of Kentucky,* published in 1896 after David Francis had achieved considerable success in business and politics, goes so far as to say, "It is to his mother . . . that Governor Francis owes his success in life. Mrs. Francis is a rare woman. As clearly as a signet makes an impression upon a sheet of white paper, she has impressed upon her children the intellectuality and strongly marked characteristics of a renowned ancestry."[6]

John Broaddus Francis unquestionably "married up" when, on December 5, 1849, he and the daughter of David Irvine Rowland were united in a Presbyterian ceremony in Richmond. But David Francis's father was not born into poverty. Like many sons and daughters of large families, he descended into it.

John Francis's parents, Thomas Francis and Polly Broaddus, had come to Kentucky from Virginia as children in the late eighteenth century. They prospered, raising cattle in the low hills and hollows south and east of Richmond. While Polly was giving birth to twelve children, Thomas Francis bought and ran a popular tavern. He became a justice of the peace, which gave him enough clout to make his twenty-four-year-old son, John, a deputy sheriff. In 1843, Thomas Francis moved up from justice of the peace to sheriff, and reappointed his son to a deputyship.[7]

As the most powerful institution in Kentucky, the county courts held sway over administrative as well as legal matters. They controlled almost everything connected with local government, from shootings and hangings to liquor licenses and ferry fees. The single most powerful political position was sheriff, nominated by the county justices from their senior members and approved by the governor. The position was also financially lucrative—the sheriff received commissions for many official acts, including collecting taxes and fees and serving summonses.[8]

The knowledge that he would have a job for at least two more years encouraged deputy sheriff/farmer John Francis to propose marriage to his cousin Susan Francis. In 1844, she became his first wife.

Three years later, John and Susan Francis had a one-year-old daughter named Martha, a 179-acre farm valued at $5,370, six horses, five cows, four slaves, and two gold watches. The future must have looked bright. And then the light dimmed. His father stepped down as sheriff in 1847, and John lost his deputyship. And Susan died. We don't know exactly when or how—death records for Kentucky before 1851 are sparse.

Late that year, on December 5, John Francis re-married. His second wife was nineteen-year-old Eliza Caldwell Rowland, the daughter of David Irvine Rowland, who had been the jailer when young John had served as deputy sheriff.

Perhaps Eliza did not want to live on the farm. Perhaps the farm reminded both of them, in different unbearable ways, of Susan Francis. Undoubtedly, it was difficult to scrape a living out of 179 acres of mediocre land, and the record suggests that John B. Francis never succeeded as a farmer.

John aspired to be county sheriff like his father, but the State Constitutional Convention of 1849 made sheriff and other important county positions elective offices, meaning that old family connections didn't mean quite so much. John Francis never held public office again.

In any event, shortly after his marriage to Eliza, John Francis sold the farm, the horses, the cows, three of the slaves, and both the gold watches. With a nest egg, he moved his family to Richmond, into Miller's Tavern, an inn on the courthouse square. Miller's Tavern had a few dozen permanent residents as well as rooms for transients—lawyers and other men with legal business who came through when the county court was in session.

Eleven months later, on October 1, 1850, David Rowland Francis was born. The census of 1850 lists his father simply as a "merchant."

John Francis was not broke, at least not then. In 1851, he was able to buy a large residential lot on Main Street for two thousand dollars. He seems to have been pinching pennies and saving his money for investment—as his son would begin doing at a remarkably early age. He certainly was not spending much on the comforts of living. David Rowland Francis spent his early childhood as a poor relative of some of the leading citizens of Madison County—the Irvines—with their large holdings of land and their plantation-style houses (including the magnificent Irvinton) just outside of town above lush pastures and large fields of corn and tobacco.

David Francis learned the thrifty ways—save and invest—that were an important part of his makeup for the rest of his life. Many years later he remarked, "A man reared in luxury or accustomed to rich environments does not feel the spirit of necessity of effort, and this is particularly so if he is not saturated with the desire or ambition to succeed."[9] From childhood on, David Rowland Francis was saturated with ambition, and he hardly was reared in luxury.

John Broaddus Francis, his young wife Eliza, their baby boy David, and four-year-old Martha lived in cramped quarters in a crowded inn and boardinghouse on muddy, rutted First Street across from a courthouse where slaves were sold. The year his first son was born, John Francis's meager possessions included one slave—an eight-year-old mulatto boy. Five years later, according to the 1855 slave census, Francis owned no one.

That year marked a seeming low point for the growing Francis family, although later events suggest David's father must have had some money tucked away from selling virtually everything he owned. His only taxable possession was a forty-dollar horse. Eliza was having babies every year or two, and by 1855 the Francises had five children to feed. They made do by working seven days a week from early to late at the inn where they lived. They scrimped and saved every penny they could.

By 1856, John Francis managed the inn, and in 1859 he bought it for $6,600 in cash, probably throwing the Main Street residential lot into the deal. He may have been helped by Sidney V. Rowland, a prosperous brother-in-law who had inherited his family shoe-making business.[10]

John Francis now owned what became the Francis Tavern, a two-story-high brick building that spread across two fifty-foot-deep city lots on the southeast corner of First and Main Streets. Running a courthouse inn and tavern was grueling work, with long days, very late nights, and little respite. Eliza must have pitched in when she was not busy giving birth to or caring for children. Courthouse inns on what very recently had been the western frontier were packed with humanity, and a constant battle was waged to keep the places marginally clean and to control the resident populations of fleas and bedbugs.[11]

The census of 1860 lists about two dozen men, women, and children as living or staying in the Francis Tavern, including Eliza's parents, Mr. and Mrs. David Irvine Rowland, both fifty-eight years old.[12]

Richmond, a notoriously wet city in the middle of a dry county, was where people came to drink, not only from outlying parts of the county, but also from the mountain hamlets to the east. They would fight over politics, with fists, knives, and sometimes guns.

David Francis grew up across from a busy county courthouse in a state known across the young nation for the intensity, and violence, of its political debate. Kentuckians traditionally had been passionate supporters of states' rights and followed Thomas Jefferson in opposing the strong central government espoused by the Federalists. Independence from federal control was a Kentucky tradition that continued into the Civil War era and long afterward, when states' rights took on a somewhat different emphasis.

States' rightists, although in a minority to "nationalists," were part of the loose grouping that coalesced together in the Whig Party, which dominated national politics in the 1840s. David Francis's father was a Whig.

The Whigs had been created, in great part, in reaction to the high-handed administration in the 1830s of "King" Andrew Jackson of Tennessee, the first Scotch-Irish president. In a burst of populist rage at eastern financial powers, the quick-tempered war hero had dismantled the existing central bank, and his tenure was marked by boom-and-bust economics. The Whigs were a party of fragmented interests, but one thing they generally agreed on was the crucial importance of a strong national bank.

Led by powerful Kentucky Congressman Henry Clay, the Whigs occupied the White House through much of the 1840s, and they held most of the power in Madison County as well. But at mid-century the party was swept into the principal issue of the times and split acrimoniously into pro- and anti-slavery wings. The divided Whigs were conquered and effectively wiped out in the Democratic landslide of 1852.

Thousands of states'-rights Whigs, including John Francis, turned to the Democratic Party, which would be dominated for a century by a coalition of Southern states' rightists and the political machines of the cities of the Northeast. Years later, David Francis said that he had been "raised a Democrat."[13]

Thousands of other Whigs, particularly those with strong feelings in favor of the abolition of slavery, turned instead to the burgeoning Republican Party. Abraham Lincoln had once been a Whig. So had another remarkable political figure from Kentucky, an angry, strongly opinionated, brilliant, charismatic man who towered over Madison County when David Francis was a boy. That man's name was Cassius Marcellus Clay.

Cassius Clay, son of the richest man in Madison County, went off to Yale University and came back filled with the spirit of abolition. He entered politics as a Whig, got elected to the state legislature, railed against slavery, and around 1844 sold his own slaves. Shortly after that, in Lexington, the center of Kentucky support for slavery, he began publishing an anti-slavery newspaper with the typically uncompromising title *The True American.*

Like his twentieth century African American namesake, Clay was quick with words and fists. In the midst of a fevered argument about slavery during the Kentucky Constitutional Convention of 1849, a pro-slavery man called Clay a "damn liar"; a fight began, and knives were drawn. Someone snatched Clay's bowie knife from his hand, and he grabbed it back by the blade, cutting three fingers to the bone. He was still able to turn the knife and stab and slash the man who had called him a liar until his intestines tumbled out.

The forces of slavery, now with a martyr to eulogize, dominated the convention and made it unconstitutional for the state to emancipate slaves without their owners' consent.[14]

In 1852, a new forty thousand-dollar Greek Revival courthouse was built across the street from the Francis Tavern. A handsome portico and four Doric columns fronted it. Rising above it, an octagonal clock tower became the symbol of the growing town.

As David Francis was growing up in the 1850s, Madison County slowly was changing, evolving from buckskin to gingham to linen, from covered wagon to carriage. The old rough-hewn pioneers—who had built log cabins and lived off the land, supplementing crops with hunting, smoking their own meat, and in many cases, making their own beer and whisky—were replaced in the countryside by planters accumulating wealth. And in Richmond, lawyers, doctors, and specialized merchants came to town. Downtown streets had been "macadamized" with crushed limestone.

Small manufacturers appeared, along with stores that sold furniture and men's and women's dress clothing and shoes. By the late 1850s, Richmond boasted more than a dozen doctors and, when court was in session, as many lawyers. Despite growing prosperity, the citizens of Madison County were notoriously reluctant to spend public money on what now would be called social services. The official history of the county comments that "Madison Countians had a great fear of having to maintain bastard children, vagrants, the aged, or the indigent poor. Their attitude was often appalling compared to the policies of neighboring counties." Paupers would be given a few dollars, if they were lucky, and ordered to leave the county.[15]

Not just the poor inspired frugality in the citizenry. In the late 1860s, Richmond lost telegraph service because the residents refused to pay for maintenance of the posts and wires put up by the government during the Civil War.

Activities that Madison Countians did support enthusiastically were agricultural fairs, the county's "largest recreational institution," according to the official history. The annual county fair in Richmond featured a small carnival midway and horse racing on a one-mile track.

But in other types of culture, the county lagged behind much of the rest of Kentucky, far from the most progressive state in the Union. The year before David Francis was born, Richmond's one-room public library was torn down to make room for the courthouse, and several years passed before it was replaced. Newspapers came and went as quickly as the azure bloom on the bluegrass. Madison Countians also lagged behind much of the rest of the state in building public schools, for decades ignoring offers of the state for land and money for that purpose.[16] Alexis De Tocqueville never visited Madison County, but he would have recognized it—his nightmare: the dictatorship of popular tastes.

By the time David Francis was ready for the first grade, Richmond had public schools, but they were terrible, and he attended private ones, beginning with the elementary grades at Madison Seminary, which had been founded in 1821 by the county squirearchy and Richmond businessmen to teach their children the three Rs, Latin, Greek, and basic science.

David's secondary education, beginning at the age of twelve, was at a private school called the Richmond Academy—more properly, the Richmond Female Academy. It offered French, painting, drawing, chemistry, and geography, as well as more basic courses, to about thirty young women and, beginning around 1862, three young men.

The principal of the private secondary school was a Presbyterian minister, the Reverend Dr. Robert L. Breck, a highly intellectual Richmond native and graduate of Princeton Theological Seminary. (A half century later, David Francis would learn that Breck had been a seminary classmate and close friend of Joseph Wilson, the Presbyterian minister and father of Woodrow Wilson.)

Breck strived for peaceful consensus at a time when a civil war over slavery seemed inevitable, and David Francis considered him to be a prime mentor, the first truly educated man he knew. Breck was a polymath who, according to published recollections by friends after his death at age eighty-eight, was a "fascinating companion, a man whose conversation was both a liberal education and a delight."[17]

Breck wanted to send his twelve-year-old son to his school, but he didn't want him to be the only boy among thirty girls, so he arranged for David Francis and another boy to enroll. There is no record of how David Francis felt about spending the schooldays of his adolescence surrounded by girls. But in later life, he very much enjoyed the company of the opposite sex.

By the time he started at the Richmond Academy, David Francis already had money earning interest in the bank. He began peddling newspapers when he was ten years old, not long before the beginning of the Civil War. The newspapers came from Lexington by stage, and the stage driver would give young David a penny apiece for selling them. Sometimes he would let "Davie" drive the stage. "At that time," Francis recalled in adulthood, "the height of my ambition was to be a stage driver and to hold the reins over four Thoroughbred Kentucky horses."[18]

Throughout the second half of the nineteenth century, both before and after the Civil War, roughly half of the population of Richmond was black. Until Francis's last year in Richmond, almost all its African Americans were slaves, including the one or two his father owned when he could afford to. As late as May 1862, slaves were sold (for about three hundred dollars apiece) at public auction on the steps of the Madison County courthouse, one of many painful sights David Francis witnessed growing up.

However, Madison County was a center of abolitionist fervor. In the 1850s, a "free"— nondenominational—abolitionist church was established in the 1850s at Berea, fifteen crooked-road miles south of Richmond. The church was built by a firebrand minister from eastern Kentucky, John G. Fee, with the financial support of Cassius Clay and the blessings of Harriet Beecher Stowe. Towards the end of the decade, an integrated school was added. It soon became Berea College, an abolitionist outpost in the midst of a county with more than five thousand slaves.

The opposition to Berea was fierce, and grew fiercer as the smouldering fire that inevitably would produce the Civil War burned hotter. Abolitionists' homes were torched, their meetings were attacked by mobs, and at least one supporter of Fee and Clay was stripped and horsewhipped. On December 23, 1859, an armed mob that included Francis and Broaddus relatives of David Francis rode south from the courthouse through a rare pre-Christmas snow and told the Bereans they had ten days to leave the state. Four days after Christmas, in a near-freezing drizzle, about three dozen men, women, and children headed to the North, where they were greeted as abolitionist heroes. Most of them did not return until after the Civil War.[19]

From that point on, outspoken abolitionists who remained or came back found themselves under attack, fired upon, beaten, and horsewhipped, their houses and barns and mills burned. Fierce little battles were fought on narrow country lanes, and men died. The Civil War came early to Madison County.

David Francis's Presbyterian preceptor, Robert Breck, although he deplored the violence, saw Fee as a dangerous fanatic, like John Brown, and the abolitionist cause as a path to chaos and disaster. As secession became imminent, Breck reluctantly chose to support the South, hoping to add a strong voice of moderation.[20]

The war officially began April 12, 1861, when Southern secessionists fired on the American flag at Fort Sumter in South Carolina. Kentucky attempted to remain neutral, and the governor, to no avail, warned both the Union and the Confederacy to keep their armies out of the state.

John Broaddus Francis was in his forties, too old to fight in the Civil War. His sympathies almost certainly lay with the South, like those of most Kentucky Democrats. Like his pastor, Robert Breck, John Broaddus Francis appears to have been a Southern moderate. His name does not appear in histories among the many dozens of those aligned with one side or another, and it would seem wise for the owner of a tavern in the middle of a town full of hotheads to avoid entering into violent disputation.

Early in the war, Confederate forces invaded from western Tennessee. General Ulysses S. Grant responded by marching in from Illinois, and the war raged across Kentucky. The "dark and bloody ground" where Indian tribes met to fight their wars was once again a battleground. About 75,000 Kentuckians—including 23,000 African Americans—fought for the Union, and between 25,000 and 40,000 for the Confederacy.[21]

Both the Union and the Confederacy claimed Kentucky. Early in the war, in a horribly bloody battle that ended virtually on David Francis's doorstep, the Confederacy prevailed.

Richmond was a Confederate stronghold, with a higher percentage of slaves even than Lexington. But many soldiers on both sides in the Battle of Richmond came from Madison County, adding to the poignant tragedy of the battle, and in some cases perhaps to its ferocity.

Ironically, by the time the war began, abolitionist leader Cassius Clay was in Russia—it is a striking historical coincidence that two nineteenth-century natives of Madison County, Kentucky, served as American ambassadors to the Tsar's court. Clay had been appointed by Abraham Lincoln, and in the summer of 1852, at Lincoln's behest, he returned to Kentucky to gauge feelings on the unresolved question of emancipation.

Clay, who held the army rank of major general from the Mexican War, heard that Confederate battalions were headed north towards Lexington. He took command of some assembled troops and marched them south, intending to make a stand on the northern palisades of the Kentucky River. But Major General William J. Nelson, commander of Union troops for Kentucky, caught up with the mercurial Clay, relieved him of his presumptuous command, joined Clay's troops with his own, and led his expanded army south to Richmond—and military disaster.[22]

The Battle of Richmond was fought on Saturday, August 30, 1862. After three months of a dreadful drought, the temperature on that sun-baked day approached one hundred degrees; the air was thick with dust from marching feet, the creeks were dry, corn was withering in the fields, and cattle were dying from lack of water. The battle began shortly after dawn six miles southeast of Richmond and from that point swept back and forth all day across the parched land, moving as steadily as an incoming tide toward Richmond. Unable to stand against the superior numbers and more experienced troops of the Confederacy, the Union men slowly fell back. By the final stage of the battle, which had begun in the late afternoon in the cemetery just southeast of town, more than half of the Union men had been killed, wounded, or captured. At that point, the Union had about twenty-five hundred troops, most of them raw recruits, and the Confederacy about four thousand, mostly veterans.[23]

The battle was joined again, and the result was one of the most thorough routs of the war.

Lucia Burnham, a daughter of the squirearchy who was about nine years old at the time, recalled the battle many years later: "We heard the great guns in the distance. All the household ran down the walk bordered by honeysuckle on trellises, beds of pansies—Johnny Jumpups we called them—columbines, moss roses and many other flowers to listen. . . ."[24]

The outmanned Union troops made a desperate last stand at the cemetery, firing muskets from behind tombstones and trees at the Confederates, who continued their advance through a walnut grove and a cornfield. The stalks crashed to the ground as the men rushed by, their muskets high. Confederate artillery shells shrieked overhead and exploded into tombstones and trees, hurling iron shrapnel and splinters of limestone and wood into the huddled Union soldiers. When the first wave of Confederate troops swept to about seventy-five yards from the first row of tombstones, the terrified Union men began to break and run toward Richmond.

Lucia Burnham recalled hearing "the cracking of bullets" and seeing mobs of federal soldiers fleeing through town. Bulky army wagons drawn by runaway mules careened down Main Street, knocking fleeing soldiers aside. The air was dense with dust, and the reaching fingers of the setting sun turned a blood red.

There are no recorded memories of the battle by eleven-year-old David Rowland Francis, but the Francis Tavern was only a few blocks from the cemetery, and the fleeing Union men and pursuing Confederates ran right past his door.

More than one thousand Union soldiers were killed or severely wounded. For days afterward, bodies littered the battlefields on the outskirts of Richmond, rotting and stinking in the intense heat. Many men who died in the cemetery were buried where they lay. More than four thousand Union prisoners were jammed together for a couple of weeks inside the wrought iron fence around the county courthouse, across the street from the Francis Tavern. Even after the prisoners left, the public buildings of Richmond—including the courthouse, churches, and schools—remained crowded with the wounded. Children brought them food and water and gifts of clothing.[25]

But the heat was terrible, and there was no escaping the constant moans of pain and pleas for water, and, as arms and legs were amputated, the screams of agony. Lucia Burnham recalled, "It seems to me now that it was an amazing thing that a child should have been taken to such a place and witness such scenes. . . . At all events, I was inured to scenes of danger and death and soldiers meant no more to me than my playmates."

Sixty years later, she still had a "vivid memory" of being taken to see a dead soldier, a Union man, laid on the grass in the shade of a grove of aspen trees. "His hands were folded on his breast and they held the daguerreotype of a woman who held a child in her arms."[26]

The Battle of Richmond temporarily secured the heart of Kentucky for the Confederacy. In October, at the Battle of Perryville, the Union took back northern Kentucky and effectively the rest of the state. Then came martial law, enforced by the Home Guard, a ragtag militia aligned with the Union. Many Southern sympathizers were beaten and several killed by the Home Guard—according to one Southern supporter, even the blacks thought of the Home Guard as "poor white trash."[27]

What were perceived as the excesses of Reconstruction kept the divisive anger alive in Kentucky and other Southern and border states long after the war ended. In January 1866, men assembled at the Richmond courthouse for an election began arguing and then firing pistols. Four of them—two Union supporters, and two Confederates—fell dead.

David Francis's mentor, Robert Breck, continually searched for ways to mediate between the two sides, and in the 1860s he fruitlessly fought to keep the Presbyterian Church from splitting into Northern and Southern branches. But when it finally did, he chose to stay with the South. In 1874, he became one of the founders and the first chancellor of Central University, affiliated with the Southern Presbyterian Church and formed as an alternative to abolitionist Berea College.[28]

In the spring of 1866, at the age of fifteen, David Francis graduated from Breck's Female Academy, apparently well versed in French, painting, drawing, chemistry, and geography—although not, as it turned out, as well versed as he thought he was. He fully expected to enter college as a junior, and he did not want to go to the local teacher's college or to the state university thirty miles away in Lexington.

"I wanted to get to a city," he said later.

"Mother had two brothers, one doing business in Cincinnati and one in St. Louis. Each had said if I would come I could have my board while I was finishing the education."[29]

Even the promise of free food and lodging did not make the decision to let young David go off to college an easy one. In March 1866, his father and mother had traded the Francis Tavern for a farm near the town of Stanford, about thirty miles southwest of Richmond. Money was tight, and hands were in short supply. John Broaddus Francis called the family together—Eliza, David, his three younger brothers, and their two sisters, Mary "Mollie" and Mahala "Hallie." Martha, David's half-sister, was twenty years old that year and no longer living at home. She married about that time and died in 1881.

John Francis said that he didn't think the family could afford to send more than one boy away to college in the foreseeable future, and he needed one of the two older boys, either David or twelve-year-old Thomas, to stay at home and work.

The father turned to Thomas and asked, "If David goes to college, are you willing to stay on the farm, take care of the horses and help me?"

"Let Dave go," young Tom replied.

Many years later, when he was fifty-five, still basking in the glow of having success-fully entertained and astonished millions of people at the St. Louis World's Fair of 1904, David Francis came back to Richmond for Madison County's Homecoming Day. He vis-ited the courthouse square, where, he said, "all the memories of my childhood cluster," and he later remarked:

> I have often asked myself what it is in Kentuckians that prompts them to take an active part in every contest that is waged and every issue that is brought up in the communities in which they live. [The] strength of character which was manifested by the pioneers who came to this state over a hundred years ago, and made for themselves homes, is felt by their descendents. . . . Those pioneers came to Kentucky, not because they were compelled to leave the communities in which they resided, not because they wanted [religious free-dom]. They were prompted by that independence of thought and action . . . which has characterized Kentuckians wherever they are found.[30]

Although he would not have realized it fully at the time, David R. Francis left Madison County both in reaction against a closed community and its provincial man-ners and as a product of it. He was imbued more with the moderation of Robert Breck than the uncompromising zeal of Cassius Clay, but he was influenced by both, as well as the yearning for culture and civilization of his mother. Like most Americans who approach or achieve greatness, he would become a walking contradiction, stubborn and idealistic by nature but with a rich strain of pragmatism and a willingness to compro-mise all but the most basic principles to get things done. He was generous of spirit but generally tight with money, his own and the public's, and inclined to save and invest rather than spend. He had much admiration for hard-working farmers and small mer-chants, little for the unemployed poor, and, in the early years of his adulthood at least, none for those who took to the streets with their grievances. He admired peacemakers more than those who made war, although he was not afraid of a fight and believed that political opinions were important and should be stoutly defended.

When he left Kentucky, he took with him the seeds of a lifelong fiscal conservatism combined with an almost mystical Jeffersonian belief in the ability of ordinary, hard-working Americans to see the truth and vote accordingly. He thought society should not support the poor, except those physically unable to support themselves, but as a young politician he came to believe in using government to help level the econimic playing field.

Young David Francis was a committed Democrat, if a conservative one, suspicious of the arrogance of wealth while determined to become wealthy. He was used to a cozy relationship between business and politics, at least on a local level, and, like most Kentuckians, deep down he was suspicious of the power of the federal government and of the rich. As a tavern keeper's son in a county seat, he was comfortable with a variety of people and a variety of points of view and inclined, through the lessons of his father and Robert Breck, to moderation and consensus. He was also comfortable with—and would grow fond of—good whisky and the men who drank it. And he liked fine horses and lavish county fairs.

When he was ready to leave for college, he went to the bank and converted the sixty dollars in gold he had accumulated into ninety-six dollars in "greenbacks," inflationary paper money that had been issued to finance the war.

Thus he learned about the "miracle" of compound interest and the dazzling power of gold.

It's easy to see why an ambitious, adventurous young man like David Francis would choose St. Louis over Cincinnati at that time in history. Cincinnati was prosperous but well established. St. Louis was still, if not quite the frontier, the gateway to it, a boom-town, the route to entrepreneurial riches.

There was a fervor about the city of St. Louis and the state of Missouri, an excited babble of voices full of money. The voices had been hushed by the war, but were rising again after it and could easily be heard three hundred miles away in Kentucky.

In the satirical novel that helped define the coming era and give it its name—*The Gilded Age*—Mark Twain and Charles Dudley Warner personified the period's frenetic entrepreneurial spirit and sheer hucksterism in the character of Beriah Sellers, who beckoned friends to join him in the new Promised Land:

> Come right along to Missouri! . . . You'll never regret it. It's the grandest coun-
> try—the loveliest land—the purest atmosphere—I can't describe it; no pen
> can do it justice. And it's filling up every day—people coming from every-
> where. I've got the biggest scheme on earth—and I'll take you in; I'll take in
> every friend I've got that's ever stood by me, for there's enough for all, and to
> spare. Mum's the word—don't whisper. . . . You'll see! Come!—rush!—hurry—
> don't wait for anything![31]

CHAPTER 2

Down Along the Levee

I N EARLY SEPTEMBER 1866, David Francis took a stagecoach up to Lexington and climbed aboard a westbound train. It carried him 350 miles to the east bank of the Mississippi River, across low hills that gradually flattened out until the train rolled across the flood plain of the biggest river in the nation. For the last few miles, he could look ahead and see St. Louis, the city he would call home for the rest of his life, rising on a series of terraces from a riverbank lined with massive white steamboats. Above the tall smokestacks of the boats, and over the city itself, hung a dome of dark smoke shaped like the cap of a vast inky mushroom.

Francis was just short of his sixteenth birthday, tall and gangly, clean shaven, with unruly chestnut hair beneath a gentleman's straw hat. With heavy suitcase in hand, he stepped down from the train onto mud flats teeming with commerce. He made his way through a thicket of railcars and wagons piled high with freight, dodging horses and mules and stevedores. This muddy riverboat landing was called the American Bottoms—the anachronistic name dated from before the Louisiana Purchase of 1803, when Illinois had been a part of the United States and St. Louis had not. He climbed up a gangplank, across a loading barge permanently anchored to the shore, and aboard a ferry.

Although the first railroad bridge across the upper Mississippi had been built in 1855 at Rock Island, Illinois—not coincidentally, 150 miles due west of Chicago—and three more with direct Chicago connections had been completed or were well underway upriver by the time Francis arrived, there wouldn't be a bridge at St. Louis for another eight years.[1] That fact would be crucial in determining the fate of the city as well as the future of David Rowland Francis.

A few miles above St. Louis, the Missouri and Illinois Rivers pour into the Mississippi, more than doubling its volume. The river at St. Louis is deep and treacherous. An eastern journalist who crossed the Mississippi to St. Louis about this time observed:

Such ferries as those by which we cross the Hudson and the Delaware are impossible upon a river so swift and capricious as this. The ferry-boat is built like other steamboats, except it is wider and stronger. With its head up the stream, it lies alongside of a barge to receive its enormous freight of coal wagons, omnibuses, express-wagons, mail wagons, cars, and loose mules enough to fill the interstices. Being let go, the boat, always headed [in]to the impetuous flood, swings across—the engine merely keeping the huge mass from being carried away down the stream.

Seen from the top of the ferry boat, St. Louis is a curved line of steamboats a mile and a half long, without a single mast or sail among them. The whole number of steamboats plying between this city and other river towns is 265, of which one hundred may frequently be seen in part at once, ranged along the Levee in close order, with their sterns slanting down the stream and their bows thrust against the treacherous sand of the shore. . . .[2]

On the other shore, a crowd of people waited at the ferry landing. Among them was David Francis's uncle, David Pitman Rowland, thirty-three years old, with a hawk nose, a slightly receding forehead, piercing dark eyes, and a flowing reddish-brown moustache and goatee. Uncle Pitt looked like a young Civil War general, although he had managed to sit out the war. Like his nephew, he was a tall, sturdy, energetic Kentuckian, proud of his Scotch-Irish/Presbyterian heritage, and healthy as a horse. He, too, had been stirred by ambition at an early age.

Born in Richmond in 1832, Rowland had quit school at fourteen and gone to work in the largest general store in town. Within a few years he ran the place. When he was twenty-two, in the booming mid-1850s, he came to St. Louis on business, took a long look around town, and decided he saw the future.

He went to work for a St. Louis dry goods company, advanced rapidly, saved his money, and soon went out on his own into the tobacco business. By that September day when David Francis disembarked on the St. Louis levee, Rowland and his older partner, W. P. Shryock, had one of the largest produce houses in the region, occupying most of a large building a block west of the levee, trading for commission in tobacco, cotton, grain, and other agricultural products.[3]

David Rowland was a Democrat with Southern leanings, and one way he had built his business was by opening up Mississippi River trade with the South in the early 1860s. The river had been blockaded during the latter part of the war, but by the summer of 1866, the paddlewheel boats steamed north again, and Rowland's warehouses were full of cotton and tobacco.

UNCLE PITT EMBRACED HIS NEPHEW and passed his suitcase to a black servant. On this side, the levee was many times more crowded than the American Bottom, quite dangerously so, with hundreds of black muleskinners cracking long whips from wagons sagging with their loads, driving horses and mules along the slippery levee.

The three men, with the servant in the lead, picked their way through the shifting mob of men, animals, and goods, heading up the slanting levee. The sloping bank of the Mississippi, the commercial nexus of St. Louis since its beginning, had been partially paved with large stones before the war, but maintenance was difficult as the river rose and fell, dislodging stones. River mud, along with horse and mule droppings, spread over every hard surface.

At the top of the levee, David Francis followed Uncle Pitt into the back of a carriage. The servant, a bright young man named George Simms who had been born a slave, stowed the suitcase behind them, climbed into the driver's seat, and snapped the reins; and with a clatter of hooves on bricks and levee stones they headed up into the city.

ST. LOUIS HAD BEEN FOUNDED IN 1764 by New Orleans fur trader Pierre Laclède and his precocious fourteen-year-old lieutenant—and stepson—Auguste Chouteau. In 1803, Napoleon sold St. Louis, along with the rest of the French land west of the Mississippi, to Thomas Jefferson for $15 million, doubling the size of the land-hungry nation. St. Louis quickly became the funnel through which westward expansion flowed, a city known for immense wealth quickly gained and even more quickly lost, on a plunge in the price of pelts or the turn of an ace. Like Richmond, Kentucky, it was a city of duels among the gentry and drunken brawls among the rabble. Much of the drinking and killing was blamed on the city's many immigrants from Kentucky and Tennessee, and an English visitor in the 1820s complained that St. Louis was dangerously dominated by "Kentucky manners."[4]

Located just below the confluence of the nation's two longest rivers, the Missouri and the Mississippi, St. Louis became the locus of trade and manufacturing for the vast central valleys of the nation, with flourishing commerce to the cities of the East Coast and Europe through the port of New Orleans, to the ironworks and steel mills of Pittsburgh through the Ohio River, to the American Southwest through the Arkansas River, and to the pioneer West through the Missouri, which ran all the way to the northern Rockies, the final killing grounds of the fur trade.

By the time David Francis arrived, St. Louis was a sturdy city of stone and brick, with an undercoating of bourgeois civilization added in great part by the emigration in the 1840s and 1850s of tens of thousands of Germans, relatively well-educated political liberals and radicals escaping oppression and civil strife back home. Many of them were skilled tradesmen and artisans, and they quickly entered the city's growing middle class.

Like Kentucky, Missouri was a slave state that nearly had been torn apart by the Civil War. About 110,000 Missourians fought for the Union, 40,000 for the Confederacy. In St. Louis, thousands of German immigrants and transplanted Yankees fervently supported the Union, and thousands of immigrants from Southern and border states as well as what remained of the old French families were equally as fanatic in siding with the Rebels. Skirmishes were fought within the city limits, and St. Louis spent the last half of the war under federal martial law.[5]

The wounds had by no means healed when David Francis arrived. "When I entered Washington University in the fall of 1866," he recalled later, "scarcely 12 months had passed since the close of the civil war. St. Louis, whose interests had been more closely allied with the South than with any other section, and which was nearer to the line of hostilities than any other city of its size, was just beginning to revive from the commercial lethargy consequent upon a community being in a high tension of political excitement."[6]

As Francis and Rowland rode west through downtown on the wide, partially paved main boulevard of Washington Avenue, the most prominent landmarks ahead were the stone and brick steeples of churches and, a few blocks to the southwest, the 198-foot-high, green cast-iron capitol dome of the main courthouse, where earlier in the decade slaves had been sold and where, in the early 1850s, the Missouri courts deliberated on Dred Scott. They passed the warehouses and offices of the river trade, including the three-story brick building that housed Shryock & Rowland, and crossed Third and Fourth Streets, which were becoming, respectively, the main banking and retail thoroughfares as the city moved slowly west away from the river. They clattered past three- and four-story brick commercial buildings, dodging streetcars drawn by horses and mules, and moved through the western edge of downtown, crossing Twelfth Street into an area of two- and three-story brick and stone houses, tree-lined boulevards and lanes, and small parks and grassy vacant lots.

At Seventeenth Street they passed, on the left, Washington University, installed in a single large brick building in an area of substantial homes and mansions that were just beginning to lose fashion, as families who could afford it moved further west to get away from the smoke and pestilence of the city. David Francis arrived at the end of a summer when the wasting effects of cholera, spread through the contaminated water supply and food in the older neighborhoods of the city, had killed thirty-five hundred people.[7]

David Rowland lived in a mansard-roofed, two-and-a-half-story brick house about two miles west of the river at 2709 Morgan Street, between Ewing and Garrison. About seven blocks further was Grand Avenue, a wide boulevard that arced across the western edge of the city. Grand was effectively the western limit of urbanization in the early days after the Civil War.

Uncle Pitt's first wife—Mattie Shackelford of Bourbon County, Kentucky, probably a distant cousin—had died in 1864, leaving a small son, W. S. Rowland, motherless. A few months before David Francis arrived for college, his uncle had married again, this time to Emma Aderton, the daughter of J. A. J. Aderton, president of the prosperous Valley National Bank. Marrying up was common among ambitious, well-spoken young men from Kentucky, Tennessee, and Virginia. David Francis was installed in an upstairs room in the house where his uncle lived with his bride and his son. George Simms lived down the hall.

Francis later recalled, "On the day of my arrival in St. Louis, I attended the closing day of the St. Louis Fair, which was held on Grand Avenue, where Fairgrounds Park is now."[8] Although the memory is probably inaccurate—he seems to have arrived in St. Louis in early September, in time for the opening of classes at Washington University, and the week-long fair did not begin until October—it's interesting that he remembered spending part of his first day in St. Louis at a fair.

The St. Louis Agricultural and Mechanical Fair spread out over more than eighty acres of lightly wooded land along Grand Avenue near Natural Bridge Road, north of the settled areas of the city. The fair combined crop and livestock exhibitions and blue-ribbon competition with demonstrations of agricultural and industrial machinery, manufactured goods, and fabrics. There was horse racing (with betting) on a half-mile "speed track," and an amphitheater that seated more than twelve thousand. Several large exhibit halls included a block-long industrial showcase and a three-story, wire-domed "Chicken Palace" for exhibiting poultry. But the most popular attractions were sideshow acts—sword swallowers, strongmen, fat ladies, and dwarfs.[9]

The fair brought in so many visitors at the time of the fall harvest that, around 1860, the prominent citizens who ran it began talking about holding a world's fair in St. Louis. The Civil War put a stop to that talk, and for a time to the St. Louis Fair itself. The fair resumed in 1866, the year David Francis arrived. In fact, it opened on Monday, October 1, Francis's sixteenth birthday.[10]

At Washington University, David Francis quickly discovered that the Richmond Female Academy barely had prepared him to enter as a freshman, much less a junior. His small class was otherwise made up of the well-educated sons of rich men or academics, and the course of study was rigorous, based in great part on Harvard's.

Washington University had been established in 1853 by Kentucky-born millionaire merchant Wayman Crow and a group of fellow Unitarians. But its intellectual and moral founder, the first president of its board of directors, was their pastor, a towering figure in nineteenth-century St. Louis, the Reverend Dr. William Greenleaf Eliot. Eliot, of the Boston/Cambridge Eliots, a magisterial, intellectually severe Unitarian cleric, had come to St. Louis and the western frontier with what he considered a mission into the wilderness. Missionaries like Eliot came, as Huckleberry Finn would later put it—half in scorn, half in fear—to "sivilize" Missouri. It could be said that the culture of St. Louis and its region has been determined to a great extent by a continuing battle between, on one side, the Southern-rooted, lusty country wit and pragmatic clarity epitomized by Missourian Mark Twain, and, on the other, the Northern, Puritanical reformist zeal of a William Greenleaf Eliot.

Francis took a horse-drawn streetcar to the university, which was small, almost an annex of the much larger preparatory schools associated with it—Smith Academy for boys and Mary Institute for girls. His freshman class began with about a dozen students, several of them from prominent St. Louis families.[11]

Required courses for the freshman class of 1866–67 at Washington University were Latin, Greek, mathematics, Roman history, English literature, French, and German. Tuition was fifty dollars a term, and there were two terms of twenty weeks each. Sophomore requirements were Latin, Greek, trigonometry, Greek history, and English, French, and German literature—the students read Schiller's "William Tell" in German and classic plays in French.[12]

Francis was lonely. He later recalled, "At the age of 15 I came to St. Louis to go to college. Homesick! Someone has written that no one but a Scotch-Irishman can appreciate the motives or understand the character of Andrew Jackson. One must have experienced homesickness to realize what it is to yearn for mother and father and sisters and brothers, and the scenes and companions of childhood."[13]

But he made friends quickly. Francis joined the Irving Union, the student debate society, and at the end of his sophomore year, on May 29, 1868, he delivered the closing oration at the Irving Union's "exhibition" in the university's main auditorium. His subject was "Change."[14]

The instruction at Washington University, and the intellectual and cultural life of the still-rough city in which David Francis was coming of age, was influenced in those days by the so-called St. Louis Movement and its formal apparatus, the St. Louis Philosophical Society. This loose group of educators and writers gathered informally at the small Viennese-style cafes downtown near the courthouse and organized night classes for adults, public lectures, and book, art, and music clubs for those desperate for culture and enlightenment. They shared a philosophical approach that blended Hegelian reason, brought to the edge of the frontier by idealists who had fled the repression and upheavals of Germany, and the neo-Platonic transcendentalism of New England emigrants.[15]

More than once in later life, David Rowland Francis expressed admiration for and quoted from the works of the transcendentalist poet-philosopher Ralph Waldo Emerson, whose writings he claimed to have read almost in entirety. The Emersonian tenet of self-reliance, both on a personal level and a national one—the notion that America must develop its own culture and ideals independent of the stifling legacy of Europe—would be among Francis's core values.

By his junior year at Washington University, Francis was reading Thucydides and Sophocles in Greek, Tacitus in Latin, and Moliere in French. He studied physics, analytical geometry, and differential and integral calculus, while continuing with English literature and European history. It was a tough curriculum, as would be expected from a college inspired by William Greenleaf Eliot and headed by William Chauvenet, a mathematician and scientist who was the first president of the National Academy of Sciences.

One important teacher was Calvin M. Woodward, a mathematics professor who took Francis and his class onto the Mississippi, where "submarines"—sandhogs—were placing footings of the Mississippi River bridge in bedrock, below twenty or thirty feet of water and fifty or sixty feet of sand. In 1867, chief engineer James B. Eads began construction on the bridge, which would not be finished until 1874. The students were able to descend into the caissons of the bridge. They walked in single file more than one hundred feet down on a long spiral staircase that lead to airlocks into one of the heavily pressurized, airtight chamber where the work was being done. There, candles burned with an eerie light and human voices sounded like shrill cries of birds. Francis would never forget the visit.[16]

In 1869, David Francis and a few friends founded the Ugly Club, with Francis as president. The Ugly Club announced it intended to recognize those who "excel in ugliness, beauty, modesty, childishness, repugnance to labour, self esteem [and] . . . love for the opposite sex." The Ugly Club threw parties and assembled annually to lampoon other students and, sometimes, faculty.[17]

He also joined the Central Presbyterian Church, then as now one of the pillars of the St. Louis establishment. Like Robert Breck's church in Richmond, Central had chosen the Southern branch when the denomination had split. By Francis's junior year, the church had imported its pastor, Robert G. Brank, from Lexington, Kentucky.[18]

Religion appeared to play a small role in David Francis's life,[19] although he would maintain his membership in the Presbyterian Church for many years. In part, he was lonely and looking for friendship in the few hours of leisure he permitted himself, as he tried to catch up with students with much better secondary educations. His church of choice was fashionable, and he became the librarian of the Sunday School, attended by children of the wealthy. A young girl named Jane Perry and her railroad-magnate father were members of the church as well.[20]

In Francis's senior year, required courses included astronomy, geology, philosophy, political economy, and Constitutional law. Grades for Francis's class are missing, but he must have done at least an adequate job—about half the class was gone by graduation. Later, George Simms, his floormate in the Rowland house, recalled that David Francis was a "hard student. He didn't go out much evenings. He would sit there at that table hour after hour and night after night."[21]

Commencement was held in the college auditorium on the evening of Thursday, June 16, 1870. The next day, the *Missouri Republican* gushed: "An audience such as we have seldom witnessed in St. Louis—composed as it was of the talent, beauty and fashion of our city—thronged the capacious hall."[22]

A band played at intervals throughout the long ceremony, and each of the six graduates spoke. David Goldsmith, who would become a lawyer and a lifelong friend of Francis, spoke on patriotism, and Francis's speech, delivered in Kentucky-twinged but perfect English, was on "The Statesman."[23]

The enthusiastic audience, in addition to friends and family, included hundreds of young women, who tossed bouquets of flowers at the graduates as they marched off the stage, diplomas in hand.

A graduation photo shows Francis clean shaven, with thick curly chestnut hair parted on his left side and curls rolling backward over his large, high-peaked ears. His deep-set blue eyes look from beneath thick lashes with confidence, and his wide mouth has a determined set to it.

After graduation, Francis went home to Kentucky, hoping to return to St. Louis in the fall. He told his father he wanted to study law. His father said he couldn't afford to support him through law school.

Francis decided this was not the time to tell his father he was already in debt—he had borrowed $450 for tuition and expenses. But he pressed his case.

"After some thought," Francis recalled later, "father said to me that if I could collect some old debts that were due him, I might take the money and go to law school."[24]

John Francis handed his son a promissory note from a farmer named Mitchell Ford, who had borrowed about $150. David Francis, note in hand, went to see Ford.

Ford took the note, looked at it and said, "Oh, that's been settled long ago. It was settled last year. Tell your father I will keep the note."

David Francis went home empty handed.

"I was very much discouraged," he recalled. "I remember that on my way home I lost my way. When I got there at last I said, 'Father, Mitch Ford said the note had been paid.'"

"No such thing!" replied his father. "Did you let him keep the note?"

"Yes," the nineteen-year-old college graduate replied reluctantly. He recalled later, "Father didn't whip me, but he was very mad."

It's hard to imagine a more valuable lesson for a future businessman, but for a while Francis despaired of ever getting back to St. Louis. He began working on the farm and quickly discovered a great deal of difference between the Jeffersonian ideal of the stout American yeoman and the reality of farm labor in rockbound hill country.

"The last time I plowed," he said later, "I went back to the house limping. I had shoes that didn't fit, and I wore the skin off one heel. I told father I wouldn't plow anymore."

A strong young man who wouldn't plow was not much use around a farm, although his brief stint at the rear of a mule would play an important role in his later life, giving him the right to tell rural voters he once had been a farmer himself. Fortunately, he didn't have to be one for very long. That summer, a letter came from Uncle Pitt, offering him a clerkship in his commission house at a salary of sixty dollars a month.

Francis leaped at the chance. He returned to St. Louis and moved back in with the Rowlands, who by then had bought a new, larger house two blocks west at 2910 Morgan Street.[25] He went to work as a "mud clerk." Mud clerks worked long days and, often, well into the night, tromping through the muck and dodging the speeding wagons along the levee, checking incoming and outgoing shipments of grain and other produce. His pocket was filled with dozens of little cloth bags for the samples of grain he would take by poking a long, narrow tube through the rough weave of the sacks. David Francis was very busy, but he was excited by his work at the busiest spot in the city and curious about every aspect of commercial life on the levee. "I was never satisfied until I understood everything everyone else was doing," he later recalled. "I don't remember having ever looked at the clock and wished that the hour of closing would come."[26]

A merchant later described activity along the levee in the early 1870s:

The levee was the busiest place in town. Between Washington Avenue and Elm street [about a mile and a half], the boats often lay three and four deep at the river front. Freight from arriving steamboats was piled as high as the houses . . . drays were coming and going in an endless stream, as fast as the drivers could make the horses trot, and to cross the levee you started in a run, ended in a jump and blessed your stars if you were still alive. In summer time the levee was as hot as Africa; in winter it felt as cold as Novaya Zemlya [in the Arctic]. But cold or hot, the sampling of grain in bags had to be done.[27]

Francis worked hard and quickly got a raise to seventy-five dollars a month. He carried his lunch in a paper bag and otherwise pinched his pennies, and by the end of his first year on the job, he had repaid the $450 loan. After that, he continued to live frugally, but he put every cent he saved into investments.[28]

CHAPTER 3

The Fourth City

D AVID FRANCIS WAS STILL LABORING AS A MUD CLERK on the St. Louis levee when the federal census of 1870 sent the city's boosters into euphoria. The population of America's westernmost major city was reported at 310,000, double the figure a decade earlier. St. Louis had leaped past Baltimore and Boston and now officially could call itself the Fourth City, lagging in population behind only New York, Philadelphia, and Brooklyn. True, upstart Chicago's population had tripled since 1860, but the young giant rising out of the marshes of southern Lake Michigan still had only 298,000 people, according to the 1870 census.

The population figures seemed to confirm the grandiose dreams of the St. Louisans who, the year before, had convinced a convention of twenty-one states and territories, from Pennsylvania to Oregon, that the United States capital should be moved to St. Louis. A prominent grain dealer was elected president of the convention, which was held at the St. Louis Merchants' Exchange, and a journalist and failed real-estate sales-man named Logan U. Reavis was placed in charge of promoting the notion in Washington. Predictably, Congress laughed and increased the funding for federal con-struction in the District of Columbia.[1]

Undeterred, Reavis wrote *St. Louis: The Future Great City of the World*, which was published by St. Louis County in 1870 and sent all over the United States. The crux of the book was the then-fashionable theory of the "isothermal zodiac," which held that great civilizations from ancient to contemporary times inevitably had sprouted in the temperate climes of the northern hemisphere on major inland rivers. St. Louis was the next in line, announced Reavis, joining other great cities of the world, from ancient Babylon on the Euphrates to modern Paris on the Seine, in "the center of equilibrium between excess of heat and cold."[2]

The flowery, pseudoscientific tome, combined with the census figures, added to the excitement, and perhaps the complacency, of the St. Louis businessmen that waited for the inevitable rebirth of Rome on the west bank of the Mississippi.

When the 1870 census figures were released, Chicago merchants and newspapers screamed fraud, with justification. Federal census officials, appointees of the corrupt administration of former St. Louisan Ulysses S. Grant, had bowed to the wishes of powerful St. Louis Republicans and waited until the Chicago figures arrived before reporting the numbers for St. Louis—a trick Chicago learned well for the future. The St. Louis census figures turned out to be phony, as will be discussed in the next chapter. In reality, by 1870 Chicago was probably already somewhat larger than St. Louis and was growing much faster. And by the early 1870s, Chicago also had surpassed St. Louis as a grain market, rail hub, and in many other measures of commercial success.[3]

There are a number of explanations for Chicago, rather than St. Louis, becoming the commercial and industrial giant of the Midwest. The Civil War's disruptive effect on St. Louis and Missouri often is blamed, and that was an important factor, but Chicago had established itself as a railroad hub to the west even before the Civil War, with lines reaching from New York to the Great Plains, thanks to copious eastern investment and the bridge at Rock Island, Illinois, spanning the Mississippi River. St. Louis languished, in part, because every item of New York finery and pot of Boston beans had to be unloaded at the American Bottoms, ferried across the Mississippi at an exorbitant cost, and reloaded onto wagons and trains. St. Louis's huge economic stake in the continued success of technology that was rapidly growing obsolete—the steamboat—didn't help, nor did the short-sighted greed of some of St. Louis's most prominent citizens.

In the 1850s and early 1860s, St. Louis business leaders wangled enormous state and local subsidies for the Pacific Railroad, a proposed major line from St. Louis to Kansas City and points west that would compete with the northern routes leading out of Chicago. When the Civil War effectively put a stop to further construction in 1861, the Pacific remained unfinished, years behind schedule, slowed in part by the weight of millions of dollars of graft and outright theft by politicians and insiders. While St. Louis awaited the completion of the Pacific Railroad, and some of its most distinguished citizens were getting rich off the boondoggle, Chicago became the major market for the farm products of the Great Plains.[4]

At the end of the war a flurry of track-laying occured in western Missouri, and by September 1865, shiny new rails finally lay unbroken from the still-bridgeless levee at St. Louis three hundred miles to Kansas City. But by May 1869, Chicago already had won the battle. A golden spike driven into the alkali soil of Utah signaled that the United States now had uninterrupted railroad tracks running from coast to coast—through Chicago and across Mississippi River bridges well north of St. Louis. The first bridge at St. Louis was still half a decade away.

During the war, St. Louis and Missouri at best marked time economically, while Chicago grew rich and powerful perched hundreds of miles north of the fighting. The war's main effect on Chicago was to inflate the prices it got for its goods.

Ironically, even the great Chicago fire of 1871 helped that city, clearing room for a vast urban renewal project. Chicago quickly was rebuilt—pushed along by millions of dollars in New York money.

To this day, a considerable argument wages among regional historians over the major causes for Chicago's emergence as the dominant midwestern city. One well-supported thesis is that St. Louis was held back by its entrepreneurial conservatism—overly cautious bankers, the exclusion of outsiders from the city's cosy financial circles, and in general an insufficiently aggressive approach to business.

Perhaps the most influential work on this subject is Wyatt Belcher's 1947 analysis, *The Economic Rivalry Between St. Louis and Chicago, 1850–1880,* which extensively documents the argument that, because of over-confidence in its economic future and the "conservative . . . business temper of its citizens," St. Louis "lapsed into commercial intertia" in the second half of the nineteenth century and was overwhelmed by Chicago and its "bulldog attitude."[5]

James Neal Primm, whose *Lion of the Valley* is the best and most thorough history of the city, has fought that conventional wisdom, and he attributes Chicago's rise, in great part, to "the Windy City's natural advantages . . . located strategically on the south shore of Lake Michigan," closer to New York and Boston, offering farmers of the upper Mississippi Valley quick access to the hungry millions of the industrial northeast.

"Perhaps the most pervasive and erroneous of the St. Louis myths," he says, "is the generalization that Creoles and genteel Southerners dominated and paralyzed St. Louis business in the 1850s and 1860s." The dominant St. Louis businessmen in the mid-nineteenth century, Primm argues, were tough, shrewd Yankees and "hawkish, hard-driving and ambitious" Southerners.[6]

There certainly were tough, shrewd Yankees in nineteenth-century St. Louis, and some of the emigres from Southern and border states—David P. Rowland and his nephew among them—were notably hard-driving and ambitious. And yet eastern visitors to St. Louis in the years following the Civil War noticed and wrote of a pervasive old-fashioned Southern genteel lassitude about the city and its businessmen, a taste—without the open hedonism—of the "Big Easy" attitude of New Orleans, whence came the city's founders.

James Parton of the *Atlantic Monthly* visited in 1867, when St. Louis probably still led Chicago in population. The writer noted:

> St. Louis is an immense surprise . . . to those who come round to it from furious and thundering Chicago. . . . If Chicago may be styled the New York, St. Louis is the serene and comfortable Philadelphia of the West. . . . There is something in the aspect of the place which indicates that people there find time to live, as well as accumulate the means of living. Chicago amuses, amazes, bewilders, and exhausts the traveler; St. Louis rests and restores him. . . . As the chief city of a State that shared, and deliberately chose to share, the curse of slavery, it has much of the languor and carelessness induced by the habit of being served by slaves.[7]

Seventeen years later, William Henry Bishop visited St. Louis for *Harper's New Monthly Magazine,* and came to similar conclusions about the negative effects of a

Southern climate as well as of a Southern mindset: "Two-thirds of all the merchants have to go away to escape the extreme heat [of summer] at what might otherwise be a favorable season," he noted, and "the sluggish influence of slave days is not wholly outgrown here."[8]

As noted in the previous chapter and above, there were strong Northern and abolitionist forces in St. Louis before the Civil War, and lumping St. Louis with the rest of Missouri as a city that had grown lazy because of slavery is perhaps unjust. But, whatever the cause, the conservatism and lack of daring of St. Louis merchants and financiers, particularly as compared to dynamic, risk-loving Chicago, is a continuing thread throughout the city's history, at least from the Civil War on. At times, when economic bubbles burst, as in the Panic of 1893 (see chapter 7), or during the savings and loan debacle almost a century later, conservatism served the city well, but in boom times it seems to have held St. Louis back. And the history of America is more boom than bust.

Blaming it on the weather is not as frivolous as it might seem today. In the summer, St. Louis is indisputably Southern, and the heat can be literally debilitating when, as often happens, the temperature shoots up into the nineties by June and stays there for a couple of months, accompanied by devastating humidity. It might be pertinent to point out that cities in the American South and Southwest—Charlotte, Atlanta, Dallas, Houston, Phoenix—did not became major metropolises until after the spread of air conditioning. By then, perhaps, St. Louis was too set in its ways to change.

Not only visitors took note of the city's economic lassitude. For well over a century, the city's most prestigious newspaper, the *St. Louis Post-Dispatch*, regularly criticized local business leaders for their conservatism. In 1880, the paper attributed the city's decline in relation to Chicago on "the conservative snail's pace" of the "fogy elements" that dominated the city's business and financial affairs.[9] And in 1998, in the midst of a boom based on personal computers and the Internet, the *St. Louis Post-Dispatch* sought to explain "Why St. Louis does not rival Silicon Valley." Yet again, the paper blamed the city's stodgy bankers and "a too-conservative financial environment."[10]

There was nothing stodgy about young David R. Francis. Soon, as both a political leader and a businessman, he would publicly battle the image of Missouri as a sleepy, backwards state, racist and violent. He and other ambitious St. Louisans of his generation were go-getters who collectively came to be dubbed "the New St. Louis" and thought of themselves as still being in a race with Chicago. But by the last third of the nineteenth century, when David Francis and his chums began to take hold of the reins of St. Louis, it was probably far too late to catch Chicago.[11]

One day in the early 1870s, David Pitman Rowland took his nephew with him into the vast Merchants' Exchange Building, where the trade of the region was conducted. One businessman took a long look at the gangly, boy-faced young man and asked Rowland, "What are you going to do with him?"

Rowland replied, "Well, if there's anything in him, I may make him president of this chamber some day."

"And what if he doesn't make good?" cracked the businessman.

Rowland smiled and replied, "Then I'll run him for governor of Missouri."[12] As it turned out, Francis would hold both offices.

St. Louis's Merchants' Exchange was a busy place, a combination commodities market, businessmen's social club, and chamber of commerce. Here's how the correspondent from the *Atlantic* described the room where David Francis would spend thousands of his days:

> The great Exchange room, where the twenty-five hundred ruling businessmen of the place daily meet for an hour and a half, is a refreshing scene. . . . Here, along the sides of the long room, are tables covered with little tin pans, containing samples of corn, wheat of all grades and colors, flour, meal, oats, barley, beans, bran, seeds, apples, dried apples, salt; on other tables are hams, samples of hemp, wool and cotton, bottles of coal oil, lard, lard oil, lubricating oil, currying oil, specimens of rope. . . .
>
> Here are the millers, with their ruddy faces and light-colored clothes. . . . Here are the buyers of grain, each in his accustomed place, to whom come sellers bearing pans of wheat, which the buyer runs his hand through, asks the price and the quantity and indicates, by a shake or a nod of the head, whether he takes or declines it.

He adds a telling characterization of the exchange, making a comparison to Chicago:

> These men of the St. Louis Exchange do not know as much, do not think and read as much, do not push and advertise and vaunt as much, as those who frequent the Exchange of Chicago; but they have that something about them which makes the charm of the farmer and the country gentleman. Evidently they take life more easily than their rivals farther north. . . . We must not omit to record that the standard of commercial honor has always been high at St. Louis, and that its merchants have rather inclined to an excess of caution than to an excess of enterprise.[13]

David Francis grumbled from time to time about the city's lack of business spunk, but, with a good poker player's combination of caution and well-timed audacity, plus a terrific line of gab, he flourished at the Merchants' Exchange, where he began as a protégé of E. O. Stanard, a former exchange president who managed to serve as a Republican congressman without losing touch with his large flour business.

While still working as a clerk for Shryock & Rowland, Francis established, according to his friend and biographer Walter Stevens, "his two primary principles in business life—saving and sticking."[14] The notion of buying and holding stock was much less proven as a way to wealth than it would become a century or so later. Francis's investments didn't always work out—early on, he bought stock in a new bank, the Clerk's Saving Bank, and stubbornly held on to it until the bank collapsed. But he had a shrewd eye for value. One of his earliest investments was a few shares of what became the Merchants-Laclede National Bank, co-founded, perhaps not coincidentally, by his future father-in-law. He kept putting money into the fast-growing bank until he was its largest shareholder.

"He did not part with a share," Stevens recalled. "He bought at all kinds of prices, below and above par. His investment more than trebled, not to count the dividends received." When a new company or financial institution would incorporate—St. Louis's first trust company, an expanded streetcar system—Francis would take a close look at it, and if he liked his prospects he would buy stock and, almost always, hold on to it. Even after he became wealthy, he was careful with a dollar—some might say cheap—in part so he always would have capital for investment.

After a long day's work, he might have a drink or two at the German bierstubes and hotel bars around Fourth and Market Streets, where stock and commodities traders drank down their adrenaline levels and sometimes joined in serious philosophical discussions with a group whose ambition was to make St. Louis the cultural center of the world. Writer Orrick Johns recalled, "In those early seventies, there was a flourishing philosophical movement in St. Louis, which afterward became celebrated and still has its niche in every history of American philosophy. . . . The St. Louis Movement bequeathed a warmth and intellectual comradeship to the town which vanished only with the First World War. The cultural climate of the city cannot be explained without it."[15]

Francis, better educated at Washington University than all but a few of his business contemporaries, in later years surprised strangers with his knowledge of literature, philosophy, and the arts.

W HILE STILL A CLERK, Francis was hired to write a weekly market report for the *St. Louis Times,* one of the city's half-dozen major daily newspapers. There, he met Walter Stevens, then a young reporter on the *Times,* and the two became lifelong friends. Stevens's viewpoint, reflected in his extensive writings about Francis, is that of a friend, but his words are invaluable because of the immense detail they provide.

Stevens tells us that one day Rowland decided to teach his nephew a lesson—"to bring his eye teeth through." Rowland was pretty certain the price of wheat was about to drop. He told a friend to sell five hundred dollars worth of wheat futures in his name. Then Uncle Pitt gave his nephew five hundred dollars and dealt him what he figured was a losing hand by telling him to buy wheat. With the market thus straddled, Rowland would break even no matter which way the price went.

The next day, after wheat had plunged as he had expected, Rowland asked his friend for his profits. The friend replied, abashed: "I'm grieved to tell it, Pitt, but I met Dave on 'change and he gave me such a plausible talk about September wheat that I violated your order and bought instead of selling. It's a shame, I know . . . but you're out $500. That nephew of yours is to blame. He could coax a bird off the bush."

Exasperated, figuring he had not hedged his losses but doubled them, he sent for his nephew. With a sigh, he asked, "Dave, how much did you drop [on] September wheat yesterday?"

"How much did I drop?" David Francis replied, "Why, nothing. I won out!"

Perplexed, Rowland asked, "You won out? Didn't I advise you to buy?"

"Yes," replied his nephew. "And I intended to buy. But at the last minute I thought it best to sell."[16] Francis was ready to graduate from mud clerk.

Francis began working in the offices a block from the levee. From the river he could see the intricate web of iron and steel that became the Eads Bridge rising from its four caissons. Only in the last months of construction could the graceful design of the bridge, with its three arches loping across the river in five hundred-foot strides, be appreciated fully.

Finally, after seven years of construction, on July 4, 1874, the double-decker bridge—with railroad tracks below, foot and horse traffic, including horse-drawn street-cars, above—officially opened. Cannons roared, brass bands blared, and a fourteen-mile-long parade moved across the fifteen hundred-foot bridge from the Illinois shore into downtown St. Louis. There were battalions of soldiers on foot and horseback, marching bands, orchestras on giant wagons, amassed singing societies, a fully rigged sailing ship on wheels, and, to finish off the parade, a locomotive pulling thirteen Pullman cars loaded with dignitaries, a numbing number of whom spoke at the reviewing stand high above the levee.

The parade lasted several hours, and David Francis probably watched the whole thing, either by his uncle's side on the reviewing stand or with a superb view from the top floor of Shryock & Rowland's five-story building just three blocks from where the bridge flowed into Washington Avenue.[17]

The Eads Bridge was, and remains, one of the most beautiful inland bridges in America, as well as a wondrous feat of engineering. This graceful triple arc of meshed metal was the symbol of St. Louis until completion almost ninety years later of Eero Saarinen's 630-foot-high stainless steel Gateway Arch, which purposely echoed the Eads Bridge. The symbolism of these two magnificent structures is not without irony for those residents who simultaneously love St. Louis for its palpable sense of history and are maddeningly exasperated by the city's death grip on the past. The bridge symbolizes grandiose failure, the inability to act on a large scale until it's too late; the glittering Arch, as contemporary *Post-Dispatch* columnist Bill McClellan is fond of pointing out, commemorates St. Louis as the Gateway to the West—in other words, it's a monument to people who left town. St. Louis was a place people passed through on their way to somewhere. Chicago was a destination.

Although the Eads Bridge came far too late to make St. Louis the transportation center of the mid-continent (ironically, the bridge was financed in part by risk-happy Chicagoans), the city was still a boomtown. In 1875, business was so good that the Merchants' Exchange moved west a couple of blocks to a huge, ornately decorated new three-story stone building that occupied the entire block bounded by Third and Fourth

Streets, Chestnut and Pine. Accepting the keys to the building from the architect was that year's president, David Pitman Rowland. The building then was dedicated by William Greenleaf Eliot—like Emerson, a New England Unitarian with a decidedly Calvinstic bent—"to the righteous use of commerce and trade."[18]

Although still living at his uncle's house, sometimes skipping lunch entirely—he once collapsed at work and a physician ordered him to eat a hot lunch every day—David Francis now worked as a broker and trader. He was a long way from the Francis tavern.

From his second-story bedroom window in his uncle's house, Francis could look west up Morgan Street across a tree-lined vacant lot and see, half a block away, the imposing new three-story home of millionaire businessman John Dietz Perry. It's difficult to believe that he couldn't also see, from time to time, Perry's young daughter Jane walk down the steps and, flashing a stocking-clad ankle, step aboard the family carriage.

The story of John D. Perry and his family is not an unfamiliar one. A Virginian of Scotch-Irish ancestry, he had begun working in a dry goods store when he was fifteen. He saved his money, went into the milling and manufacturing business, and, with a bankroll, at the age of twenty-five headed west. In the Missouri River town of Glasgow, Perry got rich in the hemp and rope business and headed up a company that built the first plank road in Missouri. In 1854, Perry and his growing family moved to St. Louis. He founded or helped found two banks and, after the Civil War, began building a railroad across Kansas—the Kansas Pacific Railroad (not to be confused with the aforementioned Pacific), which by its completion in 1870 completed a link from St. Louis through Kansas City to Denver. It was a major and daring undertaking, and young David Francis admired him for it.[19]

Perry's daughter Jane was born in Glasgow on August 18, 1854, shortly before the move to St. Louis. Her mother was Eliza Turner Perry, John Perry's second wife and the mother of four of his five surviving children. Eliza Turner's father, Talton Turner, had come to Missouri as a surveyor from Richmond, Kentucky, where he had worked for Cassius Clay's father. (It was indeed a small world. The father of John Perry's first wife had been a Broaddus from Kentucky, like David Francis's paternal grandmother.)

Jane was very pretty, with hazel-gray eyes and light brown hair. "Dainty and exquisite of stature, with the bearing of a queen," is how a woman who knew her well described her.[20] In a photograph taken around the time of her marriage to David Francis, she is strikingly attractive, with full lips, bright eyes, and a slim, aristocratic nose, her fair hair puffing above her high forehead.

"She had a very feminine figure, and she had been a beautiful young woman," recalled her granddaughter, Anne Francis Currier, who was nine years old when Jane died. Mrs. Currier remembered her as being of average height—"perhaps 5'5" or 5'6"." Photographs, however, suggest she may have been a bit shorter than that.

Neither David nor Jane documented how they met. She may well have met her future husband at the family church, Central Presbyterian—perhaps he handed her a book one day. Strong-minded, like David Francis's mother, Jane Perry Francis had been partly educated abroad. When she was in her early teens, her father had collapsed from the exhaustion of all his business activities, and the Perrys had more than enough money to spend three or four years living in Europe and going on leisurely tours of historical sites and museums, getting as far east as Asia Minor. Much of Jane Perry's secondary schooling took place in Germany, and she stayed in that country for college, majoring in architecture at a German university, highly unusual for a woman at that time, in Europe or America.[21]

By all accounts, Jane was a formidable woman, even a forbidding one. In a book on Missouri governor's wives published in 1936, twelve years after her death, historian Nettie Beauregard, who had known Jane Francis from childhood, noted that Jane, unlike her husband, "did not like people in general," was "frank and outspoken," and "possessed of a keen sense of justice."[22] Like his father, David Francis married a strong-willed, intelligent woman whose position in society was above his.

The Perrys spent much of their time in the late spring, summer, and early fall at Perry Park, a four thousand-acre family resort on a working ranch in the eastern foothills of the Rocky Mountains south of Denver, a spectacular site. The adventurous British writer Isabella L. Bird was cantering through eastern Colorado in late October 1873 when she got caught in an unexpected snowstorm. She saw a path and rode along it two miles up into the hills, through a set of gates and over a rushing creek and, she recalled, "at the entrance to a most fantastic gorge I came upon an elegant frame house belonging to Mr. Perry, a millionaire to whom I had an introduction. . . . Mr. Perry was away, but his daughter [Jane], a very bright-looking, elegantly dressed girl, invited me to dine and remain."

After a fine meal of stewed venison, served by an "adroit colored table maid," one of five former house slaves who had stayed on with the Perrys as servants after Emancipation, Isabella Bird was taken on a horseback tour of the countryside. She judged it "among the finest scenery of Colorado."

After returning from her ride, Isabella Bird sat in front of a blazing fire with Jane Perry. The writer recalled, "I passed into a region of vivacious descriptions of Egypt, Palestine, Asia Minor, Turkey, Russia and other countries in which Miss Perry had traveled with her family for three years."[23]

About two years later, Upton Smith, a man who worked for the Perrys, was introduced to David Francis by Charles Perry, Jane's beloved older half-brother. Smith was asked to have the two best saddle horses ready at once because "Miss Jennie . . . had volunteered to introduce the twenty-five-year-old Mr. Francis to the beauties of Perry Park. And this was the program for several days. The weather was ideal and Mr. Francis and Jennie Perry put in full time as lovers, billing and cooing until business required his departure."[24]

David Francis and Jane Perry were married on January 20, 1876, in a chapel at Lucas and Garrison Avenues, catty-corner from the mansion of John D. Perry. The chapel was the temporary home of Central Presbyterian Church while a new church was being built nearby.[25]

On their wedding day, David Francis was twenty-six years old, Jane twenty-two. For the first few years of their marriage, they lived in modest houses on Morgan Street near his uncle and her father and often dined with one or the other family. Their first child, John Dietz Perry Francis, was born October 31, 1876.

The next year, on April 30, David Rowland Francis left his uncle's firm and went into the grain-commission business on his own, setting up offices in the new Merchants' Exchange Building. He soon became known, according to Walter Stevens, as a "very cautious and safe trader," one whose "accumulations were made slowly." Stevens is talking in relative terms; from the beginning, Francis leveraged his grain deals by making them on margin, committing money he would have to borrow if the deal went sour. His first big profit came on the purchase, on margin, of forty thousand bushels of oats—worth, in the gyrating markets of the late 1870s, tens of thousands of dollars.

That evening, a Friday, he mentioned the deal over dinner to his father-in-law and said that he was a bit worried that he might have to come up with a lot of money on Monday if the price dropped.

"If you need any help, let me know," said Perry. As it turned out, Francis had calculated correctly on the direction of the oat market and neither then nor in the future had to ask his father-in-law for money to meet a margin call.[26]

T HE YEAR DAVID FRANCIS WAS MARRIED, the city of St. Louis opened Forest Park, a heavily wooded 1,375-acre tract just west of Kingshighway. The regally named thoroughfare, at the time a wide dirt road running north and south about four miles from the river, was destined to replace Grand as the city-spanning boulevard as the elite moved west. Also in 1876, the city limits of St. Louis were fixed at about six hundred feet west of Forest Park, or about six and a half miles from the river. The city became a county within itself, separate from St. Louis County—several hundred square miles of land surrounding the city.

At the time, the separation of city and county seemed to make sense, and not just to the city's machine politicians, who did not want their power to be diluted. City taxpayers wanted to shield themselves from the notoriously inefficient county government and the burdens of building roads and bridges and providing aid for the 26,000 mostly impoverished residents of the much larger county. And there were still thousands of acres of farmland and pasture for development within the city's 61.37 square miles.

It did not become clear that a mistake had been made until well into the next century, as the tax base drifted into the county and its population came to far exceed that of the city. By then, it was too late—the suburban residents of the county had no intention of voting themselves back into the decaying, smoke-choked, crime-plagued city.

The 1870s also brought several ugly episodes of labor strife that, at times, verged on localized class warfare. The financial Panic of 1873 had set American industry into a frenzy of cost-cutting. Thousands of workers in the country's key industries saw their wages slashed, and the size of work crews was drastically reduced. On the railroads, crews were perilously undermanned, and the workers who remained had to work long hours of overtime without pay or lose their jobs. In 1877, when more cuts in manpower and pay were announced, strikes broke out in major cities across the country, spear-headed by railroad workers, and strikers battled police and militia in the streets. By July 1877, a million American laborers were on strike.

In late July, thousands of workers amassed at the Lucas Market on Twelfth Street and marched through the downtown St. Louis business district to the ominous wail and beat of fifes and drums. Radical speakers invoked the French revolution and the guillo-tine. Black workers from St. Louis and East St. Louis were prominent among the leaders of the strike and the march, arousing racial paranoia among well-off whites.

The *Missouri Republican,* a newspaper that by the Civil War had become the major organ of the Democratic Party in St. Louis (as the *Democrat* had become the principal voice of the Lincoln Republicans), railed at the strikers and focused in part on race, reporting on "distressing scenes of terrified women, rudely handled by brutal negroes."[27]

For several days, the strikers controlled the city, until a "citizens militia" of about six hundred men, led by the mayor, police officials, and platoons of foot patrolmen dispelled the crowds, luckily without anyone being seriously injured. There is no record that David Francis, busy making money and wooing and marrying the beautiful daughter of a very rich man, a man inclined to moderation and averse to any sort of street demonstrations, was involved; subsequent events suggest Uncle Pitt was at least a sympathizer.

The following year, partly in reaction to the general strike, fourteen prominent St. Louisans, including David P. Rowland, inaugurated an elite group that became the Veiled Prophet Order. At least five of the fourteen had been leaders of the antistrike mili-tia, including Police Commissioner John G. Priest and Leigh Knapp, an owner of the *Republican.*[28]

Inspiration for the parade, and the debutante ball that would follow it, came from the Slayback brothers, Alonzo and Charles, staunch Confederate supporters who had lived in New Orleans and wanted to create something like Mardi Gras in St. Louis. The public rationale for the Veiled Prophet Parade was to promote the fall harvest fair in Fairgrounds Park, but not far beneath the surface—and sometimes heaving above it—was the desire to put the lower classes in their place, to "take back the streets" in the ter-minology of a century later. The parade was led by a phalanx of saber-bearing police, who opened a way through crowds that packed the streets in the working-class neigh-borhoods. Just behind the flying wedge of policemen, a float bore the Veiled Prophet himself, accompanied by a man outfitted as an executioner hovering over a butcher's block. The first Veiled Prophet, and the only one identified by the organization in its long history, was Police Commissioner John G. Priest.[29]

By the time of the parade, the Veiled Prophet Order had about two hundred mem-bers. David Francis was not among the seventy-three names on record, although David Rowland was.[30] Within a few years when the memory of the general strike had faded, the organization had established itself as a way for the social elite to gather and honor their daughters, as well as a celebration of the St. Louis Fair, Francis had become an important member. For many years, as the city's leading citizen, he had the honor of escorting the queen of the debutantes into the ballroom at the Merchants' Exchange.[31] By then, Francis and other leaders had transformed the VP organization into a tool of the entrepreuneurs and civic reformers called "The New St. Louis."

Men from old French Catholics families, including, inevitably, representatives of the prolific Chouteau family, were members. The great majority of members were Protestants, men who had come to St. Louis from the South and East without a great deal of money and had quickly made or married some, but there were two or three powerful German Jews, men with Gentile business partners or close associates. More than half of the founding members of the VP organization were connected to trade in farm products, as brokers, processors, transporters, or insurers.

The Veiled Prophet Order reflected not so much Southern views as those of St. Louisans from both the North and the South who embraced the Calvinistic faith that the acquisition of wealth was a sign of grace.

On May 30, 1879, Jane Perry Francis gave birth to her second child, another son, David Rowland Francis, Jr. The following year, David and Jane built a large, three-story brick house at 16 Vandeventer Place, the newest and westernmost of the exclusive, gated "private places" that St. Louis is still known for, short stretches of street owned and maintained by the residents and closed to through traffic. As with most of the private places already built and soon to come, Vandeventer Place had ornate stone gates and a wide, grassy, tree-lined mall down the center. The large houses and mansions faced it, turning their substantial backs to the city outside.

Vandeventer Place occupied a three-quarter-mile block just west of Grand Avenue in the central corridor. West of it were scattered houses and farmland. Its residents were among the wealthiest families in the city—the John Dietz Perrys were practically next door at number 12. Both the Francis and Perry homes were built to order of St. Louis brick. They were rambling, turreted, and gabled near-mansions of two and a half stories.

On Vandeventer Place, all service had to be through the back alleys. If they wished, residents could live most of their lives undisturbed by the noisy, venal city to the east, although eventually they would complain that the very population growth and industry that had made them wealthy impinged on their privacy, bringing black bituminous smoke from the east and the clang of streetcars from Grand and other nearby thoroughfares, and they would move west again.[32]

At the peak of its prosperity in the 1880s, there were eighty-six large homes and mansions of brick and stone on Vandeventer Place, all of them attended by servants. The Vandeventer Place bylaws stated that houses had to cost thirty thousand dollars, but that stopped no one from spending much more than that. One mansion, with a staff of twenty-two servants housed separately a block away, reportedly cost eight hundred thousand dollars and included stained glass windows from Tiffany and an elevator that led up to a vast third-floor ballroom.[33]

About the time he moved to Vandeventer Place, David Francis brought Sidney, his twenty-three-year-old brother, to St. Louis to work for him as a clerk. Within a year he also had welcomed to the growing business twenty-seven-year-old Thomas, the brother who had agreed to stay on the farm so David could go to college. Both brothers lived with the Francises at 16 Vandeventer Place, as David Francis had lived with David Rowland.

In 1882, Francis bought a 125-acre farm in the low hills to the north of the city, on the present site of the small St. Louis County municipality of Pine Lawn. He moved his parents there from Kentucky. His father was sixty-three, his mother fifty-two. Other rich St. Louisans had country spreads nearby, miles from the merest hint of city smoke, and a narrow gauge railroad ran into the more fashionable parts of the city.

To what they called Uplands Farm, John and Eliza Francis brought their two youngest daughters: Mary (called Mollie), who was thirty, and Mahala (or Hallie), twenty-eight. Both would soon marry well-to-do St. Louisans. The rough experiences of childhood had made David Francis determined not only to pull himself up by his own bootstraps, but to pull his family up with him, and he never forgot sacrifices they had made.

His new family had grown, too. Third son Charles Broaddus Francis was born on August 23, 1880. He was named after Jane's late brother Charles, who had died in 1876 after being kicked to death by a horse at Perry Park. Talton Turner Francis, whose name also came from Jane's side of the family, followed on July 26, 1882. And on March 26, 1883, a fifth son was born. He was named Thomas Francis, after David Francis's grandfather and brother.

In 1883, the brokerage firm was reincorporated as D. R. Francis & Bro. Commission Co. Within a few years, an enthusiastic local historian said of the firm, "The operations of the house extend over the entire country, and immense quantities of wheat, corn, oats, barley, cotton, provisions, and pork are handled. A large business is also done in futures, in addition to an immense export trade which requires the maintenance of a branch house at New Orleans as well as the commodious offices in the Gay Central Building, at the corner of Third and Pine Streets."[34]

Francis steadily grew richer. His business instincts seem to have been those of a superb poker player, basically conservative, always calculating the odds and going for the best bet, but willing to risk a great deal on those relatively rare occasions when the odds strongly favored him. In poker, a sure way to lose is to bet on every hand. Four decades later, he shared this wisdom with his son, Perry. "Keep out of the market at times," he wrote from Russia. "Continuous trading is sure to result in loss."[35]

His first big triumph came one summer in the early 1880s when wild fluctuations occured in the wheat markets. At one point, wheat prices in St. Louis soared as high as thirty-five cents a bushel over the Chicago price. Almost alone among St. Louis traders, Francis sensed the market was about to turn and began selling in St. Louis and buying in Chicago, "pressing his credit to the utmost limit," according to Walter Stevens.[36]

The bubble burst in St. Louis, and wheat plunged to five cents below the Chicago price. Francis had timed the market perfectly. By the fall, he had made half a million dollars, the equivalent of $10 million in the year 2001.[37]

After a long, tense day in a stifling-hot building packed with frantic men battling to place orders, Francis often would head for one of the many taverns and hotel bars in the vicinity of the Merchants' Exchange. Memoirist Orrick Johns has listed some of the better known downtown haunts of businessmen relaxing and reporters looking for stories: "The Planter's and Southern Hotels; Spechts, the rendezvous of the Germans, and Tony Faust's. They were all just around the corner from each other, and the current flowed among them all day long. One bar was called 'Dave's Place,' because it was the favorite of David R. Francis."[38]

One of Francis's frequent haunts—perhaps it was Dave's Place—was Tony Faust's, a lavish Gilded Age bar and restaurant where men of substance drank German beers and regularly lingered for hours over ten-course meals, one dollar cigars, and French cognac. To the wonder and delight of its patrons, Faust's was the first place in St. Louis to be lit electrically.[39]

Faust had bought an electric generator and a system of lights (at one dollar a bulb) in 1878 at the third Exposition Universelle de Paris. World's fairs that demonstrated the era's new technology were becoming all the rage in Europe. By then, two world's fairs had been held in the United States, in New York and Philadelphia. But the greatest of the American fairs were yet to come. One would be in Chicago, the second in St. Louis.

CHAPTER 4

Entering the Political Arena

*The first time I ever saw St. Louis I could have bought it for six million dollars,
and it was the mistake of my life that I did not do it. It was bitter now to look abroad
over this domed and steepled metropolis, this solid expanse of bricks and mortar
stretching away on every hand into dim, measure-defying distances, and remember
that I had allowed that opportunity to go by.*[1]
—*Mark Twain, after an 1882 visit to St. Louis*

ST. LOUISANS, WHO RIGHTLY FELT THAT THEIR CITY was growing fast and prospering mightily, were shocked when the 1880 census figures were released. The census indicated that the city had grown by only forty thousand people in the past decade, despite the fact that the core city's streets and tenements were thick with recent immigrants, new buildings were going up all over town, and St. Louis had doubled its area only a few years before. The new census showed St. Louis with a population of only 350,000, while Chicago had leapt to 500,000, with a staggering population gain of more than 200,000. Chicago was now the Fourth City, and St. Louis had dropped back to sixth. (The top five, in order, were New York, Philadelphia, Brooklyn, Chicago, and Boston.)

Chicago shouted victory, and it was St. Louis's turn to cry fraud. But the 1880 population totals quickly were judged to be roughly accurate and the 1870 figures the bogus ones. To the irritation of local boosters, this fact was pointed out again and again by the *St. Louis Post-Dispatch,* the gadfly newspaper founded in 1878 by the brilliant, cantankerous former state legislator Joseph Pulitzer. Pulitzer, who had just been hornswoggled out of the Democratic nomination for Congress by the party's slick political boss, Ed Butler, went on what many saw as a personal vendetta against his adopted city. "And now," crowed Pulitzer in the *Post-Dispatch,* "after all her brag and blow, St. Louis sits in sackcloth and ashes, gnashing her teeth as the sixth instead of the fourth city of the Union."[2]

That kind of civic slander, combined with the *Post-Dispatch*'s tough-minded reportage of scandal—and the continual heaping of scorn on St. Louis's conservative financial institutions—went against the grain of Gilded Age puffery, although the emerging middle and lower-middle classes loved Pulitzer's mix of gossip, flaying of the rich, and hard-hitting investigative journalism. St. Louis business leaders were quite vocal about their dislike for this foreigner with Jewish ancestry, and Pulitzer in turn came to detest the St. Louis establishment with a lingering, simmering resentment that would affect his view of David Francis, particularly after the young grain dealer achieved the notable success in St. Louis Democratic politics that had been denied Pulitzer.

In 1882, the publisher's unpopularity among the St. Louis establishment further increased when Veiled Prophet founder Alonzo Slayback came into the offices of the *Post-Dispatch* looking for a fight, and feisty editor John Cockerill shot him dead. Pulitzer decided to get out of town for good, in part to escape what he saw as provincial small-mindedness but more to find a larger stage for his genius. He'd had his eye on New York for a while, and in the spring of 1883 he bought the ailing *New York World* from robber baron Jay Gould, who by then also owned, among many other things, the Missouri Pacific Railroad—heir to the boodle-laden Pacific. Pulitzer retained ownership of the *Post-Dispatch* and by no means forgot about it, as his memo-blistered editors discovered regularly, but he moved to New York, where he made journalism history.

By then, Chicago was shipping almost three times as much grain as St. Louis. Cynical St. Louisans began referring to their city in snide tones as "The Future Great," and the grandiose predictions of historical and zodiacal inevitability were dismissed as "The Great Illusion."[3] St. Louisans developed a deep and abiding civic inferiority complex.

Actually, only in its race with Chicago could St. Louis be considered a loser. St. Louis was still a major grain market, the third largest in the nation, and in wheat—David Francis's specialty—St. Louis was almost even with Chicago. St. Louis was also the country's largest manufacturer of, among many other products, house paint and plug tobacco.[4] Elsewhere in the country, except perhaps in the Windy City, St. Louis correctly was perceived as a growing, thriving metropolis (albeit in a backwards "Southern" state), with a strong grip on trade to the South and Southwest. And finally, it had good rail connections to the West.

On his 1882 visit, Mark Twain found a prosperous city, with "fine new homes . . . noble and beautiful and modern" on the outskirts of the old city, "where the dwellings . . . are packed together in blocks and are all of one pattern." Twain was enthusiastic about Forest Park: "It is beautiful and very extensive, and has the excellent merit of having been made mainly by nature." Even the smoke seemed to him to have diminished somewhat from the days when it used to "hide the sky from view." Still, Twain allowed, "There is a sufficiency of smoke. . . . I heard no complaint."

Twain saw one ominous development, symbolized by the disappearance from the fancy bars and billiard rooms of the "steamboat crowd," with their "swell airs and graces, and ostentatious display of money." On the levee, he found:

Half a dozen sound-asleep steamships where I used to see a solid mile of wide-awake ones! This was melancholy, this was woeful . . . a mile of empty wharves, a Negro, fatigued with whisky, stretched asleep in a wide and sound-less vacancy, where the serried hosts of commerce used to contend!

He mused further:

The towboat and the railroad had done their work . . . the ancient armies of drays, and struggling throngs of men, and mountains of freight, were gone. . . . The immemorial mile of cheap, foul doggeries remained, but business was dull. . . . St. Louis is a great and prosperous and advancing city; but the river-edge of it seems dead past resurrection.[5]

Just a couple of blocks west of those cheap foul doggeries, on a slow Wednesday in early January 1884, the gambling instincts of several hundred bored traders turned to the current race for president of the Merchants' Exchange. A small man with a large voice broke the unusual silence by shouting, "I bet 10 to 1 on Francis!" "I take you," was the shouted reply, and the race was on.[6]

By the end of the day, more than two thousand men had voted, and thirty-three-year-old David Francis had won by 121 votes over his main opponent, a cotton dealer. His victory celebration was held that evening in the vast main hall that opened more than eight years earlier, under the presidency of his uncle.

Francis climbed the president's rostrum, an almost ludicrously elaborate mass of hand-carved mahogany and walnut, and looked down on a long table of reporters and out over the 235-foot-long floor of the exchange. His colleagues, crowded around the hundreds of marble-topped commodities tables, stood and cheered. Sixty feet above him, on the elaborately frescoed ceiling, a fourteen-foot goddess symbolizing St. Louis stretched her arms wide, gathering in and distributing the bounty of the world.

Francis's first significant victory speech was, unlike some of those to come in later years, brief and modest. He said he was "thankful to all those who have so greatly hon-ored me," and remarked, "This election is not the result on any merit I possess; it is the untiring work of my friends. I appreciate that the responsibilities of the office are great and the duties are onerous and I ask you to give me your hearty support and be to my faults a little blind."

The new president was escorted across Fourth Street to the Planter's House, St. Louis's most elegant hotel, where a feast was laid out and the toasting and celebrating went on well into the night. The position he had been elected to, while partly ceremoni-al, also carried with it considerable power and responsibility. In a nineteenth-century way that Francis was comfortable with all his life—at times, probably too comfortable—the presidency of the Merchants' Exchange mixed private and public affairs, sometimes inseparably. Francis's duties included overseeing commercial licensing and grain inspec-tion, promoting the widening and the deepening of the Mississippi River and its tribu-taries, lobbying for a national bankruptcy law, and even representing the city and region in debate on federal tariffs and trade treaties.

Francis was also becoming involved in party politics.

Like his uncle, David Francis was a Democrat. Although there was a definite Southern tinge to the party in those days, with the scars of the Civil War and reconstruction still far from faded, the party also stood for reform in reaction to the mass corruption in the 1870s of "Grantism"—of which the phony St. Louis census count had been one small example.

Before the war had hardened ideological positions, the Democratic Party in St. Louis and Missouri had included a strong "free-soil" (i.e., anti-slavery) faction, led by the state's most famous politician, Senator Thomas Hart Benton. That wing reemerged after the war, led by men like David Rowland and, soon, David Francis.

While "men of property"—industrialists and those with inherited wealth—tended to be Republican, a large number of men in "trade" were Democrats, in great part because the Democratic Party stood for lower tariffs and thus freer international trade. Low tariffs and sound money were the bedrocks of Francis's economic beliefs throughout his life. Both principles were embraced by the business, or Bourbon, wing of the Democratic Party, which also supported low taxes (to be produced by political reform) and a minimum of government control.

Party lines were in great flux in the late nineteenth century, leading to interesting anachronisms in the names of two St. Louis dailies. The city's leading Republican paper, which had begun life as a pro-Benton, anti-slavery sheet, was called the *Democrat,* and the leading Democratic organ, which had started as a Whig sheet, was called the *Republican.* In 1875, after a merger with a like-minded paper, the *Democrat* became the *Globe-Democrat.* Thirteen years later, the *Republican* was renamed the *St. Louis Republic.*

Nationally, Bourbon Democrats of the 1880s coalesced around Grover Cleveland, who became governor of New York in 1882. He fought machine corruption and "boodling" and soon gained a national reputation as a reformer. Cleveland—with his platform of clean and efficient (and thus inexpensive) government, low taxes, a minimum of government regulation of business, and opposition to giant monopolies and protective tariffs—became one of David Francis's heroes and his early political inspiration.

In 1883, the St. Louis Democratic Party had tried to nominate David Francis for the City Council, but he declined. However, the following June, at the Missouri Democratic Convention, in the midst of a battle for control of the party between Democratic regulars and the reformist Bourbons, Francis was elected a delegate at large to the upcoming Democratic National Convention, defeating reactionary Police Commissioner John G. Priest. John H. Overall, a prominent St. Louis lawyer who also lived on Vandeventer Place, had nominated Francis as the candidate of "the young, vigorous Democracy of St. Louis," in opposition to the "old lawyers."

"D. R. Francis is a merchant," Overall said, "and the mercantile class should be recognized."[7]

In July 1884, Francis took the train to Chicago as a delegate to the Democratic National Convention. It was Francis's first real taste of party politics, and the thirty-three-year-old grain dealer was busy. When a group from Indiana visited the Missouri delegation to serenade it, according to the convention correspondent for the *Globe-Democrat* (probably Walter Stevens, who began covering national politics from the *Globe*'s Washington bureau that year), "Dave Francis made a neat speech in acknowledging the compliment, and said his delegation did not feel bound to anybody in particular, but would support whoever seemed to be the best candidate for the party when the convention reached a ballot."[8] The remark could be considered either politic or disingenuous—Francis and the majority of the delegation were there to vote for Grover Cleveland.

Although it was his first convention, Francis played a key role in running the delegation and in helping steer the nomination toward Cleveland, and clear away roadblocks. The independent *Post-Dispatch* wrote: "Tally one for the President of our Merchants' Exchange. Dave Francis had to show the Convention how to get through its work of organization in a business-like way."[9]

Cleveland won the nomination on the second ballot, despite fierce opposition within his own New York delegation from Tammany Hall machine politicians. As was the tradition, the nominee was not present at the convention, and Francis represented Missouri in the forty-eight-man notification committee that, several weeks after the convention, went to the governor's mansion in Albany to "tell" Cleveland he had been nominated and "invite" him to accept.[10]

At the convention, Francis got in the middle of a testy fight—a fight, according to the *Globe-Democrat,* that "overshadow[ed] Presidential preferences and the platform" for the state's delegation—over whether or not an old-line St. Louis Democrat named Joseph "Grif" Prather should be reelected national committeeman. Opposition to Prather among the insurgent Bourbon Democrats was headed by St. Louis industrialist and streetcar magnate John Scullin, who won the post.[11]

In the tangle of political battle, Francis strengthened what became a lifelong friendship and business and political association with Scullin. Also working with Scullin were two men who would have a great deal to do with Francis's political future: Charles Chouteau Maffitt, scion of a wealthy old St. Louis family who would become Francis's main political strategist, and Ed Butler, an Irish blacksmith and Democratic power broker who was sometimes referred to in mock Hibernian urban slang as "de boss of St. Louis."[12]

A young, wide-eyed St. Louis cub reporter named Theodore Dreiser described Butler as "an amazing person with a head more or less like that of a great gnome or ogre . . . more like a great hog than anything else . . . and yet with a manner as soft and ingratiating as that of an Italian courtier. . . . What force! What reserve! What innate gentility of manner and speech! He seemed . . . like a prince disguised as a blacksmith."[13]

The convention was followed by a nasty election campaign, with the Democrats accurately accusing Republican nominee James G. Blaine of wide-ranging corruption while serving as Speaker of the House during Reconstruction and the Republicans accurately accusing Cleveland of fathering an illegitimate child. Cleveland, single at the time, cheerfully admitted the charge. He won the election, with the vociferous support of Joseph Pulitzer's newspapers in New York and St. Louis.

Francis was already rich, and he must have found that the political arena, particularly in victory, could be at least as exciting and rewarding as the grain exchange. The next time the call to political office came, he was ready.

On March 25, 1885, 162 delegates assembled for the St. Louis Democratic Convention in the large hall of the Mercantile Library, a private businessman's library and club near the Merchants' Exchange. Not until 4:30 P.M. did they finish preliminary speeches and votes and got down to the main business—choosing their nominee for mayor of St. Louis. It would be, the *Post-Dispatch* judged when it was over, the "longest, most bitter and most exciting contest in the history of local politics."[14]

There were three candidates. Representing the silk-stocking, Bourbon wing of the party was Major C. C. Rainwater, a businessman and former Confederate officer. His main opposition was Judge Edward A. Noonan, a magistrate and professional politician. Holding the balance of power was lumber merchant R. M. Parks.

Francis was in the hall not as a delegate but as an observer who, publicly at least, supported his friend Rainwater. The delegates began casting their ballots by voice vote. On the first roll call, Noonan got sixty-three votes, Rainwater fifty-seven, Parks forty-two. A second vote was held—and a third, and a fourth. No change. The delegates kept going. Votes were held every five or ten minutes, and the men refused to adjourn for dinner.

After about fifty ballots, with little substantive change—Rainwater had picked up a few votes from Parks—Francis decided to go home. It was well after 9:00 P.M., more than two hours after his normal supper time. He had a bite to eat in the kitchen and went upstairs to bed.

The convention continued through the night, with the sleepy delegates growing irritable and resisting any arguments for compromise. Around midnight, after the eighty-seventh roll call had not changed the deadlock, a delegate named Thomas C. Hennessey announced that it was time for a compromise candidate, but, he said, he couldn't think of anyone.

Shortly past 3:30 A.M., on the 133rd roll call, exhausted delegates from the posh 18th Ward, which included part of Vandeventer Place, threw in a new name. They switched their twelve votes from Parks to David R. Francis, praising the popular young president of the Merchants' Exchange who, the summer before, had shone at the party's national convention.

The president of the convention rejected the vote. He reminded the delegates that no man could be considered for the nomination unless he had submitted a pledge to support the party's nominee no matter who was on the ticket. "All through the night," noted the *Globe-Democrat*, "the warring factions obstinately refused to give up their candidates. Every attempt to adjourn was hissed down, and when morning dawned it showed the maddest lot of politicians ever seen in St. Louis. . . . Hungry, sleep and worn out, they persisted."

Boss Ed Butler, whose lawyer son presided over the convention as the sun rose, was one of the few observers who remained awake. Always willing to partner up with the silk stocking candidates when it worked in his favor, Butler supported Rainwater, at least overtly. The corpulent blacksmith was relaxing after almost coming to blows with the sergeant at arms over some overly aggressive lobbying for Rainwater when someone remarked to him, "Those Noonan fellows are town painters, and they'll wear you out."

"Not by a damned sight," Butler replied gruffly. "The town painters ain't used to this kind of medicine. They want to be out and filling up at the bars. . . . We'll stay here with 'em for a month, if necessary."[15]

About that time, a document mysteriously appeared on the convention floor and was read aloud to exhausted cheers. It stated:

> Having been raised a Democrat, and in that faith I expect to die, I pledge
> myself to support the nominee of this convention.
> —D. R. Francis

At that moment, Francis slept peacefully in the master bedroom on Vandeventer Place. Although Francis often had said that he had been raised a Democrat and expected to remain loyal to the party through thick and thin, the note itself, and Francis's signature, were forged by two delegates desperate to resolve the deadlock. The president agreed to accept it.[16]

As the morning progressed, the balloting continued, and slowly Parks and Rainwater delegates switched to Francis. The Noonan supporters refused to budge. Finally, on the 182nd ballot, a little after ten in the morning, after almost nineteen hours of voice votes, Francis went over the top with ninety-two votes, winning the nomination and the lasting enmity of Judge Noonan and many of his diehard supporters.

By then, Francis was busy in the grain-trading pit of the nearby Merchants' Exchange. A little before 10:30 A.M., there was a shout at the door of the vast room.

"Francis! Francis!"

David Francis turned toward the man at the door. "What's that?" he shouted back.

"You've been nominated for Mayor!"

CHAPTER 5

The Boy Mayor

IT WAS A WHIRLWIND CAMPAIGN, with only twelve days between Francis's nomination and election day, April 7, 1885. As would be expected, Francis got the enthusiastic endorsement of the *Republican,* which predicted he would "stand apart from all 'rings' and political cliques and . . . discharge executive duties without fear or favor."[1]

The *Post-Dispatch,* beholden to no political party but generally leaning toward the Democrats, also endorsed Francis: "Mr. Francis has the great personal advantage of having the good opinion of all men. He is, it is true, impracticed in Municipal government and inexperienced in politics, but he has become widely and favorable known to the people by an acquaintance which, for so young a man, extends through a long period of years."[2]

Even the *Globe-Democrat,* in its endorsement of Republican incumbent William Ewing, spoke favorably of Francis before noting that he was a political neophyte and predicted that he would "find the political pit to be much more troublesome than the grain pit."[3]

There were no dramatic differences between the two candidates. Francis was younger and vaguely associated with reform, a new broom that might sweep clean. The grain merchant's lack of political experience was a bonus with many voters, who were disgusted with the political corruption that seemed endemic to city government, no matter which party was in power. The main issue of debate was the high cost of gas provided by the St. Louis Gas-Light Co., which had a monopoly on service to half the city. Both candidates declared they were for "cheap gas," without going into much detail as to how they would get it. However, Francis stressed this point: "I do not own, nor have I ever owned, one share of stock in any gas company in the City of St. Louis. Nor am I interested in any corporation whose interests have ever, or will ever, come in conflict with the best interests of the city."[4]

Francis campaigned by walking through the city—paved sidewalks in silk-stocking wards and muddy tenement streets alike—shaking hands and making friends, using his considerable charm and his salesman's gift of gab. Minor political functionaries and even ordinary voters were astonished at his ability to remember their names after a single brief meeting—a talent that would serve him well throughout his business and political life.

His was a fresh voice and a fresh (and handsome) face. Tall—6'2"—and slim, Francis by his mid-thirties had sprouted bushy sideburns and a large reddish-blond mustache that was curled and waxed upward at the end. He had a wide cleft chin, a high forehead, well-trimmed chestnut hair parted just to the left of center, and thick eyebrows above empathetic blue-gray eyes.

Francis wisely attached himself to the coattails of his hero, new President Grover Cleveland. The previous fall, many thousands of "mugwump" Republicans had broken with the party to vote for Cleveland, the reform candidate. And in St. Louis, former Congressman E. O. Stanard, a Republican stalwart, announced he would cross party lines to vote for his friend and protégé David Francis and said, "I think that many of Mr. Francis's Republican friends will vote for him out of personal considerations."

Some did, but Francis still was relatively unknown outside the Merchants' Exchange Building—on election day, the *Missouri Republican,* the organ of his party, printed his full name as "David Ryan Francis." It was a very tight race, but Francis squeaked through, 20,841 to 19,314. His victory, the *Post-Dispatch* declared, "was largely due to the prevailing wish and impression that he would make Cleveland's administration in Buffalo, Albany and Washington his model."[5]

A bit later, the *Post-Dispatch* discovered, to its dismay and lingering anger, that Francis's election also was due to the wily election-day shenanigans of Ed Butler and his rowdy tribe of "Indians," who could make the dead walk—and vote. More than once.

At the age of thirty-four, David Francis, "the Boy Mayor," took over a city whose population had reached four hundred thousand. The largest ethnic group was German, making up more than 40 percent of the population. The Irish made up another 20 percent.

The "scrubby Dutch" Germans, divided between Catholics, Lutherans, and "freethinkers," leaned toward the Republican Party, which had its own political machine, led by men who spoke English with thick, low German accents rather than rolling brogues. The Irish, almost entirely Catholic, were welded into a solidly Democratic voting bloc by Ed Butler, who held the key to city offices. Both groups were inordinately fond of beer, which, as Francis would discover, was not just a cultural preference but a powerful factor in their political decisions.[6]

On April 14, 1885, David Francis was sworn in as mayor. A bright young *Globe-Democrat* reporter named Mike Fanning twitted the new mayor with "a Democratic operetta," which featured Ed Butler declaiming to Dave Francis, "I hope you're satisfied with the election. . . . Of course, you know who did the little business?"

Francis replies, "Oh yes . . . I'll see you at the bank," and goes on to sing:

Ah Fortune, you've been kind to me (the luckiest of shavers)
Most kind in thus locating me at once 'twixt fame and gain.
So while I pay my money out for all these public favors,
I can thro' my business brethern get it back again on grain.[7]

David Francis was a wealthy man, but he had grown up in the rough and tumble of a rural county seat, where he had learned to deal with a variety of human types, and he was determined not to lose the common touch. One of the first duties he chose to impose upon himself was to meet daily with his constituents.

The St. Louis mayor's office was on the second floor of City Hall at Eleventh and Market Streets, on the western edge of the downtown business district. Every morning, after taking care of pressing administrative duties, he would leave the office and stroll a few blocks south to a massive, renaissance-style, three-story structure called the Four Courts Building. In a city courtroom, with the help of a crusty old police sergeant named Alexander B. McGrew and an officious, bewhiskered secretary named Lyndon A. Smith, both of whom he had inherited from his predecessor, he met the citizenry.

The *Globe-Democrat* sat in on one of the first sessions, as the wealthy grain dealer and rising star of St. Louis society, a man who had made half a million dollars over a recent summer, earned his salary of three thousand dollars a year:

People wanting everything, from a pair of shoes to a broken heart, go to the Mayor for relief, and as a consequence his Honor is brought face to face with some very queer people and some very interesting phases of life. Mothers who want their boys released from the Work House; wives who want their brutal husbands arrested; professional mendicants who seek to gouge the city out of a living, and crazy people who imagine that they are being persecuted, all flock to the Mayor. This role of magistrate appears to be new to Mayor Francis, but he assumes it with a great show of interest every morning, and indeed does honor to himself in it. . . .

Mr. Francis was crowded to the wall with callers yesterday. Towards evening he began to give in [and retreated to his private chambers off the courtroom]. . . . Commodore Smith, his side-whiskers standing straight out with indignation, pushed an angry man back from the door that led to the mayor's private room, and then went over to his desk and swore under his breath against the infernal mob that was always piling itself against the Mayor's private door.[8]

The *Globe* suggested that Commodore Smith was simply too valuable and well-entrenched to be replaced, but Francis soon got rid of him and hired as his secretary the man who wrote the satirical operetta, *Globe-Democrat* political reporter Michael Fanning. Francis was not above co-opting the press. He once remarked, "The power of the newspaper in politics is well known and I shall spare no effort to have it used in my behalf."[9]

He also liked and appreciated journalists—at least the smart ones—for their knowledge of the way things worked and the peculiar blend of cynicism and idealism it takes for them to do their job well. Like Walter Stevens, Mike Fanning would become part of Francis's extended professional family, and the two men would work together again.

"My private interests shall be put into the background," Francis promised.[10] Although he continued to make major business decisions, he turned many of his duties of D. R. Francis & Bro. over to twenty-eight-year-old Sidney Francis, who was vice president. Sidney still livied with his brother and sister in law and their five children on Vandeventer Place. Thomas, now thirty-one, worked at the firm as a salesman and lived nearby with his wife, Belle.

Under St. Louis's weak-mayor system, Francis had little control over the police, limited budgetary powers, and even was forbidden from making some major city appointments until he had been in office two years. And the bicameral Municipal Assembly was split between a Democratic City Council and a Republican House of Delegates. Francis found power outside the traditional channels, and he scored a notable early victory because of his financial expertise and his lifelong willingness to blur the line between public and private affairs. After a well-publicized visit with financiers in New York, he managed to pressure local money men down to a remarkably low interest rate of 3.65 percent for a new bond issue to pay off city debts, partly a result of jacked-up gas rates for street lights and city buildings. The interest rate was the lowest ever paid by the city and astonishingly lower than the prevailing rate of 6 percent.[11]

After that coup, even the *Globe* supported Francis.

Francis kept the honeymoon alive by playing politics as if it were a particularly important poker game. An ordinance passed cutting telephone rates in half. The local Bell company balked at the new rates. People who refused to keep paying the old ones one day discovered that their phones were dead—the phone company had removed the boxes that connected them to the system. So Francis ordered city workers to take down telephone poles and wires in areas where service had been cut off, arguing that there was no longer any need for them. The telephone company quickly put the boxes back in and restored service, while the courts worked out a reasonable compromise.[12]

The first six months of Francis's administration went swimmingly. Then, in early October 1885, thousands of streetcar drivers and workers from the militant Knights of Labor went on strike for a ten-hour day. When the owners refused to negotiate and hired nonunion replacements, the strike turned ugly. Mobs swarmed over the horse and mule-drawn streetcars, yanking the nonunion drivers out of the cabs, turning the long wooden cars over in the street, and sometimes literally ripping them apart. Drivers and even passengers were beaten.

The strike was timed to coincide with a time of peak ridership—the week of the St. Louis Fair in Fairgrounds Park. Thousands of people had to walk home from the fair when strikers blocked the Grand Avenue line. Francis, who had become a director of the fair organization, was not the only one who found this outrageous. The fair was very important to St. Louisans.

Early in the strike, a "scab" was killed, gutted by a knife. The next day, a policeman protecting a car was surrounded by an angry mob hurling bricks and paving stones. He shot and killed a striker.[13]

Under Missouri law, the St. Louis Police Board controlled the police. The Police Board was appointed by the governor, with the mayor only an ex officio member.[14] In response to the fighting in the streets, the board appointed five hundred "special police-men" who rode the cars. They were volunteers, many of them prosperous businessmen: Francis's neighbors. Francis was not directly responsible for this move and later tried to give the appearance that he had maintained an air of neutrality, but during the heat of battle he made statements that the Knights of Labor considered tantamount to strike-breaking. For example, he said on October 12:

> I have spared and shall spare no effort to protect the property and lives of citi-zens as well as that of the different street railway companies. . . . There is a state law which calls the overturning or destroying of cars, tearing up tracks, etc., a felony for which the punishment is not more than 20 years in the peni-tentiary, and I mean that the rioters be punished for that offense.[15]

The strike dragged on. Finally, in November, after a woman passenger was shot and killed in a gun battle between police and strikers and five strikers were arrested for blowing up streetcars, the Knights of Labor called off the strike. The strikers won noth-ing, but for years organized labor nursed a grudge against David Francis.

At this point, David Francis probably did not hold a significant amount of streetcar stock (later he certainly did), but he was a friend, neighbor, and business associate of men—like John Scullin—who owned large blocks. This was not the last time that David Francis took a "pro-business" attitude in a labor dispute, although he would have con-tended that his position was against anarchy and fighting in the streets. Like Grover Cleveland, he was clearly a businessman's sort of Democrat.

In December 1885, the gas dispute that had festered for years came to a head. Under franchise agreements with the city, St. Louis Gas-Light Co.'s exclusive right to sell gas to homes and businesses in the southern half of the city included City Hall. Another local-ly owned company—Laclede Gas—had the right to provide gas to the northern half of the city, but that franchise was not exclusive.

For more than a decade, rates had been about the same in both areas, but in 1883, a third company, financed with eastern money, came into the picture. It was the St. Louis Gas, Fuel and Power Co., known colloquially as the Water Gas Co. for the new method it used to produce natural gas. It began competing with Laclede Gas in north St. Louis, driving down the price. The result was that south St. Louisans paid almost twice as much for gas as north St. Louisans. The *Post-Dispatch,* also south of Washington Avenue, the dividing line, repeatedly denounced St. Louis Gas-Light as an unjust monopoly that fleeced the public. Virtually all the press demonized owner Socrates Newman.

The eastern interlopers from the Water Gas Co. proposed to solve the problem, and get rid of all competition, by a radical change in arrangements. In 1890, when all current contracts expired, the Water Gas Co. proposed to accept a thirty-five-year grant to sell gas to the entire city at $1.25 a thousand cubic feet, lower than anybody currently paid.

Late in November, with all three companies throwing sheafs of boodle around, both houses of the city legislature approved the offer, and the bill was sent to Mayor Francis for his signature, which seemed certain to come. But Socrates Newman made a very tempting counter offer. If Francis would veto the bill, Newman's St. Louis Gas-Light Co. would reduce its rate to $1.50 on January 1, 1886, and to $1.25 on January 1, 1890.

Francis vetoed the bill in favor of Newman's offer, which would give south St. Louis cheaper gas almost immediately.[16] In retrospect, Francis's decision seems to make sense. However, at the time, "Soc" Newman and his company were so widely and fiercely detested for their gouging that much of the press and public saw Francis's decision as a sellout to the forces of evil. The House of Delegates, the lower house of the city legislature, immediately and unanimously overrode the veto, and a few weeks later the City Council voted to give the eastern Water Gas Co. the city's gas franchise in 1890.[17]

But that left four years to go. So Francis successfully pressed Newman to reduce his company's rates anyway. He may well have known that, for practical reasons, a regulated monopoly over an essential service like gas was inevitable, and he wanted it to be a locally controlled monopoly. And sure enough, in 1889, three years after all the furor and a year before the Water Gas Co. was scheduled to take over service in all of St. Louis, all the gas companies merged into one: Laclede Gas Co., which continues to hold a monopoly.

Francis had chosen a judicious, business-like compromise over an appeal to popular emotions. He also had favored local business interests over outside ones, as he would over the years, which could be considered enlightened self-interest, since what was good for St. Louis business was, directly or indirectly, good for David Francis.

No sooner had the furor over gas begun to abate than the *Post-Dispatch*, which had been in Francis's corner, began hammering him for acquiescing in voter fraud. His former opponent, William Ewing, came up with compelling evidence that in Democratic wards controlled by Ed Butler and his cronies boxes had been stuffed with phony ballots.

Eventually, a few ward heelers were charged with election fraud. Democratic lawyers, including Ed Butler's son, shrewdly kept the scandal from ever coming close to the mayor's office, at least in legal terms, and Francis maintained the high ground by refusing to dignify the charges with a response.[18]

When necessary, Francis worked with Boss Butler, just as four decades later across the state in Jackson County, administrative judge Harry Truman would work with the breathtakingly corrupt Boss Tom Pendergast. The Boy Mayor quickly learned to take a practical approach to politics, and he seems to have learned a lot from Ed Butler, although Butler never had as much power over the mayor as he sometimes boasted.[19]

Francis seems, like Truman later, to have worked with the machine without being unduly corrupted by it. He seems to have stayed clear of the boodle that flowed through the city in noisome spurts like the flood-prone River des Peres. The best evidence of Francis's clean politics is that he was not touched fifteen years later when crusading circuit attorney "Holy" Joe Folk swept like a cyclone through St. Louis and indicted dozens of politicians (including Ed Butler) and businessmen for offenses going back a number of years. Folk was no respecter of persons, and he and Francis were political enemies to boot. (For a full discussion of Francis and Folk, see chapter 8.)

Still, after the voter-fraud charges surfaced, the *Post-Dispatch* turned on Francis.

The *Post-Dispatch* was becoming one of America's great newspapers. One of its strength was its aggressive pursuit of political corruption wherever it appeared, an approach fueled in part by Pulitzer's lingering resentment of his shabby treatment by the St. Louis Democratic machine. In that strength, in a usual, paradoxical way, lay a failing—the inability, from the 1880s until very late in the twentieth century, to recognize that big-city political machines and "bosses" grew in response to real needs of poor people and immigrants and lasted in power only if they succeeded in filling those needs, whether they be for asphalt in a pothole, a leg up for a relative looking for a job at City Hall, or the kinds of giant public/commercial projects and undertakings—like rapid-transit systems and highways and world's fairs—that poured millions of dollars into the economy.

On March 6, 1886, with the *Post-Dispatch* still yelling for Francis to stop stalling and stonewalling and let the voter fraud see the light of day, the Knights of Labor called another strike, this time against Jay Gould's railroads.

A BIT OF HISTORICAL RECAPITULATION IS NECESSARY HERE. Completion of the Eads Bridge in 1874 did not put an end to the transportation of goods and passengers by ferry, but it did result in a price war between the expensive toll bridge and the ferries. At the same time, in the aftermath of the Panic of 1873, many overextended railroads went into default. In 1875, pressed by stiff competition from the ferries for declining rail traffic, the bridge company fell into bankruptcy. The company eventually was leased to the Missouri Pacific, which came into St. Louis from the west, and the Wabash, which entered from the east. Both systems were controlled by Jay Gould, a shrewd and thoroughly unscrupulous speculator whose nearly successful attempt, with Jim Fisk, to corner the market on gold had been one of the earliest major scandals of the Grant administration. Gould moved on from gold to railroads, gutting some to buy others.

By 1886, Gould controlled thousands of miles of track spreading out to the south and west from St. Louis, which he envisioned as a rail hub to rival Chicago. Pitted against Gould were the Knights of Labor, an early attempt to unite all American workers in a big national union. An ideological precursor to populism, the Knights stressed the rights of "native Americans"—not Indians, but men and women born in the United States. The Knights opposed the wave of millions of immigrants who came into the country in the last decades of the century and took jobs at radically low wages. By 1886, the year of the strike, the Knights had grown to seven hundred thousand red-blooded Americans.

The strike, triggered by the firing of a worker in Texas, began on March 6 and quickly spread north and east, shutting down Gould's operations in St. Louis and effectively cutting the city off from all rail trade west of the Mississippi. Gould's Missouri Pacific reacted by firing the strikers and hiring nonunion replacements. The Missouri Pacific asked for police protection in the St. Louis yards, and the St. Louis Police Board, with support from Mayor Francis, supplied it, providing an escort of one hundred policemen for the first train to head out of St. Louis after almost three weeks of strike. Francis said, "My course in this matter has been to assure the railroad that it could run as many trains as it desired—one every hour, if it so chose—and that it would be free from interruption."[20]

There was little violence in St. Louis, although across the river in East St. Louis, Illinois, seven men were killed in an April 9 battle between strikers and militia. After that, a congressional committee investigating the strike, asked the Knights of Labor to call it off for the public good. Losing anyway, the Knights accepted defeat—and began to die as an effective force. Not coincidentally, the same year, the more conservative American Federation of Labor began its rise.

Francis testified at congressional hearings on the labor violence and stated that "the City Government took no official action in any way terminating the strike; my idea has been that it was my duty to preserve the peace and protect life and property; the relations of employers with employees I consider beyond my province."[21]

Most union leaders, and many other working people, failed to see the difference between protecting life and property and guarding strikebreakers, and Francis soon would feel the wrath of labor. Once again, he had demonstrated his horror at disruptive tactics and violence, as well for his distaste for anything that interfered with commerce in St. Louis. But he was equally horrified by Jay Gould, and the strike had shown how easily one man could bring the city to a commercial halt.

Gould controlled not only the bridge, but also the rail terminals on both sides of the river and most of the tracks going in and out of them. He charged exorbitant rates for passengers and freight to steam across his bridge. Francis and other wealthy St. Louisans began talking about trumping Gould and his so-called "bridge arbitrary" by building a new bridge at Bissell's Point, three miles north of the Eads Bridge. The idea was that the Merchants' Exchange, or at least a large group of its members, would own the bridge, to be called the Merchants' Bridge. Francis argued that its completion would result in "abolition of the bridge arbitrary which has been one of the greatest incubi St. Louis has labored under for years, costing us about $1 million annually."[22] These words would come back to haunt Francis many years later. The Merchants' Bridge was not completed until the winter of 1889–1890, and even then, as will be explained in subsequent chapters, it did not end the bridge arbitrary.

After the strike ended, Jay Gould turned up the heat on a plan he'd been simmering for months, a plan that would further concentrate his power over St. Louis rail traffic. He proposed to build an elevated railway system through downtown St. Louis to the Union Depot, about twelve blocks from the levee. The catch was that the tracks would be controlled by the Iron Mountain Railroad, which Gould owned.

Gould's boodle flowed through City Hall, and after feasting on it, the Municipal Assembly passed a bill approving his proposal. On July 8, Francis vetoed the bill, a move that was very popular with the public and the major newspapers. The *Post-Dispatch* cheered Francis on and admonished the few naysayers who suggested Gould might retaliate: "Even Jay Gould does not revenge himself on his rebellious subjects by cutting off his own resources, and St. Louis is too important a railroad center to be ignored by any of its existing systems."[23]

In July 1886, the *Republican* barely could contain itself and stopped just short of again proclaiming St. Louis "The Future Great City of the World," thanks to the Boy Mayor:

> The administration of Mayor Francis is contemporaneous with a new awak-
> ening of enterprise in St. Louis. With new buildings going up on every street,
> a new bridge in prospect, a chance for railroad competition and the grandest
> autumnal festival ever seen in the United States [the fair], the town will be in
> a position to reach for everything in sight.[24]

Francis seemed to have regained confidence and a second wind, and he began to use his considerable talents as a speechmaker to consolidate his popularity. There were audible murmurs among the powerful that Francis would make a good governor.

In April 1887, as major city jobs came open, David Francis paid a political debt by naming James J. Butler—Boss Ed's son—city attorney. But he infuriated other party regulars by reappointing a competent street commissioner and several other Republicans to key jobs. He turned down a chance to appease Noonan, whose bitterness lingered from the long battle for the nomination, by refusing to appoint the judge's brother-in-law to the post of superintendent of the City Hospital, going so far as to describe the fellow as "a drinking man and totally unfit for the place."[25]

In response to his intraparty critics, Francis outlined what could be considered a tenet of his philosophy of government:

> Political parties have always existed in republics and they will and should
> continue to do so, but the great mass of the people in a municipality hold
> good government above party issues. A city government is a business corpora-
> tion as it were in which the citizens are the stockholder, the interests and wel-
> fare of whom should be the constant air of its officers. An administration
> should be surrounded and sustained by its friends, and there should be a
> party affinity between the head and its branches if it can be brought about
> without injuring or jeopardizing the public interest.[26]

Battles with Judge Noonan continued. Noonan ruled that the state's Sunday saloon-closing law, pushed through the state legislature by its rural majority, did not apply to the sale of beer or wine. The city, backed by Francis, appealed the ruling to a higher state court, and when the ruling was overturned, Francis strictly enforced Sunday closing. This infuriated party hacks, saloon keepers, and brewers.

Francis was hardly a prohibitionist, but he supported strong regulation of saloons. Populist Democrats called him a hypocrite. With his club memberships and the ample liquor cabinets at his house and at the homes of his friends, David Francis never had a problem getting a drink on Sunday. But working men, with what was left of Saturday's paycheck in their pockets, had to make do on their only full day off with sarsaparilla and fancy ice cream dishes (called "sundays").

Further battles with the Noonan wing erupted in the winter and early spring of 1887, and the judge scotched rumors of détente: "When you hear of an armistice being signed by Christ and the devil, you may look for a peace conference between me and Dave Francis. Things have gone too far for that, quite too far." [27]

Francis's alliance with Ed Butler helped him through these rough times in the party. Paradoxically, he was seen as battling the city Democratic machine, and that was viewed favorably in rural Missouri, where St. Louis was thought to be an unredeemable den of iniquity.

Francis also impressed Missouri and gained a modicum of national fame by taking the lead in a political dance that began in the spring of 1887. The Grand Army of the Republic (GAR), a national organization of Union veterans, had scheduled their annual "encampment" for St. Louis in September of 1887. In February, the local arrangements committee, which was headed by Francis, decided to invite Grover Cleveland to the encampment. Francis led a delegation to Washington to tender the invitation, and on March 29 the president agreed to come. But his plans ran afoul of one of the acrimonious Yankee-Rebel skirmishes that continued to break out for decades after the Civil War officially had ended.

Cleveland already was viewed with suspicion by many members of the predominantly Republican GAR for halting highly questionable medical pensions to former Union men who had left the service healthy, part of the immense pork-barrel apparatus left over from Grantism. Then, late in May, in an attempt to further heal the wounds of the war, the president agreed to return all captured Confederate flags to their home states. In response, the national commander of the GAR, Lucius Fairchild, literally cursed the president of the United States: "May God palsy the hand that wrote that order! May God palsy the brain that conceived it, and may God palsy the tongue that dictated it." [28]

Cleveland quickly rescinded the order, but that did not still the enraged protests of GAR leaders, one of whom said that if Cleveland dared to show his face in St. Louis during the encampment, "There is a good prospect of there being trouble . . . if they want fighting, by God, we can give 'em some of that."[29] In late June 1887, with many GAR posts threatening public disrespect to the president if he came, Francis returned to Washington. He proposed a stratagem to turn the embarrassing dilemma into a triumph: the president should find it necessary to delay his visit and come in early October, when St. Louis put on its annual Fair and Veiled Prophet Ball and Parade. By then, the GAR literally would have pulled up stakes and left town.

The president immediately saw the wisdom of Francis's proposal. On July 4, Cleveland wrote a public letter to Francis regretting that he had to withdraw his acceptance of the invitation, saying he wanted to avoid coming to town and stirring up "unfriendly feeling" that could disrupt "an occasion which should be harmonious, peaceful and cordial."[30]

On July 23, after rallying enthusiastic support in St. Louis and across the state for the later Cleveland visit, Francis led another delegation to Washington on a special five-coach train. The side of one of the coaches was covered with a white canvas sign that read, "The people of Missouri invite the President to visit St. Louis." Not coincidentally, most of the other men on the train were Democratic political leaders from across Missouri, and some of them were subject for the first time to Francis's considerable personal charm and persuasiveness. One of them subsequently reported that of the sixty men along for the ride, fifty-five now would support Francis for governor in the next election.[31]

Not, of course, that Francis was running for governor.

Cleveland enthusiastically welcomed the visitors from Missouri and officially accepted the invitation to come for St. Louis's fall festival, remarking to Democratic Senator George Vest of Missouri, "That mayor of St. Louis is a bright young man." Francis promised the president a relaxing visit, telling him in a follow-up letter, "My residence is in a private park and you can have all the quiet you desire."[32]

In late September, Francis welcomed the Grand Army of the Republic, fifty thousand strong, by making a plea for the "obliteration" of the sectional lines that had led to "the spilling of so much fraternal blood" and a reuniting of the country. On the evening of Saturday, October 1, Francis, in his fanciest carriage, was driven to East St. Louis and met the train bringing the huge-jowled, mustachioed president and his pretty young wife. (The previous year, in the White House, the forty-nine-year-old Cleveland had married his former "ward," Frances Folsom, who was barely twenty-one.) They all rode into St. Louis across the Eads Bridge and through downtown, mobbed with cheering people, including many former Union soldiers who had stuck around, to the tree-lined hush of Vandeventer Place. In honor of the visit, Francis had installed a gold chandelier in the drawing room of number 16.[33]

Sunday was a day of rest, with the afternoon broken by a leisurely drive a couple of miles south to the seventy-five-acre Missouri Botanical Garden. The garden was not open to the public on Sundays, so the presidential party had the garden, with its thousands of trees, shrubs, and flowers, to themselves on a lovely, blue-skied fall day—a wave of hot, stormy weather had left town with the GAR.

On Monday morning, Cleveland was greeted at the St. Louis Fair by the cheers of thousands of school children, and at the Merchants' Exchange by the huzzahs of thousands of businessmen. That evening, forty thousand Democrats paraded through downtown St. Louis. The rising young mayor of St. Louis was on the reviewing stand, by the side of the popular reformist president of the United States.[34]

On Tuesday, the last day of the visit, Cleveland viewed the floats and elaborate costumes of the Veiled Prophet Parade, and Mrs. Cleveland was guest of honor at the Veiled
Prophet Ball that followed. The Clevelands watched from a balcony box as David Francis
led the masked Veiled Prophet and his gaudily dressed entourage into the great hall of
the Merchants' Exchange.[35]

The visit was a rousing success, and much discussion followed about Francis's
potential next step, one towards the governor's mansion. Statewide support was crucial,
since no mayor of the state's dominant city ever had managed to overcome the taint of
urban sin and corruption and get elected governor in the predominantly rural "Show
Me" state. After the Clevelands had headed back to Washington, the *Post-Dispatch* sur-
veyed leading Democratic-leaning newspapers across Missouri and came up with the
"surprising" conclusion that the leading candidate for governor was political neophyte
David Rowland Francis, finishing above such other likely candidates as popular
Missouri Supreme Court Justice Elijah H. Norton and Lieutenant Governor Albert P.
Morehouse.

Francis still hedged his bets. He wrote thank you notes to the editors who had put
him in the lead, saying he appreciated the compliment but stressed that he had not
announced that he would run for governor.[36]

Privately, he worried that his growing wealth would damage his political future and
remarked somewhat defensively to a friend, "I am not a millionaire but . . . I see no crime
in it if I were and it is not my fault that I am not as I have worked hard all my life to earn
a competency and whatever I do possess I have secured by my own exertions. If that is
a crime I plead guilty." [37]

Though perhaps not a millionaire, he was very close to it, at a time when that was a
relatively rare distinction.

In December 1887, according to a letter he sent to a New York banker, his personal
holdings included seven hundred shares of Laclede Bank stock, selling at $110 a share,
and a variety of other valuable stocks and bonds, including county bonds in Missouri
and Texas, railroad and cattle-ranch bonds. His unmortgaged real estate holdings he
valued at more than one hundred thousand dollars, including the house at 16
Vandeventer Place.

In addition, D. R. Francis & Bro., which he essentially owned, was valued at one
hundred thousand dollars, had a surplus of fifty thousand dollars, and earned an average of more than fifteen thousand dollars a year, which was plowed back into the business.[38]

His total holdings, at least those he chose to report in the letter, came to about
$825,000, or the equivalent of $16 million in the dollars of 2001, remarkable for a still-
young man who seventeen years before had moved back to St. Louis with a carpetbag
full of clothes, a few dollars in his pockets, and $450 in debt.

Within a couple of years, he was unquestionably a millionaire, and by January 1893,
his fortune had reached more than $1.5 million. It kept growing.[39]

All his life, Francis, like many rich men who rose from meager circumstances, would be cheap in small ways, yet at times surprisingly generous. He constantly worried about minor family expenses, as well as Jane's not so minor pursuit of fashion in clothes, furniture, and social entertaining. He kept his sons on strict allowances and seldom picked up a drink tab. And yet, in the early winter of 1887, he decided that city employees should not be forced to wait until after Christmas for their last paycheck of the year. He loaned the city seventy-five thousand dollars of his own for a couple of weeks so their families could have a merry Christmas. It was the sort of gesture, a mixing of public and private funds, that would be repeated time and again in his political career and sometimes be misunderstood.

THE DAY AFTER CHRISTMAS 1887, the fifty-five-year-old governor of Missouri, former Confederate General John S. Marmaduke, collapsed with pneumonia. Two days later he died, and Morehouse became governor. Suddenly, it seemed, Morehouse was the leading candidate for next year's election. He would have a full year to campaign as the sitting governor, an almost unprecedented advantage, because state law prohibited elected governors from succeeding themselves.[40]

Francis, who had been on the verge of publicly announcing his candidacy, drew back to see what would happen. At the beginning of February, Judge Norton and Morehouse met, and on February 5, Norton announced the withdrawal of his candidacy. The next day Morehouse said he was running. Francis got the definite impression that Norton had promised to support Morehouse. Still, on February 15, Francis announced he would run, too, having decided that Morehouse was still beatable.

The day after his announcement, Francis left St. Louis at the head of another delegation to Washington—this time to secure the 1888 Democratic Convention for St. Louis, a project Francis had been working on behind the scenes for months. After a week of glad-handing and lobbying with the Democratic National Committee by Francis and friends, the party announced it indeed would hold its convention in St. Louis that summer. Walter Stevens was by then the *Globe-Democrat's* Washington correspondent and almost certainly the author of a non-bylined story reporting the Washington trip in great detail and remarking that Francis was taking "a considerable stride ahead of his competitors in the race for the governorship of Missouri."[41] (One of the numerous slurs against Francis in the upcoming gubernatorial election was that Francis and friends had shipped a carload of whisky to Washington to win the convention.)[42]

While in Washington, Francis visited with Grover Cleveland and gained some gawkish respect back home by escorting the vibrant young First Lady to the opera, even attracting the attention of the New York papers, one of which reported, "Mayor Francis is tall and thin, with blue eyes, red mustache, hearty manners and the air of a man at home in every possible society. He wore a rough and ready suit, shaggy overcoat with collar partly turned up behind, silk hat, black satin scarf and enameled pansy for a pin."[43]

Asked on his return if his friendship with the First Lady had helped secure the convention, he remarked, presumably stifling the urge to grin boastfully, "I don't think so. That was altogether a social matter. She was at my house when here and she knows me." [44]

On March 15, Francis began his active campaign in Springfield in southwestern Missouri, speaking to a convention of county political leaders trying to promote immigration to the sparsely populated Ozarks. He called for cheaper and more efficient transportation in general and, in particular, for using the perennial surplus in the federal treasury to build and improve roads. The speech went over well, and one listener called Francis "about the best rough-and-tumble speechmaker in Missouri." [45]

Morehouse backers spread a story that Francis had gotten drunk in Springfield. Francis had never denied his enjoyment of good Kentucky-distilled bourbon, particularly if bottled in St. Louis—he once accompanied a gift case of St. Louis–bottled Old Crow with a letter extolling it as "a beverage so delicious to the taste, so invigorating in its effect, and at the same time altogether harmless when used with discretion." [46]

Francis dismissed the drunk story as ridiculous and told a newspaper editor who had printed it, "I was not only not drunk upon that occasion but never was drunk upon any other occasion." [47] The statement that he had never been drunk in his life, one that he repeated over the years, may have been a slight exaggeration, but the evidence suggests that Francis was never more than an enthusiastic social drinker—although he was certainly that. David Francis could hold his liquor, and he had contempt and pity for those who couldn't. Toward the end of the campaign, in an apology for a Democratic supporter who had shown up drunk at a political affair, he said, "He is one of those unfortunate men who cannot drink without getting drunk. . . . I have no more use for a drinking man than you have; I was never in that condition myself." [48]

The liquor rumor did Francis little apparent harm—it may have helped with certain raffish elements in St. Louis and Kansas City. When it began to appear that Francis easily would defeat Morehouse, rumors surfaced that Morehouse might withdraw in favor of Judge Norton. Francis wrote a friend and supporter who was influential in the party, "Please do not let Morehouse withdraw from the race. Do not quote me but encourage his friends to think he stands a fair show of getting the nomination. I'm afraid if he withdraws, a stronger man might be put in his place." [49]

But another candidate suddenly announced he was running: St. Louis Congressman John M. Glover, who was two years younger than Francis (Morehouse was fifteen years older) and very popular. Glover quickly earned the support of the *Post-Dispatch,* which began referring to Francis as "a grain gambler" and "the candidate from the grain pit of the Merchants' Exchange." [50]

The *Globe-Democrat,* noting that Morehouse had stayed in the race, had a different response. It ran a cartoon of Francis standing on a platform labeled with such words and phrases as "Integrity" and "Clean Record." In front of the platform stood Glover, robed as a vestal virgin, his features grotesquely distorted, preparing to throw a clod of dirt. Behind him stood Morehouse holding a club saying, "That's right Johnny. You make faces at him and throw dirt, while I sneak around and hit him in the back." [51]

The campaign was a bitter one, filled with vituperation and sometimes disintegrating into fist fights and brawls. Francis was even falsely accused of the most horrible of sins—having voted Republican in a presidential election.[52] But slander and outrageous behavior on both sides tended to cancel out.

Francis lamented that his duties as mayor were making it "impossible for me to devote more than two or three days out of the week" to outstate campaigning, noting that "there are 114 counties in the state of Missouri and I am sadly in need of a pair of seven-league boots in order that I may get around." [53]

He managed, traveling thousands of miles by train and horse and buggy, taking time off in early June to play host to the Democratic National Convention, which renominated Cleveland. By early August, he had a commanding lead. The state convention to choose the party's candidate was on August 22 in Jefferson City. The hall in the capitol building was decorated with giant pictures of Grover Cleveland, who had stayed at David Francis's house and whose wife had gone to the opera with him. John Glover stepped out of the race, perhaps sensing the inevitable (although the fine Irish hand of Ed Butler might be glimpsed in the background, giving him a bit of a shove). By a large majority, David Francis won the Democratic nomination for governor, and one newspaper editor who had opposed him observed that the "real reason" he had been chosen was "his personal magnetism and popularity. It was hard even for Mr. Francis's opponents to keep from falling in line for him after once meeting and conversing with him." [54]

It had been a tough five months, but what followed was a political campaign so ugly and vicious that, for a time, it soured David Francis on the electoral process, and he vowed to friends he never would run for public office again.

WRITER CHARLES DUDLEY WARNER, who had first visited St. Louis in 1853, came back in 1888, the last year of Francis's mayoralty, and found the city had changed profoundly. Thirty-five years before, he had seen a poor, dirty city "hindered in municipal improvement by French conservatism, and touched with the rust of slavery. . . ."

"Now," he wrote, "everything is changed as by some magic touch. The growth of the city has always been solid, unspeculative, conservative in its business methods . . . preserving always something of the aristocratic flavor of 'old families' accounted 'slow' in the impatience of youth. But it has burst its old bounds, and grown with a rapidity that would be marvelous in any other country."

Warner had co-authored with Mark Twain the scathing satirical novel *The Gilded Age*, and his pen could wither the paper it scrawled upon. But in St. Louis he found, to his startled delight, a "cheerful town," prosperous and throbbing with "fresh energy." Industry and trade thrived, the railroads had created a vast transportation hub, and the city parks and botanical garden were a joy to visit. But, he decided, St. Louis's "chief distinction lies in its social and intellectual life. . . . I am told by men and women of rare and special cultivation that the city is a most satisfactory one to live in, and certainly to the stranger its society is charming." [55]

B Y THE SUMMER OF 1888, Francis effectively had turned over administration of the city to the president of the City Council and ran full time for governor. Mike Fanning became his private secretary and functioned essentially as a co-campaign manager, along with Francis's friend and near contemporary, the politically astute Charlie Maffitt, a wealthy descendent of the Chouteau family.

Newspaper assessments of Francis's term as mayor already had begun. They tended to be positive, no matter which party the paper favored, although attacks by Francis's enemies within the St. Louis Democracy continued unabated. A pro-Noonan sheet called "The Critic" issued a lengthy and scathing denunciation, focusing on his "betrayal" of the party by appointing Republicans to important posts. The paper contended, with some justice, that "the masses [in St. Louis] are opposed to Francis's candidacy . . . there is absolutely no enthusiasm in the city for Mayor Francis outside of the Butler ring and his own appointees." [56]

In the aftermath of the Democratic nomination, the *Post-Dispatch* said it had supported the defeated Glover because Francis's administration "was identified with the interests of ward bossism, of forged registration lists, stuffed ballot boxes, convict election judges, and political skullduggery of every kind."

However, the *Post* continued:

> We will, in justice to Mr. Francis, say that he has made a good Mayor. He
> made certain bad appointments to reward the men who put him in office. . . .
> But he showed courage of a very high character in his dealing with the gas
> question and with the terminal franchises, and if he has not introduced any
> striking reforms in municipal administration, he has enforced honesty,
> secured efficiency and avoided scandal, and he is entitled to credit for his
> active work in bringing the Democratic Convention to St. Louis.[57]

The *Post* declined to endorse either candidate at this point. Francis did receive the almost giddy endorsement of the Democratic afternoon newspaper, whose name recently had changed. In May 1888, Floridian Charles H. Jones purchased one-third of the closely held stock in the *Missouri Republican* from owner-publisher Charles Knapp. On June 1, Jones changed the name to the more logical *St. Louis Republic*. The Democratic paper remained a supporter of Francis for a time—the *Post-Dispatch* took to calling Francis "the editor's mascot"—but soon there would be a falling out between Francis and the prideful "Colonel" Jones.[58]

Francis had been a strong, pragmatic mayor, willing to compromise and work with the other party. He had drawn down the city's debt, significantly lowered the interest it paid on bond issues, and cut the budget. With the help of his Republican street commissioner, he set in motion major programs to build roads and viaducts, to pave streets, and to regularly "sprinkle" city streets that still had dirt surfaces.

Perhaps his major lasting achievement, not particularly controversial but crucial to the future of the city, was signing contracts for the Chain of Rocks waterworks, twelve miles above the Eads Bridge and several miles upriver from any city sewers. The city had suffered through several serious cholera epidemics over the past couple of decades. When the Chain of Rocks plant began pumping water about six years later, the water was finally safe to drink, although still notably murky.

Francis was not a relentless reformer, like some city officials a bit later, but he worked within the existing system without being noticeably soiled by the corruption around him. He gained experience and confidence during his years in City Hall, and his actions showed it. Some of Francis's decisions favored business and thus helped his own financial cause, since he was deeply invested in St. Louis banks and companies. But, as the major papers acknowledged, he left the city a better place when he stepped down as mayor.

Cyrus P. Wallbridge, a Republican mayor of the mid-1890s, said of Francis many years later, "His value is not to be judged by what he did in the office [of mayor] but by what the office did in him. It prepared him for the big things he has done since." [59]

FRANCIS RAN AGAINST an unremarkable country lawyer named Elbert D. Kimball, whose fervent core of support within the Republican Party came from Union veterans and their supporters—Kimball was state commander of the Grand Army of the Republic. Francis focused on the rural voters, who dominated the Missouri electorate, and often identified himself with farmers by saying, "I was raised on a farm. I have followed the plow. Today my father is a farmer. Today I am trying to farm myself, but find that farming is so unprofitable I am compelled to do something else as well in order to raise money to pay the taxes." [60]

Technically, he owned not one farm but two—in 1884, he had bought 377 acres of farmland in the southwest part of the city as a real-estate investment. But he was far from a farmer, and he took a lot of kidding about his professed closeness to the soil. Opposition papers took to calling him "Farmer Francis," and there was mock-bucolic doggerel aplenty. One satirical epic joked that Francis's farm was so small he had to bring it inside when it rained to keep it from getting wet. It was, the newspaper poet quipped, just about big enough to serve as Francis's funeral plot when the gubernatorial campaign was over. [61]

Francis deserved some of this joshing, yet it is also true that he had grown up among farmers. His brief and unpleasant stint behind the plow had, if anything, taught him to respect farmers and realize how hard they worked. Francis had a Jeffersonian faith in the small farmer as one of the keys to the success of American democracy. And he truly detested price-fixing monopolies that skinned not only farmers, but also the other group he considered to be at the core of a free and democratic society—the small merchant. [62]

In rural locales, he ran against big city corruption:

It is true that there is some opposition to me in St. Louis. I have incurred the ill will of the railroads because I have vetoed several ordinances providing for terminal roads wholly in the interests of monopolies.

I am opposed by a certain portion of the Democrats of St. Louis, because, believing them and their friends unfit to hold office, I refused to appoint them or their friends to prominent positions.

I am also opposed by the liquor interests of St. Louis because, after two years of hard fight, I have succeeded in stopping the selling of liquor on the Sabbath, and have closed on Sunday every place where liquor can be retailed, from the largest beer garden to the lowest groggery.[63]

Since St. Louis reporters followed him on his long train trips, and he knew his speeches were going to be quoted back home, Francis almost seems to have written off a large part of the St. Louis vote to win decisively outstate—more than 75 percent of the Missouri voters lived in rural areas. Francis campaigned hard, taking few breaks from his constant traveling, visiting each of Missouri's 114 counties several times. He became well known for his affable charm and his remarkable politician's memory for faces and names. He would go into a Democratic campaign headquarters in a remote county seat, meet a dozen or two people at a brief reception, and return several weeks later able to greet them all by name.

Francis came home only when he absolutely had to, as when he needed to be at City Hall for the Municipal Assembly's annual budget debate. Four weeks before the election, on October 8, 1888, he rushed home for the birth of his sixth and last son. He and Jane named him Sidney Rowland Francis.

As the days grew shorter and cooler and the leaves began to turn, the campaign grew increasingly bitter on both sides, with some political rallies broken up by fist and club-wielding thugs from the opposing party. In St. Louis, with a growing almost exclusively Republican black population and an even faster-growing population of poor Southern whites who were fervent Democrats, the fights were often along racial lines.

Francis and Grover Cleveland, who was running for reelection against Benjamin Harrison, both campaigned against the controlled high prices maintained by the trusts and monopolies that ruled the Gilded Age, as well as the high tariffs that protected American manufacturers and further inflated the prices of goods. Francis attacked restrictive tariffs in general, but he said that if "any class needs protection, it is the farming class" and noted that American farmers had to buy expensive American manufactured goods while competing against farmers in countries like Russia and India, where farm labor cost just a few cents a day.[64]

He stopped short of arguing in favor of protective tariffs for farmers, who had seen the price of corn and wheat decline by more than half in the two decades since the Civil War. But he suggested that eliminating tariff protection for manufacturers at least would put everyone on an even footing. He even suggested that farmers "could" form their own association—their own monopolistic trust—to limit agricultural production and thus drive up prices. In his standard speech, though, he ended this discussion by saying it would be wrong for farmers to do so. Francis appeared to be trying to have his cake and eat it too, simultaneously proposing radical action and then suggesting it was a bad idea. Nonetheless, as it turned out farmers were far too independent minded (as Jefferson had hoped) to do anything so concerted as fix farm prices.[65]

Francis's opposition to protective tariffs for manufacturers was, like other key positions, much more popular in rural Missouri than in the growing industrial center of St. Louis.

Election day finally rolled around on November 5, and not a moment too soon for an exhausted David Francis. Kimball had gained supporters in St. Louis with disturbing rapidity, and a couple of minor candidates, representing the Prohibition and Union-Labor Parties, threatened to siphon more votes from the Democrats than from the Republicans. And, shortly before the election, the *Post-Dispatch* decided that Francis was just too cozy with Butler and his machine to be trusted with the governorship. Pultizer's paper urged voters to split their ticket, voting Democratic in the presidential race but Republican on the state and local level.[66]

By the time the ballots were counted across Missouri, Francis had squeaked through with a tiny plurality of thirteen thousand out of more than a half-million votes cast. In the city of St. Louis, however, he lost by ten thousand out of about sixty-one thousand cast, actually polling two thousand less than Grover Cleveland.[67] (Cleveland won the national popular vote, but he lost in the Electoral College to Benjamin Harrison.)

This time, it appeared, the Republicans had won the city's battle of ballot stuffing—hundreds of transient stevedores from the levee were paid to walk up into the city and vote under phony names. But, as usual, plenty of cheating occured on both sides.

As expected, Francis received few votes from the city's growing African American population, who were loyal to the party of Lincoln. Francis also lost some of the Democratic vote in the city because of his anti-labor reputation and his opposition to Sunday saloon drinking. And the city's wealthy manufacturers, fighting to keep protectionist tariffs, spent thousands of dollars to defeat the Democratic ticket in St. Louis and Missouri.[68]

David Francis, nonetheless, became the first St. Louis mayor to be elected governor of Missouri. More than a century later, at the beginning of the twenty-first century, he remained the only one.[69] That astonishing fact suggests the enduring distrust of St. Louis politicians by voters from the rest of Missouri. Shrewdly, Francis, with the help of Mike Fanning and Charlie Maffitt, seems to have realized that the only way he could win the state was to lose the city. Still, when exactly that happened, he was deeply bitter about losing in his own hometown and remained so for a long time.

A week after the election, he wrote a political friend, who had suggested he move to friendlier Kansas City, that he would probably keep his permanent residence in St. Louis, "if for nothing else to repay the treacherous Democrats who knifed me on Tuesday last on account of personal or fancied grievances."[70] He said, "I think that the annals of Missouri politics will show that no man was ever subjected to so much abuse and made the object of so many slanderous attacks as I have in the campaign just ended."[71]

And four weeks later, he lamented, "I am not thoroughly satisfied that the game was worth the candle. The annoyances of official life, to say nothing of its labors and responsibilities, [tend] to disgust a man of business." [72]

On Christmas Day, he reacted to widespread reports that his next race would be for the United States Senate by stating, "It is my intention now to retire from political life when my term as governor expires and devote myself to my family and business."[73]

CHAPTER 6

The Youngest Governor

O N JANUARY 14, 1889, David Rowland Francis became the youngest sitting governor in the United States.[1] He was thirty-eight and still lean and lanky, with a full head of hair.

The swearing-in ceremony, at noon at the state capitol in Jefferson City, was witnessed by dozens of Francis's family, friends, and supporters, including Jane Francis, the five oldest sons, the two brothers and two sisters who lived in St. Louis, and David Pitman Rowland. They had arrived early that cold, sleety morning from St. Louis in a special train of three Pullman cars.[2]

Many years later, Francis said that he had been very nervous about public speaking until the World's Fair of 1904.[3] Still, by all accounts, he was a gifted and eloquent speaker long before that. The speech he gave that inaugural day was a brief but rousing one, and applause and cheers rose from the assembly hall, which was packed with members of both houses of the legislature, top state officials, and judges.

The predominantly rural legislators cheered as he attacked "monopolies and trusts" that "moved solely by a love of gain, unfettered by the duties of citizenship. . . . The result is the crowding out of all healthy competition and the survival of the strongest, which, under this process, is by no means the fittest."

The speech was a bit of a dancing act, as Francis slid to the left and then quickly skipped back to the right. "In avoiding the Scylla of disintegration," he proclaimed, evoking the standard Homeric metaphor of the middle of the road, "let us not run into the Charybdis of a centralized despotism. . . ." After calling for tough enforcement of liquor laws to control "the corrupting influence of the saloon on the morals of the community and the politics of the country," he added, "The broadest liberty consistent with the welfare of society, the peace and good will of the community, is the unquestioned right of the individual."

He urged electoral reform to insure that voters could cast "free, unbiased ballots"— in those days, in Missouri and much of the nation, ballots still were printed and distributed by political parties and politicians—and outlined an ambitious list of programs he wanted the 35th General Assembly to enact, from boosting education to encouraging immigration into Missouri's wide-open spaces. In conclusion, he pledged to work for "the interest and welfare of all classes" and to be "actuated by patriotic rather than partisan motives."[4]

That evening, David and Jane Francis held a reception in their new home, the executive mansion, a tall, graceful, three-story brick and stone house about two blocks from the capitol, on a bluff overlooking the Missouri River. The mansard-roofed mansion was built in 1871 in a French-Italianate style, with thick granite columns at the portico provided from the quarries of sitting governor B. Gratz Brown. It had seven bedrooms on the second floor and six bedrooms and a huge billiard room on the third. The first floor, which was entered through the seventeen-foot-ceilinged Great Hall, was devoted to reception parlors, a large library, and a magnificent dining room. Marble fireplaces were in almost every room.

Jane was "still convalescing from a recent illness" during the inauguration, according to a firsthand report.[5] Perhaps she had not recovered from the aftermath of giving birth three months before. Also, she suffered from respiratory ailments.

At 8 P.M., after she had bathed and dressed for the evening, a slight, light-skinned, blue-eyed, nineteen-year-old African American man in formal attire carried her down the gracefully curving Grand Staircase, whose railings and pedestals were wrapped in ropes of evergreen, and placed her in a chair in a reception room in the back parlor. She remained in her chair until eleven that evening, receiving guests with her husband, their families, political allies and their wives, and Mike Fanning, who stayed on as Francis's private secretary. The new governor once again amazed and delighted his hundreds of guests with his ability to remember their names.[6]

Jane Francis, who was thirty-four, was beautifully and, for mid-Missouri, daringly dressed in a low-cut, sleeveless black velvet gown with a gold thread necklace around her neck and gold pins in her hair. She held a bouquet of yellow Noisette roses. Attending her, elaborately gowned and laden with roses, were fashionable young women she had brought with her from St. Louis.[7]

At the end of the reception, when the orchestra struck up a festive tune and dancing began, the young servant with the café au lait complexion picked Jane up from her chair and, holding her in his surprisingly strong, wiry arms, carried her upstairs to the master bedroom. The man's name was Philip Jordan. He had been recommended to Francis by former governor Joseph W. McClurg, who had employed him on a steamboat.[8]

Jordan had been born in the black section of Jefferson City, a few blocks from the capitol and the executive mansion. He had grown up, either as an orphan or without noticeable parental control, in a tough back street called Hog Alley, where drinking, gambling, and fighting with fists and knives were routine. He had, in part, cleaned up his life, but still, from time to time, he would head back down to Hog Alley, a short block and a half south of the mansion.[9]

It would be several months before Jane Francis felt well enough to climb the long staircase herself. Jordan carried her downstairs for the receptions that were held almost weekly when the legislature was in session and carried her back upstairs when the last guests went home. He became deeply devoted to Jane Francis, and she to him.

Jane discovered that Jordan was illiterate, and she began teaching him to read and write. He learned quickly. Despite his youth, "Phil" quickly became the family's principal servant. In the warmer months, he prepared elaborate picnics to be served below shade trees on the banks of the nearby Moreau River, a pretty little tributary of the Missouri. Jane Francis led the way in a high-wheeled cart driven by a black coachman, followed by a hay wagon carrying the Francis boys and their friends and by Jordan riding a pony. After lunch, Mrs. Francis and the boys climbed into a small boat, and Jordan rolled up his pants, pushed the boat up the shallow, slow-moving river, and then let it drift back down to its starting point. The younger Francis boys came to adore Philip Jordan.[10]

One morning, after he had been working for the Francises for about a year, Jordan served breakfast to Francis when the governor sniffed a familiar bouquet. "Philip, do I smell liquor?"

"I guess you do, Governor," Jordan replied. Francis pressed the point, and Jordan admitted he had taken a nip that morning. He also noted that he had been drinking since he was twelve years old. Angry, Francis told Jordan he wouldn't permit servants to drink on duty and was in the process of firing him when Jane Francis, who had overheard the conversation from an adjoining room, came bursting in, shaking her head and murmuring, "What a pity, what a pity."

She asked Jordan to step into the hallway and pleaded softly, "Can't you promise to quit drinking?"

Jordan replied, "I don't know, because I never tried."

"Well, can't you try?" she insisted. Jordan promised he would try.

"Then go right ahead with your work," she said. "The Governor is master at the capitol, but I am mistress in the mansion, and I have faith in your promise."

Jordan tried to keep his drinking under control, but it seems clear now that he was an alcoholic, and he couldn't resist going back to Hog Alley from time to time, addicted not just to liquor but to the wild side of life. Francis, although also fond of Jordan, threatened to fire him several more times when he fell hard off the wagon, but Jane Francis insisted that he stay.[11]

JEFFERSON CITY was in the rural center of Missouri, about three hours by rail from both Kansas City and St. Louis. The city's dominant structures included the domed capitol and the hulking brick-and-limestone Missouri State Penitentiary. The city's dominant industry, then and now, is government, including penal work.

The capital's population in 1889 was about eight thousand. Jefferson City had very much the feel of a busy rural county seat (which it was). In the streets and cafes, particularly when the legislature was in session, the drawling Southern accents of Little Dixie, the Ozark Mountains, and the Bootheel competed with the harsher tones of recent German immigrants and the brogues of Irish politicians from St. Louis and Kansas City. Jefferson City also had a sizable black population, much of it in the old downtown within a few blocks of the capitol.

Jane Francis disliked Jefferson City. She thought of it as a backwater, with some justification. It was legal to let livestock roam free in the capital until the summer of 1888. And to her disgust the mansion was in bad shape, only half furnished, with frayed rugs, sagging floors, and water-damaged walls peeling paint. A sign on the porch read, "The bell is broken . . . walk in and touch the bell on the table."

Inviting a committee of legislators to tour the mansion, she shamed them into appropriating eleven thousand dollars for renovation. Jane planned the renovations in detail and then, late in the winter, headed for St. Louis so she and her children would not have to live on a construction site.[12]

In early March 1889, after the bulk of the renovations were completed, she moved back to Jefferson City with the two youngest children, the baby Sidney and four-year-old Charles. The other boys remained in St. Louis to attend school—Jane Perry Francis certainly would not have her sons educated in Jefferson City. They probably stayed with their grandparents, dividing their time between the city mansion of the Perrys and the north St. Louis County farm of the Francises. The boys came to Jefferson City in the summers and, often, on weekends and school holidays.

She shipped her furniture to the mansion, and the Vandeventer Place house was sold for $47,500.

Jane Francis was "a woman of the world, while in no sense a worldly woman [who was] peculiarly fitted to grace what was the most brilliant social administration in the Mansion's history," wrote socialite/historian Nettie Beauregard, who knew Jane from childhood.

"Unlike her husband, Mrs. Francis did not like people in general," Mrs. Beauregard observed. "In spite of this, she made a lasting impression as a charming hostess; she had a distinct individuality and this was stamped upon all the acquaintances she formed in the performance of the trying duties which fell upon her."[13]

When Jane moved back in, electric chandeliers had replaced old gaslight fixtures, city water and plumbing had been extended to the second floor, where the main bedrooms were, new French-glass doors had been installed at the front entrance, and the soot-covered pink brick exterior received a coat of dark red paint. A new Steinway grand piano sat in the music room.

In a portrait painted at the time and still hanging in the foyer of the mansion, Jane is quite pretty, with full, wide lips, and large luminous eyes. Her hair, reddish brown with short bangs over her high forehead, is pulled back and pinned so it almost appears bobbed in a style that wouldn't become popular for another three decades or so. Her strong chin and the somber set of her lips play off an ineffable sense of sadness in her face, as if she is resolute about heading into a future not particularly to her liking.

Jane Francis made new friends with difficulty, but she managed to find a group of a half-dozen women in Jefferson City who became what she called her "Women's Cabinet."[14] It was not easy for her to play the gracious hostess for the man she loved and had married. Jane and David were very different people. Like a lot of successful salesmen and politicians, David Francis was optimistic, outgoing, and happiest amid a crowd, preferably an adoring one. Jane loved being alone. For the renovation, she had designed two stained-glass bay windows for the Nook, a cozy alcove tucked under the curving, dark-wood stairway. She loved spending hours reading in the Nook. By the time Jane Francis had shipped all of their books from St. Louis, the main library on the first floor of the mansion contained nearly two thousand volumes.[15]

A**FTER HIS INAUGURATION**, David Francis immediately set to work on his ambitious agenda, putting in long hours in his office in the capitol while his brothers and a few trusted employees back in St. Louis ran the business. He told an associate, "I cannot afford, for six months at least, to pay much, if any attention to business affairs. After becoming familiarized with the office of governor, I understand that I shall have considerable leisure."[16]

The expected leisure never really came—in part because Francis always found new projects to fill his spare time—although his reasoning is understandable. The legislature met only every other year. He had to work fast, while the legislators were in town for the 1889 session, or wait until 1891. It wasn't going to be a cakewalk—although the Democrats held comfortable majorities in both houses, some of the most powerful Democrats, including the Speaker of the House, actively had opposed his nomination.

A quick and typically self-assured act early on seemed to have set the tone of his relationship with the legislature. He proposed sending a delegation of the Missouri National Guard to New York for the celebration of the centennial of George Washington's inauguration. The National Guard was unpopular among many of the Southern-leaning legislators, a carryover from the hatred of federal troops during the Civil War, and the house refused to appropriate the money for the puttee-clad troops they called "spider-legged dudes."[17]

Francis obviously put a lot of stock in such celebrations. As the date of departure approached, he ordered 340 members of the guard and its forty-piece band to assemble at the Union Depot in St. Louis. Francis had hoped the legislature would come through at the last minute. When it didn't, and a railroad agent demanded the fare, Francis signed a personal note for almost twelve thousand dollars in train fare for nearly four hundred people. He climbed aboard and joined the troops for the trip to New York. It was a popular move, and the statewide applause got the attention of the legislature, which quickly reimbursed Francis.[18]

Francis was attacked for this move by the *Post-Dispatch*, which promoted an alternate George Washington centennial celebration in St. Louis. He wrote the new editor of the *St. Louis Republic,* Charles H. Jones, urging that they join forces to fight the *Post.* Francis noted that the appearance of disciplined troops in the East might help to dispel the popular notion that Missouri was a lawless, sparsely settled wilderness, an attitude that rankled him greatly. Also, he remarked, "If we doggedly persist in withholding from participation in this celebration we cannot expect other states to join with us in any interstate celebration which we may originate in the future." [19]

The sort of interstate celebration Francis had in mind soon became apparent. In the summer of 1889, Francis began pushing for a world's fair, to be held in St. Louis in 1892, commemorating the 400th anniversary of the Columbus landing. He formed a committee of twelve prominent St. Louisans, including Colonel Jones, to begin lobbying for local and federal support. The seeds of the 1904 World's Fair were thus planted.

Early in his term, Governor Francis took a tough stand that cemented his reputation for independence and political courage.

He was under heavy public and political pressure to grant clemency to three convicted killers who were members of the "Bald Knobbers," Ozark vigilantes who, according to legend, met on the treeless tops of hills in the dark of night.

The Ozarks had been settled by Scotch-Irish emigrants from the Southern Appalachians. They brought with them a deep-seated mistrust of authority and a preference for settling disputes and dealing with criminals among themselves. In the lawless years right after the Civil War, the Bald Knobbers served as informal protectors of common people. But by the 1880s they had evolved into thieves and murderers, marauding nightriders who evoked frequent comparisons to the Ku Klux Klan. In 1888, a jury in the town of Ozark, Missouri, sentenced four Bald Knobbers to death for the cold-blooded murder of two innocent men during a midnight raid on their family's cabin. [20]

Francis's predecessor, Governor Morehouse, had ducked the controversy by staying the executions until he had left office. On the day of Francis's inauguration, the *Nevada* [Missouri] *Democrat* remarked, "The best part of the past three weeks has been spent by Governor Morehouse in pardoning criminals and handicapping his successor." [21]

Wives and relatives of the killers pled for mercy. They stirred sympathy across the state and particularly in southwest Missouri. An Ozark jailer purposely left a cell door open, and one killer escaped.

Francis was bombarded with clemency petitions for the three remaining Bald Knobbers signed by thousands of Missourians, including a majority of the 174 members of the General Assembly. Delegation after delegation came to his office to plead for mercy, at least once bringing tears to Francis's eyes. Even the judge and prosecutor of the original trial urged commuting the sentence to life imprisonment. So did the *Post-Dispatch.*

The executions were set for May 10. As the date approached, Francis debated the issue with himself late into the nights. He was used to making snap decisions about the price of grain, or the cost of natural gas, but this was the first time men's lives were in his hands. Finally, on the morning of May 8, after a long night's pondering, he made up his mind. Of overriding importance, he decided, was that the murders were premeditated and ruthless. The men deserved to die.

The Bald Knobbers had killed innocent people, he announced, "not in the heat of passion on the highway in open day but after apparently well-formed judgment at the solemn hours of the night, and at the fireside of the family. The sanctity of a home was invaded and the blood of those who had laid down in peaceful slumber within their own dwelling places [was shed]. The attack had little provocation, and no reasonable explanation."

Francis also argued that the time had come to make a stand against anarchy and vigilante organizations like the Klan: "The epidemic of lawlessness which has broken out in various parts of the country in the guise of self-styled regulators, and which in this state has found expression in Bald Knobberism, should be suppressed." [22]

Francis had another somewhat less noble motive. In the aftermath of the Civil War, outlaws like Frank and Jesse James had treated Missouri as their bloody playground. To encourage investment and immigration, Francis wanted to dispel the notion back East that there was no law west of the Mississippi. Some historians have criticized him for, in effect, making a decision about men's lives on economic principles. [23]

The killers were hung on schedule. The tough decision helped strengthen Francis's political hand. He became a hero to many Missourians, and the legislature was less inclined to resist a governor who was becoming so popular. Not that he abandoned political gamesmanship. He and Jane regularly had legislators over for dinner in groups of twenty, and he made a point of having lunch with key committee leaders as decisions on important legislation approached. [24]

Through a combination of firmness and charm, Francis began pushing his programs through the General Assembly, which soon approved:

- State anti-trust legislation providing fines for monopolistic suppression of free trade;
- A standardized "Australian ballot" printed by the state that would list all the candidates and make it easier to vote in secret;
- Creation of a grain-inspector's office to prevent farmers from being cheated on weights by unscrupulous operators of grain elevators;
- Stronger state supervision of such state institutions as mental hospitals and the school for the blind. [25]

But the cause that stirred him the most, from the beginning of his four years in office, was the state's public university at Columbia, thirty-five miles north of Jefferson City. Although he had graduated from a private university, Francis was always a strong supporter of public education at all levels, and he once said, "Every Missouri boy and girl should be permitted to get within the borders of the state and at the expense of the state an education as thorough and as advanced as in provided by any state in the Union or country on the globe." [26]

Throughout his political life, one of Francis's core beliefs was that capitalism could not coexist with true democracy without freedom of opportunity, the key to which was good free public education. Francis had a Jeffersonian faith in the educated common man. Many years later, from Russia, he would write a friend, "The small land owner and the little merchant are the very backbone of our institutions and the source of our strength. We are now realizing the benefit of the universal education system adopted in every one of our states. If the Russians had been better educated and less oppressed they would not have been so easily misled by the Bolshevik doctrines."[27]

When Francis took office, the University of Missouri was in turmoil. President Samuel Spahr Laws, a God-fearing Southern autocrat, hired staff and faculty on the basis of their religious beliefs and made erratic and arbitrary administrative decisions. He was disliked by professors; several prominent ones resigned during his tenure. And students hated him for his Puritanical intrusion into the minutiae of their social lives. In disgust at all the discord, the legislature virtually had abandoned the school, refusing to approve appropriations for expenses ranging from departmental budgets to the purchase and taxidermy stuffing of the corpse of a circus elephant that Laws foolishly had acquired for the university museum.[28]

Francis broke the impasse by appointing a strong new board of curators representing every part of the state and both major political parties. Previously the board had been dominated by curators from the areas of Columbia and Rolla, where the Missouri School of Mines was located. His appointment of two Republicans to the nine-member board infuriated party hacks. But the bipartisan, statewide board pushed Laws into resigning, made peace with the legislature, and after a two-year search, came up with a new president, Richard Henry Jesse, a professor at Tulane University who would be considered one of the great leaders in the history of the university.[29]

THE LEGISLATURE ADJOURNED on May 24. Francis had been so successful in his four months of dealing with this raucous bunch of lawyers, small businessmen, farmers, ranchers, and political hacks that there was already talk in the St. Louis papers of Francis running for the U.S. Senate in 1892, before his gubernatorial term expired. Still bitter about the governor's race, and with Jane Francis quietly adamant about returning to St. Louis when they finally could escape Jefferson City, Francis repeatedly denied he had any such ambitions. The election in April of his political nemesis Judge Noonan as mayor of St. Louis couldn't have helped his mood or his chances of political support in his hometown.[30]

With the legislature gone home, Francis had the time to pursue what was becoming his biggest dream: to bring the Columbian Exposition to St. Louis in 1892. He met with his committee of twelve, and they agreed to expand to two hundred. That summer, the larger group unanimously elected Francis president, and intensive lobbying began to persuade Congress to approve funds making St. Louis the site of the fair—rather than Washington, New York, or Chicago, all of which wanted it. Francis and his new friend Colonel Jones of the *Republic* went to Washington in November and opened a St. Louis headquarters in the Willard Hotel, where they lavishly entertained and lobbied members of Congress.

Francis spent much of the late fall and early winter in Washington and New York, trying to drum up political and financial support for a great fair to be held in Forest Park. In late February 1890, he was in the East when two blows struck almost at once: Congress chose Chicago to play host to the Columbian Exposition, and Edward T. Noland, treasurer of the state of Missouri, was caught dipping deeply into state funds to finance a gambling binge.

Francis took the next train back to Jefferson City, suspended Noland, took over the treasurer's office, and after ascertaining that more than thirty-two thousand dollars was missing, forced Noland to resign from the elective office. Noland claimed the charges were merely political, and Francis initially took some heat. Later, the treasurer admitted his accounts were short, and he eventually was indicted, convicted, and sentenced to two years in prison for embezzlement.[31]

In this instance, as in others, Francis's business background helped him size up and deal quickly with a bad situation, and most of the press praised him, although the *Post-Dispatch*, which had hammered away at Francis for spending all his time in New York and Washington, remarked that Noland's thefts were "a strong argument in favor of a stay-at-home governor."

The *Post-Dispatch*'s continued hectoring so angered Francis that he described the editor of the Pulitzer paper, John Dillon, as "a contemptible cur who is aggrieved at me because I declined to speak to him some years ago in a company of gentleman." And of the paper itself and its continuing "animus" towards him, he remarked, "What a pity it is that this paper has so small a circulation! . . . I observe that it is devoted almost exclusively to me and my official acts."[32]

As soon as the Noland affair had been dealt with, Francis, with typical optimism and determination, put the disappointment of losing the Columbian Exposition behind him and began talking about another celebration ten years later, one that made more sense historically for the city where the exploration of the West had begun. The one hundredth anniversary of the Louisiana Purchase, which had brought St. Louis and much of the vast territory to the west of it into the Union, was coming in 1903. With Francis as the spearhead, the fair committee that already had been formed simply shifted its focus and began working on the Louisiana Purchase Exposition.

IN THE CONGRESSIONAL ELECTIONS OF 1890, with millions of desperate farmers leading a revolt at the ballot box, voters turned on the Republicans, whose so-called Billion-Dollar Congress had passed huge pork-barrel bills and protectionist tariffs that seemed to benefit every business but farming. The Democratic landslide also increased the party's hold on the Missouri legislature.

On January 8, 1891, Francis welcomed the new farmer-elected General Assembly, and in his biennial address (six times longer than his inaugural address) acknowledged that it was a "source of regret and a cause for reflection" that farmers had "not prospered as they deserve," and he continued:

> The widespread discontent which pervades the agriculturalists of the country is a natural result of the class legislation which has been enacted at Washington during the past thirty years. . . . To the extent that the State [of Missouri] can aid, without violating the rights of others, in bettering the condition of those who contribute so materially toward her wealth and importance, all wise measures will meet my approval.[33]

His statement was intended to play to his audience, but it also reflects the "conservative liberalism" of David Francis and Grover Cleveland. Both men believed in reform that was careful of the rights of others and the law. And both feared concentrated power in the hands of any group, whether monopolistic trusts or large unions of working men or farmers.

Cautious Bourbon Democrats like Francis and Cleveland, who would be re-elected president the following year, were labeled "Tories" and soon would be replaced in party leadership by free-silver advocates, populists, and others with more radical governmental solutions to the nation's economic problems.

In his address, Francis called for cooperation with other states in establishing uniform divorce laws, because "the severance of the marriage bond has become so common in this country [that] its frequency may jeopardize the integrity of the home, which is the nucleus of our civilization and the safeguard of society." And he urged the state to make a "creditable display of her unequaled resources and wonderful progress" by "conspicuous" participation in the upcoming world's fair in Chicago.

Francis, the business Democrat, announced that the state's debt had been reduced by nearly a million dollars. By the end of his term, state property taxes had been cut by one-fourth and debt reduced by $2,845,000.

After Richard Henry Jesse was named president of the University of Missouri in late January 1891, Francis proposed that a $647,000 federal tax refund to the state be used to establish a permanent endowment for the University of Missouri. Francis received an honorary doctorate of laws, and the Alumni Association presented the university a life-sized oil portrait of David R. Francis.[34]

When the legislature approved the university endowment, the *Columbia Statesman* remarked, "It has come to us that the recent success of the University is largely due to Mrs. Francis. To this we say, all honor to Mrs. Francis and her husband. We wish there were more like her, with brainy husbands under an equally good control." [35]

Jane Francis worked almost as hard as her husband, and with little if any of his delight in the task, at courting legislators and their wives. She invited pretty, clever young women from St. Louis up to Jefferson City for parties and masquerade balls, not forgetting to send invitations to powerful politicians of both parties and important state officials.

Young men and women held competitions in waltzing up and down the long, S-curved Grand Staircase, and Francis's kid sister Mollie shone. Perhaps the grandest party came in June 1891, when David and Jane Francis celebrated their fifteenth wedding anniversary. More than five hundred guests attended, two orchestras provided constant dance music, an elaborate meal was served, and the mansion was bedecked with flowers shipped in from St. Louis.

By then, two years into Francis's term, the family was very much at home in the executive mansion. The Francises had three resident dogs, included a sickly-looking brown mutt named Calamity described by a Jefferson City reporter as "the ugliest dog in existence anywhere in North America."

That summer, the Francis boys also kept a pet goat that they permitted to run loose behind the mansion's wrought-iron fence. One evening, a St. Louis legislator named Dennis Ryan—presumably a Noonan man—came up the front walk for a reception when he saw the goat and, mistaking it in the gloom for a dog, tried to pet it. The indignant goat butted him in the ribcage and chased him off the property. Ryan drafted a bill requiring the goat to be tied up in the interests of public safety, but another legislator, one friendly to Francis, grabbed the bill, took it to the mansion, and fed it to the goat.[36]

That summer, after the General Assembly had adjourned—it was not scheduled to meet again until January 1893, when a new governor would be inaugurated—David Francis theoretically had little more to do until he stepped down. More talk circulated about him running for another office, perhaps for a new congressional seat in 1892. But Francis was more interested in world's fairs—the one coming up in Chicago and the one he hoped to land for St. Louis in 1903.

At his instigation, $150,000 had been appropriated to construct a Missouri Building at the Chicago fairgrounds, and the state secured a prime location in the Mines and Metallurgy Building, which he described to the legislature as "an unequaled opportunity . . . for a display of the mineral wealth of Missouri." Once again, the Missouri National Guard—642 strong—was sent to the dedication ceremonies in October 1892. This time, at Francis's insistence, the railroads put the round-trip train fare on the tab at a cut rate until the General Assembly got around to appropriating the necessary $3,800.[37]

ON THE EVENING OF SATURDAY, JANUARY 9, 1892, Jane and David Francis were spending a quiet evening at home when, thirty miles away in Columbia, an electric chandelier crashed to the floor of the chapel in Academic Hall, the main building of the university. Flames burst through the ceiling. The fire, apparently electrical, spread quickly through the large, domed brick building.

Students, teachers, and townspeople tried to battle the blaze, but Columbia's water system was tragically inadequate, and within a couple of hours the building was destroyed, along with almost everything in it, including the university's main library of about forty thousand books and pamphlets and the portrait of David Rowland Francis, less than a year old. By morning, all that remained of Academic Hall in a landscape of fire-blackened snow were the stone front steps and the six tall Ionic columns that rose above them. The heart of the university had been destroyed.

When Francis was notified, he immediately telegraphed Jesse: "Hold the students." Jesse did just that at a mass meeting Sunday morning, reading a message from Francis urging the students to stay in Columbia and adding his own eloquent words. Jesse arranged for classes in churches, private homes, vacant downtown storefronts, and other temporary classrooms. Meanwhile, Francis took the next train north through zero-degree weather and deep snow to Columbia, and Monday morning he spoke to a rally of students and faculty, praising Jesse for holding the university together and promising that new buildings would be constructed "at once."

He returned to Jefferson City and called an emergency session of the General Assembly to fund reconstruction of the university. Inspired by Jesse and Francis, the students not only remained in Columbia, but other young men and women joined them. By mid-February enrollment actually had increased by 25 students to 612.

Some legislators tried to use the disaster as an opportunity to move the site of the university closer to their districts, but Francis stood fast and announced that any legislator who failed to vote to rebuild the university in Columbia "will be held to strict accountability by his constituents."[38] After the city of Columbia agreed to construct an improved water supply, the General Assembly appropriated $236,600 for construction.

Within a year, six new buildings had been built around a quadrangle, with the six columns of old Academic Hall at the center. The tall, graceful columns stand there to this day, in the middle of Francis Quadrangle.[39] Preservation of the university was "the greatest achievement of my administration," Francis would say.[40]

In the spring of 1892, a group of Democrats came to the governor's mansion to plead with Francis to run that year for the U.S. Senate. After hearing them out, he asked Jane Francis to step into the library and told them to repeat the proposal.

"What do you think?" he asked her.

She said that she understood well the honor election to the Senate would confer on her husband, but she had good reasons why he should not seek the seat:

> We have several children who are almost grown and who will, for the next few years, require the care and attention of their father. . . . I have looked after them as far as I could and it is now his duty to see that they are given the right start in life. I would not under any circumstances live in Washington while they were left at home.
>
> I think it would be small compensation to my husband and myself in our old age to know that he had represented Missouri in the United States Senate, if it had brought disastrous results to our sons. I am opposed to my husband's further active participation in politics until these duties have been fully discharged, and if, after that, he has any desire to enter public life, I shall interpose no objection. Until then, I think his first duty is to his wife.

Francis bowed to Jane and told the visitors that he agreed completely with her. He added, "I will not be a candidate for any public office until the personal obligations to which she has referred have been fully discharged."[41]

Francis may have been, for the time being, through with running for political office, but that didn't mean he was through with politics. A split was widening in the Democratic Party, both in Missouri and nationwide. At the center of it was "free silver," an emotion-drenched proposal to mint millions of dollars in silver coins in an effort to spend the country out of its deepening depression.

Free silver was a popular cause with farmers, who were devastated by a long period of deflation. As the years went by, they received fewer and fewer dollars for their crops, while their long-term debts remained fixed. The nostrum of free silver would flood the country with silver dollars, purposely creating inflation. Debt-ridden farmers would get more dollars for their crops and could pay off their fixed debts with cheaper and more abundant new money.

The banks, of course, thought this was a terrible idea.

Francis's lifelong sound-money principles—and it could be argued, his considerable holdings in banks—led him to oppose the silverites. That put him at odds with many rural Democrats in Missouri, who rallied behind Kentucky-born Missouri Congressman Richard Bland, a flamboyant populist nicknamed "Silver Dick." Bland, first elected in the early 1870s, was Congress's earliest proponent of free silver, and one of its loudest.

Francis increasingly was estranged from the mainstream of the state and local Democratic Party. His old enemy Judge Edward Noonan was mayor of St. Louis and in control of the major elements of the city's political machine. And Francis gained two powerful new enemies.

Congressman William Joel Stone of Nevada, Missouri, asked for Francis's endorsement in the race for governor, which began heating up in the spring of 1892. Stone's family was from Richmond, Kentucky, and his father and Francis's father were friends, but Francis turned him down, saying he felt an obligation to another candidate, Judge James Gibson of Kansas City, a major force in Francis's campaign in western Missouri four years earlier. The enmity that developed between Francis and Stone—a shrewd and indefatigable ward-heeling politician nicknamed "Gumshoe Bill"—lasted for years, as Stone grew more and more powerful in national politics.[42]

And the volatile Colonel Jones of the *Republic* had evolved into a staunch Noonan man. He began to give full play to Noonan's attacks on Francis, as well as throwing a few editorial bombs of his own. If Jones continued as editor of the *Republic*, Francis warned, he would tear the party apart.

The animosity between Jones and Francis appears to have been partly personal. Jones recently had married a young woman with a scandalous reputation. When Colonel Jones announced that he was bringing his bride to Jefferson City to meet the governor and his wife, Jane Francis replied with a brusque note that she would not be at home for his visit. Jones, understandably, took great offense.[43]

On June 21 to 23, at the Democratic National Convention, Grover Cleveland won the nomination on the first ballot, despite opposition from Tammany Hall and rumblings from free-silver advocates. Francis was one of Cleveland's staunchest and most vocal supporters and was considered a prime candidate for the vice presidential nomination—a young moderate Democrat from a middle western state would balance the ticket nicely. But strong opposition in Missouri dissuaded Cleveland from naming Francis.[44] Instead, the vice-presidential nominee was Adlai E. Stevenson of Illinois.

A month later, back home in Missouri at the Democratic State Convention, Congressman Stone won the Democratic nomination for governor. Francis reluctantly agreed to support him as the party's nominee. Both Cleveland and Stone beat their Republican opponents in November.

Francis's governorship ended January 9, 1893. He continued to insist that he had no further political ambitions, and at the time he seems to have been quite serious. Francis took less pleasure in politics after the bitter governor's race of 1888.

Although David Francis always fought political battles with gusto, his relatively late entry into the political arena, and his fast rise to power, may have left him thin-skinned to the inevitable attacks of political and journalistic enemies, as powerful businessmen who move into politics often are. The personal attacks and vendettas of those turbulent times repelled and hurt him. By the end of his term as governor, he seemed almost literally sick of politics.

He had run a notably honest and fiscally responsible administration while taking important progressive steps. The *Post-Dispatch*, after acknowledging that it had frequently been critical of Francis during his tenure, concluded that he deserved a great deal of credit for "good intentions and really good work."

"Large reductions of public debt and taxes have been effected," the *Post* noted, "while our eleemosynary and educational institutions have been more liberally provided for than they ever were before and their public usefulness greatly increased."[45]

In his final report to the General Assembly, Francis cautioned against "excessive legislation," and in an echo of Emerson's famous dictum, "The less government we have, the better," he added: "Very few laws are necessary or advisable. . . . The liberty of the individual should be observed and his opportunities protected. . . . The people of Missouri require very little government."[46]

The Missouri House of Representatives bid Francis farewell by voting 125 to 4 to urge Cleveland to appoint the outgoing governor to the cabinet. The *Globe-Democrat* thought that was a grand idea.[47] The *Globe*'s Walter Stevens later reported that Cleveland had been seriously considering Francis for a cabinet position until "the President-elect received a message from four men, three of them holding high official position, that the appointment of Mr. Francis to the Cabinet would not be agreeable to them."[48] It's hard not to conclude that the mayor of St. Louis, the governor of Missouri, and the editor of the state's most powerful Democratic newspaper were among those sending the message, perhaps in company with Silver Dick Bland.

Cleveland asked Francis to come to Washington, and after a private conference at the White House, Francis announced that he was not a candidate for any office and that he wanted to go home and look after his business and his family.[49]

Sadly, when he and Jane moved back to St. Louis, Francis felt he was forced to leave Philip Jordan behind. He said later, "I cannot afford to take him back to St. Louis on account of my boys."[50] He feared that Jordan would influence his sons, who loved and admired the man, to become heavy drinkers—a feat several of them managed quite nicely on their own.

Jordan worked briefly for incoming Governor Stone, but he soon quit or was fired. He found a job as a Pullman porter and worked off and on at that and other service jobs, but he repeatedly went back to liquor and Hog Alley. Over much of the next decade, Philip Jordan, with quick hands and the wiry build of a flyweight boxer, earned his keep and his liquor as a saloon fighter who was renowned for his ability to lick much larger men. It would be almost a decade before he sobered up and rejoined David Francis, this time for life.[51]

CHAPTER 7

The Crucible of Silver

O N THEIR RETURN HOME, the Francis family moved into St. Louis's most fashionable new neighborhood, the West End, out near Forest Park where the air was clean and the lots were large and leafy. Francis paid $62,000 for a twenty-four-year-old gingerbread-colored brick house at the top of a low hill, on a four-acre lot at the corner of Newstead and Maryland Avenues. The Francises lived in the brick house for two years while they planned and built the mansion that would replace it.

The property, about three blocks east of Kingshighway, had been part of a small dairy farm, and among the outbuildings were a large stable/carriage house and an old stone ice house with a cellar dug deep into the rocky soil. It was a wonderful place to raise boys, with a couple of acres of yard and many large old oak and maple trees.[1]

The boys attended both public and private schools, including Smith Academy, the city's best boys' school, a part of Washington University. In the mid and late 1890s, three of the boys—David, Jr., Charles, and Talton—also spent one or two years at St. Paul's School in Concord, New Hampshire, where the Vanderbilts and the Morgans sent their sons to learn Spartan values and Yankee discipline. For the newly wealthy, St. Paul's was a doorway to the American Establishment. Only David remained at St. Paul's long enough to graduate, in 1896.[2] The others probably left more because of rebellion against the school's strict discipline than a lack of brains. The Francis boys could be an unruly lot.

It was a sad period for the Francis and Perry families. Late in 1893, David's brother Sidney fell ill and became bedridden with pneumonia. His sister Hallie, who was married to William G. Boyd, president of the Merchants' Exchange, moved Sidney into their home to care for him. She apparently became infected with his disease, and the two died within forty-eight hours of one another. Both were in their late thirties.

The following year, David's father died at the age of seventy-five, and a year after that, in August 1895, Jane's father died at age eighty. By then, David's mother already was weakened severely by respiratory ailments. She died three years later.[3]

Financially, David Francis prospered, despite a nationwide economic depression beginning in 1893. Political power, at least on its most overt level, was a different matter. Francis had clout in the local Democratic organization—"The St. Louis Democracy"—but not control of it.

At times, the Democracy was run like a secret society. In 1894, a young businessman (and future mayor) named Rolla Wells—his father, Erastus, was the city's first streetcar magnate—got a phone call after dinner one evening. The caller, an insurance man, told him that an "intimate friend" wanted to meet him at the corner of Garrison and Olive in midtown St. Louis. Wells reluctantly agreed to go.

At the corner were a half dozen of his friends, including Charlie Maffitt and Dave Francis. They took him aside, told him the Noonan and Francis factions in the party had argued for hours without any hope of resolution, and finally had chosen him as a compromise candidate for president of the Democracy. Wells said he was not interested in entering politics and did not expect to be, but Maffitt pleaded with him to accept as a personal favor. Wells finally agreed. He was escorted inside a nearby meeting hall, where several hundred Democrats immediately elected him their president.[4]

The fissure in the party soon yawned open again. Although Francis almost always voted a straight Democratic ticket, Ed Butler fought the Noonan and free-silver forces by throwing his weight behind Republican candidates for city office. As a result, St. Louis had Republican mayors for most of the last decade of the nineteenth century.

A symbol of the continuing and widening rift in the Democratic Party, at least on a local level, were the repeated attacks on Francis by the Republic and its feisty editor, Charles H. Jones. The runty forty-five-year-old Floridian had grown even more egotistical with power, so often featuring his portrait and doings prominently in his paper that his morning competition, the *Globe-Democrat*, took delight in lampooning him, running mock social notes in the manner of the *Republic*: "Among the distinguished gentlemen on the [speaker's] platform were Charles H. Jones, Benjamin Harrison and Grover Cleveland." The *Globe* also like to printed outrageous caricatures of the colonel, including one of him holding up the front page of the *Republic* to display his own bug-eyed visage, adorned with spectacular sideburns that swept down to widen the broom of a ridiculously bushy beard.[5]

Francis and Jones, formerly bosom buddies, came to detest one another. Shortly after Francis returned from Jefferson City, the two men ran into each other on a busy Grand Avenue sidewalk, began arguing, and then swinging.

The fist fight may have been the last straw for *Republic* owner Charles W. Knapp, who increasingly had been disturbed by the paper's *ad hominen* attacks on Francis. Knapp fired Jones and forced him to sell his large block of *Republic* stock—which Knapp arranged for Francis to buy. Over the next decade and a half, Francis would buy more stock until he had gained control of the *Republic*, but almost immediately the paper began to reflect Francis's political and economic views.

Jones headed for New York, where Joseph Pulitzer hired him. Pulitzer liked pugnacious editors and apparently fell for Jones's legendary gift of gab. Jones's "belief in himself was monumental and was matched by his ability to convince others," Walter Stevens remarked.[6]

At almost the same moment in the spring of 1893 that David Francis was buying Jones's share of the *Republic,* a young man named Theodore Dreiser started to work for the paper. It was housed at Third and Chestnut Streets, in what Dreiser described as "a tumbledown old building in a fairly deserted old neighborhood at the outskirts of the business heart, in that region near the waterfront from which the city proper had been steadily growing away for years . . . one of the darkest and most dilapidated portions of St. Louis."[7] Francis hoped he could pull the paper out of its long decline. "I believe I would like newspaper work," he declared, and for a time contemplated actually running the paper.[8] But he had other business to take care of.

In late spring 1893, Francis gathered together his family and took the train to Chicago and the World's Columbian Exposition, which had opened in May, a year late. The Francises rented a house in Chicago and spent a month at the fair. Francis went almost every day to the "White City," which was laid out on 600 acres along Lake Michigan and made up of some 150 monumental-appearing buildings built of staff, a cheap, disposable fiber material that looked like marble. For Francis, it was a working vacation, as he studied the fair and planned ahead, spending his own money to do it.[9]

The fair marked the end of the Gilded Age, which quickly lost its glitter as one of the worst depressions in American history hit in full force with the Panic of 1893. The Gilded Age expansion in industrial production and railroad building, and the easy credit that had helped fuel the expansion, had swollen into an economic bubble, and it burst.

Without the protections that would come in the twentieth century—a federal reserve system, federal deposit insurance—the United States' flimsy economic controls did little to stop depression and panic. By the end of the year, five hundred American banks had collapsed, many major railroads and other large employers had gone bankrupt, and at the depression's depth in 1894, some 20 percent of the work force was unemployed. Stock prices continued to slump, reaching bottom in 1896.[10]

As usual, the depression devastated the poor. In response, in his brokerage office downtown, Francis presided over the founding in 1893 of the Hospital Saturday and Sunday Association, which raised money to help seriously ill, hospitalized poor people. He was a leader in the association and its successors for the rest of his life.[11]

Still, the depression was less severe in St. Louis than in other major cities, and not just because of conservative bankers. The St. Louis economy (as well as David Francis's wealth) was based to a great extent on the sale and transportation of grain and other foodstuffs. People always had to eat. By 1894, with the worst still to come in some eastern states, the Missouri commissioner of labor statistics reported that the state's economy was already on the way to recovery, and in 1897 a visiting magazine journalist could remark that St. Louis "suffered no serious results of the panic."[12]

The Panic of 1893 did batter one of David Francis's major investments, the Merchants' Bridge. The history of the new bridge, which crossed the Mississippi three miles above the levee, would return to haunt him in years to come.

The original charter for the Merchants' Bridge had been granted by the city in 1887, while Francis was mayor. The idea was that the Merchants' Exchange as a body, or at least a large number of its members as a group, would finance the bridge as a public service that might eventually lead to some profits. The main goal was to end the "bridge arbitrary" or "kid glove bandit"—the high tariff charged for crossing the river on Jay Gould's bridge.

But the Merchants' Exchange, with typical St. Louis caution, refused to finance the bridge. Francis, by then governor of Missouri, along with his father-in-law and a few other wealthy St. Louisans, put together the St. Louis Merchants' Bridge Co. to build the span privately.[13]

A rumor spread among an understandably suspicious public that infernally clever Jay Gould would wait until the bridge was built and then get control by buying up a majority of the stock. To reassure the public, the company inserted a clause in its charter that expressly forbade selling the bridge to any other company that already owned a Mississippi River bridge.[14]

In 1889, after construction of the Merchants' Bridge had begun, Jay Gould, by then quite ill, sold the Eads Bridge and connecting tunnels to the Terminal Railroad Association, a combine of major railroads and St. Louis businessmen. The Terminal Association continued Gould's practice of charging a high premium for moving freight and passengers across the river.

The Merchants' Bridge was completed and opened for traffic in 1890, but the six dominant railroads that belonged to the Terminal Association refused to use it, and the bridge lost money from the beginning. During the Panic of 1893, Francis and the other major stockholders of the Merchants' Bridge Co., in the red and desperate to protect at least some of their investment, surrendered. In a private meeting, they gutted the no sale clause in the company charter, and then they sold their bridge to the Terminal Association. The *Post-Dispatch* understandably was outraged and charged that David Francis had betrayed the city.[15]

The Merchants' Bridge was paid for in Terminal Railroad Association stock, so David R. Francis became a major stockholder. Within a few years, he had become vice president of the Terminal Association, which continued to control most railroad entree into St. Louis from the east well into the next century. Now it could charge for traffic on two bridges.[16] St. Louis businessmen like Francis, who had fought the monopoly when it was controlled by Jay Gould, now were the monopoly.

The Terminal Railroad Association also controlled the new Union Station, one of the largest terminals in the world. The neo-Romanesque station at Eighteenth and Market Streets had been built in 1894 with considerable financial and slum-clearance help from the city. As the Gilded Age drew to a close, politics and business in St. Louis were in a very cozy relationship indeed, probably to the benefit of the city but certainly to the benefit of David Francis and his friends. They were flush.

Theodore Dreiser observed that St. Louis was "compounded almost entirely of trade and the things which related to it"; in other words, it was a city dominated by commerce rather than manufacturing. The new streets in the West End were among his most vivid memories:

> . . . in which were ranged the residences of the ultra-rich, the new rich of this comparatively young city. . . . You should have seen them—great gray or white or brownstone affairs—bright, almost gaudy, with wide verandas, astonishing doorways, flights of stone steps, heavily and richly draped windows, immense carriage houses, parked and flowered lawns, carriages and pairs of the most polished and finished character.[17]

In 1895, David and Jane Francis built their own "great affair" in the West End, a magnificent grayish-white stone mansion. The principal architect, William S. Eames, had designed many of the handsome brick buildings that graced downtown St. Louis. He was later president of the American Institute of Architects.

For the Francises, Eames tore down all but the four-room core of the old house and designed a Corinthian-columned, Renaissance-style palace. A long reception hall was divided into sections by marble pillars, with two rows of gilded Ionic pediments. Also on the first floor were a vast dining room, two living rooms, and a large drawing room with walls covered in green satin brocade chosen by Jane Francis. Elizabeth S. Benoit, who grew up near the Francis mansion, recalled that one of the living rooms was much larger than the other:

> . . . a great room, which in spite of its size was cozy and homelike, especially in the winter when the curtains were drawn and the two fireplace were lighted. . . . At one end of the living room was an enormous desk. It was here, and at the great dining room table across the hall, that political campaigns were mapped out, the Louisiana Purchase Exposition was planned, and other stirring events of the day were discussed, and more often than not, settled.[18]

A central staircase with a brass handrail led to the second floor, where a balcony overlooked the reception hall. The master bedroom and several elegant guest bedrooms were on this floor. The house held at least six bathrooms, including a private one for Francis, where a heavy porcelain cuspidor was installed. By then, he had developed a taste for good cigars and liked to chew the ends.

The third floor held extra bedrooms and a walk-in cedar storage closet.

The address was 4421 Maryland Avenue. Maryland was the street to the south, and there was a semi-circular, six-columned two-story portico on that side, but the entrance gates were on Newstead to the east. The main entry, at the top of a semi-circular drive, had a triangular pediment held up by four columns, very reminiscent, some said, of the White House—or, for that matter, of the plantation houses of Francis's rich Kentucky cousins.

The new house was fitted with the most modern plumbing and electrical wiring available, hardwood floors, and paneling of oak, cherry, and white pine.[19]

Eames had studied at the Ecole des Beaux Arts in Paris. But Jane Francis had studied architecture in Europe, too, and her husband was seldom at a loss for a word or an opinion on any subject. Years later, Francis suggested the nature of the architect-client relationship in a letter to Jane. He noted that the mansion had been built "on plans which you and I designed or outlined to William H. Eads [sic], Architect. . . . The wall surrounding it was designed by Ike S. Taylor after two plans had been made by Eads and one by [another St. Louis architect], none of which pleased you or me."[20]

While the Francises and other wealthy St. Louisans built grand new West End mansions, most of the country still struggled in a depression, and the supposed quick fix of "free silver" had become the single most important national political issue of the time.

Free silver was a simplistic, emotionally appealing scheme to deal with a very real problem—the long decline in the price of farm products, caused by the great expansion in the available land as the frontier opened up, the technological revolution that increased crop yield dramatically in the late nineteenth century, and competition with cheap farm labor overseas.

The silverites wanted to end this period of deflation by artificially creating inflation. The government would buy raw silver, then pouring out of mines in the Rocky Mountains by the ton, and flood the nation with millions of silver coins.

Inspired by populist passion, and the fat campaign contributions of powerful western silver miners, the silverites blamed the international gold standard for the plight of the farmers. They wanted to create a so-called "double standard" of silver and gold—either metal could be used as the economic base of the nation's money supply. To avoid fiscal chaos, the value of the two metals would be tied together by fixing the value of silver artificially—sixteen ounces of silver always would be worth one ounce of gold to the United States government, no matter how the international silver market fluctuated. The cumbersome slogan of the silverites became "free and unlimited coinage of silver at a ratio of 16 to 1."

At the time, the international market value of silver was closer to twenty-five or thirty to one. So the new silver dollars really would be worth fifty-five to sixty cents. Flooding the country with them indeed would cause inflation, and creating inflation to break the long deflationary slide seemed like a good idea to many sensible people at the time. And in retrospect many economists and historians have felt that the dollar in the early 1890s probably was a little too "hard" and the economy could have done with some loosening, although probably not as much as the silverites wanted.[21]

Under the Sherman Silver Purchase Act of 1890, a bone tossed to the silverites, the U.S. Treasury was required to buy 4.5 million ounces of silver every month and to issue certificates for it redeemable in either gold or silver.

The act succeeded in modestly expanding the money supply but, as the U.S. economy slid towards depression, nervous European bankers and financiers, particularly the British, exchanged silver for more stable gold and hauled it across the Atlantic to their vaults.[22]

By 1893, Washington was under heavy pressure from powerful "gold bugs"—international bankers and financiers led by J. Pierpont Morgan—to stop the outflow of gold. In October 1893, despite an electrifying three-hour speech in the House of Representatives by a young pro-silver Congressman from Nebraska named William Jennings Bryan, the Republican Congress repealed the Sherman Silver Purchase Act. The repeal bill quickly was signed by Grover Cleveland, who had spent his four-year presidential interregnum as a lawyer at a Wall Street firm with close ties to J. P. Morgan. The bill did little to stop the outflow of gold; the radical passion and large popular appeal of the silverites frightened Europeans.

Francis opposed the silverites, although not as adamantly as his hero, Grover Cleveland, who clung to the gold standard as if it was a piece of the true cross. Francis, as usual, searched for a middle ground. For example, in 1894 he urged the president to sign Silver Dick Bland's seigniorage bill, which would order the U.S. Treasury to mint $55 million in silver coins. It was, Francis argued, a concession to the silver forces that could do no economic harm and might make peace within the party and the country. But Cleveland, with typical stubborn adherence to principal over pragmatism, vetoed the bill, and Congress sustained the veto despite another rousing speech by Bryan.[23]

Throughout his career, Francis was a "pacificator"—a word applied to him by a State Department official years later in Russia.[24] He always looked for the middle ground in party strife. Perhaps he was influenced in part by the history and fate of the Whigs, the original party of his father. The Whigs had been torn fatally apart by the issue of slavery.

With silver, as with slavery, there was no tenable middle ground to stand on, although Francis continually tried to feel around for one in the shifting political currents. In a desperate attempt to smooth over deep differences within the Democratic Party, he came to espouse something called "international bi-metallism." Francis's compromise position proposed, in effect, to expand the money supply by issuing millions of dollars in new silver coins but to reject setting the exchange rate artificially low—at sixteen to one—which he felt would destroy the value of the dollar on the world market.[25]

The issue is difficult to understand now. Indeed, it was difficult to understand then. Part of the considerable confusion, then and afterward, comes from the use of terms like "bi-metallism" to describe their positions by men as opposed in economic philosophy as David Francis and William Jennings Bryan.

The country, with irreconcilable southern and western populist ire on one side and stiff-necked Yankee economic rectitude on the other, was in no mood to search for a viable middle ground with David Francis. The silverites, at least the more radical ones, were fueled by xenophobic rage against "alien" bankers and financiers, particularly Jews and the British; the more conservative anti-silverites were driven by class snobbery and fear of the mob.

For a time, heated in the dark cauldron of a great depression, the issue of free silver drew the Democratic Party apart. It was an ugly time, with millions out of work, labor unions growing increasingly desperate and driven to strike, and a Bourbon Democrat in the White House who had even less sympathy for militant labor than David Francis and was less politic to boot.

In late March 1894, as Cleveland's pen was poised to veto the Bland silver-coin bill, Ohio radical Jacob Coxey staged a march of the unemployed on Washington to demand that Cleveland issue $500 million in paper money. The ill-planned march ended in farcical disarray, but Cleveland had prepared to meet Coxey's army with military force, and he and his generals remained on alert.

About four months later, Pullman workers whose wages had been slashed to maintain high dividends shut down much of the nation's rail traffic. Cleveland's attorney general, a former railroad lawyer, issued an injunction against the strikers and Cleveland dispatched federal troops into Chicago to enforce the injunction. Among the results was the imprisonment of the leader of one of the railway unions, a young man named Eugene V. Debs.[26]

The end of the nineteenth century was a time of great turmoil and breathtakingly rapid change, as the country moved from an agricultural to an industrial base and from a rural to an urban society, one connected by vast networks of railroads and telegraph and telephone wires. Economic power became concentrated in the hands of a few men, and the struggle against them focused most intently on the battle over silver.

Silver was a particularly critical issue in Missouri, not only because it was still a predominantly farming state, but also because the first important champion of free silver was Missouri Congressman Silver Dick Bland.

Although David Francis had passed up two opportunities to run for the United States Senate in the mid-1890s, he remained the leader of sound money forces in Missouri, along with his friend and ally Charlie Maffitt, chairman of the central committee of the state Democratic Party. But Bland's free-silver supporters, led by Governor Stone, triumphed in a series of caucuses and conventions. Francis tried to accommodate some with his compromise position of international bi-metallism, but Bland and colleagues stuck to their guns, and Francis refused to compromise his basic belief that massive infusions of cheap silver money would wreck the economy.

He couldn't even win the battle to define his position—two days before a crucial Democratic primary in St. Louis, he was surprised to learn that election officials, Stone appointees, had labeled the Francis delegations "Gold Standard" rather than "Sound Money," which he preferred. Thenceforth, in the popular mind, Francis was a gold bug, and there was no crawling out from under the label. At that point, he was effectively out of power in the Missouri Democratic Party and bitter about it.[27]

In Francis's anti-silver stand, personal and political interests coincided, since he was a director and significant stockholder through investment and marriage of several large banks (i.e., mortgage-holders). Throughout his career, Francis took strong stands that could be considered either enlightened self-interest or outright conflict of interest. Or both. But there seems little question that he believed policies that benefitted commercial and financial interests also benefitted the country. He also felt that pumping silver into the economy provided a huge and grossly unfair subsidy for silver producers.[28]

Rabble-rousing Silver Dick Bland was unequivocal in blaming bankers, financiers, and brokers—men like David Francis—for creating the Panic of 1893. He lashed out at the "anarchy," the "madness," and the "panic-producing system" in the markets where Francis had made his fortune, railing that "the scene on the exchanges of St. Louis, Chicago or New York gives an immediate explanation of all that is worst and most demoralizing in our politics." He argued:

> The most dangerous element of society is seen without restraint. The mob around the call board and in what is strikingly called 'the pit' shows symptoms of more violent dementia that is seen in the insane asylums . . . scrambling as only the fiercest animals scramble when food is thrown them. . . . The confusion is anarchical and expressive of the latent fierceness of the primitive animal nature not less than is that of the average riot during labor strikes.[29]

The St. Louis silverites gained another loud voice early in 1895 when Francis's old enemy Colonel Charles H. Jones came back to town. Astonishingly, Joseph Pulitzer had made him editor of the *Post-Dispatch*.

Jones and Pulitzer were at the opposite ends of the free-silver controversy, but Pulitzer got the impression that Jones had agreed not to push his fervent free-silver position in the *Post-Dispatch*. Jones may well have told Pulitzer that, but as soon as he got back to St. Louis he began writing rousing silverite editorials. Pulitzer tried to fire Jones, but the colonel refused to leave, and he had an ironclad contract. It took a lawsuit and many months to dislodge Jones. Meanwhile, sniping at Francis—or simply ignoring his presence at major events—resumed in the *Post-Dispatch*, as did the glorification of free silver and the ridicule of gold bugs.[30]

In December 1895, Francis went East to talk the Democrats into holding their convention the following summer in St. Louis. After he failed—they chose Chicago—he shrugged and went after the Republicans. While in New York on this mission, a *New York Times* reporter spotted him and asked, "Is it not likely to be very warm in St. Louis?" Francis replied heartily, "No. It will not be so uncomfortably warm as it would be here in New York. The atmosphere is not so humid in St. Louis as it is in New York. When the thermometer stands at 90 degrees here, it is more uncomfortable than it is in St. Louis when the temperature is 110 degrees."[31]

That, to put it mildly, is humbug, and perhaps the only time in history anyone has had the gall to apply the "yes, but it's dry heat" argument to the swampy summer air of St. Louis. But the Republicans apparently bought it.

At their convention in St. Louis in mid-June, the Republicans nominated William McKinley, who supported the gold standard. An interesting sidelight of that convention is that former Nebraska Congressman William Jennings Bryan, who two years before had lost in an attempt to move up to the Senate, was there to keep an eye on the opposition. He dropped by the *Post-Dispatch* to visit Charles Jones, whom Bryan later declared to be "a very able man, entirely in sympathy with the progressive ideas of the party."

Bryan noticed that Jones scribbled away at something and discovered he was writing a proposed draft of the platform to be presented to the Democratic Party in Chicago. Bryan recalled, "I prepared a plank covering the money question and he inserted it in the platform he was preparing." Much of the Jones draft, including the silver plank written by Bryan, ended up in the final platform.[32]

Before the Democrats met, New York financier William C. Whitney, Cleveland's point man at the convention, asked Francis and other Democratic sound-money leaders to come up to Chicago to decide how to stem the silver tide. They found the hotel lobbies near the convention hall filled with an aroused and intimidating populist throng, including the Bland Silver Club of St. Louis, five hundred men dressed in identical white-linen suits.

"For the first time," a wealthy associate remarked to Whitney as he gazed upon the unruly rabble, "I can understand the scenes of the French revolution." Francis and a few other men met with Whitney secretly in what they called the "hoodoo room" of the Auditorium Hotel and later led a sound-money rally, but they saw little hope. They didn't even have a decent candidate—there was no constitutional reason then that Cleveland couldn't run for a third term, but that was out of the question. The president was in virtual disgrace within his own party, a conservative Democrat seen as a tool of Wall Street in radical times. Cleveland would be condemned in the convention hall as a tyrant.[33]

Francis realized that moderation and compromise were doomed. He resigned himself to defeat. The nomination was hotly contested, but it seemed almost certain that Missouri's Silver Dick Bland would prevail over the other silverite candidates, including William Jennings Bryan.[34]

Then, in the convention-hall debate over the party platform, Bryan took the podium to argue for free silver, and everything changed.

Francis was seated next to Mary Baird Bryan, the candidate's wife, in the folding chairs that rose in tiers behind the speaker's platform. They were chatting away when a raucous cheer went up.[35] Both turned toward the speaker's stand as the thirty-six-year-old "Boy Orator of the Platte" mounted it and proceeded to give one of the greatest of all American political speeches.

Draped in preacher's black, his arms spreading like the wings of a giant bird, he spoke in a voice that soared out over the audience. The crowd responded with repeated and prolonged cheering and applause before he reached the part of his speech that literally stopped the convention: "We shall answer their demands for a gold standard by saying to them: 'You shall not press down upon the brow of labor this crown of thorns; you shall not crucify mankind upon a cross of gold!'"

The audience leapt up, cheering and applauding. Men shook hands across the aisles and stomped their feet. The fervor caught almost everyone in the hall, not just supporters of free silver, who were in the majority, but hundreds of delegates and party regulars who until that moment had been solidly in the gold camp. The times were desperate and the party was fractured, but here, finally, was a leader who seemed to transcend politics and reach for the divine.

In the audience of twenty thousand crowding the hall sat the liberal lawyer Clarence Darrow, who would have a classic confrontation with Bryan almost thirty years later in Dayton, Tennessee. Darrow later remarked:

> I have enjoyed a great many addresses . . . some of which I have delivered myself, but I never listened to one that affected and moved an audience as did that. Men and women cheered and laughed and cried. They listened with desires and hopes, and finally confidence and trust. Here was a political Messiah who was to lift the burdens that the oppressed had borne so long.

Later, after the cheering had finally died down, Darrow's friend, Illinois Governor John Peter Altgeld, remarked to him, "I have been thinking over Bryan's speech. What did he say, anyhow?" [36]

Darrow wasn't sure. It didn't matter.

The next morning, as Francis was coming into the convention hall, the voting that would carry Bryan to victory already had begun. Some of the other leading sound-money Democrats headed home, it being clear that the party was in no mood for compromise. But Francis continued to hope a middle ground could be found, somewhere, to save the party. [37] Charles Jones avoided mentioning David Francis in his voluminous convention reports for the *Post-Dispatch*, but he did point out that the party not only had defeated the gold bugs, but also it had rejected all overtures by "the bow-legged straddle bugs." [38] Francis, although long and straight of limb, was a straddle bug.

William Jennings Bryan was by far the youngest man to run for president as the nominee of a major party, and he soon received the nomination of the Populists as well. Over the next four months, his considerable speaking talents honed to perfection by two years on the Chautaqua circuit, he rushed back and forth across the country giving hundreds of speeches, moving crowds to something close to rapture when he uttered once again the famous words, "You shall not crucify mankind upon a cross of gold."

In the immediate aftermath of the convention, despite tremendous party pressure for all Democrats to fall in line behind the party's new Messiah, Francis and Cleveland refused to either reject or support the Bryan-led ticket. Both men declined to join a group of sound-money Democrats, including Francis's good friend Rolla Wells, when they agreed to convene in Indianapolis on September 2 as the National Democratic Party, which would nominate its own candidates for president and vice president.

IN AUGUST, Secretary of the Interior Hoke Smith, the only cabinet member to openly support Bryan, resigned under pressure from Cleveland. The president, who was at Gray Gables, his summer home at Buzzard's Bay, Massachusetts, quietly asked Francis to go to Washington, where a member of the cabinet asked him to take over Interior. [39]

Francis left the capital as unobtrusively as he had come, this time taking a northbound train, and by the morning of August 24 he was in Jamestown, Rhode Island, where he recently had bought a large two-story clapboard cottage overlooking the ocean. Jane, who had been in mourning for her father, was already there, with five of the boys. David and Jane had a long talk, and finally she reluctantly agreed to spend the next six months in Washington.

Francis wired his acceptance to the president. That evening, Cleveland announced the appointment of Francis to replace Smith.[40]

The Francis family immediately returned to St. Louis, where David officially turned the business over to his brother, Thomas, and his brother-in-law, Hallie's husband, Will Boyd. Francis said he would sever all his business connections in St. Louis "as far as is practicable." The *Republic* took this occasion to summarize the major parts of his business:

> He is president of the D. R. Francis & Bro. Commission Company, receiver of nine grain elevators, composing the St. Louis United Elevator System, vice president of the Mississippi Valley Trust Company, vice president of the Merchants-Laclede National Bank, vice president of the Union Casualty Surety Company, director of the Covenant Life Insurance Company, director of the Laclede Building Company, vice president of the Rialto Building Company, director of the Merchants' Bridge Terminal Railway Company, director of the Madison County Ferry Company, director of the Insurance Exchange Building Company of the Anderson & Wade Realty Company, director and treasurer of the Venice, Madison and Granite City Street Railway Company, director in a number of real estate companies and president of the Francis-Smith Export Company of New Orleans.[41]

There was no detailing of the large and diverse stock holdings of Francis & Bro., and no mention of Francis's partial ownership of the *Republic*.

"There is no doubt in our mind that Mr. Francis will make an admirable Secretary," commented the *Washington Post*. "He is a comparatively young man [Francis was forty-six], of extraordinary ability, largely endowed with the executive faculty, self reliant, courageous and highly intellectual. We think that Mr. Cleveland has made a wise selection, and feel quite sure that even in the brief term open to him, Mr. Francis will abundantly illustrate its wisdom."[42]

And the *New York Times* noted that as governor of Missouri Francis's administration of the affairs of State was

> . . . conservative, wise and statesmanlike. . . . He has been the strong personal friend of Mr. Cleveland ever since 1884, when he assisted in nominating Mr. Cleveland for President. His position on the financial question is well know to be strongly in favor of sound money.
>
> In personal appearance, the new Secretary of the Interior is very striking. He has a pleasant face, with a frank expression. His manners are easy and genial. He is a great favorite in social life. He has amassed a considerable fortune by his business enterprises in Missouri.[43]

Francis would begin serving as secretary of the interior almost immediately, although his appointment would have to be confirmed by the Senate when it reconvened in December.

On September 2, Francis took the train to Washington. Jane was with him, and she watched on the morning of September 3 as Francis, still slim, his hair barely streaked with gray, his mustache now curled up and around at the ends, his blue eyes bright, was sworn in as the twenty-first secretary of the interior by Associate Justice of the Supreme Court John M. Harlan. After he and Jane had lunch at the Arlington Hotel, Francis went to the Interior Department and started to work.

That afternoon, Francis learned that the breakaway National Democrats, including two members of Cleveland's cabinet, had just nominated Senator John M. Palmer of Illinois, a former Union general, as its presidential candidate. Kentuckian Simon B. Buckner, a former Confederate general, was on the ticket as vice president. Francis replied that it was a fine ticket and said he would support it in November. A week later, in a telegram to the National Democrats, he said:

> Those old heroes have fought valiantly for their convictions on many battle-
> fields, but no patriot ever enlisted in a nobler cause than that which they have
> consented to lead. It is the maintenance of the country's honor and the
> preservation of the integrity of Democratic principles, on whose perpetuity
> depends the survival of our institutions.[44]

Like Cleveland, Francis declined to campaign actively for the National Democrats, saying he was far too busy trying to master the intricacies of the Interior Department and prepare its annual report, due in early December. The department was in charge of 177,000 Indians, more than 1.8 billion acres in the public domain, all government pensions, many of the affairs of the territory of Alaska, the expansion of railroads through public lands, the Geological Survey, the Bureau of Reclamation, the proposed Nicaragua Canal across Central America, and the National Parks, including Yellowstone and Yosemite, parts of which had to be guarded by troops to prevent poaching and squatting.[45]

Busy as he was, Francis took a couple of days off to ride up to New Hampshire and help Charles and Talton get settled for the school year at St. Paul's.[46] He probably stopped in New Haven, where Perry was beginning his senior year at Yale and David was a freshman. Although not exactly campaigning for the National Democrats, he couldn't resist issuing some strong political statements, including one that expressed his deep concern about radical populist rabble-rousing:

> I believe the sober second thought of the people will condemn and repudiate
> those who are trying to array classes against each other and incite the discon-
> tented to violation of obligations [i.e., debts], if not lawlessness. . . . If the
> organization calling itself the regular Democracy be successful at the coming
> election, commercial disaster, financial misery, social discontent [and] nation-
> al dishonor would ensue, and the party responsible for such conditions would
> be cursed by an outraged people for a generation to come.

Francis contended that Bryan was "too intoxicated with the belief in the divinity of his own mission, or blinded by his own conceit" to see that free silver would be a financial disaster for the nation.[47]

To defeat Bryan, Republican power broker Mark Hanna had assembled an immense campaign chest from banks, railroads, and insurance companies. The campaign was vicious and intemperate on both sides, which may have been one reason David Francis stood back after it became clear that silver would prevail among the Democrats.

Xenophobia and anti-Semitism reached the virulent stage, directed against both the Jewish tycoons who allegedly pulled the strings on Wall Street and the new wave of immigrants from eastern and southern Europe who threatened to take jobs away from "native Americans." Bryan denied that he was in any way motivated by anti-Semitism and courted Jewish voters. But many of his supporters were less careful and chose to interpret Bryan's central crucifixion metaphor in a way that made it apparent just who was guilty of nailing the hands of American farmers and workers to a cross of gold.[48]

Bryan carried Missouri and the West as well as the South, but he lost badly in the populous eastern states and in much of the Middle West, and William McKinley defeated him by a half-million votes.

Francis and Cleveland were quietly pleased with the results of the election, but Francis also was concerned that all the fury and vitriol had obscured legitimate questions about the American economic system and in particular, the barely restrained power of monopolies and trusts. When a group of gold bug Democrats got together in Kansas City in late November to celebrate Bryan's defeat, Francis sent a cautionary telegram:

> While I agree with the advocates of sound money in the fight recently made, there are many principles advocated by some of those who have been advocates of that cause to which I cannot subscribe. If some legislation is not enacted to check the growing influence of wealth and circumscribe the powers of the trusts and monopolies here will be an uprising of the people before the century closes which will endanger our institutions.[49]

The statement could almost be taken as a call to arms of the trust-busting, activist Progressive movement, which blossomed in American urban centers and, after the turn of the century, would become the dominant force in American politics.

ON DECEMBER 7, the lameduck Congress reassembled, and Francis's appointment was referred to the Senate Finance Committee.

Throughout most of our country's history, presidential appointees may have had to endure rancorous debate, but they usually have been confirmed as a matter of political courtesy. But the 1890s—like the 1990s—were not ordinary, or particularly courteous, times in our country's history.

A key member of the Finance Committee was Senator George Vest from Missouri. Vest was a silverite, as were all the Democrats on the committee. Vest kept the Francis nomination bottled up in the committee through Christmas and into the new year. At that point, Senate action in a sense would be a formality—even if confirmation was denied, Francis would be permitted to serve until the session of the old Congress ended on March 4, when the new president and the new Congress would be sworn in.[50] But Francis would be weakened in stature and would find it difficult to deal with the Congress that had repudiated his appointment.

By early January, it became clear that Vest had a serious problem back home in Missouri and that Francis would not be confirmed until it was solved. Senators still were elected by the legislatures of their states, and Vest's concern was that the sound-money Democrats in the Missouri General Assembly, men who had opposed his views fiercely in the past half year, would join with the Republicans to block his re-election. Confirmation of Francis was his hole card, but he wanted to play it wisely. "If the gold Democrats in Missouri keep their hands off the senatorial contest," the *Globe-Democrat* surmised, "Senator Vest, on his return to Washington, will withdraw his objections, and . . . the nomination will be favorably acted upon."[51]

That was more or less what happened. On January 18, having returned from Jefferson City with a deal, Vest permitted Francis's confirmation to sail through the Senate. On January 19 and January 20, Vest was reelected to the U.S. Senate by both houses of the Missouri General Assembly.[52] Now Francis could make the final push on the programs that Cleveland had appointed him to handle in the first place.

A T THE TIME OF THE APPOINTMENT, the *Republic* tried to deal with a question that many in St. Louis asked: Why would a man of Francis's stature accept a six-month appointment to a relatively minor cabinet post. The *Republic,* undoubtedly following the Francis party line, explained that duty and friendship had induced him to sacrifice his own interests to show "his esteem for the President as a man."[53]

And business historian Cosmo James Pusateri, in his thorough, insightful 1965 doctoral dissertation on David Francis, wonders why Cleveland would appoint him in the first place and concludes that the president called Francis into service either as a partial apology for not having previously named him to the cabinet or as a payment for Francis's "steadfast loyalty to the President and the cause of sound money."[54]

Certainly, loyalty and friendship played a role, but more importantly, Cleveland very much wanted two critical pieces of business finished in the last few months of his administration, and it seems likely that the president felt he needed someone he trusted, both personally and politically, to be in charge of finishing them. Francis responded eagerly to the challenge of dealing with these pivotal issues, issues that a hundred years later, still unresolved, would continue to inspire passionate national debate.

One issue was the government's treatment of Indians; the other was the preservation of the nation's forests.

The Department of the Interior governed the Bureau of Indian Affairs, and Francis strongly advocated a proposed solution to the so-called "Indian problem" that at the time seemed, at least from the nation's capital, a good idea. In retrospect, it was a terrible, even tragic idea. The story requires some historical perspective.

In the early 1830s, with former Indian fighter Andrew Jackson as president, the Choctaws, a notably peaceable tribe, had been forced to move from their Mississippi homeland to Indian Territory. In return, they were guaranteed that the land they occupied in what became Oklahoma would be irretrievably theirs. The Choctaws soon led the Cherokees, Chickasaws, Creeks, and Seminoles in the long, deadly, forced trek west along what became known as the Trail of Tears. Together the groups made up the so-called Five Civilized Tribes, with large tribal holdings and statutory independence in their territory. They developed their own governments and schools, and for a while, they prospered as farmers, ranchers, and coal miners. Over the years, a few dozen more tribes were forced to move to Indian Territory.

As the West filled up with whites, the Indian land, once considered practically worthless and quite disposable, began to be coveted by potential settlers, greedy "land-grabbers," and railroads eager to expand. The discovery of oil in the late 1880s further fed the campaign to open up Indian Territory, and the pressure became too much for politicians to bear.[55]

Beginning in the 1880s, one tribe after another was pushed into giving up its tribal holdings and permitting the land to be broken up and either "allotted" as private property to individual members of the tribe or sold at auction, with the money going to tribal members. Inevitably, much of the land ended up in white hands. The last major holdouts against the white invasion were the Five Civilized Tribes, who still owned much of the eastern Oklahoma territory.[56]

In 1893, Congress introduced several bills to simply take the land away. Ultimately, the Five Civilized Tribes realized they would lose the land one way or another, and they were forced into the arms of the Dawes Commission, which had been created to impose the allotment program.

According to conventional wisdom in the late-nineteenth century, only when Indians became land-owning, independent small farmers could they truly advance out of their pagan morass. Grover Cleveland and David Francis both were devoted to applying the Jeffersonian agrarian ideal to Indians and integrating Indians into American society by letting them participate in the educational and economic glories of white America. Both believed they had the best interests of the Indians at heart in pushing the so-called allotment system. However, both were inexcusably naive about true conditions in Indian Territory.

The accommodating Choctaws were once again the first of the Civilized Tribes to surrender to the inevitable. In mid-December, after long negotiations, Choctaw leaders in Muskogee, Oklahoma, signed an agreement with the Dawes Commission, providing for the gradual dissolution of tribal control and allotment of some of the land to members of the tribe. The rest of it, including towns, public buildings, and mineral sites, was sold and the proceeds given to members of the tribe.[57]

The Choctaw leaders then went to Washington and met with Francis, who congratulated them and added his approval to the agreement. Francis and Cleveland urged Congress to ratify it. However, seemingly reacting in pique to loud opposition among a minority of Indian leaders to the Muskogee agreement, Congress not only rejected it but turned around and passed a bill authorizing the federal government to simply take over the land of the Five Civilized Tribes.

Cleveland, with Francis's encouragement, pocket-vetoed the intemperate bill until his term expired in March.

FOREST PRESERVATION long had been a primary objective of the conservation-minded Cleveland, who had told Congress after his second inauguration, "The time has come when efficient measures should be taken for the preservation of our forests from indiscriminate and remediless destruction." [58] Cleveland's policies included adding millions of acres to the forest land held in reserve by the government and creating what became the National Park System.

In late January 1897, Cleveland's seven-man National Forest Commission, which included Gifford Pinchot, the young lion of the forest conservation movement, passed on to Francis its recommendation that thirteen new forest reserves be created. The protected land would total more than twenty-one million acres, including the Black Hills Reserve in South Dakota; the Lewis and Clark, Flathead, and Bitterroot reserves in Montana and Idaho; the Big Horn and Teton reserves in Wyoming; the Washington, Olympic, and Mt. Rainier reserves in Washington; the Uinta Forest Reserve in Utah; and the Stanislaus and San Jacinto reserves in California. Francis eagerly approved the recommendation and suggested to the president that February 22 would be an appropriate day to make the announcement, remarking, "The birth of the Father of our Country could be no more appropriately commemorated than by . . . establishing these grand forest reserves." [59]

On Washington's birthday, February 22, 1897, Cleveland proclaimed that the twenty-one million acres in seven states were now part of the nation's forest reserves, more than doubling the acreage of the existing reserves. By this time, however, weary of political maneuvering and with only ten days remaining in his term, the president had neglected to consult with the elected representatives of those seven western states, and the news hit them like a slap in the face. The "mixed-use" concept that now permits controlled logging and other commercial activities in national forests had not been worked out yet, so the bill appeared to be a blow against some of their most powerful constituents.

An outraged senator from Wyoming immediately pushed through an amendment to the Sundry Civil Appropriations Bill (a major part of the federal budget) that would nullify Cleveland's proclamation and put the twenty-one million acres back in the unprotected public domain. For the next few days, as the terms of the president, his cabinet, and much of the Congress drew to a close, the amendment went back and forth between the two houses in fierce debate. Francis was in the middle of it, lobbying for the forest reserves.[60]

Francis recalled later:

Much of these 21 million acres was used at the time by owners of mines who were felling timber thereon for supports in the mines; also used by owners of sheep and cattle for grazing; of course the Government derived no rental from such uses and the utilizers were opposed to being deprived of a great factor in their profits.

Such owners had friends in both houses of Congress and in fact some of such owners were members of Congress. . . . Threats were made to hold up the appropriations bills especially the Sundry Civil, thus necessitating an extra session of Congress. I was waited upon by members of both Houses, Republicans and Democrats, and requested to urge the President to alter his proclamation.[61]

Francis went to the White House and told Cleveland about the bipartisan request for a change in the proclamation. Cleveland glared up at him and said, "You have not changed your mind on the subject, have you?"

Francis replied that he absolutely had not changed his mind. Cleveland nodded and said he did not intend to alter the proclamation one whit.

At that point, Francis later recalled, Congress was meeting in twenty-four-hour session, cobbling together crucial measures at the last minute with the big appropriations bills still being debated. Francis met with Senator James K. Jones of Arkansas, chairman of the National Democratic Committee, and told him that the president was "immovable" and "if an extraordinary session of Congress was necessitated the blame . . . would rest with the Congress itself."[62]

About 5 P.M. on March 3, some nineteen hours before his term expired and McKinley's inauguration would commence, Cleveland told his cabinet that he still had not received the Sundry Civil Appropriations Bill and that the cabinet secretaries should be ready to come to the White House at any hour. He ordered them to follow the debate closely, so they would know what Congress was putting in the bill, and taking out.

At midnight, Cleveland informed the cabinet that the bill would not reach him before 10 o'clock the next morning.

By 9:30 A.M., the cabinet had assembled in Cleveland's office. All were standing. A few minutes later, the Sundry Civil Bill, containing $159 million in appropriations, was laid on his desk. It was fifty pages long, hastily and messily handwritten rather than typed. Cleveland showed the cabinet the sheaf of papers and shook his head, expressing his incredulity that the American people expected him to act intelligently on a bill of such magnitude with two hours left on his term. Without reading it, he went around the room, beginning, as was traditional, with the secretary of state, and asked if the cabinet members knew the contents of the bill that affected their departments and if the bill was satisfactory.

The secretary of state answered in the affirmative, followed in the traditional order by the secretary of the treasury, the attorney general, the secretary of war, the postmaster general, and the secretary of the Navy. Next came the secretary of the interior.

Francis said the appropriations bill was satisfactory except for one thing:

> They have put a rider on the amount they have appropriated for guards of the Public Domain, and that rider is that the appropriation for the guards shall not be available until the President revokes or alters his proclamation of February 22, 1897, taking 21 million acres from the Public Domain for Forest Reservations.

At this point, a messenger hurried in and told Cleveland that President-elect McKinley had arrived at the White House and was waiting to be escorted to the capitol by the president and his cabinet. Cleveland told the messenger to have McKinley shown to the Blue Room and that he would join him in a few minutes. Quickly, Cleveland asked Francis to tell him again what was in the rider. Francis did. Cleveland frowned and hurled the handwritten bill to the floor. Loose pages flew across the room. Then he heaved his great bulk up from his chair and told the cabinet that carriages were waiting to take them all up Pennsylvania Avenue to the capitol. He led the way to the Blue Room, introduced Francis and the other cabinet members to McKinley, and strode out the front door of the White House, with the president-elect and the cabinet following him.

Throwing the Sundry Civil Appropriations Bill on the floor "was the last official act of President Cleveland," Francis later remarked wryly.[63]

Most of the earmarked land was taken out of the forest reserve system during the McKinley administration, but the president who succeeded him in 1901, Theodore Roosevelt, was an ardent conservationist. Through his efforts and those of some of his successors, the great majority of the land that David Francis and Grover Cleveland had chosen to preserve for future generations ended up as part of the National Forest and National Park Systems, as a look at a current map of the United States clearly shows.

As for the Indians: In April, with the Congressional land-grab bill dead because of Cleveland's pocket veto, the Dawes Commission negotiated a new agreement similar to the one Francis and Cleveland had wanted, and the new Congress voted it into law. Francis and Cleveland, by holding to the more moderate course, had succeeded in getting the Indians a better deal than they would have received from the previous Congress, but it turned out to be far from a good deal.[64]

In 1934, a relatively enlightened new commissioner of Indian Affairs named John Collier looked back over the history of the allotment policy and charged that, through destruction of traditional tribal life, allotment had been the principal cause of the Indians losing ninety million acres of land and had created shameful conditions among Indians that included poverty so deep it bordered on starvation, 30 percent illiteracy, and a death rate twice that of the white population.[65]

FRANCIS HEADED HOME. He had been in the capital for only half a year, but as usual he managed to work his spell on journalists. A Washington correspondent for the *Philadelphia Ledger* later described Francis:

> A distinguished man, a chief among chiefs, a master of affairs, a savant in the greatest of sciences, knowledge of folks . . . he shakes hands as if he were glad to see you and talks interestingly. He is a very good speaker, especially after dinner, and is fond of giving and attending dinners. He never forgets a name or a face, and can usually remember something more about even a chance acquaintance.[66]

Including, one presumes, journalists from Philadelphia.

But Francis's political career appeared to be over, after a surprisingly fast twelve years. He accepted that fact with a combination of bitterness and relief. In the silver debate, he had made a stand on principal—not unalloyed with personal interest—and like his friend and idol, Grover Cleveland, he had suffered for it. He was virtually an outcast in his own party, and indeed it would be nearly a decade before he attended a Democratic Party meeting in Missouri. But that does not mean he disappeared from what he proudly would call public service. For the next seven years, he worked without pay for the most important project he had undertaken. Indeed, he had never really stopped working on it since that February day in 1890 when Congress had chosen Chicago over St. Louis as the site of the World's Columbian Exposition.

CHAPTER **8**

The Big Cinch

D AVID AND JANE FRANCIS RETURNED TO ST. LOUIS in the spring of 1897. He was eager to get back to his business and his dream of putting on the greatest of all world's fairs, she to her books and her rose garden and her small group of friends. Francis figured they were home for good. Friends on Wall Street sometimes urged him to move to New York, where he could become truly wealthy and truly important. But he demurred, saying he would stay where he was: "I have six boys. St. Louis is a better place than New York for raising sons." [1]

Later that spring, Perry, the oldest, graduated from Yale and went to work for his father. He moved into the Maryland Avenue mansion. David, Jr., was still at Yale, where he would be a sophomore in the fall. The four younger boys were enrolled in schools in St. Louis.

Francis was in his forty-seventh year, and even if he had been childless he would have found it difficult to leave the city where he had so much influence and privilege and over whose commercial and social life he had become such a dominant figure.

David Francis long had been a director of the St. Louis Fair, a sign of his prominence and one he was particularly proud of. In June 1898, he became a trustee of Washington University. For more than a decade, he and his brother Tom had been leading members of the most prestigious downtown clubs, the University Club and the St. Louis Club. And in 1895, when St. Louis Country Club bought a large spread at Clayton and Hanley Roads in St. Louis County and built a sumptuous clubhouse with a golf course and tennis courts, David and Thomas Francis were among the 290-odd charter members. The club was, and remains, the haven for St. Louis's white, gentile, predominantly Protestant elite; the populist *Post-Dispatch* heralded its founding with a long photo spread head-lined: "Are You In It? No? Too Bad, My Dear Fellow, Really Too Bad." [2]

David Francis quickly learned to enjoy golf, which was relatively new to America, and several of his sons came to love it. By the early 1900s, J. D. Perry Francis had become one of the best golfers in the state.

For family weekends, David Francis still preferred the quieter, more bucolic surroundings of the Kinloch Club in north St. Louis County, not far from the farm he had bought for his parents. The Log Cabin Club in west St. Louis County, a gentleman's lodge and poker den, was always his favorite when alone or with a small group of male cronies.

All in all, David Francis was probably the best-known man in town. In the O. Henry story "Seats of the Haughty," written before the World's Fair that made Francis a nationwide celebrity, two Texas cowboys, their pokes packed with yellowback bills from a big oil strike, head for St. Louis and at a posh restaurant send word to the chef that they want a meal "such as you serve to Dave Francis and the general passenger agent of the Iron Mountain when they eat here." They are served a Gilded Age feast worthy of Diamond Jim Brady.[3]

By the turn of the century, Francis was one of the leaders—according to the *Post-Dispatch*, the leader—of a powerful group known as the "Big Cinch." The *Post-Dispatch* explained the name by offering dictionary definitions of "cinch": "(1) A broad saddle-girth . . . (2) (Colloq.) Hence, a tight grip, a sure thing."[4] Francis said he was baffled by published reports that he was the head of the Big Cinch, remarking that he wasn't even sure what the phrase meant but that it seemed a slur against "public-spirited citizens who happen to be at the forefront of important financial or commercial enterprises."

He noted, somewhat defensively, "It is true, I am a director in the Merchants' Terminal Railway Co., which is part of the Terminal Association, but that is a connection dating many years back, and I seldom if ever attend one of the meetings of that corporation."

The nickname was if not coined at least popularized in print by the gadfly St. Louis journalist William Marion Reedy. Reedy, writing under a pseudonym, proclaimed shortly before the turn of the century:

> St. Louis is a close corporation. Less than twenty men run it. Jim Campbell,
> Dave Francis, Geo. A. Madill, Sam Kennard, Ed Butler, Charlie Maffitt, John
> Sculin [Scullin], Edwards Wittaker [Whitaker], Thomas H. West, Julius S.
> Walsh, George E. Leighton and a few more own the town.

The pungent screed continued:

> They dare do anything. . . . They control the banks, the trust companies, the
> street railroads, the gas works, the telephone franchises and the newspapers
> . . . . They are the local nobility. They can crush anyone who ventures to
> oppose their desires. . . . They unite against the newcomer and crush him.
> They control municipal legislation. They buy aldermen like cattle. The city is
> at their mercy.[5]

Other estimates of the size of the city's ruling elite approached sixty-five or seventy, with lists of names that varied somewhat; but Francis's was always included. The Big Cinch was divided between Democrats and Republicans. Most of them were millionaires. Almost all were WASPs, with a handful of Catholics (like Francis's buddy, streetcar magnate/banker James Campbell) and, when the list of names focused on economic power or contributions to high culture rather than social prestige, one or two Jews. The Big Cinch and the theoretically mysterious Veiled Prophet Society had overlapping memberships.

Many of the Big Cinchers, or their fathers, had come to Missouri from Kentucky, Tennessee, or Virginia, and Southern or border-state drawls—and conservative Southern ways—dominated St. Louis business. Reedy, whose weekly *Mirror* became an important national magazine in the 1890s, argued that the tightfisted, clannish Southerners who held the city's economic reins were a main cause for St. Louis lagging behind Chicago.

The Kentucky Society was particularly strong and included in its membership David Francis; his friend Breckinridge Jones, president of the Mississippi Valley Trust Co.; wealthy merchant Samuel Kennard; Francis's brother-in-law and business partner, William G. Boyd, like Francis a former president of the Merchants' Exchange; and silk-stocking lawyer and rising political star Harry B. Hawes, who just before the turn of the century molded the Democratic reform group called the Jefferson Club into a powerful political machine. By 1913, fifteen members of the Kentucky Society were officers or directors of big downtown banks.[6]

Also, like Francis, many members of the Big Cinch had come to St. Louis relatively poor and had become rich by a combination of hard work, shrewd investments, and wise marriages. One sure way to the top for these men was marrying into one of the handful of old French families whose wealth dated back to the fur trade. The model may have been Charlie Maffitt's father, Dr. William Maffitt, a Virginian who had come to St. Louis as a U.S. army surgeon, married Julia Chouteau of the founding family, and acquired great wealth. Charlie's family had owned, among other things, a large chunk of the land the city bought for Forest Park.

As the second half of the nineteenth century progressed, these men took power, creating interlocking directorates at the major downtown banks and other financial institutions. They owned public utilities, dry goods and agricultural distributors, and manufacturing firms, including steel mills in both St. Louis and across the river in East St. Louis and environs. They became known as the New St. Louis and were much resented by the old families, at least those that hadn't been lucky enough to have their daughters marry one of those slick gold-digging Southern interlopers.

These new men were mostly Protestants, although three Irish Catholics—Festus Wade, John Scullin, and James Campbell—were the principal stockholders in rapidly rising Mercantile Trust. The city was by then nearly half Catholic, but few Catholics were considered part of the social elite. For example, despite their great wealth, Wade, Scullin, and Campbell were not members of the WASP–controlled St. Louis Country Club, although they were all good friends and business associates of David Francis and other members.[7] Wade, Scullin, and Campbell all became directors of the World's Fair that Francis never had stopped promoting from the moment Chicago had gained Congressional approval for the Columbian Exposition.

Francis also had friends among prominent St. Louis Jews, including lawyer David Goldsmith, a classmate at Washington University, and Nathan Frank, a powerful Harvard-educated lawyer who had also attended Washington University in the late 1860s. In 1888, running as a Republican from the city of St. Louis, Frank became the first Jew ever elected to Congress from the state of Missouri. (As of 2001, he remained the only one.)[8] Frank was named a director of the Fair and was the key to support from St. Louis's German Jewish community, important to the Fair's success both locally and back East.

FRANCIS WENT BACK to Washington early in 1898 to lobby for congressional backing. That winter and spring, back in St. Louis, support was lined up from the Bar Association, the Business Men's League, the Merchants' Exchange, and about two dozen other business and civic organizations, plus the St. Louis Building Trades Council, an umbrella labor group.[9]

On January 10, 1899, St. Louis played host at the Southern Hotel to a convention of the twelve states and two territories in the Louisiana Purchase. After an eloquent speech by Francis, the delegates voted to back St. Louis for the celebration in 1903. A Committee of Two Hundred was formed to organize the Fair, with Pierre Chouteau, an important early backer of the Fair, named chairman. David Francis became chairman of the executive committee and banker William H. Thompson head of the finance committee.

The Fair had the slavish support of the St. Louis press, including the *Post-Dispatch*, whose feud with Francis had ended in the summer of 1897. That's when Joseph Pulitzer had finally managed to oust Charles H. Jones from the editorship.[10] Although the paper would continue to attack Francis and the St. Louis power structure, in particular for the hated "bridge arbitrary," the opposition was not the unreasoned vengefulness of Jones, and the *Post-Dispatch* was very much behind the Fair and, on the whole, effusively praised Francis for his leading role in it.

Francis made hundreds of speeches a year promoting a grand world's fair that would both look back on the exploration of the West and forward to the exciting new technology of the twentieth century. He looked for subscribers, and he tailored his speeches to his audiences. At Temple Israel, a very wealthy, very assimilationist German Jewish congregation, he focused on the cultural and educational aspects of the Fair, which would be "an exhibit of the progress of the world."

In comparison with other fairs, he stated:

The Columbian Exposition of 1893 at Chicago portrayed the progress of the world from the Dark Ages, if not from the days of Moses, to the 19th century. Since that exposition, ten years have elapsed, or will by 1903, and what a memorable decade it has been. Science has made incomparable advances. . . . New trends of thought seem to have taken hold of the human mind.

Touching on the cultural, philosophical, social, moral, political, and commercial benefits that the Fair would bring to St. Louis, as well as "the advancement of women," Francis said, "I think that all would agree that the sum of money which has been suggested as necessary to launch the enterprise may be considered as money well expended, whether those subscribing or advancing the money ever receive one cent in return or not." [11]

With other audiences, those less reluctant to focus directly on the commercial aspects of the Fair, Francis stressed the millions of dollars and tens of thousands of jobs the Fair and its millions of visitors would bring to the city. But almost inevitably he emphasized the nobility of the cause.

"Every exposition is a great peace conference," he said more than once. "Each one is another step forward in the progress of man. It is a source of growing education to the human race and brings the civilized races closer together." [12] He often concluded his pitch by quoting his favorite author, Ralph Waldo Emerson: "Trust thyself; every heart vibrates to that iron string. Accept the place the Divine Providence has found for you. . . ." [13]

O N JANUARY 31, 1900, twenty-three-year-old J. D. Perry Francis married Emilie (Mimi) De Mun Smith, a petite dark-haired young woman with a high forehead and striking large brown eyes. Like his father, Perry married well. Mimi was closely related to the Cabannes and the Chouteaus as well as the De Muns, three wealthy intermarried Creole families who had lived in St. Louis for a century or more. Mimi was "conspicuously one of the loveliest girls in St. Louis," gushed the *Globe-Democrat's* society editor, who remarked that Jane Perry Francis "looked almost as youthful as her first daughter-in-law in a beautiful gown of moonlight satin." [14]

David Francis became very fond of Mimi, who physically resembled a young Jane, and ultimately was deeply saddened that she and Perry never were able to have children.

Perry and Mimi lived for three years at 224 North Newstead Avenue, a half-block south of the Francis mansion, and then, with the help of his father, Perry bought a large, two-and-a-half-story brick house at 4510 Maryland Avenue, about a block west of the mansion.

Meanwhile, David, Jr., graduated from Yale in 1900 and joined Perry at the family investment house. On June 12, 1901, he married Sarah C. Coulthurst of Danvers, Massachusetts. Sarah and David, Jr., lived for a couple of years at the mansion and then, late in 1903, with Sarah pregnant, David, Sr., helped them buy a house at 4448 Maryland Avenue, across the street from the mansion and about a half block from Perry and Mimi's new house. [15]

With their boys at home or a few doors away, Jane and David Francis were as happy as they had ever been, each of them devoting their days to things they loved. Jane spent much of her time working in her garden or curled up in a chair in the bookcase-lined parlor at the southeast corner of the house, reading Jane Austen or the latest Edith Wharton short story, soothed by the parlor's dark green furnishings and its mahogany woodwork.

"There is an air of high breeding and dignity about her that might impress the casual observer as haughtiness," an acquaintance remarked at the time, "if it were not for the pleasant graciousness of the greeting which is sure to follow an introduction." Occasionally, Jane invited a few close friends over for private functions, which, the acquaintance observed, "she manages to keep private indeed. . . . Mrs. Francis is a most loyal friend. She has, however, the courage of her convictions, and never hesitates to express an opinion when she thinks the occasion demands." [16]

When David Francis finally arrived home around 7 P.M., there were drinks before dinner, with Jane taking a glass of sherry and Francis bourbon, and a game of anagrams with whichever boys were around. Dinner was the occasion for family debates, which sometimes grew quite heated. David Francis was an avid reader of history, Jane preferred literature and critical essays, and they both insisted their children read widely, develop opinions, and be prepared to defend them. After dinner, David headed for his smoking room, which adjoined the billiard room, for the best cigar of the day, while Jane and Perry and Mimi played billiards. Sometimes Francis put his cigar aside, attracted by the click of balls and the chat coming from next door, and joined in the game. "Dave loves an audience," said a close friend, "and he never has a more appreciative one than his own family." [17]

Sometimes in the evenings, Jane Francis organized little dances, inviting not just their friends but their sons' friends, male and female. David Francis was very fond of dancing with the girls. [18]

I N 1899 AND 1900, FRANCIS made several more long lobbying trips to Washington. In tow were prominent men from states and territories throughout the Louisiana Purchase, and under Francis's guidance they lobbied their representatives for funding the World's Fair. At a banquet attended by members of Congress, the cabinet, and the Supreme Court, Francis announced, "The city of St. Louis pledges her people to raise at least $10 million towards preparing for such an international exposition." [19]

On June 9, 1900, Francis returned to St. Louis from Washington triumphant. He, former Congressman Seth W. Cobb, and Corwin Spencer of the Fair's executive committee had secured a promise from Congress to cough up a $5 million federal appropriation for the Fair when St. Louis had raised its $10 million. Francis was jubilant—a $5 million public fund already was four-fifths subscribed, and a state bond issue for an additional $5 million was on the ballot in the fall.

"A great work is before St. Louis," he announced. "We have only three years to complete it." At that point, the Fair was still intended to begin in 1903, the 100th anniversary of the Louisiana Purchase. He said there was enough time to assemble the American exhibits, but, presciently, Francis added, "Foreign countries move slowly in such matters and we will have to be up and doing to complete the fair in the time." [20]

Francis was greeted by a welcoming parade and a bitter labor dispute. The morning before he arrived, thirty-three hundred St. Louis streetcar workers had gone on strike against the new, consolidated St. Louis Transit Co. (Although it is unclear whether

Francis directly or indirectly owned any stock in the St. Louis Transit Co. at that point, within a few years his investment firm owned a substantial amount.)[21]

The strike came after a long dispute that began when work shifts for drivers were lengthened and wages lowered by the head of St. Louis Transit, Edwards Whitaker, a West End businessman. The dispute grew increasingly contentious, coming to symbolize the wide split between blue collar and silk stocking, between business and labor, and by early June rioting occured in the streets, with workers and their supporters on one side and on the other St. Louis police and "posses" that totaled more than two thousand men, primarily businessmen, lawyers, and other wealthy St. Louisans.

Nothing in the record suggests that Francis took any role in opposing the strikers, beyond publicly deploring the violence that came from both sides and its negative effect on the city's image as it prepared for a world's fair. But his brother, Thomas Francis, along with World's Fair executive committee member Spencer Corwin, who had been in Washington with Francis, volunteered to serve on posses that guarded streetcar equipment at night from saboteurs. A board appointed by the governor controlled the police. The president of the police board was Harry B. Hawes, a powerful young Democratic lawyer, and the governor was Democrat Lon Stephens. Both Hawes and Stephens were close friends of David Francis.

Some members of the posses rode the cars during the day, with the official mission of preventing sabotage and the beating of nonunion drivers and riders, many of whom had been attacked just for taking the streetcar to work. The posse members were encouraged to carry arms.

On June 10, the day after Francis's return, a posse fired on strikers and their supporters, killing three and wounding thirteen. Decades of economic anger boiled over. One labor leader declaimed, "The shots which on Sunday sounded the death knell of innocent men also rang the death knell of the capitalistic crowd now fighting the working people of St. Louis through hired thugs."[22]

In the June 14 *Mirror*, William Marion Reedy blamed the "disgrace, the tragedy and the horror" of the strike on politics and politicians such as Hawes, who permitted armed posses to roam the streets and fire on strikers, and Governor Stephens, who refused to call out the state militia to stop the violence: "All the rottenness of our system is exposed in this strike—bribery in legislation, corruption in politics, bestowal of monopoly without compensation, concentration of power into irresponsible and incompetent hands." But perhaps, he said, the death and destruction finally would bring St. Louis to its senses as the city began planning in earnest for the Fair.[23]

Francis needed no convincing—he already believed that nothing good could come from men taking to the streets to demand their rights, and now he worried that the riots would derail the Fair by destroying the city's image. And indeed, a national magazine, *Collier's Weekly*, compared the scene in St. Louis to "the terrible orgies of riot and wantonness that characterized the early days of the French revolution in Paris."[24]

In fact, as Reedy had hoped, the strike probably provided impetus to reform—the city fathers wanted nothing like it to happen during the Fair, when St. Louis would play host to the world. The Missouri Democratic Party, meeting shortly after the strike had ended, adopted a plank that supported the right of workers to organize and called for arbitration of labor disputes. The conciliatory approach seemed to work. Some labor problems arose during the construction of the Fair but nothing even remotely comparable to the violent streetcar strike.

IN THE FALL ELECTIONS, under a barrage of support from newspapers, business, and labor, Missouri voters approved a constitutional amendment that permitted St. Louis to issue $5 million in bonds for the Fair. In addition, voters approved giving the Fair $1 million in state funds.

Nationally, the voters again rejected Bryan and reelected McKinley, who had helped himself with St. Louis and western voters by enthusiastically endorsing the Louisiana Purchase Exposition.

The depression was over, and silver had faded as an issue. Crop failures in other countries had increased the price of American grain and thus, the income of American farmers. The pay of American workers had begun rising, too, in part because labor unions had passed through their baptism of fire and emerged stronger. The Spanish-American War in 1898 had helped heat up the economy. And the gold supply—and thus the money supply—had increased greatly because of new finds in the Klondike and South Africa. America happily embarked on the road to inflation.

With a healthy economy, the more radical populists lost favor, to be replaced as representatives of the interests of ordinary Americans by the Progressive Movement. More reformist than radical, the Progressives included Democrats like St. Louis circuit attorney–elect Joseph Wingate Folk, who had negotiated an end to the bloody streetcar strike, and Republicans like Theodore Roosevelt, who was elected vice president on the winning ticket headed by McKinley.

In 1900, without undue fuss, Congress approved and McKinley signed a bill making gold the official monetary standard of the United States. By then, McKinley also had pushed Congress to pass the highest tariffs in American history. David Francis didn't like that part of the picture, but otherwise the beginning of the new century seemed a perfect time for Francis's dream of the biggest American world's fair of them all to come true.

Joseph Folk, who had won the race for circuit attorney with the help of Ed Butler and his intimidating, ballot-box-stuffing Indians, took office on January 1, 1901. He almost immediately convened a grand jury to investigate vote fraud, putting himself in the odd position of calling for the arrest of the men who had helped elect him.[25]

At the same time, Fair organizers announced that the $5 million subscription fund was completed. Nearly twenty-three thousand people had pledged almost $5.3 million. A share of stock in the Louisiana Purchase Exposition cost one hundred dollars, and many people had promised to buy more than one share. (About $4.8 million was actually collected.) St. Louis had fulfilled its end of the bargain with Congress.[26]

Two months later, Congress appropriated $5 million for the Louisiana Purchase Exposition (LPE). Senator George Vest of Missouri spearheaded the lobbying effort. David Francis was behind the scenes, working closely with the man who two years before had sat on his appointment as interior secretary. Five million dollars was the most federal money ever appropriated for a world's fair, and yet Francis would return within a couple of years to ask for—and get—millions more.

Under the bill, federal support of the Fair was contingent on the appointment of a Board of Lady Managers, with one member to serve on each of the main Fair committees to make sure that public morals were not violated by any exhibitions.

Francis and the other Fair directors might have emphasized science, education, and international cooperation, but millions of Americans went to fairs for such attractions as Fatima the hootchie-cootchie dancer who had shocked and entranced Chicago. However, the most popular attraction in Chicago, other than perhaps the world's largest Ferris Wheel, had been the "anthropological exhibit," hundreds of people from the islands of the South Seas, Japan, Africa, and South America, mixed with American Indians, all living on the Midway in replicas of their native habitats.[27]

These primitive folk were in Chicago to be contrasted with the demonstrably more civilized denizens of Western Europe and the United States, and Social Darwinism was the dominant philosophical mode, presented with scientific justification by leading American and European anthropologists with the help of the Smithsonian Institution. The exercise in self-congratulation would be expanded greatly and moved off the midway into the main exhibition areas for the St. Louis World's Fair.

Shortly after the federal funds had been committed, the leadership of the LPE was reorganized, with ninety-three directors elected by the vote of everyone who had subscribed to the $5 million stock issue. The directors, who included such friends of Francis as Pierre Chouteau, John Scullin, James Campbell, publisher Charles Knapp, brewer Adolphus Busch, and bankers Festus Wade and Breckinridge Jones, elected Francis president and banker William H. Thompson treasurer. Veteran journalist, and longtime friend of Francis, Walter Stevens was named secretary.

The Board of Directors, after lengthy debate, put together its "Plan and Scope" for the Fair, promising:

> It will aim definitely at an exhibition of man as well as the works of man. . . .
> It will comprehend man in his full twentieth century development, exhibiting
> not alone his material, but his social advancement. . . . It will embrace in its
> scope a comprehensive anthropological exhibition, constituting a congress of
> races, and exhibiting particularly the barbarous and semi-barbarous peoples
> of the world as nearly as possible in their ordinary and native environments.[28]

On June 24, 1901, with support of the city's major newspapers, the Fair's executive committee decided on a site: the heavily wooded western end of Forest Park, consisting of 657 acres—roughly the size of the Chicago fairgrounds. Within a few days, the full Board of Directors approved that site and McKinley appointed the national commission to oversee the Fair from the federal viewpoint. A few real-estate speculators, including at least one Fair director, made a bundle on property adjacent to the park. But Francis's friend John Scullin lost out—he had lobbied for Carondelet Park in south St. Louis, where he was a large landowner.[29]

Almost immediately, Francis decided the Fair needed more room, to beat out Chicago, if nothing else. The developed eastern half of the park was already in use, with its zoo, fish hatchery, cricket field, and other athletic facilities. Just west of the park, however, Washington University was building a new campus.

Francis leased land and buildings from the university for $650,000, plus an extra $100,000 if the Fair should be delayed until 1904, which, of course, it was. The $750,000 did wonders for the university's capital campaign, which was falling short of its goals, and critics at the time suggested something suspiciously cozy was going on, particularly since Francis's friend, mercantile multimillionaire Robert Brookings, was president of the university's board of curators and its principal fundraiser. Although Brookings was not a director of the Fair, at least five curators of Washington University, including David Francis, were.

The rent money went into construction of university facilities, including the athletic venues used for the 1904 Olympics during the Fair that became Francis Field and Francis Gymnasium. All in all, the deal was a classic example of getting things done by mixing public and private matters, friendship, business, and government. Everyone, Francis argued, benefitted from the arrangement, so how could there possibly be any objection?[30]

The LPE Company also leased some tracts adjacent to the new campus, and by 1903, the total area for the Fair came to 1,270 acres, a site more than a mile and a half long (east to west), and about a mile and a quarter wide. This was, as Francis pointed out regularly, about twice the size of the Chicago fairgrounds.[31]

W ITH THE APRIL 1901 ELECTION of steel magnate Rolla Wells as mayor, the Democrats of the New St. Louis completed their takeover of the city. Wells's most important supporters were emerging Democratic power "Handsome Harry" Hawes and David R. Francis. Wells celebrated his election with a grand fete at the St. Louis Club for seventy-five political leaders, business men, and journalists. He called it "The New St. Louis Banquet." The toastmasters included Francis and Reedy.[32]

Like David Francis, Wells was basically honest, in the context of the business world of mutual back-scratching that they dominated. Both men fought for reform of a flagrantly corrupt political system. But both men were very much a part of the power structure, the Big Cinch. As old-style blatant corruption fell from fashion and the World's Fair era rapidly approached, Francis and Wells represented one face of the Democratic Party—the more conservative, business-oriented one, and the evangelical reformer Folk, who idolized William Jennings Bryan, represented the other.

William Marion Reedy, not always favorably disposed toward Bourbon Democrats—he often dined with the city's financial establishment, but he wasn't afraid to take a nip out of the hands that fed him—greeted Wells's election as an end to an era of "ignorant and corrupt and uncouth" Republican city rule. The outgoing Republican mayor, a thick-headed south side German named "Uncle Henry" Ziegenhein, was best known for reputedly having replied to a citizens plea for more street lighting by saying, "Vell, we got a moon yet, ain't it?"[33]

Wells, Reedy wrote in the *Mirror*, "was a young, progressive man," untainted by the silverite heresy that had ruptured his party, and his campaign—led by Francis and a few others—was a clean one that "urged nothing but good government."[34]

Progressive muckraker Lincoln Steffens, who came to greatly admire Joe Folk, disagreed: "There was little difference between the two parties in the city; but the rascals that were in had been getting the greater share of the spoils, and the 'outs' wanted more." In St. Louis, Steffens decided, the credo was "government of the people, by the rascals, for the rich."[35]

The businessmen of St. Louis, Democratic and Republican, Bourbon and Progressive, piled onto the reform bandwagon, if for no other reason than to spruce up the city's image for the World's Fair. Rolla Wells urged the boodle-ridden Municipal Assembly to work with him to clean up the city, arguing that "St. Louis herself must constitute the greatest of all the exhibits to be displayed."

"There is a moral awakening which is all a part of the New St. Louis," proclaimed Mrs. Louis Marion McCall, a manufacturer's wife who was head of the new fifteen hundred-member Civic Improvement League.[36]

With evangelical fervor, municipal and private forces combined in preparation for the Fair. Streets were paved, street lights were installed, and public buildings were tuckpointed and renovated. Under goading from the Civic Improvement League and its Ladies Sanitary Committee, alleys were cleaned up, houses were painted, and vacant lots were turned into parks. Some slum dwellings were fixed up. Others, particularly those that might disturb visitors on the main routes to Forest Park, were torn down. A new smoke abatement ordinance was passed, and for a few years, until the Fair was over, the notorious air of St. Louis was nearly transparent.

Making the water transparent was an even knottier problem. The opening of the Chain of Rocks waterworks upriver of the city's sewers in 1895 had lessened greatly for a time the chances of water-borne diseases, but the appearance of the water had not improved signficantly from a decade earlier when young Theodore Dreiser, on his first day in town, was shocked to discover that the local faucets produced "a dark, yellowish brown [liquid] which, in a glass, as I saw, immediately deposited a yellow sediment."[37]

Also, the growth of the city and its environs meant that the bacterial count of the city water was again on the rise. Francis put heavy pressure on city officials to do something about the water, but plans were not set in motion for a purification plant at Chain of Rocks until January 1902. The problems with the water remained unsolved until about six weeks before the Fair opened. (See Chapter 9).[38]

In 1900 and 1901, David Francis and publisher and fellow Fair director, George Knapp, took advantage of several eastern trips to talk with Joseph Pulitzer, who had not been back to St. Louis for nearly twenty years. They wanted to buy the *Post-Dispatch* and make it an afternoon annex of the morning *Republic.*

At one point in the negotiations, Francis visited Pulitzer at Chatwold, his gargantuan summer chalet at Bar Harbor, Maine. Pulitzer, in his mid-fifties, gaunt from a series of illnesses, his eyesight nearly gone, asked Francis to step with him onto a second-floor balcony, "out here in the light so I can see you." Pulitzer put his hands on Francis's face and held it up to the sun, peering closely at him through his thick glasses. He shook his head and said, "I remember you as a boy; I don't see how you have ever attained any reputation, position or influence at home. You did not give much promise of that when I knew you as a boy."

Running his long, thin hands down Francis's face, Pulitzer said, "There is nothing in that"—the face—"to indicate that you have anything in you." But, Pulitzer concluded, lowering his hands to his sides, "there must be something good in you or you could not exert the influence that you are reputed to exert at home." [39]

Eventually, a deal was struck with Pulitzer at $1.5 million, but hours before papers were to be signed, Don Seitz, Pulitzer's top aide in New York, told his boss he was making "a foolish deal." The *Post-Dispatch,* Seitz argued, "would be wrecked, just as the *Republic* was being destroyed by a rich politician's ownership," and Pulitzer eventually would "get it back as damaged goods." Pulitzer immediately doubled the asking price to $3 million, infuriating Francis, and the deal fell through. [40]

By the summer of 1901, Francis had little time for matters other than the Fair. Occasionally, business would intrude. Francis was meeting with the city's House of Delegates to press for a pivotal piece of legislation permitting the LPE Company to use Forest Park when a pale-faced man came quickly down the aisle and whispered to him: "Northern Pacific has gone [down] to $1,000 a share."

"We haven't any," Francis softly replied. "What of it?"

"Everything else is down 15 to 25 points," the man answered, his voice rising. "There's a panic in Wall Street. We've been called for $450,000."

Francis sighed. "Go back and get the money together," he said. "I'll be down in a couple of hours." He waved the man away and went on with his presentation. The market panic soon subsided. [41]

Before David Francis, world's fairs had been run by a director general, a well-paid professional manager. There was no director general for the St. Louis World's Fair. The president of the Board of Directors, David Francis, ran the whole shebang and exulted in the challenge.

He quickly found out, if he hadn't known all along, that running a world's fair was better suited to his temperament than government, where positions and ranks and duties already were established. With the Fair, he discovered, he could make up the whole thing from scratch and use his powers of leadership and persuasion to make it work: "In a position like this which confronts me, one has to create the law himself; he must assemble men by personal influence, and he must adjust their duties, their relative rank and their different opinions in such a way as to produce the best result without depriving himself of their loyal services."[42] He had 1,270 acres in which to create his perfect city-state and the power of a benevolent dictator.

Francis's wealth and his stature in St. Louis and in Washington gave him a degree of independence that no professional manager could ever hope for. It helped that he worked for free. When a committee of directors pleaded with him to take a salary, he replied, "I cannot serve for a commercial reward, but the best in me will be given cheerfully to promote the success of the enterprise fraught with such consequences to St. Louis and the country."[43]

What would be the consequences to St. Louis? A broadening of vision, he hoped, and a more secure sense of the city's place in the country and the world. Implicit was Francis's belief, or need to believe, that St. Louis still actually might become one of the great cities of the world.

Francis said of the Fair, in retrospect:

> St. Louis needed something like this. We are a peculiarly self-centered people. We own our city. We have always stood ready to furnish capital to others. But we are, perhaps, too independent. We need to be brought more closely in contact with the outside world. We need to have a certain narrowness of vision altered. We need to learn something of our own merits and possibilities, so that many of our people will realize a little better than they do that St. Louis is, in its own way, as great a city as any on the Continent.[44]

On August 20, 1901, President William McKinley proclaimed:

> I do hereby invited all the Nations of the Earth to take part in the Commemoration of the Purchase of the Louisiana Territory, an event of great interest to the United States and of abiding effect on their development, by appointing representatives and sending such exhibits to the Louisiana Purchase Exposition as will most fitly and fully illustrate their resources, their industries and their progress in civilization.[45]

Seventeen days later, McKinley was dead, fatally shot by an anarchist while touring the Buffalo World's Fair. The day before, he had given a rousing speech saying that world's fairs "stimulate the energy, enterprise and intellect of the people and quicken human genius."[46]

Vice President Theodore Roosevelt ascended to the presidency. Francis attended the McKinley funeral and quickly established a friendly relationship with Roosevelt, with whom he had a lot in common—from a love of the outdoors to a conviction that unregulated trusts were a signal danger to democracy. Roosevelt became a passionate supporter of the Fair.

In the spring and summer of 1901, after the $5 million federal appropriation had been approved, Francis moved quickly to set up the structure of the Fair and bring in top executives. For the crucial post of director of exhibits, he chose Frederick J. V. Skiff, a veteran of the Chicago fair and currently director of that city's Field Museum.

For director of works he picked Isaac S. "Ike" Taylor, the architect who had designed many prominent St. Louis buildings and the iron fence around Francis's house. In September, Taylor moved into his new offices in the Odd Fellows building downtown and began hiring architects, draftsmen, engineers, inspectors, managers, and clerks. Early drawings for buildings began appearing in October.

Much of western Forest Park was covered with trees, and Taylor later made a point of noting, somewhat misleadingly, that "none of the forest trees was sacrificed, except those immediately on the sites of the buildings." There were, however, many building sites—the twelve main "palaces" alone covered 128 acres—so thousands of trees were cut down, including many venerable hardwoods a century or more old.[47]

On December 22, 1901, the 98th anniversary of the formal transfer of the Louisiana Purchase to the United States, the groundbreaking ceremony was held in Forest Park. The ground almost literally had to be broken, since a long, unseasonable cold spell had left the topsoil frozen under five inches of snow. The temperature was ten degrees below zero, and a scheduled parade had to be canceled. A log bonfire was kept roaring for most of the day to thaw the earth where David Francis, taking a firm grip on a special commemorative shovel—silver-plated, diamond-edged steel with an ebony handle—pried loose the first scoop of soot-smeared earth. The sun briefly broke through the clouds as he gave a short speech—much shorter than he had originally intended.

Then everyone adjourned to midtown for a grand public celebration at the Coliseum. Later that evening, a banquet was held at the Southern Hotel for directors of the Fair and visiting representatives of the states and territories in the Purchase.

Support poured in from the West, but Francis fretted about the lack of enthusiasm abroad. That winter, he dispatched Frederick Skiff to Europe to drum up support. In January 1902, Skiff sent a wire from St. Petersburg, the capital of Tsarist Russia, asking for help in getting the Russians to realize the importance of St. Louis's upcoming international exposition. He suggested asking American companies that held Russian notes to put pressure on the Tsar.

Francis responded by contacting John A. McCall, the president of New York Life Insurance Co., asking him to exert his influence. New York Life, which had a large presence in Russia and recently had purchased millions of dollars in Russian bonds, was a politically well-connected financial empire that functioned as a national and international investment bank, both directly and through its close ties to J. P. Morgan and Co. Francis had done a considerable amount of brokerage business with both New York economic behemoths, and New York Life became a major subscriber to the Fair. Shortly after Francis got in touch with McCall, the Russians agreed to send a large exhibit to the Fair.[48]

As Francis prepared to dazzle the world with the accomplishments and hospitality of his city, prosecutor Joseph Folk aggressively moved ahead to expose its shame. The *Post-Dispatch*, perhaps with a tad of irony, took note of this odd duality in 1903 by presenting loving cups to both Folk and Francis, noting that "on weekdays we read about the horrors Folk uncovered and on Sunday we watched the progress of the Fair."[49]

Beginning early in 1902, Folk and his grand jury issued a flurry of subpoenas to politicians and to the businessmen who had bribed them. Initially, Folk targeted Municipal Assembly approval of line extensions by the Suburban Railway Co., one of St. Louis's two streetcar companies. Folk showed that Ed Butler had promised to ram through an extension bill for $145,000, which would be spread around among members of the so-called "Combine" in the city's bicameral legislature.

Once Folk's investigation got up a head of steam, it roared ahead on multiple tracks, spotlighting widespread and massive corruption. One member of the House of Delegates admitted to the grand jury that he had netted twenty-five thousand dollars from the boodle combine in one year; another, a key member of the City Council, said he was paid fifty thousand dollars for his vote on one measure.[50]

Folk's grand jury proclaimed, "Although there may have been corruption in other cities as great as we have had here, yet in no place in the world and in no time known to history has so much official corruption been uncovered."[51]

Folk issued sixty-one indictments, many of them hastily and, it turned out, sloppily drawn. In the end, he got only eight convictions that stood, all of minor figures.

That is not to suggest that many others, including prominent politicians and businessmen, didn't deserve to go to jail. Folk was so zealous in his fight against the forces of corruption that he sometimes plowed blindly ahead without sufficiently preparing his cases, leaving room for findings of error. And the Missouri Supreme Court, three of whose members were beholden to Ed Butler for their election, was preternaturally alert to error. The court overturned several major guilty verdicts, including Butler's conviction for bribery to get city contracts for his garbage hauling business.[52]

In his muckraking articles, Lincoln Steffens made Folk a national hero of the burgeoning Progressive Movement. Under heavy scrutiny, St. Louis did clean up its politics and revoked Butler's lucrative garbage-hauling contracts. Rolla Wells and Harry Hawes were now in control of the party, with David Francis pulling strings behind the backdrop of the Fair.

Joe Folk was no respecter of persons, and it's probably a commentary on David Francis's ethics—or his shrewdness—that he emerged unindicted and unscathed, even after he became an outspoken political opponent of Folk. Some of Francis's friends were indicted, and one, wealthy brewer Ellis Wainwright, who had attended Washington University with Francis and was a director of the Suburban line, conveniently was touring Europe when his indictment was handed down, and he simply didn't come home. He lived most of the rest of his life in Paris. At least two other indictees fled to Mexico.

By EARLY 1902, it was time to let contracts for construction on the Fairgrounds. The first one, signed January 6, committed $125,000 to rerouting the park's flood-prone, sewage-filled River des Peres. It took about five months to accomplish this Herculean task by digging deep ditches and lining them with wood, creating large conduits that carried the main flow of the river underground and accommodated floods. By the time the Fair opened, a clean, gentle stream flowed over gravel above the filthy underground river.

As contracts were let for other work, a major problem—and a potentially damaging conflict of interest—appeared. There were no switching facilities for rail traffic into the park, and only one railroad, a "dinky" short line of about one hundred miles called the Colorado, had tracks that led to the park. The Colorado was owned by a partnership of two men—steel and streetcar magnate John Scullin, and his close friend, David Rowland Francis.

The matter of the Colorado Railroad needs to be dealt with here, although full public discussion did not come until 1910. That's when the *Post-Dispatch* ran a novella-length investigative series charging that Scullin and Francis bought the Colorado cheap with the private knowledge that Forest Park would be chosen as the site of the Fair, giving them a lucrative monopoly on freight-switching at the Fair, a monopoly they later sold at great profit. By 1910, David Francis was running for the U.S. Senate, and the time long past when attacking him would interfere with ballyhooing the Fair.

In the fall of 1900, Francis and Scullin bought the fifty-five-mile Colorado—officially, the Kansas City and Colorado Railroad—from the Santa Fe for about $480,000. During the year and a half the two friends owned it, they extended the tracks forty-five miles further to the west, and put forty to fifty additional miles under construction. The *Post-Dispatch* failed to determine from a scouring of public records exactly how much had been spent on these extensions, and neither Francis nor Scullin volunteered a figure.

According to a report by Director of Works Ike Taylor:

> In the winter of 1902, the first contracts for construction of the World's Fair were let. There was no railroad connection with the World's Fair grounds. There was one single wagon road leading into the site. . . . The Executive Committee was asking the railroads to form an organization, lay tracks on the World's Fair grounds and operate them jointly. The railroads offered to build to the boundary of the World's Fair, but maintained the position that the Exposition company should build and operate its own terminals. . . .
>
> With contractors pressing and valuable time passing, the director of works urged that at least a temporary railroad connection be furnished. . . . The only road which touched the World's Fair boundary was the Colorado.[53]

The situation was desperate, Taylor said, so William Thompson sent for Scullin and:

> . . . asked him as a favor to the Exposition company to build a spur from the Colorado across the corner of Washington University and into the northwest corner of Forest Park, where contractors were clamoring for material.

Mr. Scullin demurred, pointing out the difficulties. Mr. Thompson urged. Mr. Scullin yielded. The spur was put in and as needed, additional trackage. On the 18th of March 1902, the first car was switched into the World's Fair Grounds. The charge for switching into the grounds was $4 per car, of which 25 per cent, or $1, was paid into the treasury of the Exposition. The charge was not sufficient to pay for the cost of services. . . . This arrangement continued for five weeks.[54]

Then, on April 23, Scullin and Francis sold the Colorado to the Rock Island for roughly $4.25 million in cash and stock. According to sworn testimony by a Rock Island attorney in a later civil suit, the price was based on $750,000 for terminal facilities in St. Louis, $30,000 a mile (or $3 million) for about one hundred miles of completed railway, and the remainder (about a half million) for "the cost of construction [of the uncompleted stretch] with a reasonable contractor's profit."[55]

The switches Francis and Scullin had installed, which were the crux of the *Post-Dispatch*'s case, were not part of the deal with the Rock Island, and for a good reason: The Rock Island did not want them. As the *Post-Dispatch* itself noted, the switches "would have been so much junk on the Rock Island's hands when the World's Fair closed."[56]

In July 1902, John Scullin turned the switches over to the Fair and asked, in a letter, that he and Francis be reimbursed for their construction cost. The records are unclear as to how much, if anything, was paid to Francis and Scullin for the switches. Scullin complained later that he and Francis had not been reimbursed fairly, and Director of Works Taylor said that Scullin and Francis had lost money on the switches.[57]

All that being said, there is no question that Francis once again had mixed public and private business in a manner that appeared unseemly. But it's hard to believe, both from the facts and from knowledge of Francis's priorities, that he would have taken a chance on tainting his great dream with a shady financial deal.

ONE DAY IN 1902, PHILIP JORDAN, now thirty-three years old and sober, showed up at the mansion on Maryland Avenue and asked for his old job back. He said he had never been happier than when he worked for the Francises, and he intended to stay as long as they permitted. When he swore that he was on the wagon for good, the Francises hired him, aware that they would need extra help soon, when distinguished guests began arriving for the World's Fair. Much to the delight of the Francis boys, he moved into servant's quarters on the large city estate and remained an employee of the Francis family for the rest of his life.[58]

Through the winter and spring of 1902, what came to be called the "Ivory City"—as if it were an even richer white than Chicago's White City—grew in the park, with hundreds of workers now living in makeshift quarters on the Fairgrounds. The main construction materials were wood and staff, plaster reinforced with hemp fiber and hair.

Burlap-based staff, which could be polished to resemble marble, had been used successfully for building exteriors and statues at Chicago. In the decade since, staff mixing had been improved and made cheaper with the use of hemp and hair. There was no reason, Francis was told, that staff, if painted once a year, could not hold up for ten to twelve years. Francis didn't need nearly that long.[59]

There were twelve major Fair buildings. The largest was the Transportation Building, which was 1,300 feet long and 575 feet wide, covering nearly seventeen acres. The most striking building was the domed Festival Hall, laid out along the crest of the highest hill in the western end of the park, its wide arms, meant to evoke St. Peter's in Rome, reaching northeast to embrace the central square of the Fair. Behind it, on what became known as Art Hill, was the double-winged Palace of Fine Arts, the only major building that was made of stone and meant to last—it needed to be sturdy and fireproof to protect its valuable contents.

Below the arms of the Festival Hall was the Grand Basin, a waterfall and fountain-fed lake, and the long Plaza of St. Louis, which was flanked on each side by four major buildings: Mines and Metallurgy, Liberal Arts, Education and Social Economy, and Manufactures to the east; Electricity, Varied Industries, Machinery, and Transportation to the west. This area became known as "The Main Picture." Farther west, across Skinker Road on and near the new Washington University campus were the Agriculture, Horticulture, Forestry, and Fish and Game Buildings.

The average building, according to the official Fair history, was 1,200 feet long by 525 feet wide, covered about 14.5 acres, and contained seven million board feet of lumber and 445 tons of iron and steel. The manpower for each building included 80 diggers and laborers for the foundation, 140 carpenters, 100 plasterers, 100 staff workers, 200 nailers and helpers, 50 roofers, and 100 painters.[60]

These twelve enormous display and convention buildings, constructed by the LPE Company, were just the core of the Fair. Eventually, more than nine hundred buildings stood on the grounds, many of them built by states and foreign countries.

The Fair was an immense undertaking, and by the spring of 1902, it became clear that it could not possibly be completed in a year. Francis breathed a deep sigh of relief and made the announcement. Chicago had celebrated the 400th anniversary of Columbus's voyage in 1893, a year late; St. Louis would follow suit and deliver its fair on the 101st anniversary of the Louisiana Purchase, in 1904.

Postponing the Fair meant that Francis had a shot at fulfilling another dream—to have both of the quadrennial national political conventions in St. Louis during the Fair.

With the opening of the Fair delayed until 1904, a potentially damaging conflict became apparent. In 1896, the ancient Olympic Games had been revived in Athens. Four years later, the games were held in Paris. The third modern Olympiad was scheduled for the summer of 1904 in, of all places, Chicago.

Francis appointed a committee, headed by businessman A. L. Shapleigh, to look into prying the games away from Chicago. A number of meetings, most of them attended by Francis, were held with members of the Chicago Olympic Committee. At the same time, St. Louis–based athletic equipment magnate A. G. Spalding was assigned to push for the change with leaders of the American Athletic Union, which sponsored the games in the United States.[61]

With or without the Olympics, St. Louis planned on having an array of athletic events at its Fair, and representatives of both cities felt that having similar events in St. Louis and Chicago at roughly the same time would be harmful to both. Some directors of the Chicago committee, like the wealthy manufacturer Charles Crane—Crane would reappear more than once in Francis's life and already may have been a friend—were more favorably disposed than others to turning the Olympics over to St. Louis.[62]

Finally, late in 1902, Henry J. Furber, Jr., president of the Chicago Olympic Committee, tossed the controversy to Baron Pierre Coubertin, the French president of the International Olympic Committee. Furber recommended that the games be moved to 1905 and remain in Chicago. If that was impossible, he wrote in a cable impatiently pushing for a solution to the dilemma, "we consent to transfer to St. Louis."

Coubertin was miffed at the squabbling Americans. He threw the ball back across the Atlantic to President Roosevelt, whose embrace of "the strenuous life" had helped revive interest in athletics and physical culture in this country. Roosevelt chose St. Louis and the Louisiana Purchase Exposition as the best showcase for the Olympics and the notion that physical well-being was necessary to the well-rounded human being. In February 1903, Coubertin approved the move to St. Louis in a terse telegram: "Transfer accepted."[63]

Roosevelt was named honorary president of the 1904 Olympics, and Francis the president.[64]

In mid-1902, Francis moved into the new offices of the Fair, in the castle-like Administration Building (now Brookings Hall) of the just-completed Washington University campus, on a low rise overlooking the Fairgrounds to the east. But much of the early planning was done late at night over drinks and cigars in the great dining room of the Maryland Avenue mansion, with plans spread out over the huge dinner table.

Francis also traveled extensively across the United States to promote the Fair.

Long before the first building was completed, stories ballyhooed the Fair in the St. Louis papers virtually every day. Even the haughty *Post-Dispatch* had assigned a reporter to work full-time coming up with regular stories about the Fair, even when nothing much was happening.

Most of the coverage was favorable, but not all. As construction proceeded apace in 1902, the *Globe-Democrat* decided butchery was being done to the forest that had given the park its name. A *Globe* photographer was assigned to set up near the middle of the park and point his lens to the west, across a vast wasteland of tree stumps and swampy ditches stretching a mile or more to the brand new towers of Washington University rising in the western distance. Smoke from burning logs and blasted stumps hung like a pall over the western end of the park.

The *Globe*, along with Mayor Wells and other city officials, fretted that Forest Park never would be properly restored. In January 1903, a landscape architect estimated that it would cost at least $1 million to restore the park after the Fair. The city asked that $550,000 be added to the $100,000 bond that guaranteed the park's restoration. For the time being, Francis ignored the board and kept the work moving forward.[65] Trees were felled, swampland drained, hills molded, and ravines filled in, brush and undergrowth cleared out, sewer, water, electric, and gas lines installed.

Meanwhile, the publicity machine was rolling across America, with Francis so busy making public appearances that William Marion Reedy remarked, tongue in pudgy cheek, "In after years we shall see organizations of citizens placing a memorial tablet on the spot where David Francis was not photographed."[66]

Francis was becoming very well known across the United States, but he began to worry about Europe, China, and Japan. He was, after all, planning on a *world's* fair. In the summer of 1902, he received a disturbing letter from brewer Adolphus Busch, who was spending the summer at his mountain villa in Germany. Busch warned that there was "not much enthusiasm for our Fair here" and recommended that "men of stature" were needed to promote the Fair overseas. Full of recently acquired noblesse oblige, the brewery magnate noted that, unfortunately, "good men have to do all the work," a sentiment Francis was prone to agree with.[67]

Late in 1902, Francis eagerly accepted an invitation to be the main guest at a Washington's birthday dinner to be given by the American Society of London on February 22. But, as the winter rolled along, with the inevitable bad weather delaying construction, and the Dedication Day of April 30 approached, Francis began to worry about leaving town. The executive committee agreed he needed to stay in St. Louis, perhaps bending to Francis's will and his need to oversee the driving of every nail.

On February 1, 1903, he cabled his regrets to London. There was a quick and anguished reply from his hosts, pointing out that many important Britishers already had accepted invitations. A flurry of transatlantic cables concluded on February 9, when the American ambassador in London settled the matter by cabling that "the interests of the Exposition demanded that its President accept the invitation."

Francis's personal secretary, J. Collins Thompson, Jr., frantically checked sailing schedules and discovered that only one ship could get Francis to London in time for the dinner. The next day, Francis and Collins Thompson took the train to New York, where they were met by several directors of the Fair, including Rolla Wells. Francis sailed on February 12, 1903, on the French Line steamer *La Bretagne,* bound for Le Havre. Mayor Wells stood on the pier at Tenth Street and, according to Francis, "waved bon voyage as long as a human form could be distinguished on the shore."[68]

The day after embarkation, in calm seas under sunny skies, Francis, in an expansive mood, wrote a letter to President Theodore Roosevelt asking him to declare April 30, 1903, Dedication Day, a national holiday.

Two and a half days out, with the winds rising and the waves crashing against the windows of his stateroom, Francis's optimism had vanished with the sun, and he worried that the ship might be delayed by foul weather. "It would indeed be unfortunate to travel nearly five thousand miles to attend a banquet and reach my destination after the feast was over," he remarked.[69]

He quickly became bored with his daily games of backgammon with Thompson. His stomach was too queasy for whisky. None of the other twenty passengers in first class, he complained, was "sufficiently attractive or interesting to divert my thoughts from the interests of the Louisiana Purchase Exposition or the stupendous work" ahead. He complained about the plainness of the women aboard—"no man of good taste would desire" them, he grumbled.[70]

For a man of action like Francis, few places are worse than a ship in the middle of the ocean. He poured out his frustration in a lengthy, scolding missive to the executive committee that began, "I have had more time for reflection during the past three days than during any similar period within the past ten years."

As he obsessed about the coming fourteen months until the opening of the Fair, he despaired that the work would never be done in time:

> The plans projected and the scope adopted will require almost superhuman effort from this time forward. . . . The attendance, however, of the Executive Committee upon its sessions has been so irregular that I have concluded, upon reflecting upon conditions, to endeavor to arouse you to a realizing sense of the labor and the sacrifices your position entails.

He went on for several pages, pressing a long-standing argument that another $1 million in subscriptions needed to be raised. He asked the board members to pledge an additional ten thousand dollars apiece to their subscriptions, because, he said, he was willing "to exceed the $15 million limit if we find it necessary to do so." The letter must have hit finance director/banker William Thompson like a blow to the solar plexus, confirming his long suspicions that Francis had no real intentions of sticking to the budget.[71]

FRANCIS'S SHIP ARRIVED AT LE HAVRE on the evening of February 20, and at midnight he sailed across the channel for Southampton. His train arrived in London at 11 A.M. on the twenty-first, a Saturday, and he checked into a suite at the Claridge in time to join the American ambassador and his top aides for lunch. He discovered that the Washington's birthday dinner had been moved to February 23.

The tall, handsome, eloquent fifty-two-year-old midwestern American was a hit in London. On the morning of Sunday, February 22, he spoke of the wonders coming to St. Louis in interviews with the English newspapers and the London correspondents of the major American and European papers and wire services. That evening a dinner was held in his honor at the Carlton, attended by a flock of generals, admirals, industrialists, and members of the nobility. At the dinner, and for the remainder of his visit, he talked almost nonstop about the World's Fair.

The next day, he met King Edward VII, Prime Minister Arthur Balfour, and the top members of the government, and he attended a session of Parliament. That evening, he greeted about four hundred dignitaries, including the lord mayor of London and the president of the Royal Academy, at the delayed Washington's birthday dinner at the Hotel Cecil. Francis spoke for twenty minutes, dwelling at some length on American assumption of the White Man's Burden, so long and valiantly borne by the British. "After subjugating the savage," he proclaimed, "we are engaged in his education and elevation."

He paused momentarily in his boasting to insist, "But I have not come here to boast," and then he urged the British to participate lavishly in the Fair because "the citizens of every civilized country on the globe will visit us. . . . You do not need to be told that of the millions who will visit the Exposition Grounds almost every one will ask to be shown the building of the country on whose possessions the sun never sets."[72]

On February 25, to the irritation of haughtier members of the peerage, he was invited to a thirty-minute private audience with Edward VII. The well-connected London journal *Lloyd's* reported that King Edward had been informed that Francis was "one of the most likely future Presidents of the United States."[73]

The king told Francis he had decided to send to the Fair the glittering array of jewels and other gifts that his late mother, Queen Victoria, had received for her 1897 Jubilee. (Although not usually given credit, Florence Hayward, a Washington University graduate whom Francis had appointed as a roving commissioner to promote the Fair in Europe, had planted and nurtured the seed of Edward's decision to send Victoria's jewels into the wilds of America.)[74]

According to a humorous summary of his trip in the American monthly *Everybody's Magazine,* Francis's visit seemed to fill a need in Europeans to "seize on" American visitors "as a method of testifying to that love for America and American institutions which it does not feel." The well-publicized audience with the king set off a chain reaction, not only among journalists and the high-born English, who clamored to play host to Francis during the remainder of his visit, but also among other royalty. "When the King of England gave Mr. Francis that interview," *Everybody's Magazine* remarked, "every other crowned head made ready to follow his suit."[75]

The invitations came pouring in. He had planned on returning to New York on February 28, but he couldn't really turn down an invitation to have lunch on March 1 with the Lord Chief Justice of England or to dine with Melville Stone, manager of the Associated Press, who had come from Berlin to meet him. By then, Francis already had received an invitation to visit from the government of France, and Stone told him he would miss a magnificent opportunity if he didn't continue his trip to the continent. The word went out through diplomatic channels, and quickly Francis had enough engagements on the continent to more than occupy the time until March 10, when he could sail from Bremen.[76]

On March 2, after an uncomfortable overnight trip across the channel and through northern France, he arrived at the Ritz in Paris, where he was entertained by the mayor, the president of the French Republic, and a cadre of French politicians and industrialists. His Grand Tour continued to Madrid, where he met leaders of government and industry and got commitments for significant Spanish representation at the Fair—in itself remarkable considering that the Spanish American War was still fresh in the memories of the losers and diplomatic relations had not returned to normal. While in Madrid, he went to the theater at 11:30 p.m. with a group of Americans, including Maddin Summers, a special envoy investigating Spanish war claims. He quickly came to like Summers, who shared his optimism, enthusiasm, and tireless dedication to his work. Summers would appear again in his life.[77]

Then it was on to Berlin, by way of Paris, where he paused long enough for breakfast at the Hotel Continental with an array of French ministers and dignitaries. Francis read aloud, in French, a lengthy speech that praised his hosts for their pioneering success in international expositions, noting that the Fair in St. Louis would embrace four times the acreage of the most recent Paris World Exposition. He left with a loving cup and commitments for major French representation at the Fair.

After another overnight train trip, Francis reached Berlin on the morning of March 8, where he met with the chancellor, the foreign minister, and, in private session at the royal palace, Kaiser Wilhelm II. The *Post-Dispatch* later remarked that the Kaiser had not only followed the example of his relative King Edward but had "overpowered" it: "King Edward had given Mr. Francis 30 minutes; the Kaiser gave him an hour, and asked more questions than a divorce lawyer on cross examination. In the end, the Kaiser exuberantly promised the German favor to the Fair. . . ."[78] The *New York Times* reported, "Considerable astonishment is expressed at the length of Mr. Francis's interview with the Emperor, as such audiences rarely last more than a few minutes. . . . It is not remembered that any other person ever asked for an audience and named the time for it."[79]

Then it was on to Brussels, where Francis met, among others, the head of the Rothschild banking operation in Belgium, and King Leopold, with whom he spent an hour.

Francis later described Leopold as "a progressive monarch, who is said . . . to be imbued with the American instinct of trade and accumulation." He did not mention, and may well not have known, that Leopold's "instinct of accumulation" was causing the enslavement and murder of millions in Belgium's African colonies.

After thanking the Belgian Parliament in person for appropriating five hundred thousand francs for the Fair, Francis headed back to France. Collins Thompson had figured out that they could stretch Francis's time in Europe by catching the Kronprinz Wilhelm at Cherbourg rather than Bremen, and they arrived on the afternoon of March 11, just in time to climb aboard.[80]

As Francis had sped across Europe, meeting presidents and prime ministers and kings, the Associated Press and other American news outlets reported on his trip. He was becoming a hero back home. The *Globe-Democrat* reacted to the national furor by evoking that blend of pride and defensiveness with which St. Louisans and midwesterners in general often react to slights, real or imagined, issued from the great metropolises of the East:

The effete East, voicing itself in some of its newspapers, marvels that Mr. Francis carried himself 'well in the presence of King Edward VII.' . . . Evidently there was fear and trembling, in the East, lest the man from St. Louis should be so overcome by the royal presence that he would appear awkward, clumsy and altogether unpresentable. It is clear that some of them were expecting on their next 'run over' to have to apologize for Mr. Francis as 'a man from the provinces.' . . . Those who know Mr. Francis better would wonder, rather, if the king could come through the ordeal without flinching. . . . The East, which is not well acquainted with Mr. Francis . . . styles as 'graciousness' what we who know Mr. Francis well can only consider a mental attitude of deference toward an American citizen who is always as cocksure of himself as any sprig of royalty who ever sat on a throne.[81]

F RANCIS LANDED IN NEW YORK on March 17, and despite a six-hour delay in quaran- tine because of a case of smallpox on board, when he walked down the boarding ramp a flock of New York reporters met him. One reporter asked if he was planning on running for president in 1904. He replied, "Count me out. . . . My work is to be devoted to the success of the St. Louis Exposition."[82]

By then, enough talk swirled in the national press about Francis running for either president or vice president that the *Republic* issued, surely at Francis's request, a state- ment that was picked up across the country:

The World's Fair must be kept free from associations of partisan politics, and since Governor Francis is so thoroughly identified with the Fair, he cannot be regarded as a political candidate without enveloping the enterprise in a dam- aging tinge of partisanship. . . . [St. Louis] must insist that he is president of the Louisiana Purchase Exposition and will not be a political candidate until the gates of the enterprise are closed.[83]

After disembarking in New York, Francis champed at the bit to get home and check on the progress of construction, with Dedication Day less than six weeks away, but again he had invitations difficult to turn down.

The next day, Francis had lunch at the University Club with the editors and pub- lishers of seventy national magazines. After he spoke about his Grand Tour, the audience gave him three cheers, the editor of *Harper's* proposed everyone in attendance give him a complimentary subscription to their magazines, and someone in the jovial crowd shouted, "Where do you live?" Before Francis could reply, someone else shouted, "The Governor's address hereafter is America."[84]

After the luncheon, Francis was escorted to the New York Press Club, where he met with more than one hundred newspaper and wire-service reporters, editors, and pub- lishers. Finally, on the morning Saturday, March 21, he took the train to Washington and had lunch at the White House with Theodore Roosevelt, an enthusiastic supporter of the Fair (although not quite enthusiastic enough to declare Dedication Day a national holiday).

Roosevelt kept Francis for an extra hour and a half after the dishes had been cleared to continue discussing his trip. After visiting cabinet members, including John Hay, the secretary of state, and Elihu Root, the secretary of war, he rejoined the growing group of St. Louisans who had come east to greet him.

The groups included more than a dozen people, including his son, Perry, his brother, Thomas, his early mentor, E. O. Stanard, and Charles Knapp of the *Republic*. That evening, in a private car, the group headed home, arriving on the evening of Sunday, March 22, to a tumultuous greeting by thousands of people at Union Station. He announced to exultant cheers that "all the great powers of the earth" would come to St. Louis for the Fair.[85]

The *Globe-Democrat* observed that Francis "looked the picture of health and seemed to have taken on a little flesh as the result of his strenuous journey to the capitals of Europe. His face was ruddy from the sea breezes and his step quick and buoyant. Every action bespoke the fact that he was hugely glad to get home again."

His reputation for having an eye for beauty led to a discussion with a reporter about European women. He replied that he had seen "many women of great beauty and grace," he said, but none of them could top Natalie Townsend, the wife of the American ambassador to Belgium. It may or may not be relevant that her husband, Lawrence Townsend, was a rich and influential Republican.

St. Louis reporters repeatedly brought up the presidential race, and he repeatedly insisted that he was not a candidate and that all his energies would be devoted to the Fair. One reason the question kept coming back was William Jennings Bryan, who believed that talk of running Cleveland for a third term was a smoke screen for a Francis candidacy. "Cleveland will probably allow the talk of his nomination to run for a while," Bryan remarked in May 1903, "and then, knowing that he has no possibility of election, refuse to be considered, and Francis is likely to be the next man taken up by the reorganizers." And Francis, Bryan charged bitterly, was on the wrong side of the "great war between plutocracy and democracy, and there is no middle ground." Bryan saw Francis as among those "trying to increase the hold that organized wealth has upon the government."[86]

Francis struggled to appear as nonpartisan as any outspoken, fervent, lifelong Democrat could. He still had hopes of snaring both national conventions, and he counted on a coup for the upcoming Dedication Day: appearances by the both the Republican president of the United States, and the only living ex-president, Democrat Grover Cleveland.

With five weeks to go to Dedication Day, Francis settled once again into his offices at Fair headquarters. Every few days, the local papers carried bulletins such as this one, from the *Globe-Democrat*:

> PEKIN, March 22—The dowager empress has ordered an appropriation of half a million taels (about $275,000) to be made for the Chinese representation at the St. Louis exposition.[87]

By early April, seven thousand men worked on the Fairgrounds, many of them from dawn to dusk. Isaac Taylor announced that the Liberal Arts Palace, where two days of dedication ceremonies would be held, was ready. Three additional major exhibition halls—Education, Varied Industries, and Electricity Palaces—now were being painted a creamy off-white and would be finished just in time for Dedication Day. He promised that the remainder would be completed before the next winter set in.[88]

But as the month progressed, heavy rains fell, the rivers and creeks rose, and Forest Park was awash in spring muck and debris. As if St. Louis's own sewage was not enough of a problem, Chicago dumped so much into the Illinois River that the water was still virulent with bacteria when it reached the Mississippi just above St. Louis, three hundred miles downstream. At least, that's what St. Louis health authorities maintained, and they feared an outbreak of typhoid fever just as thousands of visitors would be arriving.

Then, the Board of Lady Managers rose up in arms about reports of "indecent dancing" and even bullfighting coming to the Fair's midway. And hundreds of laborers and railroad track-layers walked off the job, demanding that their wages be raised and their workdays cut from nine to eight hours a day.

And then it rained some more.[89]

CHAPTER 9

He Invited the World

Ain't you glad it's over?
Ain't you glad it's done?
Teddy's gone and Grover—
Every blessed one. . . .

Noise to beat creation!
Noise you couldn't stand.
Glorious dedication!
Finest in the land!
—St. Louis Post-Dispatch, *May 2, 1903*

I**N THE DAYS LEADING UP TO** A**PRIL** 30, Francis managed to placate the unions and pacify the Board of Lady Managers. He accomplished the latter by announcing that the Louisiana Purchase Exposition would not have a "Midway" at all. Instead, it would have a "Pike," which would stretch for about a mile along the north side of the Fair and feature such innocuous exhibits as "The Streets of Cairo." The *Globe-Democrat* was not fooled:

> When the gates at last are opened
> And the bands begin to play;
> When the hootchie-kootchie dancers
> Wriggle in the same old way;
> When they show the howling Zulu,
> Who is known at home as "Mike"—
> Oh, the rapture! Oh, the glory,
> Of a canter down "the Pike."
>
> Oh, the "congresses of beauty"
> And the freaks will all be there—
> Known by any other name, a
> Midway's still the same affair. . . .[1]

The rains slackened, the swollen rivers subsided, the typhoid scare abated, construction sped along, and, with four thousand soldiers already bivouacked in Forest Park
for the big parade and eight thousand more on the way, Francis looked forward to a singular success on Dedication Day. Chicago had managed to snare only a U.S. vice president, Levi Morton, for its dedication. Francis had two presidents coming for his, and
both were staying at his house. The *Globe-Democrat* declared grandly, "For the time that
President Roosevelt is in St. Louis, the seat of the national government will be at the
northwest corner of Maryland and Newstead avenues."[2]

Teddy Roosevelt and Grover Cleveland both arrived on Wednesday afternoon, April
29. Roosevelt reached St. Louis first. His train bypassed Union Station and stopped near
the new World's Fair station on the north side of the park. Grinning like the Cheshire
Cat he had already become in editorial cartoons, eyes flashing with energy behind his
steel-rimmed glasses, Roosevelt trod off the train about 4:30 P.M. and was met by
Francis and Thomas H. Carter, president of the national commission for the Fair. They
took him to the Odeon, a large assembly hall on Grand Avenue, where he enthralled the
national convention of the Good Roads organization.

Leaving Carter with Roosevelt, Francis hurried in his carriage to Union Station in
time to meet a special train carrying Grover Cleveland. In the ex-president's party,
Francis was pleased to see his friend Oscar Straus, a Democratic businessman, diplomat,
and statesman who had served both parties and knew both Cleveland and Roosevelt
well. He soon would become the first Jew to join a presidential cabinet when Roosevelt
named him secretary of commerce and labor. Straus, a brilliant, versatile man who
moved easily between politics and commerce, would be a significant figure in Francis's
life in later years.

Francis took Cleveland home, among the tall cedars, oaks, and maples. The mansion's wrought iron fence now was backed by a lush green hedge. Bright daffodils
bloomed in beds along the sides of the house and roses swarmed in the back.

President Roosevelt soon joined them. No introductions were necessary. Cleveland,
sixty-five, and Roosevelt, forty-four, both from centrist wings of their opposing parties,
had worked together cleaning up New York state government in the 1880s, when
Cleveland was the governor and Roosevelt the popular young minority leader of the
state assembly. Bitterly fought national campaigns had taken a toll on their friendship,
and Francis, while willing to risk some discord to get the two living presidents of the
nation at his Dedication Day, worried they wouldn't hit it off. They got along just fine, at
least that evening, as the honored guests at a dinner party at the Francis mansion that
included, among others, Secretary of War Elihu Root, Missouri Governor Alexander M.
Dockery, Mayor Wells, Nicholas Murray Butler, the president of Columbia University,
and Oscar Straus.[3]

Roosevelt, later known as the "first environmentalist president," was restoring
Francis and Cleveland's initiatives to protect millions of acres of wild America, with
Gifford Pinchot as his chief forester.

The next morning at 9:30, Francis, Roosevelt, and Cleveland were photographed on the front steps of the mansion in their Prince Albert coats, silk hats in hand. The photograph appeared in newspapers across the country. Although he is about halfway between the two men in age, Francis looks the youngest of the three. Yet only Francis is wearing the standup collar that was fast losing fashion in this new century. He would wear the high-collar of his youth for formal occasions for the rest of his life.

A gun fired to begin a loud salute, and a half-dozen carriages drawn by teams of festooned horses rolled out of the gates of the Francis mansion. In the lead was the president, with David Francis by his side. Cleveland and other dignitaries followed to Grand Avenue, where the parade began.

On this cold, damp, gloomy, November-like day, between two and four hundred thousand people turned out to watch the parade.[4] The crowd, a "living wall" according to the *Globe-Democrat,* jammed the sidewalks and side streets and lawns along Lindell Boulevard, which runs from just east of Grand to Forest Park. Thousands stood on roofs and limbs of trees and telegraph poles to watch the parade as it made its way west. It was about four miles from Grand to the Fair's entrance, and at its fullest the parade, whose marchers included seven thousand Fair workers, twelve thousand officers and troops, and more than a dozen military bands, stretched for more than two miles along Lindell.

The parade ended at the St. Louis Plaza, the central square of the Fair, beside the one thousand-foot-long mudhole that would become the Grand Basin and beneath sixty-foot-high Art Hill, with mysterious, scaffolded edifices rising upon it. Francis, Roosevelt, and Cleveland disembarked and walked up onto a large reviewing stand, followed by hundreds of other dignitaries, including almost two hundred members of Congress, the governors of nineteen states, most of the president's cabinet, and dozens of members of the diplomatic corps, including the ambassadors from France, Italy, Great Britain, and Russia. They all spent the next two hours watching the rest of the parade pass by. Then, the doors of the nearby Palace of Liberal Arts were thrown open. Between thirty-five and fifty thousand people crowded into the vast shell of a building, which covered nine acres. A one hundred-piece orchestra and a chorus of twenty-eight hundred provided patriotic inspiration as the dignitaries crowded onto a speaker's stand at one end of the five hundred-foot-long building.

Among them was Jean Jules Jusserand, the recently appointed French ambassador to the United States, who treated the whole affair in his memoirs sardonically, with mock awe at America's grandiose ways—his attitude fueled in part, he admitted, by quite justifiable feelings that Jefferson had euchred the French in the Louisiana Purchase.

About 2 P.M., Francis rose to stand at the podium, a small portable desk resting on a large, sturdy table. In his right hand was a minor national treasure, a gavel that had been used by George Washington. "Mr. Francis called the assembly to order," Jusserand recalled, "with such a masterly hand that he broke at one stroke the gavel and the desk."[5]

Only momentarily flustered, Francis called for the invocation, although almost no one could understand a word that was said in the cavernous hall.

Jusserand observed:

Nothing had been neglected to prevent anyone from hearing anything. . . . The place, hastily constructed in boards, thick-packed with people . . . was of vast immensity; it had many doors, some of which remained opened all the time; a quantity of broad strips of bunting, stretched from one side of the hall to the other, efficiently stopped the sound of the speakers' voices and prevented their reaching anywhere.

Not that anyone cared about that. Jusserand had been warned ahead of time that no one would be able to hear any of the speeches but that Americans "love to be in a place where speeches are made."

When Roosevelt rose to speak, Jusserand continued:

His stentorian voice was of no avail. . . . He asked that the ruins of the desk be removed, and leaped upon the table where it had been; thunderous applause greeted this feat of agility. From that place of vantage he renewed his efforts, but in vain, he remained inaudible. Now and then a ray of sun piercing the overcast sky lighted the hall for a brief moment; it was received with pro-longed cheers and applause, in which the orator good-humoredly joined.

After him spoke former President Grover Cleveland, lustily cheered by an assembly in which the [D]emocratic element predominated. He did not jump on the table . . . but read low and quickly, as if for himself, a long paper. The hearers, who heard nothing, continued to show that good will characteristic of American audiences. . . . As he resumed his seat, the former President turned to me and said, 'When your turn comes, don't make a fool of yourself, and don't strain your voice.' I was not as yet Americanized enough to reply, 'You bet,' but I answered something to that effect.

Predictably, both Cleveland and Roosevelt spoke, into the vacuum, of the vast possibilities for American expansion that the Louisiana Purchase had made possible, with Roosevelt invoking the glories of Greece and Rome and Cleveland concluding his speech by proclaiming, "It is a solemn thing to belong to a people favored by God."[6]

Years later, David Francis would recall that Grover Cleveland "delivered an excellent address and received the lion's share of the applause. . . . You can imagine how Pres. R. was piqued at this and is said to have stated that he would not attend any more public function in which Mr. Cleveland should participate."[7]

Roosevelt left that evening, after a thirteen-course Frenchified banquet for four hundred in the Hall of Congresses, the main convention hall on the Fairgrounds. The president sat at Francis's right hand. On his left was Cleveland, who had arrived tired and looking worn, but he seemed to gather in the energy of the enthusiastic crowd, as politicians will do. He canceled his plans to hurry home to New York and stayed for several more days, attending all the ceremonies, which stretched through Friday and Saturday, with two more parades, two more nights of fireworks, the laying of several cornerstones, more speeches, more music, more banquets, more invocations, and a closing benediction by Rabbi Leon Harrison of Temple Israel.[8]

About seventy-five thousand people had come to St. Louis for Dedication Day, including several hundred journalists who were wined and dined for three days at Tony Faust's and the Planter's Hotel.[9] Although the resulting press was overwhelmingly positive, so much so that literally thousands of applications for exhibition space at the Fair began pouring in from across the country and around the world, a few important journals judged that St. Louis was not ready for a World's Fair. The *New York Times* correspondent reported, "The hotels are extortionate in their charges, the transit facilities are vile, and the celebration lacks . . . ginger and snap." There was, the correspondent opined, a "lack of cohesiveness in the management," and the managers would "have to do some hard work from now until the great show opens."[10]

Honored guests, like the governor of New York, were forgotten and left standing bewildered in the mobs at Union Station. There were not nearly enough cabs for those who could afford them, and few could, since many drivers were guilty of outrageous overcharging. Perhaps the most egregious case was that of the wife of the governor of Colorado, who was charged fifteen dollars (three hundred dollars in the year 2001) for the three-mile trip from the station to the Fairgrounds.[11] Streetcars got jammed up at intersections and sometimes took two or three hours to go the fifty-odd blocks from downtown to the Fairgrounds.[12]

Worse, Teddy Roosevelt reportedly said that he "got nothing fit to eat in St. Louis," despite the Aiquillette de Bass aux Eperlans Dauphine at the Hall of Congresses, not to mention dinner and breakfast from Jane Francis's kitchen. The *New York Times* used Roosevelt's alleged remark, which apparently originated with a Kansas City tabloid, to lead into an unfavorable comparison of St. Louis's Dedication Day to Chicago's, where visitors "found themselves very well taken care of."[13]

Francis was furious, and not just at the messengers. If he could "identify the hackmen who demanded the outrageous rates," he declared, he would try his utmost to get their licenses revoked. He agreed that cab service in St. Louis was "very inadequate," noting that most people in St. Louis rode the streetcars or had their own vehicles, but he promised to work on the problem.[14] Francis also put pressure through the city on hotel owners not to gouge, although he hoped competition would solve that problem. Major new hotels and hotel expansions were in the works, including a large inn being built on the Fairgrounds itself, and many homeowners planned on taking in boarders.

Despite the complaints, Francis continued to work his spell on journalists. Even the *New York Times*, on its editorial page, expressed full confidence that David Francis, with his "extraordinary energy," could be counted on to make sure everything was working smoothly by opening day.[15]

In the final year of preparation, Francis routinely worked eleven to twelve hour days and often stayed at it well into the night. His long day began over breakfast at 7 A.M., when personal secretary Collins Thompson arrived and Francis put on his gold-rimmed reading glasses, read his mail, dictated letters, and took phone calls while he ate his oatmeal and fruit. After Jane had gone outside to talk with the gardener and cut fresh flowers for the house, he lit the first of the fifteen to twenty cigars he smoked every day and sipped his coffee while he continued reading and dictating.[16]

About 7:45, he was driven by carriage the two miles to the new Washington University campus, and he and Thompson continued working on correspondence as the wheels rolled westward. By 8 A.M., he sat at his desk on the second floor of the Fair's Administration Building, with two immense overhead fans stirring the hot, humid St. Louis air.

Lunch in the Fair's private dining room was a working lunch with Fair officials, most often Skiff, the director of exhibitions; Walter Stevens, who had become director of exploitations (press agentry) as well as secretary of the Fair; and Director of Works Isaac Taylor. Often they were joined by visitors: Fair representatives, public officials, and businessmen from across the country and from Europe and Asia. After lunch, Francis generally toured the grounds, checking on progress. He didn't leave for home, drinks, and dinner until around 7 P.M.

Jane spent her days reading, cultivating her garden, and preparing for that evening's entertaining. In the last year before the Fair, she was often the hostess at small dinner parties and dances that were as much to promote the Fair as to provide entertainment—although for a political animal like David Francis, little difference stood between the two.[17]

That summer, Francis stayed in St. Louis while Jane and the younger boys, accompanied by Philip Jordan, spent much of July and August in Colorado, at a resort at the foot of Pikes Peak (Perry Park had been sold).[18] After Jane left, the nights were long and lonely, and Francis often headed out west from Washington University to the St. Louis Country Club for nine holes of golf or took the streetcar to his favorite spot, the Log Cabin Club, where he could eat dinner, sip whisky, smoke cigars, and play cards with friends like Rolla Wells and fall asleep surrounded by the sounds and smells of the countryside. On other nights, there was simply too much to do, and after dinner with Collins Thompson the two worked late into the night. He read himself to sleep with the latest political biography. Seven hours later, he was up and ready to go again, impatient for Thompson to arrive.[19]

There was never enough time. William Marion Reedy remarked in wonder and exasperation that Francis wanted to be "the whole thing. He is a wonderful worker, but no man living can do as many things as he tries to do at once."[20]

Reedy affirmed:

Mr. Francis is an iron man. . . . He never wearies. He never utterly neglects his own business. He will buy or sell a million bushels of wheat in the midst of a discussion in the executive committee as to the kind of gargoyles that ought to decorate the Fisheries Building. He jumps out of town at the drop of the hat, and doesn't know when he's coming back, and he banquets at least once every evening, with telegrams, cablegrams, and long-distance 'phone messages punctuating the courses. . . . He soothes the angry concession seeker. He consults the architects and then turns to deliberate with the board of Lady Managers. He sees men who want police jobs on the grounds and then he dictates a cablegram to a representative of the French Government. . . . And he does it all with a smile. . . . He is never ruffled. . . . He does not appear to be conscious that he is doing a giant's work. He can talk with three men about three different things at once. He never forgets a man's name, or when or where he met that man. He appears to consult everybody, but the consulta- tion usually ends in the decision being that for which Francis has contended . . . . He has absolutely 'corked up' all the big papers in St. Louis, so that never a line of criticism has appeared. . . .

It is said he is always out for 'Number One,' but his 'Number One,' even his enemies must admit, is the success of the Fair. Mr. Francis is not a man given to giving away his money, but he gives himself completely to a cause, and his time is worth more than most people's money. . . . One thing all must admit. He 'gets there,' and he does it with fine aplomb. . . . He aggrandizes himself, but he does not crush others. If he dominates his town and that town's greatest undertaking, he does it by virtue of his character. The men in St. Louis who have given him his free hand and his supreme authority, even while they resent some of the results of their surrender to him, agree that it's the best thing they could have done.[21]

In August 1903, after a long search, the Fair hired a director for the critical Department of Anthropology. He was W. J. McGee, former head of the Bureau of American Ethnology at the Smithsonian. Although he had left the Smithsonian under a shadow after being accused of misappropriation of funds, McGee came highly recom- mended by distinguished scholars, including Franz Boas of the American Museum of Natural History, probably the most influential anthropologist of his time. Francis looked favorably upon McGee's support of government Indian schools, which the anthropolo- gist called "America's best effort to educate the lower races."

After arriving in St. Louis, McGee announced, "The aim of the Department of Anthropology at the World's Fair will be to represent human progress from the dark prime to the highest enlightenment, from savagery to civic organization, from egotism to altruism [using] living peoples in their accustomed avocations as our great object les- sons." "Living displays" of cultures from around the world would educate fairgoers by showing the "upward course of human development beginning with the Dark Ages of tooth and claw and stone and tools, and culminating in the modern enlightenment illustrated in the great exhibit palaces and the International Congresses."[22]

As summer turned into fall, and fall into winter, Francis pushed forward, past labor disputes and recalcitrant public officials and frozen ground that melted into mud and then froze again in deep, axle-snapping ruts. Sometimes he forged ahead without pay- ing much attention to legalities. When landowners on the perimeter of the Fairgrounds stalled on granting permission for roads or sewer lines to run through their property, Isaac Taylor, with Francis's approval, would appear at midnight with a work crew and simply start digging.[23]

SERGE A. ALEXANDROVSKY, the Russian commissioner general for the Fair, arrived in the summer of 1903 and rented a large house at 4946 Berlin Avenue, about two blocks from the Francis mansion. He told Francis of the glorious palace Russia would build and the astonishing exhibits that would fill it, including "a steam engine made a hundred years before the time of Watt."

Over the next half year, the Russians, in person and by cable, kept asking for even more space for their exhibitions. Then, in early February 1904, the Japanese attacked the Russian naval base at Port Arthur, and the Russo-Japanese War began. Almost immediately, Russia notified the Fair that they would be unable to finish building or occupy the one hundred thousand dollar exposition hall they had agreed to, nor could they send any of their planned exhibits for other halls.[24]

The large Japanese delegation at the Fair hurried en masse to Francis's office. Francis said he certainly hoped they were not about to drop out, too. On the contrary, the Japanese replied. They had come to ask for the space the Russians had given up.

The Japanese, Francis mused later, "are good bluffers and always have been." He responded with a noncommittal nod, saying he would think it over. That's all he did, and eventually, as will be discussed in the next chapter, there would be Russian exhibits at the Fair, including a superb array of traditional and contemporary paintings.[25]

On January 10, 1904, much to the delight of David and Jane Francis, Sarah Coulthurst Francis, the wife of David, Jr., gave birth to the first grandchild, Alice Pepperell Francis.[26] By then, Perry and David both worked for their father and lived within half a block of the Francis mansion, Talton and Tom were Yale students who spent the summers at home, and Charles, who had graduated from Yale in 1902, had moved back into his parent's house. Charles drifted from job to job. A brilliant student but a highly impractical human being, Charles already exhibited signs of the mental instability that would worsen as the years grew.

Sidney, the youngest at sixteen, was still in high school.

By early 1904, it had become clear to Francis and to finance director Thompson that there was not enough money to complete construction of the Fair, despite the fact that they and many of the other directors had kicked in an additional ten thousand dollars apiece. In late January 1904, with the cash situation growing desperate, Francis and Thompson went to Washington to ask Congress for a $4.5 million loan. Two weeks of intense and sometimes angry debate ensued over this unprecedented request, with Republican Congressman E. J. Burkett of Nebraska railing about "the gall" of the St. Louisans asking for more money. If they got it, he said, they would have received more than the federal government had given to the seven previous American expositions combined.[27]

But Francis kept bending ears and, one suspects, elbows. Some of the more puritanical congressmen acquiesced after one hundred thousand dollars was added to fund the Board of Lady Managers in their battle against vice. The loan bill passed Congress and, on February 18, was signed by President Roosevelt. One Washington journalist, quoted anonymously by Walter Stevens, enthused:

> There never was anybody in American affairs quite as clever, in the Yankee sense of that word, as David R. Francis of St. Louis, Mo. He has just wheedled the American Congress out of more than $4,580,000 on a little talk that must excite the admiration of all spell-binders from Kamloop's Kootenay to Key West. He borrowed it on gate receipts not yet received at a world's fair that may possibly burn down or be blown away before the day of dedication. He borrowed it in the face of an opposition based almost entirely upon the feelings of men in Congress who had hoped to have received concessions or appointments from the fair for their friends. . . . He put up the finest and most meritorious confidence game that ever was played on this country. . . . Of course, it was all done in a good cause, but for all that, it stands forth . . . as the most neatly contrived and brilliantly executed raid upon the Treasury that this country of 'smart' men has ever known.[28]

Francis rushed home with little more than two months to go until opening day, April 30, 1904. In the final weeks of preparation, Francis and his key directors worked deep into the night, shoving plans and cost estimates and balance sheets across the waxed surface of the huge mahogany table in the main dining room of the Maryland Avenue mansion.

Francis aged perceptibly in the last year of preparation for the Fair. By the spring, his hair and mustache were splashed with gray and white, and he seemed to be wearing his small, round, gold-rimmed glasses more often. (By the time the Fair was over, Francis's hair would be mostly white.)

Still, he continued to look younger than his years. One 1904 visitor observed:

> Francis is a tall, slender, handsome man who hardly looks 40 of his 54 years. His sandy hair is streaked with gray, it is true, but it seems to add dignity, not age to the man. His face is calm and time has put few lines on it. These but accentuate the kindly mouth and firm jaws. His eyes are gray and piercing— but not unkindly. They are penetrating and look you squarely without a movement of the lids. His nose is aquiline and rather large. The man is the personification of conscious power. His movements are rapid with all the appearances of deliberation; yet he does not impress you as an emotional man. If he had not nerves of steel he would be a mental wreck long before this. He sits squarely and aggressively at a flat library desk in his office at the Administration Building.[29]

That spring, in a brief *Everybody's Magazine* profile, Alfred Henry Lewis wrote that Francis had "toiled like a galley slave, and the victory of the enterprise will be more than one-half due to the industry and wise forces which he has thrown into its destinies."[30]

As spring approached, Mayor Wells repeatedly told Francis his Fair could not open until an additional $550,000 bond was posted, guaranteeing the park would be restored after the seven-month-long party was over. Francis kept stalling, correctly figuring that Wells was bluffing about shutting down the Fair. He quickly would change the subject to St. Louis's murky water supply. Wells understood the problem well. As he explained in his 1933 autobiography:

> The main spectacle of the World's Fair was to be cascades at the summit of Art Hill, tumbling down masonry courses to the valley, and there forming lagoons, which would become an integral part of the landscape and of the architectural arrangement. It would not be satisfactory or picturesque to attempt this grand display with Mississippi water as it was; and the settling of the substance contained in the water would rapidly fill up the lagoons.[31]

The water presented another problem, usually glossed over in public discussions at the time. In 1901, four thousand cases of typhoid, resulting in two hundred deaths, had been reported in St. Louis. A primary cause of typhoid is contaminated drinking water, and in 1902 the city health commissioner warned that water in some parts of the city needed to be boiled before it was drunk.[32] One of Francis's worst fears was an outbreak of a deadly epidemic at the Fair, and he hardly wanted to put cards in hotel rooms warning guests not to drink the odd-looking tap water.

"Don't worry, Dave," Wells would say. "St. Louis will have clear water by May of 1904." Francis, hedging his bets, installed a thirty thousand-dollar filtration plant on the Fairgrounds. By then, Wells had done considerable research and settled on a combination of settlement ponds and a treatment of ferrous sulfate and milk of lime. On March 21, 1904, less than six weeks from opening day, the new system went into full operation at the Chain of Rocks water plant, and clear, clean water flowed for the first time from St. Louis taps. Francis never had to use his auxiliary system for the twenty million gallons of water a day pumped through the Fair's fountains and lagoons.[33]

The foci of the spectacular water display at the Fair were the Cascades, three stair-stepped waterfalls, laid out in the shape of a giant inverted trident, that flowed down Art Hill to the Grand Basin. The Cascades were tested successfully several times in April. The first night test, with the waterfalls and basin illuminated by tens of thousands of electric lights, occured only eleven days before the opening. An onlooker marveled as the water from the central Cascade "burst out from the mouth of a dark cavern . . . and, rolling like a mass of molten silver, slowly found its way over the cascade steps to the basin at the foot. . . . Simultaneously, the four fountains in the basin spouted forth like geysers, and the spray, caught up by the wind . . . appeared as a thin veil thrown across the row of lights."

Standing beside the Grand Basin, Ike Taylor turned to Francis and said, "If anyone has ever seen anything like this, I would like him to tell me where and when it was." Francis grinned and shook his head in wonder and delight.[34]

By the time of the Fair, the air over Forest Park was nearly as clean as the water flowing into it. Rolla Wells kept pressure on the city's industries to install and maintain filters on their smokestacks, and smoke content of the air in 1904 decreased by 70 percent from the turn of the century.[35]

In March 1904, another episode occured in the long-running comic opera of Russian participation in the Fair. Edward Grunwaldt, a Russian fur manufacturer and high official in the Ministry of Finance, cabled Francis that he would put seventy-five thousand dollars of his own money into helping his country participate in the Fair, but only if additional room could be found for more exhibits. Francis scrambled for space and came up with more than twenty thousand square feet of display area in four exhibition palaces. The Russians said they would take it.[36]

Every day, dozens of carloads of building material and tons of exhibits, human and otherwise, arrived in St. Louis, and by the early spring of 1904, St. Louisans visited the Fairgrounds by the thousands every day to gawk at the Graeco-Roman fantasy city emerging from the muck. The biggest attraction was the Philippine Reservation, on forty-seven acres of gently rolling farmland west of Forest Park and south of David Francis's office. More than eleven hundred Filipinos, from primitive tribespeople to soldiers and schoolteachers, came to St. Louis for the Fair.[37] But it was not the schoolteachers who drew the crowds to the Philippine Reservation.

In early April, the *Globe-Democrat* reported, the "savage headhunters" of the Philippines had begun spring plowing for their rice and sweet potato crops, accompanied by well-attended ancient rituals. The story was headlined:

Dancing Girl Leads Squad of
Toilers, All Singing Weird
Chant To Weather God.[38]

And there was much fascination with the diet of some of the tribes, particularly the Igorots, who, after much behind-the-scenes maneuvering, finally were allowed to celebrate their arrival with a celebratory dog feast, gorging on animals from the city pound poached in an iron kettle over a campfire. Francis was conspicuously absent from the feast, although he sent his son, David, Jr., to represent him at the post-prandial exhibition of dance.[39]

Interest in the Filipinos was also a reflection of national pride, since the Philippines had become de facto American colonies after the war with Spain. In retrospect, it is clear that among the things celebrated by the Louisiana Purchase Exposition were American imperialism, colonial paternalism, western superiority, and the assumption by the United States of the White Man's Burden.

The whole notion of exhibiting human beings as if in a zoo seems cruelly arrogant today. But Francis, like most educated people of his time, seemed to see it as an uplifting experience for all concerned. The irony was not lost on Mark Twain, whose greatest novel ended with Huck Finn heading west to avoid well-intentioned efforts to "civilize" him, and who angrily opposed American armed occupation of the Philippines.

In a letter from Italy to David Francis, Twain sent his regrets at being unable to attend the Fair, noting, "It has been a dear wish of mine to exhibit myself at the great St. Louis Fair and get a prize, but . . . I must remain in Florence." Instead, he said, he was sending a portrait, cigar in hand, by an Italian artist. "You will find it excellent," Twain wrote. "Good judges here say it is better than the original. They say it has the merits of the original, and keeps still, besides."

Twain added a personal note to Francis, whom he knew from visits to St. Louis: "I suppose you will get a prize, because you have created the most prodigious and in all ways wonderful Fair the planet has ever seen." [40]

Arriving early for the Fair, along with the Filipinos, was a pioneering thirty-three-year-old photographer named Jessie Tarbox Beals. She had been working for the small *Buffalo Herald* and had the credentials and the scrapbook to prove it. But at first she couldn't get anyone in the Fair publicity office to take her or her paper seriously. Up to that point, there had been a few celebrated female newspaper correspondents but no women photographers of any note.

Refusing to go back to Buffalo, she laid siege to the Administration Building and finally managed to get through to Stevens and eventually to Francis, both of whom admired her persistence. She received a press pass, signed by Francis, and during the Fair she became a familiar sight, trotting in her long skirts across the Fairgrounds with her assistant, a young man known as "Punkin," tagging along behind her. The two of them looked like a circus act, lugging her large box camera, its heavy tripod, a case of her photographic plates, and the twenty-foot-high ladder she used to shoot over crowds.

Francis soon came to know her well. She took hundreds of pictures of him, many of them as he greeted well-known visitors, and at times he seems to be helping her by keeping them still until the shutter has clicked shut. By the end of the Fair, she had gained a national reputation, particularly for her candid photographs of tribal people in the anthropology exhibits, who seemed particularly comfortable with her. Many of the best photographs that have come down to us from the Fair are by Jessie Tarbox Beals, and after it was over Francis presented her with one of the eighteen-carat-gold commemorative medals he also gave to presidents and kings. [41]

On the Fairgrounds, diplomatic crises, both internal and external, arose almost daily. The British ambassador to the United States protested to Francis that the South African Boer War exhibit planned for the Fair—a thrice-daily restaging of two climactic battles—would tend to cast ridicule on the British Army, which had won using notably cruel tactics, including putting women and children in concentration camps. [42] Perhaps fearful of losing Queen Victoria's jewels, Francis strongly suggested to the South Africans that their war might better be staged outside the official Fairgrounds on the Pike. (After the furor had settled down, the reenactment ended up on the Fairgrounds after all, but off in the southwest corner near the livestock pens.) [43]

By the last weeks of preparation for the April 30 opening, the work force had risen to fifteen thousand and included hodcarrier and Yale graduate Charles Francis, who had gotten himself hired without his father's knowledge. One day, Francis was taking his daily inspection tour of the grounds when a tall, broad-shouldered, well-tanned work-man in a slouch hat shouted hello. Francis, distracted, touched his hat in response, and his carriage had rolled on before Collins Thompson, who was seldom away from Francis's side, told him the workman had been his son.[44]

About this time, Francis began referring to his six tall sons, all sworn Democrats, as "Thirty-six feet of Democracy." Francis assiduously avoided partisan controversy, but sometimes his hot-tempered sons found themselves in the middle of it, as they did on March 12 when voters went to the polls in the Democratic primary to choose their can-didate for governor. The race was between Holy Joe Folk and Handsome Harry Hawes.

Hawes, a Bourbon reformer like Francis, had the support of the regular Democratic machine. The Progressive Folk was favored by much of the gentry, particularly idealistic younger college-educated voters. Some of Butler's Indians, tough mugs from the river wards, were dispatched to the West End to keep people they suspected of being Folk supporters from reaching the ballot box. Spotting a couple of tall, sturdy, collegiately dressed young gentlemen with cleft chins standing in line to vote at Taylor and Delmar, they rushed over and pushed them out of line, assuming they were Folk voters.

Perry and David, Jr., who were there to vote for Hawes, didn't bother with explana-tions and fought back. Burly David, according to an observer, "using football tactics, tackled low in the crowd to force his way back into line." Eventually, they forced their way into the voting booths and marked their ballots for Hawes. Hawes won in the city but lost statewide to Folk, who would become governor.[45]

By March 18, the major Fair buildings essentially were completed, but many of the hundreds of other structures, including state, foreign and Pike attractions, lagged behind, and a few hadn't even been started. Francis ordered that no new buildings could begin after April 1, and all construction must be completed by April 29.[46] He didn't quite get his wish, but the announcement resulted in a nervous flurry of work.

Ten days before the opening, with construction proceeding at a furious pace, six inches of snow and sleet fell on St. Louis, an April record. The snowstorm, and the rivers of mud that quickly appeared as temperatures rose and cold rain fell, virtually halted construction for a day or two.[47] The rain kept falling through the last week of April. The Mississippi rose above flood stage, ripping through a dike on the Illinois side of the river, but the River des Peres stayed out of sight in its underground wooden channel, and work resumed.

On Thursday, April 28, Prince Pu Lun, nephew of the emperor of China, arrived with a large entourage. Francis, Rolla Wells, and Adolphus Busch met them at Union Station and took the prince to a fancy West End wedding and reception. That evening, with about thirty-six hours to go, Isaac Taylor announced that all the principal buildings for the Fair were completed.[48]

This was not entirely true. Construction work still went on in roped-off sections of several exposition halls, and the exhibits still came in. The roofs of some of the build-ings leaked, although none as badly as the U.S. Government Building, which was pocked with holes from the hobnailed boots of the electricians who had wired the place.[49]

Some fifteen thousand workmen labored all Friday night to get the Fairgrounds ready for Saturday morning's ceremonies. The thirty-four miles of asphalt and gravel walkways were not finished until midnight, after which thousands of workmen grabbed brooms and began sweeping the grounds.

On Friday evening, Secretary of War William Howard Taft, President Roosevelt's official representative to the opening, arrived at Union Station on a train full of important visitors. Francis and D. C. Nugent, Taft's intended host, were there, but somehow the two lost him in the huge crowds and the maze of unfinished renovation. Francis and Nugent were not quite sure what to do until Nugent's name came booming over the station's loudspeakers. Nugent's wife was calling frantically to inform her husband that Taft had arrived by cab at their West End home, and suggesting he and Francis get on out there.

On the whole, however, with a year to work on it, most of the foul-ups of Dedication Day had been eliminated, including the transportation snarls—at least Taft had been able to find a cab.

After tucking in Taft, Francis headed to Forest Park for one more tour of the Fairgrounds, and then he went home for a quick meal and another late-night planning session over the dining room table.

The forecast for Saturday was cloudy skies and, by afternoon, more rain. When Francis finally fell asleep, clouds obscured the full moon, but his eyes opened to the rays of a rising sun. The clouds had scattered, and the sun shone on opening day of the Louisiana Purchase Exposition.

Francis, Taft, Fair officials, and honored guests gathered at about nine in the morning at Francis's office in the Administration Building. Horse-drawn carriages began pulling up, taking on passengers, and swaying down the slight incline into the Fairgrounds. The towers and domes of the Ivory City gleamed in the morning sun. The crowd cheered and shouted huzzahs as the lead carriages rolled to the Louisiana Purchase Monument. At 10:25, to a great cheer and the waving of thousands of men's hats and ladies' handkerchiefs, Francis climbed the gleaming white steps to a speaker's platform on the side of the monument, facing the crowd in the Plaza of St. Louis. Behind him, rising up Art Hill, were the bare stairsteps of the Cascades.

Nearly one hundred thousand people were there for the opening ceremony, most of them dressed to the nines, the men in dark suits with high-cut coats and bowlers or crisp fedoras, the women in long white dresses or full dark skirts and white shirtwaists, their hair tucked under fashionable wide-brimmed hats. Seated just beneath the one hundred-foot-high Louisiana Monument were representatives of twenty-seven foreign countries, and more than one hundred governors, senators, congressmen, and other top American officials.

"For more than a generation to come," Francis proclaimed, the St. Louis World's Fair would be "a marker in the accomplishments and progress of man. So thoroughly does it represent the world's civilization that if all man's other works were by some unspeakable catastrophe blotted out, the records here established would afford all necessary standards for the rebuilding of our entire civilization." [50]

By the time Francis finished his opening address, the program already was running long. Then Isaac Taylor spoke, followed by Director of Exhibits Skiff. Mayor Wells took his turn on the podium, as did a Minnesota congressman, two U.S. senators, representatives of France and Mexico, and railway magnate Edward H. Harriman, who was supposed to represent the state of New York but spent much of his time defending railroad mergers and angrily denouncing "obstructive," "destructive" government antitrust meddling.

Francis must have been amused, knowing exactly what had stuck in Harriman's craw—the month before, in the most important trust-busting move of Roosevelt's first administration, the Justice Department had forced the breakup of Northern Securities, a vast railroad combine of which the stubby, pugnacious Harriman was a principal owner.[51]

Then came the jovial, rotund, handlebar-mustached Taft, the former colonial governor of the Philippines. He dwelled at length on America's newfound Pacific stepchild, echoing Roosevelt's paternalistic policies: "We find ourselves burdened with the necessity of aiding another people to stand upon its feet and take a short cut to the freedom and civil liberty."

The speeches went on long past noon St. Louis time (1 P.M. Eastern Standard Time), when Roosevelt in the White House was scheduled to touch a golden telegraph key and open the Fair. The Fair was important to Roosevelt, but so was another meeting he had scheduled for early that afternoon. At 12:15 P.M. St. Louis time, with the end of the speechifying not in sight, Roosevelt pressed his key and made a brief speech, remarking, with his usual zest for displays of physical prowess, how pleased he was that the 1904 Olympics had been made a part of the Fair.

It was not until about an hour later, at around 1:15 P.M. St. Louis time, that the speeches were finally over in St. Louis and Ike Taylor signaled Francis that it was time to open the Fair. By then, it was 2:15 in Washington, and Roosevelt had been gone from the White House for almost an hour.*

At Taylor's signal, Francis raised his arms high in the air and shouted, "Open, ye gates. Swing wide, ye portals. Enter herein, ye sons of man, and behold the achievements of your race. Learn the lesson here taught and gather from it the inspiration for still greater accomplishments."

Bells rang in towers and belfries across the wide grounds, motors at industrial exhibits all over the Fairgrounds rumbled into life, and the earth trembled as huge pumps began working beneath the Cascades. The three giant mouths gurgled and spat and water burst forth and rolled down the sea-green stone steps. Fountains spewed water high in the air and the spring winds blew the mist across people standing on the edge of the Grand Basin. John Philip Sousa's band, two hundred strong, and a chorus of a hundred voices launched into "The Star Spangled Banner," and the huge crowd

---

*The delay of almost exactly an hour between Roosevelt's pressing the key in Washington and the actual opening of the Fair in St. Louis, combined with the hour's difference in time zones, has led to confusion over the years, confusion that, in most newspaper accounts and in the official Fair history, has events that happened an hour apart in St. Louis and Washington seeming to occur simultaneously. However, the *New York Times* of May 1 got it right.

cheered and clapped and sang along. David Francis looked out at the jubilant mass of people celebrating his most prodigious feat, and for just a moment he was speechless.[52]

That evening at dusk, the full moon shone low on the eastern horizon as one hundred thousand people waited for the lights to be turned on.

Some 125,000 electric bulbs had been installed along the building lines, cornices, and arches of the main buildings of the Fair and beside and beneath the bubbling Cascades. The illumination was a stunning, magical sight that would take place six nights a week until the end of the Fair.

St. Louis author Sally Benson, who turned five that summer, described it several decades later in *Meet Me in St. Louis*. As it began:

> Tiny sparks of light outlined the Cascades, Festival Hall, and the Colonnade of States. . . . Suddenly the outlines of the columns, the arches, and the great statues were obliterated entirely. The lights glowed in dull redness and expanded into white light. It was as though the picture had been rebuilt in a minute, not of substance but of light. The successive falls of the Cascades shone in the brilliance. The white lights faded out and from bottom to top, from end to end, the Festival Hall, the Colonnade, and the Pavilions stood out in carmine.
>
>   Everyone stopped talking, and Rose drew in her breath sharply. 'There has never been anything like it in this world,' she said. 'There never will be.' . . .[53]

Benson continued:

> The miracle of the World's Fair in St. Louis rising as it did out of the wilderness, stunned everyone. It seemed impossible that only two years before, Governor Francis . . . had driven in the first stake with a silver ax while crowds walking through the briers and coarse grass to witness the ceremony carried heavy sticks to protect themselves from snakes. . . .
>
>   To the people of St. Louis, the Fair was finished, perfect. It was the cream of everything in the world. There was nothing better to come. Only the visitors complained of the mud. . . .[54]

This time, visiting correspondents were virtually unanimous in their praise of the ceremonies and the city. The *New York Times,* in a long, top-of-the-front-page story, reported that "the handling of the crowds, the guarding of the enclosures sacred to the participants in the exercises, and the police work generally could not have been better." Further inside, on the editorial page, the *Times* noted, somewhat edgily, that every American should wish the Fair success, since "more nearly than any of its predecessors, it has been nationalized."[55]

The *Post-Dispatch*, not for the first (or the last) time, noted that David Francis had become the most photographed man in America.[56] And about the same time, Joseph Pulitzer said, "I know of no man today so well entitled to the admiration of the citizens of his state or who is doing more enduring work for the city of St. Louis than Gov.

Francis." After watching Francis in action all day, Taft remarked, quoting a famous description of Daniel Webster, "What an engine in breeches [britches]!" [57]

Francis announced that about 190,000 people had gone through the turnstiles on opening day from 8 A.M. until closing at 11 P.M. Francis was pleased. Only about 140,000 had attended opening day in Chicago.

This time, there were few complaints of gouging, either by cab drivers, who had been warned they would lose their licenses if they overcharged, or by hotels. Competition had come from several large new hotels, including the 2,257-room Inside Inn on the Fairgrounds. Also, dozens of private homes had been converted into boardinghouses.

Inevitably, there were a few glitches. The drinking fountains didn't work. Nine elephants, being unloaded near the Philippine Exhibit for Hagenbeck's Zoological Paradise and Animal Circus on the Pike, apparently were spooked by all the noise and stampeded through the compound, knocking over and trampling fences and huts. No one was seriously hurt. And, of course, many of the buildings were not finished. There was so much sawdust and waste lumber lying around that Francis forbade smoking on the Fairgrounds.

The World's Fair social season began Monday night, with a reception and banquet at the Planters' Hotel. The guests of honor were Governor James H. Peabody of Colorado and his wife, who had been gouged by a cab driver at Dedication Day. David and Jane Francis stood at the head of the reception line.[58] The social pressure on Jane Francis was intense and sometimes unpleasant, but at least now she had the help and support of Mimi and Sarah, her young daughters-in-law, both of whom had grown up accustomed to the duties and rewards of social prominence.

Now that May had arrived bringing the sun, the rains and snows of April were a boon, as trees budded and shot out leaves, and spring flowers bloomed. On May 12, Francis decided that the Fair was near enough to completion for him and other Fair officials to tramp through the lingering mud on an official inspection. Prince Pu Lun, in ermine robes, tagged along.

The eleven-mile tour, which passed through every area of the Fairgrounds, took five hours, and at the end of it Francis pronounced that the Fair's exhibits "present the most marvelous collection of the accomplishments of mankind ever witnessed." In an act of generous self-interest, Francis declared that it was now okay to smoke.[59]

On the outside, David Francis's Ivory City was a compact metropolis of obelisks and minarets and pediments and friezes and colonnades. It was neo-Egyptian, neo-Greek, neo-Roman, neo-Byzantine, neo-Renaissance, neo-baroque, neo-anything but twentieth-century American, as if the voluptuous exteriors redolent of the past, the fake marble solidity, and the painted-on patina of the massive buildings anchored the Fair to earlier eras of glory, right in the heart of the new Roman empire. Inside the steel-beamed palaces was the first, and ultimately the largest, celebration of the astonishing technological progress of the second half of the nineteenth century and the first few years of the twentieth.

On display at the Fair, among myriad inventions, were the light bulb (by the hundreds of thousands), the refrigerator, the phonograph, the motion picture, the diesel engine, the Bessemer steel-making process, the radio, the telephone, the automobile, the airplane, and a Swedish invention called the "statisticum," a forerunner of the computer.

The Louisiana Purchase Exposition was a combination of a vast amusement park, on a scale never seen before, a giant international trade fair, a human zoo, and the Smithsonian Institution. It was a twelve hundred-acre preview of what came to be called the American Century.

CHAPTER 10

The New American

STILL DETERMINED TO GET TEDDY ROOSEVELT TO THE FAIR, Francis invited the president to speak to the World Press Congress, one of several large gatherings of editors, publishers, and reporters that he and Walter Stevens had shrewdly scheduled for the first weeks of May. The president declined, but he dispatched Secretary of State John Hay to represent him. The venerable Hay arrived on May 13 with a large party that included his friend Henry Adams.

In his famous memoir, *The Education of Henry Adams,* Adams said he believed religiously in world's fairs as crucial to education and international understanding. The trip from the East alone was, for him, an education. It had been a decade since he had traveled so far west, and as his train rolled toward St. Louis, Adams was dismayed to see that "agriculture had made way for steam" and "tall chimneys reeked smoke on every horizon."

"The new American," he observed, "was the child of steam and the brother of the dynamo. . . . The new American, like the new European, was the servant of the power-house, as the European of the twelfth century was the servant of the Church. . . ."

Adams spent ten busy days at the Fair. It was, he decided,

[the new American's] first creation in the twentieth century, and, for that reason, acutely interesting. One saw here a third-rate town of half-a-million people without history, education, unity, or art, and with little capital—without even an element of natural interests except the river which it studiously ignored—but doing what London, Paris, or New York would have shrunk from attempting. This new social conglomerate, with no tie but its steam-power and not much of that, threw away thirty or forty million dollars on a pageant as ephemeral as a stage flat. The world had never witnessed so marvelous a phantasm; by night Arabia's crimson sands had never returned a glow half so astonishing, as one wandered among long lines of white palaces, exquisitely lighted by thousands on thousands of electric candles, soft, rich, shadowy, palpable in their sensuous depths. . . .

The prospect from the Exposition was pleasant; one seemed to see almost an adequate motive for power; almost a scheme for progress. In another half-century, the people of the central valleys should have hundreds of millions to throw away more easily than in 1900 they could throw away tens; and by that time they might know what they wanted. Possibly they might even have learned how to reach it.

This was an optimist's hope, shared by few except pilgrims to World's Fairs, and frankly dropped by the multitude, for, east of the Mississippi, the St. Louis Exposition met a deliberate conspiracy of silence, discouraging, beyond measure, to an optimistic dream of future strength in American expression.[1]

Adams was right about the lack of attention paid to the Fair in the East—press coverage had dropped off a cliff after the initial flurry of stories heralding the opening. Early attendance was very disappointing. Ticket sales and concession revenues were far less than Francis hoped, not just to outdo Chicago but to keep up with the five hundred thousand dollars he had agreed to send the federal government twice a month to pay off the loan.

By late May, perhaps in part because of the publicity generated by the large press gatherings, the crowds began to grow markedly, with paid admissions more than doubling from the first week of the month to the last. About 450,000 people visited the Fair during the last week in May, and attendance on the first Saturday in June, for the first time since opening day, exceeded one hundred thousand. Attendance continued to grow.[2]

Back in Washington, over dinner at the White House, Henry Adams urged his friends, the Roosevelts, to visit the Fair. The president demurred, but his fiery daughter, Alice, began packing steamer trunks full of clothes and shoes and boxes full of hats.

Barely twenty years old, Alice Roosevelt was an athletic, intellectually and verbally acute young woman, flirtatious, saucy, and impatient with convention. She hit St. Louis like a firecracker on the afternoon of Thursday, May 26, and stepped off the train beneath an enormous plumed hat to be greeted by a crowd of reporters, photographers, and about two thousand gawkers, mostly girls and women. Some of the mob followed her out to Vandeventer Place, where she stayed with Miss Irene Catlin, the young daughter of a old St. Louis family.

After an early evening reception, Alice and a group of young people crowded into two automobiles—she loved automobiles, the faster the better—and headed to Forest Park. She toured the Pike from end to end and, as dusk arrived, clapped her hands in delight when the lights were turned on and the illuminated Cascades rolled toward the Grand Basin.[3]

The next morning, after slipping through the throngs that crowded around the house, she spent the day tramping tirelessly through the Fair, wearing a daringly short white skirt that revealed her black-stockinged ankles, on her head a white-veiled Italian straw hat the size of a sombrero. At the Philippine Reservation, she was cheering at a sham battle among barely clad Igorots when she looked over her shoulder and, at least pretending to be surprised, spotted a familiar face in the crowd. "Hello Nick," she cried, reaching over the heads of her entourage to shake the hand of a handsome mustachioed man in his mid-thirties. "Nick" was Ohio Congressman Nicholas Longworth.[4]

Longworth immediately joined the party and was seen with her often for the rest of the trip. In 1906, the two married in the White House, and Alice Roosevelt Longworth began her decades-long reign as the doyenne of Washington society.

That weekend, she toured the Fair with David Francis, who had to increase his usual long-legged gait to keep up with her. Everyone else trailed in their wake. Postponing her scheduled departure twice, she stayed until June 5, tromping through the Fairgrounds and the Pike during the day and being the life of the party at night.[5]

Alice spun around the St. Louis social circle faster than anyone had before, and she charmed David Francis, who took her for a gondola ride on the Grand Basin, and the younger members of the Francis family, who accompanied her to parties and on Ferris Wheel rides. On Saturday, June 4, with David Francis beaming approval, Alice gave away trophies at an American Athletic Union track and field meet, a prelude to the August Olympic Games. Then, on Sunday, she slipped out of town, proclaiming to the small group of friends who saw her off that she had had "such a delightful time."

"The people of St. Louis have been kind to me," she said. "Only I wish they wouldn't crowd so."[6]

For David Francis, the Ivory City was as close as he could come to the sort of place he longed to govern, a city of one hundred thousand people who were, almost always, polite and well-behaved and attentive, well-dressed and well-fed, interested in music and art and science and beautiful buildings, and kind enough to go home no later than midnight. It was a city where the trains ran on time, children played together on the Model Playground without regard to race or color, all the guns fired blanks, nations competed on the athletic field rather than the battlefield, the air was clean, the water pure, the litter was picked up immediately, and the police were honest, polite, and subject to the law like everyone else.

However, societal storm clouds hovered over the fantasy city, clouds that Francis could not always see. Social historians now see the American expositions of the late-nineteenth and early twentieth centuries, and St. Louis's in particular, as metaphors for and a demonstration of Western territorial aggression, unfettered capitalistic acquisitiveness, racism, and Social Darwinism. Phillips Verner Bradford and Harvey Blume powerfully humanize this attitude in their superb 1992 book *Ota Benga: The Pygmy in the Zoo*, the tragic story of an African pygmy on display at the St. Louis Fair, and later at the Bronx Zoo.

W. J. McGee, director of the Department of Anthropology, believed that human history was "a trend of vital development from the low toward the high, from dullness toward brightness, from idleness groveling toward intellectual uprightness." And, he proclaimed, "The burden of humanity is already in large measure the White Man's burden—for, viewing the human world as it is, white and strong are synonymous terms."[7]

McGee's anthropological "exhibits" in the western end of the Fairgrounds included some fifteen hundred men, women, and children living in replicas of their native dwellings, people ranging from African pygmies to South American Indians billed as "Patagonian Giants"—they were, at their largest, about the size of David Francis.[8]

There were Indians from at least two dozen North American tribes, including the legendary Apache warrior Geronimo, and Chief Joseph, the wise and dignified Nez Perce chief. The largest national group consisted of eleven to twelve hundred Filipinos.

"Chief" McGee, as he liked to be called, had offices and laboratories in Cupples Hall in what became the Washington University quadrangle. Here and on the nearby athletic fields, McGee conducted extensive psychological and physical testing. One of McGee's favorite tests was the careful measurement of cranial capacity—basically, hat size—of almost all the native peoples at the Fair. But McGee's theories of white superiority ran afoul of fact when many members of the colored races—including the lowly, half-naked Igorots—turned out of have, on the average, larger heads than whites.[9]

At one point, McGee was asked how he reconciled his theories of the superiority of the white race with the undeniable facts that the Japanese had one of the largest and most sophisticated exhibits at the Fair and were beating the tar out of the Russians in their current war.

"It's the complexity of the blood," he replied. "The more strains of blood a nation has in its veins, the more powerful it becomes." The Japanese, he argued, were "the most complex nation of the Orient, just as the Anglo-Saxons, through the waves of successive populations that swept over the continent, were made the most complex nation of the Occident."[10] In other words, the Japanese were the Aryans of the East.

How did Francis feel about all this racial and ethnic stereotyping? It was, after all, very much his Fair. There is no evidence that he fought the preponderance of conventional academic wisdom as represented by Harvard, Columbia, and the Smithsonian, nor the implicitly racist colonial notions of Progressives like Theodore Roosevelt.

He has little to say on the matter in the official history of the Fair, which bears his name as sole author. It can be assumed that a detail-obsessed man like Francis, supervising the history of what he considered to be his greatest triumph, wouldn't let anything be published under his name that he had not approved. The anthropology exhibits are described briefly as representing "the slow, tedious evolution of civilization," and inclusion of the pygmies is said to have "brought the collection of primitive races down to the lowest known human stage."[11]

Although McGee's advocacy of these ideas, as well as Francis's implicit acceptance of them, were commonplace at the time, Mark Twain was not the only 1904 observer who thought that there was something at the least odd and ethnocentric in putting people on display. "FHC" (veteran reporter Fred H. Collier), the *Globe-Democrat*'s daily Fair columnist, remarked:

> I was thinking what a queer thing it would be if things were reversed and . . .
> it should be the Chinese or the Turcomans or the Burmese [who] were powerful and civilized and they should desire an anthropological village on their

midway, and should import a hundred or so of us to show in the American village of St. Louis by Gaslight. . . .

The barker would . . . say, 'Ladies and gentlemen, you see them dressed in the peculiar and amusing costumes of their native land. These tall hats that you see are universally worn by the American on festal occasions. They are peculiar to religious worship in that country, and are always worn when they go to their temples on what they call Sunday.' . . . He would tell them that our principal habits are making money and riding in automobiles.[12]

The pygmies—actually the group of eight included five true pygmies and three other Congolese men—shared FHC's sense of absurdity. Inspired by the regular marching drills of the Fair's Indian School, the pygmies formed their own marching company. Carrying long sticks in place of rifles and swords, they began marching in tight formation and then, on command, scattered. "The company kept perfect time to the music of the Indian band," the *Post-Dispatch* reported, "in spite of the fact that they were marching in any and every direction."[13]

When the pygmies finally returned to Africa with Samuel Verner, the missionary-explorer who had contracted to bring them to the Fair, they had difficulty explaining to other villagers what they had done. Because of the Belgian colonial terror, their fellow tribe members certainly could understand imprisonment and even torture, but the notion of putting human beings on display made no sense to them at all. Finally, the pygmies who had been to the Fair demonstrated by erecting a wooden pen in a clearing and sitting Verner inside it at a desk piled with books. He smoked his pipe and read and wrote—doing what he normally did, in a replica of his native habitat, observed by strangers on another continent. The other pygmies laughed and laughed, and at last they understood.[14]

As for Americans of African ancestry, in general, their status in the Ivory City was liberal by the standards of the time, particularly considering St. Louis's Southern roots. As early as 1901, Francis and the directors of the Fair insisted that "the Negro has been so important a factor in the development and cultivation of the Louisiana Purchase and is now an element of such great importance in the industrial, political and social life of the Union that he cannot be omitted from the great exposition." One St. Louis black leader heralded black participation in the Fair as "a momentous event in the history of St. Louis."[15]

Officially, there was no color line at the Fair, whereas other fairs in the same period in Southern cities had a "Negro Building" where blacks could eat, drink from the water fountains, and use the toilets. Any black person with the fifty-cent admission could enter the Fairgrounds and visit all the major exhibits. Black children in their segregated St. Louis schools were encouraged to create exhibits for the Palace of Education, and St. Louis's black newspapers appeared in the journalism display in the Missouri Building. Still, not many exhibits by or about blacks could be seen on the Fairgrounds, and blacks routinely were denied admission to cafes and shows on the Pike, where the Exposition Company had, or claimed to have, limited power. Blacks also had trouble finding hotel rooms off the Fairgrounds. In June, after hearing numerous reports of discrimination, the Fair directors issued an official statement disapproving of it but went no further.

On June 30, Booker T. Washington spoke to an integrated gathering of the National Education Association. A week later, his wife introduced the Fisk University Jubilee Singers, who performed spirituals and other music to a large and enthusiastic mixed crowd at Festival Hall.

Concessionaires continued to discriminate, and few blacks were employed by the Fair. By July, the many negative reports caused the National Association of Colored Women, led by an angry Mrs. Booker T. Washington, to change their minds about holding part of their annual convention on the Fairgrounds.

A Fair spokesperson told the black *St. Louis Palladium* newspaper that management had done everything it could to halt discrimination on the Fairgrounds and that "President Francis, in several instances when complaints had been made by Colored people, made a personal investigation, and caused the discriminations to be stopped." Francis personally pledged that the Fair's management would "do all within its power to prevent race discrimination." But the discrimination continued, and by October other black events had been canceled, in part in fear of racist attacks from white fairgoers. By then, the *Palladium,* which long had supported the Fair, had reversed course and suggested that blacks "with any pride" would stay away.[16]

John Philip Sousa, who spent the first month of the Fair in St. Louis, had promised that a lot of ragtime—a form of music created by blacks—would be played during the Fair.[17] It was played but almost entirely by whites.

Scott Joplin, who lived in St. Louis and wrote "The Cascades" for the Fair, was not invited to perform it on the Fairgrounds and had to settle for playing it on the Pike. He was joined there by the great St. Louis and Sedalia ragtimers of the period, almost all of them black, while less innovative white musicians dominated the official bandstands. Joplin very much wanted to be taken seriously as a composer, and his failure to break into the main Fairgrounds was one of the great disappointments of his life.[18]

A FTER THE FAIR GOT UP AND RUNNING, Francis started his weekday mornings at his desk in the Administration Building by picking up a phone, a private line to what now was known as Francis, Bro. & Co. six miles away. He would talk fast, asking about the opening prices of stocks, commodities, and foreign exchange, and then bark out a rapid series of orders for the day. This flurry of trading lasted about five minutes, and then he set the phone down and turned to the business of the Fair. Sometimes, when the daily pressure got to him, he made another call and did some more business. Surely this was one of the rare occasions in which a busy man sought relaxation from stressful tasks by speculating on the future price of winter wheat.[19]

Francis was so busy that Philip Jordan, who had become his valet, received the duty from Jane of making sure that Francis always had clean suits and shirts, along with twenty dollars in spending money in his pocket. Jordan was becoming an increasingly important part of Francis's life, and as time went along he would take on more and more of the duties of a personal assistant.[20]

Several hundred conventions, congresses, and formal meetings were held in St. Louis, all or in part on the Fairgrounds, during the seven months of the Fair. Alienists and dentists convened, as did physicists and physicians, the deaf and the blind, the Daughters of the American Revolution and the Colonial Dames, bankers and union members, firemen and librarians, dog lovers, real-estate salesmen, teachers, plumbers, and lumbermen, who had their own building, the House of Hoo Hoo. The National Federation of Women's Clubs met for a week in May, with almost two thousand women gathering to discuss matters ranging from healthy menus to women's suffrage—it would be another decade and a half before women could vote in the United States. Among the speakers was child-welfare leader Jane Addams.

For David Francis, the most important convention took place downtown at the Coliseum beginning on July 6. Some twelve thousand Democrats met to nominate a presidential candidate to run against Teddy Roosevelt. He had been re-anointed the month before by the Republicans, who literally had been burned by Francis's forecast eight and a half years earlier of cool breezes and low humidity in mid-summer St. Louis and had chosen to meet in Chicago.

Francis was on the speaker's platform when the convention was called to order but only to issue an invitation to the delegates to come to the Fair to celebrate what he described as "the acquisition of an empire by peaceful negotiations and the extension of the jurisdiction of democratic principles from the Atlantic to the Pacific."[21]

He stayed out of the wrangling over a platform and a candidate, perhaps in part because, by then, the horse he backed was a sure winner. A fiscally conservative New York judge named Alton Parker, who led the opposition to the Bryan forces, took the nomination on the first ballot.

F AIR ATTENDANCE FOR THE FIRST FULL WEEK in July exceeded 600,000, pushed by a record 179,000 for the big Fourth of July celebration. But Francis remained concerned about paying off the government loan every fifteen days, particularly if crowds dropped off precipitously in the fall, as expected. He and treasurer Thompson visited every major bank and trust company in St. Louis and got almost all of them to agree to jointly loan the Fair an emergency $1 million if necessary. He also trimmed salaries, the cuts ranging from 5 percent for the lowest-paid workers to 20 percent for the highest.[22]

At the same time, in response to constant pestering by Rolla Wells, Francis finally agreed to increase the bond for restoration of the park by $550,000. Francis and seven other directors, including his close friends John Scullin and Jim Campbell, promised to be responsible for one hundred thousand dollars, with the Palace of Fine Arts put up as security for the rest.[23]

To boost attendance even more, Francis expanded the hours of popular shows and laid on more fireworks. In late July, one spectacular fireworks show concluded with portraits of the two presidential candidates outlined in lights in the night sky.

By then, the Russian exhibits finally had begun arriving. Rather than the great pavilion that had been promised, Russia ended up constructing a small log hut, decorated with folk designs, in the Transportation Palace. Russia's contribution to the Fair was relatively minor, with one exception: the 112 cases of paintings it shipped to the Palace of Fine Arts.[24]

Most of the art that was displayed at the St. Louis World's Fair was undistinguished. The Russian contribution was the major exception. There were works by Ilya Repin and other members of the mid-nineteenth-century "Wanderers," whose folk-influenced work was rediscovered in the late twentieth century, as well as dozens of pieces by contemporary Russian artists from the Mir Iskusstva ("World of Art") group that gathered around the St. Petersburg impresario Sergei Diaghilev.[25]

On August 12, in "a cloud of glory and gasoline" as the *Globe-Democrat* put it, 285 automobiles rolled up Lindell and through the Fairground in what was said to be the largest automobile parade ever held west of the Mississippi. Many remarked on the fact that two of the drivers in the open cars, which had come from all over the East and Midwest, were women.[26]

August 13, a Saturday, was the sixth anniversary of the fall of Manila to the American military. Philippine Day was one of the major productions of the Fair. Roosevelt once again sent William Howard Taft, who praised the administration's aggressive colonial policies and insisted that, regardless of party politics, "no man would deny the duty of the country to take up the white man's burden."[27]

As part of that burden, Roosevelt and Taft had reacted to complaints from prudish visitors by urging that the loincloth-wearing Igorots be induced to don pants. Francis initially bowed to the wishes of the federal government, and the Igorots were persuaded to wear shorts. But the tribesmen complained so often and so loudly that Francis put the question to the final arbiters of decency, the Board of Lady Managers.

Despite the multitude of sexist jokes routinely reprinted in the local press, the Lady Managers tended to be better educated and, in general, more sensible than any number of male Fair visitors and directors, not to mention the president of the United States and his secretary of war. The Lady Managers announced that there was nothing indecent about a loincloth if that was the proper dress in the Igorot's society. With that unimpeachable support, Francis let the Igorots go back to their rear-revealing attire.[28]

Francis kept pushing for more attendance. He played host to barbecues and watermelon feasts, increased the number of simulated battles and fireworks displays, and scheduled more "special days" for professions, grand and humble, and for cities, large and small. He leaned on the railroads to cut fares for World's Fair specials. He and Walter Stevens increased the promotions staff, bought more billboards across the country, and boosted the budget for newspaper advertising.

Crowds continued to grow. By August 15, when the Fair was officially half over, total attendance had reached well over seven million, and a visitor who had been an official of the Chicago World's Fair told Francis that he could expect many more people in the second half. Francis hoped so; he was nowhere near halfway to Chicago's 27.5 million.[29]

THE 1904 OLYMPICS, which got underway in St. Louis on August 29, were only the third held since the revival of the ancient games, and the first in the United States. The track and field events were held west of the Washington University quadrangle at the thirty-five thousand-seat Olympic Stadium and at the nearby Palace of Physical Culture, now Francis Field and Francis Gymnasium.

Athletes came from eight European countries as well as Australia, Canada, Cuba, and South Africa, but most of the competitors, all male, were American. By today's standards, they were strictly amateurs, in both senses of the term. The names and achievements of only two athletes are of much interest today. George Coleman Poage finished third in the 200-meter and 400-meter hurdles and became the first African American to win Olympic medals. And then there was Fred Lorz, who briefly won the marathon.

The marathon, which began and ended in the stadium, proceeded over an agonizingly hilly course of about twenty-five miles (the race was not standardized at 26 miles, 385 yards until 1908). About thirty men, including two Zulu tribesmen from the Boer War extravaganza, took off when David Francis fired the starting gun. The temperature was in the nineties, and the humidity was literally staggering. The dirt roads in the western part of the course were soft from lack of rain and horses' hooves, and the runners struggled, kicking up choking clouds of dust that plastered the profuse sweat on their bodies. A half-dozen runners collapsed with severe cramps and had to be taken to the infirmary, and one man almost died from stomach hemorrhaging.

About three hours after the start, the stadium crowd of nearly ten thousand let out a cheer as a runner ran slowly onto the track, took a lap, and crossed the finish line, raising his arms in victory. Francis picked up the Francis Cup, which he had donated, and stepped onto the track to hand it to the runner, Fred Lorz. A judge rushed over and stopped him.

A quizzical, murmuring hush fell over the crowd as the judge told Francis the story he quickly had pieced together from reports of other officials. Lorz had collapsed, exhausted, about ten miles out. He had been helped into a car and driven back to the stadium. On a sudden impulse, excited by hearing the hum of the crowd inside, the New Yorker trotted through the gate and took his victory lap, drinking in the cheers. He was, of course, disqualified.

A few minutes later, the real winner, British-born Thomas J. Hicks of Cambridge, Massachusetts, came into the stadium at a half-trot and barely managed to stumble around the track and across the finish line before he, too, collapsed. He was taken off to the hospital with his hands wrapped around the Francis Cup.[30]

The Olympics drew huge crowds. By the end of August, paid admissions, concession revenues, and bookings for the fall had grown to the point that Francis felt confident he could make the federal loan payments until the end of the Fair. He notified St. Louis banks that he would not need the $1 million loan he had asked them to hold ready.[31]

September 15 was designated St. Louis Day. Francis talked city and state politicians into declaring the day a holiday. The Fair laid on more parades, including one featuring prize-winning cows.

The weather was pleasantly cool and sunny for St. Louis Day. Trainloads of visitors rolled into St. Louis, the turnstiles clicked madly, and by the time the light of the last of the aerial rockets had faded from the night sky and everyone went home, about 385,000 people had attended. That was not just a single-day record, but also it was far more than the weekly attendance in the first month of the Fair. Francis was everywhere, making speeches, shaking hands, and handing out blue ribbons to ecstatic cow owners.[32]

Two and a half weeks later, Francis was hit hard by the death of David Pitman Rowland, the uncle who had made it possible for him to attend Washington University and had gotten him started in business. The Fair still had four weeks to run and allowed little time for mourning.[33]

Early on the morning of October 17, one of the few American women as famous as Alice Roosevelt arrived at Union Station. Helen Keller, the extraordinary blind and deaf writer and lecturer, barely twenty-four years old, was the first person to be given her own day at the Fair, and at that point she was scheduled to be the only one. She arrived with her teacher, Annie Sullivan, and stayed with Mary Perry, Jane's half sister, at their late father's mansion at 12 Vandeventer Place.[34]

Helen Keller spent three days visiting the Fair, walking through the entire Fairgrounds. Escorted by David Francis and followed, like the president's daughter, by a large crowd, she exclaimed with delight at exhibits she could only see and hear through the touch of Annie Sullivan.

On Helen Keller Day, October 18, she spoke at the national conference of superintendents of schools for the deaf. David Francis led her through the crowd that packed the Hall of Congresses to the platform, where he introduced her. The crowd went silent as she began to speak in her high-pitched, wavering voice, barely audible beyond the first few rows. Annie Sullivan repeated her words, louder but not loud enough to be heard in back, and finally Francis, in his powerful voice, began repeating the words, too. When Miss Keller got to a passage where she praised the "distinguished founder" of the exposition. Francis blushed and hesitated, and one of the educators on the podium picked up the sentence. Francis resumed his broadcast as she said words he believed in deeply: "God bless the nation that provides education for all her children."[35]

The Louisiana Purchase Exposition was, at times, a manic sweep from the sublime to the ridiculous. Helen Keller's visit preceded the arrival of what was trumpeted as "the smallest dog in the world"—Chiquita, a twenty-three-ounce Chihuahua who lived in a cigar box. And about the same time, the *Globe*'s FHC claimed that Fair vendors at the height of summer had invented the ice cream cone.[36]

Attendance peaked in September and October, with nearly 3.5 million visitors pushing through the turnstiles each month. In late October, anticipating a slackening of attendance as the weather worsened, Francis sent out letters asking that all departments trim staff by November 1.[37]

Roosevelt was reelected on November 8, and Francis finally convinced the president, jubilant in victory, to visit the Fair. President and Mrs. Roosevelt, Alice, and about a dozen high government officials arrived in their special train at the World's Fair Station early on the morning of November 26, which had been declared President's Day.

Beginning shortly after 9 A.M., Roosevelt, accompanied most of the way by David Francis and trailed by everyone else including Alice, began a whirlwind tour of the Fairgrounds. With an hour out for lunch, the president was on the go until 6:30 P.M., hopping in and out of his carriage, walking fast through exhibits, glancing approvingly to the left and the right, occasionally startling the Secret Service escort by darting away from them to eyeball something up close, and constantly smiling his huge smile for the crowds that pursued him.

Roosevelt kept moving until he had covered all the major exhibits and some ten or eleven miles. He visited or at least glanced at several hundred exhibits, pausing for a few minutes to review a parade or ninety seconds to watch the Igorots dance, occasionally exclaiming to Francis, "This is marvelous. . . . Why this is wonderful!" Stopped momentarily by a reporter as he hurried through the U.S. Government Building, Roosevelt answered the question before it had been uttered fully, shouting, "It is magnificent. . . . Yes, it is stupendous. The memory of it will live with me always!" And he hurried on.

One of the few places he didn't visit was the ornate building erected by New York, his home state. It seems likely that he had been warned that E. H. Harriman, the ill-tempered railroad magnate whose woes at the hands of this trust-busting president were by no means over, lurked inside, red-faced with furious anticipation, waiting to ambush him. The president's carriage just clattered on by.[38]

Alice Roosevelt later said that her previous visit, which had been "fairly active work," seemed like "loitering compared to the two days I spent scuttling in Father's wake."[39]

As the president's carriage sped through the Fairgrounds, Jessie Tarbox Beals and her assistant hurried ahead on foot with their cumbersome equipment, cutting through exhibits and across lawns, and were often set up and ready to take the next picture when Roosevelt arrived. Roosevelt was amazed at seeing the woman photographer in her voluminous dress at almost every stop he made. Francis told him who she was, and after seeing the results of her work—she got thirty-two separate shots of him and his family—the president arranged for her to take official photographs at his inauguration.[40]

That evening, at a banquet for six hundred at the huge restaurant cum bierstube beneath the Tyrolean Alps on the Pike, Francis toasted Roosevelt, proclaiming that in one day he had "seen what no other man could see in six months." Roosevelt replied:

> This marvelous Exposition [was] in very fact, as you, President Francis, have said, the greatest exposition of its kind that we have ever seen in recorded history. As I walked today through and among the buildings. . . . I had but one regret, and that was a deep regret—the regret that these could not be made permanent. The regret that it is impossible to keep these buildings as they are for our children and our children's children and all who are to come after as a permanent memorial to the greatness of this country.

"This country is under a great debt of obligation to you and your associates.[41]

Francis took no chances with the food, which was supervised by two of the most famous restaurateurs in the country—August Luchow of New York and Tony Faust of St. Louis. The menu included German beer and wine, blue point oysters, salmon soufflé, medallions of beef, risotto with truffles, quail, French ice cream, and biscotti. This time Roosevelt had no complaints.

Sunday was a much less strenuous day, beginning with church at Second Presbyterian and ending with the Roosevelts and their party having dinner with the Francises and top Fair officials at the Maryland Avenue mansion. At midnight, shortly before the train pulled out, Roosevelt stood on the rear platform of his special car and looked out over the Fairgrounds as the myriad lights went out. The palaces and towers and fountains, the giant Ferris Wheel and the tumbling Cascades, slowly disappeared from view. A correspondent traveling with the president asked how he had enjoyed his visit. Roosevelt looked silently out over the darkened Fairgrounds for a moment and then said, softly, "Why, my boy, I've had the time of my life."[42]

While in St. Louis, Roosevelt had suggested to Fair directors that they close the exposition with a day dedicated to Francis. At a directors' meeting Francis was not told about, they decided to do just that.

December 1 was designated Francis Day. Public and Catholic schools and state and city offices were officially closed, and the mayor and the governor, despite the short notice, urged business to close, too. Most larger firms complied. In either an act of generosity or to swell the crowds, the Fair announced that Francis Day would be "free to the poor."[43]

Francis Day began at 8:30 A.M., when Mayor Wells and a committee of Fair directors arrived at 4421 Maryland Avenue and escorted Francis on a private trolley car to the Administration Building. The corridors and stairwells had been decorated overnight in red, white, and blue bunting. Along the walls were pictures of Francis and the flag of Kentucky, and the seal of Missouri had been hung in his office.

At 10:30 A.M., Francis led a procession of Fair directors and officials down the long stone steps of the Administration Building and along a walkway to the Plaza of St. Louis and the Louisiana Purchase Monument. According to the *Globe-Democrat,* the Plaza "was a human sea" when Francis arrived:

> The sound of music and marching feet brought people running from every
> part of the grounds. They were pouring through the gates at [the] Lindell
> entrance in steady streams that flowed unceasingly to joined the sea of faces
> surrounding the monument. As President Francis appeared . . . the bands
> struck up 'Hail to the Chief' followed by 'Dixie.' The crowd went wild. Hats,
> gloves and handkerchiefs went into the air, while the noise of the demonstra-
> tion brought other thousands running from the Pike.[44]

A considerable amount of speechifying ensued, and Jessie Tarbox Beals captured the scene on the speaker's platform as Francis sat, half-listening, his eyes drifting towards the photographer, slumping in his chair, looking untypically exhausted. With bags under his eyes, and his hair turned white, he appeared to have aged ten years in the seven months since she had photographed him touching the golden telegraph key that set in motion the grandest world's fair of all.[45]

Wells went on for a bit, praising everyone who had worked on the Fair, and then he declared, "Above all, we admire and applaud the forcible leadership of our president, David R. Francis, under whose ceaseless energy, courteous demeanor and superior intelligence success has been achieved. . . . Long live David R. Francis!"

Governor Alexander Dockery introduced Francis as "the executive genius who made the Fair." Francis stood and, as the crowd gave him a three-minute ovation, looked out over the cheering crowd and the Main Picture, with its tumbling Cascades and its gleaming neo-classical buildings, perhaps realizing he was seeing it for the last time in all its glory, and tears came to his eyes. Finally, hesitantly, before the applause had entirely died down, he began to speak, his voice quavering with emotion. "I am dazed," he said, "if not dumb from the manifestations and expressions of this day."

He spoke for seven or eight minutes, pausing occasionally to catch his breath and rub his eyes, or to still the quaking hand that held the list of people he did not want to forget. He thanked the directors, the department heads, the federal government, foreign and state governments, the mayor, the governor, and "all who have shared in the spirit of the undertaking."

He continued:

Speaking for myself, it has been the work of my life. The duties of the position I have held not only claimed my entire time and thought, having not failed to be on the grounds from six to 14 hours each day since the opening . . . but the performance of those duties have been so pregnant with pleasure and interest that it has dispelled all feelings of weariness, and its cessation will seem like the severing of beloved ties. . . .[46]

Ceremonies went on all day. Then, at 5 P.M., Francis was picked up by the Yellowstone Park stagecoach, pulled by six beautifully groomed white horses, and driven on a tour of the grounds, with crowds cheering as he passed through. A rowdy mob in a Mardi Gras mood greeted him along the Pike, celebrating the final night of the Fair by blowing horns and waving canes and poking each other with feathered ticklers and stretching ropes across the walkway to stop the tormented from escaping. Tons of paper confetti and feathers were tossed into the air and lay on the pavement of the Pike like a layer of snow.

The day ended at the Plaza St. Louis. David and Jane Francis and Director of Works Isaac Taylor, after a long banquet at the Tyrolean Alps, arrived at the Louisiana Purchase Monument at 11:30 P.M. A crowd of about one hundred thousand cheered as the

Francises stood together at the speaker's stand, and David spoke for a few moments, his voice at times trembling.

"I am about to perform a heartrending duty," he said, and swept his hand across the horizon, where hundreds of thousands of lights outlined the great palaces of the Fair and the Ferris Wheel and lit the roaring Cascades. He said he wished the Fair might live forever, but that was not to be.

He turned and put his hand on the arm of Jane Francis, and said, "Here stands the partner of my life," and the crowd cheered for two minutes. As the clock in a nearby tower rang midnight, he walked across the stand to a large electric switch. Raising his hands toward the Cascades and Art Hill, he said, "Farewell, a long farewell to all thy splendor." He paused for a moment to take it all in for one last time and then threw the switch.

The lights dimmed and flickered and went out, the water stopped rolling down the Cascades, and, as a thousand machines slowed to a halt, the earth gradually stopped rumbling. Rockets shot into the air, gushing smoke and showers of sparks, and Francis's face appeared, in lines of fire hundreds of feet high, in the western sky above the towers of the Administration Building. On one side of the Plaza, rockets exploded and formed the word "Farewell." On the other side, the clear night sky was lit with the words "Good night."[47]

CHAPTER 11

After the Lights Went Out

"They won't ever tear it down will they?"
"No," Tootie said. "They will never tear it down. It will be like this forever."
—Meet Me in St. Louis[1]

O F COURSE, THEY DID TEAR IT DOWN, beginning in earnest the morning after Francis Day. Indeed, part of the Fair's sentimental appeal had come from the inevitability that the Ivory City would not survive the winter. The ephemeral, summer-dream quality of this fantasy city was part of its deep and enduring emotional power; millions of Americans left the Fair with a wistful, half-understood sense of nostalgia.

The wrecking crews rolled into Forest Park. Fifteen million dollars worth of Fair-owned buildings, all the major ones except the Palace of Fine Arts, were sold for $386,000 to a salvage company. The Inside Inn was quickly torn down and scrapped. Hundreds of pianos, and thousands of other items large and small, from china teacups to horse-drawn carriages, went on sale in St. Louis. Within six months, all that remained from the grandest world's fair of them all were piles of rubble, fields of bare earth, the Palace of Fine Arts, the giant iron bird cage, and the twenty-six-story-high Ferris Wheel, which was finally dynamited into a forty-foot-high pile of scrap metal and hauled away.[2]

Although plenty of international expositions would follow, the St. Louis World's Fair was a pinnacle, the biggest and most elaborate of its kind, the climax of an exuberant tradition of the late nineteenth century and early twentieth. The St. Louis Fair would be remembered longer than any before it and probably any since (the 1939 New York "World of Tomorrow" Exposition might be the exception), in part because it was the setting of one of the most popular movie musicals of all time.

The World's Columbian Exposition in Chicago had summed up the nineteenth century. The Louisiana Purchase Exposition marked the beginning of the twentieth. A new technology was on display, but so were new ideas, or at least old ones empowered with new intellectual constructs. These ideas would dominate political and cultural thought for the wonderful and horrible century to come. The Louisiana Purchase Exposition was rich with paradox. It celebrated America's proud assumption of the white man's burden as well as its dream of ending centuries of racial, ethnic, economic, and religious prejudice. It trumpeted unfettered capitalism and ruthless expansionism as well as universal education and social welfare. It showcased post-Darwinian ways of thinking about human societies that would hover over the century, for good and for evil. It even marked the dawning of the nuclear age.

"Modernism Comes to Middle America" is the title of the chapter on the St. Louis World's Fair in William Everdell's intriguing 1997 book, *The First Moderns.* The Fair comes between chapters on motion picture pioneer Edwin S. Porter and on Albert Einstein. Everdell pays particular attention to the International Congress of Arts and Sciences, held in late September and featuring brilliant thinkers who would come to influence twentieth-century thought in philosophy, psychology, sociology, political science, history, genetics, chemistry, physics, and even U.S. politics. The idea of the congress was to sum up nineteenth-century thought in a wide spectrum of fields and look ahead to the twentieth. One organizer said that the ultimate aim was *"a weltanschauung,* a unified view of the whole of reality." [3]

Participants included historian Woodrow Wilson, the new president of Princeton; lawyer and educator A. Lawrence Lowell, president of Harvard; sociologist and social theorist Max Weber; moral philosopher Josiah Royce; John Watson, who would found behavioral psychology; Oskar Drude, a pioneer in the new science of ecology; and Harald Hoffding, a Danish philosopher of psychology whose widely read works brought to the United States and the rest of Europe the ideas of his obscure countryman Soren Kierkegaard—ideas central to the distinctly twentieth-century philosophical movement called existentialism.

At the congress, important European and American alienists fought over Freud's concepts of the unconscious mind, and a number of influential physicists and mathematicians, including several Nobel Prize winners, presented pivotal work on atomic theory and on newly discovered subatomic particles. They pushed hard on the limits of classical physics, limits that a young clerk in Switzerland named Albert Einstein soon would break through entirely with his 1905 Special Theory of Relativity. The theoretical physicist and philosopher Ludwig Boltzmann, who greatly influenced Einstein, described the St. Louis congress as "a flood . . . a Niagara of scientific thought."

Many who saw the Fair would never forget it. Thomas Wolfe, who turned four at the end of that summer of 1904, typically remembered in great detail visits to the Fair with his brothers and his mother, who ran a boarding house near the Kingshighway streetcar line that summer. Wolfe described the visits in *Look Homeward Angel* through his alter ego, Eugene Gant:

> Once in a huge building roaring with sound, he was rooted before a mighty
> locomotive, the greatest monster he had ever seen, whose wheels spun
> terrifically in grooves, whose blazing furnaces, raining hot coals into the pit
> beneath, were fed incessantly by two grimed fire-painted stokers. The scene

burned in his brain like some huge splendor out of Hell; he was appalled and
fascinated by it. Again, he stood at the edge of the slow, terrific orbit of the
Ferris Wheel, reeled down the blaring confusion of the midway, felt his
staggering mind converge helplessly into all the mad phantasmagoria of the
carnival. . . .

His last remembrance of the Fair came from a night in early autumn; with
[sister] Daisy again he sat upon the driver's seat of a motor bus, listening for
the first time to the wonder of its labored chugging, as they rolled, through
ploughing sheets of rain, around the gleaming roads, and by the Cascades,
pouring their water down before a white building jewelled with ten thousand
lights.[4]

Many years later, Wolfe returned to St. Louis to reclaim his memories. Inevitably, he
was disappointed. St. Louis was only "a big, hot, common town upon the river, swelter-
ing in wet, dreary heat, and not quite South, and nothing else to make it better." He visited Forest Park, trying to slip back into "the vast and drowsy murmur of the Fair," and
he later found the house where the family had lived and his beloved older brother,
Grover Cleveland Wolfe, had died. At the end of his visit, "he knew that he would never
come again, and that lost magic would not come again." The St. Louis World's Fair was
the perfect metaphor for Thomas Wolfe's lifelong, epic sense of loss.[5]

THE FAIR MADE MONEY. After some knuckle biting and belt-tightening in the spring
and early summer, David Francis had kept up with his payments to the federal government, and he paid off the final installment of the loan on time, on November 15.[6]

However, St. Louis did not come close to beating out Chicago for attendance. Its
final admission total came to about 20 million (12.8 million paid), as opposed to 27.5
million (21.5 million paid) for Chicago.[7] But it must have been somewhat gratifying to
Francis when the *Chicago Tribune* hailed the St. Louis Fair as "the greatest of expositions" and said the main reason for its success was the LPE president's "personal force,
his unfailing energy, and his fund of good natured persistency."[8]

At the end of the twentieth century, according to the *Post-Dispatch*, the Louisiana
Purchase Exposition remained the only American world's fair to have turned a profit.[9]
Depending as it does on the vagaries of accounting, this contention is virtually impossible to prove or disprove. In any event, a year after the Fair had ended, when the great
majority of accounts had been settled, the LPE Company had about $850,000 in the
bank—or rather, in the banks that had put money into the Fair—drawing interest at 3
to 4 percent.[10]

In the short term, at least, the Fair benefitted St. Louis in its economic competition
with other cities. Commerce rose 25 percent in the year following the Fair, local industry boomed, and real-estate prices soared.

"Nothing ever contributed so much toward bringing the people of St. Louis together and inspiring a consciousness of strength and mutual confidence as did the World's
Fair," Francis contended later, with some justification, although in the long term the Fair

may well have lingered so long in the local memory that it led to complacency or resignation, both qualities already abundant in St. Louis. Visitors at the end of the twentieth century are often astonished at how St. Louisans born long after 1904 speak with loving memory and pride of the Fair and describe it as the city's finest moment, as if nothing could ever top it.

William Marion Reedy proclaimed that the "beauty" of the Fair had "sunk into our hearts. . . . It is part of the city's life, of the life of all of us, and it shall be a legacy of our descendants, with whatsoever else of good and true and beautiful we may bequeath them in the very fibres of their being."

Reedy also was enthusiastic about the broadening effects of the Fair on midwesterners:

> The Exposition has . . . made for a broader tolerance, a keener appreciation of
> the good in all the world . . . [and] awakened in us a poignant sense of our
> shortcomings, and those shortcomings we must obliterate. We have learned
> to be humble before the achievements of other people whom we fancied we
> long ago left behind in the march of progress.[11]

The park itself took several years to restore, after a considerable amount of squabbling between two contingents. One wanted a wild, unmanicured park, a restoration of the Wilderness. The other wanted to keep more buildings from the Fair, and provide more sites for recreation.

Francis had contracted with landscape architect George E. Kessler, who had landscaped the Fair, to draw up a plan for the future of Forest Park, and Francis went with the compromise Kessler proposed—a pastoral escape from the city, with vast lawns and grassy hills and few buildings.[12] What eventually emerged was modern Forest Park, with long, green, tree-shaded expanses suitable for picnicking, open fields for kite flying, art and regional-history museums, a celebrated zoo, a planetarium, golf courses, tennis and handball courts, softball, soccer, and cricket fields, a system of lakes, ponds, and canals, some stocked with catchable fish, and a large outdoor amphitheater. It's all encircled by an almost dangerously popular six-mile bicycle path.

Washington University tells prospective students that the campus is right across the street from one of America's finest urban parks. In the end, the cozy deal David Francis and Robert Brookings made at the beginning of the century has greatly benefitted both the city, whose most prosperous neighborhoods tend to be those near Forest Park, and the university, which by the 1990s had evolved from a streetcar college to a nationally prominent institution, with an endowment among the top ten in the United States.

In January 1905, after the first heavy snowfall of the year, children discovered that Art Hill was a wonderful spot for sledding. David Francis stood at the crest, watching with delight as children belly-whopped down the hill on their wooden sleds, and someone asked him if he would like to have a go at it. He politely declined.[13]

The following year, Francis and the Exposition Company made a gift to the city for the crest of Art Hill: a bronze replica of the Fair's landmark statue of King Louis IX, the city's patron saint, on horseback as if ready to ride off to the Crusades. By then, Francis was not just president of the LPE Company but its treasurer. William Thompson died in December of 1905.[14]

IN MAY OF 1905, halfway around the globe from St. Louis, the Russian fleet was destroyed by the Japanese, and in September Teddy Roosevelt negotiated an armistice.

The humiliating defeat in the Russo-Japanese war helped fuel anti-Tsarist agitation among the Russian people. Some leaders of "zemstvos"—local and regional councils—called for a constitutional, representational, parliamentary government to end centuries of despotic reign by the Tsars. Tsar Nicholas II made some half-hearted concessions to raging democratic sentiment, but he repressed any real reform. As revolutionary groups sprang up, his Cossacks and his vast cadre of secret police cracked down on dissent and, in what seemed an inevitable part of Russian political repression, increased the persecution of Jews.

In the next few years, many prominent Russians, including the impresario Diaghilev, the dancers Nijinsky and Pavlova, and the composer Stravinsky, left St. Petersburg for Western Europe. Among them was Edward Grunwaldt, who had checked the Russian art for the St. Louis World's Fair through customs and who, as far as this country was concerned, held legal claim to it.

Some of the paintings had been sold at the Fair, not necessarily with the artists' permission—one, a huge painting called "Forest Fire," had been purchased by Adolphus Busch, and until the 1970s, when Busch's grandson, August Busch, Jr., gave the painting back to the Russian government, it hung in the reception room of the Anheuser-Busch brewery.

For several months after the close of the Fair, seventy-two cases of paintings sat in storage at the Palace of Fine Arts. Finally, in the spring of 1905, Grunwaldt shipped them to New York, where he set himself up as an art dealer and sold several hundred pieces. After paying off debts and custom fees, Grunwaldt kept most of the money that was left. Few of the artists saw a ruble. In 1910 the venerable and revered Russian painter Ilya Repin swore that he would "never send another thing to America," which was a country of "barbarians."[15]

Francis had hoped to make another grand tour of Europe to thank the leaders who had sent exhibits to the Fair. But he decided he needed to attend to business, which was booming. In February he did manage to take a couple of weeks off to join his friend, railroad magnate Sam Felton, and the Commercial Club of Chicago on a brief cruise to sunny Havana. And in June, after being invited to a VIP tour by the private company that ran Yellowstone Park—Francis had been the park's defender as secretary of the interior and its host at the Fair—Francis headed west for a vacation. With him on a private railroad car were Jane Francis, their sons Charles and Sidney, and Philip Jordan.

Years later, Jordan set down a vivid description of the trip, a description that provides the earliest look we have at the unusually close relationship that was developing between Francis and Jordan.

While the group was visiting Old Faithful, Francis said to Jordan, "Philip, I am going out on the lake this afternoon and catch some lake trout. Get your hat and I will show you how to fish."

Jordan replied, "No, Governor, I appreciate your kind offer, but I don't care much for fishing. I can take ten cents and buy all the fish I want."

"You don't understand," said Francis. "It is the sport of catching them."

"You go ahead and I will be waiting when you return," said Jordan.

A guide picked Francis up in a small boat and headed out on the lake. Jordan waited until the boat was out of sight and strolled away to look at the spectacular scenery. About an hour later, he returned to the landing just as the boat was coming in. Francis was terrifically excited, and he stood and said, "You see these?" and held up a stringer of lake trout. "They are fine," said Jordan, reaching for the stringer as Francis clambered off the boat. "Give them to me and I will have them fixed up for your dinner."

Francis said to the guide, "Well, my man, what do I owe you?"

"Eighteen dollars."

"WHAT?" shouted Francis.

"That's what we charge per hour," said the guide.

"All right," said Francis, his face red, "but the next time I want to go fishing, I will do like Philip—take ten cents and buy them."

Typically, Francis complained loudly about the outrageous expense, and the park company returned his eighteen dollars before the group left Yellowstone.[16]

IN JANUARY 1906, on behalf of the Merchants' Exchange, Francis presented a loving cup to his mentor, former governor and exchange president E. O. Stanard, on his seventy-fifth birthday. He said he would never forget the influence the Republican businessman/politician had exerted on him, beginning in 1870, when he had begun his business career as a mud clerk and messenger for his uncle. "It is rare indeed that for half a century a man can point to a record in which there is not a blemish," Francis said. "I know of none whose character has exerted more influence. . . . Never a breath of suspicion; never has the tongue of slander assailed him."[17]

Six months later, Francis symbolically returned to politics—after almost a decade of absence—by appearing before the Democratic state convention in Jefferson City to call for party unity. By 1906, free silver had waned as a divisive issue, and William Jennings Bryan, although he still yearned for the presidency, had moved onto other causes, some of them—like low tariffs—important to David Francis.

While emphasizing that he disagreed with some of Bryan's positions—such as the need for public ownership of railroads—he said that he had great admiration and respect for Bryan and felt Bryan would follow the will of the majority of the party on major issues.

The split in the party over silver, he announced, had led to the Republican near-sweep in 1904, and that was "an outrage. . . . It will be to our everlasting disgrace if we permit it to occur again." He brought the already cheering assembly to its feet by endorsing William Jennings Bryan as the Democratic nominee for president of the United States in 1908.[18]

About a week later, he boarded an eastbound train for a sentimental journey to his hometown of Richmond, Kentucky, for its Homecoming. It was forty years since he had left to attend Washington University and thirty-six years since he had last visited Richmond.

Now fifty-five, his hair and mustache white, his frame thickened, gold-rimmed glasses over his still-bright eyes, he met with friends and relatives, men and women whom he had known as children, and he took a slow stroll around Courthouse Square, where he had spent much of the first years of his life. He saw where he was born and had grown up, where he had gone to school, and where he had watched the bloody aftermath of the Battle of Richmond, with wounded soldiers limping through town, pursued by their advancing enemies. He visited the cemetery where his grandparents were buried, and where the tombstones still bore the scars of battle.

The main ceremonies were at Eastern Kentucky State Normal School, on the green and leafy campus of what had been Central University—founded by his mentor, Robert Breck, now nearly eighty and retired to Pasadena, California. People had been coming in from the countryside for several hours, and when the band struck up "My Old Kentucky Home," thousands sang along and then listened as Francis spoke emotionally. He said that he had "been honored by audiences with crowned heads of Europe" and had "addressed national and international assemblages," but in all his travels, never had his "feelings been so deeply touched as they are today."

Francis quoted Emerson: "The presence of a rich man in his community helps the credit of every man and every institution in it." He added that it was difficult to overestimate the influence over a community and its sons and daughters of a citizen with strong character and high standards. He said, "I think one of the most potent incentives to effort that can be instilled into a young man is his pride of ancestry. If you can imbue your children with the conviction that they have a family name and reputation to uphold and maintain, half of your duty is accomplished."

Later that day, he announced the gift of a monument of Missouri granite to be placed at the southeast corner of the courthouse square, across from his childhood home. The monument, to honor Kentucky pioneers, would be a shaft topped by a bronze bust called *The Typical Pioneer*. The sculptor would be George Julian Zolnay, who had been chief sculptor for the World's Fair and whom Francis had brought to the Homecoming. Also at the Homecoming were two of his sons, David, Jr., and Talton, and his sister Mollie Ellerbe.[19]

By the summer of 1906, despite his thriving brokerage business, his various directorships, and his civic obligations, Francis found himself with time on his hands. In mid-July, he and three friends—Fair executive committee members Breckinridge Jones and

L. D. "Bud" Dozier, and Chicago railroad magnate Samuel Felton—set sail from New York on the luxurious *Kaiser Wilhelm* for a two-month tour of Europe, scheduled to get them back home in time to get ready for the Veiled Prophet celebration in October.

After landing in Cherbourg, Francis was tireless in tracking down monarchs and prime ministers and handing them eighteen-carat gold World's Fair commemorative medals and diplomas honoring them for their contributions to the Fair. He managed to pin a medal on the president of France, King Oscar II of Sweden, King Frederick of Denmark, Kaiser Wilhelm of Germany, Emperor Franz Joseph of Austria, and King Leopold of Belgium.

The "World's Fair cowboys," as the *Post-Dispatch* called them, made a side trip to London, where they discovered that King Edward VII was vacationing on the continent at an unrevealed location. Francis managed to track Edward down at Marienbad, the Austrian spa. He was registered as the Duke of Newcastle, but that didn't fool Francis. Francis spotted the king and shouted, according to the *Post-Dispatch*, "Hands up! I'm going to decorate you!"[20]

On September 19, they sailed for home. "KINGS GRIEVE" the *Post-Dispatch* proclaimed. "Gloom Settles Over Abode of Europe's Royalty as Ship Bears World's Fair President Toward His Native Shores."[21]

A week later, he arrived in New York, where he was met by Collins Thompson. He was eager to see Jane Francis, who had been relaxing by the sea in Massachusetts and whom he had expected to come to New York to meet his ship. Thompson said he believed she had returned to St. Louis. Francis was disappointed—he had been looking forward to spending a few days with her at the Waldorf-Astoria. Instead, he checked into the Waldorf alone and proceeded to entertain the press with his remarks on his trip and on William Jennings Bryan's nearly permanent campaign for the presidency, assuring the newspapermen that Bryan was not about to do anything radical.[22]

At the end of 1906, Francis was elected a director of New York Life, a position he held until 1925. (Nicholas Murray Butler, the president of Columbia University, who had stayed at Francis's house for Dedication Day, was also a director.) Francis almost certainly was recommended by, among others, Oscar Straus, who had been a director between political appointments since the early 1890s. Rising to the top of the vast financial network of New York Life, which was very close to and partly owned by J. P. Morgan and Co., signified like almost nothing else his entry into the upper levels of the American establishment.[23]

The directorship of New York Life was an almost entirely WASP institution dominated by powerful men in New York and Chicago, captains of industry and members of the top law and banking firms, men named Innis and Milliken and Steele and Abbott and Aiken and Snow who had attended the best Ivy League colleges and dined at the best New York clubs.

Also in 1906, Francis and a few friends bought, for $2 million, a small, failing railroad they hoped to turn into a large one as population and markets expanded in the

Southwest. Francis became chairman of the board of the Missouri and North Arkansas Railroad Co., with his close friend, industrialist John Scullin, as the president and banker Festus Wade a large investor. Over the next few years, they would pour several million more into extending and improving the line south and eastward from western Missouri through the mineral-rich Ozarks into the fertile cottonlands of eastern Arkansas. But Arkansas failed to develop its natural resources as rapidly as Francis and his partners had hoped, and the Missouri and North Arkansas became one of Francis's few long-term bad investments and would nag at him for years.

Although he later complained that corporate meetings left him little time for other things, Francis thrived on being busy, and during the Fair he had learned how his adrenaline raced when he was working at his limit, with more to do than the average man could possibly accomplish. In November 1906, he added to the load. At a meeting in Kansas City, with Secretary of State Elihu Root, William Jennings Bryan, E. H. Harriman, president of the Union Pacific Railroad, and Leslie M. Shaw, the secretary of the treasury, looking on, he took over the presidency of the Trans-Mississippi Commercial Congress, which represented all the states and territories in the Louisiana Purchase. It was, in effect, a chamber of commerce for two-thirds of the United States.

The feisty, bantamweight Harriman, in a rambling speech, said that he had gotten to know David Francis through the World's Fair. He initially had declined an invitation to speak at opening day, he said, but that spring he happened to be passing through St. Louis on a business trip, and had stopped to "simply shake hands." At that point, Harriman said with a grin, "he had me." There was much knowing laughter and applause.

Bryan, tall and magisterial, noted that fifteen years before, as a young man who had just been elected to his first term as U.S. Representative from Omaha, he had been turned down in his attempts to speak to the Trans-Mississippi Congress. Finally Francis intervened and got him a place on the program. "There were many who wanted to speak and I was almost a stranger," Bryan said. "I have never ceased to be grateful to him for the time that he gave me then when I was a young man."

Francis made a lengthy speech in praise of the Monroe Doctrine, typically managing to bring in his private audience with the Kaiser. Then, introducing Treasury Secretary Shaw, Francis described himself as having been, for many years, "one of the largest borrowers west of the Mississippi." He assured his listeners that, thanks to the gold standard and the man he was introducing, "today money can be borrowed cheaper in this country than it can in London." He added, "I know because I am borrowing in both places."[24]

The Trans-Mississippi Congresses were important to Francis in keeping up his contacts with the men who ran the United States, many of whom, like Francis, had grown up in rural America. The following year, at the Trans-Mississippi Commercial Congress in Muskogee, Oklahoma, Francis played to that audience skillfully in a speech about country boys and the American dream:

I remember a great many years ago of a country boy who went to town with his clothes on the end of a stick, which he carried over his shoulder. He saw pass by him an equipage that contained some of the rich people of the city. He looked on in admiration if not with envy, but in the course of time that young man was leading all of the interests of the city and so it is in almost every city; the men who do the things, the men who build up the city are the boys that come from the country.

Francis was given a long ovation by the large audience. Several men went on to tell the congress that David Francis would make an excellent candidate for president of the United States.[25]

For Francis, business trips and vacations often were indistinguishable. In mid-February 1907, after Sam Felton of Chicago had made arrangements, Francis and other leaders of the Commercial Club of St. Louis joined the Commercial Clubs of Boston, Chicago, and Cincinnati in a four-week Caribbean cruise. In theory, the eighty-six men, in their blue blazers and sailing caps, made an official fact-finding trip to Panama. Roosevelt and Taft had assured them that their observations of progress on the half-finished canal across the isthmus, as well as the galvanizing effect of their very presence, would be immensely helpful. But February was also a very good month to be out of St. Louis, Boston, Chicago, and Cincinnati.

Their main stops were at two theoretically independent countries—Cuba and Panama—that were very much under the control of the United States, control enforced by the presence of garrisons of American troops. At the Culebra Cut through the mountainous spine of mid-Panama, the visitors received a long and detailed VIP tour by chief engineer John F. Stevens, who would reappear in Francis's life. In Havana, Francis spoke approvingly of the Monroe Doctrine and the stability that came from being under the protection of the United States. He suggested that if he were a Cuban political leader he would think seriously about organizing a drive to become an American state.[26]

The travelers barely had returned when the financial balloon that had swelled on Wall Street for years began leaking air. The Panic of 1907 was in full swing by the fall, with seventy-year-old J. P. Morgan virtually taking over the country's financial affairs, bringing smaller financiers into line by threatening them with ruin unless they went along with his program to stop the Panic. To prop up the economy, Morgan loaned out so many millions, both of his own money and that of the federal government's, that he became, in effect, the country's central bank.

Roosevelt was grateful to Morgan and came to believe that there actually were "good trusts." He blamed the Panic on the bad ones, "malefactors of great wealth" among a new generation of potential robber barons, and he eyed them balefully and took a tight grip on his big regulatory stick.[27]

David Francis, who was moving into the mainstream of the new Progressivism, became much more willing to see an increase in the power of the federal government. At national and regional commercial conferences, he urged federal regulation of the enormous corporations that were consolidating their hold over such major American industries as steel and oil. Unless the trusts were controlled, he argued, the result would be "almost absolute power for a comparative few."

"The conditions thus established," he said, "are but one step from socialism, and the indignant masses, if their spirit is not entirely broken, will inevitably conclude that such powers are the function of the State only. Monopoly and socialism in America are step-systems, if not relatives of full blood." [28]

The link between monopolistic oligarchy and one-party socialism, between the dictatorship of the right and that of the left, became an enduring theme for David Francis, one that would influence his reactions in a world crisis to come.

And Francis saw eye to eye with Teddy Roosevelt on the need, in the wake of the Panic of 1907, for some government control of the nation's banks. There had been no true national bank since Andrew Jackson, in full populist fury, had closed down the Bank of the United States in the early 1830s. Presidential candidate William Jennings Bryan didn't think a central bank was a good idea—like Old Hickory, Bryan was certain a national bank would be run by his arch enemies, the fat cats in the financial capitals of the Northeast.

In time, the Panic of 1907 would lead to the creation of the federal reserve system and a Federal Reserve Bank in St. Louis, with strong and significant support from David Francis and what was becoming his newspaper, the *St. Louis Republic*. As often was the case, Francis's position had an element of self-interest—he saw the federal reserve system and the positioning of its banks in St. Louis and other cities across the country as an aid in wresting financial control away from a few New York banks and investment houses. [29]

I N 1907, Talton became the fourth Francis son to graduate from Yale. (The other two, Tom and Sidney, also attended Yale, although neither came close to graduating.) [30] Talton went to work for Francis Bro. & Co., and moved into a small house just across Newstead from the Maryland Avenue mansion.

Anne Francis Currier recalled in a 1997 interview with the author that her grandfather, David R. Francis, "gave each of his sons a house. He seemed to want to have them all right across the street." At one point or another, four of the sons, including Sidney, lived within a block of the mansion, while Charles lived at the mansion.

According to Mrs. Currier, Tom, her father, stubbornly resisted his father's considerable pressure to live near the mansion and spent much of his young adulthood in north St. Louis county, at Uplands Farm. Tom broke away in another way, too, leaving the family brokerage to start his own real-estate business.

Around that time, with the presidential election a year off, speculation again grew that Francis might be a fine candidate for president or vice president. But in the campaign of 1908, ongoing among the out-of-power Democrats since 1906, Francis remained solidly behind Bryan.

Francis wanted no repeat of the debacle of 1904, when millions of Bryan Democrats sat out the election or voted for the candidates of smaller parties. However, as Collins

Thompson was careful to point out in a letter to a Wisconsin man who had written to urge Francis to run for president:

> Among the newspapers of the country, the Governor has many ardent admirers, and after Mr. Bryan I think no one's name is mentioned more frequently in their columns than his. If Mr. Bryan should not be elected as the nominee of the Party at the next election, certainly there is no one in its ranks more entitled to consideration and who would prove a better standard bearer than Gov. Francis.[31]

Francis not only supported Bryan in 1908, he campaigned with him, perhaps in part to keep reminding the Great Commoner that he needed to appear moderate if he wanted to beat the Republican nominee, William Howard Taft. In an almost condescending address at Carnegie Hall a couple of weeks before the election, Francis acknowledged that Bryan was "the same man" whom he had actively opposed in 1896 and been unable to support in 1900. But Bryan had grown, Francis said. He added, "A man may, by a brilliant flight of oratory, attract admiration of the masses and hold it for a time, but no man in this free and intelligent country can for twelve years continue to maintain his influence as William J. Bryan has without possessing character and merit."[32]

Bryan lost. Taft promised to carry on the legacy of Roosevelt. But many of his decisions on such matters as protective tariffs and the private exploitation of public lands aligned him with the right wing of the party and infuriated Progressives, including former President Roosevelt and David Francis. Francis began to contemplate a run for the United States Senate.

THE SURPLUS CONTINUED to grow in the World's Fair treasury, and Francis committed money to construction of what became the World's Fair Pavilion, a large gazebo where park visitors could cool off and buy snacks and drinks. In April 1909, the city announced it would consider the park to be "restored" if the Exposition Company would spend an additional two hundred thousand dollars on a monument to Thomas Jefferson.

Francis liked the idea, and after months of wrangling, the Exposition board and the city came to an agreement. In April 1910, at a dinner marking the sixth anniversary of the Fair, Francis announced that a statue of Thomas Jefferson would be the centerpiece of an arched entrance to the Jefferson Memorial, which would be built near the site of the main entrance to the World's Fair.

By then, Francis was in the midst of a heated political race for the Democratic nomination for the Senate. State legislators still chose senators—the 17th Amendment to the Constitution, transferring election of Senators to the voters, was not ratified until 1913—so the important race was the primary, which was held that year on November 8.

In the weeks leading up to the election, the *Post-Dispatch* attacked Francis on several fronts, including his profitable participation in the "bridge arbitrary" that he had once so roundly condemned. More potently, the *Post* dug up all the details it could on the Colorado Railroad deal and charged that Francis and John Scullin had made a couple of million dollars by owning the tracks and switches that carried thousands of tons of material into the Fairgrounds.

Francis refused, as he often did, to go into details on his financial dealings, and public disclosure laws were much more lax than they are today. But he angrily denied the charges, saying that anyone who said he had "made anything, directly or indirectly, out of my connection with the World's Fair is a liar, and anyone who reports that charge is a liar." [33] (See chapter 8.)

The affair represented the only time that Francis was linked publicly with any degree of credibility to a political scandal, and he was furious. A number of Fair directors and others with political and economic power complained about the series to the *Post-Dispatch*, which took the unusual step of running several explanatory editorials, saying essentially that Francis was a fine man and had done great public service but that his actions called into question his attacks on predatory trusts, railroad monopolies, and the influence of special interests on government. [34]

The charges were over-reaching, as sometimes was the case in those days, when *Post-Dispatch* owner Joseph Pulitzer was helping define "yellow journalism"—and beginning what became a highly respected tradition of fearless investigative journalism that helped uncover such legitimate scandals as Teapot Dome. To both the credit and the shame of the *Post-Dispatch*, its series contains sufficient information, in details deep within the stories, to refute the most important of the charges made in its inflammatory headlines and lead paragraphs. [35] In some cases, the *Post* seemed to purposely misinterpret its own evidence against Francis. On the other hand, underlying the *Post-Dispatch* series was a good point—Francis was hardly innocent of the slick, competition-strangling practices he so resoundingly attacked in his railing against trusts.

Francis lost the primary election to James Reed, a tough, eloquent former Kansas City mayor and prosecutor, in part because of the *Post-Dispatch*'s charges. But Reed's victory also was a demonstration of the growing power of the Pendergast machine in the western half of the state. Also, Reed got some mileage out of the not-entirely absurd charge that Francis wanted the Senate as a national stage to run for the presidency two years later.

"Fighting Jim" Reed, with considerable help from Boss Tom Pendergast, went on to serve three terms in the United States Senate, preceding Harry S Truman as what came to be called "The Senator from Pendergast."

Although the *Post-Dispatch*, no friend of political bosses, had been rough on Reed, too, Francis always blamed the paper for his defeat and emerged from his final political campaign once again deeply bitter about attacks on his personal and professional integrity. The animosity between Francis and the *Post-Dispatch* spilled over into St. Louis polite society. Orrick Johns, whose father, George, was the crusading editor of the *Post-Dispatch*, wrote in a memoir that 1910 "was a difficult and anxious time for many people. . . . Feeling ran to white heat among the powerful followers of Francis, and threats of vengeance filled the air." [36]

"Father had known Francis nearly all his life," Johns wrote, "knew him well and liked him. He had a great admiration for his abilities, but he believed him too rich for legislative office, too much entangled with large business interests, a man of the school that drew a rather vague line between business and politics."

Charges and curses were hurled back and forth, with Francis's friends and his enemies both going on the attack. From Europe, Joseph Pulitzer, by then an admirer of Francis but who also trusted Johns, cabled his editor to be sure of his facts and "be just, be fair." After the series had run, Pulitzer cabled, "I hope you have been generous to him."

Orrick Jones recalled being introduced at a St. Louis Symphony concert to Francis. When Francis heard the name Johns, "his smile turned to a glowering stare" and he turned away.

During the brouhaha, according to Orrick Johns, his father "expected to be shot but refused to carry a gun."

"As all the world knows," Orrick Johns concluded, "Francis became Wilson's ambassador to Russia. He forgave, and before his death he and father had several long and friendly conversations."[37]

Perhaps, in the last year or two of his life, when Francis was ill and enfeebled and making his peace with the world. But eight years after the series ran, as he stood in the fire of Bolshevik Russia, Francis remained bitter about the 1910 Senate race and told a friend the attack was personally motivated by the fact that George Johns had once been passed over for the editorship of the *Republic*. (If that was true, George Johns was a lucky man to become editor of the *Post-Dispatch* instead.)[38]

"MY GRANDMOTHER said she had always wanted a farm by the sea," recalled Anne Francis Currier. So in the spring of 1909, David Francis bought Jane a lovely summer house in New Hampshire. "She loved it," Mrs. Currier recalled. "You could see the ocean from the second floor." Almost the first thing Jane Francis did after the family moved in was start a rose garden.

The house, built in the late eighteenth century, was white clapboard with green shutters and a large screened-in porch. It sat at the end of a spruce-lined drive on a bluff overlooking Rye Beach. The eleven-acre tract of fields, pastures, and woods adjoined a private golf course. Francis could walk to the first tee, usually accompanied by Philip Jordan carrying his golf bag. Someone—perhaps Jordan—took symbolic possession of the place by hanging a poster in the barn. It showed what a later owner, Louise H. Tallman, described as "a knight on horseback" (Louis IX) and was emblazoned with the words "ST. LOUIS 1803–1904."[39]

Francis continued to make regular public appearances at important national events, keeping in the public eye and maintaining his contacts with politically powerful men.

In March 1911, for example, Francis, President Taft, former President Roosevelt, and Woodrow Wilson, by then the governor of New Jersey, were among the featured speakers at the Southern Commercial Congress in Atlanta. Francis extolled the South as a vast area of untapped natural resources, with particular attention to the mineral-rich mountains and fertile river plains of Arkansas.[40]

In this period, Francis strengthened a friendship with Charles R. Crane, a wealthy Chicago businessman and world traveler who shared Francis's belief that free trade would lead to a better, more peaceful, and more democratic world. Crane was also a friend of Woodrow Wilson.

THE CHARTER of the Louisiana Purchase Exposition Company expired in the spring of 1911, and before it did the company contracted for the construction of the Jefferson Memorial. One wing would house the permanent collection of the Missouri Historical Society, already the main repository of records of the exploration of the West, and the other the records and artifacts of the World's Fair. Ground was broken on April 8, and the cornerstone officially was laid on May 1, at a ceremony presided over by Francis.

The two-story, neo-classical building of granite and white limestone was dedicated on April 30, 1913. As Karl Bitter's nine-and-a-half-foot-high marble statue of Jefferson was unveiled in the rotunda, there was a twenty-one–gun salute, and, Walter Stevens recalled, "a mighty shout went up." Gesturing toward the statue, Francis reminded the crowd that Jefferson's greatness had come in the midst of revolution, and that the third president had been "a bitter foe to tyranny, whose hostility to every form of oppression was deep rooted and unwavering."[41]

By then, Francis had majority control of the *Republic*. Circulation and net earnings had been declining for years, and in 1908 the *Republic* quit paying dividends, never to resume. Its morning competitor, the *Globe-Democrat*, took a big leap in circulation and ad revenue at the time of the Fair, presumably because it covered the Fair more thoroughly, more entertainingly, and more perceptively than the *Republic*.[42]

David Francis probably was destined to fail as a newspaper man. Despite his democratic instincts and his relatively poor upbringing, he never really understood the average working person. And, unlike Joseph Pulitzer and the men who ran the *Globe-Democrat*, he didn't love newspapers as he seems to have loved the trading floor. He loved owning one, but that is quite a different matter.

By the early 1910s, he pretty much controlled the *Republic*'s editorial positions. He was not just bragging—although he was doing that—when he wrote to Missouri Congressman and Speaker of the House James Beauchamp "Champ" Clark, another prominent Missourian born in Kentucky:

My Dear Champ:
I suppose you read the *Republic* regularly and trust you are pleased with its views on public questions. You can always tell my position on any question by reading the editorial columns of the *Republic*—but, of course, this is confidential.[43]

Champ Clark was a friend as well as a political ally, and when Clark decided to run for president in 1912, Francis gave up his own designs on the White House and supported Clark, perhaps deciding two men from Missouri couldn't run at the same time. At the National Democratic Convention that summer in Baltimore, Clark was pitted against the scholarly governor of New Jersey, Woodrow Wilson, a deceptively shrewd politician. The race between the two men was extremely close and balloting went on well into the night, with Clark holding a majority of votes but not the two-thirds needed for nomination. (According to Walter Stevens, in the midst of the fight a compromise ticket with Francis as vice president was proposed to break the deadlock, but Francis turned the offer down.) The turning point came when William Jennings Bryan, alleging that Clark had sold his soul to the demons of Wall Street to get the New York vote, switched his support from Clark to Wilson.[44]

Wilson won the nomination and ran on a basically Progressive platform, enthusiastically supported by David Francis, that included reducing tariffs, vigorously enforcing antitrust laws, and reforming the banking system. During the campaign, Francis worked with Charles Crane, who was vice-chairman of Wilson's finance committee. Francis (and Champ Clark) campaigned vigorously for Wilson in Missouri, a key state that Wilson carried in winning the close election. Then, as Missouri looked expectantly towards Washington for its reward, Wilson named William Jennings Bryan his secretary of state and announced that all high-level presidential appointments would have to be approved by members of the cabinet.

A twitting story quickly appeared on the front page of the Sunday New York Times, headlined, "Wail From All Missouri." The Times reported that important Missouri Democrats, including both U.S. senators and the speaker of the house, were furious at Wilson. Missourians, the Times speculated, asked, "Doesn't the President know that we want an Ambassadorship for our State? Have we got to kowtow to that Nebraska person who put Champ Clark out of the running at the Baltimore convention?"

The Times commented:

Gradually, it seeped through their minds that . . . before they could land David R. Francis in any post, they must go to Secretary of State Bryan, the man who at the Baltimore convention prevented Clark's nomination and handed the Presidency to Wilson. . . . Missouri is pained, and will stay pained until she wakes up to the realization that we now have a President of the United States who does not do things in the same old way, but has a track of his own.[45]

Wilson moved forward quickly with his programs and in December 1913 signed into law the Federal Reserve Act, which set up twelve federal banks across the country to control the flow of currency. The legislation had been hammered and pounded and molded for months to satisfy most important opponents, including William Jennings Bryan. Francis cheered and immediately began scheming with his friends to get one of the banks located in St. Louis—and not just a bank but one of the four largest.

Madison County Courthouse, Richmond, Kentucky. This postcard view, circa 1900, still shows the wrought iron fence that confined the Union prisoners of war after the battle.
Eastern Kentucky University Archives.

The inn run by David R. Francis's father, now an annex of the Madison County Courthouse, as seen from the courthouse steps. Francis Fountain is in the foreground.
Talton Ray, 1997.

Cassius Marcellus Clay, prominent eastern Kentucky politician. This engraving was made from a photograph taken in 1864 in St. Petersburg while Clay served as U.S. ambassador to Russia.
Geo. Perine, N.Y./University of Kentucky Libraries Special Collections.

David R. Francis on his graduation from Washington University, 1870.
Talton F. Ray Collection.

David Pitman Rowland.
Western Bank Note Company, 1876/MHS Library.

This 1874 illustration from *Picturesque America* shows
the hustle and confusion of the riverfront found by the new mud clerk, David R. Francis.
A. R. Waud/MHS Library.

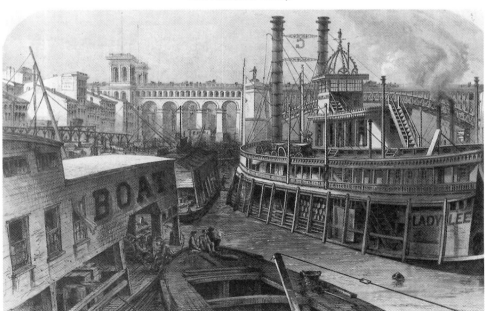

Construction view of Eads Bridge, February 1874.
Boehl and Koenig, 1874/MHS-PP.

Interior view of the Merchants' Exchange Building, scene of Francis's early trading triumphs.
Emil Boehl, 1875/MHS-PP.

This cabinet card portrait of thirty-five-year-old David R. Francis was part of a collection of the organizers of the National Convention of Cattlemen, held in St. Louis in 1884. It was the stock portrait of Francis during his campaign for mayor in 1885.
Fitz W. Guerin, 1884/MHS-PP.

THE DEMOCRATIC CANDIDATE ON THE WAR PATH

Francis's whirlwind 1885 campaign for mayor was not kindly depicted by a cartoonist in one local paper, as he is shown gladhanding caricatured Irish voters. The cartoon was preserved in one of Francis's scrapbooks.
MHS Library.

Ed Butler, livery stable owner, leader of St. Louis's First Ward, and "boss" of St. Louis. Francis's perceived compromises with Butler helped his political career but made reformers suspicious.
MHS-PP.

E. O. Stanard, Francis's mentor at the Merchant's Exchange and a political supporter. The Republican Stanard crossed party lines to support Francis in his 1885 bid for mayor.
Samuel Sartain, 1883/MHS-PP.

THE GUBERNATORIAL SITUATION.

MOREHOUSE (disguised as a granger to Glover disguised as a Vestal Virgin): "That's right, Johnny. You make faces at him and throw dirt, while I sneak around and hit him from behind."

The St. Louis Spectator touted Francis's virtues over scheming outstate politicians as Francis was boomed for governor in 1888.
Dana, 1888/MHS Library.

Outstate newspapers had a far different view of Francis, the big city mayor, as shown in this cartoon from a Phelps County newspaper.
MHS Library.

Farmer Francis—Why, how are you, Farmer Jones?
Farmer Jones—My name ain't Jones, and ye can't come any of your bunco rackets on me; you may be a farmer, but hang me if you don't look more like a city shark.

The doggerel poem under this cartoon showing both mayoral candidates attacking the Laclede gas monopoly claims that both are on the right side; the side taken by the *St. Louis Post-Dispatch*. This cartoon was also in the Francis scrapbooks.
St. Louis Post-Dispatch, 1885/MHS Library.

THE GAS MONOPLY MUST GO!

Jane Perry, the future wife of
David R. Francis, ca. 1875.
Talton F. Ray Collection.

John Dietz Perry, Francis's father-in-law.
Williams, NY, 1898/MHS-PP.

David and Jane Francis with their six sons, 1894.
J. C. Strauss, 1894/MHS-PP.

David R. Francis and his sons, 1904. Left to right: David, J. D. Perry, Charles, DRF, Talton, Sidney, Thomas.
Official Photographic Company, 1904/MHS-PP.

Governor Francis
with his family and friends
on the steps of the Governor's Mansion. DRF on the far left, Mike Fanning on far right.
MHS-PP.

The ruins of "Old Main" on the University of Missouri campus in Columbia
after the fire of January 9, 1892. One of Francis's greatest achievements as governor was
the prompt rebuilding and expansion of the campus. The pillars are still a campus landmark.
Credit: MHS-PP.

In 1895, David and Jane Francis moved their family into this new mansion in St. Louis's Central West End. The house at 4421 Maryland Avenue was their home until 1918 and was last used by the family for David's funeral in January 1927.

George Stark, 1903/MHS-PP.

Charles H. Jones, journalist and newspaper editor, was first a friend of Francis's political career, and then his bitter enemy.

J. A. Scholten/MHS-PP.

Joseph Pulitzer, in 1882. Pulitzer's *Post-Dispatch* regarded Francis with suspicion because of his ties to Butler. Francis's relations with Pulitzer and the *Post-Dispatch* were never warm, but eased during his leadership of the World's Fair.

MHS-PP.

Secretary of the Interior David R. Francis. His short term in the Interior Department at the end of Cleveland's second term helped set the stage for the National Forest Service.
Charles Ayer Whipple, 1900/U.S. Department of Interior, Washington, D.C.

William Jennings Bryan, at far right, arriving at session of 1916 Democratic National Convention, St. Louis, June 11–14, 1916. Former Mayor Rolla Wells is beside him in the back seat, and Democratic National Committee member Edward F. Goltra is in the front.
J. C. Strauss/MHS-PP.

Joseph Folk, a crusading reform Democratic politician, vigorously pursued the St. Louis "Big Cinch" political/business alliance. His successful prosecution of such former Francis allies as Ed Butler catapulted Folk to the Missouri Governor's mansion in 1904.
J.C. Strauss, 1905/MHS-PP.

William J. Stone succeeded Francis as governor in 1893 and moved to the U.S. Senate in 1902. "Gumshoe Bill" and his faction often fought Francis over the years.
J. C. Strauss, 1905/MHS-PP.

William Marion Reedy, publisher of the literary/political St. Louis weekly, *The Mirror,* allegedly coined the term "Big Cinch," but in general he backed Francis.
J. C. Strauss, 1904/MHS-PP.

David R. Francis joined Mark Twain in 1902, during Twain's last visit to St. Louis, to dedicate a memorial plaque for St. Louis–born journalist and children's poet Eugene Field at Field's birthplace on Broadway.
MHS-PP.

The *St. Louis Post-Dispatch* celebrated Francis's successful tour of Europe to promote the World's Fair with this cartoon.

St. Louis Post-Dispatch, March 17, 1903/Washington University Libraries.

Walter B. Stevens, St. Louis journalist and friend of David R. Francis. Stevens served as Director of Exploitation for the Louisiana Purchase Exposition and later wrote a biography of Francis that was never published in book form.

J. Edward Roesch, ca. 1904/MHS-PP.

Grover Cleveland, Theodore Roosevelt, and David R. Francis pose at the door of the Francis mansion at 4421 Maryland Avenue before the Louisiana Purchase Exposition Dedication Day Ceremony, April 30, 1903.

Murillo Studio, 1903/MHS-PP.

Opening Day:
David R. Francis
touching button
opening Fair.
Jessie Tarbox Beals,
1904/MHS-PP.

View west from Restaurant Pavilion,
Palace of Electricity at right, Palace of Machinery in center background.
F. J. Koster, 1904/MHS-PP.

Presentation of silver service to Francis by Festus J. Wade at the closing ceremony for the Louisiana Purchase Exposition.

Jessie Tarbox Beals, 1904/MHS-PP

The final fireworks of the World's Fair, 12:01 a.m., December 2, 1904.
A portrait of David Francis is picked out in fireworks, with the messages, "Farewell" and "Good Night."
MHS-PP.

Cocopa Indian group in front of their habitation. W. J. McGee, Director of the Department of Anthropology, is at center.
Official Photographic Company, 1904/MHS-PP.

Alice Roosevelt watching a performance in the Philippine Reservation, Louisiana Purchase Exposition.
Jessie Tarbox Beals, 1904/MHS-PP.

Lousiana Purchase Exposition President Francis fires the starter's pistol for the marathon, 1904 Olympics.
MHS-PP.

The Francis family in Yellowstone Park, 1905. DRF and Mrs. Francis are in the carriage. Left to right: Maid, Charles and Sidney Francis. On the seat, the driver, Philip Jordan, and Collins Thompson.
MHS-PP.

Francis with Philip Jordan playing golf at Lake Champlain, N.Y., September 1912.
Talton F. Ray Collection.

Francis presents the key to the Jefferson Memorial to St. Louis Mayor Frederick Kreismann, February 8, 1913. Left to right: William K. Bixby, Missouri Historical Society; Mayor Kreismann; Francis; Isaac Taylor, architect; Charles Scudder; Walter B. Stevens.
F. D. Hampson, 1913/MHS-PP.

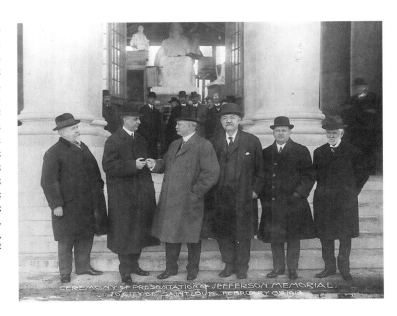

On January 21 and 22, hearings were conducted in St. Louis by Secretary of the Treasury William G. McAdoo and Secretary of Agriculture David Houston, who was on leave as chancellor of Washington University. They were met with a hero's welcome on the front page of the *Republic* and wooed without surcease, during the day at hearings packed with St. Louis boosters and in the evenings at private dinner parties with Big Cinchers like David Francis, Rolla Wells, Breckinridge Jones, Festus Wade, and Robert S. Brookings.

Brookings, in effect, had built Washington University's new campus, with help from Francis, and both were trustees, information that must have been prominent in Houston's mind as he listened to the arguments. Wade, Wells, and a few others were in charge of laying out the figures, and Francis was in charge of flash, regaling visitors with tales of meeting the crowned heads of Europe and insisting that, because of the Fair, St. Louis was better known in Europe, China, and Japan than any other American city.

St. Louis seemed like a shoe-in. There was only one problem—Kansas City had a considerable amount of clout in the Democratic Party, too, and Senator Reed was a power on the Senate Banking Committee. Surely, if you were only going to have twelve federal reserve banks, you couldn't have two of them in the same state.

Apparently you could, if the state was Democratic Missouri. Thus St. Louis, again the country's fourth-largest city, got one and Kansas City, ranked nineteenth, did too.[46]

As the years went by, Jane suffered more and more from the cold weather. Newspaper stories and letters of the period increasingly referenced Jane's "illness," and she seems to have been suffering from a combination of respiratory problems, heart congestion, and high blood pressure, perhaps mixed with the depressive moods that she now seemed to sink into easily, particularly in the cold, drab St. Louis winters, when the rose bushes were bare and the lawn turned brown.

In late January 1914, with David scheduled to be in San Francisco in a few weeks, he and Jane headed for the winter resort of Pasadena, California. Jane immediately took a turn for the worse and spent the next six or seven weeks recuperating. Francis went up to San Francisco to speak at the opening of yet another World's Fair, telling the audience that St. Louis had benefitted from the Fair by acquiring sophistication: "Traveling orchestras have to play a better kind of music now," he said.[47]

Then he headed south to be with Jane. They were back home by May 1914, for the birth of Anne Waters Francis, later Anne Francis Currier. David and Jane Francis now had five grandchildren, with more to come.

In October, the peripatetic Sidney got married in California, where his father had set him up with a job as a New York Life representative. Francis must have hoped the marriage, to Julia Holmes of St. Louis, would help his youngest son settle down: a couple of years earlier, Sidney had decided to take a trip around the world. He got as far as the beaches of Hawaii, where he spent a year before coming home.

Now five of his six boys were married, and Francis long ago had reconciled himself to the fact that the erratic Charles probably never would marry.

Late that August, a few weeks after war broke out in Europe—a war Woodrow Wilson was determined to stay out of—the president personally offered Francis the recently created ambassadorship to Argentina, apparently bypassing Secretary of State Bryan, who later denied that Francis had ever been considered for the job. In any event, Francis politely declined Buenos Aires, citing the press of business. Actually, he was deeply disappointed—he had hoped for London.[48]

Still, as he headed into his middle sixties, the traditional time for sitting back, taking it easy, and reflecting on the past, David Francis should have been a happy man, living in one of the biggest mansions in the city, surrounded by adoring progeny, respected and honored by his peers, and having accomplished wondrous things.

He hadn't been president of the United States, but he had been mayor of his city, governor of his state, and a member of the presidential cabinet; he was rich and getting richer, busy with his directorships and his civic duties, regularly traveling the country to speak to large audiences and meet with other powerful men, who were his friends. He had been lucky enough to marry a woman who, despite her own fierce intelligence and need for privacy, had loved him enough to sacrifice a large part of her private life to his public one. And, of course, there was the Fair, which at that point he considered his greatest triumph. David Francis had built his own city and ruled over it with a strong but benevolent hand.

Even if, as with most men his age, his days of conquering new challenges might be over, he could bask in the glory of a full, rich, successful life. But there was more to come.

BOOK
TWO

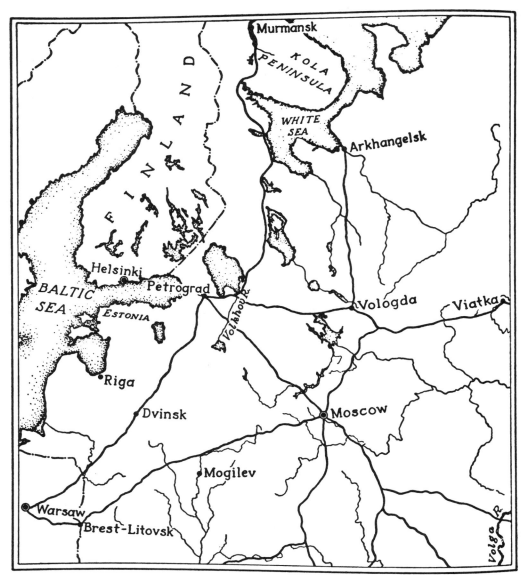

NORTHERN RUSSIA

CHAPTER 12

A Missouri Democrat in Tsarist Russia

WOODROW WILSON quickly grew disenchanted with the stiff-necked William Jennings Bryan. Wilson remarked of Secretary of State Bryan, "He suffers from a singular sort of moral blindness, and is as passionate in error as in the right courses he has taken."[1]

The two became irreconcilably at odds over the proper American reaction to the war in Europe. While publicly professing neutrality, in crucial decisions Wilson leaned toward England and the Allies. Bryan was more adamant about remaining truly neutral and conciliatory toward Germany and the Central Powers; above all, he wanted to avoid being sucked into the war.

The ongoing disagreement came to a head in May 1915. A German U-boat sank the British luxury liner *Lusitania* off the coast of Ireland, killing nearly 2,000 passengers, including 128 Americans. The Germans argued that the *Lusitania* was carrying war materiel and was fair game. Over Bryan's strong objections, Wilson made an angry, saber-rattling protest to the German government, demanding reparations. Bryan resigned.

Relieved to be rid of the Great Commoner, Wilson filled the post with Bryan's second in command, Robert Lansing, who had consistently sided with the president in calling for a hard line against Germany. Wilson admitted more than once that he preferred to act as his own secretary of state, and Lansing, a prominent international lawyer without a political constituency, seemed an apt tool to that end.

Early in 1916, George T. Mayre, the American ambassador to Russia, asked to be recalled for health reasons. For his replacement, Wilson and Lansing wanted someone who combined a commercial background with a political one. The new ambassador's main task would be to renegotiate the abrogated trade treaty with Russia, a vast potential market for goods as well as a rich source of agricultural and mineral resources.

Wilson's first choice for the Russian post was wealthy Slavophile Charles R. Crane, whose son, Richard, was Robert Lansing's private secretary. Crane, the vice chairman for finance in Wilson's 1912 campaign, declined but strongly recommended his old friend David Rowland Francis. Asked if he had any other suggestions, Crane replied, "Not any nearly as good as Mr. Francis."[2] Francis, Crane told Woodrow Wilson, was "the man to put our relations with Russia on a better basis than they have been on for half a century."[3]

Wilson responded enthusiastically to the recommendation. Francis seemed to Wilson and Lansing, as he had to Crane, an excellent choice for a position that required a combination of business acumen with negotiating and diplomatic skills—Francis's celebrated wooing of European leaders on his two grand tours. Francis also shared Wilson's pro-Allied position on the war, as was clear from his public statements and from his newspaper—the *Republic* was so firmly anti-German that St. Louis German-Americans by then had organized a boycott of the paper.[4]

Samuel Harper, a University of Chicago professor of Russian languages and institutions who became, at Crane's suggestion, an advisor to Francis, said later that Wilson chose Francis "because of his well-known liberal tendencies." He was apparently referring to a general dedication to the Progressive principles of the Wilsonian Democratic Party—from federal control of banking to free trade—as well to the belief shared by Wilson and Francis that the American government should actively support self-determination and democracy abroad. Possibly, he also had in mind Francis's friendship with prominent Jews.[5]

In mid-February 1916, Wilson summoned Francis to Washington and offered him the ambassadorship, one of only thirteen the United States maintained at that time. Excited and somewhat daunted by the challenge, the sixty-five-year-old Francis called Jane, who had escaped wintertime St. Louis to rest with friends in Florida.

Jane Francis told her husband she had little desire to move to a place that had even worse winters than St. Louis, but she encouraged her husband to go, to accept what he came to see as his last great challenge as a public servant.[6] Francis seemed relieved at Jane's decision not to undertake the arduous wartime journey to a near-arctic climate. He later told a friend that Jane "could not" go to Russia, "as she is not strong and for several years has been threatened with a nervous breakdown," and he wrote a State Department superior that "she has a very weak throat which is likely to be made worse by [the Russian] climate."[7]

On February 22, Francis returned to the White House and told Wilson he would accept the ambassadorship. He was accompanied by the two Democratic senators from Missouri, James Reed and William J. Stone. Former Governor Stone had risen to the chairmanship of the Senate Foreign Relations Committee. With those powerful men—both former political opponents—behind him, senatorial approval was almost certain. [8]

Wilson and Lansing made it clear that his principal mission was to renegotiate the trade treaty. The old treaty had been abrogated four years before, to a great extent in protest against Russian anti-Jewish policies. Russian refusals to grant routine entry visas to Jews who held American passports was particularly galling. The abrogation had been strongly supported by Woodrow Wilson, who was running for president.

Despite the lack of a treaty, trade between the two countries had grown prodigiously during World War I, much of it through the intermediaries of two of Russia's traditional trading partners, England and France. Russia needed arms, agricultural machinery, cotton, and food; businessmen in neutral America happily supplied them. Trade between the two countries almost doubled in 1915, the first full year of the war. In 1916, it rose to $310 million, and in 1917 it reached almost $560 million. [9]

Enormous profits could be envisioned, both in selling products to Russia and in financing the sales. The New York branch of J. P. Morgan and Company had loaned Russia $96 million to purchase war materiel, and Morgan's powerful London office loaned another $86 million. Some large American manufacturing firms, such as Westinghouse, International Harvester, and the Singer Sewing Machine Co., had substantial operations in Russia, and these companies were pressuring the federal government for a new trade treaty that would make it easier and more profitable for them to distribute their products to the Russian market.

With France, England, and Germany busy with the most devastating war in history, American business and political leaders saw a fine opening for the United States to step into the vacuum, eliminate the European middle men, and lock up the bulk of Russia's trade. A new commercial treaty would bring lower tariffs and simplify trading. But powerful Jewish leaders were outraged at any suggestion of a new treaty that would permit the continuing discrimination against Jews traveling on American passports. Russia should not be granted any trade benefits until it began to treat Jews "like citizens of the most-favored nation," businessman-diplomat Oscar Straus insisted in a letter to his old friend and World's Fair host, David Francis.[10]

FRANCIS'S APPOINTMENT WAS POPULAR with the press. The New York Times responded enthusiastically: "Mr. David R. Francis is admirably fit to be Ambassador to Russia. He is worthy of a great post in the public service. He has had a long experience in public affairs and with public men. . . . [He is] a man of cultivation and leisure, a man of judgment and discretion who knows how to hold his tongue, a man of the world, urbane, traveled, capable, he has both force of character and personal charm."[11] However, the Times warned, "The renewal of a commercial treaty with Russia can [only] be brought about when Russia is ready to abandon the passport denunciation of the former treaty."

In the Mirror, by then distributed nationwide and at major hotels and newsstands in Europe, William Marion Reedy called the appointment "good news," remarking that he had watched Francis develop "from a business man into no little of a political philosopher. . . . He has [a] statesman-like mind." And, he noted, "If there is one quality in Mr. Francis more conspicuous than any other it is his genius for negotiation."[12]

The Senate confirmed the nomination on March 6. After more meetings with Lansing and other top State Department officers, Francis returned to St. Louis to prepare for the journey.

He gave his power of attorney to his sons, Perry and David, Jr., and he made out a will, leaving the Rye Beach farm to Jane and $150,000 apiece to his seven beneficiaries— his wife and six sons. He noted somewhat wistfully, that the will was written "on the eve of my departure for Russia" and that "it is possible I may not return [for] a year or more. In fact, it is possible I may never return." [13]

Before Francis left the United States, he and Perry spent several days in New York. On Sunday, April 2, they attended a small luncheon given at the Lotos Club by twelve prominent New York Jews worried about how far Francis might be willing to go to get a new treaty. Their demand was quite simple: a country with a trade treaty with the United States must honor all United States passports.

Although the widespread slander that Jews dominated New York finance was untrue—indeed, most of the major financial houses excluded Jews from their top ranks—there were a few powerful Jewish financiers who also had considerable political power. These included two men who could not make the meeting but made it clear they supported its goals: Oscar Straus and financier Jacob Schiff, who had been a significant contributor to Wilson's campaign and whose hatred of Russia was so strong that he had helped finance Japan, through the firm he headed, Kuhn, Loeb & Co., in the Russo-Japanese War. [14]

The Jewish leaders at the meeting pressed the passport issue and told Francis the facts of life for Russia's five million Jews: they frequently and almost randomly were slaughtered or burned out of their homes and businesses in pogroms that had the tacit approval of the anti-Semitic Tsar Nicholas II. Subject to more than fourteen hundred laws restricting their activity, Jews could not own land and rarely lived outside areas known as "the Pale."

Unspoken at the meeting was the desire of the prosperous German Jews of New York to cut back on the flow to the city's crowded ghettos of poor, badly educated Jews fleeing anti-Semitism in Russia and Russian-occupied areas of Eastern Europe, including Poland. These shabbily dressed, Yiddish-speaking, often dark-complected newcomers were considered an embarrassment by the more haughty German Jews, as well as a growing financial burden through Jewish relief charities.[15]

David and Perry Francis were the only gentiles present. One of the men asked Francis how the Jewish group could help in his mission. Francis asked if he could be candid. When he was assured he could, he said, "By not talking so much."[16]

David Francis sailed from Hoboken on Saturday, April 8, 1916, on the small Swedish steamship *Oscar II.* Among those sailing with him were Philip Jordan; Arthur T. Dailey, Francis's new private secretary supplied by the State Department; Edward C. Riley, an executive of the New York Life Insurance Co. on his way to the company's Petrograd office; and Professor Samuel Harper.

A few weeks earlier, after assigning the young Russia scholar to accompany Francis and help him unravel the Byzantine intricacies of Russian politics, Lansing or a top aide had suggested that, as Harper put it in his memoirs, "it would be very useful if I could get the governor to propose that we take the same boat to Petrograd." On a weekend visit to St. Louis in March, the thirty-four-year-old Harper and Francis, now sixty-five, had hit it off, and Francis said he hoped that Harper would sail with him for Russia. Harper later described his sea voyage as a "delicate mission," and it appears that one of his tasks was to keep a close eye on the inexperienced diplomat, who was known for speaking his mind and going his own way.

Harper recalled that there were basically three groups on the *Oscar*: American businessmen interested in munitions contracts with Russia who hoped to cultivate the friendship of the new American ambassador; YMCA workers going to Russia to do relief work among German prisoners; and spies. In this regard, Harper recalled:

> Before Francis and I sailed from New York, a prominent American businessman who had extensive interests in Russia had come to the boat to see the new ambassador off and had pointed out to me a charming woman and warned me to keep the governor out of her clutches. She was a Russian, and I was not sure whether she represented a firm competing with that of my friend or whether that implied that she was in the intelligence service of some country other than her own. She had a German name; but the husband to whom she referred rather casually was, we were told, a Russian officer. . . . Of course, many Russians in high military and civilian positions, especially those from the Baltic provinces, had German names.[17]

After introducing himself and his wife to Francis, the Russian officer, whose name was Edgar de Cramm, stayed ashore, and the wife got on board. Her name was Matilda de Cramm,* although Francis came to know her by the diminutive "Meta." She was pretty and curvaceous, with an oval face, brunette hair lightly streaked with gray, strikingly large, dark eyes, and dramatically swooping eyebrows that she emphasized with makeup. She had a kind and vivid smile. Matilda de Cramm "was an exceedingly bright and attractive person about forty, but seemingly much younger," a colleague of Francis later observed.[18]

Harper, who must have known by then that Francis enjoyed the company of attractive younger women, kept a watch out for Madame de Cramm. "The lady was not a good sailor," he wrote, "and we saw little of her during the voyage." Francis later claimed that he had met only once with Madame de Cramm after the ship had left New York, and then only for about two minutes. Otherwise, he said, she "stayed in her stateroom."[19] But, as will be discussed, Francis may have seen more of Madame de Cramm than he admitted, or than Harper realized.

---

*The name is often spelled "de Cram," most notably by George Kennan (see bibliography), and also appears as "Cramm," "Cram," "Kram," "de Kram," and even "de Cramme." But Francis usually spelled the name of both husband and wife "de Cramm." He had been told, presumably by Madame, that her husband's name initially had been "von Cramm" but that he had changed it to the less Germanic "Cramm" and then to the Frenchified "de Cramm." (See Francis's letter to Col. James A. Ruggles, March 15, 1918, MHS.) "De Cramm" is also the spelling used more than any other in correspondence and reports by the State Department, U.S. military intelligence, and other official agencies, and we have chosen to go with that version of the name.

As the ship sailed east through choppy early April seas, Harper gave Francis a crash course on what he might expect in Russia. The vast country was in turmoil because of massive losses in the war, extreme and growing poverty, and the refusal of the autocratic Tsar to give up any significant amount of his God-given powers. And Francis wrote a flurry of letters to be mailed on the other side of the Atlantic: letters to Woodrow Wilson, to Robert Lansing, to his son Perry who ran the brokerage business and the family back in St. Louis, and to numerous friends and business associates, categories difficult to separate in Francis's case.

He complained to both Wilson and Lansing about J. P. Morgan and Co., arguing that the financial giant had changed for the worse since the death in 1913 of J. Pierpont Morgan, Sr., whom Francis described as "a thorough American . . . who through several trying ordeals in our financial history deservedly commanded the respect of all who followed his career." The demise of the old lion had left what Francis considered to be lesser young men in control of the House of Morgan, men whose main goal was the accumulation of capital in their New York and London coffers, without regard to the national interest.[20]

It may well be that with Pierpont Morgan's death, Francis and his firm had lost their old-boy connection to the powerful international cartel. Prior to departure, Francis had spent four days going to luncheon and dinner meetings with businessmen, financiers, and politicians, but representatives of J. P. Morgan and Co. politely avoided talking about anything of substance.

Francis railed against the House of Morgan's powerful English branch. He contended:

> [The Morgan company was] so thoroughly English in sentiment that they look with solicitude, and in fact with suspicion, if not fear, upon any movement to promote commercial relations, or even closer social relations between Russia and the United States. . . . Their desire and plan is to have whatever Russian financing is done in this country to come through the intermediary of London. They also seem to think that any direct commercial relations between this country and Russia is an approach on their preserves.[21]

In his correspondence, Francis compared Morgan unfavorably to the competing National City Bank of New York, which with the help of Rockefeller money had become New York's largest bank and was contemplating not only investing in Russia, but also opening branches there. Francis noted in a letter to Woodrow Wilson that he had "talked with the National City Bank people, who thoroughly agree with my plan to promote direct commercial relations between Russia and the United States without the interruption of any other country or influence."[22]

Wilson had run for president in 1912 against J. P. Morgan and the "Bank Trust." At the time, Morgan owned a considerable stake in City Bank. In January 1914, the Morgan partners, attempting to placate themselves with Wilson's trust busters, had divested themselves of their holdings in City Bank. Wilson was pleased, although not necessarily in the way the Morgan company had wished, and his secretary of commerce, William Redfield, urged City Bank to open a branch in Petrograd, which it did.[23]

Further encouraged by Francis's enthusiasm for the development of Russia, City Bank would expand its operations in that country and play an important role in the relationship between Russia and the United States during Francis's tenure as ambassador. After the Bolshevik Revolution of November 1917, the bank became an American conduit for Francis and others to funnel aid to counter-revolutionaries. [24]

Francis also wrote Wilson about a pet plan for improving direct relationships between his country and the Tsar's: "I have visited the Western Union Telegraph Company and I think I have induced its president . . . to take under serious consideration the laying of a cable from this country direct to Russia."*

In the same letter, after acknowledging rumors that his predecessor had been replaced for being too openly anti-German, he told the president, "It goes without saying that my official conduct and personal utterances will be carefully guarded at all times, as will become a representative of a neutral government."[25] One reason it was important for Francis to avoid publicly favoring the Allies was that the neutral United States had agreed to provide diplomatic representation for German and Austrian interests in Russia.

Francis also fretted about business back in St. Louis, as he would throughout his years abroad. He wrote John Scullin that their mutual investment—the Missouri and North Arkansas Railroad—had "for a long time been a source of great concern to me, in fact, I have never made so large an investment that provided to be so unfortunate." In this same letter, he showed, as he would time and again, that he continued to mix his eye for private gain with his public responsibilities. Scullin and Francis were partners in a business that pressed briquettes out of coal dust and pitch. Francis had heard that Russian cities were short on coal and suggested Russia would be a terrific place to sell briquetting machines.[26]

And, in a letter to Paul W. Brown, editor of the *Republic,* Francis suggested "a number of editorials, not too long," be written about the "the possibilities the Russian field offers by the immense resources of the country." Russia, Francis contended, "has been liberalized very materially during the past five years and the process is still going on at a rapid rate."[27] The statement, in line with the views of Samuel Harper, presented a laughably rosy view of life in Tsarist Russia. Francis followed it with a lengthy pronouncement that is remarkable for what today would be considered its shockingly offensive anti-Semitism:

> The main obstacle to a commercial treaty with Russia is the Jewish question. . . . There was no good judgment in the abrogation of our commercial treaty with Russia. . . . The entire action was for political effect. . . . The Jews compose but 3 percent of the population of Russia and but 2 percent of the population of the United States. . . . They are very aggressive and, at the same time, shrewd and unscrupulous, as you know, but of course such statements must

---

*There were a surprising number of similarities between Francis and his fellow Madison Countian Cassius Clay as ambassadors to Russia. Among them were an unshakable American hostility toward English arrogance, a rejection of diplomatic pretense and finery, and big plans for a direct undersea cable between the United States and Russia.

not be publicly made. The prejudice against them is not confined to Russia, but exists in every land where they live. This is attributable in great part to their claimed superiority and to the fact that while in many instances they have been good citizens of the countries in which they live, still they have never thoroughly assimilated with the peoples thereof. . . . They still consider themselves the chosen people of God and believe that eventually they will come into control of the world. . . .

If Russia . . . should enact laws permitting the Jews to live beyond what is [now] known as the pale to which they are presently confined, and granting them greater privileges in the professions and in the high schools . . . that would not satisfy the radical Jews whose hatred of Russia is deep-rooted, nor would it be acceptable to the Republicans.

A further obstacle to a treaty, he wrote, was that "the Russians say that the Jews sympathize with Germany in the war." Before the United States entered the war, many Jews of German ancestry quietly cheered for Germany to defeat Russia.

Of course, Francis wrote, "there were many Jews who have done good work." He quoted a popular saying that since has acquired even more sinister overtones through its association with the Nazis: "We all have our pet Jews."

The next day, Francis wrote to Oscar Straus, saying he was sorry that Straus had been unable to attend the "delightful luncheon" in New York. He said he had been told that, in Russia, "a more liberal spirit prevails [in] the empire of the Czar than has exist-ed at any time in the past" and remarked that there was "a decided inclination on the part of the government to put an end to the discrimination practiced in the past." He noted that Russia had "more than once expressed willingness to negotiate a new treaty provided the subject of passports should not be included" and asked Straus to tell him, in a personal and confidential letter, how he would react if the Russians, without chang-ing their passport policy, quietly took such liberalizing steps as agreeing to let Jews live outside the Pale. (Harper had told him this might well come about.) It would be a month before Francis's letter reached its destination, and another before Francis received a reply.[28]

When he wasn't writing letters, Francis "spent much of his time in the smoking room, playing bridge and talking with all sorts of people," Harper observed. "I felt it was not my job to listen in to all these conversations; but I heard enough of them to realize that our new ambassador was a very blunt, outspoken American, who believed in speak-ing his mind regardless of the rules of diplomacy."

The ship was met by British boats patrolling the coast and escorted through mine fields to the Scottish port of Kirkwall in the Orkney Islands, where it remained for five days while the British checked the passenger list. "While we were interned in the Orkneys," Harper recalled, "Francis went ashore for a day. He was not supposed to men-tion to a soul where he had been, but soon the whole boat knew that he had been shown Scapa Flow [Naval Base] and the British fleet lying at anchor there."

After the boat was released to continue to Scandinavia, several passengers were missing, presumably taken off by the British. But one passenger whom Harper had "regarded with some suspicion"—Madame de Cramm—was still aboard.[29]

After docking at the port of Christiania (now Oslo) about April 22, Francis and Harper and Matilda de Cramm took a train to Stockholm and spent several days there before proceeding by rail on the long northern loop to Russia. In Stockholm, Harper recalled:

> Representatives of all the belligerent countries called on the governor, and the Germans were particularly active. I kept on the lookout for any contact between them and our charming Russian lady who stopped, as we did, at the Grand Hotel. Until that time she had done little more than exchange greetings with Francis. . . .
>
> I thought I had handled the situation well, until just before our departure another American who had attached himself to our party told me at the last minute he had been able to secure accommodations for our Russian lady on the train we were taking. By the time we reached Petrograd, this lady and the governor had become very friendly.

In their chats on the long, looping train ride up through Sweden and down through Finland to Petrograd, Francis learned that Matilda and Edgar de Cramm, a chemist now in the import/export business, both had been married before. She had two sons by her first marriage, both of them now in the Russian Navy, and her husband had a son by his first marriage. That son and his wife now were being held prisoners in Germany, where they had lived when the war broke out.

Edgar de Cramm, Francis learned, was about ten years older than his wife, had a wandering eye, and was not pleased by her independent, feminist notions. The bloom was clearly off their romance.[30]

The Stockholm Express pulled into the Finland Station in northern Petrograd at two o'clock on the morning of April 28. By the Russia calendar, it was April 15.*

Francis, Jordan, and Harper were met by several members of the staff of the American Embassy, who drove them by car across the Neva, the wide, dark river that runs westward through the city and flows into the Gulf of Finland. The American Embassy occupied a long, two-story, ornately facaded, late-nineteenth-century building at 34 Furstatskaya Street in a fashionable district where many foreign diplomats and Russian officials lived. A large gate opened into a courtyard, at the rear of which were stables. The offices and living quarters were mostly on the second floor.

---

*Until February 1918, Russia clung to the Julian (or Old Style) calendar, which was thirteen days behind the Gregorian (New Style) calendar used in Western Europe and the United States. To avoid shifting back and forth between calendars, all dates unless otherwise indicated will be the New Style, which was generally used in international matters. In most of his correspondence, Francis followed the common practice of giving both dates, with the Old Style preceding the New Style and a slash separating them: "February 1/14." When necessary for clarity, we will give both dates.

The embassy was about four blocks from the Tauride Palace, a two-story green-domed stucco building inspired by the Pantheon, where the Duma, the elected legislature, sporadically met to listen to angry men like socialist lawyer Alexander Kerensky excoriate the Tsar and his minions and call futilely for a new government.

Madame de Cramm went to the best hotel in town, the Hotel d'Europe off Nevsky Prospect, where she spent the next few weeks. Then she moved into an elegant apartment, number eighteen, at 81 Sergeivskaya Street, about two blocks from the embassy.

PETROGRAD, FOUNDED IN 1703 by Peter the Great as his new capital and "window on Europe," was called St. Petersburg until the summer of 1914. After Russia entered the Great War, the name was changed to the less-German sounding Petrograd—"grad" is a common condensation of "gorod," the Russian word for "city." (In 1924, the city became Leningrad and now is once again St. Petersburg—or, as Russians affectionately call it, Petersburg or simply "Peter.")

The city of broad boulevards and large, low granite and stucco buildings is near the sixtieth parallel, like Anchorage and Oslo. When Francis first saw Petrograd, it was just struggling out of its thick winter blanket of snow. Fyodor Dostoevsky, one of many writers who have called the city home, described the onset of spring in the capital of Russia as "inexplicably touching." The city, he wrote, "puts on a gaudy mantle of flowers [and] somehow reminds me of that sick and consumptive girl . . . who will suddenly, for one isolated moment, somehow become ineffably, miraculously beautiful, leaving you to ask yourself, thunderstruck and intoxicated, what force has made these sad, reflective eyes glitter with such fire."[31]

Built on vermin-infested marshland over imported rocks and timber and the bones of many thousands of serfs and prisoners of war, Petrograd was—and is—a beautiful, majestic city, defined by its great river, the Neva, a mile wide as it flows past the old Winter Palace of the Tsars and divides into broad channels on its course to the Bay of Finland. Tributaries and granite-lined canals wind through the "Venice of the North," making it possible to travel within a few blocks of almost anywhere in the main part of the city by boat. The colors of the northern water and sky, and the shades of the earth and its fruits, are picked up and heightened in the profusion of painted stucco buildings, with the predominant colors a dark mossy green, an almost Mediterranean but icy blue, a rich coral, an earthy yellow/ochre, and a stunning plummy red. These colorful stucco buildings scattered throughout the city give it an airy feel that counteracts the solidity and weight of its massive, low-slung palaces and government buildings of dark granite. It's as if the city is simultaneously anchored by the stone and lifted by the stucco, a slightly unsettling, almost vertiginous contradiction that, in mid-summer, can lead to the manic gaiety of the White Nights celebrations and, in the seemingly eternal dark and cold of winter, to the jittery depression and sense of longing that marks the work of its most famous writers, from Gogol and Dostoevsky to Maxim Gorky and Anna Akhmatova.

The major buildings, sometimes a block long, are generally between three and five stories high—in the first half of the nineteenth century, Tsar Nicholas I decreed that no building could rise higher than the cornice of his Winter Palace, which was seventy-seven feet above the plaza below—and the boulevards are long, wide, and straight, so the central city feels like the more elegant parts of eighteenth- and nineteenth-century Paris. A few gold spires and domes rise high above the low skyline, outlined against the watery blue sky or hovering in the mists and fogs that hang over the city much of the year.

The Russia David Francis entered in the spring of 1916 was becoming a vast keg of powder, and Petrograd the fuse. Russia was filled with thousands of angry revolutionaries, fiery political evangelists whose flock comprised the many millions of peasants who had left the land or been forced off it and congregated in the cities and towns. The Russian "serfs"—the word loosely means "slave"—had been emancipated by Alexander II, grandfather of the reigning Tsar, Nicholas II, in 1861. But the terms of their emancipation were severe; they received long-term mortgages on the land they farmed, and the obligatory payments to the gentry almost guaranteed to keep them in poverty and servitude or drive them off the land. In the first decade and a half of the twentieth century, millions of impoverished peasants had succumbed to the latter.

The population of the capital was 2.2 million, half of which had arrived from rural areas in the past twenty years. There was little work, and what there was barely paid a living wage. The average working-class family crowded six to a room in rodent and bug-infested flats. And those were the lucky ones—many thousands of workers were forced by economics to live in factory barracks, where men, women, and children slept together, with only their filthy, ragged work clothes for bedding, on rows of wooden planks. The writer Maxim Gorky, who lived in Petrograd at the time, compared workers' barracks to "dwellings of a prehistoric people."[32]

The anger of the displaced peasants, living within a short walk of palaces as glittering and opulent as anything at Versailles, was shared by the thousands of soldiers who roamed the city. Many of them had deserted the front, where they had been ill-equipped, badly fed, and led by incompetent officers whose main qualifications for rank were their aristocratic connections.

Russia mobilized twelve million men for World War I, more than any other nation. About 1,700,000 Russians were reported killed and 4,950,000 wounded, higher totals in both categories than those of any other combatant. Much of the understandable bitterness of the returned soldiers focused on the Tsar, who periodically rode to the outskirts of the front to take personal command of the army and drive it on to further disaster.

The Duma, the elected legislature, was a farcically weak and ineffectual version of the British House of Commons. Nicholas II had reluctantly established it during the so-called Revolution of 1905, when hundreds of thousands of Russians took to the streets, burning and pillaging the homes of the wealthy, demanding political and economic freedoms. But once the crisis had passed, Nicholas, who believed his authority absolute and that it flowed from the hand of God, used the Duma solely to rubber-stamp his proposals. He regularly dissolved the body when it seemed to be drifting towards an independent act, and in the summer of 1914, when Russia entered the war, the Duma helpfully had dismissed itself for "patriotic reasons," announcing, in effect, that it didn't want to distract from the war effort with republican quibbling.

Nicholas's imperial government met efforts to move toward a constitutional monarchy by throwing radicals and even liberals into jail, exiling them to Siberia or, in thousands of cases, simply having them hanged or shot. Many political prisoners ended up behind the thick stone walls of the St. Peter and Paul Fortress, which was just across the Neva from the Winter Palace, visible from much of the city. In the minds of common people, the fortress became the Russian equivalent of the Bastille.

At the same time, members of radical revolutionary groups went on a reign of terror. Radicals killed or wounded more than seventeen thousand people in the last twenty years of the rule of the Romanov Tsars. As seems almost inevitable, terror and repression escalated in a fearful dance between two increasingly irreconcilable parties, and liberal reformers found themselves isolated from both sides.

Among the nineteenth-century martyrs of the political left was Alexander Ulyanov, who had participated in a failed plot to assassinate Alexander III, the father of Nicholas II. Ulyanov was executed in 1887. His younger brother, a radical law student and son of the gentry who took the revolutionary name of Vladimir Ilyich Lenin, was even further radicalized. By the time David Francis arrived in Petrograd, Lenin, who had spent a year in prison and three years in Siberia for his political activities, was in voluntary exile in Switzerland, in constant communication with leaders in Russia of the political sect he had helped found—the Bolsheviks, a left-wing branch of the Marxist Social Democratic Party.

Lenin was an implacable revolutionary and believed that the means of revolution, no matter how cruel, were justified by the end. During the Great Famine of 1891–93, he opposed the shipping of food to starving peasants because feeding them might prevent their continuing to move en masse into the cities and create anarchy. Ultimately and inevitably, the revolution would come, in accordance with the teachings of Karl Marx. Lenin didn't expect the revolution to come any time soon, so he, like David Francis, had quite a surprise in store.[33]

DAVID FRANCIS'S PETROGRAD DATEBOOK, purchased in Russia, has the months and days in Russian, and the dates in both Old Style and New Style, divided by a slash. The page for his first day, Friday, April 15/28, begins: "Arrived Petrograd 3 A.M. Took charge 10:30 A.M." His first visitor, significantly, was H. Fessenden Meserve, who represented the National City Bank in Russia.[34]

In an interview Francis gave to *Russkoe Slovo*, the country's leading official paper, he said he could not speak officially until he had presented his credentials to the Foreign Office and been received by the Tsar. He then proceeded to speak anyway, causing some grumbling in the State Department. After he properly tried to duck the question of whether the United States leaned toward the Central Powers or the Allies, he unwisely muttered that neither Germany nor the twenty million German-Americans in the United States, despite their "bellicose frame of mind," could afford to antagonize the United States of America.[35]

Eager to get started on his main task, Francis sent a note to the Russian foreign minister asking to be received. The next day, a Saturday, he went to the Foreign Office, in a large granite building across Palace Square from the Winter Palace, and met in the late afternoon with S. D. Sazonov, the beleaguered veteran foreign minister.

Francis immediately liked Sazonov, a thin middle-aged man who, despite the obvious strain of long and frustrating hours in service of the Tsar, seemed alert and highly intelligent. But Francis spent a disappointing hour and twenty minutes with him, and his heart must have sunk as Sazonov put the damper on Francis's naive dream of getting the commercial treaty signed, the undersea cable underway, and the briquette machines humming so he could go home a hero in time for Woodrow Wilson's fall campaign.

Sazonov, Francis said in his Russia memoir, "was extremely cordial, but said that Russia was not prepared at this time to negotiate any commercial treaty with our country or any other country until all of the Allies arrived at some understanding on economic issues." The foreign minister seemed to suspect, not without cause, that the United States and the Allies, excluding Russia, had been talking among themselves as to just how the pie of conquest was going to be sliced up once the war was over. An economic council of all the Allies was scheduled to meet in Paris in June. No commercial treaty between the United States and Russia was possible, it appeared, until the conference had ended.[36]

Francis sent a cable to Secretary Lansing to that effect, also reporting that a "gentleman who has had a great deal of experience in Russia" had suggested that Sazonov was under the thumb of the British.[37] If this tip came from Meserve of City Bank, as seems likely considering the timing, it hardly could be considered objective.

At the request of the Russians, Francis also met with Baron Boris Sturmer, a corrupt high bureaucrat whom the Tsar had named prime minister in January and who was rapidly acquiring nearly dictatorial power—subject at any time, of course, to overrule by the Tsar or Tsarina. Baron Sturmer was outwardly cordial and told Francis he was anxious for closer relationships with the United States, but Francis disliked his looks and his manner: "His appearance was as German as his name. His mind worked slowly and his temperament was phlegmatic. In short, he impressed me as a dull man." Francis could not help noticing that Sturmer had a long mustache that he waxed and turned up at the ends, just like the Kaiser.[38]

The new American ambassador, who had promised friends that he would be "on the lookout" for German spies, was not alone in suspecting that Sturmer's Teutonism ran deeper than his name. As the bread lines in Petrograd grew longer, a rumor spread that Sturmer was working for the Germans, intentionally trying to starve the peasants to death. And Sturmer was not the only high-ranking Russian linked in the public mind to the Germans. Like other women who had married Tsars, including Catherine the Great, Tsarina Alexandra had been a German princess. And the Tsar himself was Kaiser

Wilhelm's nephew. Both were also close relatives of the British royal family, and Alexandra had, to a great extent, been raised by her grandmother, Queen Victoria. But it was the Teutonic connection that set tongues wagging. The Tsarina's advisor, the charismatic monk Rasputin, was thought to be a tool of the Germans as well.

Francis arrived in the Russian capital in the middle of the "Tsarina's Rule," the eighteen-month period beginning in September 1915, when the Tsar, enraged at the catastrophic defeats Russia had suffered in the first year of the war, fired his top generals and war ministers and took command of the Russian army himself. When the Tsar was at the front, Rasputin, as much as anyone, ran the country. Nicholas periodically returned to the capital, where, egged on by the Tsarina to "show your fist!" he fired more government leaders or closed down the Duma.

Tsarina Alexandra, who liked to gaze at a large portrait of Marie Antoinette as she dawdled at her dressing table, was, if anything, more autocratic by temperament than her husband. She listened to every word from Rasputin, who had a kind of hypnotic power over her, in part because he alone seemed able, miraculously, to stop the bleeding of the frail, hemophiliac Tsarevich Alexis, the presumed heir to the Tsardom.

Shortly after Francis arrived in Petrograd, he received word that Nicholas was at his country estate at Tsarskoe Selo—the "Tsar's Village"—about fifteen miles south of central Petrograd. The Tsar and the Tsarina received the new American ambassador on Friday, May 5, 1916.

Francis had a lot of work to do before that occasion. But first, on Sunday, April 30, he played golf at what he described as "a very indifferent course about ten miles out." He was joined by two executives of the New York Life Insurance Co., general manager Frederick Corse, who was considered the dean of the American colony in Petrograd, and new arrival Edward C. Riley, whom Francis had met on the boat coming over.[39]

One of Francis's first official duties was to check on the condition of the old German Embassy, a hulking brownstone building facing the large plaza of the majestic, golden-domed St. Isaac's Cathedral. After the Tsar had declared war on Germany, mobs had stormed and ransacked the embassy. Francis found the building ruined, but that was the least of his worries. He was "appalled at the enormous amount of work and responsibility entailed by my uncongenial task as the representative of German and Austrian interests in Russia."[40] Some 1.5 million Austrian and German war prisoners were being held in Russian prison camps, which also held 250,000 interned civilians. The enormous responsibility forced Francis to devote several hours of each day to supervising the treatment of these men and woman.

Francis also was appalled at the rundown condition and inadequate furnishings of the rented American Embassy, which was described by an American visitor as looking more like a warehouse than a residence.[41] Francis had his office on the second floor, near two small private rooms that Philip Jordan, with the help of Madame de Cramm, had furnished as his bedroom and sitting room.

His predecessor had let work pile up, and the staff was demoralized and in disarray. Several top positions were unfilled. Fred M. Dearing, who held the diplomatic rank of first secretary, had worked to exhaustion as charge d'affaires, but the load was almost unbearable. Francis worried that Dearing, a small, slim man in his middle-thirties, would break down from the strain. But Dearing, Francis was to note approvingly, "was a Missouri boy" who had worked his way through the state university in Columbia.

Francis almost immediately began a campaign to move to better and more appropriate quarters. He wrote to Perry, "It is a large house and susceptible of being made very attractive, but it is out of repair and has little furniture and no furnishings whatever. Phil and I are sleeping here and I get breakfast in my room, furnished by the wife of one of the messengers; it has so far consisted of coffee, not very good, and ham and eggs."[42]

Fortunately, one always could go to the elegant Hotel d'Europe, about a mile and a half away, just off the Nevsky Prospect, Petrograd's Fifth Avenue. That's where Dearing and his wife had a suite and other embassy people lived. Francis frequently dined there.

The combined American staff of the embassy and the American consulate, which worked mainly out of leased offices in the Singer Building on the Nevsky Prospect, consisted of about two dozen foreign service officers at any given time, with eight or ten of them serving as secretaries or in other top diplomatic positions.

On Friday, May 5, Francis and the nine ranking members of the embassy staff boarded a special train for the twenty-five-minute trip to Tsarskoe Selo. The Tsar's estates there consisted of two stunning eighteenth-century palaces: the magnificent, neoclassical, ochre Alexander Palace, which the Tsar and his family had moved into when the mobs in Petrograd became unruly, and the even more magnificent, dazzlingly baroque, blue, white, and gold Catherine Palace, which was used mainly for royal receptions. Francis's first meeting with the Tsar probably took place at the Alexander Palace. His second, on the Russian New Year, would be at the Catherine Palace.

Members of the royal staff in uniforms glittering with braid and brass met the Americans at the Tsar's private railway station. Francis wore a dress suit, with a high-collared white shirt. On such occasions, his predecessors had worn the official diplomatic uniform, with its gold-striped knee breeches, gold-buckled shoes, silk stockings, and tall-plumed hat. Francis had not bought one and wasn't at all sure he ever would.[43]

The ten Americans rode about a half mile down a tree-lined lane in six carriages, "vehicles so rich in gilt finish that they had better be termed chariots," Francis recalled. He was in the lead carriage, drawn by six horses with an outrider on the lead horse.

At the palace, the wide doors were swept open and inside were more uniformed servants than Francis could readily count. The other Americans waited outside while Francis was conducted to a room where the Tsar awaited in the dress uniform of a military commander, with gold-fringed epaulets and ribbons and medals sweeping across his chest. He shook Francis's hand and the two sat down for a private talk that lasted about thirty-five minutes. The Tsar spoke excellent English. [44]

Nicholas II, Tsar since 1894, was thirteen days shy of his forty-eighth birthday. He and the Tsarina had five children, four daughters and his son and heir, twelve-year-old Tsarevich Alexis. The Tsar, elegantly bearded and mustached, was small-boned and slim; his powerfully built father, Alexander III, had thought him "girlish" and teased him with cruel feminine nicknames.

After handing the Tsar a sealed message from President Wilson, Francis launched into his main topic. The Tsar smiled and replied that Russia also wanted a new trade treaty, and he trusted there would be no difficulty in negotiating one. Francis mentioned that the embassy had received many complaints that German and Austrian prisoners were being mistreated. The Tsar said he was sorry to hear that but added that a "prisoner's lot at best is hard to bear." He smiled again. Francis quickly learned that the Tsar was skilled at noncommittal pleasantries.

Francis drew another smile when he complimented the Tsar on his "vodka edict." At the outbreak of the war, Nicholas II had prohibited the sale of vodka, a government monopoly. The edict did nothing to stop the sale of more expensive imported liquors, but it added another coal to the fire of the people's burning anger against the Tsar.

After Nicholas said he was particularly interested in the relationship between Germany and the United States, Francis went on at length about America's difficult position as a neutral country and noted that as a representative of that neutral country—one looking after German and Austrian interests in Russia—he needed to be "discreet." The Tsar smiled and nodded, and his smile increased and his nods became more empathetic as Francis said, not very discreetly, that his "personal sympathies were with the Allies." (If Francis's conversation with the Tsar seems a bit one-sided, we can perhaps partly blame the narrator for focusing on his own words. However, it seems likely that the Tsar did let Francis do most of the talking, which fit the nature and disposition of both men.)

Francis recalled, "As my conversation with the Emperor was drawing to a close my attention was attracted by a very fine life-sized portrait. I remarked to His Majesty that it was a very fine likeness of him. He smiled and replied, 'It is not me at all, but my cousin, King George.'"

The blood relationships between the rulers of Europe on both sides of World War I helps explain why many people of radical bent, including Lenin, as well as many internationalist liberals, felt that millions were dying in the trenches for what was basically a family feud among cousins.

After getting permission to bring his nine staff members in to meet the Tsar, Francis was taken to another room in the palace where Tsarina Alexandra waited to receive him.

He recalled, "She very gracefully advanced with extended hand and, after a genuine American handshake (I think I forgot to kiss the hand of royalty), she conducted me to a seat."[45] He spent about fifteen minutes with the Tsarina, apparently chatting about nothing of consequence.

Later, in reflecting on his first visit with the Tsar—and his only visit with the Tsarina—Francis decided that the best way to describe the royal couple and their relationship was to pass on a story told him by an Englishman who was well versed in Russian ways:

> Once a nobleman of great experience and progressive tendencies was received in audience by the Tsar. He laid before the sovereign the wretched state of the peasantry, the resulting general unrest and the strong necessity of remedying it by a modification of the political machinery of the Government. The Emperor, after listening very attentively and approvingly to his visitor, said 'I know. Yes, yes. You are right, quite right.' The nobleman retired well satisfied with his interview and feeling certain that the monarch would mollify his policy.
>
>   Immediately afterward, a great landowner, also a member of the nobility, was ushered in and he unfolded a very different story. He sought to show that affairs were quite satisfactory with the exception of the leniency of the throne toward peasants. 'What is needed, Sire, is an iron hand. The peasants must be kept in their place by force, otherwise they will usurp ours. . . .'
>
>   Nicholas II . . . said, 'Yes, yes I know. You are right, quite right.' The second visitor departed as pleased with his interview as the first had been. A side door opened, the Empress entered and said to the Tsar: 'You really must not go on like this, Nicky. It is not dignified. Remember you are an autocrat. You should show a will strong enough to stiffen a nation of 150,000,000 people. . . . You must learn to have a will of your own and assert it.'
>
>   'You are right, dear, quite right,' was the reply of the Tsar. [46]

CHAPTER 13

The Gathering Storm

T HREE REGIMENTS OF SOLDIERS were stationed within a few blocks of the embassy, and at nine in the morning recruits began drilling on Furstatskaya Street, their shoes tramping in uncertain rhythm on the cobblestone surface of the wide thoroughfare. From the bay window of his second-floor office, Francis saw them marching, and he heard them singing Russian airs that he found "plaintive but enchanting" and that lingered in his mind long after the final notes had faded.[1]

Sometimes, to see and hear what was going on in the street, he stepped onto the balcony that extended over the sidewalk. To either side of the balcony, large American flags flapped in the gusty spring winds. The snowcover finally had melted, and spring flowers bloomed in plots along the boulevards. In the Tauride Gardens, a large, graceful park about a block and a half east of the embassy, the poplars and birches swarmed with buds, and nightingales sang.

Madame de Cramm's flat was near the gardens, a few minutes from the embassy. Soon after their arrival in Petrograd, she and Francis began taking long walks and carriage rides together through the gardens and along the tree-lined streets nearby. She became friends not only with Francis, but with Arthur Dailey, Francis's secretary, and particularly with Philip Jordan, helping him learn how to shop at the open street markets near the embassy.

Francis often described Madame de Cramm as "my French teacher," although there is little evidence that the aging ambassador ever achieved much more than a rudimentary grasp of French—a drawback, since it was the diplomatic language of the period and often was spoken in high social circles as well. However, someone helped Philip Jordan with his Russian. Not long after Francis and crew had arrived in Petrograd, an embassy aide noticed that Jordan already went shopping alone and came back with food. "Well, Phil, how do you get on?" the man asked. Jordan replied, "I'm making out pretty well since I learned the language."[2]

The diminutive former street fighter eagerly and fearlessly plunged into this busy cosmopolitan capital city, a roiling mix of people from across an empire that stretched east to the Pacific and south to the Black Sea. He soon was eavesdropping on the dissident political assemblies in the streets. Also, Jordan accompanied Francis on jaunts through the city to look for a new embassy and for long walks after dinner, accompanied by various members of the staff.

As usual, Francis worked hard. He wrote Jane, "I come to my office every morning about ten o'clock, sometimes take no luncheon—If I lunch at all it is in the Embassy—and then return to the office where I remain until about seven o'clock and later if I do not have to dress for dinner."[3]

Francis quickly grew frustrated with the long delays in communicating with the United States; ordinary letters took four or five weeks, and even the diplomatic pouch could take three weeks. Cables took five or six days. They were routed through England, where, Francis came to believe, they were intercepted and read or even purposely lost—particularly if they threatened British dominance of trade with Russia. As the dream of a quick commercial treaty faded, his idea for a direct cable was the enduring accomplishment he wanted to "mark my incumbency of this place."[4]

On May 9, 1916, he dictated a letter to Jane that began with an apology for not having time to write her an "autograph letter." He complained, "I have not had a letter from home since I left home six weeks ago today." Both the apology and the complaint would become familiar elements in Francis's letters over the next two and a half years.

He suggested Jane come for a visit in June, when a subordinate would be returning from a visit to the United States. But he warned her that she would not like "the official life" of the embassy. Inviting Jane to Russia while laying out reasons she shouldn't come also became a theme in his letters. He sent her two photographs of himself taken in Russia and attached a list of things he wanted, including a porcelain picture of her from his bedroom and a group photograph of the family in front of the mansion.[5]

Francis, accustomed to being surrounded by friends and family, made a point of frequently dining with American businessmen—including, fairly often, executives of the National City Bank—or with his staff members in their apartments and hotel rooms and suites. And at least once a week he played host at embassy dinner parties. Thanks to Philip Jordan, the dining room now held a large table that could hold eighteen or twenty, with two at either end.

At the head sat Francis and a woman guest, usually the wife of one of the men who worked for him, sometimes Madame de Cramm or one of the American women who lived in Petrograd and were married to aristocratic Russians. Francis had arrived with effusive letters of introduction from his friend Natalie Townsend, the ambassador's wife he had been so charmed by on his first grand tour of Europe. He became particular friends with Princess Julia Grant Cantacuzene, a granddaughter of Ulysses S. Grant.[6]

Early on, he was invited to tea at Princess Cantacuzene's suite at the Hotel d'Europe. There, he met six women married to Russian noblemen, each of whom commanded troops at the front. He soon had formal dinner invitations almost every evening.[7] This notably convivial man seems to have badly missed the company of family and friends, and he tried to fill the vacuum—in part, with his friendship with the vivacious Madame de Cramm and his deepening personal relationship with Philip Jordan.

After a brief experiment with a Russian cook, Jordan took over cooking breakfast for himself and Francis. On June 1, they hired a black cook from the Caribbean, and Jordan again devoted much of his time to furnishing the place, again with considerable help from Madame de Cramm.[8] Typically, Francis was too impatient to wait for the bureaucratic mills to grind out money, and he advanced his own cash to pay for a dining room suite, kitchen utensils and supplies, curtains, and shades. Meanwhile, he lobbied the secretary of state for $250,000 to buy and equip a new embassy.

The first letter from St. Louis arrived on May 14 and was dated April 18. Perry had forwarded financial statements that Francis reacted to immediately, writing to complain about such expenditures as ten dollars for two portraits: "Did you have to pay $5 apiece for these pictures? Don't do so any more."[9] Like many self-made men, he could not resist the need to micro-manage.

On Sunday, June 25, after lunch, Francis and Arthur Dailey took Madame de Cramm to the horse races. This was noted in one of the few datebook references in 1916 to Madame, although there is no question that he saw her frequently. That same day, in writing to a friend at the Mallinckrodt Chemical Co. in St. Louis, he made what appears to be his first reference of her in a letter, although it is an indirect one: "I saw a letter a few days ago written by yourself to Dr. de Cramm, in which you complimented him on an article he had written and published in some periodical, the name of which I don't recall. [De Cramm was, by training, a chemist.] I told the person who showed me the letter that I know you personally and that any statements you might make could be thoroughly relied upon." He warned his friend not to mention to de Cramm that Francis had "written anything about him whatever."[10]

Charles F. Lewis, an American in partnership with Edgar de Cramm in the import-export business, called on Francis several times in the early months of his ambassadorship. Lewis claimed to be a friend of Elihu Root, a former Republican secretary of state. Madame de Cramm's brother, a Moscow businessman named Weyde, had at least two meetings with Francis. We have no indication of anything substantive Francis discussed with either man on their visits.[11]

The Allies concluded their Paris conference in mid-June with no change in Russia's official position on the status of Jews. By then, in any event, the Russian government was in disarray, apparently being run as much as anyone by a brilliant, devious, and possibly crazed Siberian monk. Francis began to realize that no progress could be made on the treaty until the government stabilized and, perhaps, until the war was over. Still, he was enthused about Russia's potential. He wrote Perry, "The resources of Russia are so enormous and the opportunities for development so numerous and apparent that I now feel inclined to remain here after my official duties are completed for a few years anyway."[12]

On June 12, Francis finally received a reply from Oscar Straus to his April 16 letter suggesting that treatment of the Jews in Russia was improving. Straus said that was absurd; he had it on reliable testimony that the "persecutions and horrors" that Jews had suffered in Russian-controlled Poland were comparable to the infamous slaughter and oppression of the Armenians by the Turks. He was adamant that any trade treaty specifically must provide equal protection for Jews or it would not be acceptable to American Jews, nor for that matter to Woodrow Wilson or Robert Lansing. Straus emphasized that there was no finessing the matter, even if the Russians unofficially let up on severe restrictions on where Jews could live or how they could make a living.[13]

In heated moments, Francis continued to partly blame American Jews for his inability to get the Russians to talk about a new trade treaty. The most shocking document in this regard was a letter written by Francis to Frank L. Polk, counselor of the State Department. The letter, not a cranky, informal note to a business crony but an official letter to a top representative of the United States government, strongly suggests that anti-Semitism was casually accepted in the Protestant-dominated upper levels of the State Department, even under a liberal Democratic president elected with considerable Jewish support. Or at least David Francis must have assumed that was the case when he stated: "As I have written heretofore to either you or Secretary Lansing, there is not doubt that if the Jews were given absolutely equal rights of residence, profession, etc. in Russia and the right to own land, they would become possessors of the entire Empire within a comparatively short time. . . . The peasant would stand no show whatever with the designing, usurious and pitiless Jew."[14]

Francis may well have had a point about the gullibility of Russian peasants, but wealthy men of Slavic ancestry needed no help in bilking them out of their land. Francis continued, predictably, "I have no prejudice against the Jews as a class nor as a race; in fact, many of them, like Oscar Straus, I admire, and some of my personal friends are Jews."

He did continue to raise the Jewish issue with Russian officials. In a letter to Darwin Kinglsey, president of New York Life, he reported:

> The minister of foreign affairs, M. Sazonov, said to me the other day, 'Why do you Americans bother us so much about the Jews? You are the only country that does. The Jews love Germany better than they do America. There are 2,000,000 Jews in Austria and nearly as many in Germany and neither of those countries ever annoyed us about the Jews before the war began. There are many Jews in France, and nearly 1,000,000, in England; both of those countries are Allies but neither one has ever mentioned the Jewish question to us.'

Francis's conclusion, not completely irrational, was that America was the only country that would make any effort at all to secure passport rights for Jews.[15]

Francis had been assured by Sazonov, whom he trusted, that Jews with American passports would not be excluded from doing business in Russia or restricted to the Pale, "unless they are agitators or otherwise objectionable."[16] Then, on July 22, Francis received shocking news—the veteran statesman was out as foreign minister, forced to resign by the increasingly erratic Tsar under pressure from the Tsarina and Rasputin.

Civil unrest was growing as it became apparent that the Russians were in real danger of losing the war to Germany. Official corruption and war profiteering sapped the country's will to fight. In the cities of Russia, supplies of food and fuel grew short, even in midsummer, and inflation drove prices beyond the range of ordinary people. Thousands of wounded men came limping home, many of them missing the hands, fingers, or toes they had shot off to escape the horror of the blood-drenched trenches. The crime rate soared. The Tsar's name was cursed openly on the street, and revolution was in the air.

Shocked and saddened by the departure of Sazonov, Francis then was horrified by his replacement—the autocratic prime minister, Baron Sturmer, who added foreign minister to his pocketful of titles, which included minister of the interior and supreme minister for state defense.

Francis strongly believed that the Russian aristocracy and upper-middle class had to force a move to a constitutional democracy, both for moral and practical reasons. The alternative was a cataclysm and the collapse of the Russian war effort. By this time, three months after he had arrived, Francis seems to have achieved, with the considerable help of Samuel Harper, an essentially accurate understanding of the situation.

"Universal regret is expressed at the retirement of Mr. Sazonov," Francis wrote the secretary of state on July 25. Sazonov had been a "statesman and a liberal" while Sturmer was "looked upon as a reactionary. . . . I have had two conferences with him, and must say that he did not impress me as a man with breadth of view or imbued with high ideals." He passed on to Lansing the remark Sturmer was overheard to make after a rare Russian victory at the front: "One or two more such victories and we can do away with the Duma."[17]

Francis also reported that Russia was said to be exploring the possibility of a separate peace with Germany. Meanwhile, the Tsar's government continued to call up men. The new troops flocked into Petrograd, swelling the crowds of recruits that Francis could see every morning from his office window, and mobbing the city's train stations:

> I have seen thousands of them coming into Petrograd in obedience to a call. Fresh from the fields, boys who had never before seen a village of over 2,000 inhabitants, with sunken chests, slip-shod gait and careless carriage. After three or four weeks of drill, equipped with military clothing, including boots of which they were very proud, they march singing through the streets with swinging gait, heads high in the air, chests out-thrown, and their very countenances manifesting pride in their country and consciousness of their own power.[18]

Francis may well have seen pride on the faces of these new recruits, but they were probably proud less of their ill-defined and chaotic nation than of their own survival and accomplishments, as is common among soldiers who have just finished basic training. Francis did understand that these strong and vital young men, if properly armed and organized, could present a real menace—and not just to the Germans and Austrians. He wrote, "It may be that the supporters of an absolute monarchy in Russia are asking themselves what such an army, well disciplined and conscious of its strength, will do in Russia when there are no more foreign enemies to fight."

Through Samuel Harper, Francis already had developed contacts among dissidents and revolutionaries. Still, his main sources of information at this point were with the snobbish Russian elite. He wrote to Lansing:

> When I asked the president of a large bank in Petrograd, a man who is said to be the ablest financier in the Empire, what he thought of Baron Sturmer's appointment to the Foreign Office, he said, 'It is just as appropriate as would be the appointment of a tailor to the place I occupy.' . . . I do not think there will be a revolution immediately after the close of the war; that would be premature, but if the Court Party [the nobility] does not adopt a more liberal policy by extending more privileges to the people and their representatives in the Duma, a revolution will take place before the lapse of even a few years. [19]

In the uneasy summer of 1916, the wealthy, some of who entertained David Francis in their marble palaces on the Fontanka Canal or in their suites in the grand hotels near Nevsky Prospect, adopted an attitude of *carpe diem,* drinking up their wine cellars, spending thousands of rubles on black-market caviar, gambling all night and sleeping all day. A British intelligence officer, Sir Samuel Hoare, remarked that the wealth of the aristocracy "and the lavish use they made of it dazzled me after the austere conditions of wartime life in England."[20]

Early in July, Francis was happily surprised to hear from Hugh H. Moran, a grandson of Robert Breck. Moran worked in Siberia with war prisoners for the YMCA. After remarking to Francis that "your name has been a household one with us since I can remember," Moran asked for help with a passport problem and informed Francis that his aunt, Belle Breck, was in China, on her way around the world, and she would spend several months with him in Siberia. She ended up staying much longer, doing relief work for the YMCA as well.[21]

Francis responded eagerly to this surprise and was anxious to see these relatives of his childhood preceptor. They became frequent visitors to the embassy during stays in Petrograd, beginning with Moran's arrival in the capital in November. Francis, figuratively and literally, embraced them as friends from home at a time when he trusted few people.

One of the people he did trust, Samuel Harper, left at the end of August 1916. Francis would miss the young professor. They had spent a great deal of time together, and Francis found him to be smart, trustworthy, and honest, with "a very valuable acquaintance among men of influence in Russia."[22] Francis regretted losing a vital contact with influential leaders on the Left. Harper later noted that Francis quickly had "interested himself in the work and views of the people's organizations, whose leaders were soon to head the revolution of March, 1917."[23]

"In his official position," Harper wrote, "he could not, of course, spend too much time with these leaders, but I could and did see them freely and frequently." This was not the last time that Francis would depend upon an American associate in a semi-official capacity to maintain contact with revolutionary leaders, while maintaining appropriate diplomatic distance.

Hopes for a commercial treaty continued to fade. On August 18, State Department Counselor Frank L. Polk warned Francis against trusting any commitments the Russians made amid the shifting fortunes and alliances of war. Polk wrote, "I want to suggest that for the present you confine yourself to maintaining pleasant relations with the Foreign Office and the various officials and do not attempt anything more than the routine work of the Embassy. In other words, I think it would be well to show no interest whatever in a new treaty or in closer commercial relations."[24]

That seems to have closed the door temporarily to what Francis (and Woodrow Wilson) had perceived as his principal mission. He turned his focus to the scheme for a direct telegraph cable between the United States and Russia, a project that was also doomed to be lost in the turmoil of war, intrigue, and, soon, revolution. But he never stopped thinking about trade between the two countries, and sometimes that obsession spilled over, as it would with Francis, into pure business.

In the spring, Francis had recommended that National City Bank loan $50 million to the Russian government to help it fight the war. He argued that the loan would be a step toward closer commercial relations between the country and suggested to Perry that it be mentioned favorably in the *Republic*.[25] Early in the summer, a syndicate formed by Samuel McRoberts of National City Bank, and including its sometime rival J. P. Morgan and Co., made the $50 million loan. Francis wrote the president of the New York Life Insurance Co., which had a large presence in Russia, "I think the loan absolutely good and offers promise of good profit; so much was I convinced of this that I made a personal subscription."[26]

Francis long ago had made his fortune, and most of his adult life had been devoted to public service. But Russia thoroughly excited his commercial instincts. Sending Francis to Russia was like showing an old war-horse a new field of battle. Understandably, some of Francis's professional colleagues looked askance at the ambassador's multifaceted role in the Russian bond deal. Early the following year, Francis received a letter on this point from fellow New York Life board member Oscar Straus, a former ambassador to Turkey:

> With a sense of appreciation, because I too had the privilege (or call it the responsibility) . . . of representing the country at a distant post, I will bring to your attention a matter which I hope will be received by you in the same spirit of friendship which prompts me to offer it. Numerous letters have reached me and friends calling attention to the fact that your firm, Francis, Bro. & Co., is advertising in the daily paper the sale of Russian Loan, as appears in the *St. Louis Republic* and also by circulars from your firm upon which your name

appears. In fact, information reaches me that an effort was on the way to make a protest to the President of the impropriety of an Ambassador being interested in banking or commercial transactions of his own with the government or of the government to which he is accredited. I think I have been able to prevent any such action being taken, as I felt that if this matter were brought to your attention you would be the first to recognize the impropriety [and] the unpleasant criticism it would subject you to. There is a saying, which is attributed to Socrates, to the effect that in private life it is our duty to do that which is right; in public life, it is not only our duty to do that which is right but to avoid doing that which may appear to be wrong. I would feel that I was lacking in candor and in the duty which friendship imposes should I decline . . . to bring this matter to your attention . . . knowing as I do your high sense of public duty.[27]

Francis forwarded a copy of Straus's letter to Lansing and wrote, "I was not aware that my house had any interest in this loan until the receipt of this letter from Mr. Straus. . . . Personally I would have preferred that my house had taken no interest in this Russian loan as they have no doubt been unable to place it all and what they hold now will undoubtedly show a loss."[28] All this was untrue, including the part about the difficulty of placing the bonds—they were snapped up quickly.

In the meantime, he continued to mix commerce and diplomacy, although not always for personal profit. He was admonished at least twice by the State Department, once by Lansing himself, for using diplomatic pouches for sensitive communications between American companies working in Russia and their home offices. He remarked in one letter to the State Department, "All other embassies and legations do not hesitate to use their respective pouches to promote commerce for their countries." Francis had been sent to Russia by Woodrow Wilson to foster commerce, and that is what he intended to do.[29]

He continued to fret over business at home. He despaired over the *Republic*, which was losing one hundred thousand dollars a year, and even worried about the financial future of St. Louis itself. Perry had reported an offer to buy the home at Maryland and Newstead, and Francis replied that, although it would break his heart to sell the house, he was tempted, because he was "by no means pleased with the progress St. Louis is making. It does not seem to me there is any prospect for values in real estate lines to show any improvement in the near future, or even for some times after."[30] He now doubted he would live to see St. Louis become the great city he still hoped it could be, nor was he sure his sons would live to see that day, either.

Another reason to sell the house, Francis said, was that Jane was "inclined to give up the labor and responsibility of keeping house. She is not strong, her tastes are peculiar to herself. . . . I have written her a number of times in regard to coming here, but really there is no reason why she should from her own point of view, as I am sure she would not like it."[31]

FRANCIS WORKED SIX DAYS A WEEK and played golf on Sundays, when he wasn't taking Matilda de Cramm to the horse races. His usual companion on the golf course on the outskirts of the city was Frederick M. Corse, the head of New York Life in Petrograd. The tall, fifty-one-year-old Vermonter was fluent in Russian and considered to be the dean of the American colony in Petrograd. He was Francis's closest male friend, with the possible exception of Philip Jordan.[32]

The long trip to the golf course got a little easier towards the end of the summer, when the car Francis had ordered several months before arrived at the White Sea port of Archangel and was shipped south to Petrograd. It was a Model T Ford, which he may have chosen in stubborn rejection of diplomatic elegance, but which turned out to be perfect, high-riding and tough, for the rough roads of the countryside around Petrograd.

Philip loved driving it, his large white military-billed cap perched jauntily on top of his head, an American flag tucked into the brace of the left headlamp, fluttering past the brass radiator. The car attracted a lot of attention as it cruised down the Nevsky Prospect. Typically, Francis complained about the $440 shipping cost, although he wrote Jane, "I understand I can sell it here for much more than it cost, after I have finished using it."

He also informed Jane, "We have a negro cook who is very black, a West India negro named Green. Phil does not associate much with him on the streets because, I think, Green is so black, and Phil is almost white enough to pass for a white man." In fact, with his tan skin and his large, Arabic-appearing nose, Jordan easily could have been mistaken for an émigré from one of the southern regions of the Russian empire. That must have helped him as he roamed the streets and haggled at the markets, mixing in with the multiracial, polyglot crowd, fascinated by what he saw. "It is very difficult to procure food here," Francis wrote, "and Phil and Green are always scheming to get food for me."[33]

As the very long days of summer shortened and the chill and fog of fall crept into the air, crucial shortages became more and more severe in Petrograd, and many feared there wouldn't be enough food or fuel to get the city through the upcoming winter—the third one of the war and, as it turned out, the coldest.

However, fall was also ballet season in Petrograd. Francis informed Jane that he had bought a season box for the ballet, which he described as "by all odds the finest ballet I have ever seen and I think it is the best in the world." He was referring to the ballet of the Mariinksy Theater, where Pavlova and Nijinsky had danced a few years earlier. It is now better known as the Kirov. For the opening ballet of the season, Francis's guests included Minister of Finance P. L. Bark and his wife, and "a very pretty young woman," the daughter of National City Bank's Meserve.[34]

He complained that it was "almost impossible to get food in Petrograd, so dinners [at restaurants] are very infrequent." However, the rich seemed to be able to put food and wine on the table, and so did Philip Jordan.[35]

By midsummer, reports had reached the State Department in Washington that Francis was not only spending much time with Madame de Cramm, but also writing her personal letters. The diplomatic pouch of August 26 arrived with a month-old letter from Frank Polk, expressing concern about "a certain lady you and I discussed, whom you met some time again when you were in New York."

"I strongly urge you to be very cautious," Polk admonished him, "as some people close to the other side seem to know you are writing her. You really cannot be too careful in this matter."[36] Unstated was that Edgar de Cramm was under surveillance as a German agent, and there was a growing suspicion at the State Department and among the Allied diplomats in Russia that his wife was working for the Germans as well. Francis's reply, marked "personal and confidential," read, in part:

> I thank you for the personal suggestion. . . . It was very surprising as the correspondence I had with the party you designate was purely romantic, if not sentimental. If I did not fear giving you the wrong impression concerning the relation, I would say that this reminds me of an experience of Alexander Hamilton who, in order to exculpate himself from a charge of malfeasance in office, had to betray his relations with a very attractive lady. I am very curious to know who it was that discovered or suspected this strictly personal correspondence of mine.[37]

As Francis apparently realized, there is something outlandish in his excusing an affair with a suspected spy by explaining his motives as "purely romantic." Over the next few months Polk continued to warn him about the association and Francis continued to dismiss Polk's concerns, at one point saying that "the fears you express are somewhat amusing," while pressing Polk for his sources.[38]

A State Department inventory of photographs in Francis's Petrograd office, probably taken in the fall of 1916, shows that he had a small picture of Matilda de Cramm near his desk. However, among the thirty-odd photos in the office were also pictures of a half-dozen wives of his staff members, of Princess Cantacuzene, Countess Nostitz—another American woman married into the Russian aristocracy—President Wilson, Secretary Lansing, and Jane Perry Francis.[39]

Francis liked women who were both pretty and smart. Madame became his closest Russian friend, and it's hard to imagine him being so fervent about the friendship if she were a man. Francis was, as he admitted to Breckinridge Long, a State Department official from Missouri, "fond of ladies' society."[40]

Madame de Cramm began spending a great deal of time at the embassy, sometimes staying until after midnight, and other Allied diplomats, according to many reports, became reluctant to speak to Francis of confidential matters, particularly involving the Great War. Witnesses later said that Francis was so careless as to read aloud in her presence confidential cables that had just been decoded.[41] Francis later would argue that the United States had nothing to fear from Madame de Cramm and that he depended upon her and their close friendship to gain a knowledgeable understanding of the Russian makeup. But even if she was innocent of espionage, Francis was arrogantly insensitive to the negative effect appearances had on political realities.

David R. Francis and Philip Jordan aboard the Swedish ship *Oscar II*, traveling to Russia in April 1916. Jordan wrote to Perry Francis on the back of the photograph: "This was taken at about the same place that Lord Kitchener was when his ship went down. . . . This was the only time we felt uneasy because we were in the North Sea and always has floating mines. It was awful rough and cold about this time."
Philip Jordan/MHS-PP.

President Woodrow Wilson and his cabinet, 1917. Front row, left to right: William Redfield (Commerce), Robert Lansing (State), David Houston (Agriculture), Woodrow Wilson, William McAdoo (Treasury), A. S. Burleson (Postmaster General); second row, left to right: Josephus Daniels (Navy), William Wilson (Labor), Newton Baker (War), T. W. Gregory (Attorney General), Franklin Lane (Interior).
Library of Congress.

Oscar Straus, former U.S. ambassador to Turkey, advisor to Presidents Cleveland and Wilson, and a director in the J. P. Morgan–connected New York Life Insurance Company. Straus was a friend of Francis who adamantly insisted that Francis not yield on the question of equitable treatment of Russia's Jews in negotiating the commercial treaty with Russia.
Library of Congress.

Alexander Kerensky. This photograph, published in Francis's book, *Russia from the American Embassy*, was inscribed to Francis: "In memory of friendly conversations through bright but difficult days."
MHS-Library.

Madame Matilda De Cramm and her sons, April 1918.
MHS-PP.

The United States embassy in Petrograd. From Francis's book, *Russia from the American Embassy* (1921).
MHS-Library.

Ambassador Francis in sleigh in the courtyard of
the U.S. embassy, inscribed to Betsey [Mrs. Talton Francis].
Talton F. Ray Collection.

Philip Jordan, as he often did, captured on film this dramatic funeral procession in Petrograd moving along the Nevsky Prospect.

Philip Jordan, 1917/MHS-PP.

Ambassador Francis and Mikhail Rodzianko, president of the Duma, addressing a crowd from the balcony of the U.S. embassy, April 1917. Philip Jordan/MHS-PP.

Celebration in the Duma on Eleventh Anniversary of First Duma, April 1917. Ambassador Francis acknowledges applause on the announcement of American declaration of war on Germany. On the balcony with Francis are Italian Ambassador Carotti, M. A. Thomas, and British Ambassador George Buchanan. MHS-PP.

Members of the first Provisional Government: (counterclockwise) Prince G. E. Lvov, A. I. Konovalov, A. F. Kerensky, A. I. Guchkov, V. N. Lvov, P. N. Milyukov, M. I. Tereshchenko, F. I. Rodiehev [not a member of the cabinet], N. V. Nekrasov, A. A. Manuilov, A. I. Shingarev, and I. V. Godnev.
Hoover Institution, Stanford University.

Leon Trotsky arriving at Finland Station, Petrograd, May 14, 1917.
David King Collection, London.

Ambassador Francis, Philip Jordan, and Counselor J. Butler Wright in Francis's Model T Ford on their way to the Winter Palace to meet with the Root Commission, June 2, 1917.
MHS-PP.

The Root Commission in the Winter Palace.
Elihu Root is just to the left of Ambassador Francis. Seated, second from the left, is Charles R. Crane, the Chicago businessman who suggested Francis for the ambassador's post.
MHS-PP.

V. I. Lenin, speaking at the unveiling of
the Marx-Engels monument in Moscow,
November 7, 1918.

David King Collection, London.

Note from V. I. Lenin to
Ambassador Francis, January 14, 1918
(old calendar, January 1).

David R. Francis Papers, MHS-Archives.

Francis and aides with the Red Cross representatives.
Left to right: Red Cross Colonels Anderson and Billings, Red Cross Major Peabody, Francis, J. Butler Wright, Colonel Thompson, Minister Volhicka of Roumania, and General Judson.
MHS-PP.

Red Cross representatives with the Socialist Revolutionaries: left to right seated: William B. Thompson, George Lazarev and Catherine Breshkovskaya. Standing: N. V. Chaikovski, Frederick M. Corse of the New York Life Insurance Company, Victor Soskice (Kerensky's personal secretary), and Raymond Robins.
State Historical Society of Wisconsin.

Relief Division conference, Moscow, January 11, 1917. Seated from left are North Winship, William Sands, DRF, Basil Miles, and Maddin Summers. By the window are Earl Johnston (left) and Norman Armour. MHS-PP.

R. Bruce Lockhart, ca. 1922. David King Collection, London.

Edgar De Cramm and his adopted daughter, Marion, October 1917. National Archives.

The clubhouse in Vologda
that served as the American embassy in 1918.
MHS-PP.

Ambassador Francis and staff on the steps of the Vologda embassy. Philip Jordan
is at the top left with flag, Earl Johnston and Colonel James A. Ruggles are standing to the right of Francis.
MHS-PP.

Last meeting of the diplomatic corps in Vologda, Russia, July 23, 1918.
Seated, left to right: Italian Chargé Torretta, French Ambassador Noulens, DRF,
Serbian Minister Spaleikovich, Japanese Chargé Maruono, British Chargé Lindley.
Standing, left to right: Brazilian Chargé Kelsch, French Counselor Dulcet, and Chinese Chargé Chen-Yen-Chi.
MHS-PP.

Georgi Chicherin, center, in uniform, with Soviet Foreign Ministry officials, ca. 1925.
David King Collection, London.

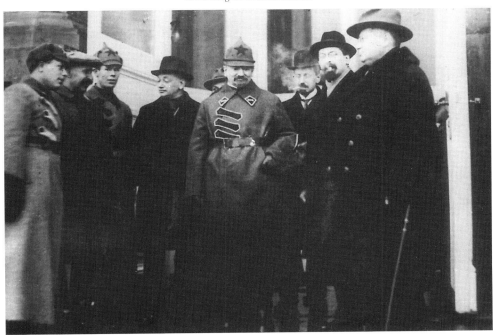

Karl Radek, 1920.
David King Collection, London.

David R. Francis and President N. V. Chaikovski of the
Supreme Soviet of the Northern Region, Archangel.
Philip Jordan/MHS-PP.

David R. Francis in his hospital bed at the U.S. Naval Hospital in London after his operation, 1919.
Philip Jordan/MHS-PP.

J. D. Perry Francis, his wife Mimi, Philip Jordan, and Francis in London, 1919.
MHS-PP.

The Francis family at Uplands Farm, 1919.
Back, L to R: Thomas and Leila, J. D. Perry; David, Jr., and Nina; Julia and Sydney; and Betsey and Talton.
Middle: Mimi (J. D. Perry's wife); Charles; Alice (daughter of David Jr.); Jane and David Francis.
Front row: grandchildren Miriam, David III, Anne, Sidney Jr. and Jane.
Talton F. Ray Collection.

Francis posing for sculptor Julian Zolnay, 1925. The bust was given to the Missouri Historical Society.
MHS-PP.

Author Harper Barnes and his wife, Roseann Weiss, posing in front of the old Vologda embassy, now a museum, 1997.
Alexander Bykov/Harper Barnes.

Philip Jordan surrounded by memorabilia in his apartment in the carriage house of J. D. Perry Francis. This was probably taken on the occasion of his sixtieth birthday in 1929.
Sid Aschenbrenner/MHS-PP.

IN October, embassy counselor Fred Dearing left Petrograd for an extended leave. In response to Francis's frantic pleas for more help, Polk had promised him a good replacement. Although left even more short-staffed, Francis was not unhappy to see the high-strung Dearing go. He groused that Dearing treated him patronizingly, as if "I knew nothing about the duties of an Ambassador nor good form of diplomacy because I had not been trained in the service."[42]

This almost inevitable chafing between professional diplomats and a political appointee was made worse by Francis's sometimes foolish outspokenness, his close friendship with Matilda de Cramm, and his casual Kentucky-Missouri style, as opposed to the Ivy League propriety of most of his aides. Francis's refusal to obtain a diplomatic dress uniform, thus forcing his aides to keep theirs in the closet, was an irritant, and so perhaps was his choice of a plebeian Model T, as opposed to the elegant limousines of other ambassadors.

Much to Francis's relief, an old Russia hand, thirty-nine-year-old Basil Miles, a graduate of the University of Pennsylvania and Oxford, arrived in October to take over the heavy burden of the Second Division, which was responsible for German and Austrian prisoners of war. It was housed in the Austrian Embassy, about three blocks from the American Embassy.[43] And in November, Francis got a new personal secretary, twenty-six-year-old Earl M. Johnston, another Missourian, who would be with him for more than two years and become a close friend and golfing crony.

Francis's former secretary, Arthur T. Dailey, along with the embassy accountant, George W. Link, went to work for the new Petrograd branch of National City Bank, strengthening its ties with the U.S. government and David Francis.[44]

On November 18, Joshua Butler Wright arrived to take over the vacant position of counselor. For the next year and a half, Wright effectively would be Francis's second in command. The thirty-nine-year-old Princeton graduate, a former banker, broker, and rancher, had entered the diplomatic service in 1909. He resembled a British colonel, with a stiff dark mustache and a formal, almost military bearing.

Sizing Francis up as knowing little about the polite rules of diplomacy, Wright took on the job, vacated by Harper, of keeping Francis out of trouble. Unlike Harper, Wright sometimes accomplished this by leaving his boss in the dark on important matters, but his intentions seemed to have been wholly honorable. Indeed, Wright's personal diary, and the commentary of others, suggest that Wright remained loyal to Francis long past the time when other aides and colleagues were deserting him and calling for his recall. To a great extent, the difficulties to come between Francis and the buttoned-up J. Butler Wright seem to have sprung from differences in temperament.

Wright had been in Petrograd less than a week when he wrote in his diary: "DRF very kindly. Great sense of natural good business and common sense-but very little concept of the social amenities as regards the diplomatic service. Ergo, H. (wife Harriet) and I will have to coach him and it will not be hard." A few days later, he wrote, "The Ambassador himself is anxious to reduce the burden of his office. I think he is right, for he has been overworked. The column of correspondence is stupendous and I am rather overwhelmed by it." He later noted, "The detail of the work of this Embassy is really enormous, embracing, as it does, relief disbursements amounting to over six million roubles a month [and] the direction of a staff of over fifty persons."[45]

In early December, Francis reported that Counselor Wright was "proving to be a very efficient aid" and that he and his wife were "delighted with Petrograd." Wright's thirteen-year-old son, a bright boy who had grown up in Europe and already was fluent in French and German, was quick to learn Russian, and he and Philip Jordan became great friends. Jordan thought Butler Wright, Jr., looked exactly like David Francis, Jr., as a boy.[46]

Francis was deeply relieved to have a proper and competent staff in place, even if he still chaffed at the size and condition of the embassy building. But he was not totally trusting of career diplomats. He wrote Frank Polk, "I do not believe in the Civil Service to the extent of including therein ministers and ambassadors, as residence abroad for a protracted time places a man out of touch with his own country, and so incapacitates him from properly representing his country."[47]

As time went by, and Francis discovered what he considered to be treachery by some of his top aides, he developed that notion further. With some justification, Francis felt that the counselors and top secretaries in the American diplomatic service, those "society men" as he called them, with their impressive family connections and prestigious eastern educations, looked upon ambassadors as an imposition. He fumed, "Their constant effort is to demonstrate to the appointee who has not been trained in the service not only their superior knowledge of the forms, but his want of knowledge and utter helplessness without their assistance and guidance."[48] His top aides sometimes went so far as to change the wording of his cables, emphasizing caution and diplomatic language over frankness and decisive action. And they would put diplomatic documents in French on his desk for his signature. He soon began to send them back and say he wanted them in English.

I N EARLY NOVEMBER, heavy blizzards blew across northeastern Russia from the Arctic Circle, increasing fears that a rugged winter was on the way. And food was already in short supply.

Francis reported to Washington:

> There have been manifestations lately of unrest among the workers in the factories and also among the long lines of people waiting to be served small amounts of sugar or meat. . . . I have heard it rumored that these rumblings are instigated by German money. . . . The Duma will meet . . . on Nov. 1st/14th. Today's papers state that Prime Minister Sturmer will be unable to address the Duma because of illness. He is not seriously ill and the meeting is one week off. It would seem that he fears to go through the ordeal.[49]

By then, the Tsar had briefly raised the hopes of the liberals by appointing A. D. Protopopov, deputy chairman of the Duma and a supposed moderate, the acting minister of the interior. But Protopopov, a favorite of Rasputin and the Tsarina, turned out to be a fanatical mystic whose belief in the Tsar's right to rule was absolute. The Duma's liberals were further radicalized, convinced that reform was not possible as long as the Tsar, the Tsarina, and Rasputin ran the country.

Most important among the dissidents were socialist lawyer Alexander Kerensky; Prince Georgi Lvov, who, like Tolstoy, had worked in his fields side by side with his peasants; and Paul Miliukov, a professor and leader in the moderate Constitutional Democratic or Kadet Party. At the opening session of the Duma on November 14, Miliukov electrified the Great Hall of the Tauride Palace with a passionate attack on the revolutionary climate that had been created, either through "folly or treason," by the government. The speech, Miliukov later ruefully admitted, became an unintentional "storm-signal for the revolution."

In his Russia memoir, Francis described Miliukov's speech as "suggestive of the old Hebrew prophets or of Cicero's attack on Cataline," and he quoted it in full.[50]

As delegates packing the large hall repeatedly cheered, Miliukov railed against powerful forces that seemed bent on making a separate peace or even acquiescing to a German victory. "Unless you act now," he shouted, "unless you do your very utmost, the name of Russia will stink in the nostrils of humanity. . . . Russia is about to betray the trust of her Allies . . . the oldest civilized countries in the world, the oldest democracies . . . are to be betrayed. Judas has closed the bargain! Judas is the traitor amongst us."

He was not afraid to identify the Russian Judas: "Sturmer is in negotiation for separate peace. Sturmer has betrayed Russia. . . . Sturmer is doing it for German money."

Miliukov charged that Prime Minister Sturmer and his cohorts were "traitors and spies" and that Sturmer's repressive measures were designed to create "dissatisfaction of the masses" and "Red, bloody revolution," tying up the homefront and forcing Russia to agree to a separate peace.

"Gentlemen, this traitor, this German, must go," he railed. "The people stand helpless awaiting your lead. . . . You must act!"

The speech was banned from the press, but copies were spread by hand throughout Petrograd. Members of the aristocracy, including the Grand Duke Nikolai, the Tsar's uncle, begged the Tsar to avert disaster by letting the Duma appoint a government. Instead, a week after Miliukov's speech, the Tsar fired Sturmer and, bending to the will of his wife and Rasputin, appointed a new prime minister, A. F. Trepov. Once again, the Tsar had replaced a bad choice with an even worse one. Francis observed, "Trepov, although opposed to a separate peace, was also a reactionary and was not satisfactory to the Duma. He was, moreover, a man with deep convictions and iron nerve, and on that account more dangerous than Sturmer, who was venal."[51]

Trepov made some halting attempts at accommodation with the Duma, but Kerensky and other deputies responded with angry and embittered speeches calling for an alliance with "the masses" in preparation for a revolution. The Duma was becoming increasingly divided. In the middle, moderates who hoped for change without revolution were shrinking in number and influence as the war dragged on, and the Tsar seemed unable to govern. Russian casualties were now in the millions, the food lines were growing longer, paranoic rumors and terrible truths flew through the populace, and a hard winter approached.

Shortly after Trepov's appointment, Francis attended a turbulent session of the Duma in the Grand Hall in the center of the Tauride Palace. The Italian, British, and French ambassadors joined him in the diplomatic boxes.

Premier Trepov tried to begin a speech. He barely got a word out before his voice was drowned out by shouts of derision, loud staccato clapping, and bootheels pounding the floor. Francis recalled:

> [Three times] the Premier's efforts to be heard were drowned in the uproar. . . .
> Finally, after the expulsion of a half dozen of the most obstreperous dis-
> turbers, he . . . read his address, and received a perfunctory hearing. He denied
> that Russia had sought a separate peace, and said that no peace would be
> concluded that did not give Russia control of the Dardenelles and added that
> Russia's Allies had agreed to this. At this point a number of the members
> looked curiously toward Sir George Buchanan, the British Ambassador, who
> sat next to me, but his expression showed no trace of dissent."[52]

Several less provocative speakers followed the premier, and the fury on the floor of the Duma abated somewhat. Then General V. M. Purishkevich rose to speak.

Purishkevich had been a founder a decade earlier of the far right, fervently nationalistic, pro-Tsar Union of the Russian People, a proto-fascist group known popularly as the Black Hundreds. But, deeply patriotic and disgusted with what was going on in the government, Purishkevich had turned against the Tsar and had become a hero of much of the Duma. The general's speech that day created a sensation by charging that the Germans held sway over the Tsarist court, the military, and even the banks. "Dark forces" surrounded the Tsar, he proclaimed to a thunderous ovation from the delegates and the mob of onlookers.

At the end of his speech, Purishkevich turned toward the boxes where the Allied diplomats sat. A majority of the delegates followed his lead, and cheers for the Allies echoed off the dome of the Great Hall.

Samuel Hoare, a British diplomat and sometime spy who sat behind Francis and Buchanan, recalled that the Westerners were "greatly moved by the scene." He added:

> We were also diverted by the American Ambassador, who, understanding no
> Russian and thinking that the demonstration was in honour of the United
> States, started bowing right and left to the upturned faces. Poor man! He was
> greatly disconcerted when Buchanan turned to him and said he would imme-
> diately telegraph to the Foreign Office the news that America had joined the
> Allies.[53]

As the year drew to a close, after Perry mentioned that he hadn't gotten a letter from his father in three weeks, Francis became seriously concerned that some of his letters to the United States were not getting through. He complained to Perry that he had not received acknowledgments for small gifts of lace and spoons he sent home to female relatives and friends. Part of the complaint can be traced to querulousness, abetted by loneliness for his family, but mail was uncertain and about to get more so.[54]

Back in St. Louis, on Christmas Eve, as the lights were lit on the City Hall Christmas tree, a man dressed as Santa Claus appeared with a deed to sixty acres in south St. Louis. The land, part of the Francis Farm, was Francis's Christmas gift to the city. He sent a message from Russia: "St. Louis has done everything for me; I'd like to do a little for St. Louis." The land became Francis Park.[55] Francis also sent back gifts to his family, including, for Jane, a silver box, a salt cellar, and a souvenir cider cup from Kirkland, Scotland.

About that time, the patriotic zealot Purishkevich, who had roused the Duma with his attack on the dark forces at work in the royal court, was a conspirator in a shocking event—the murder of Rasputin. Purishkevich was joined in the conspiracy by three wealthy young members of the Romanov court who were outraged by Rasputin's control of the Tsarina and the Tsar and by rumors that he was the prime mover behind talk of a separate peace with Germany.

Rasputin was not an easy man to kill. Invited by the conspirators for a soiree at Prince Felix Yusupov's palace on December 29, 1916, he drank several glasses of poisoned madiera and ate one or two sweets crammed with cyanide. The huge doses of poison seemed to have little effect, so Prince Yusupov went upstairs, got a pistol, came back to the basement salon, and shot Rasputin, aiming for his heart. The monk screamed and fell to the floor. The conspirators thought he was dead, and they left the room for a moment. Rasputin staggered to his feet and lurched out the door into the snow-covered courtyard, heading for the gate and shouting, "Felix, Felix, I will tell the Tsarina everything!"

Purishkevich took over, shooting Rasputin two more times and then, to make sure he was dead, kicking him repeatedly in the head as he lay spurting blood into the snow. The corpse was wrapped in heavy chains and dumped into a hole in the ice that already covered most of the Neva.[56]

Francis and all of Petrograd got the report of the murder two days later, on Sunday, December 31 (December 18 by the Russian calendar), when Rasputin's body was found washed up in a half-frozen inlet. The beleaguered Tsar, who came back from the front at the news of Rasputin's death, reacted by banishing the conspirators and resisting reform even more fiercely, as he and the Tsarina enclosed themselves behind the ochre walls and towering white columns of the Alexander Palace.

Rasputin's death was the main topic of conversation among the sixty guests, mostly Americans, at the fancy New Year's Eve party at the American Embassy. Philip Jordan had managed to scrounge up an adequate buffet, and after the Americans had toasted the new year with quite acceptable Russian champagne, they rolled up the rugs and danced until the wee hours of the morning.[57]

By early January, several top government ministers had been fired or had resigned in anger at the autocratic policies of the Tsar's appointees. "The Emperor," Francis reported to Washington, "has been undoubtedly very much provoked by all these hostile demonstrations, and in his appointment of reactionaries is showing a defiant attitude."[58]

Despite the furor, Francis was notified on January 10 that the Tsar would receive the diplomatic corps on the afternoon of January 14—by the Russian calendar, January 1, or New Year's Day.

This time, the reception was in the magnificent Italian baroque Catherine Palace, the gold-bedecked Russian equivalent of the Sun King's palace at Versailles. The visitors, about eighty of them, were led down a gravel path past the lawn, a field white with snow and Greek statues, up long marble stairs to the magnificent Grand Hall, which was dazzlingly lit with huge clustered gold chandeliers reflecting off gold-framed mirrors and long rows of windows.

All of the ambassadors except Francis were knickered and plumed in full diplomatic uniform. The Americans wore dress suits or, for the military attachés, dress uniforms.

The Tsar came in, dressed in a Cossack uniform, with an open greatcoat that reached almost to his ankles. Though a man of medium stature, Francis remarked later, he seemed much larger and gave the appearance of having supreme confidence in himself. Making his way slowly down the reception line, beginning with the British and Sir George Buchanan, dean of the diplomatic corps, the Tsar paused to speak for a few minutes with each delegation. When he got to the Americans, he shook hands with Francis and, in excellent English, said that he was glad to see him again. Francis replied that, since their meeting in May, "I have learned a great deal more about his country and his people, and have found much in both to admire."

Nicholas said he was gratified to hear that. Francis said, "I have also been endeavoring to promote closer relations between Russia and America." The Tsar smiled and replied, "Yes, I have heard of your actions in that line and think considerable progress has been made."

Francis later observed, "We were all impressed with the cordiality of His Majesty's manner, by his poise and his apparent excellent physical condition."

The whole ceremony took about an hour and twenty minutes. This time, the Tsarina did not appear.

Everyone was back in Petrograd by 6 P.M. During the day, Francis learned, the Tsar officially had announced the names of new members of his Imperial Council. They were, as far as Francis could tell, almost all reactionaries. Francis saw the appointments as "but another indication that His Majesty is not yielding in the slightest degree to the liberal sentiment . . . spreading throughout the Empire."

Years later, looking back on his meeting with the Tsar on the Russian new year, Francis wrote in his Russian memoir:

Little did any of us who were present at this reception know that we were witnessing the last public appearance of the last ruler of the mighty Romanov dynasty. And as I look back on it I am convinced that just as little did the central figure, the Czar of all the Russians, realize that within sixty days he would be compelled to abdicate the throne of his ancestors. . . . This complacent monarch had no premonition of the storm that was brewing . . . no idea that he was standing on a volcano.[59]

CHAPTER 14

The First Revolution

B Y January 1917, Petrograd was in the lock of one of the bitterest winters in its history. "It's as cold here as in Lapland," wrote Maxim Gorky, as fierce Baltic winds smothered the city in blizzards and unrelenting sub-zero temperatures, shutting down factories and forcing thousands more out of work. Food lines grew so long that women, at the end of ten-hour work days, would go immediately to the nearest market and queue up, spending the night shivering on sidewalk pallets or standing beside street fires of scrap lumber, to be in line for the meager dole of bread or sugar that might be available in the morning.[1]

In February, the mercury plunged to Arctic depths and stayed there. The average temperature for the month was fifteen degrees below zero Fahrenheit, or more than thirty degrees below normal.[2] Workers by the thousands in ragged bundles of clothes marched in the streets, calling for revolution in explosions of frozen breath, and soldiers garrisoned in Petrograd rushed out of their barracks to cheer the workers on, heaving bricks and paving stones at police who tried to block the marching men and women. As Francis had predicted, turning oppressed peasants into soldiers had dangerous consequences.

Soon, no force short of mounted Cossacks—fierce warriors from southern Russia and the Siberian steppes who served the Tsar as elite cavalrymen—was sufficient to stop the growing and increasingly militant crowds. Meanwhile, at the front, although Russia won an occasional victory, the overall tenor was of defeat, and masses of veterans limped back to Petrograd and Moscow, bringing with them anger and bitterness.

On February 3, in response to a German threat to torpedo ships without regard to whose citizens were aboard, Woodrow Wilson broke off diplomatic relations with Germany. The next morning, a Sunday, the news broke in Russia, and the American Embassy was besieged by reporters. Under specific instructions from Washington, Francis gave out a cautious statement, insisting that the breach did not mean the United States had declared war on Germany. Privately—and sometimes not so privately—Francis was eager for America to enter the war, which he called "just and inevitable." In a subsequent telegram to Lansing, he expressed anger that Senator William Stone, chairman of the Foreign Relations Committee, led the congressional opposition to a bill to arm American merchant ships, and said he had cabled the *Republic* to support the administration's position.[3] He also urged Woodrow Wilson to send American troops to war against Germany, typically arguing that if the Allies won without the United States, "England would attempt to dominate the commercial world and would come near doing so for a generation or perhaps for a century."[4]

On February 25, shortly before Wilson's second inauguration, Francis cabled the president: "Understand customary to tender resignation on beginning of new term. Mine is herewith presented. Thoroughly reconciled to return or entirely willing to remain or to serve in any position where you think can be effective. Personal interest and inclination subordinated to country's welfare at this critical junction."[5]

He waited for many weeks for a reply to his resignation. Meanwhile, as Francis clearly could see from his bay window, the capital of Russia was coming apart.

"Long breadlines were constantly seen," he later reported, "one of them being just across the street from the Embassy. The women formed these at four or five in the morning and sometimes waited for hours with the thermometer eight or ten degrees below zero, and then on reaching the point of distribution, after enduring such hardships for so long, they were told there was no more bread or sugar."

Even rough black bread, the staple of peasant life, disappeared from the markets. There was a general belief in Petrograd, Francis reported, that the Tsarist government had engineered the shortage of this final weapon against starvation. The intent: to create so much internal dissension that Russia could justify negotiating a separate peace with the Central Powers.

Across the street from the embassy, the women screamed in fury, and around the city men walked off their jobs at factories and gathered in the streets, demanding bread and, in some cases, peace. Francis watched as the Cossacks dispersed "several thousand hungry people" on a street near the embassy. This time, however, the Cossacks broke up the crowd without using clubs or swords and, Francis noted, were "advising the people, while dispersing them, to demand bread or the cessation of war."

At first, Francis—like most Western diplomats, including Sir George Buchanan, who had been in Russia since 1910—felt that the crowds in the streets would grow tired of marching and slowly disappear. But the demonstrations continued, and they grew so tumultuous that late in February Francis asked the Russian Foreign Office to place a military guard in front of the Austrian Embassy on Sergeivskaya Street, one block north of Furstatskaya. The Americans, short of space, used the building as the headquarters for its second division. It took almost a week for the guards to appear, and then there were only two. Francis kept pushing the Foreign Office, fearful of what the mobs would do to anyone found in the Austrian Embassy, and finally one day eighteen guards appeared—still not nearly enough, as it turned out.

In early March, with sporadic gunfire echoing in the streets, Francis gave a dinner for Baron Uchida, the new Japanese ambassador and his wife, a Bryn Mawr graduate, Francis noted approvingly.

"It was the last function of its kind to be attended by Ministers of the Russian Empire," he recalled. "When bidding my guests good night, I expressed the hope that they would reach their homes safely. As they departed they made jesting references to the disturbances and were inclined to accept my solicitude about their safety as a conversational pleasantry."[6]

Few of the diplomats, Allied or Russian, realized that revolution was imminent. Neither did the major radical leaders in Petrograd, nor Vladimir Lenin in Zurich, nor Leon Trotsky in New York. Buchanan thought the crowds soon would settle down. Francis expected revolution would come only after the war ended and millions of trained, disillusioned soldiers came home. Lenin had predicted about a month earlier that "we older men perhaps will not live to see the coming revolution." Sergei Mstislavsky, a leader of the Socialist Revolutionary Party, later said, "The revolution found us . . . fast asleep, just like the Foolish Virgins in the Gospel."[7]

THE RUSSIAN REVOLUTION—THE FIRST ONE—began on Thursday, March 8 (February 23 by the Russian calendar) when the sun finally broke through the clouds and the temperature soared almost to zero. It was International Women's Day on the socialist and feminist calendars, and thousands of women from all circles, from well-dressed aristocrats and students to ragged-scarfed peasants, began marching for equal rights. Women textile workers protesting against the shortage of bread soon joined them. They marched from the fringes of the city toward the Nevsky Prospect, passing factories whose workers spilled out the doors to join them. Soon, one hundred thousand workers were on strike.

Police at the Liteiny Bridge, a few blocks from the American Embassy, blocked a large contingent from crossing the Neva into the city center, but thousands of men and women slid and scrambled down the frozen embankment and walked across the frozen river itself. They reassembled on the French Embankment, in sight of the Winter Palace and about three blocks from the American Embassy, and continued their march toward the commercial center of town, chanting "Bread! Bread! Bread!"

That evening, the fashionable literary and artistic crowd paused for a theatrical production at the Tsar's Alexandrinsky Theater that had been five years in the making—the three hundred thousand-ruble *Masquerade,* based on Mikhail Lermontov's nineteenth-century drama about decadence and murder among the city's mad, doomed aristocracy. Cast members nicknamed the lavishly costumed production "Sunset of the Empire." After the performance, poet Anna Akhmatova recalled, it was almost impossible to get a droshky—a horse-drawn taxi—to take her across the Neva into the working-class Vyborg area where she lived. "There were shots on Nevsky Prospect and horsemen with bared swords attacked passersby," she recalled. "Machine guns were set up on roof tops and in attics."[8]

The next day, more than 150,000 workers took to the streets, joined by people from all walks of life, some of them just out for a stroll in the rare sunlight. Observers described it as "an enormous circus," and a British newspaperman said it was "like a Bank Holiday with thunder in the air."[9]

The Tsar, who was five hundred miles south of Petrograd at the front, sent word that evening that he had once again shut down the Duma. "The effect," Francis said, "was like throwing a burning match into a powder magazine."[10] Political leaders of more than a dozen parties, factions, and splinter groups tried to grab hold of the reins of the stampede. Their activity centered on the meetings halls of the Tauride Palace. But, for a few days, events moved too fast for the leaders, and the action was in the streets, not in the smoke-filled caucuses and vast central hall of the Tauride Palace.

On Saturday, March 10, 1917, all the major factories in the city were struck, and two hundred thousand workers marched down Petrograd's main "prospects" (boulevards). They were growing more political by the day. Homemade red flags appeared everywhere, and there were new, more daring demands shouted from the streets: "Down with the War!" and "Down with the Tsar!"

In Petrograd, as at the front, military officers found it more and more difficult to get soldiers to follow orders, and many men in uniform joined with crowds to battle the mounted Cossacks and the police. In some places, the Cossacks turned on police trying to beat back crowds, chasing policemen away with their sabres drawn. Soldiers abandoned their regiments en masse and joined the mobs in the streets. Court buildings were torched and thousands of prisoners, most of them simply criminals, were freed from jails. Radicals commandeered cars with mounted machine guns and drove through the main streets, killing policemen and Cossacks. Looting and mugging became common, and by the middle of March, nearly fifteen hundred people had been killed. Gorky, himself a revolutionary, decided what he was witnessing was not a revolution but "chaos," and he predicted that events would "probably collapse in ruin worthy of our Asiatic savagery."

"Much blood will be spilled," he predicted, "much more than has ever been spilled before."[11]

On Sunday, March 11, huge crowds desparate for leadership gathered in front of the Tauride Palace. The political leaders inside, from radical Bolsheviks to moderate Kadets, feared anarchy and fought through the chaos to organize some sort of government. Out of the turmoil, over the next thirty-six hours, three thousand delegates were elected, or elected themselves, to the Petrograd Soviet (Council) of Workers' and Soldiers' Deputies. At the head of the Soviet was an executive committee made up of about thirty representatives of a half-dozen socialist and revolutionary parties.

The three most important parties were the predominantly agrarian Socialist Revolutionaries, whose leaders included the charismatic lawyer Alexander Kerensky; the Mensheviks, who included the exiled intellectual Leon Trotsky, although Trotsky's positions sometimes veered from the Menshevik mainstream, and the Bolsheviks, the party of the firebrand Lenin.

The Mensheviks and the Bolsheviks were contentious factions of the Marxist Social Democratic Party. Although their disputes were, in part, based on personality clashes—particularly between Lenin and those who refused to accept his imperious ways—the parties also differed on several key issues.

Throughout their disputes, both had continued to adhere to some version of the Russian Marxist doctrine that an initial bourgeois revolution, similar to ones that had already occurred in the West, would be followed by a proletarian socialist revolution, but they differed markedly on the timetable, and on the nature of the initial revolution.

The Mensheviks, who tended to be more moderate in their attitudes and strategies, believed that a democratic revolution should be headed by an alliance of the liberal bourgeoise and the proletariat. The Bolsheviks, more radical and authoritarian, scorned the bourgeoise. Their position on the current (and to most of them quite unexpected) revolution would not become clarified until the middle of April (see chapter 15), when Lenin returned and called for an alliance of workers and peasants to create a "democratic dictatorship" that would be poised for the second and final revolution, ending capitalism forever.[12]

The Bolsheviks and Mensheviks also differed in their attitude toward the Great War. Like other Russian socialists, including the Socialist Revolutionaries, most of the Mensheviks came to the support of the Motherland when war broke out in 1914. Lenin, however, railed against the war and called for soldiers of all nations to turn their guns on their rulers and destroy imperialism.

The Mensheviks and their allies the Socialist Revolutionaries dominated the Soviet in its initial stages.

The main assembly in the vast Catherine Hall was as chaotic as a beer hall on payday, with mobs of soldiers, who by now made up two thirds of the delegates, standing on stools and waving rifles as they pledged their regiments would support the Soviet, while other delegates tried to shout their proposals through the roar. Nothing could be accomplished in the mass meetings. Instead, the executive committee of the Soviet, made up mainly of socialist intellectuals, most of them more moderate than the soldiers and workers in the Catherine Hall, made decisions in private caucuses in a large room in the left wing of the palace.

The Soviet and its executive committee were only half the story. In the right wing of the palace, some members of the old Duma, ignoring the Tsar's order to disband, formed something called "The Temporary Committee of Duma Members for the Restoration of Order in the Capital and the Establishment of Relations with Individuals and Institutions." As the unwieldy name suggests, these moderate delegates were mainly interested in restoring order, not seizing power. The sitting president of the Duma, Mikhail Rodzianko, was one of many who still hoped that reform was possible without unseating the Tsar.

By the evening of March 11, the roots of what became known as the "period of dual power" had been planted. On the right was the Temporary Committee of the Duma; on the left, the multiparty Petrograd Soviet. Revolutionary leader Sergei Mstislavsky later described the two very different groups as united from the first hours of the revolution "by one single characteristic which determined everything else . . . fear of the masses."

He wrote:

As recently as yesterday, it had been relatively easy to be 'representatives and leaders' of these working masses; peaceable parliamentary socialists could still utter the most bloodcurdling words 'in the name of the proletariat' without even blinking. It became a different story, however, when this theoretical proletariat suddenly appeared here, in the full power of exhausted flesh and mutinous blood. And when the truly elemental nature of this force, so capable of either creation or destruction, became tangible to even the most insensitive observer—then, almost involuntarily, the pale lips of the 'leaders' began to utter words of peace and compromise in place of yesterday's harangues. They were scared—and who could blame them.[13]

The marble hallways of the elegant neoclassical palace, built by Catherine the Great and given to her lover Prince Potemkin, were packed with unkempt soldiers from nearby regiments, ready to defend the palace from counterrevolutionary forces. Soldiers stationed in Petrograd had been joined by others just passing through on their way to the front.

The leaders of both the Duma committee and the Soviet despaired of ever getting the unruly soldiers back to their barracks. To speed their return and to alleviate their fears of punishment for their mutiny, the full Soviet, by acclamation, approved "Order Number One." The order, which would have profound implications for the future of Russia and the Great War, greatly limited the privileges of rank of officers and greatly expanded the rights of soldiers, loosening military discipline to the point of disorder.

Francis visited the Tauride Palace several times in the early days of the March Revolution, accompanied by Philip Jordan and Earl Johnston, and gave thorough daily reports to Washington. And he passed on information picked up by Jordan, who freely roamed the city, blending in with the mobs of angry, hungry people.

Francis became more and more dependent upon Jordan, and in the midst of a generally testy letter to Senator Stone, he wrote, "The colored valet or 'body servant' whom I tried to transfer to you when you succeeded me as governor and who has been living with me continuously since 1902, is living here with me—in fact, I don't know how I could get along without him. He is loyal and honest and efficient and intelligent withal."[14]

On March 12, at the end of a long, exhausting day, Francis sent a lengthy dispatch to the State Department, one that took him several hours to dictate to Johnston. Every time Francis thought the report was finished, some new horror would be reported to him, and he would update the dispatch.

He reported:

Yesterday, there were soldiers in the streets and perhaps 50 people were killed or wounded, but most of the firing was with blank cartridges. . . . About ten o'clock this morning a regiment of 1,000 to 1,200 men stationed in barracks about two blocks from the Embassy mutinied and, according to reports, killed their commanding officer because he would not join them.

At 11:30 A.M., Mr. Miles phoned me from the Austrian Embassy that some of the mutineers accompanied by many revolutionists had visited the munition factory adjoining the Austrian Embassy; they killed the officer in command there, and had ordered the men to quit work . . . many of the employees and one lieutenant had come into the Austrian Embassy, crawling through the back windows to seek protection from the angry crowd. I telephoned to the Foreign Office and was assured that the guard would be strengthened if possible. . . . That was the last communication I had with the Imperial Foreign Office.[15]

From his office that evening, Francis could see crowds of people moving along dimly lit Liteiny Prospect, the busy thoroughfare a half block away. James G. Bailey, one of his top aides, had reported earlier that he had seen four dead and five wounded men lying on Liteiny.

All afternoon, he reported, as Johnston furiously took notes, armed men walked back and forth along Furstatskaya, and at one point about one hundred men dressed in civilian clothes but carrying muskets marched down the middle of the street: "They observed no order of marching and appeared to have no commanding officer."

From 4 to 5 P.M., a long line of motor cars filled with both civilians and armed soldiers rolled down Furstatskaya. At about 6 P.M., Captain Newton A. McCully, the American naval attaché, telephoned that in his mile-long walk from the embassy to his apartment he had watched as a thousand or more cavalrymen rode toward the Neva, apparently abandoning the streets to the revolutionaries. Francis reported:

About 6:30 P.M., the telephone connection of the Embassy was severed. Between 7:30 and this writing, 9:30 P.M., many rumors have come to the Embassy through the Secretaries and other attaches. Mr. Basil Miles, director of the Second Division, took the women employees from the Austrian Embassy to the Hotel de France, where they are quartered for the night. The city seems entirely quiet but absolutely under the control of the soldiers who have mutinied and of the revolutionists. . . . One rumor [basically true] is that the Duma, after being dissolved, assembled notwithstanding the royal decree, and declared the [Tsar's] Ministry deposed and made the President of the Duma, Rodzianko, the President of the Council of Ministers. . . .

I had a telephone talk with Moscow today about noon and Consul-General [Maddin] Summers reported that everything was quiet in the city; the [proroguing] of the Duma, however, will arouse every section of the empire.

At about midnight, with the long report finally finished, Francis and Johnston decided to go for a walk and look around the neighborhood. They were less than a block from the embassy when they saw a mob in an intersection ahead and heard rifle shots. They decided to head back to the embassy. On the way back, Francis later recalled:

We came upon about fifteen soldiers carrying guns, but not in formation and evidently under the influence of liquor. As we passed one of them held his gun in very uncomfortable proximity to my secretary's stomach. We heard no further disturbances during the night. The twelve or fifteen members of the staff who lived in the Austrian Embassy, after two or three successful attempts to reach that building, which is only three blocks away, decided to spend the night with us.[16]

The next day, Tuesday, March 13, was the last day of February in the Russian calendar. By then, the revolution was a *fait a compli*, although most Russians—even those intimately involved—didn't realize it at the time amid the chaos. (This revolution, the first of two in 1917, was generally referred to by Russians as the February Revolution, and by westerners as the March Revolution.)

Gunfire awakened Francis, and he heard firing all day. Armed revolutionaries patrolled the streets, looking for officers and policemen. When they found an officer, they demanded he give them his sword, and if he refused they shot him. Police were simply shot on sight. A cook from the consulate on Nevsky Prospect was walking about two blocks from the embassy when he saw a revolutionary cut off a policeman's head with a saber. The cook ran to the embassy in hysterics.[17]

Francis spent the day in the embassy, gathering tales of slaughter from throughout the city. A Russian general and military attaché that Francis knew and liked was killed in a gun battle with soldiers who then rode their horses over his body and, reportedly, cut off his head, put it on a spike, and used it for target practice. Late that evening, Francis went for a walk. About a block from the embassy, at the intersection of Liteiny and Sergeivskaya, revolutionaries had put up a barricade and rolled three cannons behind it.

During the night, the gunfire was continuous. On Wednesday, March 14, firing continued. In his daily dispatch to the State Department, Francis reported, "Desultory parties from two to a dozen armed men wandered about without restraint of any kind. They were fired at from windows and from housetops as they passed, supposedly by policemen, and whenever this occurred the bands would fire back wildly."[18] Armed sentries appeared at intersections, and for several days men who worked at the embassy could not get through the sentry lines to their apartments, and they slept on sofas and tables in the embassy.

Most of the top ministers of the Tsarist government, including Prime Minister Sturmer, were among four thousand officials who were tracked down by revolutionaries, arrested, and thrown into the St. Peter and Paul Fortress, which had just been vacated by a previous round of political prisoners. Many officials were killed. Other aristocrats, including many top military officers—such as General/Count Nostitz, whose American wife was a friend of Francis—were captured but bought freedom by swearing allegiance to the Duma.

In a dispatch to the State Department, Francis reported, "During the day, March 14, the Duma commission, headed by its President, Rodzianko, made considerable headway toward asserting its authority and restoring order. That commission was empowered by the Duma to name a Ministry. . . . The members of that Ministry are men of education, of good records, some of them possessed of great wealth, and their selection does great credit to the judgment of the Commission."[19] Shortly after midnight, deciding that the firing in the streets had slackened, David Francis went for a reconnaissance walk in the blocks around the embassy, as he had the night before. His young secretary and friend, Earl Johnston, accompanied him.

In a message to the State Department, Francis stated:

> We met a body of armed men, two or three hundred in number, marching qui-
> etly down Sergeivskaya and apparently commanded by non-commissioned
> officers. . . . As we were returning to the Embassy we were stopped by two very
> alert soldiers and asked who we were. Our reply appeared unsatisfactory and
> they called the non-commissioned officer commanding them. Upon his
> approach, I advanced toward him and pointing to myself said in Russian:
> 'Amerikanski Pasol—American Ambassador.' Thereupon he saluted me,
> motioned Mr. Johnston and myself to proceed and directed the two soldiers to
> pass on. In the light of subsequent events I must admit that these midnight
> walks of Tuesday and Wednesday were more reckless than discreet.[20]

The next day, Thursday, March 15, under intense pressure from his top military leaders at the front, the Tsar abdicated the throne and handed the empire over to his brother, the Grand Duke Mikhail. The Tsarina, at a country home, telephoned Rodzianko, asking for protection. Later in the day, the Grand Duke Mikhail was sum-moned by leaders of what came to be called the Provisional Government and issued a manifesto accepting the authority transferred to him, on the condition that the people of Russia wanted him as their royal leader.

That evening, Francis reported, "During this day comparative quiet prevailed. The abdication of the Emperor was authoritatively announced . . . and published in circular form and distributed in the streets—no newspapers had been published since the morning of Saturday, March 10."

In the meantime, several manifestos and orders had been issued

> . . . by a committee calling itself 'Commission of Workingmen and Soldiers'
> Deputies' [the Soviet; "Workingmen" was more usually translated as
> "Workmen"]; these publications were violent in tone and tended to alarm all
> law-abiding citizens, as they advised the soldiers, of whom there were thou-
> sands walking the streets, that they were not compelled to salute their officers
> and that they could by a vote select their own commanders.
>   This commission is still professing or attempting to exercise authority
> and is in almost continuous session in the Duma building—in fact they were
> meeting in the Duma hall last evening when I went to the Duma building
> unofficially, accompanied by my secretary and [my] colored valet, Philip
> Jordan.

This visit was made incognito, but in order to gain admission to the building I was compelled to reveal my identify to the guard, and upon doing so was shown every courtesy.

The three Americans were led to the door of the Duma hall, where they saw "a large audience composed of soldiers and agitators or workingmen's delegates listening to a speaker in the Tribune who wore a soldiers uniform."[21]

By the next morning, the Provisional Government, an extremely loose and contentious alliance of the Soviet and the temporary committee of the Duma, began taking control of the city. Francis recalled:

A few parties of armed men were still walking the streets and an occasional shot was heard, but the new Ministry had assumed authority. . . . Reports came to Petrograd from Moscow, Kiev and other cities to the effect that the authority of the Provisional Government was being accepted and its representatives installed without bloodshed or opposition of any kind. . . . The commanders of two of the Russian fronts under whom were hundreds of thousands of soldiers publicly announced their allegiance to the new government and it began to appear as if the revolution was successful in every respect.[22]

The March Revolution came as a revelation to David Francis. At sixty-six, he was not too old and set in his ways to learn that something good could, after all, come out of men demonstrating and even fighting in the streets, if that was the only way to rid themselves of cruel unyielding oppression, and if good men rose to control. He was cheered when men like the liberal leader Prince Lvov were named to positions of power, and on March 16, he wrote to Maddin Summers, consul general at Moscow, that he had been delighted to hear that Summers was related by marriage to the prince: "I have been of the opinion that it would be unwise to attempt to establish a republican form of government in Russia just now, but if such men as these are put at the helm, it is possible that they may be able to steer through the breakers that beset its course."[23]

On March 15, Francis reported to the State Department:

This is undoubtedly a revolution, but it is the best managed revolution that has ever taken place, for its magnitude. . . . Upon the whole Russia is to be congratulated in my judgment on the prospect of getting through an important change in government with so little bloodshed and without material interference with the war she is waging with powerful antagonists. One cause of this revolution is a suspicion on the part of the army and of the people who call themselves true Russians, that the Empress and those surrounding her have been planning a separate peace.[24]

And late on the evening of March 17, before he went to bed, Francis dictated a cable to Lansing reporting that the Duma committee, under the leadership of Rodzianko, had tightened its control, was forming a Provisional Government in a coalition with "social democrats," and a functioning cabinet had been assembled. "City is now quiet," he wrote, "and situation apparently under control, only menace being possible socialistic demonstrations of minority socialistic group."[25]

Reluctantly following the concerted advice of his staff, Francis stopped just short of recommending recognition of the new government. Wait a while, they advised. See who emerges in control. Make no official commitment. A week from now, the Tsar could be back on top and the new leaders dead or locked away in the St. Peter and Paul Fortress.

As was his nature, Francis wanted to leap right in and embrace the revolution, which to him was the equivalent of the American one almost a century and a half before. Washington offered no help as he struggled to make up his mind to defy his staff—he had received no instructions since the revolution had begun a week before, and he wasn't even sure all the cables were getting through. The telegraph office was in chaos, and sometimes it simply would close for a day or two.

On the morning of March 18, Francis awakened after his usual six hours of sleep and lay in the dark, his mind riddled with thoughts. Angry at most of his aides, he found himself depending more and more on the few men he trusted—mainly Earl Johnston and Philip Jordan. He found himself half wishing that Dearing was still around, bad ear, pregnant wife, and all. At least the man was from Missouri.

He fumed as he thought about the actions of Counselor J. Butler Wright and his underlings: changing the wording of his dispatches to avoid offending anyone, persistently asking him to sign documents written in French, and insisting that he purchase one of those idiotic diplomatic uniforms with knee breeches—at least there was no need of that now that the Tsar had abdicated. He was sick of his underlings going around him while outwardly maintaining every appearance of deference and loyalty. They sabotaged him at every turn, he decided, and it was time for a change. If a man couldn't, by his actions and manner, impress his subordinates that he was their chief in merit as well as title, he didn't deserve the title.[26]

Fueled in part by anger and resentment, Francis decided to break away from his subordinates and their cautious State Department ways and do what he was certain was the right thing. As the sky grew light, he sat in his bedroom planning his day. Philip Jordan called him down for breakfast. He ate quickly, his mind still working, and then went to his private office and called Mikhail Rodzianko. Francis admired and respected the Duma president and found him affable and approachable. The two men had dined together and had become acquainted during the tumultuous last few months. Rodzianko was desperate for support from the West—none of Russia's allies in the war yet had been bold enough to recognize the fledgling Provisional Government. He eagerly agreed to meet Francis in private. There was no need for an interpreter; Rodzianko spoke English well.

Francis left the embassy quietly and rode by sleigh over frozen snow to Rodzianko's mansion, which was a few hundred yards east at 20 Furstatskaya. Rodzianko essentially lived at the Duma building, catching a few hours of sleep when he could, and the night before—Sunday—was the first one in a week that he had spent in his own bed. Francis looked for reassurances that the Provisional Government was in control, and the fact that Rodzianko had felt confident enough to finally leave the Duma building was good news.

Francis recalled:

> [Rodzianko] was a large man, over six feet in height and very heavy, weighing almost three hundred pounds. . . . He was an eloquent speaker and had a great voice that could reach thousands of auditors in the open air . . . his speaking qualities had made him quite prominent during the previous six days in addressing soldiers who left their barracks and marched to the Duma in bodies of a thousand or more.[27]

Rodzianko, Francis soon learned, was not as strong in principles and backbone as in oratory, and he later speculated that a stronger man might have made the Duma committee a more powerful moderating force in the anarchy to come. At their half-hour meeting, Rodzianko waffled when Francis pushed him for specifics on the new government's plans and said the man to see was Paul Miliukov, the new foreign minister and leader of the moderate Kadets, the man whose speech attacking Baron Sturmer had so electrified the Duma the previous fall.

Francis told Rodzianko he had intended to see Miliukov next. Wanting to make sure his visit appeared unofficial, Francis suggested meeting Miliukov at the foreign minister's home. Rodzianko picked up the phone, called the Foreign Office and spoke with Miliukov, and then handed the phone to Francis. Miliukov said he would not be able to leave his office and get home before 11:30 that evening. Francis did not want to wait until then, and the two men agreed to meet at Miliukov's office at the Mariinsky Palace on St. Isaac's Square. The imposing palace was now the headquarters of the Provisional Government.

Miliukov, a trim, distinguished-looking man in his fifties with white hair and a sweeping white mustache, was an intellectual who spoke excellent English and had lectured at American universities. He emphatically assured Francis that the Provisional Government was firmly established and could hold on to power and administer the government until a new legislative assembly was elected and seated. "As I looked at him and heard his prompt replies to my questions," Francis recalled, "the thought passed through my mind that here was the real leader of the Revolution; here was a deep thinker and a real Russian patriot."[28]

Miliukov told Francis confidentially that Buchanan, the British ambassador, had authority from his government to recognize the Provisional Government, but that he was waiting until the other principal Allies, the French and the Italians, gave their approval so the three could act in concert. Francis left the brief meeting, he said, "more convinced than ever that the rule of the Romanovs was ended and that those entrusted with the administration of the new Government were right-thinking, sincere and determined Russians who would prosecute the war fearlessly regardless of its cost in blood and treasure."

These "patriotic men," he was certain, "deserved the support of all foreign governments that favor law and order and especially of that government represented in Russia by me."[29] And he also saw an opportunity to steal a march on the punctilious British.

Before he left, Francis made an appointment to see Miliukov again that evening. He told the foreign minister he had an important cable to send to Washington, and Miliukov agreed to expedite the cable. There is no record that Francis told Miliukov the subject of the cable, but it's hard to imagine that Miliukov didn't have a pretty good idea, and he must have been overjoyed to help however he could.

It was about 3:30 P.M. when Francis returned to the embassy. Brushing off questions from his top aides, whom he had kept in the dark about his meetings, he took Johnston into his office, closed the door, and dictated a telegram. Johnston gave the telegram to the embassy's code clerk, who spent three hours encoding it. The clerk finished at 7 P.M. and brought the coded transcript to Francis. Deeply curious about what was going on and worried about the intentions of their hot-headed boss, top aides Basil Miles and Norman Armour followed him in. On their heels were William Sands, Miles's assistant, and Lieutenant E. Francis Riggs, military attaché. Butler Wright apparently had gone home to dinner.

Before the four men could sit down, Francis said that he was sorry that he didn't have time to meet with them just then.

"I'm going to meet the new foreign minister," he announced. "He has promised to expedite for me a cable to the Department that I prepared, and that has just been enciphered. I will read it to you."[30]

To the astonishment of the four men standing in his office, Francis read a cable that began: "The six days between last Sunday and this have witnessed the most amazing Revolution. A nation of two hundred million people who have lived under absolute monarchy for more than one thousand years and who are now engaged in the greatest war ever waged have forced their emperor to abdicate. . . ."

The cable went on to say that there was no significant opposition to the Provisional Government, which had the support of the legislature and the army. "This," it stated, "is official information obtained by my personal unofficial calls today on Rodzianko at his residence and Miliukov, minister of foreign affairs, at his office."

His listeners were astonished and aghast to hear of these visits, but Francis wasn't nearly through:

> Miliukov tells me confidentially that Buchanan has authority from his government for recognition but is waiting till Italian and French Ambassadors are likewise authorized. I request respectfully that you promptly give me authority to recognize Provisional Government as first recognition is desirable from every viewpoint. The revolution is the practical realization of that principle of government which we have championed and advocated, I mean government by consent of the governed. Our recognition will have a stupendous moral effect especially if given first. Rodzianko and Miliukov both assure me that Provisional Government will vigorously prosecute the war.

He concluded on a triumphant note:

The third of the eight principles in the manifesto issued announcing the new
Ministry and signed by the President of the Duma and all of the ministers is
'abolition [of] all class, religious and national limitations.' Answer. Francis.[31]

Francis glared up at the four aides, all momentarily speechless, and then told Philip
Jordan, who was standing nearby, to bring his coat, cap, and galoshes. Jordan already
had made certain Francis's sleigh was waiting outside.[32]

Francis walked to the door of the office, where Jordan helped him put on his heavy
fur-collared wool coat. He asked the four men if any of them would like to go with him
to see the new foreign minister. Still taken aback, they mumbled that they would if he wished.

"I don't want anyone of you to go unless he wants to," Francis replied. He turned to
Miles, who as the leader of the second division had worked most closely with the
Russians, and asked if he wanted to go.

"Yes," said Miles cautiously, "I would be very glad to go."

"Come on, then," Francis said, heading down the stairs followed by Miles and by
Jordan, who carried Francis's fur cap and galoshes. As they descended the stairs, Miles
asked, "Has Butler Wright seen that cable?"

"No, he has not," Francis said over his shoulder.

"I think he should go with you," said Miles.

Reaching the door and putting on his cap and galoshes, Francis replied that it was
almost 8 P.M., and he did not have time to wait for anyone. Miles then suddenly remembered that he had an "engagement."

The other three men came down the stairs. Francis asked if any of them would like
to go. Armour, second to Butler Wright in the hierarchy of those present, said he would.

When Francis and Armour arrived at the Mariinsky Palace, about a mile and a half
way, they discovered Miliukov was in a Council of Ministers meeting, but he had left
word with the soldier at the door to the meeting room that an important visitor was
coming and to interrupt the meeting.

Miliukov came right out, smiling in welcome. Francis handed him the encoded
telegram. Miliukov said that he would see that it was transmitted immediately and sent
a soldier for the superintendent of the telegraph office. Then Francis told Miliukov that
he had asked the State Department to authorize recognition of the Provisional
Government. Miliukov responded with a huge smile.

Back at the embassy, Francis went inside. Armour immediately headed for Butler
Wright's apartment, about two blocks away. Within a few minutes, Wright came hurry-
ing up the stairs to Francis's office, flustered. Before he could say anything, Francis said,
"I'm glad you've come," and handed him a copy of the cable.

Without reading it, Wright said, "I was at the embassy at three o'clock and asked
you if there was anything wished me to do."

"Yes," Francis said. "I remember, and you will also recall that I made the reply that I
had something on my mind in connection with the revolution which I was trying to
whip into shape and after I had accomplished it I would inform you."

"Yes, sir," Wright said, and sat down to read the cable. He then asked, his voice shaking but still deferential, why Francis had not called him to help with the cable.

"Because I wished to do it myself," Francis said. "I wished to do it expeditiously and thought that the calling in of any other man or men would cost time and result in delay. To sum up, I wished to do it myself and in this way."[33]

The next day, Wright entered this in his diary: "The Ambassador, in a very astute way, got in touch with the new Minister of Foreign Affairs yesterday and saw him twice, the result being a telegram to the Dept. giving a remarkably concise resume of the situation and advising that we recognize the Government."[34]

Less than two days later, at noon March 20, Secretary of State Robert Lansing sent a cable to Francis:

> Please call on Miliukov, Foreign Minister of the new Government, and ask for an appointment with the head of the Provisional Government to acquaint him with the desire of this Government to open relations. . . . At your interview state that the Government of the United States recognizes the new Government of Russia, and that you, as Ambassador of the Unites States, will be pleased to continue intercourse with Russia through the medium of the new Government.[35]

Francis received the telegram on the morning of Thursday, March 22, and he immediately made an appointment with Miliukov to deliver the news in person. By 11 a.m., he was in Miliukov's office. The foreign minister was delighted with the news. The men agreed that Francis and his top aides should immediately make a formal presentation of the recognition to the Council of Ministers and the new prime minister, Prince Lvov, who had been chosen as a compromise candidate between the two real powers in the ministry, Miliukov and the minister of justice, Alexander Kerensky.

Francis then met separately with Rodzianko and Mikhail Tereshchenko, the new minister of finance, and at 4:30 that afternoon, in formal dress, Francis, Counselor J. Butler Wright and four other top civilian aides, the military and naval attachés, a commercial attaché, and two special attachés rode up the Nevsky Prospect in carriages with liveried coachmen to the Mariinsky, where the recognition was formalized in a brief ceremony.

After being introduced to Prince Lvov and the other ministers, Francis read his statement:

> I have the honor as American Ambassador and as a representative of the Government of the United States accredited to Russia, to state in accordance with my instructions that the Government of the United States recognizes the new Government of Russia and that I, as Ambassador of the Unites States, will be pleased to continue intercourse with Russia through the medium of the new Government. May the cordial relations existing between the two countries continue to obtain and may they prove mutually satisfactory and beneficial.[36]

A few days later, Francis wrote to Perry and Dave telling the whole story, adding, "I took some or many chances in taking this stand and in taking it in the manner above described, but the outcome has been all that I could have anticipated and even more. The Department not only granted my request, but promptly, and in a most sweeping way." The reply came with "remarkable speed, not only for the cable but for action of the Department."

Francis went on to say, "You can imagine what effect all this has had on the staff. . . . The situation in this embassy is no different from that in London and Paris and Berlin and Vienna and elsewhere so I am told where the Ambassadors are all having their first experience in diplomatic service." He went on to reiterate his belief that career diplomats should not as a rule become ambassadors:

> If I had been out of America for 15 or 18 years of the last twenty, I would not only have lost touch with the affairs of my own country but would have been so thoroughly absorbed with the forms and habits of diplomatic usage that I would have been un-American, timid, and would have asked the Department at Washington for instructions before taking any step whatever. . . . As I am six thousand miles away from home and communication is slow and unsatisfactory, and as I am better acquainted with the local situation that anyone in Washington can be, I will take the responsibility of acting and reporting to the Department instead of asking for instructions.[37]

The last statement is a concise summary of the philosophy and circumstances that underlay many of his subsequent decisions as ambassador.

America was the first country to recognize the Provisional Government, two days ahead of the other Allies, and Francis was always very proud of that. Wright was proud too, particularly since the United States had beaten the British to the punch. In his diary for March 23, he wrote:

> The fact that our Government was the first to recognize formally this Government has created a very favorable impression here (save for certain of our diplomatic colleagues. . . .) Twice yesterday an American woman who was treated with a decided lack of courtesy when the proprietor of an establishment thought she was *English*, was greeted with honor and congratulations when she stated that she was an American.

And a few days later he noted:

> It is positively amusing to see the way in which our British diplomatic colleagues are squirming in an attempt to balance on the tight wire of reconciling their present attitude toward the new order of things, and their fabulous praise of the Czar not so long ago. It is certainly not adept diplomacy. In addition, the people are beginning to grow restive under the British control and to lean more and more toward us.[38]

Walter Page, the distinguished American ambassador to Great Britain, shared in the delight. "The whole world congratulated you on your 'scoop,' at the time of the Revolution," he wrote Francis that spring.[39]

In his Russia memoir, Francis contended that America's recognition of the Provisional Government

> . . . followed as it was within forty-eight hours by like action on the part of the British, French and Italian Governments, undoubtedly gave strong moral encouragement to the new Government which . . . was in a situation of extreme peril. It was menaced on the one side by forces desiring the restoration of the Monarchy and on the other by the threat of the Workmen's and Soldiers' Deputies [the Soviet] to take the administration of affairs into their own hands. If either of these hostile elements had succeeded, an armistice with the Central Empires would have followed immediately and consequently Germany would have sent her hundred-odd divisions from the Eastern to the Western Front almost a year sooner than they were sent and at a time when the Allied Armies were particularly ill prepared to resist them.[40]

The March Revolution, and the swift recognition and legitimizing of the Provisional Government, gave Woodrow Wilson a stronger hand as he prepared to bring United States into the war in reaction to the sinking of American merchant ships. "There can be no doubt," Francis remarked, with reason, "that there would have been serious opposition to our allying ourself with an absolute monarchy to make war."

On April 2, eleven days after the United States recognized the Russian Provisional Government, Woodrow Wilson asked a joint session of Congress for a declaration of war. Now that Russia was, or promised to be, a revolutionary republic, like the United States, Wilson could tell Congress, without undue hypocrisy, "The world must be made safe for democracy."

CHAPTER 15

A Continuing Disorderly Meeting

"It seems to me Petrograd is the stage for the most interesting game in the world's history, and . . . you are playing one of the big hands."
—*Princess Cantacuzene to David Francis, May 1917*[1]

DAVID FRANCIS, LIKE WOODROW WILSON, saw Russia in the late winter and spring of 1917 through the lens of the American summer of 1776. In an impassioned draft of a cable to Washington, written heatedly in his own hand, Francis exulted, "No people so circumstanced have ever made greater sacrifices for freedom. . . . Our form of government is their model."[2]

Princess Cantacuzene, (Julia Cantacuzene-Speransky) the American-born wife of a Russian aristocrat and colonel, found her friend Francis to be a bit naive about her adopted country. "The brave American ambassador," she wrote, "judged the spirit of our nation to be about that of the American colonists after their revolt, and the first establishment of a new republic. He counted on our people (ignorant as they are) to fall into line . . . establishing law and order and to carry on the war, 'since they must surely realize their life as a great power depended upon such action!'"

As a giddy revolutionary spring stampeded toward a summer of anarchy, Princess Cantacuzene and her friends tried to argue Francis out of his upbeat view of the revolution. "A reign of terror must come," she argued, "and then Russia would emerge strong and powerful, but with entirely new ideals and desires." Like her husband and many officers, she also thought, from the earliest days of the revolution, that the only way to "save Russia's army for the war was to have Allied troops called in."[3]

On the other hand, Matilda de Cramm—or "Mati," as Francis now called her—fervently defended the Provisional Government. By then, she had dinner at the embassy at least once a week and often stayed afterwards, sipping cognac with Francis, who some-times enlivened their chats by reading aloud confidential telegrams fresh from decoding.[4]

Counselor J. Butler Wright, the ambassador's chief advisor, also spoke optimistical-ly of the future. In late March, Wright had told Francis that "the uprising was undoubt-edly popular and practically unanimous," and estimated that 80 percent of the Russian populace supported the Provisional Government, with the remainder being Reds. He also was convinced that there was great public enthusiasm for keeping Russia in the war. In his diary for April 1, he noted that Rodzianko toured Petrograd speaking to cheering crowds whose enthusiasm "actually reached the pitch of throwing hats in the air. . . . Can this be Russia?"[5]

Having overcome a lifetime of belief that mob action in the street was not a pro-ductive means of political discourse, Francis may have gone overboard in the other direction, as converts will do. He overestimated the strength of the Provisional Government and failed to understand the degree of real power held by the Soviet, and he failed to realize that the system of shared power between the liberal Duma commit-tee and the radical Soviet was unstable and almost inevitably would blow apart. But it is also inaccurate to say, as historians and a few members of Congress later would, that Francis failed to provide Washington with any sense of what was coming. He sent out warnings, but Washington didn't listen.

On the day he formally recognized the Provisional Government in the name of the United States, Francis met with Alexander Guchkov, the new minister of war, and Guchkov informed him that powerful radicals were encouraging soldiers to revolt against the rank system in the military. Francis passed this information on to Robert Lansing, along with Guchkov's warning that "the principal menace to a vigorous prose-cution of the war was the socialistic element among the workingmen" and his concern that the leaders of the Soviet "had greater control over the soldiers than the [War] Ministry itself."[6]

Lansing said in his memoirs:

> In spite of the information which came out of Russia as to the political group-ing by classes, I do not think any of us in Washington appreciated the real menace that the bloc system was to the establishment of a republic based upon the principles of representative democracy. I conferred with several men who knew Russia and the Russian people, such men as Charles R. Crane, Professor Samuel N. Harper and Stanley Washburn [who had been a war cor-respondent in Russia for the *London Times*], and I found them optimistic as to the success of the Moderate or Constitutional Democrats and of their abili-ty to control the situation.

Indeed, Charles Crane, Wilson and Lansing's first choice for ambassador to Russia, made the new Russia sound like paradise on earth. After a visit to Russia in early May, Crane reported to his son Richard, Lansing's private secretary, there was "absolutely no class feeling and no bitterness or resentment against the old functionaries" and that "even the great landed proprietors unhesitatingly staked all their possessions on the result." He described the new government as "practically a peaceful anarchy" supported by nearly everyone, without the need for soldiers or policemen.[7]

Also, almost no one among the American officials in Russia understood the explosive nature of the concept of dual power. One exception was young North Winship, U.S. consul at Petrograd since 1914. He was in a different office from Francis—the consular staff was based in the Singer building on Nevsky Prospect—and he reported directly to Lansing. On March 20, Winship warned the secretary of state that during the revolution there had been "immediate danger of civil war in Petrograd between the Duma and the Council of Workmen's and Soldiers Deputies" and that continuing shortage of food would "cause further serious disorders capable of developing into new revolutionary movements with greater socialistic tendencies than before."[8]

Winship's cable did not arrive on Lansing's desk until April 26, but it probably would have had little effect even if Lansing had seen it weeks earlier, before the country declared war. The United States had little choice but to support and pray for the success of a government of educated liberals and socialists who wanted to keep Russia in the war, no matter how precarious their hold on power might be. And Woodrow Wilson was strongly influenced by the enthusiastic assessments of close advisors like Crane, who said the Russians would "teach the world democracy"; Harper; unofficial cabinet member Colonel Edward House; and Lansing himself.

Francis *was* guilty of falling prey to wishful thinking in his conviction that revolution was good for the Russian war effort, his reasoning being that it had rid the leadership of pro-German elements and given the common man a real reason to fight. Again, he was not alone: his top deputy Wright felt the same way and refused to believe what he called "rumors" that men were deserting en masse from the central and northern fronts.[9]

In his request for a declaration of war, Wilson praised "the great generous Russian people" for adding their "might to the forces that are fighting for freedom." He remarked that "Russia was known by those who know it best to have been always in fact democratic at heart." And a few days later, Lansing cabled Francis to tell the Russians that as the United States entered the war its people "rejoice that the great Russian people have joined the powerful democracies who are struggling against autocracy" and that Americans hoped that "a Russia inspired by these great ideals will realize more than ever the duty which it owes to humanity and the necessity for preserving internal harmony in order that as a united and patriotic nation it may overcome the autocratic power which by force and intrigue menaces the democracy which the Russian people have proclaimed."[10]

After the United States declared war, Francis received enthusiatic ovations when he spoke to large gatherings of Russians. He was elated that his barely hidden enthusiasm for America entering the war now could be public. Indeed, he was enthusiastic about the war, period, and wanted his sons to feel the same. He wrote Jane, "I am looking forward anxiously to letters from you or others as to which if any of our boys have gone in the army."

He added:

I regret being separated from you and never cease to miss you and have not since coming here but am so thoroughly occupied with official duties that I have not the time to get lonesome, and never cease to be thankful that I have been so fortunate as to perform some part in this struggle which is so historic, so unprecedented and which is destined to effect a revolution not only in government but in society itself.[11]

Like many of his countrymen, the ambassador had an inspiring vision of free Russians fighting side by side with free Americans to defeat the Central Powers. America's entering the war, he maintained, had infused the Russians with "a confident spirit and imbued them with a firm determination. They ask for no soldiers but have an army unequalled in number, unexcelled in courage."[12]

He was right about the numbers, and perhaps about the courage, but the will to fight was another matter. In early April, thousands of Russian soldiers were permitted to go home for a few days of Easter leave. Many of them never returned to the front. In the tumultuous six months following the March Revolution, as many as one million Russian soldiers deserted and wandered home, swelling the ranks of the strikers and antiwar demonstrators who crowded into the streets daily. Russia, one observer remarked, was in that period "a continuing disorderly meeting."[13]

Prince Georgi Lvov, the prime minister of the Provisional Government, a liberal aristocrat and former gentleman farmer, seemed quite Jeffersonian to Francis. Lvov described the Russian soul as "a democratic soul" and said, "I believe in the great heart of the Russian people, filled as it is with love for their neighbors, and convinced that it is the foundation of our freedom, justice and truth." The prince trusted the Russian peasants, as Jefferson had trusted the independent American farmer. But a world of difference stood between the two, as Lvov would learn. A year and a half later, not just out of power but having spent three months in a Bolshevik jail, the prince traveled through the United States looking for support for a war against the Bolsheviks and spoke in anger and despair of the "base and anarchistic instincts" of the Russian people.[14]

In the weeks following the March Revolution, the leaders of the Provisional Government worked to stabilize the nation in their new headquarters at the Mariinsky Palace, south of the great golden dome of the Cathedral of St. Isaac, while several miles across town in the Tauride Palace, the Petrograd Soviet of Soldiers and Deputies wrangled over the future of the revolution.

On April 16, a wild card shoved itself into the deck. Vladimir Ilyich Lenin, head of the Bolshevik Party, arrived from Zurich, riding with a group of compatriots in the single passenger car of a German train that was "sealed" for much of the journey—no one could get on or off, and it went through borders without customs checks. The train rolled for seven days across bleeding Europe and when Lenin arrived at the Finland Station in northern Petrograd he was greeted by a huge, cheering crowd and an armed Bolshevik escort.

The stocky, balding professional revolutionary, his fury honed by almost seventeen years of exile, set the radical crowd of soldiers and workers on fire with a speech based on ten "theses" that he had refined on the train. In what came to be known as the April Theses, Lenin called for a worldwide socialist revolution, the "democratic dictatorship of the proletariat and the poorest peasants" and an end to the "shameful imperialist slaughter" of the Great War. The next day, he repeated it all at the Tauride Palace. The Mensheviks booed and hissed as he called for further revolution to establish quickly the dictatorship of the proletariat. Now was the time to strike, he proclaimed, now when Russia had just become "the freest of all the belligerent countries in the world."[15] As the spring progressed into summer and the days grew longer and warmer, Lenin's Bolsheviks sucked in power.

David Francis may have seen the Russian situation in terms of the American Revolution, but the Russians in the middle of it, revolutionaries and aristocrats alike, tended to think more in terms of France. That was true of Princess Cantacuzene, with her expectations of a democratic nation emerging from a reign of terror; of Prince Lvov, who liked to use the phrase "liberte, egalite, fraternite" in his speeches; and of Lenin himself, who was pleased to be greeted at the Finland Station by a band that played the Marseillaise. Lenin readily accepted, or ruthlessly grabbed, the role of the chief Jacobin.

By mid-summer, at least twenty thousand armed workers and former soldiers had been called together into what became the Red Guard, most of them anarchists or Bolsheviks, all of them impatient with liberals who seemed to do little but talk. The fury of the soldiers and workers grew as the men in the Tauride Palace wrangled endlessly over the exact composition and methods of choosing of the "Constituent Assembly"— the elected legislature that had been promised in March.

Still, Francis was surprised and heartened to learn that many of the revolutionaries were friendly to America. The ambassador often was asked by groups of Russians, on the spur of the moment, to make speeches. On the last Sunday in April, a cold, dreary morning, a huge and nervously anticipated demonstration took place in the wide street in front of the embassy, and Francis interrupted his breakfast to greet the crowds marching by from the embassy's second-floor balcony.

Butler Wright jotted in his diary:

> About 20,000 people perfectly orderly, with ban[d]s and mounted officers . . .
> troops, laborers, women, trade unions and wounded from the various
> Lazerets and Hospitals filed by with red flags and inscribed banners, halting
> by divisions in order to be addressed by the Ambassador, who made five
> speeches. The enthusiasm was intense, particularly when Rodzianko (the pop-
> ular hero) was discovered in the crowd and brought on the Embassy balcony.
> The people were all pro-war to a victorious conclusion, anti-separate peace
> and pro-Republic.[16]

Philip Jordan, who had become very adept with a camera, took a photograph from a window of the embassy, and the scene is dramatic: Francis—bundled up in a fur-collared overcoat, a Russian black sheep's-wool hat high on his head—speaks to the marchers below, who pause briefly to listen to him and then continue walking. The balcony is packed with well-dressed Russians, including Rodzianko, and Francis stands straight and tall, but in the cold and gloom of late April in Petrograd, he looks every one of his sixty-six years.

A few weeks later, Francis and Wright attended a mass meeting of the Russian Baltic fleet. Catherine Breshkovskaya, the "Grandmother of the Russian Revolution" who had been in exile in Siberia for almost forty years, had returned to an ecstatic welcome. According to Wright, "The Ambassador's speech on the forceful persecution of the war brought the entire audience of sailors to their feet."[17] However, not all the crowds were so friendly. On April 22 came the famous incident involving the revolver and the mob, touched upon in the prologue.

There are several versions of the story, but only Philip Jordan and David Francis really were in a position to tell it accurately. Here's Francis's version. It's the least heroic telling of the tale.

"On Sunday evening . . . while I was entertaining some guests at the Embassy, my colored valet, Philip Jordan, came to me and said that the police official in charge of the district had called me up to warn me that an anarchist mob was gathering with the intention of attacking the Embassy." Francis later found out that the rally in front of the Kazan Cathedral, the meeting place for large political gatherings since the first revolutionary stirrings of the nineteenth century, had been called to protest the death sentence given to radical firebrand Tom Mooney for bombing deaths during a San Francisco labor protest.

Francis recalled:

> I instructed Jordan to reply to the police officer that I thanked him for his warning, but considered it was his duty rather than mine to protect the Embassy. I then told [Jordan] to load my revolver and bring it to me. In a few minutes the police official who had telephoned arrived at the Embassy with a squad of police. Revolver in hand I went to meet the police officer, and told him to station his men at the Embassy gate, with instructions to shoot anyone who tried to enter the building without my permission. I stated I would take my stand inside prepared to shoot anyone who attempted to cross the threshold.

The mob, Francis wrote, never reached the embassy, probably because Cossacks or police scattered it. He continued:

> I later learned that some of my friends had circulated a very much more sensational version of this episode [in which] the angry mob did reach the Embassy where I met them with a threat to shoot the first man who crossed

the threshold and thus violated American territory, and that thereupon the mob shrunk away. . . . I tried to correct it, but with little success. Everyone seemed to prefer the more sensational story, so I suppose I shall have to resign myself to this heroic role. It, at any rate, truthfully represents my intentions. All I lacked was the opportunity to carry them out.[18]

Sadly, Philip Jordan's letters home from his first year and a half in Petrograd have not survived, so we don't have his full account of the incident. But years later, he did comment on the story. He remarked that after Francis had told him to get the gun, "I got it, but I asked him please not to fire it. He had never fired a gun in his life, so far as I knew, and I knew if he fired at that crowd, it would probably be the end for both of us."[19]

Charles Crane later told Woodrow Wilson one of the more heroic versions of the story, with Francis, gun in hand, standing down the angry Russian bear. Wilson was delighted and repeated the story at a cabinet meeting.[20] It is unclear exactly what version Minister of Justice Alexander Kerensky heard, but on April 23, one hundred Russian school children were sent to the embassy to apologize for their countrymen's rudeness, and then Kerensky appeared in person to express the sympathy and indignation of the Provisional Government.[21]

Kerensky was a rising power, the only committed socialist among the twelve ministers of the Provisional Government and the only one who had the confidence of the Soviet. Francis first met Kerensky when, as Francis put it, "I formally recognized the Provisional Government."[22] They became quite friendly. Decades later, when Kerensky was at Stanford University's Hoover Institution, an undergraduate introduced himself as the great-grandson of David Rowland Francis. "Kerensky's face lit up, and he spoke warmly about the ambassador," Talton Francis Ray recalled.[23]

A former student radical whose dream of revolution had come true, Kerensky had more mass appeal than any other leader of the Provisional Government. Francis was sufficiently aware of Kerensky's growing importance. They met frequently, both at their respective offices and at less formal lunches and dinners, and Francis was positioned to deal personally with Kerensky, as the charismatic young socialist moved up the ladder of power in the next two and a half months.

As David Francis described him, Kerensky was:

> . . . a young man, thirty-four years of age [actually he was thirty-five], with a smooth-shaven face, not over five feet ten inches in height and of extremely nervous temperament. He had been the leader of the Socialist Revolutionists in the Duma . . . his speeches always commanded attention, because they were logical and delivered in a good voice, and they were always characterized by a vehement opposition to the Tsar's government.[24]

Meanwhile, Lenin moved to consolidate his control over the Soviet, and no one had the strength or the will to stop him. Francis wrote Perry that "an ultra-Socialist named Lenin has been doing a great deal of foolish talking and has advised his hearers to kill all people who have property and refuse to divide." And, he noted with concern, the government "has not asserted its authority with any force."[25] Within a few days of his return, Lenin and his followers "requisitioned" a mansion from Matilda Kchessinska, a famous ballerina who had been the Tsar's mistress. Every day, the Bolsheviks gave speeches and handed out pamphlets in front of the house, which was north of the city center on Petrograd Island, near the St. Peter and Paul Fortress. Supporters of the Provisional Government gathered in front of the house to argue with the Bolsheviks. These vocal liberals, it turned out, included a close friend of David Francis.

On May 2, in a letter that seems bizarre out of context, or even within it, Francis wrote to Minister of Justice Kerensky:

> This will introduce Madame Mati de Cramm, the lady who addressed the crowd in front of Lenin's house last Sunday [April 29] afternoon and preached the doctrines for which you stand and which you so ably advocate. She is a Russian by birth and thoroughly Russian in sentiment, and she is a great friend and champion of the revolution. I commend her to your favorable acquaintance. She is willing and desirous to aid you in the work in which you are engaged and asks no compensation therefor.[26]

Francis handed Madame de Cramm a personal check for five thousand rubles (by then, worth at the most one thousand dollars) to give Kerensky to use for Russian relief programs.[27] We have no record of how the meeting between Madame de Cramm and Kerensky went, if it occurred. But that would not be the last time she would ask Francis to help her meet with Kerensky. (See chapter 16.)

Despite his friendship with Matilda de Cramm, David Francis very much missed his wife. In a letter to her, he complained about receiving so few letters from home and wrote:

> You say in one [letter] that you wish you were here, which is the first expression of that kind you have made since I left home. I have often wondered whether you miss me as much as I do you. It is true I am very busy and haven't time to get lonesome, and it is also true that I have never had you here and consequently do not expect you at the table or at any place or upon any occasion. It is different there however. We have lived together forty years and have never been separated for more than two months. If you have missed me however, I have never known it from anything you have written.[28]

IN EARLY MAY, Foreign Minister Miliukov publicly reaffirmed that Russia would remain loyal to the Allies and would not make a separate peace. Francis was delighted, but large peace demonstrations broke out in the streets. Francis grew increasingly concerned as the rallies grew larger and more violent, sometimes blocking the Nevsky Prospect for hours and erupting into small riots between competing radical groups. Meanwhile, reports of violence and disintegration of government control came in from throughout Russia. Consul General Maddin Summers, with his aristocratic Russian in-laws, wrote Francis from Moscow:

While, under your guidance, we are duty bound to do everything possible to encourage a free government here, yet there is a limit to everything, and this is being reached rapidly. The soldiers are plunging the country headlong into anarchy and civil war, and the army as a fighting force no longer exists. This is the unanimous opinion of everyone who returns from the front. The situation in the provinces is still worse. Estates are being sacked and the owners beaten and murdered. Drunkenness is rampant and the soldiers and plundering everywhere. . . . In every province there are riots and murders daily. . . . The time has come when strong representations will have to be made to avoid one of the bloodiest situations in history.[29]

In the capital, demonstrations against the government grew larger and more ferocious. Alarmed, Francis met on May 3 with Miliukov and Minister of War Guchkov and told them bluntly that he had risked a great deal in asking for recognition of the Provisional Government, and he hoped his faith in them would not be betrayed. He told the Russian leaders that he felt "a considerable official and personal responsibility concerning a stable Government in Russia" and "if more satisfactory evidence were not given of such government, I should feel compelled to advise my Government not to extend the aid which I had been continually recommending."[30]

That evening, Miliukov spoke to large crowds in front of both the Mariinsky Palace and the Tauride Palace and won their cheers and applause with strong, patriotic calls for order. In a subsequent report to Lansing, Francis said, with some pride, "How much influence my talk with the Ministers had upon their assuming for the first time a rather independent position I cannot say but the report has gained circulation and credence that the stand taken by the [Foreign] Ministry was inspired if not demanded by the American Ambassador's." At demonstrations over the next few days, he noted, "Opponents of the anarchistic and extremely socialistic expressions of Lenin gained courage to such an extent that whenever a Lenin banner appeared on the streets it was captured and torn to shreds."[31]

In regular private meetings with Kerensky and other officials, and in his frequent public speeches, Francis urged the Russians to stay the course. That spring, Counselor Butler Wright wrote in his diary, "The constant, wearing calls upon this Embassy are almost more than anyone less Herculean in mental and physical force than the Ambassador can stand. I wonder more and more at the way in which he thrives under the fearful strain and keeps the threads of all the complex questions clear in his mind." Butler Wright laid out the details of the daily work of the embassy: "Commissions, visitors, commerce, publicity, railroads, extraditions, land values, military preparations, naval statistics, finance, passports, prisoner relief, moving picture propaganda, capacity of printing presses, house furnishing and repairing, lost passports, censorship, mail inspection, wharf and port capacity and dues, relief ships, food supply, strikes, coal mining operations, couriers for mails, ocean cables, etc. etc. etc."[32]

Still, Francis had time to fret about business matters back home. He wrote Perry that he kept up with stocks through the *London Times,* which arrived several weeks late,

244   Standing on a VolcanoStanding on a Volcano

and had noted that stocks and grain prices were depressed: "It requires eternal vigilance even to execute orders when such abnormal prices prevail. I hope you boys have followed my advice in regard to keeping out of the market at times as continuous trading is sure to result in loss."[33]

O N MAY 8, Petrograd Consul North Winship warned Robert Lansing, "The power which the Temporary Government now administers is fictitious to a certain extent. . . . If this power is not handled with the greatest versatility and tact it will pass to the leaders of the Council of Workmen's and Soldiers Deputies who openly profess and personify the expectations of the majority of the lower classes." Insistence on full Russian participation in the war was dangerous, Winship contended, because it led to tremendous resentment at "being forced to continue a distasteful and irksome war" and could backfire on the Allies.[34]

Francis came to realize the political situation was tenuous, and sometimes his natural optimism was overcome by a darker vision. In mid-May he remarked:

> There is a feeling of uneasiness generally prevalent because the Provisional Government, composed of eleven able men . . . is not looked upon as sufficiently strong or stable. This view is not attributable to any want of confidence in the men composing the government but is due to the existence of what is called a Workmen's and Soldiers Deputies Committee, which assumes to visae [review] and at times to veto the decrees of the Provisional Government. A test of the powers of these forces must be made very soon. . . . I trust it will not result in bloodshed but such an outcome would not surprise me.[35]

As the power of the radicals grew, along with public opposition to the war, the Provisional Government made a desperate attempt to placate the left. More representatives of the Bolshevik-infused Petrograd Soviet were invited to join the Provisional Government, resulting in the formation of what became known as the Coalition Provisional Government. On hearing this, Francis remarked approvingly that "the surest way of making a man conservative is to give him administrative duties."[36]

In the Coalition, Kerensky replaced Guchkov as minister of war, probably in hopes that the popular socialist could sell an unpopular war with the sheer force of his eloquence and personality. He called for a new offensive and toured the front to raise morale. His speeches were received enthusiastically but had no real effect. By then, the Russian army had little discipline and no will to kill anyone but its own officers.

Mikhail Tereshchenko, formerly minister of finance, replaced Miliukov as foreign minister. Francis liked and approved of the new foreign minister, describing him as "a young man who inherited a fortune but has improved his time and opportunity."[37] Francis met daily with Tereshchenko, whose English was excellent, and the two became friends. The new foreign minister publicly reaffirmed Russia's commitment to the Allies and the war. Other names and faces in the government changed in the spring and early summer of 1917 as the Provisional Government futilely struggled to pacify the radicals.

Kerensky was the dominant figure in the new government, although he was not actually named prime minister until July, and Francis clung to their close relationship.

In late May, Samuel Harper returned to Petrograd and resumed advising Francis. With his excellent Russian, he acted as interpreter on Francis's private talks with Kerensky and other leaders of the Provisional Government and in his public speeches. On May 19, a mass rally was held at the Ciniselli Circus, a huge auditorium on the Fontanka Canal, a few blocks north of the Nevsky Prospect, to stir up support for the war. Francis spoke, as did Bernard Pares, British liaison official and writer who had spent many years in Russia. Francis, Pares recalled, "spoke through an interpreter—but very loud, with a gap between each word: 'I have telegraphed to my Government that Russia will not desert the Allies—tell 'em that. . . . My Government has replied, putting one hundred thousand dollars . . . at the disposal of the Russian wounded—tell 'em that.'"[38]

The United States, in line with Francis's recommendations, had by then earmarked at least $100 million for Russia, with one condition—the money had to be spent on American products. With Francis's encouragement, the line of credit for the Provisional Government in the next few months was raised to $325 million, as the Central Powers won battle after battle in France and Belgium. The United States felt it was crucial to prop Russia up, hoping to keep as many enemy troops as possible tied up on the Eastern Front.

Francis's impassioned speeches were making him a hero. In a front-page story, a Russia correspondent for the *New York Times* enthused, "Since the revolution our Ambassador Francis has come into the highest usefulness. Autocracy somewhat cramped the style of this old-fashioned Missouri Democrat, but under the new regime he has become a real power. His oratory is a rare treat to the Petrograd population, who gather in great numbers to listen to him and though not understanding his words, greatly enjoy his earnest delivery."[39] And Russia veteran Frederick Corse of New York Life remarked, "The Governor, under present democratic conditions, finds himself very much at home. His counsel is widely sought and I must say he has surprised us all by the apparent grasp which he has on the movement and influence which he has achieved in government spheres. We pronounce him the right man in the right place."[40]

Francis's diplomatic skills and political acumen further were tested with the arrival, on June 12 and 13, of two groups of important American citizens, both bent on assessing the situation in Russia and helping the Provisional Government cope with disorder. They were, in order of arrival, the Stevens Railway Mission, whose formation Francis had encouraged, and the Root Mission, of which he was quite wary. Both groups, he remarked to Jane shortly after their arrival, "will be on my hands now for I don't know how long and they will largely increase my work as well as my anxiety and will not lessen my responsibility in the slightest degree."[41]

The United States government had sent the Stevens Railway Commission to help improve the flow of Russian rail transportation, both for the war and for the commercial cornucopia Francis believed would flow once peace came. The commission was assigned to pay particular attention to the Trans-Siberian Railway. Because of the increased German submarine activity in the North Atlantic, the safest way to get to Petrograd was to sail from the American West Coast to Vladivostok and then take the so-called "Siberian Express" across all of Russia.

The train, which ran once a week, took ten days to two weeks to make the five thousand-mile journey from Vladivostok to Petrograd, swaying and bouncing over poorly maintained tracks, with the frequent, often inexplicable stops typical of Russian rail travel. Almost from the beginning of his tenure, Francis had been concerned about the Trans-Siberian Railway, and America's entry into the war had lent an urgency to his requests to the government for help with the railroads as a crucial military resource. He welcomed the commission and its head, John Stevens, the engineer he had met and been impressed by on his visit to Panama a decade earlier.

The five-man Stevens Commission ultimately would prove of value in helping the Russians, but initially it got underfoot at the embassy and accomplished nothing in its meetings with government leaders. In Petrograd, in the words of Butler Wright, the commission was "having a typically 'Russian' time of it—finding that these people are long on talk and very short on practical ideas."[42]

Woodrow Wilson sent the Root Mission to spread goodwill among the Russians, to water the extremely shallow roots of Russian democracy, and to see how America and Russia could cooperate on waging the war. Elihu Root, a former Republican secretary of state, headed the bipartisan commission. Wilson and Root thought the group should appeal to the revolutionary Russians by including a couple of members of the American left.

They chose James Duncan, elderly vice president of the American Federation of Labor, and a mildly socialist writer named Charles Edward Russell, suggesting how little the Wilson Administration understood the truly radical nature of the Russian political situation. Russian socialists considered both men to be right-wingers. Others members included John R. Mott of the Young Men's Christian Association and Cyrus McCormick of International Harvester. Charles Crane, already in Petrograd, joined the group when it arrived.

The nine-man Root Mission stayed for about a month. Francis, short of staff and hours in the day, did his best to help them, and after Root had returned to the United States, he thanked Francis for being "so kind to the wandering amateur diplomatists." The seventy-three-year-old Root reported to Wilson that the solidity of the Provisional Government had encouraged him and opined that the spine of the Russian army was stiffening.[43]

The Root Mission left behind Colonel William V. Judson, who assumed the posts of military attaché and chief of the American military mission, and soon was promoted to general. As attaché, he served under Francis. As mission chief, he reported directly to Washington. This ambiguous situation further confused the prickly tangle of crisscrossing authority.

The third important delegation sent that summer was the American Red Cross Commission, which showed up in early August and will be discussed in detail in the next chapter.

"Soviets" modeled after the one in Petrograd sprang up all over the country that spring. On June 16, the first All-Russian Congress of Soviets convened in Petrograd. The Socialist Revolutionary Party claimed the allegiance of the largest bloc of delegates, followed by the parties that had been formed from the division of the Social Democrats: the Mensheviks, whose increasingly radical leader, Leon Trotsky, had come back to Russia a month earlier, and Lenin's Bolsheviks.

The presence in Petrograd of radicals from throughout Russia only added to the city's chaos. On June 27, novelist-revolutionary Maxim Gorky wrote, "This is no longer a capital, it is a cesspit. No one works, the streets are filthy, there are piles of stinking rubbish in the courtyards. . . . There is a growing idleness and cowardice in the people, and all those base and criminal instincts which I have fought all my life . . . are now destroying Russia." About the same time, Gorky also said, "I think the crazy politics of Lenin will soon lead us to a civil war."[44]

By then, Kerensky was at the front, trying to stir up a new offensive on the Eastern Front. He had little success. The Germans kept advancing toward Petrograd, and the "democratization" of the army had left it impotent. And many soldiers wanted nothing to do with the Provisional Government.

On the evening of July 17, a block from the American Embassy, Cossacks loyal to the Provisional Government battled radical soldiers in the street. Philip Jordan described the clash to Jane Francis:

> The Cossacks as you know always fight on horse back. they made a charge on the Soldiers who was in the middle of the street with machine guns and cannons. My oh my what a Slaughter. After 30 minutes of fighting [I] counted in half a block 28 dead horses. when the Cossacks made their charge the Soldiers began to pump the machine Guns and you could See men and horses falling on all sides. after the dead was carried away and it was quiet again we all went to bed. well at 5 minutes to twelve the Guns and Cannons began to roar again. I jumped out of bed and rushed to the Winter Palace bridge [more than two miles away] and oh such a Sight. the Bolsheviks had started to come on this Side of the town and the Soldiers was waiting for them at the foot of the Bridge. Just as they were about on the middle of the Bridge the Soldiers opened fire with machine Guns and cannons. It was one grand Sight. The sky was full of the prettiest fire works you Ever saw. . . . I was laying flat behind the man that was pumping the machine gun.[45]

Jordan described in his vivid prose a Bolshevik and Anarchist-inspired insurrection that came to be called the July Days.

Princess Cantacuzene recalled:

I had been dining [one mid-July] evening at the American Embassy. Two or three days after the uprising, it was, and as the town was only superficially quiet, and the night splendid and warm, Mr. Francis proposed when we left, about ten o'clock, to drive another guest and myself home; affording us the protection of his carriage, with its American flag. It was still twilight, with a splendid after-glow fading on the horizon, and the charm of the soft July sky caused the Ambassador to say as we settled into our seats: "It's early yet, and we have all been shut up for so long. I haven't left my desk today. Shall we go round by the Quai, and admire the river on the way to your hotel, Princess? . . ."

I naturally gave an affirmative reply and we all drew a deep breath of pleasure as we turned out on to the Quai, the most beautiful street I know, with its great palaces on one side and the swift, vast expanse of river on the other. Soon we were passing the Summer Garden, and the British Embassy stood up in front of us, while the long elegant curves of Trinity [or Troitsky] Bridge, clear against the sky, spanned the river, and joined the Field of Mars [a parade ground and park] to the Fortress of St. Peter and Paul.

"It doesn't seem possible we have been so agitated these last days," I said.

"No," said Mr. Francis, "certainly this time the provisional government has held its own."

"See, there are the fortresses of the government and of Lenine [a common English transliteration of Lenin] standing opposite one another, and at peace," I said; and then we both noticed a light playing on them.

"What do you suppose that light means? A signal?" said our host. "Or perhaps one of the naval searchlights being tried," I answered. Suddenly, the silence across the river was broken, a shot was fired, and then an avalanche of them rang out, and the whole space between Peter and Paul and the Kchessinska Palace was alive with soldiers and with guns, flashing and banging—bedlam let loose again!

"Hello, that looks serious," said Mr. Francis.

The coachman, without asking for orders, whirled his plunging horses completely round, and started back in the direction whence we had come.

When she arrived at her hotel, the princess discovered that General A. A. Polovotsov, head of the Petrograd Military District, had made a raid on the palace the Bolsheviks had commandeered and found gold he identified as coming from Germany. In the aftermath of the raid, he ordered the jailing of hundreds of Bolsheviks.[46] Leon Trotsky, who by then had divined the future and switched from the Mensheviks to the Bolsheviks, was arrested as one of the ringleaders of the July uprising and jailed for two months. Lenin slipped out of sight and soon fled across the border into Finland. He would be back.

After three days of bloody street fighting, the revolutionary soldiers and sailors were stopped, but the Provisional Government once again was torn apart. Prince Lvov resigned as prime minister and named as his successor Kerensky, who was thought to be the only man with the popular support to prevent the Petrograd Soviet and the increasingly powerful Bolsheviks from simply taking over.

At the time, Francis complained to Tereshchenko, the foreign minister, that the Provisional Government had not responded to the attempted coup forcefully enough. Later, with the benefit of considerable hindsight, he wrote:

> Had the Provisional Government at this time arraigned Lenin and Trotsky
> and the other Bolshevik leaders, tried them for treason and executed them,
> Russia probably would not have been compelled to go through another revolu-
> tion, would have been spared the reign of terror, and the loss from famine and
> murder of millions of her sons and daughters. . . . I doubt whether two more
> as strong characters as Lenin and Trotsky could have been found among the
> Bolsheviks of the entire world.[47]

Francis continued to fret about the dearth of instructions from Washington and focused on Woodrow Wilson's failure to respond to his letter of resignation. As the months went by, he wrote both Polk and Lansing, wondering if the resignation had been accepted, and on July 13 he wrote Polk again, saying, "I have not had a word concerning my resignation which was tendered by cable February 25th . . . suppose the policy of the Department and of the Administration is to express disapproval only."[48]

On Sunday, July 22, Francis sat in the dining room of the embassy before dinner, lis-tening to new records from Jane on the Victrola that Jane had sent him. Jordan was in charge of changing records. Occasionally, gunfire rang in the distance.

With Earl Johnston taking down his words, Francis dictated a long letter to Jane. He told her that at least 470 people had been killed in riots on the night of July 17 and the thousands of soldiers returning from the front magnified the difficulty of maintaining order. "There are no police in Petrograd now," he said, "but the streets are patrolled by what is called militiamen, who wear citizens' clothes, carry guns, and have on their left arms white bands with red letters."[49] These men—by July, twenty thousand of them were in Petrograd alone—were the Red Guards, and their allegiances were primarily with the Bolsheviks. (Also a strong force within the July insurrection were several thousand mili-tantly left-wing sailors from the Kronstadt Naval Base near Petrograd.)

Francis's leisurely dictation was interrupted by the foreign minister, Tereshchenko, who stayed for almost an hour and discussed the current political situation. Then Charles Crane came by, and the two men had a late supper.

Afterward, puffing on one of his last cigars of the day, Francis resumed dictating. He thanked Jane for the records and reflected on his earlier recommendation that she close the house on Maryland Avenue and take an apartment when she returned to St. Louis from Rye Beach in the fall.[50] Assuming she would do as he suggested (she did), he said he hoped "there will be room enough for Phil and myself if we should return . . . but don't make any provisions for us until you hear we are coming. Phil, who heard this [dicta-tion], said that we are having so many revolutions here now that it is too interesting for us to think of leaving."

A few weeks later, Earl Johnston reported to Perry:

The Governor's health is apparently as good as usual, though he doesn't get enough exercise by any means. . . . He went to Finland [to the beach] for a couple of days two weeks ago and I noticed much improvement, as he had been under great mental strain for a number of days prior thereto. He does three times as much work as any two of the Secretaries and from all reports that come here he is surely making his record felt in the states. I have heard him mentioned several times as a possible 'dark horse' nominee of the party in 1920 for president.[51]

Colonel Judson went along on the trip to the Finnish seaside villa of Count and Countess Nostitz, where the two men mingled with wealthy Russians and expatriates. "The Ambassador is a good old sport," Judson jotted in his diary.[52]

Toward the end of July, Francis, Judson, and Jordan attended a mass funeral at St. Isaac's Cathedral for twenty Cossacks killed in the July Days. The enormous funeral itself spilled out onto the large square in front of the cathedral in the heart of the city. Many mourners were quite jittery for fear that terrorists would hurl bombs into the crowd.

In a letter home, Philip Jordan wrote, "The funeral was the largest that was ever in Russia and I believe the largest in the world. the press Said Over one million people. . . . Miss Annie think of such a large crowd and all frightened half to death. every time the man would strike his base drum the crowd would Shiver."[53]

CHAPTER 16

The Second Revolution

O N August 7, the American Red Cross Commission invaded Petrograd. Its main force was about forty men in the uniforms of colonels, majors, captains, and lieutenants. All had American military commissions.

"We dubbed the outfit the 'Haytian Army' because there were no privates," remarked George Gibbs, an engineer with the Stevens Railway Commission. "They have come to fill no clearly defined mission, as far as I can find out. In fact Gov. Francis told me some time ago that he had urged that they not be allowed to come, as there were already too many missions from the various allies in Russia. Apparently, this Commission imagined there was an urgent call for doctors and nurses in Russia; as a matter of fact there is at present a surplus of medical talent."[1]

Although Chicago physician Dr. Franklin Billings was the titular head of the group, the strong man was copper magnate, stock promoter, and financier William Boyce Thompson, who thought he should play a major role in world affairs and was convinced, on evidence that appears vague today, that Woodrow Wilson agreed with him. Thompson's biographer, Herman Hagedorn, who knew him well, has described his state of mind:

> Thompson no longer found promotions and stock operations stimulating enough for his imagination. The world was the chess board over which he dreamed. . . . The overthrow of the Tsar startled and thrilled him. . . . If Russia could be held firm, Germany would be defeated. . . . It was of the highest importance to have a forceful mind on guard in Petrograd in behalf of the United States. The American ambassador's, it happened, was not that. The amiable and aging Missourian, David R. Francis . . . was filled with good intentions but no one looked to him for vision or initiative. Since it appeared impractical to supplant him, the only alternative was to send an . . . unofficial envoy.

Hagedorn remarked, "How much of all this was reduced to definite instructions and how much remained a matter of hints and hopes; how much the Red Cross, the President or the State Department were involved or only certain individuals who happened to be both Thompson's friends and executives of the Red Cross, no document revealed then or thereafter." In any event, it was clear to Thompson, if to no one else, that he was in the Russian capital as a second ambassador, with the main task of propping up the Provisional Government and energizing its military forces.[2]

Thompson, an arrogant Taft-sized man, was close to the J. P. Morgan Co., which did not help to endear him to Francis. Still, the ambassador held a small embassy luncheon for Thompson and Dr. Billings, inviting Kerensky. To make them feel welcome, Philip Jordan baked biscuits and corn bread. Harper was there to translate. Thompson startled Francis, and probably Kerensky as well, by offering to personally loan the Provisional Government one hundred thousand dollars.[3] A few days later, after Kerensky arranged for him to meet the heroic Madame Breshkovskaya, Thompson drew $1 million from his account with J. P. Morgan and gave it to the Little Mother of the Revolution and her allies in the pro-Kerensky Socialist Revolutionary Party.[4]

Thompson and his principal aide, Colonel Raymond Robins, a founder of the American Progressive (or Bull Moose) Party, intentionally kept Francis in the dark about much of their efforts to bolster the Provisional Government and keep it in the war. "There had been leakage from the embassy," explained Thompson's biographer. "The aging and not too wide awake ambassador had a French teacher, a woman of charm and culture, in whose discretion he had a childlike trust. . . . The work, [Thompson] told the Ambassador, might develop into something which it might be better for him to know nothing of. The Ambassador agreed and told him to go ahead."[5] This was not the first or last time that David Francis would give his private approval to unofficial contacts and assistance that could embarrass the United States if officially linked to its embassy. Sometimes using others to enter realms he needed to stay clear of was misunderstood as weakness or indifference.

In the days leading up to Thompson's arrival, the Provisional Government had barely survived another crisis. Kerensky, in despair at not being able to control events, had resigned as prime minister. After a long night of entreaties from his colleagues, he finally agreed to rescind his resignation and restructure the government. On the day Thompson arrived, Kerensky formed the so-called Second Coalition Provisional Government, with a cabinet dominated by socialists. David Francis and Matilda de Cramm may have been partly responsible for Kerensky reconsidering his resignation and forming a new government.

Madame de Cramm had become friends with Mrs. Emmeline Pankhurst, a British suffragist who had spent most of the summer in Russia, trying to convince influential Russian liberals to rebuff the Bolsheviks and stay in the war. Mrs. Pankhurst tried to get an audience with Kerensky. British Ambassador Buchanan had refused to help. Many British political leaders considered the feminist a dangerous nuisance. Madame de Cramm asked Francis to intercede.

Francis heard Mrs. Pankhurst speak and discovered, apparently to his surprise, that her remarks "were extremely sensible." But he said he could not help her because she was not an American citizen. However, as Francis soon discovered, and reported to his oldest son, "Mrs. Pankhurst and another bright energetic woman can accomplish almost anything they take in hand."[6]

By then, the Provisional Government had moved its headquarters to the grand neo-baroque Winter Palace, whence Tsars once had reigned. On August 1, Francis and Harper were descending the steps of the Winter Palace after meeting with Kerensky when Francis heard someone call his name. It was Matilda de Cramm, who had been waiting out front, trying to get an appointment with Kerensky. Francis and Harper were talking to her when a Russian officer walked down the stairs. She spoke briefly with him and then accepted Francis's offer of a ride home in his carriage.

Much to Francis's surprise, Madame de Cramm said the young officer had agreed to ask Kerensky to meet de Cramm and Pankhurst soon—at the American Embassy. Francis, taken aback, asked why the American Embassy had been chosen, not the British, and Madame de Cramm said she thought Kerensky would be more likely to accept a meeting there.

Francis figured nothing would come of the request. To his surprise, he soon got a call saying that Kerensky would "receive" the two women the next day at the Winter Palace. The turmoil in the cabinet delayed the meeting by a day, but on the afternoon of August 3, Madame de Cramm came to the embassy in a state of high excitement. She told Francis that Kerensky was "nervous, determined, and angry," and that she feared he would resign. She urged Francis to contact Paul Miliukov immediately and convince him to stop Kerensky from resigning.

Miliukov, no longer foreign minister but still associated with the Provisional Government, was about to leave for political meetings in Moscow when Francis called. At Francis's request, Miliukov came by the embassy and Francis repeated what he had heard, wondering rhetorically who possibly could replace Kerensky. Miliukov replied that Kerensky was the only man who could save Russia from the Bolsheviks. In that case, Francis said, it was imperative that Miliukov postpone his Moscow trip and attend a meeting of top government ministers at the Winter Palace that night. Francis surely would have mentioned, as he had before, that American support for the Provisional Government—political and financial—depended in part on faith in the men who led it.

Miliukov stayed in Petrograd. That evening, Kerensky resigned and the Council of Ministers stayed up all night debating the issue. Under the influence of Miliukov, they finally agreed to ask Kerensky to form a new government. He wearily accepted and began reshuffling the deck of the Provisional Government. His most important step was to appoint General Lavr Kornilov, a tough Cossack, as commander in chief of the army. Kornilov vowed to restore military discipline, and Francis immediately asked the United States to loan Russia an additional $60 million.[7]

By then, however, it probably didn't make any difference who was at the head of the Provisional Government or how much money the United States pumped into it.

Francis staked everything on Kerensky, although privately he worried about his imperial tendencies. To a friend, Charles Moser, the American consul in Harbin, China, Francis remarked, "Kerensky is undoubtedly the most influential man in Russia; some of his own people say he has it in mind to be a second Napoleon, consequently effort is being made to undermine him . . . if his head is not turned by the adulation he is receiving he is indeed a wonderful man. He is now living in the Winter Palace and sleeping in the bed of [Tsar] Alexander the Third, which is not good politically to say the least."[8]

On August 13, the Kerensky government invited the Allied ambassadors as honored guests to a large political rally at the Narodni Dom ("People's House"), a theater usually devoted to popular entertainment. Francis was greeted warmly by Kerensky and Miliukov. Miliukov made what Francis was told—presumably by Harper—was an eloquent speech, and when he praised America's entry into the war, he pointed to Francis seated in the loge. The audience rose to its feet and gave the American ambassador a long standing ovation.

After the shakeup in the military, General Kornilov tried to make good on his promise to restore discipline. He ordered that one hundred deserters be shot and their bodies propped up by a roadside bearing placards that read, "I was shot because I ran away from the enemy and was a traitor to Russia." On August 16, Kornilov made a daylong political visit to Petrograd. Francis and his military attaché, Judson—who had just received a promotion to Brigadier General—caught up with him that evening at the Tsarskoe Selo railway station, where Kornilov held court in a special car before speeding away to the front. Francis and Judson were very favorably impressed with the proud, sinewy, erect-postured Cossack: "He appears a soldier without apparently making any effort to do so," Francis noted.[9]

Francis, Judson, and others at the embassy, including Samuel Harper, soon came to believe that the government would be better off with Kornilov in charge. However, as the gulf grew between the malleable liberal intellectual Kerensky and the tough, uncompromising soldier Kornilov, Francis argued persuasively within the inner circles of the embassy that the representatives of the United States should remain neutral, despite his growing concerns about the power of the Bolsheviks.

Kornilov's tough policies, although they had little ultimate effect on the Russian war effort, endeared him to the Russian right wing, and as he became more popular and Kerensky's cult faded, his supporters urged him to lead troops into the capital and take over the government. Kornilov resisted these entreaties. But in Petrograd's turbulent atmosphere of political intrigue and widespread paranoia, Kerensky became convinced Kornilov was planning a coup de etat. He fired him as supreme commander and took the post himself.

Kornilov angrily decided he needed to seize control of the government to save Russia from anarchy. He ordered a march on Petrograd. Kerensky countered by entering into a coalition with the Soviet and the Bolsheviks, permitting them to issue military weapons to thousands of Red Guards, leftist workers, and army deserters to defend the capital.

On September 12, shortly after Kerensky had armed what inevitably became his opposition, Philip Jordan and Francis went to the Nikolai railway station on the Nevsky Prospect to see off Dr. Frank Billings of the Red Cross Commission. The station faced on a square dominated by a hulking statue of grim-faced Tsar Alexander III astride a broad-shouldered horse, the capital's most potent symbol of Tsarist repression. Pouring out of the station and across the cobbled square, Jordan wrote, came "thousands and thousands of soldiers [who] had Just arrived from the front. the report was out that Genl Kornilov was comeing to take charge of the Government. they marched out to the end of the Nevsky whare they began to dig trenches. Just think of diging trenches in the heart of the city."[10]

In the face of such resolute partisan force, and lack of popular support, Kornilov's offensive collapsed. To further appease the left, Kerensky ordered that leading Bolsheviks be released from jail, including Leon Trotsky. Lenin, from across the border in Finland, was crying for the violent overthrow of the Provisional Government, and now his supporters in Petrograd were on the loose with thousands of guns at their command. As Francis observed years later, Kerensky had "found himself in the predicament where he had to arm one group of virtual enemies of his Government in order to prevent its overthrow by another and more immediately threatening hostile group."[11]

However, in September and October 1917, despite a growing feeling among his aides that the Provisional Government would not make it through the fast-approaching winter, Francis remained doggedly optimistic. In one letter, he opined that the disintegration of the Kornilov Revolt had resulted in "strengthening Kerensky," although he made it clear that Kerensky had to get control of the army away from the Soviet or he was doomed.[12]

Meanwhile, in Washington, Lansing had been receiving reports from other diplomats and returning visitors that were highly skeptical of Kerensky's ability to hold on. On September 28, he cabled Francis and asked his reaction to an assessment by the American minister to Stockholm that the Provisional Government was doomed. Francis replied by cable on October 4 that there were serious difficulties, exacerbated by the release of Trotsky and continuing German intrigue, but that he remained convinced that Russia would "survive [the] ordeal and be safe for democracy if we and other Allies are patient and helpful."[13]

Lansing decided that the United States had little choice in the matter. After the failure of Kornilov, he felt, "there was no practical course for this government to take other than with loans, experts and publicity to assist Premier Kerensky in his endeavors to keep control and bring order out of disorder."[14]

As usual, Francis received no specific instructions from the State Department. He worried that he had misled Washington about the prospects of the Provisional Government. He wrote a friend:

I am feeling tonight as if some expressions I have made to the government within the past few days might possibly result in my being looked upon as persona non grata. Being over six thousand miles away from Washington with very irregular cable connection and most unreliable and uncertain mail communications I am often compelled to act solely upon my own judgment. I always cable to the Government what I have done but sometimes act without instructions.

Still, after a long talk with the foreign minister, Tereshchenko, Francis decidedly had "not yet lost all hope for Russia, as the Provisional Government can still save the situation if it takes prompt and decisive steps to restore the discipline of the army and navy."[15] It didn't and doubtless couldn't.

General Judson was more pessimistic. As an experienced career military man, he understood more than Francis the need for a thoroughly disciplined army in wartime. On August 7, Judson cabled Washington, "It is at least an even chance that coming events may take Russia out of the war within the next few months. Our larger war plans should be made accordingly." Judson repeatedly pushed the issue of the disintegrating Russian army with Francis. Francis replied, "Why, Judson, I can understand how soldiers feel on this subject, but an old politician like me understands human nature much better, and I can assure you that the Russian army will never quit but will fight like lions."[16]

Yet, the two Americans had an amiable relationship, taking weekend trips, enjoying bridge and idle chat on Saturday afternoons, meeting for a cigar and a glass of bourbon in the evenings. Francis was used to the give and take of politics, in which men of good will could disagree, sometimes effusively, and yet remain friends, and some of Francis's other top aides and colleagues might have done well to be as open and honest with him as Judson was.

It helped that the two men agreed on the overriding need to prevent Russia from leaving the war. Francis, in a late-September letter that once again urged that at least one of his sons enlist, wrote, "If Russia should conclude a separate peace (which God forbid!) or if the Russian army should refuse to fight and Russia be overrun by German and Austrian hordes, the brunt of the war will fall on the United States and this conflict may be prolonged for two or three years and if so will cause us to lose millions of lives and untold billions of money."[17]

That same day, Butler Wright wrote in his diary what seems to be his first negative comment about his boss: "Rumor has it that the 'Bolshevik' sentiment is growing in strength through the country. . . . *Everyone*, with the only exception of D.R.F., believes that a clash—and a serious one—is bound to occur soon. We fervently wish that it would come and get it over with."[18]

Francis had staked his reputation, and hundreds of millions of American dollars, on the success of the Provisional Government. As his staff and other Allied diplomats soured on Kerensky and his ministers, Francis clung to the upbeat prognoses of Matilda de Cramm, an upper-middle-class liberal who identified strongly with sophisticated men like Kerensky. It was no secret that she and Francis were, at the very least, close friends. He invited Thompson and Raymond Robins, men he had little reason to trust with his private life, to join him and Madame for lunch. And he wrote a note to the venerable

Catherine Breshkovskaya introducing Matilda as "a Russian lady of character and intelligence . . . who desires to meet you and is inspired with a commendable desire to help Russia and to contribute her bit in the great struggle in which the world is engaged."[19]

Francis continued to shrug off suggestions of impropriety in his relationship with Madame de Cramm. He spoke freely around her, sometimes of very sensitive matters. Allied diplomats became reluctant to discuss with him any official secrets. He was typically insensitive to the negative effect appearances had on the realities of the situation. Even if the relationship did not seriously compromise security, it had a devastating effect on his dealings with his Allied peers.[20] Francis fretted about people talking behind his back, yet he did nothing about the cause of all the talk—his relationship with Madame de Cramm. Instead, he brooded about the talkers. He wrote to Washington:

> I heard in confidence today and from a source which I think reliable that Mr.
> Fred A. Sterling, who is chief of the bureau in the [State] Department in which
> Russia is one of the countries, has been talking disparagingly concerning
> myself and has made some expressions which show unfriendliness if not ani-
> mosity. This surprises me greatly as I have known Sterling from his boyhood;
> he and two of my sons having gone to school together when they were under
> twelve years of age, and for the further reason that he professed to feel other-
> wise when serving under me as he did for about three months after I took
> charge of this Embassy. I cannot imagine why he cherishes such feeling and it
> would not concern me at all if the dispatches from the Embassy and the
> instructions to it did not pass through his hands. . . . You would do me a great
> favor if you would . . . write me whether my fears concerning him are
> correct.[21]

In the spirit of brilliant amateurism that dominated high-level British espionage in both world wars, the writer Somerset Maugham was sent to Petrograd in the late summer of 1917 as a spy. Although he worked for the British, it appears that Woodrow Wilson's ubiquitous advisor Colonel Edward M. House also had approved the mission and expected it would result in valuable information. Maugham's ultimate goal, under the cover of gathering material for stories, was to try to prevent the Bolsheviks from seizing power and yanking Russia out of the war. His instructions were to "guide the storm."[22]

Maugham arrived in Petrograd on September 1 and stayed about six weeks. One of Maugham's goals, it appears, was to ferret out the truth to the rumors that the American ambassador was having an affair with a German spy. He seems to have decided that Francis was romantically linked with Madame de Cramm, but she wasn't a spy. In the process, Maugham came up a striking portrait of David Francis and his relationship with British Ambassador Sir George Buchanan. The writer's World War I espionage became the basis for his 1927 book *Ashenden; or, The British Agent*, which Maugham described as "a work of fiction, though . . . not much more so than several of the books on the same subject . . . that purport to be truthful memoirs."[23]

In the book, the British ambassador had been instructed to let Ashenden operate independent of the British Embassy and to forward his coded cables unread. He was furious and did as little as possible to help the writer. After being dismissed by "Sir Herbert Witherspoon" politely but with "a frigidity that would have sent a little shiver down the spine of a polar bear," Ashenden proceeded to the American Embassy:

> The American ambassador was Mr. Wilbur Schafer; he came from Kansas City and had been given his post . . . as a reward for political services. He was a big stout man, no longer young, for his hair was white, but well-preserved and exceedingly robust. He had a square, red face, clean-shaven, with a little snub nose and a determined chin. His face was very mobile and he twisted it continually into odd and amusing grimaces. . . . He greeted Ashenden with cordiality. He was a hearty fellow.
>
> After the greetings, the ambassador said, 'I suppose you've seen Sir Herbert. I reckon you've got his dander up. What do they mean in Washington and London by telling us to despatch your code telegrams without knowing what they're all about? You know, they've got no right to do that. . . . Well, what is this mission anyway?'

Ashenden did not intend to answer that question:

> He had already made up his mind from the look of him that Mr. Schafer, though doubtless possessed of the gifts that enable a man to swing a presidential election this way or that, had not, at least nakedly for all men to see, that acuteness that his position perhaps demanded. He gave you the impression of a bluff, good-humored creature who liked good cheer. Ashenden would have been wary when playing poker with him, but where the matter in hand was concerned felt himself fairly safe. He began to talk in a loose, vague way of the world at large and before he had gone far managed to ask the ambassador his opinion of the general situation. It was the sound of the trumpet to the war-horse: Mr. Schafer made him a speech that lasted without a break for twenty-five minutes, and when at last he stopped in exhaustion, Ashenden with warm thanks for his friendly reception was able to take his leave.

At this point, Ashenden informs the reader that the American ambassador had "succumbed to the fascination of a Swedish lady of undoubted beauty [whose] relations with Germany were such as to make her sympathy with the Allies dubious." The reports note "a leakage of very secret information," and "the question arose whether Mr. Schafer did not in these daily interviews inadvertently say things that were promptly passed on to the headquarters of the enemy. No one could have doubted Mr. Schafer's honesty and patriotism, but it was permissible to be uncertain of his discretion . . . the concern was as great in Washington as in London and Paris, and Ashenden was instructed to deal with it."

Ashenden recruited the Swedish lady's maid to be his spy, and every two or three days he received "a neat report upon the goings-at this charming lady's apartment."

Nothing in the reports confirmed "the vague suspicions" that the lady was a spy, but Ashenden learned "something else of no little importance":

> From conversations held at the cosy little tete-a-tete dinners that the countess gave the ambassador it appeared that his excellency was harbouring a bitter grievance against his English colleague. . . . In his blunt way he said he was sick of the frills that damned Britisher put on. He was a he-man and a hundred per cent American and he had no more use for protocol and etiquette than for a snowball in hell. Why didn't they get together, like a couple of regular fellows, and have a good old crack? . . . They'd do more towards winning the war by sitting down in their shirt sleeves and talking things out over a bottle of rye than by all their diplomacy and white spats.

So Ashenden, hoping to end the impasse between the two men, again visited the British ambassador and told him what he had learned. With "a hint of a smile," the ambassador asked Ashenden, "What does one do to become a regular fellow?'

"I'm afraid one can do nothing, Your Excellency," Ashenden replied. "I think it is a gift of God."

"You did quite right to come and tell me this," the British ambassador says. "I have been very remiss. It is inexcusable on my part to offend that inoffensive old gentleman. But I will call at the American Embassy this afternoon."

Francis met Buchanan at the British Embassy at least twice in a three-day period at the end of September and beginning of October.[24] So perhaps Buchanan tried to patch up his relationship with Francis. But it's hard to imagine they ever got along very well. Buchanan's daughter Meriel, who was with him in Petrograd, described her father as a terrible snob who couldn't help treating people he considered beneath him with "a certain distaste and fastidious disapprobation."[25]

B Y MID-SEPTEMBER, with shadows lengthening and a chilling hint of winter already in the air, the situation in Petrograd grew increasingly dire. Bread lines had formed again on Furstatskaya Street, and Francis could look out of the bay window of his second-floor office and see hundreds of people waiting four to six hours for a food shop to open. Many of them were sent away empty handed when the loaves ran out. Walking through the city one day, Francis overheard a woman say, "I have asked for bread so often and been refused that now I am going to demand it."

Francis wrote a friend:

> The air is full of rumors and general fear is entertained of a Bolshevik outbreak. The British Embassy and Consulate are said to have given notice to all British subjects to leave Russia. . . . Many Americans are frightened and that condition prevails somewhat in the Embassy and in the Consulate also. I do not partake of it in the slightest degree, as I feel no concern about my personal safety, nor do I anticipate that the Embassy itself will be attacked. In compliance with . . . repeated appeals. . . . I have, however, chartered a small

steamboat upon which Americans who so desire can take refuge in the event disturbances should occur. I shall remain in Petrograd as long as the Government does, and perhaps longer.[26]

A few days later, Philip Jordan wrote Jane Francis:

I believe their will be more people starve to death here in Petrograd than they will kill with Bullets. it does certainly look might bad right now and think what it will be when She drops to 38 and 40 below . . . some days and nights you will See on the Nevsky Prospect ten or twenty thousand marching with black flags and banners reading we are on our way to kill all Americans and all rich people—that includes me and [whoever] has on a White shirt. I will tell the Gov. that they are on the way again to kill us. The Gov will Say all right are you ready. I will say yes I am all ready so the Gov will tell me to load the Pistol and see if She is in working order. he Says that he will get to or three before he goes.[27]

Jordan found it more and more difficult to find fresh food, no matter how much American money he had to spend or how far he went in search of the impromptu little markets that sprang up around farmers' wagons. He told Jane, "I know a Very Rich family with the finest furnished house I was ever in worth millions and can not get any thing to Eat. . . . I have a woman who brings Milk and Cream from the county and I take them a bottle of milk and cream once a week . . . this Ford Automobile is certainly a life Saver. I go all through the villages and buy chicken and Vegetables."

On September 13, an attractive if somewhat disheveled young American couple arrived at the embassy with a letter of introduction from what Francis described as "a prominent federal official of New York." The letter read, "I want to present to you my old friends, Mr. and Mrs. Jack Reed, both of whom are of the American newspaper world and are visiting Russia with a view to studying conditions. Any courtesy at any time which you and the gentlemen of the Embassy may extend to them will be deeply appreciated."[28] There is no record of how the meeting with John Reed and Louise Bryant went, but shortly afterward Reed's wallet showed up at the American Embassy, and it contained notes that convinced Francis Reed was a dangerous Red.

Francis claimed the wallet was lost and returned to the embassy. Some scholars believe Francis, already suspicious of Reed, had an agent pick his pocket.[29] The latter version is certainly a possibility. There is no question that Francis and his aides were conducting espionage from the embassy, probably a considerable amount of it. Francis dispatched an agent to keep an eye on Reed as he waded into the middle of the revolutionary fury.

Reed correctly decided that the Allied embassies were trying to steer Russian internal policies. Francis, for all his undiplomatic bluntness, was actually more cautious in this regard than his colleagues. On October 9, Francis refused to join the British, French, and Italian ambassadors when they met with Kerensky and handed him a note threatening to cut off all military aid to Russia unless the country took immediate, harsh steps to restore order both at the front and in the cities. Incensed by this Allied ultimatum, Kerensky handed the note back to British Ambassador Buchanan, the senior envoy, and suggested that he pretend it never existed. Apparently, that was what happened: in his Russia memoir, Buchanan mentions the meeting but says nothing about the threat to cut off money. Immediately after the three ambassadors left, Kerensky recalled, "I went to see David Francis, the U.S. ambassador, and asked him to send President Wilson a cable thanking him for not associating the United States with this unfriendly act."[30]

On October 8, a startling story appeared on the front pages of the *Washington Post* and the *New York Herald,* one that further stirred up the suspicions around Matilda de Cramm. The headline in the *Post* read:

RUSSIA BETRAYED HERE
BY WOMAN AGENT WHO
SOLD SECRETS TO FOES

The story, by correspondent Herman Bernstein began, "On October 25, 1915, Mme. Mirolubskaya, accompanied by a Mathilda Cramm, arrived in New York on board the Norwegian steamship Christianiafjord." No further mention of Madame de Cramm appears in the story, and the only connection apparent between the two women was that they were both Russian and had struck up a brief friendship on the long sea journey two years earlier.

According to Bernstein's story, Alexandra Petrovna Mirolubskaya was a spy and saboteur. For several hundred thousand dollars, she sold the Austrians and Germans military secrets obtained from members of the Russian Military Commission, a liaison group that had been sent to the United States to represent Tsarist Russia in connection with the war. Many tons of war materials meant for the Russians were delayed or destroyed by saboteurs, and ships containing guns and other supplies were blown up, the story charged, "as a direct result of information given by traitors on the Russian commission to the German agents." Saboteurs who were part of the ring blew up a $40 million munitions plant manufacturing arms for Russia on Black Tom Island in New Jersey.[31]

The charges against Mirolubskaya, who had returned home to Russia in 1916 and was arrested and prosecuted by the Russians for revealing state secrets, appear valid. No evidence ties any of her activities to Matilda de Cramm. But on the basis of the story, the Russian Espionage Committee investigating Mirolubskaya called in Madame de Cramm and interrogated her for four hours. No charges were ever filed.[32]

The Mirolubskaya story did not mention Edgar de Cramm, but it inevitably cast further suspicion on him. A New York–based commercial attaché of the Russian Embassy already had reported to U.S. Military Intelligence in August that Edgar de Cramm had been "travelling through the United States, Cuba and Brazil, pretending to be closely connected with the Russian Government" but was "in fact a dangerous German spy."[33]

Edgar de Cramm well may have been a German spy; he was unquestionably a philanderer.

In December 1916, a business acquaintance of the fifty-year-old de Cramm introduced him to his baby sister, Marion Lyon, who had just turned eighteen. She was tall and buxom, with strikingly large grey eyes and long chestnut hair, and de Cramm apparently fell for her right away. They began an affair. In March, Edgar went to Havana on business, and Marion went along. In April, they returned to New York, and he rented a large apartment on 152nd Street so Marion could live with her brother and his wife and he could visit her.[34]

Marion Lyon's parents were dead, and on May 23, 1917, in a Staten Island courtroom, Edgar de Cramm adopted her. A few months later, he sailed for Central and South America, purportedly to engage in the import-export business. Marion was with him. They traveled for six or seven months, and by late October or early November American agents were keeping an eye on them.[35]

In Petrograd, Allied intelligence agencies intensified their investigation of Madame de Cramm. In October or early November, General Judson received a joint dossier from the U.S. Secret Service and the French Counter-Espionage Bureau at Petrograd about Madame de Cramm. It included the information that she had arrived in America with "a Russian woman who was well identified as an important Central Powers spy" and that Madame de Cramm had made a point of traveling on the same ship and same train as Francis on her way to Petrograd.

Judson became deeply concerned about Francis's friendship with Madame. He later wrote, "She was an exceedingly bright and attractive person about forty, but seemingly much younger. Her influence over the Ambassador seemed vastly greater than that of all the Embassy Staff and Military Mission combined."[36]

Judson personally appealed to Francis to stop seeing Madame de Cramm and showed him the dossier. "Thus," he recalled later, "I was the only one who personally approached the Ambassador [about] Madame de C."

Over the summer and fall, Francis wrote several times to his friend Breckinridge Long, now third assistant secretary of state, asking about reports that scurrilous rumors about Madame de Cramm were being circulated by men who had returned from Russia. One letter also complained that "some liar has industriously circulated the report in Washington that I am drinking too much," which Francis strenuously denied, saying, "I have never been drunk in my life nor have I ever been charged with being so."[37]

In mid-October, Long finally responded to Francis's concern:

As to the personal remarks which have been made about you, and which you indicated in your letter have come back to you, they need not worry you in the slightest degree. . . . The record which you are making at Petrograd speaks for itself. . . . I know the way that you are handicapped there and I know the influences which cause it, but a man of such resources as you need not be more than inconvenienced by such circumstances. That you have successfully overcome these obstacles is only too well demonstrated by the results which you have obtained and are obtaining. . . . All the world appreciates the magnificent work you are doing.

He urged Francis to concentrate on keeping Russia in the war:

> We are very much worried about the situation on the eastern front. . . . I sincerely hope that during the winter Russia will be able to draw herself together and will assume a united and aggressive attitude by spring. It is almost too much to hope, in view of the circumstances there, but if even she could assume a united defensive attitude, and draw the attention of the German troops in sufficient numbers, that would be doing a great service.[38]

The situation in Petrograd continued to deteriorate. Political wrangling in the government again had delayed the election of a Constituent Assembly, promised right after the March Revolution, and balloting now was set for the last week in November. On October 18, Kerensky summoned Somerset Maugham and gave him an urgent verbal message for Prime Minister David Lloyd George, a message so secret Kerensky would not put it in writing. He said that he could not hold out without Allied guns and ammunition. And he wanted Buchanan replaced. Maugham left that day for London to deliver the message.

Lloyd George replied to Maugham, "I can't do that." Maugham asked for clarification and wondered what he should tell Kerensky. The prime minister, before hurrying off to a meeting, replied impatiently, "Just tell him I can't do that." The events of early November prevented Maugham from returning to Russia and delivering the message.[39]

William Thompson kept trying to prop up Kerensky. Francis worried that he was getting out of control. On October 26, he wrote Lansing that Thompson was "spending a great deal of money, considerably over $1,000,000 of his own funds. . . . Col. T's advisor in the expenditure of the money is Raymond Robins of Chicago; I did not know him until his arrival here, but he impresses me as being sincere, although decidedly progressive. I understand Robins has converted Thompson to progressivism." Francis soon became much more familiar with Raymond Robins.

In mid-October, Lenin returned from Finland, slipping back into the country in disguise—he had shaved off his mustache and goatee and wore a wig on his bald head. He slipped in and out of meetings at the Smolny Institute, a former girls' boarding school a few blocks east of the Tauride Palace that had been taken over by the Soviet. On October 23, in a heated ten-hour meeting that lasted into the night, Lenin swayed the central committee of the Bolshevik Party to issue a call for an armed insurrection. Certain victory, he said, would come with "rivers of blood." Those who argued against him, he contended, were "miserable traitors to the proletarian cause."

"We are on the eve of a world revolution," he argued. For the Bolsheviks not to act would be "utter idiocy or sheer treachery," which would destroy the party and "ruin the revolution." The time to strike was now, while Kerensky was still reeling from the

Kornilov affair. The central committee voted to approve Lenin's scribbled declaration that "an armed uprising is inevitable, and the time for it fully ripe."[40] The next day, Kerensky delivered an impassioned speech pleading for support. By then, the prime minister had taken on several additional ministerial posts and was in the ironic position of being a virtual dictator, at least on paper, with no real power.

Kerensky proclaimed:

> Waves of anarchy are sweeping over the land. The pressure of the foreign
> enemy is increasing, counter-revolutionary elements are raising their heads,
> hoping that the prolonged governmental crisis, coupled with the weariness
> which has seized the entire nation, will enable them to murder the freedom of
> the Russian people. . . . The Provisional Government presumes that all citizens
> of Russia will now rally closely to its support for concerted work, in the name
> of . . . the defense of the fatherland from the foreign enemy, the restoration of
> law and order and the leading of the country to the sovereign Constituent
> Assembly.[41]

Zealous young John Reed, in his stirring revolutionary diary, *Ten Days that Shook the World,* describes with eloquence and accuracy the early fall of 1917, when even Petrograd's grim weather seemed to conspire against order, and the Germans advanced past Riga, less than two hundred miles southwest of Petrograd:

> Under dull grey skies, in the shortening days, the rain fell drenching, inces-
> sant. The mud underfoot was deep, slippery and clinging, tracked everywhere
> by heavy boots, and worse than usual because of the complete breakdown of
> the Municipal administration. Bitter damp winds rushed in from the Gulf of
> Finland, and the chill fog rolled through the streets. At night, for motives of
> economy as well as fear of Zeppelins, the street lights were few and far
> between. . . . It was dark from three in the afternoon to ten in the morning.
> Robberies and house-breaking increased. . . .
>   Week by week food became scarcer. The daily allowance of bread fell
> from a pound and a half to a pound, then three quarters, half, and a quarter
> pound. Towards the end there was a week with no bread at all. . . . For milk
> and bread and sugar and tobacco one had to stand in queue long hours in the
> chill rain. . . . I have listened in the breadlines hearing the bitter, acrid note of
> discontent.[42]

Power inexorably shifted from the ever-changing Ministry of the Provisional Government to the Soviet. In Smolny, Reed wrote, "The long, vaulted corridors . . . were thronged with hurrying shapes of soldiers and workmen, some bent under the weight of huge bundles of newspapers, proclamations, printed propaganda of all sorts. The sound of their heavy boots made a deep and incessant thunder on the wooden floor."

Downstairs in the large former school, thousands were fed cabbage soup in long cafeteria lines. Upstairs, in what once had been the school's ballroom, under the soft glow of alabaster chandeliers, a thousand men and women crowded together for raucous meetings that went on around the clock as the overthrow of the Provisional Government was planned. Reed wrote:

> Petrograd presented a curious spectacle in those days. In the factories the committee-rooms were filled with stacks of rifles, couriers came and went, the Red Guard drilled. . . . In all the [army] barracks meetings every night, and all day long interminable hot arguments. On the streets the crowds thickened toward gloomy evening, pouring in slow voluble tides up and down the Nevsky, fighting for the newspapers. . . . And in the rain, the bitter chill, the great throbbing city under grey skies rushing faster and faster towards—what?

Princess Cantacuzene and her husband fled the city in October, out of fear of both the Bolsheviks and the advancing German army. In those terrible days, she recalled, she "found no optimism except in the heart of the brave American Ambassador. Each time I met him, I admired his energy and indomitable will to help Russia, and to believe in her powers, when to us she seemed done for. Nothing one could say gave him the least alarm, any more than threats against him personally inspired him with fear; and his embassy was a citadel of strong warm comfort to me, and to many others."[43]

On November 5, Francis cabled Washington, asking for an additional emergency loan of $100 million. But it was too late for Kerensky's speeches, or America's money, to stop the tidal wave in the streets.

Kerensky tried to get tough. On November 6, he closed down several Bolshevik newspapers, succeeding in merely increasing the anti-government fervor in the streets. That afternoon, David Francis made his customary daily call on the Foreign Office and had a long talk with Tereshchenko. While they were talking, Francis walked to a window and gazed out at a thousand soldiers drilling in the vast square between the Foreign Office and the Winter Palace. There was a long silence, broken by Tereshchenko: "I expect a Bolshevik outbreak tonight."

Francis replied, "If you can suppress it, I hope it will occur."

"I think we can suppress it," the foreign minister said, momentarily appearing calm, and then he turned red and said with a fury: "I hope it will take place whether we can or not—I am tired of this uncertainty and suspense." Francis was taken aback. He did not realize until later that Tereshchenko had lost faith in Kerensky, and as Francis put it, "undoubtedly felt that the chief responsibility for saving his country from the terrible fate that threatened her rested upon his shoulders."

Gesturing toward the window, Francis asked, "Whose soldiers are those?"

"They are ours," the foreign minister said wearily. Francis left, hoping that would remain the case.

Francis recalled:

> As I stepped to my victoria, drawn by two gray horses with small American flags attached to the rosettes of their bridles, I directed my coachman to drive by the soldiers who had stacked arms and were talking in little groups. I saluted as I passed and the men under their non-commissioned officers

promptly came to attention and returned my salute with all proper military precision. I wanted to impress these men with the fact that America and her Ambassador were back of the threatened Provisional Government.[44]

All afternoon and evening, Francis could hear gunfire and see gangs of men, many of them armed, rushing through the streets. Cossacks battled mobs trying to cross the bridges from the working-class and factory neighborhoods on the islands north of the central city. That evening, Francis cabled Lansing and for the first time proposed that America intervene militarily. If the Provisional Government approved, Francis said, dispatching two or three American divisions via Vladivostok or Sweden could be a great help to the morale of Russian troops on the Eastern Front and would focus opposition to the Bolsheviks and their radical allies. "Millions of sensible Russians only need encouragement to organize," wrote Francis.[45] Like so many of his countrymen, he confused the mass of angry, illiterate, impoverished Russians, just a few decades out of virtual slavery, with iconoclastic, well-fed American farmers taking up arms to drive the British from American shores.

As the fighting outside intensified and explosions lit the sky to the west, he wrote to his son, Perry, "It is reported that a Bolshevik uprising or 'demonstration' is beginning on the other side of the river. The immediate cause is the suppression of the four Bolshevik newspapers, one of them Maxim Gorky's. These papers have been advocating a separate peace and supporting extreme socialist doctrines."[46]

That evening, Lenin moved into Smolny, where the Second Congress of Soviets was set to convene, to begin the revolution. The next morning, November 7, Francis got a call from the Foreign Office. Because of pressing matters, he was told, his daily meeting with Tereshchenko had been called off. As he was digesting this news, Sheldon Whitehouse, second secretary of the embassy, came rushing in and, out of breath from hurrying on foot from near the Winter Palace, told Francis excitedly that Kerensky had commandeered an embassy car to leave the city.

There are several different versions of the story of Kerensky and the American car. Here is the gist of what seems to have happened:

During the night, the Bolsheviks had sabotaged the fleet of cars the Provisional Government kept near the Winter Palace. Two Russian officers were sent looking for available vehicles and spotted a chauffeured car waiting in front of Whitehouse's home. It was a Renault that flew an American flag. The Russian officers knocked on the door and told Whitehouse and his Russian brother-in-law, Baron Ramsai, that Prime Minister Kerensky needed the car immediately to go to the front. Whitehouse and Ramsai were understandably suspicious but finally agreed to accompany the Russian officers to General Headquarters, across the vast Palace Square from the Winter Palace and the seat of the Provisional Government. Kerensky, who was living at General Headquarters, surrounded by his staff, confirmed that he wanted the car to take him south a couple of hours to Luga, where he would gather loyal troops and return and reclaim the capital.

Whitehouse replied, "This car is my personal property and you have thirty or more automobiles waiting in front of the palace." Kerensky answered that all his cars had been "put out of commission during the night." He added, "The Bolsheviks now command all the troops in Petrograd, except some who claim to be neutral." Whitehouse and Ramsai, a Russian officer loyal to the Provisional Government, decided that they had no choice but to turn the car over to Kerensky. They tried to remove the American diplomatic flag, but Kerensky's bodyguards would not let them.

Kerensky instructed Whitehouse to tell Francis that he was going to the front and that he would return with an army to overthrow the usurpers. In the meantime, he asked that Francis not recognize any Soviet government that might be established, as the whole ugly affair would be over in five days.

That evening, at 5 P.M., Francis cabled Lansing telling him of the commandeered car and noting that Kerensky had "acknowledged that Bolsheviki control city and that Government powerless without reliable troops as there are few here of that nature."[47]

That night, and early the following morning, November 8, Red Guards and other armed Bolsheviks, with support from the guns of warships and cannons booming from the St. Peter and Paul Fortress across the Neva, fought their way through several hundred weakly resisting "Junkers"—military-academy cadets, sons of the aristocracy. They stormed the Winter Palace, rushing up the wide marble steps through vast, gold-encrusted rooms and dazzling mirrored hallways into a study glittering with gilt and green malachite. The Bolsheviks arrested the ministers who had been meeting there night and day and dispatched them under guard to the Fortress. With surprisingly little bloodshed, the Bolsheviks took control of the Russian government.

Philip Jordan, as usual, began running for the scene as soon as he heard the sounds of battle. He wrote:

> The Bolsheviks shot Petrograd all to Pieces. All the ministers was Supposed to be hiding in the Palace. at 1235 am the machine guns and cannons began to roar. When I was in two blocks of the palace I Saw about 12 or 15 machine guns turned on that beautiful building. Out of all the noise now and then you could hear a cannon shot . . . the first thing I must tell you is that we are all seting on a bomb Just waiting for some one to touch a match to it. if the Ambassador gets out of this Mess with our life we will be awful lucky . . . these crazy people are Killing each other Just like we Swat flies at home.[48]

Lenin was still in Smolny, about three miles away from the Winter Palace and General Headquarters, but if anyone was in charge, he was.

On the eve of the Bolshevik Revolution, Maxim Gorky wrote in the November 7, 1917, edition of his newspaper *Novaya Zhizn* (New Life), soon to be closed for good by his onetime comrades: "Lenin and Trotsky do not have the slightest idea of the meaning of freedom or the Rights of Man. They have already become poisoned with the filthy venom of power, and this is shown by their shameful attitude towards freedom of speech, the individual, and all those other civil liberties for which the democracy struggled."[49]

At 6 P.M. on November 7, David Francis drafted a cable for Washington that laid out simply, clearly, and accurately what had happened so far. It read, in part:

> Bolsheviki appear to have control of everything here. Can not learn whereabouts of any Minister. Two reported arrested and taken to Smolny Institute which is headquarters of Bolsheviki. . . . No government here at present. Little firing on the street but no armed contests, some streets guarded. Majority of soldiers claim to be neutral but nearly all here are with Bolsheviki who say will form new government and notify Allies Russia cannot fight more and announce peace terms to Germany and if not accepted will then fight desperately for Russia. Many newspapers, perhaps all, suppressed.

At 10 P.M., before the cable was sent, he added this note:

> Reported all Ministers arrested except Kerensky who has gone to Luga about 80 miles toward north front.
> FRANCIS[50]

CHAPTER 17

Lenin Takes Control

B Y THE TIME THE SUN HAD CLEARED the morning fog off the Neva on November 8, the Red Guards reigned in the Winter Palace, and the Bolsheviks and their allies, the left wing of the now-fractured Socialist Revolutionaries, controlled the Second Congress of Soviets. Convened at the Smolny Institute, the congress overwhelmingly had approved the seizing of political power. The slogan, "All power to the Soviets," endlessly chanted in the halls of Smolny over the past few days, was becoming a reality.

Lenin, now forty-seven years old, had been elected chairman of the Council of People's Commissars, and Trotsky soon was named foreign minister. That evening, after another long day of battle in caucus, Lenin appeared at the podium to the raucous cheers of a thousand delegates beneath the alabaster chandeliers of the main assembly hall. He read his soon-famous Decree on Peace, calling for "all the belligerent peoples and . . . Governments to begin immediate negotiations for a just and democratic peace . . . without annexations and without indemnities."

The phrase "without annexations," as the rest of the speech made clear, called for an end to colonialism, past, present, and future. The Soviet government, he declared, believed that continuing the war "in order to permit the strong and rich nations to divide among themselves the weak and conquered nationalities" would be "the greatest possible crime against humanity."

Lenin, hoarse from days of arguing, leaned forward over the podium to roar out his declarations. With, as John Reed put it, "a thousand simple faces looking up in intent adoration," Lenin called for the abolition of "all secret treaties confirmed or concluded by the Government of the landowners and capitalists"—the Provisional Government. And he tossed a flaming torch to workers "in all the belligerant countries," who needed to "understand the duty imposed upon them to liberate humanity from the horrors and consequences of war" and begin the prophesied revolution. Soldiers burst into tears, and a young workman shouted, "The war is ended, the war is ended," as the assembly burst into the stirring words of the "Internationale." Finally, when the pandemonium had died down, the congress unanimously accepted the Decree on Peace.

The Allies were horrified, which is what Lenin had expected and wanted. As the distinguished diplomat-historian George Kennan noted, "This was the first example in Soviet diplomacy of what was later to become known, in Soviet usage, as 'demonstrative diplomacy,' i.e., diplomacy designed not to promote freely accepted and mutually profitable agreement as between governments but rather to embarrass other governments and stir up opposition among their own people."[1] Later in the day, Lenin threw another bombshell: the Decree on Land, which stated that "All private ownership of land is abolished immediately without compensation."

That morning, Philip Jordan went out, as he put it, "to See how much damage was done." He saw, "in the middle of the Never river . . . two large battle ships [with] their big guns trained on the palace. I can't describe the damage done but you can guess about what happened to that building."[2] Bullet gouges pocked the green stucco facade and the white columns of the Winter Palace on the south side, facing Palace Square. On the north, facing the river, cannonballs had deeply dented the walls. Inside, looting and vandalism had reigned, fed in part by the discovery of thousands of bottles of the Tsar's vintage French wine in the cellar. Drunken mobs, including criminals released from prison, roamed through wealthy neighborhoods, beating and sometimes killing well-dressed people and looting their homes.

The first week and a half of the Bolshevik Revolution—"Ten Days that Shook the World"—was a time of both joyous celebration and, as Maxim Gorky put it, "a pogrom of greed, hatred and vengeance," fueled by "all the dark instincts of the crowd irritated by the disintegration of life and by the lies and filth of politics." The angry masses, Gorky moaned, had been joined by "adventurers, thieves and professional murderers," men who saw the revolution as an unrivaled opportunity for crime.[3]

In the uncertainty of the morning after the storming of the Winter Palace, Francis called the Foreign Office and could not get an answer as to who was in charge. Finally, an official of the Department of Agriculture came by the embassy and told him that the Foreign Office was closed because "it was impossible to do any business with the Ministers in prison." Later that day, Francis got reports that Trotsky was the new commissar of foreign affairs, but that he and Lenin were tied up in meetings at Smolny.[4] The meetings went on for days, with Lenin occasionally taking a few hours off to sleep in the small cot he had installed in his spartan office.

Francis gathered together what information he could, and by the evening of November 8, he sent an encoded cable to Robert Lansing describing in detail the capture of the Winter Palace, the arrest and imprisonment of most of the leaders of the Provisional Government, and the abrupt departure of Kerensky. "Quiet on streets today," he reported, "but Petrograd Council Workmen-Soldiers have sent bulletins throughout Russia that Soviet in control and Government deposed."[5]

He sent a copy of the cable, probably by train messenger, to U.S. Consul General Summers, four hundred miles away in Moscow, and asked him to forward it to Washington because he was not sure cables from Petrograd were going through—the

Petrograd Soviet had taken charge of the post office, the telegraph office, and the telephone system. Francis wrote:

> Kerensky left yesterday morning for Pskov in an automobile and sent me word
> before leaving that he expected the situation to be liquidated within five days
> and also expressed hope that if the Soviet government should be installed
> here, we would not recognize same. . . . All of the ministers are said to be
> imprisoned in St. Peter and Paul fortress. . . . In my judgement, this situation
> here is another step toward clearing the atmosphere in Russia.[6]

Francis felt that the Bolsheviks could not last and that a stronger and more popular government would succeed theirs. He was not alone in this feeling, which was shared by most of the men, in Russia and the United States, who advised the U.S. government at high levels. For example, on November 17 old Russia hand Arthur Bullard wrote his boss, American war-propaganda chief George Creel, that the Bolsheviks would lose their power "because they are in a hopeless minority. . . . You've got to have not only a majority, but an overwhelming majority, to put through any revolutionary change." As evidence, thinking like an American, Bullard cited the Bolsheviks' relatively weak showing in recent municipal elections. Bullard also said that in his judgment "nothing we could have done in the last six months" could have changed the outcome.[7]

Not until the morning of Saturday, November 10, did Francis's November 7 and November 8 cables from Russia go through to Washington.[8] Francis later was much criticized for leaving Wilson and Lansing in the dark during the early days of the revolution, but he actually seems to have reported promptly and, considering the chaos, with surprising accuracy.

On November 10, Francis cabled Washington again, recommending that "we should make no loans to Russia at present." A few days later, he reported:

> The Embassy has never received any official notice that there has been any
> change in the government but the departments are all closed or operating
> only partially and without chiefs. The Lenin-Trotzky Ministry has not sent any
> written or oral communication to the Embassy. . . . When a government is
> formed and I am officially advised, I shall confer with the heads of the Allied
> Missions and the Department upon a course of action. Of course, we would
> not, or I would not, recognize any Ministry of which Lenin is Premier or
> Trotzky Minister of Foreign Affairs.[9]

Philip Jordan, as usual, kept Francis informed of what was going on in the streets. Slipping in and out of crowds, anonymous, Jordan was quite possibly a better observer of the mood of the people than any of the hundreds of spies who flocked to the Russian capital. At the end of November, he wrote:

> After living in a wild country like this for 18 months it makes you feel like
> there is only two decent places to live one is heaven the other is America. We

have no Government no law and no Protection of any Kind. All the convicks and thugs in Russia are walking the streets with rifles. Tuesday [November 27] I went to the market with the Ford to buy what I could. . . . Just as I started to gather up what I had bought about three hundred Bulsheviks rushed in the market with cocked rifles. . . . [One of them] said no one can buy anything more in this market . . . because we are going to take it all for our friends . . . he said you get out of here and be dam quick about it. I Said I will not leave this place until my money is returned. he then tol the Clerk to give me my money. they then began . . . Shooting to frighten the people and took every thing in the market. . . . they will take all this and give it to the other Bolsheviks but they wont give the other people any.[10]

Two days after the revolution, Jordan recalled:

[I] was going across the [Liteiny] Bridge with the best friend that we have I mean the Ford on my way to the country to see what I could buy to eat. Just as I got across the Bridge was opened and 4 large Battle Ships passes up the Neva on their way to Pavloosk to meet Kerensky who was comeing to Petrograd on his way from the front with an army. they had an awful battle for three days but the Bolshevicks was the strongest and drove them back.

Kerensky tried to fight his way back into power at the head of three to five thousand Cossacks, but his troops were stopped about fifteen miles from the city by a force of about twenty thousand, including several thousand armed workmen. As Francis observed later, "It is not improbable that their arms had been furnished by the order of Kerensky himself when he armed the workmen of Petrograd in order that they might aid in repelling Kornilov's army."[11]

In the next few weeks, both Francis and Jordan observed, and reported home in detail, the harsh realities of the revolution. On November 18, Jordan wrote Jane:

The Bolsheviks got the city in their hands and I want to tell you it is Something awful. Streets are full of all the cut throats and robbers that are in Russia. you can hear the machine guns and cannons roaring all night and day. thousands are being killed. why we are alive I can not tell. they break into private homes and rob and kill all the people. in a house not very [far] from the embassy they killed a little girl and 12 rifle baynets found stuck through her body. oh the horrible Sights that is to be seen. Petrograd is all shot to pieces but it is not nearly as bad as Moscow. the report received this morning is that over twenty thousand have been killed. I have fond out that the best thing to do right now is keep your mouth shut and look as much like an American as you can. . . . All the thugs that have been turned out of prison was armed with a rifle. . . . we cant tell at what minute the Germans will take Petrograd. If they come right at this time I dont know what we would do because we cant get out. we are like a rat in a trap. the Bolshevicks have torn up all the rail roads. I can't tell but this Ford might be a life Saver. . . . the Ambassador told me two days ago to be packed with as little as possible because we might have to go and leave it all behind.

Jordan asked Jane to thank her cousin, Annie Pulliam, for a long letter and said he would "answer it by the next pouch if the Germans the Bolshevik or the Zeps don't get us. . . . today is the first snow. we all want to see bad weather because it will hold the Germans back especially the Zeps."[12]

This time, there was no haste to be first among nations to recognize the new government. Francis refused to have anything directly to do with the Bolsheviks, at least until they officially notified him that they had formed a government. Buchanan and the other Allied ambassadors maintained the same position. But, almost from the first day of Bolshevik power, Francis authorized unofficial and clandestine contacts with them, a fact obscured or lost in most histories of the period. Throughout November and early December, Francis, without instructions, kept up these unofficial contacts, particularly through his military attaché, General William V. Judson. Judson was responsible for, among other things, making sure that Americans were not mistreated. As Francis reminded Judson in a November 20 memo, however, he wanted it to be clear that the attaché should take no steps that could be construed as direct or indirect recognition of the Bolshevik government.[13]

On November 19, Francis issued a statement that he hoped would get into the newspapers and to the Russian people. Like Lenin and Trotsky—and indeed like American diplomats from Cassius Clay in the nineteenth century to Secretary of State Madeleine Albright during her 1997 visit to the Middle East—Francis sometimes would make statements that attempted to go over the heads of the government to the people. Clearly, however, he also hoped to catch the ear of the government.

In his statement, released in both English and Russian, Francis said he was speaking directly to the people of Russia because "there is no official in the Foreign Office with whom I can communicate and all of the members of the government or ministry with which I had official relations are inaccessible, being in flight or in prison." He reminded Russia of America's "prompt" recognition of the Provisional Government, of the $256 million in American credits Russia had received, and of the relief and aid missions that had been dispatched. He stressed his concern about the advancing German army:

> The Russian people are engaged in fratricidal strife and are paying no attention to the approach of a powerful enemy who is already on Russian soil. There is no power whose authority is recognized throughout Russia; your industries are neglected and many of you people are crying for food. This need can be supplied if you will permit the American railway commission to continue its helpful work, as there is sufficient food in Russia to feed all her people if properly distributed. . . . Food conditions or the scarcity of bread is the greatest menace confronting you at this time, and America is making every effort to improve the situation.

I have not lost faith in the ability of the Russian people to solve their own problems. On the contrary, I believe that your patriotism, your pride, your sense of right, and your love of justice will remove the difficulties that beset your pathway. But the time you have therefor is extremely limited. A powerful enemy is at your gates. A desperate foe is sowing the seeds of dissension in your midst. A hostile, unscrupulous imperial government is maintaining a well-organized espionage throughout the land. Your liberties are threatened. Your beloved land is in danger.[14]

It was not only the advancing army that caused Francis to worry that the Germans were about to take control of Russia. Like his friend Kerensky, he long had suspected, with reason, that the Germans were financing the Bolsheviks.[15] At the very least, he felt, the Bolsheviks by making a separate peace would serve the German cause, whether or not that was their intention.

On November 20, he wrote Lansing:

The situation here is extremely critical. The army is without bread, and many of the soldiers are likely to come to Petrograd in quest of food. When they arrive, it is possible they may indulge in excesses. I have a strong suspicion that Lenin and Trotzky are working in the interests of Germany, but whether that suspicion is correct or not, their success will undoubtedly result in Germany's gain. . . . You do not need to be impressed with what it means for Germany to get possession of Russia.[16]

The next day, Francis received a shocking cable from Lansing. It arrived with the instructions "to be deciphered by the Ambassador." Instead, Francis handed the cable for decoding to Butler Wright, who, according to Judson, had expected it to arrive. The cable read:

Department informed Matilda Cramm is employed in some capacity in Embassy. As Department has reason to suspect this woman, you are directed to take immediate steps to sever her connection with the Embassy as Department would not be justified at this time in permitting her to be in a position to get any information as to what goes on in the Embassy. Please report.[17]

As he heard the cable read aloud, Francis's face turned red and he shouted that he would "get the son-of-a-bitch who had caused it to be sent." Wright quickly (and inexcusably, Judson thought) denied having any foreknowledge about the cable. Francis blamed Judson, the only subordinate who had approached him directly about de Cramm, although it later appeared that the main source of Lansing's information had been Wright. "I'm quite sure," Judson remarked later, "this message did not have the desired effect."

Francis dashed off an angry cable and a follow-up letter, both saying essentially the same thing: that he was "astounded" at the suspicions, insisting that Madame de

Cramm was "not employed by Embassy; never has been" and never had been paid a cent by the embassy directly or indirectly, and said he couldn't understand why she was under suspicion at the State Department, although he acknowledged that her husband was "probably under suspicion of Russian secret service."

Confidential information had "never been accessible by party," he said. He asked for the source of Lansing's information, and said:

> I have seen Madame Cramm often during the past year and a half and have been accompanied by her in drives and walks, consequently I am inclined to the belief that the Department's suspicion of her being guilty of espionage— there is no other ground for suspicion—is inspired by someone unfriendly to myself. . . . I am disposed to thing that someone here who professes friendly feeling for myself is disposed to 'stab me in the back.' A secret enemy is the only one I fear; a man who opposes you openly is entitled to respect for his courage if not for his judgment.[18]

The next day, Counselor Butler Wright recorded in his diary, "I am becoming much concerned about DRF's health."[19]

Francis also sent a note to Madame de Cramm, with the semi-formal salutation of "Dear Madame." It stated:

> I am greatly surprised to hear that your loyalty to Russia is doubted by anyone and equally surprised and somewhat amused to learn that one of the causes of this suspicion is your acquaintance with me and your visits to the American Embassy. I therefore hasten to write you and to cheerfully testify that my confidence in your devotion to Russia has been contemporaneous with my acquaintance with you. . . . I know of no Russian whose patriotism exceeds that of yourself.[20]

On December 3, Francis got a reply from Lansing:

> Department information came from several sources, believed to be reliable. Further information received since our November fourteen [cable] which convinces me that it is not desirable that such a person should be in a position where she can secure any information whatsoever. Under circumstances consider it will be safer for your reputation and for safety of Government not to take any chances and hope you will act immediately.[21]

The next day, still steaming, Francis wrote a long, angry letter to his old friend Breckinridge Long. He said, among other things:

> You are aware that no member of my family, female or male, has been with me in Petrograd. You also know that I am fond of ladies' society. This lady, Madame Cramm, has given me French lessons and been patient enough to be considerate with my attempts to converse with her in French, which have been made on many and diverse occasions. You are aware how important it is

for one in the Diplomatic Service to be able to converse in French. . . . If this lady has been sailing under false colors or in other words if she is a German spy I am as desirous to know it as anyone.[22]

The same day, he labored over another long, self-justifying letter to Lansing, noting that Madame had been "of great assistance to Philip after our arrival in furnishing the kitchen and the two rooms I occupy in the Embassy" and protesting against any slurs on his own or her integrity. Nonetheless, he said, he would "inform Madame Cramm not to visit the Embassy again." Rather foolishly describing her apartment as "well-furnished containing many works of art," he said she was "a lady of refined tastes, of excellent character" who seemed to have enough money to live on and had "a country residence some 20 versts or 15 miles beyond the [city] limits at which she spent several months in the summers of 1916 and 1917." He added, "I have never visited it."[23]

By then, according to Judson, among the numerous Americans in Petrograd who were convinced that Madame de Cramm was a German agent assigned to Francis were Counselor J. Butler Wright, William Boyce Thompson, and Colonel Raymond Robins.[24]

I N THE EARLY MONTHS of the November Revolution, with the support of David Francis, Raymond Robins was the American with the best contacts among the Bolsheviks, thanks in great part to his aide and translator, a very bright Russian-speaking pragmatic intellectual named Alexander Gumberg. (Gumberg was described by one American in Petrograd, Propaganda Chief Edgar Sisson, as "a New York Jew with melancholy eyes, sensitive features, and a mind crammed with resources."[25])

Through Gumberg, who had known Trotsky in New York, Robins met with the Bolshevik leaders much more frequently than any other American of even semi-official standing. Robins's contacts began on November 10, three days after the revolution, when he and Gumberg met with Trotsky, whose main task at the time was trying to keep the exceedingly shaky Bolshevik government from being toppled from power either by troops loyal to the Provisional Government or by simple anarchy.[26]

Robins, a fervent liberal and evangelical Christian in his mid-forties, was bright and mercurial, bursting with ideas sometimes untempered by judgment. He and Trotsky, both idealistic zealots, seemed to have hit it off immediately. Trotsky urged Robins to stay in Russia and pulled strings to get Red Cross supplies moved quickly to where they were needed. As fall deepened, and the long, dark northern winter approached, Robins continued to meet regularly with Trotsky. He kept Judson informed of his actions, and by late November, he was working quietly but closely with Francis as well.

Thompson went home on November 28, leaving Robins in charge of the Red Cross in Petrograd. Francis later remarked, with some relish, that Thompson, who "spent over a million dollars supporting the Provisional Government and in an effort to obliterate the Bolsheviks . . . was very much frightened [after the Bolsheviks took control] and for several days or weeks took up his quarters at the Military Mission, with whose Chief, Judson, he was very close."[27] Thompson was not alone among Red Cross officials in having the jitters. "The members of the Red Cross Mission here have a case of nerves," observed propaganda agent Arthur Bullard from Moscow. "It's rather too bad as they ought not to have dolled themselves up in uniform if they were going to be so impatient to get out of the sound of guns."[28]

Before he left, Thompson tried with little success to reach an accommodation with the Bolsheviks. The arrogant multimillionaire proclaimed that his intention was to "make them our Bolsheviks," which greatly amused left-wing journalist Albert Rhys Williams and his friend, Alexander Gumberg. Gumberg wondered how David Francis would react to the idea of "making them our Bolsheviks" and asked his friends rhetorically, probably in a fake Missouri twang, "What if in making them ours, before we succeed in changing them, and bringing back law and parliamentarianism and all that, they bolshevize *us?*"

Williams passed that remark on to John Reed and added, "Francis himself doesn't dare go near Smolny. They're not going to bolshevize *him!*"

"And right he is!" Reed responded. "There's too much at stake. For what would he do with Madame de Cramm then?"

"There's the Winter Palace," Williams joked. "Why should a lot of rough workmen have it all to themselves?"[29]

The joking dialogue suggests a couple of interesting points: knowledge about Francis and Madame de Cramm was widespread among Americans in Russia, and American leftists who embraced the Bolshevik Revolution were not particularly concerned about things that the bourgeois democrat Francis considered crucial—"law and parliamentarianism and all that." Certainly, those were not among Lenin's concerns.

FRANCIS'S LIFE AND WORK became even more complicated with the arrival in Petrograd on November 25 of Edgar G. Sisson. Sisson, a small, wiry man of great enthusiasm, was sent by the Wilson administration to head up the Petrograd office of Creel's Committee on Public Information. His main task, as he defined it, was to see if the Allies could work with the Russians against Germany. Sisson joined the proliferating number of Americans—official, semi-official, unofficial, and downright clandestine—who set about making American policy, often without consulting the American ambassador.

A former Chicago newspaper reporter, Sisson had met Francis at the 1904 World's Fair and had been quite impressed by him. In the fall of 1917, Sisson decided that, despite his age and the turmoil of the past few weeks, Francis had "retained his native energy, seasoned just now with an angry disdain of the Bolsheviks. Of a sanguine temperament, he had placed his faith in the stability of the Kerensky Government. Chaos had come instead. He had reason for the depth of his present feelings."[30]

Shortly after they met at the embassy, Francis growled, "I never will talk to a damn Bolshevik." Sisson thought, "His situation is different from mine. I will have to talk to them."

Francis tried to find out exactly what Sisson's mission was. Sisson was evasive. "The situation was equivocal, without blame to either of us," Sisson said. "I was not sent to work under him, and was independent of him, in powers and in funds. War, not I, was the intruder." Sisson felt that these "invasions into the diplomatic zone" by men such as himself were necessary in wartime, but he also realized that an ambassador "would not be human if he did not feel that he should be in chief command of all the governmental units in the country."

O N NOVEMBER 26, David Francis wrote Perry, "The Department has given no instructions concerning recognition of the Lenin-Trotzky government, nor have I made any recommendation toward such recognition."[31] In fact, neither the secretary of state nor the president of the United States were quite sure how the Bolsheviks should be dealt with, if at all.

Before meeting with Wilson in early December, Robert Lansing wrote down his feelings on Russia so that he could clearly express them. Lansing wrote, in part:

> The conclusions and opinions are almost as many as the advisors. . . . I have yet to find one who, pinned down to the application of his theory, is able to furnish a plan that is practical except one who frankly asserts that the best thing to do is to let things alone as far as it is possible to do so. With this latter policy I am in entire accord. The Russian situation is to me an unanswered and unanswerable Riddle. None of our observers, some of whom are well trained, has been able to find a way out or to advise a course of action leading to satisfactory results. . . . Of one thing I am convinced, and that is that it would be unwise to give recognition to Lenin, Trotsky and their crew of radicals. . . . It seems to me that Russia is about to be the stage on which will be acted one of the most terrible tragedies of all history. . . . I believe that the Russian 'Terror' will far surpass in brutality and destruction of life and property the Terror of the French Revolution. . . . 'Do nothing' should be our policy until the black period of terrorism comes to an end and the rising tide of blood has run its course.[32]

For David Rowland Francis, a man of action, doing nothing was deeply frustrating. For that reason, among others, the last eight weeks of 1917 were probably the most difficult period of his life, and he almost broke under the strain.

The democratic revolution that he embraced had collapsed and had been taken over by men he considered to be the worst sort of opportunists. He received little direction from Washington, other than being ordered to cut off contacts with Madame de Cramm. He was surrounded by rivals for his authority, men who radically differed in agenda— personal, political, and ideological—from him and from each other. Some of them, he was discovering, went against him behind his back. He began to perceive that he was surrounded by enemies. And he was lonely; he had been away from his family and his old friends for a year and a half, far longer than at any time in the past. Desperate for friends and allies, he found them in two unlikely people—a once-illiterate although highly intelligent African American valet and chauffeur and an attractive Russian woman who was widely suspected of being an enemy spy. And he developed an odd symbiotic relationship with that fireball from the upper Midwest, Raymond Robins.

After the Bolshevik Revolution, the dour-faced, passionate Robins became what he later described as "the American ambassador's 'unofficial' aide in all dealings with Smolny."[33] While authorizing regular contacts with the Bolsheviks, Francis insisted there be nothing even hinting of official recognition of what he considered to be an illegitimate government, established by force and guile against the will of the Russian people. Sisson, who participated in several meetings with Robins and Francis in that period, recalled that "the only injunction that the Ambassador laid was that the Red Cross in whatever contact it had with Bolshevik officialdom must avoid committing the Embassy to any seeming sanction of the new regime."[34]

At the time, the most immediate pressing issue was the meeting about a possible ceasefire scheduled to begin December 1 between Trotsky and the Germans. General Judson made some suggestions to Robins about ways to make the proposed armistice less toxic to the Allies. On November 30, Robins met with Trotsky and brought up Judson's suggestions. Trotsky said he would like to talk to Judson in person. Robins said he would try to set that up.

The French and British, when asked how they would feel about contact at such a high level, adamantly opposed it. In a subsequent long meeting at the embassy, Robins and Judson argued that it was crucial for Judson to meet with Trotsky. Sisson and Butler Wright agreed. The Bolsheviks were, after all, the only government Russia had, and negotiations with the Germans were imminent. Francis agreed that there should be some contact but said he preferred that it be at a lower level—perhaps Judson could send a subordinate. Captain E. Francis Riggs was agreed upon, and the meeting adjourned on that note.

That evening, his mind rapidly going over his options, Judson went to a dinner party at the British Embassy. He talked to diplomats there, and the general alarm at the idea of the Russians abandoning the Eastern Front increased his sense of urgency. A meeting between Trotsky and Riggs could very well open up crucial issues that, Judson decided, only he as head of the military mission could deal with. Judson decided he had to be ready, at a moment's notice, to go to Smolny.

About midnight, Judson stopped by the embassy on his way home. Francis was still up, sitting in the dining room. Judson and Francis again discussed whether Judson should meet with Trotsky. Judson left the meeting believing, he said later, that Francis had agreed he would meet with the Bolshevik foreign minister if that became the only way to make any progress on the armistice. Francis's recollection was that he had not changed his stance. Both men's recollections seem to agree on one point: Judson would not meet with Trotsky without talking to Francis first.

The next day, Robins and Sisson tried to arrange a meeting between Riggs and Trotsky. Around noon, Sisson reported that Trotsky would meet only with Judson.

Deciding there was not a moment to lose on the eve of the foreign minister's departure for Brest-Litovsk, Judson hurried from the military mission to Smolny, where he met with Trotsky for forty minutes. Judson said later that he had tried to contact Francis before he went but was unable to.[35]

The whole affair is mired in confusion, in part because various people—including Sisson and Wright, who were not even present at the post-midnight meeting in the embassy between Francis and Judson—presented differing versions of what commitments Francis had made.[36] Francis later muddied the waters even further by sending Lansing contradictory cables about the matter, as we will see.

The December 1 meeting between Judson and Trotsky was the first substantive contact between high-ranking official representatives of the Bolsheviks and the United States. Judson emphasized to Trotsky that the Russians and the Allies had parallel interests. If there was to be an armistice, he argued, it should be "of long duration, with enemy troops remaining in position." That way, of course, hundreds of thousands of German troops would not be released to strengthen attacks on the Western Front. Judson argued that Russia could thus achieve peace without damaging its national pride—it was agreeing to an armistice, not a surrender. Judson came away from the meeting believing Trotsky agreed with that idea. He immediately cabled Washington a brief description of the meeting, saying he had gone with Francis's "assent" and that he had been careful to emphasize the "non-official character" of the visit.[37]

Judson then went to the embassy, told Francis about the meeting, and showed him the cable. That evening, perhaps trying to present a unified front and allay any suspicions that he was losing control of his staff, perhaps simply trying to support his colleague in a crisis, Francis cabled Lansing: "Judson saw Trotzky today with my approval."[38]

The next morning, Petrograd newspapers printed Trotsky's account of the meeting. The Russian foreign minister had told the papers that Judson had said that "the time of protests and threats addressed to the Soviet Government has passed, if indeed there ever was such a time." And, according to Trotsky, while making it clear that he was not speaking for the American government, Judson said he had come "in order to start relations." A few months later, Francis would astutely dismiss Trotsky's statement as one of many instances in which he tried to "make the impression on the public mind that the recognition of the Soviet Government was desired by the subordinates of the American Embassy and that either the American Embassy or his Government was standing in the way."[39] But on the day Trotsky's statement appeared, Francis worriedly cabled Washington: "Judson's visit to Trotsky exciting comment, especially among Allies missions who consider it a step toward recognition. . . . I consented that Judson should send subordinate to discuss armistice provisions only and was not aware that Judson had gone himself until after visit was made."[40]

Even if we put the kindest interpretation on these events—Francis initially tried to cover for Judson, but quickly felt the need to set the record straight—the American ambassador blatantly contradicted himself in cables to the State Department. It seems apparent, both from his actions and from the observations of his colleagues, that he was not thinking clearly. In early December, Judson wrote in his diary, "Mr. Francis . . . Seems to me completely exhausted and overwrought by the strain he has recently been under. This circumstance is most distressing. The American Ambassador never required more than now to be able to act with cool wisdom and vision."[41]

On December 6, Lansing cabled Francis: "President desires American representatives withhold all direct communication with the Bolsheviks."[42] At the same time, the State Department issued a statement saying that Judson had "acted without government instructions" in meeting with Trotsky. And Lansing and Wilson had a fifteen-minute meeting, the main topic being whether Judson should be immediately recalled.[43]

On December 9, Francis cabled Lansing, "Judson's personal call on Trotsky was without my knowledge or approval . . . and I was compelled so to state to my [Allied] colleagues at meeting of December 5 when they remarked that it was understood we should act in union and in any case Judson's visit to Trotsky was a violation of such understanding."[44]

There is no question that Francis presented more than one version of the facts. Perhaps he misguidedly tried to give the U.S. government what at a later point in history would be called "deniability." In any event, he was backing and filling in a clumsy way, at least in part trying to justify his own actions, and he certainly did Judson no service.

In late November and early December of 1917, Francis seems to have briefly lost his moorings. Events and circumstances conspired with his own personality and experience to undermine his confidence in himself and his judgment. Used to being the chief executive—of a multimillion-dollar business, a large city, a state, a world's fair—he had trouble acting as a subordinate under any circumstances. And even in Petrograd, where his leadership should have been unquestioned, he found himself surrounded by visitors who presumed to act as if they were the real ambassadors. Primary among these men was the overbearing William Thompson, who threw so much money and weight around that, intentionally or not, he undermined Francis's position and, perhaps, his confidence.[45]

Always ticklish about criticism, particularly when it touched on his personal standards, he found himself under attack from Lansing and other men in the State Department whom he respected for his relationship with Madame de Cramm, which he had stubbornly (and perhaps guiltily) decided was none of their business. And there was little support, political or moral, from his top advisors, official and unofficial, who tended to disagree strongly with his bedrock position—the United States should not give official recognition to the Bolsheviks. These were men he respected, men with greater experience in diplomacy than he, and when they coalesced in opposition to his instincts, he began to have doubts and become defensive about his positions. He veered between being bullheaded and being indecisive; he had often in the past been the former, but seldom the latter.

DeWitt Poole, a thirty-seven-year-old member of the consular staff at Moscow, met Francis for the first time in early December and decided that the ambassador was "mentally fatigued and incapable of grasping what was going on around him."[46] Poole may have overstated the case, under the influence of some of his colleagues, but there is no question Francis was working to the point of exhaustion. Philip Jordan wrote on November 30 that while "The Ambassador" was "in the best of health," he never went to bed "during these terrible times until 2 & 3 o'clock in the morning." Jordan took personal responsibility for fending off official visitors so Francis could get more than five hours of sleep.[47]

Francis also missed Jane's sober, steadying hand.[48] He sought out the advice, and comfort, of Madame de Cramm, continuing to visit her apartment late at night even after he finally stopped inviting her to the embassy in early December.[49] But that was a relationship fraught with worry. He must have known at some level that their closeness was, at the least, imprudent, but he would not be the first man or woman to be undone by romantic feelings when far from home.

Francis became convinced that his close associates were scheming against him— not without justification. One day, at the end of November or the beginning of December, he walked into Wright's office and discovered Sisson, Judson, and Wright speaking in low, excited tones. They stopped talking as soon as Francis entered the room. Francis brought up a minor matter of contact with the Bolsheviks, and in the ensuing discussion about how to bring the embassy closer to Smolny, Francis said, "I am doing nothing."

Sisson snapped, "That is exactly what we are complaining of and it is what is leading us to perdition." Francis snapped back that he was the American ambassador and responsible for policy. His remark was greeted by silence, and Francis turned and stalked out of the room.[50]

Butler Wright, who was growing weary of what he called Francis's "singular stubbornness," seems to have finally decided to go along with what was becoming an organized opposition to Francis in the Petrograd embassy. On December 3, the heretofore dutiful Princetonian wrote in his diary, "The air is big with possibilities of every kind!! And in our own official circle an axe seems about to fall! . . . I am increasingly worried about DRF's health."[51]

The next day, Edgar Sisson drafted a long and incendiary cable that would stir up a storm in both Washington and Petrograd. Not yet aware of Wilson and Lansing's negative reaction to the Judson-Trotsky meeting, he began the cable by taking credit for it, and adding to the confusion as to exactly what Francis had told Judson prior to his trip to Smolny: "Risked using what pressure I could muster, helped to secure from Ambassador wavering consent to a single conference between Judson and Trotsky. Judson has reported to Washington the satisfactory results of his conference. . . . I recommend . . . immediate establishment of working, informal contact with de facto power by official representatives."

Sisson had much more to say. His encoded cable was sent December 5 by a roundabout route, avoiding the embassy code office and, with the help of U.S. Consul Roger Culver Tredwell, going through the consulate on Nevsky Prospect. It read, in part:

Found Ambassador without policy except anger at Bolshiviki. . . . Have been reluctantly convinced that no fruitful work can be done here . . . as long as Francis remains in charge of Embassy. Not only does he impress every one as a sick man absolutely unfitted to the strain physical and mental of his great post, but he also has allowed himself to become subject of public gossip and investigation by the secret police of the Allied nations because of open association with a woman suspected, perhaps without sufficient evidence, of espionage. [She has] free access to the Embassy, where the Ambassador lives alone . . . on the day I arrived, the Department of State reminded Francis that this woman was an undesirable person to have in the 'employ' of the Embassy and that the connection should be severed at once. Yet she was in the Embassy on Sunday December second one week later and was alone with the Ambassador until after midnight. It is possible that the Ambassador's erratic actions of the past few weeks is due to the disturbing force of this personal entanglement . . . an exceedingly humiliating scandal is momentarily imminent. There will be no frank interchange of views between the Allied Ambassadors and Francis. . . .

I therefore urge that to prevent public humiliation formal orders be sent to Ambassador to hasten to Washington via Japan to report in person to the President on Russian situation and that Embassy be left with Charge d'Affaires. Then while he is enroute make inquiries. There is not a boat for a month or more and it is all important that he should leave here at once with the least possible scandal.[52]

Lansing saw the telegram on December 7 and passed it on to the president, who jotted down a reply: "This despatch disturbs me. Have you heard from any other source of such conduct on the Ambassador's part?"[53]

Of course, Lansing had heard plenty. At this point, the secretary of state and the president decided they had to recall at least one of three men: Francis, Judson, or Sisson. They chose to bring Judson home and informed him of that two weeks later. And, through his boss, Creel, they chastised Sisson, letting him know they wanted him to keep working at what he was supposed to work at—propaganda and a little light espionage—and let Washington worry about its ambassadors. Creel cabled Sisson, "President insists that you avoid political entanglements and personal matters."

In his Russia memoir, Sisson said he later regretted sending the impulsive cable: "I had no business to take the burden of the battles of others." Besides, as December wore along, Sisson found that he and Francis developed "terms of working amity in which General Judson was included," and his later memories of Francis were fond and admiring ones.[54]

Despite the unsettling events of late November and early December, Francis pressed ahead on matters he considered crucial. With Lansing having forbidden official contact with the Bolsheviks, Francis decided it could and should continue unofficially through Robins. On December 12, he cabled Washington asking if the prohibition included members of the American Red Cross.[55]

He hadn't heard back by December 15, when the Russians and Germans announced they had agreed on a month-long ceasefire, with peace negotiations to continue. Francis decided it was urgent to get details of the agreement directly from Smolny. The next day, with Francis's approval, Robins went to see Trotsky, who assured him that the recently negotiated ceasefire included a commitment that troops would stay in place.

After that, life at the American Embassy seemed to have calmed down for a few days. Then, shortly after midnight, December 20, all hell broke loose. Bolshevik Red Guards burst into the apartment of a former Tsarist official named Andrei Kalpashnikov, now working for the American Red Cross. Kalpashnikov, a personal enemy of Trotsky, was charged with planning to ship eighty Red Cross ambulances and trucks from storage in Petrograd to counterrevolutionaries in the Ukraine. Found in Kalpashnikov's apartment were several letters that indirectly tied the American Embassy into the scheme, although how much Francis knew and did remains unclear.

Kalpashnikov and other Red Cross officials apparently wanted the vehicles shipped south for use as a road flotilla to rescue the fabled Queen Marie of Rumania, a heroine of the Allies whose country had been overrun by the Germans. According to Robins's 1920 Russian memoir, Francis "gave himself" to Kalpashnikov's "little plan" and thus "found himself the shipwrecked mariner in the wildest teapot tempest of Petrograd's wildest diplomatic days."[56]

After hearing of the arrest of Kalpashnikov, Robins rushed to Smolny to see Trotsky. What was said is unclear, but that evening Trotsky made a speech at the Alexandrovsky Theatre and railed against the conspirators. The fiery, notably eloquent thirty-eight-year-old foreign minister said that Robins "has been loyal and correct with regard to us in all his dealings." Then he launched an attack on the American ambassador, in a voice, according to Sisson, that "swelled with indignation."

Waving pieces of paper, Trotsky shouted:

> And now this Sir Francis will have to break the golden silence which he has
> kept unbroken since the revolution. These documents will force him to
> unloose his eloquence. Our dignity as a government, our dignity as a revolu-
> tionary government, is of the highest importance to us. We shall prove it to all
> who think they can tread on our toes with impunity. Let them understand
> that from the moment they interfere in our internal affairs they cease to be
> diplomatic representatives. They are then private counter-revolutionaries, and
> the heavy hand of the revolution will fall upon them.[57]

Trotsky was speaking for effect, trying to rouse the audience to unity against a common (and perfidious) enemy. The crowd responded by leaping to its feet and shouting, "Arrest Francis! Hang him! Shoot him!" After the speech, Robins jotted in his pocket diary that Trotsky "was fair to me" and added, "Extraordinary the whole affair."

Meanwhile, Lansing finally had cabled back to Francis, with a copy to Robins, that the prohibition against direct contact with the Bolsheviks "certainly included" the Red Cross.[58] The morning after his meeting with Trotsky, Robins went to the embassy to brief the ambassador. Francis asked Robins to meet again with Trotsky and explain that the embassy had not been involved in the attempted diversion of the trucks. But, Robins asked, how could he meet with Trotsky in light of Lansing's most recent cable?

"What?" said Francis. "Pay no attention to it."

"But it's an order," replied Robins.

"I'll take the responsibility," Francis snapped back. "You keep on going to Smolny. Tear the order up."

"Well," Robins said, "Will you cable Washington to change the order?"

"Certainly."

"All right," said Robins, pleased and astonished.

"And now," said Francis, "What can we do at Smolny about this Kalpashnikov business?"[59]

Francis issued a statement that "instructions from my government are very definite and positive prohibiting any interference by any American representative in Russia on the internal affairs of this county. I have observed these instructions scrupulously." And, with Francis's unofficial blessings, Robins went to Smolny and insisted that Francis had had nothing to do with the trucks. Apparently, Trotsky believed him, if indeed he had ever truly thought Francis was involved. After that, according to Robins:

> The Kalpashnikov business was filed and forgotten. The only difficulty in explaining it was the truth about it was more romantic than Smolny's theory about it.
>
> The truth was that for Colonel Anderson [head of the American Red Cross Mission to Rumania] and for Mr. Francis, it was not an anti-Bolshevik business at all. . . . Colonel Anderson and his colleagues were pure knights-errant. They were about to rescue a lady—a fair and noble lady—a queen.

The Kalpashnikov storm blew over and, on Christmas Eve, in response to pleading from Robins, the Bolsheviks released a Red Cross train they had held up. It contained food and clothing and other relief supplies for Rumania, although not Kalpashnikov's trucks. That evening, seeing the positive results of Robins's visits to Smolny, Francis sent a coded telegram to the secretary of state announcing his willingness to effect a major change in policy toward the Bolsheviks:

> This is revolution but the fact remains that the Bolsheviks have maintained themselves in power in Petrograd and Moscow and are the de facto governments in those cities and although there are opposition movements in Ukraine and elsewhere Bolshevik power is undoubtedly the greatest in Russia . . . . Soviet Government has survived about seven weeks during which period German Government has made great progress toward re-establishing her influence here. . . . I am willing to swallow pride, sacrifice dignity and with discretion do all necessary to prevent Russia from becoming an ally of Germany. Possibly by establishing relations with Soviet Government, allied representatives could influence peace terms and in that way preserve Russian

neutrality, thereby preventing war munitions stored in Russia being acquired by Germany, also preventing immense Russian resources becoming available by German for conflict with Allies.

I have not spoken to my colleagues on these lines, but if you approve I am willing to do so. Such course mildly speaking would be exceedingly distasteful but may be advisable. You are better circumstanced than myself to know what the effect in the United States would be of such course.[60]

It would be early January before he received a reply.

Right before Christmas, in a holiday message, Philip Jordan wrote to Jane Francis:

This is to let you know that we are still alive but can not tell you how long we will be. do you know that at the present time that Petrograd is . . . full of Germans [freed prisoners of war] Struting around the Streets as proud as peacocks. all the Russian people are quite happy that the Germans are here. [Presumably Jordan was referring to the upper crust, with whom he identified]. they Say that when the Germans do take Petrograd that we Shall have some kind of law and order to live under. Every thing is shot to pieces in Petrograd Stores and houses. Monday Night [December 17] the Ambassador left the embassy at 830 pm to dine with Princess Cataquzen. I went with him and went for him at eleven oclock. On my way down to the hotel I passed great crowds of Soldiers Standing on each Corner. I told the Ambassador about it and he said to go home by Some other street which we did. when we got in one block of the Embassy we heard two or three Shots. by the time we got in the house you could hear Shooting all around. Next morning at 8 I went out to See what had been going on and Just one block from the Embassy the Streets was full of drunken Soldiers. they broke in the corner grocer Store whare thousands of bottles of wine was and oh my Such a Scene. the Streets for blocks was full of broken bottles. the Soldiers all being drunk began to fight with each other. they also began to Shoot and Several was killed and wounded. last night at 12.55 I can always tell Just what time these raids take place because they wake me and I look at my watch. I heard an awful thumping and then heard the glass break. this took place Just 3 doors from the Embassy. Just think about 8 or 9 hundred drunken Soldiers had battered their way in to this wine Store and all got as drunk as they could. it is between 18 and 20 below zero but the next morning the Street for one block was full of drunken Soldiers Some Sleeping in the Snow Just as you could in bed. And Mrs Francis think. no law not a poliseman or any one to say Stop. . . .

I am all packed up ready to fly at a minutes Notice. At times I wish the Ambassador did not have So much of that Kentucky blood in him and then mabe he would not take Such chances. I may be wrong and I might not be but at times it does Seem that the Ambassador will remain in the city Just a little longer than he ought to. . . . this is not to frighten you but Simply to let you know Just what the situation is. I will put in the daily News. A Merry Christmas and a happy New Year to all of you.[61]

By Christmas, the streets of Petrograd had grown relatively peaceful. A British journalist named Arthur Ransome arrived on December 25 and recalled the scene:

> Heavy snow had fallen repeatedly on snow that had never been cleared away.
> The tramlines ran between deep walls of snow. In the main streets the sledge
> that took me from the station . . . had to weave a twisting, bumping course
> among hummocks of snow as hard as icebergs. But the city was quiet. I heard
> no shooting. Some of the street-lamps were lit. There were armed patrols at
> the street corners, mainly 'Red Guards' in ordinary workmen's clothes, with
> leather belts and bandoliers of cartridges and rifles slung on their backs.[62]

The embassy held an open house on Christmas day, and that evening Fred Corse of New York Life gave a dinner and dance at his apartment. Francis provided a rare treat, white flour and sugar for white bread, cakes, and pies—undoubtedly scrounged by Jordan. According to fellow guest Sisson, Francis showed himself "the equal of any as a forager."[63]

Everyone was getting along much better by then, and Francis appeared to have weathered the storm. After Christmas, with Francis's approval, Robins continued to meet almost daily with Trotsky and report back to Francis on what was discussed. And Francis, as he and Robins agreed he should do, continued to broadcast the false impression that Robins was acting entirely on his own. Corse wrote a friend that "our Red Cross representation, with which I broke connection several months ago, have been disposed to have conferences with Lenin and Trotzky. . . . This action . . . has been, I think, severely disapproved by the Governor."[64]

At this point, Judson recommended both to Washington and to Francis that the United States "enter into helpful, sympathetic and friendly relations" with the Bolsheviks to prevent the country from falling into German hands. Losing Russia, he argued, probably would result in "the death of hundreds of thousands of young Americans."[65] Francis was inclined to agree, and he was not afraid to move ahead without Washington's approval.

The day after Christmas, in a cable, Francis presented Lansing with a *fait acompli,* one that clearly went against the secretary of state's orders: Robins was meeting regularly with the Bolshevik Government, with Francis's consent. The cable stated, "If you do not approve, please instruct by wire."[66]

In effect, Francis forced the secretary of state to choose between approving the unauthorized meetings *ex post facto* or disrupting the process that had helped defuse the Kalpashnikov brouhaha and that might help strengthen the Allied position in an armistice. On December 29, an exasperated Lansing replied that Robins was "to understand explicitly that he acts for and represents Red Cross and not Embassy, Red Cross being an organization maintained by private subscription and not United States Government. Robins may therefore continue measure to distribute supplies, specially as supplies continuing to come forward."[67]

Francis received the cable on December 30 and was elated. Audaciously, he decided to assume that Lansing's very carefully worded cable gave him and Robins wide authority to steam ahead. Robins, ecstatic after talking to Francis, wrote his wife, boasting, "I, a Red Cross man, am the only person in any authority that is permitted by our government to have any direct intercourse with the de facto government that has complete control over three-fourths of Russian territory."[68]

The next day, December 31, Trotsky told Robins that the Bolsheviks were breaking off the peace talks because the Germans had refused to surrender occupied territory in Poland and other countries bordering Russia. Robins rushed back to the embassy, stopping by the nearby military mission to pick up Judson. He excitedly told Francis the news and passed on a question Trotsky had presented: What would America do if the armistice completely fell apart and fighting resumed between Russians and Germans? Francis immediately told Robins to go back to Trotsky and tell him that he would recommend that the United States offer "prompt effective assistance." He then cabled the State Department explaining his actions.[69]

As it turned out, Robins, Judson, and Francis had overestimated (or were fooled about) the Bolsheviks' willingness to resume all-out war. Trotsky—whose ironic watchwords were "neither war nor peace"—was stalling, in part hoping that the imminent worldwide revolution would make the war wither away. He soon was back at Brest-Litovsk, and negotiations resumed. Trotsky, who seems to have known a thing or two himself about high-stakes gambling, had increased his odds in his game with the Germans. He was now holding the American card.

Over the years, Francis frequently has been criticized for his open hostility toward Bolshevism both before and after the Reds took power, making it impossible for him to deal with them in a practical way. But he did try to deal with them, repeatedly—at more than one point going against Lansing's specific instructions to do so. Other more experienced Allied diplomats on the scene did much less than Francis to maintain contact, or failed to act entirely, in part because they found it exceedingly difficult to make major decisions without clear instructions and policies from home. Francis was eager to make independent decisions, even snap ones. Despite his stumbles in the month following the Bolshevik Revolution, he quickly regained his footing and moved ahead on his own to do what he thought was right—and probably, given the circumstances, was about the best that could have been done.[70]

It is true that Francis misjudged the staying power of the Bolsheviks, but so did many more experienced diplomats. Butler Wright wrote in his diary on December 4, "These people are *not* going to remain in power long."[71] And Robert Lansing told Woodrow Wilson that it defied logic that such "unorganized and undirected physical power as now dominates affairs in Petrograd can continue. It has in itself every element of destruction."[72] Even the Germans predicted an early overthrow of Bolsheviks, despite doing everything they could to put them in power and keep them there.[73] And Lenin himself, by 1918, had serious doubts that his government could survive the year.[74]

After the initial confusion in the first weeks of Bolshevik power—confusion abetted by Francis's contradictory cables—the secretary of state and the president came to approve of the way Francis had decided, almost independent of Washington influence, to handle things—standing back from official recognition of the Communists while exploring various unofficial contacts. It could be said that he forced them to accept that approach, which in retrospect seems the wisest route that could have been taken in what turned out to be an impossible quest. Wilson, on January 1, asked Lansing what would be "the most feasible and least objectionable way (if there is any) in which we could establish . . . unofficial relations with the Bolsheviki."[75] By then, of course, Francis and Robins already had established unofficial relations with the Bolsheviks.

In the crucial weeks following the Bolshevik Revolution, Woodrow Wilson could have replaced Francis at any time. Influential voices in Russia and the United States urged him to do just that, and Francis's contradictory cables and his refusal to toe the line on contacts with the Bolsheviks certainly gave Wilson and Lansing reasons to get rid of him. Yet they kept Francis in place, backed him against his attackers, and occasionally praised him and the job he was doing. Mostly, for better and for worse, they left him alone.

CHAPTER 18

Leaving Petrograd

It is doubtful whether the diplomats of the allied nations could have done anything to help Russia in this stupendous revolutionary upheaval. Perhaps the kindest thing would have been for them to go home and to leave the Russians to their own resources.
—Arthur Bullard[1]

O N THE FIRST MORNING OF 1918, America's top representatives in Russia—official, quasi-official, and unofficial—met at the embassy over one of Philip Jordan's famous breakfasts to discuss what to do if fighting should resume on the Eastern Front. The Germans were within two hundred miles of Petrograd. If they launched a rapid thrust toward the capital, Edgar Sisson argued, there could be only one outcome: Petrograd would fall. If that happened, the American ambassador might well be captured, which should be avoided at all costs.

Francis, Sisson recalled, "was for staying and sitting under the flag. We convinced him, however, that the useful place for him would be wherever the Bolsheviks picked a new capital, if they lasted long enough to make a choice. Where the Ambassador went, General Judson perforce must go. The rest of us could fend for ourselves. . . . We resolved that under no circumstances would we leave Russia."

That sounded fine to David Francis. "Like most men of action," Sisson continued, "the Ambassador was exhilarated by the prospect of having something positive to do. He began to plan a request for the movement of supplies to what he trusted would become again a fighting Russia; and that afternoon in fine fettle he received New Year's callers at the Embassy."[2]

That evening, Judson was stunned to receive notice from the War Department that he had been relieved as military attaché. Lieutenant Colonel Monroe Kerth, his second in command, would replace him and report to Francis. There was no mention of Judson's additional post, independent of Francis, as chief of the American Military Mission to Russia. In other words, the top American military official in Russia would be completely under the supervision of the ambassador. There seems little question that Judson's meeting with Trotsky in early December triggered the dismissal; Judson blamed the distorted press reports of that meeting, and David Francis.[3]

The next morning, Francis finally got a response from Lansing to his Christmas Eve telegram, which had suggested the United States establish a closer relationship with the Bolsheviks. Lansing insisted, "Department desires you to continue the course you have pursued in the past and which it has approved. Department relies on your good judgment to persevere in difficult situation."[4]

Taking Lansing at his word—keep doing what you've been doing, "persevere"—Francis encouraged Robins to continue to meet with Trotsky. That evening, Robins came to the embassy with handwritten documents that he wanted Francis to sign, documents that authorized Robins to continue to deal semi-officially with the Bolsheviks and made certain vague commitments in Francis's name. Francis agreed to sign them but added codicils. From Francis's viewpoint, the documents were conditional and subject to change, but Robins chose to interpret them as giving him virtual carte blanche; he sometimes seemed to forget about the codicils, both when meeting with the Bolsheviks and later when writing his memoir.

One document was addressed to the Commissar for Foreign Affairs (Trotsky). It read, in part: "At the hour when the Russian people shall require assistance from the United States to repel the aggressions of Germany and her allies, you may be assured that I will recommend to the American government that it render them all aid and assistance within its power."[5] *Raymond Robins' Own Story* quotes this passage, but it fails to mention that the document also included the line, "I am not authorized to speak for my Government on the question of recognition," nor that it was signed, "OK, DRF, Subject to change by Dept., of which Colonel Robins will be promptly informed. 1/2/18."[6]

The other document read, in part: "If the Russian armies now under command of the People's Commissairies commence and seriously conduct hostilities against the forces of Germany and her allies, I will recommend to the American government the formal recognition of the de facto government of the People's Commissairies."

Robins's memoir quotes that section but again neglects to mention an added statement from Francis: "Nothing that I [Francis] shall do will in any event give formal recognition to the Bolshevik Government until I have explicit instructions, but the necessity for informal intercourse in the present hour is so vital that I should be remiss if I failed to take responsibility of action."

Francis was criticized for not trying hard enough to get along with the Bolsheviks. Yet, in apparent defiance—or at least Jesuitical reading—of State Department orders from Washington, he was trying to keep the channels open between his government and the Bolsheviks, giving Robins as much leeway as possible in a delicate situation while keeping the U.S. government out of it. Robins and Francis agreed that the situation was so uncertain and liable to sudden change that they had to be able to act immediately, without waiting days to consult Washington.

After another meeting with Robins, Trotsky returned to Brest-Litovsk on January 6 to resume peace talks—or at least to keep the German negotiators occupied and their troops in place until their workers united and overthrew the Kaiser. He again may have pulled out the American card. But it probably didn't matter; the Bolsheviks were too eager for peace, and too obviously holding a losing hand, to bluff the Germans for very long.[7]

Also on January 6, Sir George Buchanan was recalled to London, making David Francis, as the ambassador with the longest tenure in the capital, dean of the Petrograd diplomatic corps. Buchanan was soon taking a very hard line back home, publicly advocating withdrawing the British Embassy from Petrograd and breaking all ties, formal and informal, with the Bolsheviks. He spent the next year traveling across England, calling openly for armed intervention to expel the Bolsheviks and prevent Russia's "vast man power and untold mineral wealth" from falling into German hands.[8]

Buchanan's extreme anti-Bolshevism hardly had been a secret while he was in Petrograd, and London had recalled him to clear the air and try to find a way to deal with this new government, which didn't appear to be going away any time soon. It's ironic, although typical of the confusion of the time and situation, that Judson was recalled for being too close to the Bolsheviks, and Buchanan for being too distant from them.

The British had decided to establish contact with the Bolsheviks through unofficial agents, much as Francis had done with Robins. The man the British chose as their unofficial liaison was thirty-year-old R. H. Bruce Lockhart, their former acting consul general in Petrograd. The wily, flamboyant Lockhart, who unlike most of his Allied counterparts, official and unofficial, spoke Russian, arrived back in Petrograd on January 28, adding more spice to the stew. He and Robins hit if off immediately. In his 1932 autobiographical thriller, *Memoirs of a British Agent,* Lockhart approvingly described Robins as "a philanthropist and a humanitarian rather than a politician" and "a wonderful orator."

"Although a rich man himself," Lockhart said, "he was an anti-capitalist. . . . Robins had a similar mission to my own. He was the intermediary between the Bolsheviks and the American Government and had set himself the task of persuading President Wilson to recognize the Soviet regime. . . . I liked Robins. For the next four months, we were to be in daily and almost hourly contact."[9]

At that point, there was also close and harmonious contact between Robins and Francis, and even Francis and Judson, who stayed on as military attaché for a while at Francis's request.[10] Arthur Bullard, who returned to Petrograd in January after a long stay in Moscow, found "intense harmony prevailing among those who when I saw them last were at swords point. The incident of the [Kalpashnikov] motor trucks had caused the miracle."[11]

On January 8, Woodrow Wilson delivered his famous, and enigmatic, Fourteen Points speech, which laid down guidelines for a settlement to World War I. Point six was that Russia should be free to decide its future without foreign intervention. He called for "the evacuation of all Russian territory."

Wilson seemed to speak directly, and hopefully, to the Russian people, whom he credited with "a largeness of view, a generosity of spirit, and a universal human sympathy which must challenge the admiration of every friend of mankind." He continued, "They have refused to compound their ideas or desert others that they themselves may be safe. . . . Whether their present leaders believe it or not, it is our heartfelt desire and hope that some way may be opened whereby we may be privileged to assist the people of Russia to attain their utmost hope of liberty and ordered peace."

This supremely Wilsonian speech could be, and was, interpreted either as a forceful repudiation of the Bolsheviks, or as its opposite, a warm and welcoming embrace. When a copy arrived by cable in Petrograd on January 10, Sisson and Robins saw an opportunity to move closer to the Bolsheviks. They arranged a meeting for the next day with Lenin—their first—to take him a Russian text of the speech.

Lenin eagerly read the Fourteen Points speech and decided that all of it should immediately be sent to Trotsky at Brest-Litovsk saying, "It's a great step toward the peace of the world." He added, with a smile, throwing up his arms in mock exasperation, "Yet I have been called a German spy." According to Sisson, Lenin was "joyous as a boy . . . . He grabbed the copy and sprinted for the telegraph office himself."[12]

George Kennan suggests, probably accurately, that Lenin was acting, and that neither he nor Trotsky really believed that America's goals were anything but ruthlessly imperialistic. But Lenin decided that his new friend Robins represented the "liberal American bourgeois" and would be, for a time, a valuable ally. After that, Robins met often with Lenin.[13]

Bruce Lockhart said of Robins, "In spite of his sympathies for the underdog, he was a worshipper of great men [and] Lenin had captured his imagination. Strangely enough, Lenin was amused by the hero-worship, and of all foreigners Robins was the only man whom Lenin was always willing to see and who ever succeeded in imposing his own personality on the unemotional Bolshevik leader."[14]

With Francis's approval, Sisson and Robins arranged for thousands of copies of Wilson's speech, in German and Russian, to be sent to soldiers at the front, and for handbills reprinting the speech to be plastered on walls all over Petrograd. Ironically, in rehashing the meeting with Lenin, in the fever of intrigue that infected Petrograd, Sisson decided that the truth may have welled up from Lenin's subconscious during their meeting—perhaps he was, indeed, an agent for the Germans. Robins believed Lenin to be, pure and simple, an ideologue, beholden to no one or nothing save world revolution, and Robins's relationship with Sisson began to deteriorate as they fought over the matter.[15]

In Washington, on the same day that the president delivered his Fourteen Points speech, Basil Miles, who was now in charge of Russian affairs for the State Department, expressed concern to Lansing that Francis was becoming too involved in the peace negotiations. Influenced by a recent meeting in which William Boyce Thompson had disparaged Francis, Miles recommended that more power be given to other American representatives in Petrograd, such as Robins, Sisson, and Counselor J. Butler Wright.

Echoing Sisson's cable of early December, Miles wrote Lansing recommending "the withdrawal of the American Ambassador at Petrograd to this country, either on grounds of health or for purposes of consultation, leaving Embassy under Chargé d'Affaires."[16]

Lansing ignored Miles's recommendations, and subsequent events suggest that he and Wilson were more concerned with all the surrogate ambassadors running around Petrograd than with Francis's mental state or his sub rosa contacts with the Bolsheviks. However, the secretary of state did remain troubled about Madame de Cramm and again warned Francis that the relationship was dangerous. In reply, Francis fumed that he was "being attacked by professed friends" and insisted that

> . . . anyone charging improper relations with party named is a willful liar and anybody who repeats such rumors after hearing of this denial by myself is also willful liar. Person named has not visited Embassy since receipt of your [cable of] November 14, 4 P.M. If this statement does not put an end to gossip, I shall demand names of those responsible. . . . Both you and I have matters of too much import on our minds and hands to be annoyed or diverted by such personal gossip.

Francis wrote:

> Person named has long desired to go to America with her son. . . . Know her to be guiltless of espionage. Have hitherto hesitated to recommend admission to America but desire now to do so unless you know entrance will be denied. . . . Having . . . learned she is under suspicion in America, Madam Cramm determined to go there in order to clear her reputation. She is thorough Russian and has been of assistance to me in imparting information concerning Russian sentiment toward German and toward Bolshevik Government and concerning Petrograd conditions. [At the bottom of the telegram from Francis, the State Department telegrapher apologized for a delay in decoding it, and blamed the delay on "inexperience on the part of the person encoding it. It was probably encoded by the Ambassador personally."][17]

Francis's statement that Madame de Cramm had not visited the embassy since November 21, when he received Lansing's coded cable of November 14 telling him to "sever" the relationship, is not true.[18] Not until his cable of December 4 to Lansing did he agree to stop her visits to the embassy, and apparently he did so.

He may have been confused about dates. More to the point, however, even after Madame stopped coming to the embassy, Francis saw her at her apartment and on evening walks and drives. He admitted as much in a January 8 letter to journalist Herman Bernstein, who had established the tenuous two-year connection between Madame de Cramm and the spy Mirolubskaya. His meetings with Madame, Francis insisted to Bernstein, were purely for "diversion from the arduous duties which sorely tax my endurance, and for the purpose of practicing French." He asked for Bernstein's help in clearing Madame's name so she could get a visa to go to America with her son.

Francis said he worried about Matilda, who looked "worn and worried, has lost flesh and the gray in her hair has visibly increased." She had written him, he said, "most pathetically about this suspicion upon her loyalty to Russia, saying, 'Don't you see how I am changed now? How bad I look? And Heaven knows how bad I feel! . . . I am so serious in all of my feelings that sometimes I feel a pity for myself.'"[19]

Francis put the letter to Bernstein in an envelope addressed to the politically powerful Colonel Edward House. He included a note to Colonel House, saying he would trust him to decide whether or not to forward the letter to Bernstein, saying he did not want Bernstein to turn it into another "sensational newspaper story." He mentioned wanting to help Madame de Cramm get to America and seemed to be trying, not very subtly, to enlist House's aid.[20]

There is no evidence that House forwarded the letter to Bernstein. He may well have shown it to Lansing or his good friend Woodrow Wilson, however, and in late January acting Secretary of State Frank Polk cabled Francis outlining the department's position on Madame de Cramm, acknowledging that she might well be the subject of "unjust suspicion," but that the threat of scandal existed just the same, and thus it was very important that Francis sever his connections with her. "We are glad to hear that her visits to the Embassy have ceased," Polk said. "No objection will be made to her entrance into this country."[21]

No doubt Matilda de Cramm desperately wanted to get out of revolutionary Petrograd, where people were being killed daily in the streets, the Bolsheviks were throwing monied families out of their houses and apartments, and it had become exceedingly difficult to find anything to eat. Through Philip Jordan, Francis sent her food, but she feared that Francis soon would be forced to leave Petrograd. And she knew that even if he stayed their relationship was under attack and could end. On January 25, she cabled a business associate of her brother in New York, "Horrible times desire meet husband cable where." She received a remarkably fast reply telling her that Edgar de Cramm would be in Yokohama at the end of February.[22]

On February 7, before Edgar could sail for Japan, he was arrested in San Francisco on charges of espionage. For the next six months, until he was pressured into leaving the country, he was either in jail or under close government surveillance. Matilda de Cramm remained in Petrograd.

The winter of 1918 was another terrible one for Petrograd. Amid a horrendous January Arctic blizzard that smothered the city, Philip Jordan wrote to Jane Francis:

> This is to let you know that the Ambassador is well but is Still Very bussy. things has quieted down a little and we do not have any more fighting. It makes us all feel a little lonesome not to hear the cannons and machine guns any more. the weathr has changed from warm to awful cold. to day it is 18 below zero. we have had the biggest Snow that Russia has had in 50 years. for 48 hours it has been Snowing as it never Snowed before. all traffic is at a Stand Still. No Street Cars or Automobiles or R. R. trains have moved for 24 hours. the streets are like tunnels. the Snow is piled up 8 and 10 feet high. the

Ambassador goes out in all of this in the Sleigh and also for a walk. . . . the city is full of [Germans] and more coming all the time. the hotels and restaurants are full of them. it looks like poor Russia is through as far as the war is concerned. you can See thousands of Soldiers and Sailors returning from the front. food is Still very Scarce and hard to get. . . . Some people will send their maids out in the Streets at 6 oclock in the morning to Stand in line for 6 to 8 hours in 20 degrees of cold. . . . I have Seen these poor Servants Standing in line so long without anything to eat that they would drop in the streets. . . . at times it looks as if we will all be killed and then all will quiet down again.[23]

The blizzard barely had ended when on January 13 another political crisis erupted. Count Constantine Diamandi, the Rumanian minister in Petrograd, was arrested, allegedly in retaliation for anti-Soviet propaganda and attacks on Soviet soldiers by members of the Rumanian army at the front. Diamandi and several of his aides were jailed in the St. Peter and Paul Fortress. Sisson believed, with reason, that the Bolsheviks were trying to force the Rumanians to hew to the Bolshevik line in the Brest-Litovsk peace negotiations and that Lenin also had his eye on the millions of dollars in Rumanian gold that had been moved to Russia for "safe keeping" during the war.[24]

Francis and Judson were at the Mariinksy Ballet when they got the news. Francis was outraged that a man supposedly protected by the rules of diplomacy had been arrested, and he worried about who would be next. On the morning of January 14, as diplomatic dean, he convened the heads of the nineteen other missions in Petrograd, both Allies and neutral nations. They hashed out a protest note. The first draft, according to Sisson, "contained a sentence that if the Rumanian was not released they would all call for passports at once [i.e., head home]; but Francis, knowing that the President didn't want the United States to cut its relations with Russia, kicked hard and wisely. So the final form [of the note] was protest but not ultimatum."[25] The note expressed the diplomats' deep indignation at the arrests in violation of diplomatic immunity and called for the immediate release of Diamandi and his aides.

Francis wanted to present the protest to Lenin in person. Sisson, with the help of Alexander Gumberg, got through to the Soviet leader.[26] Early that afternoon, a signed note from Lenin on the stationery of the Petrograd Peoples' Soviet was hand-delivered to Francis. It read:

Mr. David R. Francis
American Ambassador
Petrograd

Sir;
Being unable to connect with you by telephone at 2 o'clock as agreed, am writing in order to inform you that I shall be pleased to receive you at my office, Room 81, Smolny Institute, at 4 o'clock P.M. today.

Respectfully Lenine[27]

Some members of the diplomatic corps wanted to send a representative delegation, but Francis argued they should all go in a body, and the others agreed. When other Bolshevik leaders heard the diplomats were coming, there was considerable agitation. The visit seemed to imply recognition. At the least, as Sisson put it, "It certainly was recognition that the Bolshevik Government had an official call from the representatives of the countries that refuse to concede its existence."[28]

The ambassadors arrived in a long row of black limousines and proceeded through Smolny's high stone arches. In his memoirs, French Ambassador Noulens recalled the "state of indescribable disorder" that the diplomats walked through to get to Lenin's second-floor office in the imposing, neoclassical building that less than a year before had housed and schooled the daughters of the aristocracy:

> Military camping gear, kettles in which was prepared the soup which the Red Guards and the People's Commissars shared fraternally, wooden bowls encrusted with grease, were mingled with cannons, machine guns, and rifles, some stacked, others leaning against the walls or lying around the floor among every possible sort of debris. . . .
>
> The building was vast. We had to pass through a whole series of halls before, at the end of a corridor and under the shadow of a doorway, there appeared a little man with an enormous head and with the smiling eyes of a Tatar: it was Lenin. The face, dominating and powerful, was indeed that of genius, but the semi-flat nose, the mouth and chin gave him the disturbing aspect of a barbarian.

When Lenin saw the previously elusive diplomats approach, according to Noulens, he smiled, "triumphing at the idea of seeing these Ambassadors who, up to this time, had refused to have anything to do with them."[29]

Francis took the lead and introduced himself and the other members of the delegation. Lenin, who was standing at the doorway of his office, then invited the twenty men and their aides to cram themselves into the twelve-by-fifteen-foot room and take seats on wooden chairs and a bench.[30] Inside waited Zalkind, Trotsky's assistant in the Foreign Office, and a stranger—Soviet Central Committee member Joseph Stalin.[31]

Francis, standing, read the statement in English. Then Livingston Phelps, the French-born third secretary of the American Embassy, translated into French. (Butler Wright once again missed a pivotal historical moment—he was cross-country skiing at his country place near Tsarskoe Selo.)

Lenin responded that Rumanian "counterrevolutionaries" had been killing Russian soldiers. Francis replied, "We will not discuss causes or justification but only the principal involved." He insisted that "the person of a diplomatic representative was inviolate and was immune" according to long-established principles of international relations. Francis and Noulens demanded the immediate release of Diamandi.

Francis said, "You are trying to establish a government here. Consider that the arrest of the Rumanian Minister instead of avoiding war will render it all the more certain. . . . The arrest of Mr. Diamandi will affect you possibly very unfavorably not only in Russia but throughout the world."

Lenin agreed to reconsider the question. If Diamandi were released, he asked Francis, could he guarantee that Rumania would not make war against Russia? Francis said he could give no such guarantee.[32] Lenin said he would discuss the matter with the Soviet of People's Commissars—in effect, his cabinet—and would call Francis that evening.

Francis remarked after the meeting that he found Lenin "agreeable and friendly." Of that judgment, Sisson remarked, "I do not think so, but I would sooner have the Ambassador on easy terms with a government that has to be dealt with every day in some way or other than to have him take the old stand that he would be 'damned if he would ever talk to a Bolshevik.'"[33]

Later that day, Robins and Gumberg came to the embassy to find out how the meeting with Lenin had gone. Francis told them that if the Bolsheviks released Diamandi he would "see what he could do to bring about better relations between the Rumanian Government and the Soviet." His intention, he later recalled, was to "advise the Roumanians not to kill Soviet soldiers." But he considered the conversation confidential and not to be repeated to the Bolsheviks.[34] Gumberg, whose brother was a Soviet official, apparently passed on the gist of the conversation. Around midnight, Lenin called Francis and told him that Diamandi had been released.

The next day, Francis was outraged to discover that *Pravda*, the official Bolshevik newspaper, had reported that he had met with Lenin and agreed, in return for the release of Diamandi, to make a formal protest to the Rumanian government over the treatment of Russian troops at the front. In a public announcement, and in a letter to Diamandi, he said he had made no such commitment.

About a week later, Francis received a terse telegram from Lansing, commenting on his confrontation with Lenin. "Press reports show your efforts successful," Lansing wrote. "Department approves your course thoroughly."[35] Shortly afterward, the Rumanian ambassador was forced by the Bolsheviks to leave Russia and barely escaped assassination. Lenin kept the gold.

The long-awaited, long-promised Constituent Assembly had planned to meet, at last, in December, but Lenin had cancelled the session when it became clear that more moderate socialists had the majority. To change the balance of power, the Bolsheviks arrested Constitutional Democrats who had been elected to Duma seats. Then Lenin agreed to let the assembly convene on Friday, January 18, 1918, in the Tauride Palace. The Bolsheviks were ready with armed men in the streets and warships in the Neva, their cannons pointed at the palace. Philip Jordan spent most of the day near the palace, and he described the scene to Jane:

> To day is the day that the Constituent Assembly will open. it is now 330 pm and it has not opened. at 11 am a crowd of about 2000 with banners reading long live the assembly was fired on Just one block from the Embassy and ever

so many was Killed. I have just returned from the Street where the firing is
going on and people are running for their lives. I could count at least ten dead
ones but the machine guns was turned in my direction and Just about this
time I had business at the embassy. All over town you can See men on top of
houses with machine guns. over at the palace where the assembly will meet
they have Soldiers on top of the palace and on the ground with machine guns.
we are looking for one of the worst battles to take place at night. the ice
breaker [Ermak] steamed up the Never river on tuesday and broke the ice so
that 4 battle Ships could come up. they are now at anchor Just below the winter Palace where they are all ready for business. . . . they can tear Petrograd to
pieces in a few hours. . . . things are getting worse instead of better. I will have
to finish this letter because Mr. Johnston has Just Sent word that the pouch is
ready to go. I can hear the cannons roaring. people are running by the
Embassy. the Very best luck to you all.
Respt Philip
[p.s.] A Soldier has Just fell dead across the Street. Philip[36]

About 4 P.M., with the cannon fire still echoing in their ears, the delegates inside the
Tauride Palace went into session. The first vote, which rejected the radical Declaration
on the Rights of Working People by 237 to 146, showed the moderate socialists still held
the majority. Lenin ordered the assembly closed, and the Red Guards cleared the hall,
signaling the end of anything approaching Western-style democracy in Russia for three-
quarters of a century.[37]

That day, Philip Jordan wrote to W. H. Lee of the Merchants' Laclede Bank:

When we have battles we do not have them out in the open but right in the
heart of the city, just the same as having machine guns and cannon in front of
the Merchants Laclede and at Broadway and Washington. I have watched
these battles for 20 or 30 minutes and after it was finished you could not see
anything in the streets but dead soldiers and horses. . . . the Italian embassy
was broken into. It looks like they don't respect foreign embassies any more.[38]

Jordan was right about the growing lack of respect for foreign embassies, including
the American one. Francis had begun receiving anonymous threats, one of which said,
"You irritate the nerves" and advised him to "pack the trunk" and get out of Russia.[39] On
January 19, a virulently anti-American article appeared in a Petrograd anarchist newspaper. The next day, Francis was presiding over a meeting of Allied chiefs of mission
when he got an urgent telephone call. A woman said she had some important information and wanted to meet someone from the embassy at an intersection about eight
blocks away.

Francis sent Earl Johnston and Dr. William Huntington, the commercial attaché,
who came back with a disturbing tale. The woman said a soldier had tried to sell her
some wine that he said had been looted from the Italian Embassy. The American
Embassy, he had told her, was next. It would be attacked that night and burned to the
ground. The ambassador would be killed.

That evening, a Sunday, Francis had arranged a reception for two hundred people to say farewell to General Judson, who was leaving for America in three days. Judson, with Francis's approval, used his contacts in the Bolshevik military to get ten soldiers assigned as guards. The soldiers arrived about 9 P.M. "They did not look or deport themselves as soldiers," Francis noted. "But I told Phil to give them cigarettes and tea, soup and bread. . . . They consumed that rapidly and asked for more."[40]

Guests began arriving about 9:30. Among them were two Russian officers in full uniform. When they took off their winter coats and exposed epaulets with insignia of high rank, the Bolshevik soldiers threatened to rush upstairs and rip away the epaulets. The outnumbered servants tried to keep them from climbing the stairs. Consular officer DeWitt Poole feared that if the Bolsheviks reached the officers they might kill them.

Then, Poole recalled, "The ambassador walked out. He was dressed in full evening clothes. He walked . . . to the top of the stairs, and these soldiers were down there. This fine-looking old man demanded in Missouri English, 'What do you fellows think you're doing in here?' They turned and walked out."

"The old governor," Poole wrote, "was absolutely fearless. . . . He, just by his impressive physical appearance, bluffed out a squad of Bolshevik forces."[41]

After a long argument, Judson and Norman Armour persuaded Francis to leave the embassy and spend the night in Johnston's apartment nearby. The next day, Francis assigned four American marines, who had been serving as couriers and scheduled to go home, to stay and guard the embassy. He was determined to spend his nights in his own bed.

The threatened anarchists never showed up. Lenin sent a messenger to the embassy to tell Francis that Trotsky had prevented them from attacking the embassy. Robins, who continued to visit Smolny almost daily, told Francis he didn't think an attack ever had been planned. In any event, Francis assured Perry in a long letter, he was ready: "as you know I don't scare easy. On the contrary I have wired the Department not to permit consideration for my safety to influence the action of the Government." After a lengthy recital of Bolshevik horrors, he remarked, "It is fortunate that your Mother never came to Russia."[42]

On January 23, General Judson left for Washington, blaming Francis in part for his recall. And he remained deeply offended by the de Cramm relationship. Judson later wrote:

> For a long time she spent nearly every evening at the Embassy. I was frequently present at their tete-a-tetes and able to study the woman and her influence over the Ambassador. . . . Her influence over the Ambassador seemed vastly greater than that of all the Embassy Staff and Military Mission combined. He made it a practice to talk over the public business with her. She knew the contents of many if not most of his cables.[43]

Francis would miss Judson, his experience and his counsel, and the ambassador's extensive reliance on the experienced military attaché right up to the moment of departure suggests he knew it. To the extent that his contradictory cables of early December were responsible for Judson's recall, he had blundered.

Colonel James A. Ruggles replaced Judson as head of the American Military Mission. Lieutenant Colonel Monroe Kerth was loyal to Judson and returned with him. Ruggles took his predecessor's place in Francis's regular bridge and poker games, but he knew little of Russia and was an inadequate replacement for Judson or Kerth. By then, communication between Petrograd and Washington had become even more difficult because civil war between Red and White armies had broken out in Finland, the usual route for couriers carrying diplomatic pouches.

Letters by post often were delayed for months and sometimes lost, increasing the isolation of Petrograd from Washington. Butler Wright, whose wife and son already had been sent home, wrote in his diary, "Personally, there is nothing in the world that I want more than to leave this filthy place; patriotically, I think we . . . should stay as long as possible."[44]

And in Washington, the wheels of statesmanship continued to grind slowly. On February 9, Lansing sent a memo to Woodrow Wilson:

> Recently, the Ambassador has used Mr. Robins, the head of the American Red
> Cross Mission in Russia, as a channel of information. In a telegram dated
> January 31st, Mr. Francis says that he is endeavoring through Mr. Robins to
> have Lenine revoke the appointment of John Reed as Bolsheviki representative
> here. [Reed had left Petrograd on February 6.] In order to save the Roumanian
> Minister, it appears that Ambassador Francis went directly to Lenine and
> again to the Foreign Office. . . . The Ambassador, therefore, has begun on his
> own initiative to make use of Robins further than to secure information and
> is also finding it necessary to come in touch personally with the Bolsheviki
> authorities. As we have never modified our instructions to him and it is evi-
> dent that he feels the necessity of keeping in touch with the authorities, it
> might be wise to instruct him accordingly, leaving to him the selection of the
> channel through which he may desire to communicate.

Wilson must have reacted positively, because five days later Lansing cabled Francis an expansion of his earlier "stay-the-course" instructions: "Department approves your course and desires you gradually to keep in somewhat closer and informal touch with Bolshevik authorities using such channels as will avoid official recognition. This government is by no means prepared to recognize Bolshevik Government officially. Department's previous instructions are modified to this extent."[45]

Meanwhile, in Petrograd, David Francis got his hands on what seemed to be proof of what he long had suspected—that the Germans and the Bolsheviks were not only in bed together but were planning to elope. On the evening of Monday, February 4, Francis received a visit from Russian journalist Eugene Semenov, editor of a soon-to-be sup-pressed anti-German newspaper. Semenov had a photostat of a letter that he said was from the Soviet files at Smolny. The lengthy letter suggested that the Bolsheviks were scheming with the German High Command to betray the Allies.

The next morning, Francis showed Sisson the letter. Sisson decided it "implied the continuation of a German-Bolshevik bond after the Revolution. . . . The horrid point, both to the Ambassador and me, was that the communication before us presented Trotsky as conniving at precise military advantage for Germany against the Allies, against the United States." It appeared the Bolsheviks were not only eager to sign a separate peace, thus releasing hundreds of thousands of German troops for the Western Front, but also they were willing to spy on the Allies.[46]

Sisson then told Francis about a sheaf of documents Robins had shown him on February 2, letters, circulars, and memos suggesting that the Germans had been funneling money to the Bolsheviks from the very beginning of the Great War. Shortly afterward, copies of the documents, in English, arrived at Sisson's office near the center of Petrograd. Robins was convinced they were forgeries. Sisson wasn't so sure. If legitimate, the documents showed that Lenin, Trotsky, and other Bolshevik leaders had been, as Sisson put it, "accredited and financed agents of Germany" for at least two years, and that the Bolsheviks had been acting under orders from the German General Staff to disrupt the Allied war effort.

Francis and Sisson agreed that Washington needed to be notified. It took several days to encode the voluminous documents. They were cabled to Washington in five sections from February 9 to February 13. By then, copies in Russian and English were all over Petrograd.[47]

In the meantime, Francis asked Sisson to check on their validity. After talking to E. T. Boyce, head of British Intelligence in Petrograd, and other intelligence officers, Sisson concluded that at least some of the documents were valid, confirming his deepening distrust of the Bolsheviks. Robins insisted they were forgeries. He said later that "there were more forged papers . . . in Russia than ever before in human history" and claimed he could have found documents to prove almost anything.[48]

Francis agreed with Sisson, and on February 8 he cabled Lansing: "Have absolutely reliable evidence that Lenin, Trotsky accepted German money from June to October professedly for peace propaganda and army demoralization but I have not shown to Robins as [that] might impair his effectiveness by weakening his implicit confidence in their sincerity."[49]

Disagreement over what came to be called the Sisson Papers flared into angry arguments between Robins and Sisson. The two men began passing one another without speaking. Robins frequently complained about Sisson to Francis and, Francis said later, "became quite confidential with me."

At one point, desperate to maintain favor with the ambassador, Robins told Francis about Sisson's December cable calling for Francis to be removed from his post and brought home. This was news to Francis. Angry, he called in all the top members of his staff and asked if any of them had known of the Sisson cable. All said they had not. Francis temporarily may have dismissed Robins's sensational charge as a lie, intended to inflict damage on Sisson. "Probably Sisson and Robins both influenced by pride of opinion and mutual animosity," Francis noted a bit later.[50] He mentioned nothing about the cable to Sisson, at least not immediately. Meanwhile, Sisson's disillusionment with the Bolsheviks deepened.

As to the validity of the Sisson Papers, George Kennan has argued persuasively that for reasons of typing, handwriting, use of language, historical implausibility, and "contradiction of known facts and other reasons," most of them were "rather obvious and clumsy forgeries."[51] But, as Kennan acknowledges, Lenin had strong links to the Germans, going back to the early days of World War I, when he had called for victory by Germany as a step toward revolution in his native land. German Foreign Ministry records that came to light in the 1950s show that the Germans worked hard in 1917 and 1918 to bring the Bolsheviks to power and keep them there, allocating forty million marks for that purpose as late as June 1918, and avoiding moves on the battlefield that would weaken the Bolsheviks.[52]

Although some of that information from the 1950s has come under question, Russian documents released since the end of the Cold War confirm that the Germans subsidized Lenin in 1917 and 1918. He used the Germans for his own ends and detested the Germans as much as he did any other capitalist power. His attitude was typified by a 1918 note to a Swiss Communist who served as a conduit for German money. "The Berliners will send some more money," Lenin wrote. "If the scum delay, complain to me formally."[53]

In cables to Lansing that February, Francis said he was "satisfied" that Lenin and Trotsky received money from the Germans and that they were "willing to sacrifice any country," including Russia, to "promote the chances of their world-wide social revolution."[54] And in March 1918, Francis told Lansing that the Bolsheviks "could not have better promoted the interests of Germany if they had been paid agents."[55] His main advisor, Butler Wright, was at least as suspicious of the Germans as Francis, writing in his diary in late January, "I have yet to find one conclusive proof that these Smolny elements are not in German pay."[56]

At midnight on February 13—January 31 by Russian reckoning—the Bolsheviks added thirteen days to their calendar. The next day was February 14 in both Russia and the West. "This is the sole reasonable thing the Bolshevik rule will leave to Russia," was the remark of Count Dmitri Tolstoy, director of the Hermitage Museum.[57]

Sisson finally had finished transmitting the coded documents that bore his name and had little time for relaxation with his new friend, David Francis. They dined together at the embassy, and Philip Jordan miraculously continued to discover food. Sisson, who had a sweet tooth, wrote in his log of February 8, "A real dinner, white bread, wine, cookies." In the absence of cookies—sugar was very hard to come by—Sisson discovered that "a drink of whiskey sent the sugar haunt scurrying away."

Francis, Sisson noted, was a "careful doler" of whiskey, sharing "with the utmost fairness, warning that the stock was getting lower. The final courier of the last day of January, happily, brought a new supply from far-off St. Louis, replenishment from the old man's thoughtful sons. Not until the old stock was gone did the Ambassador tell gleefully about the new. A welcoming drink and a good dinner following was mighty cheer."[58]

Robins and Sisson still were not speaking. Francis met separately with both men and let them continue in their separate directions, both of which he found useful. The feud grew more intense after February 10, when Trotsky announced that the Russians would neither fight the Germans nor give in to their demands. There would be "neither war nor peace," as Trotsky put it. The Soviet delegation marched out of peace talks in Brest-Litovsk and headed back to Petrograd, throwing the Allies into even more confusion and fearful speculation. On February 18, Francis received word that the Germans were on the march, advancing up through Estonia and down through Finland, and could be in Petrograd in a few days. That evening, the Chinese ambassador came to the embassy for a bridge game and announced that he expected to leave Petrograd quite soon. Sisson recalled that the remark "left us thoughtful, indeed."[59]

Sisson and Robins separately urged Francis to get out of Petrograd. Even if the Bolsheviks did make a last-minute peace with the Germans, they argued, Lenin was reportedly preparing to move the government inland to the ancient Slavic capital of Moscow and away from effete, Westernized Petrograd, a city he detested. With the top Bolsheviks gone, Robins warned, "great disorders were likely to prevail," leaving little respect for the rights of foreign diplomats.[60]

On February 21, after a meeting of the Allied ambassadors, Francis cabled the secretary of state:

> Germans still advancing. Five allied ambassadors have agreed to prepare for departure on short notice. British going via Murmansk, Japanese and myself via Vladivostok, French and Italian undecided. Trying to secure special train for Japanese Chinese Americans. Planning to stop enroute Vologda and other places if safe. . . .
>
> Unwilling to absolutely abandon Russia to Germans. . . . Don't know when Germans will take Petrograd but such is their intention and any hour may see uprising here in German interest—sufficient German Austrian prisoners available to form larger army than Red Guard. Petrograd garrison numbering fifty thousand or more refused to oppose German advance.[61]

Although emergency preparations were made for a departure by train across Siberia to the Pacific port of Vladivostok, Francis wanted to stay in Russia. His aide Norman Armour explained later, "So long as the war with Germany continued, [Francis felt] it was his duty and an important contribution to the war effort, for him to remain in Russia and try to keep up some semblance of a front there."[62] Francis said, "I did not like to abandon the Russian people, for whom I felt a deep sympathy and whom I had assured repeatedly of America's unselfish interest in their welfare."[63]

Francis talked to his advisors, and studied the map, and his eye fell on Vologda, a small inland city of about fifty thousand people that was at the juncture of major north-south and east-west railroad lines. It offered escape, if necessary, to the east through

Vladivostok and to the north through the White Sea port of Archangel. Francis decided to leave Petrograd but stay in Russia, and at a late February meeting, he urged his diplomatic colleagues, both Allies and those from neutral nations like Sweden, to do the same.

"Where are you going?" one of them asked him. He replied, "I am going to Vologda."

"What do you know about Vologda?" he was asked.

"Not a thing except that it is the junction of the Trans-Siberian Railway and the Moscow-Archangel Railway and that it is 350 miles farther away from the Germans."

"Well, if it is unsafe there, what are you going to do?"

"I am going east to Vitka, which is 600 miles east, and if it is unsafe there, I am going to Perm. If it is unsafe there, I am going to Itursk, and if it is still unsafe, I am going to Chita, and if necessary from there I am going to Vladivostok, where I will be protected by an American man-of-war, the Brooklyn."[64]

Raymond Robins agreed that relatively placid Vologda would be a good destination and persuaded a reluctant Lenin to let the diplomats go. He remarked later:

> The question of American interests remaining in Russia was of real concern to the Ambassador and myself. We wanted to stay there and play the hand out and re-win it if it was possible. . . . Vologda was selected because transportation was good . . . communication was good [because] the English controlled the cable to London. . . . Vologda was far enough north, at least, to be out of range of any expected German advance. Petrograd could fall and Moscow could fall and Vologda would still be free.[65]

Butler Wright also approved of the move to Vologda and admired Francis for taking the initiative to go there. All of the Allied diplomats, he noted in his diary, "are 'muddling,' I think, except our chief."[66] And, in connection with the move, Wright maintained that the American Embassy under Francis had "earned the reputation of being the best informed Embassy in Petrograd."[67]

The Japanese and Chinese were willing to join Francis and go east to Vologda, which was on their way to Vladivostok and home. Most of the Western diplomats chose to leave Russia by the most direct route possible. On February 24, the British, French, Italians, Belgians, Serbians, Portuguese, and Greeks began leaving on trains from the Finland Station, hoping to escape through Finland. They found themselves amid a civil war between White and Red Finnish armies, and only the British managed to slip through. The other diplomats were held by Finnish Bolsheviks for several weeks; eventually most of them were sent back to Russia, and they ended up in Vologda with Francis.

Shortly before departing for Vologda, in a secret cable to Lansing, Francis made what appears to be his first unambiguous endorsement of American military intervention, to keep Russia from becoming a "German province." He wrote, "I earnestly urge that we assume control Vladivostok and British and French take control Murmansk and Archangel in order to prevent supplies thereat falling into German hands. History shows

Russians incapable of great movements or great achievements as whatever creditable has been accomplished can be credited to foreign inspiration and leadership. Now is time for Allies to act." He added that he had no intention of leaving Russia "unless so ordered which trust not be the case."[68]

On Sunday, February 24, at Francis's orders, most of the embassy staff left for Vologda under the direction of the secretary of the embassy, James G. Bailey. The majority would continue to Vladivostok and sail for home.

Francis wrote his son that weekend:

> My plan is to stay in Russia as long as I can . . . if any section of Russia refuses to recognize the authority of the Bolshevik Government to conclude [a separate peace] I shall endeavor to locate in that section and encourage the rebellion . . . if there are any people organizing in Russia for armed resistance to Germany, I shall encourage them and recommend our Government to assist them. You may not conclude therefore that I am planning to return to America.[69]

Before turning the embassy over to the neutral Norwegians, Francis and the handful of Americans remaining spent February 25 and 26 packing and going through files. Confidential papers for the past ten years were burned in a bonfire in the courtyard.[70]

Phil Jordan described for Jane Francis his last day in Petrograd:

> Thousands are Standing in line all day and all night begging for tickets to get out of the city. the soldiers try and keep the croud from getting to large [and] have Started to turn the machine guns on them and hundreds are being killed every day. they kill from 3 to 4 hundred horses every day try to keep the people from starving. the Ambassador told me at ten oclock in the morning that we would have to leave by Six oclock as the Germans Was not Very far away and from whare they was they could reach Petrograd in 6 or 8 hours. he Said not to try and take every thing but only what I could carry and also to have the Ford in good Order because we might be cut off and that will be the only way to get away. well I got busy and at 430 I was loading all we had on the Sleighs to go to the Station. I had to leave the Ford and all the wine behind but brught every thing else.[71]

Francis took his golf clubs.

On February 26, Francis, Counselor Butler Wright, Second Secretary Norman Armour, Military Attaché Colonel James A. Ruggles, Ruggles's aides, Captains E. Francis Riggs and Eugene Prince, Private Secretary Earl Johnston, four marine guards, and Philip Jordan were taken with their baggage by sleigh to the Nikolai Station, where five months before Jordan and Francis had seen Bolshevik soldiers digging trenches in Nevsky Prospect. The diplomats had been allotted a special train. Accompanying the Americans were chiefs of mission representing Japan, China, Siam, and Brazil, as well as a few people from the American Red Cross Mission. Raymond Robins had decided to stay behind.[72]

By then, the Germans had advanced to near Pskov, about 150 miles south of Petrograd. Francis was anxious to leave, but the train just sat for several hours in the open shed of the station. He discovered that the Bolsheviks had changed their mind—the departure of the Americans, by suggesting lack of faith in the Bolsheviks, might trigger the forces of anarchy that constantly threatened to consume the country.

Robins, who was at the station, hurried to Smolny, about three and a half kilometers away, and confronted Lenin himself, telling him "it is worse to keep that train there than to send it out." If, Robins said, a mob should storm the American Embassy and "want to kill the American Ambassador, you might not be able to protect him, and then there would be a blot on the soviet in Russia from which it would never recover."[73]

Lenin reluctantly agreed. Robins returned to the station and decided to board the diplomatic train to make sure it got through. His friend and translator Alexander Gumberg joined him.

At 2 A.M. on Tuesday, February 27, the train pulled out of the station, headed briefly south toward Moscow, and then turned to the east in the direction of Vologda. Skirting the southern edge of Lake Ladoga, the source of the Neva, it headed slowly east across the flat marshlands. The departure ended 108 unbroken years of American diplomatic representation in the capital of Russia that went back to the days of John Quincy Adams, the first American ambassador.[74]

Russians trains, then and now, move slowly and stop often, and the 350-mile trip took twenty-six hours. The night temperature was below zero but birch-fired stoves heated the wooden cars, and as the winter dawn finally broke the Americans looked out over a vast snow-covered landscape, sometimes open to the horizon, sometimes hemmed in by tall, narrow, leafless stands of birch and thick green forests of spruce and Norway pine.

At every stop along the way, swarms of Russians clambered to get aboard, desperate to get inland and away from the Germans. Peasants in ragged army uniforms stuffed themselves into cattle and freight cars and clung to the outsides, even piling themselves on the buffer bars that angled down from the front of the train. "Every station was like an opened hive of grey-brown bees . . . and stank like a vast latrine," recalled Arthur Ransome, a British correspondent who was on the train, sharing a compartment with Gumberg. He described the scene as "aimless self-demobilisation": "I saw rolling stock, field-waggons and engineering plant evacuated from the Baltic front. Much of it had just been dumped by the side of the line, and would surely rot, but the fact that it was there at all was proof that an effort was being made to keep it from the Germans."[75]

THERE IS NO RECORD of when and where David Francis and Matilda de Cramm said goodbye. Later correspondence suggests they decided it would be unwise for her to go to Vologda with him. At some point, Francis must have gone to 81 Sergeivskaya Street for a farewell dinner or at least a glass of sherry. They wrote from time to time, and he appears to have missed her, as he appears to have missed Jane.

CHAPTER 19

The New Diplomatic Capital

Vologda, Russia. March 9, 1918

Mrs. Francis
You will see from this that we are still in Russia but not in Petrograd. the Ambassador has been in Vologda for 10 days. . . . we left Petrograd on a tuesday night and the next day the Germans began to bombard the city with airplanes. we did not get out one hour too Soon. poor Petrograd and the people. the People are Starving. they have Nothing at all to eat. . . .

when we arrived in Vologda the Ambassador lived on the train for a few days. on Wednesday [February 28] the Mayor of Vologda called on the Ambassador at the Station and welcomed him to the city. he also wanted to know if he could do any-thing for the Ambassador. the Ambassador said Something about getting a house to live in while here and the Mayor told him if he had the time to Spare he would like to Show him a large club house that was not in use at present. the Ambassador went with him and oh my what a dandy house he gave the Ambassador. It is all furnished . . . and as clean as it can be. we have a man cook . . . and chamber maid. the mayor has Sent all the Supplies that we will want for one month and we are now keeping house and living in grand Style. Now Mrs. Francis . . . I want to ask you if you dont think it was awful nice the way the Mayor has treated the American Ambassador. Of course you must take into consideration that the U.S. does not reconize these People or have any thing to do with them. the Mayor of New York City could not have done any more than this poor Bolshevik Mayor did. . . .

Just think next month we will be in Russia two years and it looks like the Ambassador will be here two more years. I don't See how he can get away until the war is finished. I think he is Satisfied because he never Says any thing about return-ing home. My Self I must say that I dont care how long he remains over here because I like it Very much. I have not had one lonesome day Since we have been in Russia. So much to do and See that you do not have time to get lonesome. . . . I will Stop because the Ambassador has Just Called Me to go with him for a walk. . . .

Respt. Philip.[1]

DAVID FRANCIS AND PHILIP JORDAN were still living on the train on March 3, when the Russian leaders signed the Treaty of Brest-Litovsk, bringing what Francis called "a disgraceful peace." The Bolsheviks, with Russia having suffered millions of casualties and its army in tatters, agreed to give up most of Russia's colonial territory in Europe. They granted "independence" under German protection to Poland, Finland, Estonia, Lithuania, and the Ukraine —in sum, the Russian empire lost about one-third of its population and half its industry. The treaty also exempted German property from nationalization by the Bolsheviks.

By the morning of Monday, March 4, word of the treaty-signing had penetrated to Vologda, and several reporters showed up at the diplomatic train. Francis issued a statement:

> While the present Soviet Government has never been formally recognized by my government nor by any of the Allied governments, both President Lenin and Commissaire Trotsky are aware, because I have so advised them, that I would recommend to my government the recognition of any government the Russian people might select and would also earnestly urge that material assistance be rendered such government provided it would continue the war against the Central Empires. . . . I should like to remain in Vologda as long as it is consistent with the interests of the trust I hold and as long as it is safe for me to do so—not meaning that I fear any harm or menace from the Russian people but only from our common enemy.[2]

The next day, Francis sent J. Butler Wright east to Vladivostok and then home to explain in detail to the State Department the unprecedented situation in Russia. Wright was to check on the condition of rails across Siberia, and learn what he could about Japanese forces in and around eastern Russia. Japan was also at war with Germany and alarmed by the increasing German presence in Russia, and it had been threatening to invade its old enemy through Vladivostok and northern Manchuria.[3]

Francis and the other Americans moved into the former clubhouse, welcomed not only by the mayor but the president of the city Duma and the head of the local Soviet. The two-story, twenty-room wooden house also became the home of the Brazilian chargé, the Siamese minister, his three-year-old son, and the boy's nurse. Four tall wooden pillars out front supported a wooden Grecian pediment, familiar architecture to Francis. It was a few blocks east of the city's bustling haymarket and two blocks north of the gentle, curling Vologda River, at a busy intersection on what was still called Ekaterininsko-Dvoryanskaya Street (Catherine-Nobility Street—the name was later changed to Herzen Street.)

Vologda was an ancient city, founded, like Moscow, in the twelfth century. Scattered throughout the main part of town were several dozen classic onion-dome churches, including Vologda's centerpiece, St. Sophia, established by Ivan the Terrible. St. Sophia had been the center of Vologda's old kremlin, or citadel. Inside, the church displays startlingly well-preserved, dramatic seventeenth-century frescoes rising up its high interior walls and covering the ceiling. The frescoes, in the style of the early Italian Renaissance, depict Roman Catholics and other non-Orthodox Christians burning in the leaping fires of hell.

"Beautiful churches and the climate is Just grand," exclaimed Jordan. "So different from that dirty Petrograd. We have Something here that we hardly ever had in Petrograd and that is nice bright Sun Shine."[4]

Arthur Ransome, the British correspondent who accompanied the diplomats to Vologda, found it to be "a little, simple country town, white with snow":

> There was hardly a brick building in the place, but little log-houses of one or two stories, broad untidy squares and street-markets, with churches in every open space, white churches against the blue winter sky, churches capped with towers of every kind of intricate design, showing the great bronze bells hanging in their airy belfries beside domes of gold and green, of plain grey lead and of violent deep blue, thickly sown with golden stars.[5]

On March 29, French ambassador Joseph Noulens and his party, unable to escape through war-clogged Finland, showed up at Vologda and moved into an abandoned school building a block from Francis's clubhouse. The Italian chargé, Marquis della Torretta, and the Serbian minister, Miroslav Spalaikov, were on the train with Noulens. They lived in parked railroad cars until they found homes. David Francis soon said, with justice, that Vologda was the diplomatic capital of Russia.

As Jordan quickly discovered, the markets of Vologda offered plenty of meat, winter produce, and canned goods. Francis had brought whisky with him, and more arrived from time to time from friends and relatives back home, sometimes accompanied by boxes of cigars. The makeshift American Embassy became, in the evenings, a kind of impromptu, well-provisioned men's club, with poker and cigars and whisky and, in a pinch, cheap local vodka and Russian champagne. When not sipping liquor and playing cards, or flirting with the local women, the diplomats dealt with affairs of state and, under the watchful eyes of the fledgling Bolshevik secret police, encouraged and funded local spies and counterrevolutionaries. In this regard, it helped greatly that National City Bank had a branch and about fifteen employees in Vologda. The bank almost certainly acted as a conduit for secret dispersions of large sums.[6]

In general, a casual male comaraderie prevailed, with a bracing whiff of intrigue and danger, and Francis was much more comfortable with his situation than with the carefully patterned diplomatic dance of official Petrograd. Francis's and Jordan's letters from Vologda show a sense of relief at being out of Petrograd, in part at having escaped with their lives but more at being away from the city's hunger, the night-long gunfire and the bodies revealed in the streets by the dawn, and the sheer physical and emotional stress of the beleaguered capital. Even the weather was better in Vologda, inland away from the cutting sea winds and the grim Baltic fogs mixed with acrid city smoke. The days were cold but crisp and sunny, and at times in the late winter you already could sniff spring in the air.

On March 15, Philip Jordan wrote Jane Francis:

> To day is a beautiful bright Sun Shiney day. it is Nice and warm. the
> Ambassador and I have just returned from the telegraph Station where he
> talked with Col Robins who is in Moscow attending the peace conference [to
> ratify the Brest-Litovsk Treaty]. of course poor Russia will Sign any thing
> because She has no army or no Soldiers to fight. . . . the Ambassador is Still in
> the Very best of helth. eats and sleeps well. I do not take any chances with
> these Russian cooks but cook for him as much as I can. this morning I gave
> him bacon and eggs, fried corn meal mush and hot cakes with Strawberrie
> Jam. . . . I am very sorry that I have no News for you. in Petrograd I could
> always go out and find plenty of News but here in this Village it is different.[7]

Raymond Robins and some of his Allied colleagues, including Bruce Lockhart, continued to cherish the illusory hope that the Fourth All-Russian Congress of Soviets,
which would meet in the new capital of Moscow, would reject the Brest-Litovsk Treaty
and that Russia could then be convinced to get up and fight again. Francis doubted that
anything like that would happen, but he was open to the possibility. Robins was not his
only emissary to the Bolsheviks. After receiving hints through the French that massive
Allied aid might revive Russia's bellicosity, he sent two military attachés, Colonel James
Ruggles and Captain Francis Riggs, to discuss the possibilities with Soviet military leaders. But any plans were contingent on the congress rejecting the treaty, a slim possibility since Lenin and, reluctantly, Trotsky already had approved it.

Robins pinned his hopes on his knowledge that Trotsky seethed at the treaty's
humiliating terms. On March 5, pushed by Robins, Trotsky had written down for Francis
a series of hypothetical questions on U.S.–Russian relations. Although the excitable
Robins felt he had achieved a breakthrough with the "what-if?" message from Trotsky,
in retrospect it appears so vague and conditional as to be almost meaningless. The central question asked by Trotsky was: If the Soviet Congress refused to ratify the treaty,
could the Russians "rely on the support of the United States?"

Robins, burning to get a quick and decisive response, ran into problems getting
Trotsky's questions properly coded and wired to Francis, so he took the train to Vologda
on March 8 and laid them in front of the ambassador. Late that night, Francis cabled
Washington, giving the gist of Robins's message. He stressed Trotsky's argument that the
threatened Japanese invasion of Siberia made quick ratification of the treaty with
Germany almost inevitable. Trotsky wanted the United States and the Western Allies to
stop Japan from invading. Francis noted in his cable:

> Trotsky told Robins that he had heard that such invasion was countenanced
> by the Allies and especially by America. [That] would not only force the
> Government to advocate the ratification of the humiliating peace but would
> so completely estrange all factions in Russia that further resistance to
> Germany would be absolutely impossible. Trotsky furthermore asserted that

neither his government nor the Russian people would object to the supervision by America of all shipments from Vladivostok into Russia [to block shipments of German war materials] and a virtual control of the operations of the Siberian railway, but a Japanese invasion would result in non-resistance and eventually make Russia a German province. . . . In my judgment a Japanese advance now would be exceedingly unwise and this midnight cable is sent for the purpose of asking that our influence may be exerted to prevent same. Please reply immediately. More tomorrow.[8]

Francis later was criticized by Robins, among others, for not taking Trotsky's questions more seriously, but in light of this cable and subsequent messages and actions, Francis seems to have taken them at least as seriously as intended. Trotsky wanted the aid, but he knew the treaty would be ratified, and he had no intention, as he put it at the time, of letting the Allies "drag us into the war" with promises of "millions of blessings."[9] The social historian Christopher Lasch, a perceptive critic of the shibboleths of the American Left, has commented that Robins's naive version of "the events of March, 1918, became an article of faith among American anti-imperialists. They now added to their indictment of American and Allied policy the blame for having left Russia with no choice except to sign a separate peace."[10]

Lenin and Trotsky were not averse to accepting American and Allied aid, even if they had to swallow a few soldiers in the bargain. And they by no means trusted the Germans. With Trotsky's approval, in early March, barely a week before the treaty with Germany was scheduled to be ratified, a small contingent of British troops went ashore at Murmansk on the Barents Sea at the northern tip of Russia. Their mission was to protect the crucial port and its railway lines from the Germans. Trotsky and the British had agreed that Russian and Allied troops would work together under joint command. French troops soon joined them, and Trotsky told Military Attaché Ruggles that American troops and officers also would be welcome, as would American railroad experts.[11]

Francis wired engineer John F. Stevens, who was now in Japan, to send him twenty railroad engineers for the rail lines to the north. "It was my intention to improve the transportation facilities of Russia," he recalled later, "with a view to assembling all supplies at Archangel and Murmansk to prevent the Germans from capturing them." Lansing was worried that these engineers would help the Bolsheviks more than the Allies and delayed sending them, a decision Francis came to agree with. Eleven engineers eventually arrived at Vladivostok on May 12, but by then the Trans-Siberian Railway was blocked by civil war.[12]

Francis had learned a great deal since his early fumbling relations with the Bolsheviks. He realized how important it was to keep open the doors of communication while always remaining suspicious of Bolshevik intentions. And having observed the shocking disarray of the Russian army in Petrograd and on the trip to Vologda, he also was aware that the people of Russia did not want to continue the war. He believed that only large-scale American aid, including troops fighting side by side with the Russians, could forestall the dangerous embrace of the Russian bear and the German wolf.

Woodrow Wilson, however, was almost viscerally opposed to any significant support for Bolshevik Russia. On March 11, he issued a statement to the Russian people:

> Although the Government of the United States is unhappily not now in a position to render the direct and effective aid it would wish to render, I beg to assure the people of Russia through the Congress that it will avail itself of every opportunity to secure for Russia once more complete sovereignty and independence in her own affairs. . . . The whole heart of the people of the United States is with the people of Russia in the attempt to free themselves forever from autocratic government and become the masters of their own life.

The message, much less ambiguous than the Fourteen Points speech, was cabled to Robins, who had followed Lenin to Moscow. On March 12, Robins personally handed it to the Soviet leader. It was read to the Congress of Soviets on March 15, the day the treaty of Brest-Litovsk was approved. The aroused congress drafted a spirited reply that also spoke over the heads of government to the "toiling and exploited classes of the United States." It expressed "firm confidence that the happy time is not far distant when the toiling masses of all bourgeois countries will throw off the yoke of capitalism."

Washington was not aware of Trotsky's queries about possible American aid, and Francis's plea for an urgent response, until March 19, through the arrival of the ten-day-old midnight cable from Francis. The State Department cabled Francis that the "President's message to the Russian people" was "adequate response."[13]

On March 16, after the peace treaty with Germany had been ratified, Francis issued an address, which he had translated into Russian and which appeared in papers in some cities, although not in Moscow where the Bolshevik grip was tight. Francis repeatedly referred to America's commitment to "the Russian people" and pointedly ignored the Russian government. He warned that the treaty could make Russia "virtually a German province." And he went on to say:

> I shall not leave until forced to depart. My government and the American people are too deeply interested in the welfare of the Russian people to abandon the country and leave its people to the mercies of Germany. . . .
> My Government still considers America an ally of the Russian people, who surely will not reject the proffered assistance which we shall be prompt to render to any power in Russia that will offer sincere and organized resistance to the German invasion.

Two months later, he learned through an Associated Press story that the State Department had "thoroughly approved" of his statement.[14]

Francis continued to send people home, and the Vologda staff soon was whittled down to about fifteen people. "The only secretary [of embassy, a diplomatic rank] with me is Norman Armour, who is faithful and efficient," he remarked in a March 17 cable to Lansing. The thirty-year-old Armour, a graduate of St. Paul's and Princeton with a law degree from Harvard, became one of Francis's most trusted and valued aides. Francis wrote:

> He and my [personal] secretary Johnston and myself have been doing all the work since Counselor Wright left . . . The Siamise minister, nurse, and child of three years, Brazilian Charge and Mr. Johnston and myself live in the building. Armour takes his meals here; also Colonel Ruggles the Military Attaché and his two assistants, Lieuts. Bukovski and Packer. Lieutenant Klieforth, who married a Russian lady of wealth and culture several days before we left Petrograd is looking for a house in Vologda, as are also four women of our staff, Miss [Jennie] Woodworth an American, Miss [Minnie] Knox an English woman and Miss [Bertha] Katz and Mrs. [Zenaida] Kennedy two Russian women.[15]

He also sent home the marine couriers who had become guards after the January anarchist threats. "I really suspect we will be as well if not better off without them," Francis remarked in a letter to Perry. "If a shot were fired by any of us at an angry crowd, four men would not be of much service to us and we would be far better off if the shot were not fired."

At that point, no angry crowds were in bucolic Vologda. There were wood fires glowing in the brick heating stoves and plenty of food and drink in the pantry. Francis described himself as "comfortably situated," explaining:

> The atmosphere is better here than Petrograd; the climate seems drier and the sun is shining a great deal more than there; also there is an air of quietness and order here which reminds one of a little village after the turbulent days in Petrograd; and the relief is a welcome one. In addition, we have plenty of good food, an excellent cook, and the company here in the clubhouse is congenial.
>
> My daily program is to rise at 9 A.M. breakfast at 10 and then go over cables etc. with Johnston for possibly an hour or more. Sometime we have pretty full days and work taking time only for meals. Other times while the work is going on or getting started I go to the billiard room of which there is one and play pool or billiards with the Siamese minister or the Brazilian Charge. In the evenings we play poker or bridge or go to concerts . . . so time does not hang heavy on our hands. I am getting more exercise here than in Petrograd and believe it is good for me. Am in perfect health and feeling more rested than in Petrograd.[16]

The proud, blustery old capitalist had developed a comfortable relationship with the local Reds. Francis remarked:

> I have never recognized this Bolshevik Government, but have established a quasi business or working arrangement with it, and to that do I attribute the courtesy shown by the municipal authorities and by the local Commissar and

by the President of the local Soviet. . . . Last night I entertained the local
Commissar, the Mayor, President of the Local Soviet, President of the City
Duma, and five other officials, at a dinner in the club house, which has
become known throughout the town as the American Embassy.[17]

The mayor had assured Francis that he and the Vologda Duma would protect the
Americans and their clubhouse embassy. Francis's declaring Vologda to be the diplomatic capital of Russia had stirred local pride. David Francis had been an ambassador
for less than two years, but he had been a successful politician for most of his life.

Edgar Sisson left Russia on March 4. By then he had owned up to sending the cable
urging Francis's recall. He wrote, "I had avowed to the Ambassador my responsibility for the dispatch and my reason for sending it. The measure of the man was that I
could do so." Francis quizzed Robins about the cable, and according to Francis, Robins
said that "Sisson had asked him to join in the recommendation [that Francis be
recalled] but that he had declined to have anything to do with it."[18]

If Robins said that, he was lying. He had been in the thick of the plot to have Francis
recalled and even bragged in his diary about helping encode the recall cable.[19] But he
was eager to stay on good terms with the ambassador. He reported to Francis by
telegram daily, having arranged with the Soviet government to have access to a direct
line between Moscow and Vologda at 11 o'clock every morning. Francis noted that
"Robins has been very profuse in his expressions of admiration of my course, having
remarked to some one that he would get up at any hour of the night to serve me."[20]

Francis may have believed Robins about the cable at first, but not after a mid-March
visit by Arthur Bullard of the Committee on Public Information. Bullard, a socialist, was
becoming strongly anti-Communist as he watched the Bolsheviks at work and was suspicious of Robins's close ties with Trotsky and Lenin.

Francis pressed Bullard for the truth about the Sisson cable. Surprised, Bullard
asked who had told him about it. Francis refused to say. But he told Bullard he was certain Sisson was influenced by others, since he had been in Russia for only a week or ten
days before sending the cable. Bullard told Francis the truth: Raymond Robins—with
William Boyce Thompson and the entire Red Cross mission—had been feeding Sisson
negative information and opinions about Francis from the moment the mission arrived
in Petrograd.[21]

Bullard was disgusted at Robins's treatment of Sisson and Francis. Bullard wrote his
boss, George Creel, that Robins had been "one of the worst personal disappointments of
my life . . . having written as strongly as I did in his favor, I must give you the tip now
that I have been forced by circumstances to alter my opinion of him entirely. God save
us from Sky-Pilots [evangelists], say I."[22]

Francis was devastated. And he was puzzled and hurt that Washington had not
informed him that he was under attack from men he trusted. Francis cabled Lansing:

Learned recently that Sisson very early after arrival cabled a note through
Military Attaché urging my recall, for reasons grossly absurd, recommending
that counselor take charge with Sisson as mentor. . . . As you have cabled
approving my course several times since, I conclude you were not influenced
thereby and [I] think Sisson changed his opinion; I am, however, desirous to
know whether any member of the Embassy staff knew of cable. Can you
inform me?[23]

Lansing, through Polk, replied that he had "no reason to believe any member of
Embassy knew of Sisson's cable." That almost certainly was not true, although perhaps
at that point a kind and harmless lie. The brief cable concluded, "You can have every
confidence in the Secretary's friendly and sympathetic attitude toward you."[24]

In mid-March, Military Intelligence in Washington notified Colonel Ruggles that
Edgar de Cramm had been arrested a month before in California and charged with
being a German agent. Ruggles passed the information on to Francis, who wrote
Lansing on March 20, "If that is so suppose the wife does not longer desire to proceed
to America. . . . I am still of the opinion that . . . she is not a German spy but a loyal
Russian." He noted that she had stayed in Petrograd when he left and, he added, "I suppose has remained there."[25]

He supposed? Matilda de Cramm had already corresponded more than once with
Philip Jordan, who was passing on her letters to Francis.[26] On March 22, Francis wrote
her. He began, as he had many times in correspondence with Jane, "I would write you an
autograph letter but have not the time." He said:

I read your letter to Philip and regretted to learn that you are not well and by
no means happy—I can understand why a person unwell in Petrograd should
not be happy. It strikes me that between the lines of your letter to Philip there
is an implied criticism of myself or certainly an indication of disappointment.
If this is true I'm sorry because if I do say so myself it is my opinion that you
have no occasion to find fault with my treatment of you. I have always been
very considerate of you and have attempted to be kind and liberal in my treatment. You have expressed yourself as appreciative and grateful. I could not
agree with your view that my ceasing to invite you to the Embassy to dinner
in connection with the French lessons you were giving me was a reflection
upon you. . . .

    I miss you greatly and often wish you were in Vologda but it would be
exceedingly unwise for you to come here and would be greatly embarrassing
to myself as every Attaché of the Embassy would immediately conclude that
you had come here on my request and that would lend color to the talk or
gossip about your relations to me. Furthermore I don't know how long I shall
remain here—in fact may depart on 24 hours notice and don't know at this
writing in what direction I will go. . . .

You are very profuse and no doubt sincere in your expressions of grati-
tude to Philip for sending you or bringing you [presumably before the departure for Vologda] provisions which you could not procure elsewhere; of course
you know that the provisions were mine, that I knew of Philip taking them to
you or that in every instance I directed him to do so and that he would not
have done so without my direction. Don't understand that I object in the
slightest degree to your feeling grateful to Phil. . . .

I was, I admit, provoked when I heard through the Embassy that you had
written to the Norwegian Minister that I had promised you the use of my
horses and sleigh and consequently you requested the use of same for one
hour daily. I do hope you have written the Minister that you did so through a
misunderstanding. If I told you that Andrea would take you driving occasionally and I probably did, I forget to tell him to do so; upon reflection however
am glad that I did forget as your being seen in my sleigh . . . would tend to
increase the gossip which was already embarrassing to you and not agreeable
to myself.

I hope you understand this letter which is meant in all kindness. I would
send you some food which your letter requests Phil to send—of course you
expected to pay for it and in fact said so in your letter—but it is impossible to
send anything from here to Petrograd in the shape of provisions.

With kind remembrances to your son George who I suppose is still with
you and hoping that when you receive this you will have entirely recovered
from your illness, I am
Yours sincerely,
[no signature on carbon]
P.S. This letter is sent sealed to Miss Sante to the Embassy with instructions
to send the same to you by messenger.[27]

As far as we know, this is the first time he wrote Madame de Cramm from Vologda.
Three days later, he sent her another long letter. He had just learned that the French
Espionage Bureau had resurrected the old charge that she had held a reception for
German diplomat Count Wilhelm von Mirbach during an official visit to Petrograd on
December 23. When Francis had asked her about this charge earlier, she had denied it,
and Francis had satisfied himself that it was not true. (It does seem unlikely that a spy
would hold a reception for the leading representative of the country she was spying for.)

He said, "I will never think you have lied to me unless you so admit yourself having
done so." However, he continued:

It is advisable . . . that you ascertain if possible whether Mirbach ever came to
your building and if so whom he visited and the number of the apartment. Do
not under any circumstance mention having been charged with his having visited you because that would give circulation to the report and what is more
important to me would betray that I have given you information concerning
the French espionage records. . . . Be sure to write personal and confidential
on the envelope so that no one will open it except myself; in fact you might

address such a letter to Earl M. Johnston Care of American Embassy Petrograd and put personal on that envelope also. You can see what pains I am taking to clear your reputation of being a disloyal Russian and you can also see how dangerous it would be for you to come to Vologda or to any place to see me.[28]

Two days later, he sent her a short note, saying, "I do hope this letter will find you in good health and spirits. Wish I could see you but don't think of coming to Vologda. . . . Have heard nothing more about the Doctor—have you?"[29]

Matilda de Cramm responded to this brief flurry of correspondence, but we have no copies of her letters. On April 18, Francis wrote that he had received three letters from her since the first of the month and remarked, "You state someone has told you that I am very happy and contended—one is always so when occupied so thoroughly as I am at Vologda. You know however that it is not my disposition to be depressed; if I don't have duties requiring my entire time and thought I initiate objects requiring effort and objects that I think merit accomplishment. In these times it is not difficult to do that especially in Russia."

He said that he had heard that Edgar de Cramm had been "charged with violating one of our national laws called the 'Mann Act' [which] prohibits a man taking a woman who is not his wife from one state into another state for illicit purposes."[30]

Edgar de Cramm, indeed, was charged with violating the Mann Act. His adopted daughter, Marion, was pregnant, with the child due in May. She told investigators that de Cramm was the father, although later she recanted and they both said she had been raped.

De Cramm, who was described by Military Intelligence officers as "a bad egg" and "a dangerous German agent," had made an unsuccessful attempt to bribe his way out of the arrest. In a statement to MI on February 11, he noted that his oldest son was a prisoner of the Germans and his two stepsons were Russian naval officers. "When all the 3 boys grew bigger," he said, "the troubles between my wife and me begun, she demanding equal rights for all. . . . Well I expected to get divorce year by year, but for the children's sake we left everything pending, until after her last visit to NY in Oct 1915, she, after 3 months declared, she has to go back and stay with her sons."

He said he had "introduced her to Mr. Francis, new Ambassador to Russia," who was sailing to Russia with her, and he later heard "they became good friends, she being as the lady of reception in the Embassy at the Thanksgiving day, working translations for the Embassy, etc."

The only letters Edgar got from his wife, he complained, asked for money: "I, being lonesome, having a son and his wife prisoners in Germany, where I have to send money for their existence, a wife and stepsons, to whom I also have to send money and money, have I no right to think upon my old days and to have somebody young around me, taking care of me in exchange for giving to a poor creature a quiet and secured life?"[31]

IN THE PRE-DAWN HOURS of March 21, six thousand German guns began a devastating barrage against the British who were dug in in northern France, and the fearful spring offensive was underway. Because of the armistice and peace treaty with Russia, the Germans had been able to move hundreds of thousands of troops to the Western Front. The Americans had sent six divisions to Europe, but by the time of the spring offensive, they had just begun to get into the war.

Over the next forty days, as the Germans pushed north and west toward the sea, Britain suffered three hundred thousand casualties, more than one-fourth of its total force, in the largest single military operation every mounted to that point. For a time, the Germans appeared to be rolling toward victory, and resuscitation of the Eastern Front seemed one way out of the impending tragedy. Francis kept lines of communications open through Robins and through the French, among others, although by this time he had little hope that Russia would turn its back on its peace treaty.

Still, life was peaceful in Vologda, even plentiful. The diplomats got together in the living room of the clubhouse embassy for "five o'clocks": drinks and diplomacy. The main topic of conversation, other than the food and drink and the startling blue-eyed beauty of the local young women, was the possibility of Allied intervention in Russia.

Francis and his French and Italian counterparts agreed that Japanese intervention in the East was necessary because of the growing German presence there, but that such intervention, to work, needed the support of all the Allies and acceptance, albeit reluctant, by the Bolsheviks. The thinking was that Trotsky might acquiesce if the troops came bearing material aid, and if they helped organize and train the new Soviet Army that Trotsky was trying to create.

Francis authorized his military attachés to work with the French and Italians in helping organize the new Red Army. He was thinking ahead, quite unrealistically, to a time when the Red Army would have saved Russia from Germany and could be prodded by its Allied advisors into turning against the Bolsheviks.* He mentioned this "strictly confidential" notion in a cable to Lansing, but Lansing was not convinced that the Red Army would fight the Germans, much less the Bolsheviks. The State Department instructed Francis to back off from any promises to help the Soviet military and to continue to "feel your way to certainty before making positive recommendations."[32]

Cooperation between the Allies and the Bolsheviks, prickly in the best of circumstances, took a hard blow on the Pacific Coast of Russia in early April. After men in Russian uniform killed some Japanese shopkeepers, five hundred Japanese troops went ashore at Vladivostok, purportedly to protect the Japanese Consulate and other nation-

---

*Underlying what now seems to be extremely wishful thinking—that the Bolsheviks would ever agree to the presence of large numbers of Allied troops on Russian soil to fight the Germans, troops that might well turn on their hosts—was a basic misunderstanding of Bolshevik goals and core principles that colored much of the thinking of the time. The Bolsheviks did not think in old nationalistic ways. The Russian people may have hated the Germans on a visceral level, a factor Francis and Lockhart were counting on to strengthen their case, but the Bolsheviks believed with fervent conviction that the false national antagonisms of the decaying capitalist system would collapse under worldwide socialist revolution, and Germany would soon be a brother revolutionary socialist republic. Indeed, as discussed in Chapter 18, early in the World War, Lenin had hoped that the Germans would defeat his homeland as a step toward revolution in Russia.

al interests. But Soviet Commissar for Foreign Affairs Georgi Chicherin proclaimed that the Japanese intended "to strangle the Soviet revolution, to cut Russia off from the Pacific Ocean, to seize the rich territories of Siberia, and to enslave the Siberian workers and peasants."[33]

Chicherin held a tense meeting with Raymond Robins, and Robins responded by cabling Francis, pressing him to repudiate the Japanese invasion. Francis replied, "Soviet government attaching undue weight to landing of Japanese. . . . There is no intention or desire on the part of any of Russia's allies to attach any of Russia's territory or to make an invasion of conquest. On the other hand the Allies desire to see the integrity of Russia preserved and are willing and desirous to aid the Russian people to that end." A couple of days later, Francis issued a public statement that repeated some of the points of the message to Chicherin but cautioned that the Japanese invasion was "not a concerted action between the Allies."

At best, Francis was using language imprecisely, seemingly trying to have it both ways. In the first statement, he angered Washington by suggesting that the Allies were working together on plans for intervention, and in the second he angered the Japanese by suggesting that they were not. Washington quietly rebuked him.[34]

In the midst of the muddle, one thing at least was clear: zealous Raymond Robins, at most a semi-official diplomat in the Russian capital, appeared to be doing all the things that would seem to be the purview of the top American official—Consul General Maddin Summers. Summers was in failing health, and the considerable pressure he was under became almost unbearably heavy when the government of Russia moved to Moscow in early March, and Raymond Robins followed.

A gentlemanly Tennessean, the forty-one-year-old Summers had been in the foreign service since 1899, serving in Latin America and Spain, where he met Francis in 1903. The veteran Summers, whose aristocratic Russian in-laws had lost land and property in the revolution, detested the Bolsheviks. He believed even more strongly than Francis that they were German agents, and unlike Francis felt that no good could come out of working with them. He mistrusted Robins, whom he suspected of revealing confidential information and misrepresenting the American position in his daily chats with the Reds.[35]

Raymond Robins was one of a triumvirate of Allied unofficial ambassadors—the other two being Bruce Lockhart of Britain and Captain Jacques Sadoul of the French military mission—who had slipped into the vacuum left by the absence from Moscow of true ambassadors. Sadoul, a socialist, disagreed as vehemently with his supposed superior, Ambassador Noulens, as Robins did with Summers. Robins, Sadoul, and Lockhart formed what might be called the left wing of thought in dealing with the Bolsheviks.

Though March and April, Robins and Summers sniped at each other in telegrams to Francis. Robins had one advantage—a direct telegraph line every morning to Vologda, courtesy of the Bolsheviks. Summers had to wait his turn on the wire, adding to his anger and frustration.

Francis tried to smooth things over, recognizing, as was habit in such situations, that the two opponents were valuable in different ways. He told them they needed to get along for the sake of American policy, at one point saying to Robins, pointedly, "Of course you are doing nothing to impair Summers' efficiency as consul."[36] Francis also was a politician, and while he could stubbornly stick to core values even in the face of certain defeat, he also was accustomed to compromise, to working out seemingly irreconcilable differences. He was a "pacificator." Also, as an elected public official, he was used to working with people he disagreed with, or who disagreed with one another.

In early April, frustrated with his inability to force his case by wire, Summers took the 250-mile train ride from Moscow to Vologda to push his concerns about "dual representation of the United States" in Moscow. He complained that the Moscow newspapers, mostly controlled by the Bolsheviks, repeatedly referred to Raymond Robins as "the official representative of the United States in Moscow."

Following up his visit with an angry letter, Summers wrote, "My position is extremely delicate in this particular. And I have no other remedy than to clear the situation with the Department, giving reasons for my complaints." If the matter was not settled, he insisted, he would ask for a leave of absence or resign and "return to Washington where I shall give ample explanation of the situation."

Summers continued:

> I should regret extremely to give up my work, but at the present moment the
> Department of State considers the Consulate General as the only representa-
> tive in Moscow, and I cannot consent that a person in no way connected with
> the Government shall compromise this office or interfere with its work in any
> way whatsoever. I can assure you of the serious displeasure of the Department
> and of numerous friends of this office should I take this step. . . . I am sure
> you will appreciate my viewpoint, and will take the necessary steps to relieve
> me of being forced to ask for a transfer.[37]

Francis was in turmoil. He considered Summers to be a friend, and Francis was loyal to his friends. He thought about asking that Robins be sent home but decided to try once more to make the best of the present situation. He no longer trusted Robins but felt he needed him.

On April 14, he wrote Summers acknowledging receipt of his letter, which, Francis said, "must have been composed when you were tired or provoked, as I don't think you meant it in the threatening tone expressed therein."

Francis wrote:

> We understand each other so thoroughly, and are so fully in accord that we
> must not have any misunderstanding. . . . The situation in Russia is so critical
> now that I am not jealous of my prerogatives but am willing to accept the aid
> of anyone who can render assistance. My desire and plan is to bring about
> Allied intervention but to induce the de facto government to request it if

possible or certainly to offer no opposition thereto consequently you will see the danger of having opposition from an American who is as close to the Soviet Government as Robins is. . . . Forget your letter dear friend and don't think of leaving your post at this critical time. You know me and I think I know you—we should serve harmoniously in order to give the best results.[38]

The next day, he scribbled a note addressed to both Summers and Robins: "If you both knew how difficult and unpleasant you are making it for me and how your disagreements are detrimentally affecting Embassy efficiency think you would make effort to work harmoniously. Francis."[39]

A few days later, after Summers again pushed the issue, Francis said he had hoped he had reconciled Summers to "endure present conditions for a while longer. . . . The Government and the Department has directed me to establish and maintain working relations with the Soviet Government and I have done so to the best of my ability disagreeable as it is."[40]

By then, Francis knew that Robins had lied to him about his role in the Sisson recall cable, but he stifled his anger and continued to use the intense Red Cross man to maintain contact with the Bolsheviks. Francis wrote Perry, "I feel that I myself am entitled to much credit for suppressing my anti-bolshevik feelings in an effort which may eventually prove futile to prevent the bolsheviks from becoming German allies. I am hoping that every day will bring from the Soviet Government an invitation for the Allies to come to their aid against Germany."[41]

IN WASHINGTON, on April 14, Francis's old Missouri foe, Senator William Stone, died. On April 20, Frederick E. Gardner, governor of Missouri, cabled Lansing: "I have decided to tender the appointment of United States Senator to the Honorable David R. Francis, Ambassador to Russia, provided in your judgment you can release him from present post."[42]

Two days later, Lansing replied:

At the present time it would be most unfortunate for the Government to withdraw Mr. Francis from Russia. No man has the experience to take his place in that difficult post. The extraordinary ability which he has shown in conducting affairs in Russia and his full grasp of the present situation make him of inestimable value to this country as its Ambassador. While I appreciate that personally his appointment as Senator would be most attractive to him I feel myself that it would be a real loss to this country if he should be called away from Russia during these critical times.[43]

By the time Francis heard about Stone's death, he was in bed under a doctor's care and Philip Jordan's stern discipline, burning with fever and unable to keep food in his stomach. Beginning the morning of April 19, he was bedridden for ten days. The first day of the illness, he reported home, he "went to stool twenty times and the second and third day ten times each."[44] At first he thought to have ptomaine poisoning, but later he was diagnosed as having an inflamed prostate and bladder stones.

His Russian physician, Dr. Gortaloff, who spoke as little English as Francis spoke Russian and communicated through an interpreter, seemed vague about the cause of the illness. Jordan tried to get a precise diagnosis, and the doctor explained to him that the problems were caused by "something bursting on the inside." Jordan pushed the doctor to name the illness, and the doctor insisted it had "no special name."[45] The doctor told Francis he needed plenty of bed rest and put him on a diet of two soft-boiled eggs a day.*

Philip Jordan wrote Jane, "This is the Worst Spell of Sickness the Ambassador ever had in his life." Jordan gave his boss a rubdown every morning and watched while Francis, on his doctor's instructions, exhausted himself with a few minutes of exercise in the evening. After a few days, Francis began to rebel against being kept in bed, but he was very weak—he blamed the weakness, with some justification, on the diet. Francis lost so much weight that Jordan told Jane she couldn't imagine how thin her husband had become. Still, he fought to get out of bed and get back to his post.

One day, the much-missed Ford arrived by rail from Petrograd. Jordan went to the train station to pick it up, and when he returned to the embassy, Francis had climbed out of bed, gotten dressed, and was ready to go to work. Jordan had to plead and push to get him back into bed. He wrote Jane that he had then "locked the door and told all ministers and the Secretarys that no one was to enter his room until I Said So. they Said we have Some Very Important messages for him. I Said those messages will not Spoil."[46]

From his bed, Francis continued to issue daily cables to the State Department and dictate notes and letters to family and friends. He complained to friends about his isolation from Washington: "I have never received any commendation from the President or from the Department other than when I asked what to do the reply generally comes 'Follow your own judgment,' 'as in the past.' Think I have outraged diplomatic customs in many ways since I came here and am truly glad that I did not have a diplomatic training as I think it pays more attention to the form than the substance."[47]

Francis had plenty of time to contemplate how weary he had become of Raymond Robins, and on April 22 he cabled Robins, "Do not feel I should be justified in asking you to remain longer in Moscow to neglect of the prosecution of your Red Cross work, but this does not imply any want of appreciation of the services you have rendered me in keeping me advised . . . as well as being a channel of unofficial communication with the Soviet government."[48]

Robert Lansing, already disturbed that Robins was working on his own without consulting the ambassador, had further reason for concern when he received a copy of

---

*After his daily visits with Francis, Gortaloff stopped downstairs in the living room and had a glass of whisky with Military Attaché Ruggles. According to Vologda historian Alexander Bykov, a specialist on the city's diplomatic era, Gortaloff later was questioned by the Bolshevik security police for consorting with a foreign military officer, charged with espionage, and died in custody.

an April 22 message from Edgar Sisson to Creel. Sisson recommended that Bullard and the other American propaganda workers in Russia be ordered home, and he suggested that the Red Cross and the remaining representatives of the American Embassy be brought out as well. He commented in his memoir:

> After analyzing all data. . . . It was apparent to me that the intent of the Bolsheviks was to keep Ambassador Francis—and the Allied nationals—in Russia as long as possible, practically as hostages, and to make a public show of their helplessness, thus exploiting before the Russian masses their ability to insult with impunity the representatives of powerful peoples. It was an advertising method potent toward consolidating internal power, aimed to impress the fatalistic Russian millions with the sense of helplessness under rulers strong enough seemingly to defy the great nations of the world.[49]

Sisson sent a copy of his cable to Francis, hoping the ambassador would realize the danger he was in.

On April 23, Count Mirbach arrived in the capital as the German ambassador. Three days later, the Germans became the first foreign ministry to be accredited by the Bolsheviks, and Robins despaired, blaming lost opportunities for close cooperation between the United States and the Bolsheviks.

Sensing the inevitable, Robins cabled the Red Cross in Washington that his relief work in Russia was "practically complete." He recommended that the entire Red Cross mission return to America, beginning about May 15. Almost simultaneously, Red Cross headquarters was drafting a telegram telling Robins to come home.[50]

On April 25, almost certain he was leaving, Robins wrote a fawning note to Lenin: "Your prophetic insight and genius of leadership have enabled the Soviet Power to become consolidated throughout Russia and I am confident that this new creative organ of the democratic life of mankind will inspire and advance the cause of liberty throughout the world." Lenin responded to the note by saying he was confident that "proletarian democracy" would "crush . . . the imperialist-capitalist systems in the New and Old Worlds."[51]

The last week in April, as Francis was recovering from his illness—the doctor had increased his ration to three soft-boiled eggs and a few glasses of milk a day—press reports from Moscow gave him even more reason to worry about Raymond Robins. The stories added strength to rumors that Francis had been hearing for several weeks: that it was not Raymond Robins who was going to be sent home but David Francis, with Robins to be named ambassador.

Trying to head off the inevitable explosion from Vologda, Robins wired Francis on April 26, "Moscow press this morning carries several stupid stories evidently prepared [to] produce dissension and suspicion among American representatives in Russia. Confidently expect your understanding to give you untroubled mastery of the situation. Your proved strength sufficient guarantee against absurd stories both Washington and Russia."

Reaching deep for flattery, Robins told Francis in a follow-up letter, "Evidently your management of the situation troubles our enemies and they would have you out of the way or get me out of the way or both if possible. I have given no interviews and of course will not give any."[52]

On April 28, still in his sickbed, Francis issued a statement:

> I have paid no attention to the false rumors that have been circulating concerning the Embassy and myself for the past three weeks, but have been curious to know their source and their object. . . . I only notice them now because the name of Colonel Robins has been mentioned in connection therewith. Colonel Robins and I are friends and understand each other thoroughly; we have the same object in view which is to make the world safe for Democracy, and we agree that such desirable end cannot be accomplished without the defeat of Germany. It is unnecessary to state that the only authoritative expressions concerning American policy in Russia are given out by myself.[53]

With the help of Philip Jordan, Francis slowly recovered from his illness, although it appears that he never fully regained his health. For the first four days of the illness, Jordan stayed by Francis's side twenty-four hours a day, and now that he was improving, Jordan had to fight to keep his boss from getting out of bed:

On Thursday, April 25, the Siamese Minister told Jordan a photographer was coming to take some pictures. (We don't know why.)

"That will be very nice," said Jordan.

"Have the Ambassador ready, will you?" the minister asked.

Jordan said that the Ambassador was not well enough to leave his room.

"Do you think it would be against the doctor's orders?" the minister asked.

"It would not only be against the doctor's orders," replied Jordan, "but strictly against mine."

Twenty minutes later, Francis called Jordan into his bedroom. Five or six aides were already there. Francis said he wanted to get up and get dressed. Jordan said, "Governor, do you think if Mrs. Francis was here today that she would allow you to get up and dress?" Francis replied that he thought she would.

Jordan shook his head and said, "As you told these gentlemen, Mrs. Francis sent me over her to look after you and I have made Mr. Perry a promise just before we sailed to do all in my power to bring you back home all well and sound. So please don't think about getting up today."

Francis sighed and finally said, "Gentlemen, there will not be any pictures taken today."[54]

On April 27, Francis felt well enough to resume his Saturday afternoon receptions, which attracted, according to Francis, "all of Vologda." It was the final reception for the Siamese minister, who left on May 1, with his son and nurse, headed east for home. By then, Francis increasingly had become disturbed by the growing German presence in the capital. Perhaps the last straw was an intelligence report that the Bolsheviks, under

Mirbach's influence, were about to prohibit the sending of cipher telegrams out of Russia by the Allies. Francis had gotten over his brief, hopeful delusion that the army Trotsky was organizing would be used to fight the Germans. Instead, he realized, the Red Army was intended to be a tool, as he put it, of "world-wide social revolution against existing governments including ours."

On May 2, Francis cabled Lansing, "In my judgment time for Allied intervention has arrived."

In amplification, he wrote, "Have been hoping for request therefore by Soviet and have been discreetly working to that end first by remaining in Russia with your approval when all colleagues departed second by cultivating close unofficial relations with bolsheviks and encouraging Robins to remain Moscow for such purpose." But another tack was necessary because Mirbach now was "dominating Soviet government and is practically dictator in Moscow. . . . Russia is passing through dream or orgy from which awakening is possible any day but the longer we wait . . . the stronger foot-hold Germany will secure." Francis was particularly concerned about protecting the northern ports of Murmansk and Archangel from German occupation.

In the lengthy cable, Francis assessed the supreme Bolshevik leader:

Lenin is dominating bolshevik spirit and in every speech justifies Brest Treaty by calling it breathing spell in world-wide social revolution which he affirms is sure to succeed as proletariat in warring imperialistic countries will soon assert itself as in Russia. In speech of [April] twenty-eighth he apparently justified slaughter at western front as weakening imperialistic governments engaged in struggle for territorial supremacy and thereby brought nearer the dictatorship of proletariat throughout the world. Lenin's last written and spoken expressions are devoted to what he calls the danger from the small bourgeois which he thinks greatest menace to proletariat as rich bourgeois effectively exterminated. He is able, far-seeing and anticipates revulsion against bolshevik principles from desire of peasants to own and cultivate small tracts of land.[55]

This last was almost prophetic, considering Lenin's upcoming attack on the people he called "bloodsucker kulaks,"[56] or what Francis might call family farmers, the core of the Jeffersonian democracy he believed in so deeply. Francis concluded his cable: "Shall patiently await instructions or information."

A month passed before he got an answer.

CHAPTER 20

High-Stakes Poker

As April slowly brightened into May, David Francis could look out the window of his bedroom at the back of the makeshift American Embassy and see the winter cover of snow and ice finally melt from the courtyard and the first buds of spring peek out from the cold, wet soil. Francis still had not recovered from his illness, but Philip Jordan was finding it increasingly difficult to keep the ambassador from responding to the latest diplomatic crisis.

Maddin Summers continued to complain about Raymond Robins. On May Day, Summers wrote Francis that he was "disgusted" with Robins, who had "decidedly undermined the work of the Embassy and Consular service." If nothing was done, he said, as he had before to Francis and Robert Lansing, he would resign.[1]

Meanwhile, Lansing had cabled Summers that the department very much wanted him to stay, promising, "The conditions which have embarrassed you will unquestionably show early improvement. Meanwhile keep in close touch with Ambassador."[2] And on May 3, Francis wrote Summers that he had strongly suggested to Robins that he go home and that Robins planned on leaving Moscow almost immediately.

"Of course, you will not think of resigning at this juncture nor asking for a transfer," Francis said. "I know you are not made of that kind of stuff. . . . We are going through trying ordeals and must be reconciled to having our pride hurt and our feelings outraged."[3]

Summers never saw that message. On May 3, after a bitter argument with Robins, he grew dizzy at work and went home to lie down. He sank into delirium and the next afternoon, convinced he had been poisoned by the Germans, he died of a brain hemorrhage. He was only forty-one years old. The State Department announced that he had "collapsed under long months of strain and overwork."[4]

Francis blamed Robins, at least in part, for Summers's death, which came as a hard blow. He long had admired and liked the courtly Tennessean, and he felt it was very important that he got out of his sick bed and attend and speak at the funeral.[5] Although he was still shaky, and on a diet of soft foods, David Francis left for Moscow on May 5.

Just before his departure, he received a telegram from Robins saying he was on his way to Vologda. It was too late to stop him.

A few hours later, the southbound train carrying David Francis passed the northbound train carrying Robins, Gumberg, and Arthur Bullard, head of the American propaganda office in Russia who was homeward bound. Perhaps it had not occurred to Robins that Francis would get out of his sickbed for the funeral of his friend, and perhaps no one had informed Robins that the ambassador was making the trip. However, Francis suspected Robins simply had wanted an excuse to be out of Moscow, either to avoid the embarrassment of Summers's funeral or because he had heard through his Russian sources that Sisson's prediction about the Bolsheviks taking Allied hostages was about to come true.

Not for the first time, Robins had a document burning a hole in his pocket. This one was a letter from his British friend and cohort Bruce Lockhart, decrying the notion that the Bolsheviks were German agents and asserting that "a policy of Allied intervention, with the co-operation and consent of the Bolshevik Government, is feasible and possible."[6]

The funeral of Maddin Summers was held on a cold, overcast Wednesday at the Little English Church next to the American Consulate, the church where, a few years before, Summers had married into the Russian aristocracy. Francis, a pallbearer, spoke at the services, and he said, in part: "Maddin Summers yielded his life in his country's service and did so as effectually as if he had been taken off by the enemy in ambush and as courageously as if he had fallen in attack on the enemy's works. He realized as fully as does an officer leading his troops in a battle that his very life was in jeopardy and that realization nerved him to renewed effort."[7]

A top official of the Russian Foreign Office named Arseni N. Voznesenski also spoke at the funeral. Publicly, he expressed the government's "profound sorrow" and the "warm sympathy and sincere friendliness of the people of Russia for the American people," and said he hoped "that the mutual regard and hearty cooperation of both peoples will be an essential factor of future progress and development of the great popular masses of the world." Privately, he urged Francis to move the American Embassy to Moscow.[8]

Summers was succeeded as acting consul general by DeWitt C. Poole, an astute thirty-two-year-old former newspaperman who was recommended for the position by Francis.

Francis stayed at the consulate. He had trouble sleeping, and his strength must have been coming back, because he took Poole on long midnight walks through the streets of Moscow as they discussed the diminishing options for the future. Francis was "a great nighthawk," Poole recalled later. "He and I had extended talks, and he designated me his political agent with the Bolshevik government." Poole would meet frequently with Georgi Chicherin, Soviet commissar for foreign affairs, and develop a friendly personal relationship.[9] In effect, Poole replaced both Robins and Summers, keeping close contacts with the Bolsheviks while, as Francis had instructed, establishing relationships with the underground opposition.

Among the many other people Francis met with in his four days in the new Russian capital were the top representatives of the Allies in Moscow; his friend from New York Life, E. C. Riley, now living in Moscow; and E. A. Weyde, Matilda de Cramm's brother.[10] Francis also met with Lockhart, describing him in a report to the State Department as the "only diplomatic representative his country has here." Francis reported that "Lockhart strongly favors allied intervention with or without Soviet Government approval but says approval desirable." Francis agreed on both points, but he added that if, as he feared, approval was "securable only by promise to sustain even secretly Bolshevik domination," the "cost would be too dear."[11] The cable, in which Francis described and commented on his experiences in Moscow during his four-day visit, was forwarded to Lansing from Basil Miles, head of the State Department's Russian desk, with the comment that it "shows much keen insight and contains valuable comment bearing on the position of the Bolshevik Government."

Bruce Lockhart seemed to be simultaneously fond and contemptuous of Francis, and much of the portrait of Francis woven through the many accounts over the decades comes from the writings of this brilliant, self-aggrandizing British agent. In *Memoirs of a British Agent,* Lockhart described the sixty-seven-year-old ambassador as "a charming old gentleman of nearly eighty—a banker from St. Louis who had left America for the first time to be plunged into the vortex of the revolution."

In fairness to Lockhart, Francis may well have looked nearly eighty in the aftermath of his illness, his face pale and drawn and his clothes fitting loosely on his bones. Francis admitted at the time that his illness had "left its mark upon me—in other words I look much older than I did before the experience."[12] In any event, the image of Francis as a tottering, naive old man who never had been out of the United States before has persisted over the decades.

"He was a kind old gentleman, who was susceptible to flattery and swallowed any amount of it," said Lockhart, perhaps under the mistaken belief that his friend Robins's fawning letters and cables had sucked Francis in. "His knowledge of anything beyond banking and poker was severely limited."[13]

Francis also met with Captain Jacques Sadoul, Lockhart's French counterpart, who told Francis that Bolshevism was "dead" and that the only way to prevent restoration of the Tsardom would be to aid a "socialistic democratic and anti-monarchical" coalition government in forming an "extremely liberal republic." Sadoul went on to spin a true pipe dream—that Lenin considered moving away from militant Communism by, among other steps, denationalizing banks. Incredulous, Francis asked Sadoul if he really believed that Lenin would compromise his radical Bolshevism, and Sadoul's affirmative answer came so promptly that Francis wondered if Sadoul might not be a Soviet agent sent to sound him out.[14]

Meanwhile, Raymond Robins reached Vologda, was informed that Francis was in Moscow, and caught the next southbound train. He found Francis at the American Consulate and told him it was very important to meet again with Voznesenski, who had been trying to schedule a second meeting. Francis finally agreed, and Robins set up a conference between the two men at the Foreign Office on May 10, shortly before Francis left to return to Vologda. Voznesenski again encouraged the American ambassador to move his embassy to Moscow. Francis replied that the other Allied missions had joined him in Vologda, and all concerned thought they were "safer from German interference" there.

After the meeting, Robins told Francis he also thought coming to Moscow would be a good idea and once again tried to flatter Francis by saying he thought the move would put him in the "forefront" of the Allied chiefs of mission. Francis, who was already in the forefront, argued that breaking ranks with the other top Allied diplomats would disrupt the alliance he had crafted—indeed, he suspected that was the result Voznesenski hoped to achieve. Francis later said, "It began to dawn on me that Robins was treacherous and while professing loyalty was making persistent efforts to undermine me."[15]

In his long report of the trip to the State Department, Francis expressed the hope that "we have been making all possible preparations for Allied intervention as I have recommended for months past."[16]

Bruce Lockhart, in describing Francis's visit to Moscow, told a story that has gained much currency. It is entertaining but probably a fable. Lockhart wrote:

> He had a traveling spittoon—a contraption with a pedal—which he took with him everywhere. When he wished to emphasize a point, bang would go the pedal, followed by a well—aimed expectoration. . . . One afternoon [during the Moscow visit] Norman Armour, the efficient secretary of the American Embassy, came into the Ambassador's room.
> 'Governor,' he said, 'would you like to go to the opera tonight?'
> 'Nope,' was the reply. 'I think I'll play poker.'
> 'Do come, Governor,' said Armour. 'You really ought not to miss it. It's Evgenie Onegin.'
> 'Evgenny what?' said the Ambassador.
> 'Oh! you know,' replied Armour. 'Pushkin and Chaikovsky.'
> There was a crash from the pedal of the spittoon.
> 'What!' said the Ambassador ecstatically. 'Is Pushkin singing tonight?'[17]

There are a few problems with the story.

First, although Francis frequently attended the opera and ballet in Petrograd, it's barely possible that he didn't recognize the name of Tchaikovsky's great tragic opera, but it is even more implausible that he could have lived for two years in Petrograd without knowing the name of its most celebrated literary hero—a large equestrian figure of Peter the Great, which inspired Pushkin's famous poem "The Bronze Horseman," is the local equivalent of the Statue of Liberty.

Second, Norman Armour was not even in Moscow with Francis; he stayed behind in Vologda to mind the store.[18]

As for the spittoon, it, like Francis's erroneously advanced age, would stick in the minds (or perhaps the craw) of future chroniclers. Francis loved cigars and sometimes chewed on them and spit out the residue, a common American practice looked upon with horror by the British. Spittoons were common in places of business and even on the floor of the U.S. Congress, and Francis probably took one with him to Russia, but no other contemporary chronicle of those days in Russia—and dozens of them discuss Francis in some detail—mentions the ornate traveling version.

ON THE MORNING OF MAY 10, as he prepared to return to Vologda, Francis was at the Moscow consulate when a telegram arrived from the Red Cross in Washington ordering Robins home. Robins, Francis noted, was "very much cast down and when I asked what it meant he said it was the work of the State Department."[19]

Four days later, Robins headed north to Vologda, where he transferred to the Siberian Express for Vladivostok on the morning of May 15. Francis met him at the train station. According to Francis, Robins remarked to the ambassador that as he had approached Vologda he thought that fate had favored Francis, having removed either by recall or death the four men who had plotted to have him recalled, while Francis remained.

Startled to hear what he thought was a rare burst of unadorned honesty from Robins, Francis thought the man referred to himself as one of the four who had conspired on the Sisson recall cable. He asked who the plotters were, and Robins specifically named Sisson, General Judson, Butler Wright, and Maddin Summers. Francis was infuriated, particularly by the reference to Summers, just buried, his blood, Francis believed, on Robins's hands. Francis held his tongue and remarked that, of course, he knew that Sisson had sent the cable, but that this was the first time he had heard that the other three men were involved.

Francis later told Consul DeWitt Poole about the conversation, and Poole angrily responded that as far as Summers was concerned the statement was "a damned lie," because Francis "never had a more loyal friend than Maddin Summers." Francis also asked Norman Armour about the charge. Armour replied that Robins had lied when he implicated Wright, who had been loyal to Francis.[20]

Before he boarded the Siberian Express, Robins told Francis he had been surprised to be recalled and blamed it on Sisson. He didn't mention that he also blamed it on Francis. According to his biographer, Neil V. Salzman, Robins's "anger and distrust" led him to neglect to mention what he had in his pocket this time—a new letter from Lenin proposing commercial cooperation between the United States and the Bolsheviks, permitting American capitalists to participate in the reconstruction of Russia and the exploitation of Siberian coal, hydroelectric power, timber, and other resources. Such cooperation, Lenin suggested, only could hurt the Germans.[21]

Robins thought that the letter was another prime, and ultimately lost, opportunity for Soviet-American friendship. George Kennan, in a lengthy analysis, persuasively argues that Lenin held economic cooperation out as bait to the capitalistic United States in return for keeping Japan from further incursions into Siberia. Lenin also hoped to divide the Allies by playing on their competing economic self interests.[22]

Washington dismissed Lenin's letter. After learning about the letter from an American journalist in Vologda, Francis remarked ironically to Lansing, "I do not understand Robins's failure to inform me of his plans as he has continually . . . expressed friendliness and admiration of my course." He added, "May I suggest advising Red Cross and [YMCA] to instruct their representatives to confine their activities strictly to their line of work?"[23]

Francis continued to correspond with Madame de Cramm. On May 13, he sent her twelve pounds of bread, and five days later, he wrote to make sure she had received it, saying, "Your [most recent] letter states that you had planned to come to Vologda in order to be at a place that you considered safer than Petrograd but that you are prevented from coming here by my being here; I very much regret this is so as it probably is. I see your photograph every day with your two sons and admire you more and more."[24]

A few days later, Military Attaché Riggs told him that the "Russian Espionage Bureau" had described Matilda de Cramm as the "mistress of the American ambassador." Francis furiously denied the allegation, and fearful that the report was widespread in Petrograd, he wrote to Robert Imbrie, the American vice consul there: "If anyone charges that I have improper relations with Madame Cramm he is a liar and anyone who repeats the rumor after hearing this denial from myself is a liar and I am in every sense responsible for this statement."[25]

By then, an explosive new factor had been added to the volatility of Russia: the Czechoslovak Legion.

Some thirty-five thousand strong, the legion had begun as a special unit of Czechs and Slovaks formed in the Ukraine to fight on the Eastern Front as part of the Russian army. As the Russian army disintegrated, the troops grew restless to join the Allies and fight the Germans on the Western Front. In late March, deciding the legion would be decimated if it tried to fight its way westward through German lines, its leaders came up with a bizarre-sounding plan: they would head east and go almost entirely around the world to join the Allies in France. Initially, the Bolsheviks approved the plan, hoping to rid the Ukraine of a large body of potential counterrevolutionaries—the legion's commanders tended to detest the Bolsheviks.

The Czech Legion began moving east on the Trans-Siberian Railway. But local Soviets, mistrustful of these armed foreigners, stopped the trains and tried to confiscate their weapons. The Czechs resisted, and by the middle of May the well-trained Czech Legion was fighting the disorganized Red Army in towns all along the Trans-Siberian Railway.

Meanwhile, in Moscow, Poole followed Francis's instructions and kept in close contact with anti-Bolshevik groups. In mid-May, he wired Francis that Kerensky secretly had been in Petrograd and Moscow, organizing opposition to the Bolsheviks. Francis decided the time was ripe for intervention. He and Noulens wired Lockhart, still the top British representative in Russia (the British chargé d'affaires, F. O. Lindley, would not return until July), suggesting he come to Vologda to discuss a concerted plan of action.[26]

On May 28, Lockhart took the train to Vologda, met briefly with Noulens, and then went to the clubhouse embassy for dinner and lodging. Over cocktails, Lockhart met the leaders of the Vologda diplomatic corps.

"Mr. Francis was a charming host," he recalled. "We sat up late into the night, but Russia figured hardly at all in our conversation. From Francis I gathered that President Wilson was strongly opposed to Japanese intervention. Otherwise, he did not seem to have any decided views about Russia. Knowledge of Russian politics he had none. The only political entry in my diary for the evening is the laconic note: 'Old Francis doesn't know a Left Social Revolutionary from a potato.'" This oft-quoted judgment must be considered hyperbole—Francis may not have had a precise mental map of the complex and ever-changing Russian political spectrum, but the Left Socialist Revolutionaries were too important for him to miss, initially the major ally of the Bolsheviks in their shaky ruling coalition, later the Bolsheviks' implacable enemies. On May 3, in a letter to Maddin Summers, Francis mentioned the "Socialist-Revolutionary organization . . . planning to overthrow the present government." Summers's successor, Poole, reported to him on opposition groups in Moscow, and in a few weeks, Francis would meet with leaders of the Left Socialist Revolutionaries.

Lockhart also said of Francis, "He was as simple and fearless as a child. It never entered his head that he himself was in any personal danger." As soon as dinner ended, Lockhart recalled, "Francis began to fidget like a child who wishes to return to its toys. His rattle, however, was a deck of cards, and without loss of time they were produced. The old gentleman was no child at poker. We played late, and, as usually happens when I play with Americans, he took my money." It may well be that the poker game began before Lockhart realized it, as Francis let Lockhart do all the talking and feigned ignorance, much as he would do in the future when officious Bolsheviks came to Vologda to probe Francis's mind.

Politics must have been discussed at some point, because Lockhart left Vologda in despair, realizing interventionists outnumbered him. Lockhart later suggested ironically that having the Western nations' top diplomatic representatives in Vologda was as if "foreign Ambassadors were trying to advise their governments on an English Cabinet crisis from a village in the Hebrides."[27]

The season's last dusting of snow fell on Vologda on May 22 and quickly melted, and by the end of the month the sun was shining almost every day, the daytime temperatures were in the fifties and lower sixties, and the nights were without frost. Francis and his chums, including Earl Johnston and members of the French and Italian contingents, packed into the Model T. With Jordan at the wheel, they tooled around the countryside and found a large open field suitable for a few holes of makeshift golf near the village of Oranova.[28]

Every Saturday afternoon from five to seven, Francis hosted a tea for the diplomatic corps. He also invited local officials and prominent citizens, including Princess Lvov, sister-in-law of the former premier, who frequently visited the embassy with her three attractive daughters. Another visitor was a beautiful teenage girl, the daughter of an old Russian general named Misener. She had a stunning singing voice, according to Johnston, who thought that she would "be a star some day."[29] Predictably, Francis found himself charmed by Miss Misener and decided he needed a new French teacher. He wrote Perry:

> I have another diversion at Vologda which I hesitate to write about lest it may be misunderstood—I have made the acquaintance of a young girl just approaching or turning 17 who has great musical talent and lives about three houses from the Embassy. . . . She is bright, pretty, has a charm of manner and is very responsive but does not speak English and as I do not speak Russian and do not attempt to do so, I am compelled to carry on my conversation with her in French—but don't tell this as I don't speak French sufficiently well to have the credit of being able to carry on a conversation in that tongue. I read it readily and as I am now daily practicing speaking it have hope of being able to master it ere long.[30]

In the summer evenings, with their long twilights, as the sun sank beneath the poplars, the Allied men got together at the spacious clubhouse embassy for bridge and poker. Francis liked to play the wild variations of poker he and his friends engaged in at the Log Cabin Club, although he complained to Perry that he was having trouble teaching such complicated variations as "skip straights around the corner." Francis noted, "My mathematical turn of mind always gives me an advantage in skip straight."[31]

By early June, Francis and his French and Italian colleagues became convinced by reports from their agents in Moscow, Petrograd, and the Ukraine that the Bolsheviks were on the ropes. On June 3, he sent a cable to Polk in Washington asking for instructions in case the Bolsheviks fell. He noted, "Russian people require guidance, are helpless without it; we are decidedly most popular of Allies not only because Russians are satisfied we have no territorial designs but because of President Wilson's eloquent, impressive utterances of sympathy and interest and probably because American Embassy was first to recognize the Republic and is only one that never left Russia or planned to do so."

Francis recommend that he be authorized to recognize "that Government which will be adopted by the people through their representatives chosen at an election duly called and held under safeguards which will insure an honest expression of the popular will."[32]

That evening, Francis set off for Petrograd, accompanied by Military Attaché James A. Ruggles, Second Secretary Livingston Phelps, Earl Johnston, and Philip Jordan, as before leaving Armour in charge. Reports had reached Francis that trouble was brewing for the Bolsheviks in the former capital, and Francis wanted to establish personal contact with organized opposition to the Bolshevik Government, including leaders of the

Czech Legion. And he wanted to see for himself how much cooperation was taking place between the Bolsheviks and the Germans.[33]

Francis was itching for Allied troops to march into Moscow and Petrograd, taking control from the disintegrating Reds. On the long train trip, Francis wrote Perry that he thought the time was ripe for Allied intervention because the Russians were sick of the Bolsheviks:

> It would not surprise me if the bolshevik government would collapse before you received this letter. I am doing all I can to prepare for such a contingency. . . . I am now planning to prevent if possible the disarming of forty thousand or more Cheko-Slovak soldiers whom the Soviet Government has ordered to give up their arms under penalty of death. . . . I have no instructions or authority from Washington to encourage these men to disobey the orders of the Soviet government. . . . I have taken chances before however and another little chance will do me no harm.[34]

By then, the Czech Legion had joined forces with the moderate socialist "Komuch"—the Committee of Members of the Constituent Assembly, many of them Right Wing Socialist Revolutionaries who wanted to resurrect something roughly like the Provisional Government. The Czech Legion and the troops of the Komuch occupied increasingly large chunks of territory in eastern and southern Russia. By the end of June, fifteen thousand Czech and Komuch troops had reached the Pacific and taken control of Vladivostok.

As the train to Petrograd rattled along, with the frequent lurching stops and starts typical of Russian trains, Francis grew garrulous, and Johnston scribbled frantically to keep up with him. He complained to Perry:

> I am entirely out of whiskey, and unable to procure any in Vologda or Moscow . . . no wine not even champagne can take the place of Scotch or good old Kentucky Bourbon. . . . You may therefore tell the Log Cabin members and also your chums in the Racquet Club (with whom I fear you crook your elbow very often) that if I were not abstemious by choice I would be compelled to be so, circumstanced as I am in Russia. I do not miss this stimulant however as new conditions arise daily and sometimes oftener requiring vigorous attention. . . . I am willing to sacrifice not only all my worldly possessions but life itself in this cause in which our country is now engaged.[35]

Francis spent four days in Petrograd, moving back into the old American Embassy. He was greeted enthusiastically by the three servants still on duty and immediately had one of them take down the Norwegian flag and raise the Stars and Stripes. Petrograd seemed deserted now that the government had moved to Moscow. Many shops were closed along the Nevsky Prospect in what had been, in Francis's words, "the gayest city in Europe."[36]

In Petrograd, he met with the leaders of the Czech Legion and several underground counterrevolutionary groups, including members of both wings of the Socialist Revolutionary Party—the right wing, allied with the Czech Legion, and the leftists. He also met with a group of industrialists who wanted to establish a constitutional monarchy. He now believed even more strongly that the Bolsheviks were on the verge of collapse, and indeed one Bolshevik official told him, "We admit we are a corpse but no one has the courage to bury us." Francis took this as further evidence that only the little push of intervention would depose the Bolsheviks. He remarked, "Sometimes a corpse becomes so putrid that it should be removed in the interest of public health."[37]

While in the former capital, Francis authorized giving money to the Bolsheviks to, as he put it, "hasten the evacuation" from Petrograd large stores of strategic metals and other supplies "lest they fall in the hands of the Germans."

He also dropped in on Madame de Cramm, probably bringing her some food. We don't know what they talked about, except she apparently asked him to inquire of the State Department the whereabouts of her husband. He did that, in a cable to Lansing after he had returned to Vologda, informing the secretary of state that he had seen her and insisting, "She is a loyal Russian, hates Germany and is very desirous to serve the Allies, especially America."[38]

In late June, back in Vologda, he wrote the sixth and last known letter from him to her in Russia, mentioning that he had received two letters from her in the past week. He said he would try to get some more food to her, and added, apparently in response to a question, "Of course I want you to continue to write to me but not at any risk to yourself. You should be exceedingly careful as your acquaintance with me is known and I suspect you are closely watched. You should destroy this letter immediately after reading."[39]

About the same time, in a letter to the estranged wife of young Second Secretary Livingston Phelps, Francis provides some insight into his views on marriage and implies he had been giving the subject some thought (perhaps on long sleepless nights, when the sun barely sank beneath the northern horizon). Francis wrote a fatherly letter to the wife, urging her to give up her decision to seek an annulment of their marriage: "If you separate from Livingston now you will never cease to regret it. You will ruin his career and render his entire future existence unhappy . . . women and men . . . sometimes imagine they have ceased to love their chosen life-mates and after reflection and separation learned they were mistaken."[40] He granted Phelps a leave to try to win her back.

By the middle of June, Georgi V. Chicherin, Soviet Commissar for Foreign Affairs, had become convinced—with good reason—that the United States was moving, in cooperation with the other Allies, toward landing troops in Russia. Chicherin sent his aide Voznesenski, described by Francis as "a shrewd, talkative little Russian," to Vologda on what Francis later called a "fishing expedition" to find out if Allied intervention was likely. Francis said he didn't know, maintaining a poker face as he told the man from the Foreign Office that sometimes he thought Allied intervention would take place and other times thought otherwise. Sometimes, he said, not afraid to play dumb to win a hand, he changed his mind "several times a day during these long Russian days." Francis later described Voznesenski as "a shrewd Jew" who had, "as we used to express it in Kentucky immediately after the Civil War, 'the cheek of a government mule.'"[41]

Voznesenski met with Francis several times. The American ambassador continued to deny any knowledge of plans for intervention.[42] At the same time, Francis was cabling the State Department, urging large-scale intervention and organizing meetings of the Allied representatives to plan their actions when—increasingly, "if" was not a consideration—Allied forces came ashore in numbers and occupied significant segments of Russian territory. As Francis was well aware, a few hundred British marines already had gone ashore at Murmansk in March, and a small contingent of American marines would join another group of British troops in landing at Murmansk on June 27.

By then, in addition to his meetings with counterrevolutionaries in Petrograd, Francis authorized widespread espionage and other covert anti-Bolshevik activities across western Russia. The Americans recruited dozens of agents among anti-Bolsheviks Russians, and their reports were forwarded to him. Poole in Moscow, Vice Consul Robert W. Imbrie at Petrograd, and other American representatives elsewhere maintained close contact with anti-Bolshevik forces and reported regularly to Francis. With Francis's support and aid, the U.S. Treasury helped the British fund anti-Bolshevik forces, and Willoughby Smith, the Russian-born American consul in Tiblisi, quietly funneled two million rubles to counterrevolutionary soldiers in the south of Russia.[43]

Francis also dispatched covert agents, including a representative of the YMCA, to the north to gather information, and he was informed that opposition to the Bolsheviks was strong in the key port of Archangel, although weak elsewhere. Francis authorized Felix Cole, consul in Archangel, to give money to anti-Bolshevik organizations in the north.[44]

In Vologda, Captain Eugene Prince was placed in charge of identifying promising routes of Allied occupation and getting copies of German and Bolshevik battle plans. Prince and Military Attaché Ruggles worked with the French military mission to sabotage property taken over by the Germans and to funnel financial aid to the Czechs fighting the Red Army. Their agents, mostly Right Wing Socialist Revolutionaries who hated both the Germans and the Bolsheviks, organized strikes and sabotaged railroads in German-occupied parts of the Ukraine and eastern Russia, as well as in Siberia.[45]

In the late spring and summer of 1918, the Bolsheviks reeled from multiple blows, with civil war heating up in the north, south, and east, increasingly incendiary opposition growing on the right and the left, and a terrible famine already spreading across much of Russia. To many government leaders in both Russia and the Allied nations, it appeared that the Reds were finished or soon would be. Even Lenin later admitted that he thought his government would not survive the attacks and woes of 1918, and Mirbach and other top-ranking Germans in Russia were deeply pessimistic: "The Bolsheviks are extremely nervous and can feel their end approaching, and all the rats are therefore beginning to leave the sinking ship," one of the top German diplomats in Moscow reported to Berlin in early June.[46]

In late June, as Bolshevik power decayed and Allied intervention seemed inevitable, a political commissar was sent from Archangel to Vologda, rightly considered to be a nest of foreigners and counterrevolutionaries. The commissar threw out pro-Allied municipal officials, officials with whom Francis had cultivated close relationships. And he brought in members of the Bolshevik's fledgling corps of secret police to keep an eye on the rebellious citizenry.[47]

On July 4, Francis held an Independence Day reception for the diplomatic corps and local dignitaries. Philip Jordan once again surprised and delighted Francis by coming up with the makings for a heady punch and tasty sandwiches. The old Victrola was hauled into the garden for dancing.

Francis decided to use the occasion to make one of his periodic addresses to the Russian people. He compared the current struggle in Russia to the American war of independence 142 years before, pointing out that a long period of "internal dissension" occured that "ended in the adoption of a Constitution and the formation of the Government which exists today." After a nod to Ambassador Noulens for French support of the American Revolution, he moved to the main subject, the world war:

> My country and all of the Allies consider the Russian people still in the struggle. We do not observe the Brest-Litovsk peace. Surely no Russian who loves his country is going to submit tamely to her dismemberment and humiliation.
>
> President Wilson has said feelingly and impressively on several occasions that he has no intention of deserting Russia, in fact that he is resolved not to do so. That means we will never consent to Germany making Russia a German province; that we will never stand idly by and see the Germans exploit the Russian people and appropriate to Germany's selfish ends the immense resources of Russia. We take this stand not because we ourselves seek territorial aggrandizement; not because we have commercial ambitions in connection with Russia; nor because we wish to dictate to the Russian people or to interfere in the internal affairs of Russia. We assume this position because we wish the Russian people to have the right to dispose of themselves and not be compelled to submit to the tyrannical rule of Germany, even though such a disposition might result in a temporary peace. . . . Therefore, on this day, which is celebrated in every city, in every village and in every hamlet in America, I appeal to the Russian people to take courage, to organize to resist the encroachments of Germany. The Allies are your friends and are willing and able to assist you notwithstanding your superb army has been demobilized.[48]

Chicherin sent a congratulatory message, also comparing the two revolutions, saying he hoped for "intimate cooperation of your people and ours." Francis sent a note to Poole, asking him to thank Chicherin for his warm message, saying he wanted "to preserve the record of never having addressed Chicherin directly."[49]

And on July 4, the fifth All-Russian Congress of Soviets opened at the Grand Theater in Moscow. Although there was strict security, an American secret agent managed to slip in and reported on the meeting to Francis. A bitter fight took place between the Bolsheviks and the second-strongest party, the Left Socialist Revolutionaries, who kept shouting "Down with Mirbach! Down with the Germans!" From then on, Francis cited the split between the Bolsheviks and the Left Socialist Revolutionaries to bolster his arguments for intervention.[50]

Two days after the shouting match at the Congress of Soviets, German Ambassador Mirbach was murdered. The Bolsheviks blamed the assassination on "Russian-Anglo-French Imperialism" and more specifically—and accurately—on the Left Socialist Revolutionaries, who hoped simultaneously to inspire popular uprisings and provoke Germany into attacking Russia and restarting the war.

Disorganized anti-Bolshevik actions erupted in Moscow and in several other near-by cities, and the civil war in the provinces heated up and spread. Allied diplomats feared that German troops would march into Petrograd and Moscow and take over the government. Francis held daily meetings of the Allied diplomatic corps in Vologda, and on the night of July 7 he sent a cable to Washington urging that the landing of a sizable contingent of American troops at Archangel, already planned, be completed as soon as possible.

The cable never arrived. Civil war cut off telegraphic communication between Vologda and the State Department. Francis, who had been sending cables to Washington almost daily that spring and summer, later would discover that many of them never reached their destinations. Francis truly was isolated. Beleaguered rebels in Yaroslavl, a town on the Volga about halfway between Vologda and Moscow, appealed to the Allies for help, but all Francis and his fellow Allied diplomats could do was try to forward the request to the British Navy at Murmansk and hope it reached London.[51]

On the morning of July 10, Francis received a telegram from Chicherin. It was addressed to the "Dean of the Diplomatic Corps" and marked urgent. The foreign minister wrote:

> Taking into consideration the present situation and possibility of dangers for representatives of Entente powers Soviet Government looks upon Moscow as town where security of named representatives can be assured. Considering as its duty safeguarding ambassadors' security Government sees in their coming to Moscow a necessity. We hope that highly esteemed American Ambassador will appreciate this step in friendly spirit in which it is undertaken. In order to execute this measure and to remove any difficulties People's Commissariat for Foreign Affairs delegates to Vologda its representative, Citizen Radek.

Francis immediately convened the chiefs of the Allied missions, which now included British Chargé d'Affaires F. O. Lindley, who had arrived on July 7. The men agreed that

Moscow, where the German ambassador had been assassinated four days before and which, by many reports, soon would be occupied by German troops, was not a safe haven. In his memoirs, French Ambassador Noulens referred to the telegram as a "burlesque document" that "invited us to entrust our security to the place where circumstances demonstrated it would be the least assured."[52]

Even Lockhart, who had said more than once how absurd it was to try to conduct foreign policy from Vologda, decided now that it was "probable" that the Bolsheviks, "realising that intervention was now inevitable . . . desired to hold the Ambassadors in Moscow as hostages."[53]

Hoping to forestall the coming of "Citizen" Karl Radek from the Soviet Foreign Office, Francis telegraphed Chicherin, inquiring why he thought staying in Vologda would be "unsafe or inadvisable." He remarked archly:

> We have no fear of the Russian people, whom we have always befriended and whom we consider our Allies, and we have full confidence in the population of Vologda. Our only anxiety is concerning the forces of the Central Empires with whom we are at war and, in our judgment, they are not more dangerous at Vologda than elsewhere. At Moscow, on the other hand, we hear that the Germans have already received permission to introduce their troops to safeguard their representatives, and in any case the town is directly threatened by the Germans. If you mean by your message that the government of Soviets has taken without consulting the Allied Missions the decision that the latter should come to Moscow and that you are sending Mr. Radek to carry such a decision into execution, we desire to inform you that we consider that would be offensive to us and we would not comply therewith.[54]

Francis gave his telegram to the press, and that evening a Vologda paper featured it in an extra edition. His message was received enthusiastically, appealing to the pride and strongly anti-Soviet feelings of the majority of Vologdans.

Meanwhile, Allied intervention was proceeding in the north and east of Russia, and Francis knew it. In a July 8 letter to Vice Consul Imbrie at Petrograd, he noted that "Allied intervention has not been announced formally but it has taken place nevertheless and British troops are being landed at Murmansk. French troops also and a contingent of American troops. . . . The Soviet rule in Russia is about finished in my judgment."[55]

Radek arrived in Vologda on July 12. Accompanying him was Russian-speaking, pro-Bolshevik British newspaperman Arthur Ransome. Ransome had been shocked to overhear Radek say on the trip north, "If they won't come to Moscow of their own accord, I'll put them into cattle-trucks and bring them!"[56]

Radek stepped off the train dressed in a brown military uniform with a large pistol strapped to his waist. (Ransome contended that the gun, which Radek usually carried, was an intellectual revolutionary's affectation and not a specific threat.) A short, ugly, fringe-bearded man—Lockhart described him as "the Bolshevik Puck"—Radek must have looked a bit comical. He immediately ordered that the local press be censored and that no more statements issuing from the clubhouse be printed. Members of the Vologda Soviet took Radek and his retinue, including Ransome, to the clubhouse in a large American car and they arrived shortly after 5 P.M., just as the daily cocktail-hour conference of Allied diplomats was commencing in the drawing room.[57]

The visitors were told to wait in the front parlor, a large room with long rows of books and bound journals in the bookcases and portraits of Gogol, Dostoevsky, and Chekov on the walls. After a long wait, Francis came out into the reception room. He was startled by Radek's gun.

Francis asked Radek to come into the drawing room and meet all of the Allied diplomats, but Radek refused to deal with any group that included Noulens, whose early, fierce, and unrelenting anti-Bolshevism had made him *persona non grata* with the Soviets. So Francis and Radek sat down in the parlor to talk, with Ransome as interpreter. A long and heated discussion about moving the Allied embassies to Moscow ensued, with Radek puffing furiously on his pipe. Francis repeated that the diplomats would not move and asked if the telegram about moving back to Moscow was an invitation or an order.

Radek insisted it was an invitation and that there was no intention of forcing the diplomats to move to Moscow. If the Allied representatives insisted on staying in Vologda, Radek said, he would demand a statement in writing absolving the Soviet Government of all responsibility for their safety. He pointed out that Mirbach had been assassinated by Socialist Revolutionaries, who were no friends of the Allies and might try to "demonstrate their impartiality by murdering an American Ambassador." And he said the countryside was thick with thousands of freed Austrian and German prisoners who might avenge the murder of Mirbach by taking the life of an Allied ambassador.

Francis excused himself, went back into the drawing room, and reported the conversation to the assembled diplomats. They agreed that as the dean Francis should tell Radek they stood by the statements in the telegram to Chicherin, at least until it was clear what Germany planned to do in the wake of the assassination of Mirbach. Then the other diplomats left, and Francis resumed his meeting with Radek.[58]

Arthur Ransome, who still thought a move to Moscow would be wise, described Francis in the context of this meeting as an "elderly, uncompromising man, anxious to make no mistake, perplexed between his sense of his own dignity as Dean of the Diplomatic Corps and his over-humble submission to the stronger will of the Frenchman [Noulens]." In fact, there is no evidence that Francis ever seriously considered altering his refusal to move to Moscow, with or without the influence of Noulens. And Francis, not Noulens, had chosen to move to Vologda in the first place.

Francis told Radek he and his colleagues had decided to "refuse the invitation." The gnomish Radek, glaring up at the tall ambassador and puffing on his ever-present pipe, replied, "Then I will station guards around all of your embassies. And no one will be permitted to go in or out without a passport."

"We are virtually prisoners, then?" asked Francis.

"No," Radek insisted, "you are not virtually prisoners, you can go in and out and the chiefs can all go in and out, but when you desire anybody to come in here, you will have to tell the local Soviet the name of the man and they will give him a pass to enter through your guards."[59]

The long meeting ended "with the definite impression that the diplomats had no intention of leaving Vologda," recalled Ransome. As he and Radek drove away, Radek began muttering about rounding up "the whole menagerie" and taking them forcibly to Moscow.

That evening, Radek and Ransome met separately with British Chargé Lindley in the "British Mission"—an unpainted, one-story wooden house. When they arrived, several members of the mission were sitting around a table on the verandah, enjoying the long July twilight. They were "an easy mark for any Social Revolutionary who might feel inclined to put his party in the right by demonstrating its impartiality in the assassination of foreigners," noted Ransome, who seemed convinced that the diplomats were in much more danger in peaceful Vologda than they would be in tumultuous Moscow. Radek had a long and intense conversation with Lindley, listing a number of reasons that a move to Moscow made sense, but Lindley refused to break with the group.[60]

Radek telegraphed Chicherin a description of his meeting with Francis. The telegram was intercepted by a British agent in Moscow and given to Lockhart. He passed it on to American Consul Poole, who sent a translation to Francis. According to Lockhart, who presumably heard the details from one of the Brits in Vologda, Francis pulled the telegram out at the daily conference of diplomats. "Gentlemen," he said, "I have received an interesting document from Moscow. It is Radek's account of his negotiations with ourselves."

Fumbling with his pince-nez, according to Lockhart, Francis read the first sentence aloud: "Ambassador Francis is a stuffed shirt."

Lockhart commented later, "It was only too true, but, coming from the Ambassador's lips, it was a little startling. Richer jests followed, and the climax came with the closing sentence: 'Lindley is the only man who has any sense. He practically admits that he considers Noulens' behaviour childish in the extreme.'"

"Lindley has faced many difficult situations with unfailing courage and equanimity," Lockhart remarked. "I doubt, however if he has ever felt quite so awkward as at that moment."[61]

Lockhart contended that Francis had not read the telegram before presenting it aloud to the conference, which seems highly unlikely—curiosity alone, and Francis had an abundance of that, would have made reading the document immediately upon reception irresistible. It is much more likely that Francis was trying to make a dramatic point. The morning after Radek's meeting with Francis, Soviet guards showed up at the embassy. Francis recalled that "they did not disturb us. They were hungry and we gave them food." George Kennan, who became American ambassador to the Soviet Union in 1952, noted that the posting of guards in Vologda "inaugurated that curious system of personal supervision, designed to serve simultaneously the purposes of protection, surveillance and isolation from the local community, without which no American ambassador was permitted to exist in the Soviet Union until after the death of Stalin in 1953."[62]

Under orders from Chicherin, Radek stayed in Vologda for several more days. According to Francis, he "made a bad impression on the people of Vologda, who showed their opposition to him and their preference for the Allies against the Germans in many ways." Angry at the lack of support among Vologdans, Radek and the Soviet summoned about two thousand railway employees and other workers for a speech intended to stir up animosity toward the Allies. According to Francis, Radek went so far as to urge the assembled men to unite with German troops to fight English and French troops, who already were landing in the north of Russia. The workers roared in disagreement, shouting that they would rather join the Allies and fight the Germans. Radek became enraged and threatened that the Bolsheviks would destroy Vologda, as they were destroying Yaroslavl.[63]

Chicherin and Francis continued to spar by telegram about moving the embassy, with the Russian foreign minister stopping just short of ordering the Allied diplomats to Moscow. Meanwhile, Allied troops continued to come ashore.

By early summer, Woodrow Wilson had decided that America should intervene in Russia with a substantial commitment of troops. The growing heroic stature in America of the Czech Legion, which Francis had been rebuked for supporting, made Wilson's decision easier. Despite murderous opposition from a large force of German and Austrian prisoners of war commanded by German officers, the Czechs had captured Vladivostok, introducing what Robert Lansing described as a "sentimental element into the question of our duty."

On July 6, Wilson quietly authorized American troops to go ashore in the East. By early September, between six and seven thousand Americans had joined an Allied force, including seven thousand Japanese, in support of the Czechs in Vladivostok and eastern Siberia.[64]

Wilson contended the intervention was intended only to help the Czechs defend themselves and to protect military supplies from the Germans. But he listened when important foreign-policy advisors, including Charles Crane, as well as Russian Ambassador Boris Bakhmeteff, a holdover from the Provisional Government, argued that the people would rise up and throw out the Bolsheviks if the American, British, and French flags appeared in Russia.

Later in July, Wilson authorized American troops to go into the northern ports of Murmansk and Archangel as well. On July 22, three battalions of American infantry were dispatched by ship to northern Russia. They arrived in early August. Once again, the stated intent was to help the Russians with self-defense, but the underlying motive was to aid in the overthrow of the Bolsheviks. Captain Hugh S. Martin, an assistant military attaché in northern Russia, said later, "The real truth was, we were waging war against Bolshevism. Everybody knew that. Yet no Allied government ever stated that that was its policy in intervening."[65]

On the morning of July 17, a British captain named McGrath came down to Vologda from Archangel. McGrath told Francis that the Allies, operating out of Murmansk under the command of British Major General F. C. Poole, soon would move south to take control of Archangel. He proposed that the Allied diplomats leave Vologda for Archangel, about four hundred miles to the north. General Poole had planned on reaching Archangel by the first week in August, but he would happily speed the advance to meet the Allied ambassadors when they arrived and protect them from Bolshevik hotheads.

Meanwhile, reports reached Vologda of brutal deeds in the town of Ekatarinburg in the Urals.

The Tsar and his family had been held prisoner in a brick manor house in Ekatarinburg. Fearful that the Romanovs would fall into the hands of advancing White Russian troops and become a rallying point for counterrevolutionaries, the regional Soviet of the Urals, apparently with the approval of Moscow, decided to wipe out the royal family. On the night of July 16 and the morning of July 17, guards took the Tsar, the Tsarina, their five children, and their four servants into the basement of the brick house, where they were shot and bayoneted to death.

The slaughter reaffirmed the Vologda diplomats' disinclination to trust the Bolsheviks to protect them in Moscow. They still thought they were safest remaining in Vologda. Then, about noon on July 23, a telegram marked "Urgent" came for Francis from Chicherin. This one read: "I entreat you most earnestly to leave Vologda. Come here. Danger approaching. Tomorrow can be too late. When battle rages, distinction of houses cannot be made. If all smashed in your domiciles during struggle of contending forces responsibility will fall upon you making deaf ear to all entreaties. Why bring about catastrophe which you can avert?"[66]

The insistent nature of the message convinced the diplomats the time had come to leave immediately for Archangel, where they hoped that General Poole and a friendly local Soviet could protect them. Francis had made sure that the railroad cars that many of them had lived in when they first arrived still waited on a siding at the Vologda station, and on the evening of July 23, the diplomats packed their bags and moved back into the cars. Francis sent a purposely misleading wire to Chicherin: "Thank you for your telegram. We fully appreciate the uninterrupted interest you have taken in our personal safety and have decided to follow your advice and are leaving Vologda." That was the first of a series of telegrams that went back and forth between Vologda and Moscow over the next thirty hours, with the Allied diplomats waiting anxiously in the hot, stuffy railroad cars.

Francis had hoped to pull out by 8 P.M., but he discovered that the stationmaster could not provide a locomotive for the train without approval from Chicherin. Through an interpreter, Francis told the man to submit the request for a locomotive to his superiors in Moscow.

The reply came from Moscow: "Who wishes the locomotive?"

Francis told the man to say, "The American Ambassador."

The answer came immediately: "Where does he wish to go?"

"To Archangel," Francis replied.

By the next morning, Francis had received a long telegram from Chicherin. It said, in part:

> If your intention is to leave Russia, we are powerless to hinder you in doing so, but we express our sincerest regrets at your departure from our soil together with our hope to see you soon in our midst. . . . It is unfortunately necessary to inform you that in the expectation of a siege Archangel cannot be a residence fit for Ambassadors. . . . I cannot but repeat that under the present conditions when our foes . . . seek to conspire and to create artificial outbursts and to provoke civil war, we can, with complete earnestness, point to Moscow, where . . . our forces are and cannot but remain in undisturbed control of the city and to its peaceful gay suburbs with their splendid villas as an appropriate abode which our government deliberately proposes to the Ambassador of friendly America. We must at any cost avoid the danger of your departure being misinterpreted in the eyes of our great masses and of American public opinion. The special train is at your disposal, but we do not lose hope that your decision will be to come to Moscow.

Francis replied with an even longer cable. In part, he wrote: "Permit me to say to you that while your message is appreciated because expressing friendly feeling for the people I represent and a desire on your part to maintain relations with them and with my government, your treatment of me as their representative does not accord with such expressions."

Rather disingenuously, Francis said:

> While refraining from interfering in all internal affairs in Russia, I have considered that the Russian people were still our allies, and have more than once appealed to them to unite with us in resisting a common enemy. I have further recommended to my government many times to send food to relieve the sufferings of the Russian people and to ship agricultural implements to meet the requirements of Russia. . . .
>
> Your telegram to me states that if permitted to go to Archangel it would be only for the purpose of [our] leaving Russia, which you are 'powerless to hinder.' . . . Speaking for myself I have no desire or intention of leaving Russia unless forced to do so, and in such event my absence would be temporary. I would not properly represent my government or the sentiment of the American people if I should leave Russia at this time.
>
> The Brest-Litovsk peace the Allies have never recognized, and it is becoming so burdensome to the Russian people that in my judgment the time is not far distant when they will turn upon Germany and by their repulsion of the invader from the Russian borders will demonstrate what I have continuously believed, and that is that the national spirit of great Russia is not dead but has only been sleeping. . . . The Allied Diplomatic Corps of Vologda await your immediate approval of the locomotive to draw their train to Archangel.[67]

By then, Chicherin and his superiors must have wished that the Allied representatives simply would go home, where they could stir up no more trouble with the populace and fund no more counterrevolutionary activities. Shortly before midnight on July 24, Francis received a cable from Chicherin: "We will give instructions that a locomotive be put at your disposal at Vologda and that a boat should be prepared for you in Archangel." Chicherin clearly wanted all the Allied diplomats out of Russia as soon as possible. But Francis had other ideas.

Instructing Norman Armour, an assistant military attaché named Earl Packer, and a clerk, Zenaida Kennedy, to stay in Vologda "to show the Russian people we are not deserting them," Francis prepared to leave with about a dozen members of his embassy and the rest of the Allies.[68] About twenty other Americans, including fifteen National City Bank employees, also were left behind.

About 140 people were with Francis, including French Ambassador Noulens, British Chargé Lindley, Italian Chargé Torretta, the Brazilian chargé, and representatives of the Japanese, the Chinese, and the Serbians.[69] When a locomotive appeared, there was considerable suspense as to which end of the train it would be attached to. Finally, it backed into place at the north, much to the relief of Francis and his colleagues. About 2 A.M. on July 25, the Allied train pulled out of Vologda station, heading north toward the glow on the horizon as the mid-summer sun briefly sank and rose again. The train pitched and swayed through the marshy lowland fields and the stands of birch and spruce north of the small city, marking the end of the strange and dangerous period when Vologda was the diplomatic capital of Russia because David Rowland Francis wanted it to be.

Francis later remarked that Chicherin "seems to have been under the impression that after our departure from Vologda the Soviet Government had disposed of the American Ambassador."[70]

But David Francis had no intention of leaving Russia.

CHAPTER 21

Into the North

BY LATE JULY 1918, U.S. MILITARY INTELLIGENCE in Washington and New York had interrogated Edgar de Cramm and held him at Ellis Island. There was some question as to exactly what to do with him. One MI report in the thickening de Cramm file, from Major Nicholas Biddle, noted that de Cramm "stated that it was his understanding or at any rate that it had been intimated to him that the State Department did not wish proceedings continued for the reason that I have explained to you over the telephone."[1] Why the State Department might not want de Cramm prosecuted for espionage or Mann Act violations will become clear.

The federal government had contemplated deporting de Cramm, but legally he would have to be sent either back to Cuba, the last country he had visited, or home to Russia. Havana was already a viperous nest of German spies, and Russia did not want Edgar de Cramm back. An American intelligence report explains why:

> Up to the latter part of 1915, De Cramm was Counselor of State under former Czar Nicholas, and was banished because of financial transactions carried on by him for Russians and Germans after the outbreak of the war, thus abusing the trust placed in him in his official capacity. De Cramm acted as an agent for Germans who had money invested in Russia by assisting them to transfer their money to Germany through Sweden by drawing a draft on himself in Sweden, after which he would go there and then forward the money himself to the proper person in Germany. He reversed this procedure for Russians who had money invested in Germany.

De Cramm was banished from Russia, and he and his wife came to the United States. At a Russian consulate, he signed over to his wife all his Russian property, including the Petrograd apartment, so that the Tsar's government could not confiscate it.[2]

At the least, Edgar de Cramm was a double-dealer, a war profiteer who used his government position to enrich himself from both sides. Top MI officials, based on information from their own agents as well as from the French and the British, were certain that de Cramm also spied for the Germans while traveling through North and South America.[3] In mild dissent, one MI officer noted, "There appears to be no direct evidence that de Cramm is anything more than a plain crook, who would willingly serve Germany if he had the opportunity and if there was money in it for him. . . . There is more reason to believe his wife is more dangerous."[4]

Crook or spy, de Cramm apparently had a hole card to play against the Americans— letters from his wife about David Francis. According to a statement by de Cramm, a lawyer named Kinzler who represented him had suggested that he "use" the letters. De Cramm agreed the letters would be helpful "should I be mistreated by the Government" but also thought he should "do everything to protect my wife's name, which is my name also."

Then another lawyer, John Maher, appeared, compliments of the Russian consulate. He told de Cramm that the United States and Kinzler were playing a treacherous game, trying to get him to turn over the incriminating letters and sign a statement disavowing any knowledge about an affair between his wife and Francis. He would then be "lost": no longer able to defend himself against prosecution and imprisonment. Sign nothing, Maher insisted. And if he *was* forced to turn over the letters, make photographic copies.[5]

On July 24, Edgar de Cramm received permission to leave for Japan on a ship sailing from San Francisco on July 31. He was sent under guard to San Francisco, where he was to be put aboard his ship. The MI office in San Francisco was told: "Before leaving he should be thoroughly searched for documents on his person and in his baggage. Any suspicious documents as well as all documents of a personal nature, should be retained, particularly letters from his wife, Matilda or Meta de Cramm, or any letters from others concerning his wife or copies or photographs of same. . . . Avoid irritating him unnecessarily."[6]

Edgar de Cramm left San Francisco as scheduled and arrived about two and a half weeks later in Tokyo, where he seems to have had too many financial problems of his own to worry about sending any money to his wife in Russia.[7] Somehow, either through a deal with de Cramm or in the search at departure, Military Intelligence ended up with two letters in ungrammatical English from Matilda de Cramm to her husband.* The letters now are filed with July 1918 correspondence in the Military Intelligence section of the National Archives. No explanation is filed with them. As far as we know, they have never before been published.

---

*It's quite possible that the multilingual Madame de Cramm wrote to her husband in English. They both would have been practicing their English, she to converse with Francis and others at the American Embassy, he to live and work unobtrusively in the United States. The appearance of phrases in French could mean that she was trying to clarify English statements through the use of a language they were more familiar with, since French was in common use by educated Russians. Or, Edgar de Cramm may have translated the letters himself from French or Russian to use in bargaining with the Americans. Or he may have simply made the letters up, but they have the ring of truth about them in their quirky details and forms of expression.

The letters appear to have been typed on two different machines. The first letter was written from Sweden:

Haparanda 24 April 1916

Dear Lu [Ludwig],
At last I arrived here, the last station before entering Russia. What is awaiting me in Russia? How are my sons? After all, I do not know myself about my feelings.

I wrote you from Christiana and from Stockholm.

During the trip on the boat I tried to be separated from the other passengers, but Francis, as well as the others, his aids, started from the first sight to court me, regardless my immediate announcement, I have two big grown up sons, officers in the Russian Army.

The worsest of all was Francis himself. If he will be occupied as energetically as he does in courting me with the Embassy business, he will be the right man on the right place.

He is 64 years of age, but he is looking as 45, to wit, how he feels himself.

He is married but left his wife in America. He wants to be free, as he said it to me.

He has heard a great deal about the wonderfull russian women_but his first acquaintance with the first, he met _he means me _has surpassed all his expectations.

At first he did not pleased me at all, a regular Yankee, directly smelling from him of dollars and cents, but the more I know him, the more he pleases me and I think we will be good friends later on.

This morning, for instance, he entered my room here and made to me a scene of jealousy, accusing me of being friendly with one of his secretaries Baily.

I am writing you openly, according to our mutual agreement, to remain good friends after we have mutually decided to cancel our sexual relations.

But divorce. What for we need same? Surely nobody of us both, after having had so many dissapointments, will start again to be bound.

And therfore "What is the woory? Let us go,"

You are now free and you may arrange your life as you please, let me therefor do what I want to and I shall always be thankfull to you for your love and faithfullness in the education of my sons.

Let us remain friends.
Best recollections

Me. [Meta]
I hope you will always supply me with the necessary funds to cover my expenses.

The second letter was written several months after Madame de Cramm and Francis had arrived in Petrograd.

Petrograd Sept. 8th 1916

Dear Lu,
Well it is settled. I cannot come to you any more. The Fate herself has decided.

You doubtless guess right, what reason has kept me back and has compelled me for ever to cancel every matrimonial relations with you.

I have now a friend, who understands me and who understands how to handle me.

You see, that not only the wish to be embraced by another man, physically, was the reason, because Francis is 65 years old and therefore the sexual relations play only the second violin.

However I have always looked upon another man for his soul, do you understand, the soul. first of all.

But, it is no use to talk with you about that. you will not understand it, all the same.

You, of course, have long forgotten me. now beeing in Amerika you are in your element, I am for you a passed passion (une passion passee). commerce and trade that is all you need and which interests you more than anything else. The studying of a womens hearth is to tiresome for you? isn't it? (Tant de bruit pour une omelette.) You have sent the divorce papers and says if I shall not agree you will force me to that.

Drop this, Lu, because it is better for you and you will some day be very thankfull to me, I have prevented you to enter to new marriage and a new dissappointment.

No Lu, you must not marry again, because every woman will put horns on you, as do not occupy with her enough. And (bien decore) "nicely decorated" you have been enough.

Georg also entered the Fleet, now serving together with Egon. Egon distinguished himself for bravery and is presented for reward. The Minister of the Marine personally has congratulated him.

Therefore (sans rancune et sans reproche) "without wrath and reproache.

Me

Were Dave and Meta having a love affair? In an emotional sense, they undoubtedly were. No question he found her charming and attractive, and more than one old friend has commented on Francis's attraction to pretty women. She was his closest Russian friend, and it's hard to imagine him being so fervent about a friendship with a man.[8]

Was the relationship physical? The only evidence we have are the intriguing letters Madame de Cramm apparently sent her husband in 1916. But in them she says the physical "played second violin." At this point in his life, despite his constant protestations of good health, Francis was in his mid-sixties and his prostate already bothered him, which would have hampered sexual relations.

At the least, he had an old man's crush on this younger, attractive, intelligent woman, and she was fond of him. (Francis, to his credit, seems to have enjoyed the company of smart, independent-minded women, Jane being the prime example.) This affectionate relationship with Matilda de Cramm was, from a diplomatic sense, stubbornly foolish, but the man was lonely for female companionship and not used to accounting to anyone for his actions.

D AVID FRANCIS'S FOUR HUNDRED-MILE TRIP north from Vologda through the Russian taiga ended at about 11 A.M. on Friday, July 26, when the train carrying 140 Allied diplomats and staff arrived at the Bakarista terminal across the Northern Dvina River from the White Sea port of Archangel. Archangel had been Russia's major port until Peter the Great, in the early eighteenth century, had built St. Petersburg (Petrograd) on the Baltic and was a strategic site in the Great War, particularly after the Germans effectively gained control of the Baltic.[9]

More than two days of waiting and wrangling ensued, with the diplomats able to see the domes and steeples of the city of about seventy thousand but unable to approach it. Hovering over events was the knowledge that the Allies already held strategic ports to the north of Archangel and were moving rapidly toward landing thousands of troops at Archangel itself.

At the railway station, three officials of the local Soviet met Francis and his colleagues. Francis invited the officials into the dining car, where they met with the other seven Allied chiefs of mission and the French and American consuls at Archangel.

Francis had been notified at a stop along the way that a steamboat awaited him at Archangel. The Russian chief commissar, a military-clad man named Popov, pointed out a window at a boat docked on the river and said, "We are instructed to direct your attention to that boat, to put you on that boat and to say you can use that boat to go where you wish."[10] Francis took a long look at the small boat, his mind working fast. He wanted to make sure he knew where the boat was headed before he got on it—he had no intention of leaving Russia. And he wanted to talk to Washington before he went anywhere.

"We refuse to go on that boat," he told the Soviet officer.

"Why?" was the perplexed reply.

"We do not intend to leave Russia until we can communicate with our own governments. Cable communication has been severed for three weeks." He demanded that Popov provide cable service through Murmansk, where a line was still open to the West. If Popov couldn't—or wouldn't—do that, Francis insisted that an armed Allied vessel meet the ship where the Dvina entered the White Sea, about twenty-five miles downstream from the station, and escort it to its destination. At that point, the diplomats were undecided on their destination—to Kandalaksha, across the White Sea from

Archangel, or directly to Murmansk, at the northern tip of the Kola Peninsula. Both
Kandalaksha and Murmansk were under Allied control.

Archangel is icebound almost six months of the year. The port at Murmansk, about
three hundred sea miles northwest of Archangel on an estuary of the Barents Sea, benefits from the Gulf Stream's sweep around northern Scandinavia and generally is open
year round. During the Great War, Murmansk became part of the "northeast passage,"
created in response to the German blockade of the Baltic.[11]

Popov said the local Soviet wanted the Allied diplomats out of Archangel immediately because it was "unsafe," although Popov refused to specify where the danger would
come from. All he could do, Popov insisted, was carry out his orders from Moscow: to
get the diplomats on the boat and out of Archangel.[12]

Francis again looked out at the harbor. "That boat is not big enough for all of us," he
said. Popov replied that he could supply two boats. Francis insisted that no one would
leave the train until he had direct cable communication or an Allied warship.

Exasperated, Popov and the other two Bolshevik officials argued among themselves.
Finally, Popov asked Francis, "What are we to do?"

Francis said, "I do not know what you are to do except to go and report what we say
to the people at Moscow, to Lenin, Trotsky and Chicherin."[13]

The officials finally left, stationing guards around the train. Through a local spy,
probably recruited by the British, Francis learned that cables were flying back and forth
between Moscow and Archangel as the Bolsheviks tried to figure out what to do with
140 foreign dignitaries in a port that was soon to be invaded. The spy told Francis that
the top government officials in Moscow, while openly professing the desire for the diplomats to leave Russia as soon as possible, contemplated holding them as hostages. In any
event, they would not be permitted to wire their governments.

By Saturday afternoon, when the Bolshevik officials returned to the train, Captain
McGrath, still in charge of the small British military contingent at Archangel, visited
Francis and his colleagues. McGrath told them that Russian counterrevolutionaries
planned to stage a coup in Archangel on the following Monday. He planned to send a
message by a fast motorboat, one that could slip through the Russian ships that loosely
blockaded the Archangel harbor, to Major General F. C. Poole, commander of Allied
forces in northeast Russia, who was either at Murmansk or Kandalaksha. McGrath
would recommend that Poole wait until after the coup had been effective and then
immediately lead his troops ashore.[14]

McGrath suggested to Francis that it might embarrass the Russian counterrevolutionary leaders if the Allied diplomats and military attachés were in Archangel as the
coup was taking place. Francis and the other diplomats agreed and decided that they
did not want to be in the midst of a battle in the Russian civil war. They decided to cross
the White Sea to Kandalaksha.

Francis told the Soviet officials where the Allies wanted to go. Many hours of wrangling ensued over matters like passports and baggage. "They did nothing to actually
detain us," he recalled later, "but they threw all the obstacles in the way they could."
Apparently, the local Bolsheviks were stalling while waiting for Moscow to make up its

mind. Around two in the morning on Monday, July 29, Francis and Lindley agreed that they would wait until 7 A.M., and if nothing had happened by then, they would simply walk over to a British merchant ship docked nearby on the river and tell the captain to take them to Kandalaksha. At 4 A.M., the Bolshevik officials came back and told the Allies they could leave.

One of the Bolsheviks handed Francis a telegram from Commissar Chicherin expressing his "profound regret and sorrow" at his departure: "Best thanks for your kindness and courtesy and for your good feeling toward the Russian popular masses whose most adequate and faithful representatives are the Soviets, the councils of the poor and of the toiling. Please convey our affection and admiration in the messages you will send across the ocean to the great people of pioneers on the new continent and to the posterity of Cromwell's revolutionaries and of Washington's brothers in arms."

Francis later remarked, "This telegram was evidently meant for consumption by American pacifists, and fearing it would be given to the American people by the Department of State, I failed to transmit it."[15]

That morning, the Allied diplomats sailed out of the mouth of the river in two Russian steamships, escorted by an armed military ship. They steamed about 250 miles across the White Sea to Kandalaksha, just north of the Arctic circle. There, Francis discovered that General Poole was in Murmansk. He decided to head north again to join the general. Some of his companions strongly disagreed. The 150 miles of track between Kandalaksha and Murmansk were rough, even by Russian standards, and the trains were not designed for passenger travel. British Chargé Lindley aroused Francis's fury by stubbornly arguing against going to Murmansk.

"He said I would be subjected to great inconvenience in travelling to Murmansk," Francis wrote Perry. "I told him I didn't give a damn about hardships and inconveniences and that I was going to Murmansk on the freight train that was on the track." Francis remarked that he felt "very close to the English people but cannot become accustomed to their stubbornness and to their selfishness." Francis prevailed in the argument. Before he left Kandalaksha, he cabled Washington, saying again that his "intention and desire" was "to remain in Russia," and promising he would advise the Department of further developments.[16]

About fifteen weary travelers joined Francis for the July 31 trip up the Kola Peninsula, including Lindley, Noulens, and Torretta. Philip Jordan reported the trip to Jane:

> [They all] pilled in box cars and went to Momansk . . . over the roughes R. R. I was ever on except the missouri and north arkansas. I had 6 in my party to cook for and only a Small Spirit lamp to cook on . . . some heavy pine boards was put from one end to the other and that was the only bed we had. of course you never traveled this way but you know while the train is running it is impossible to go from one box car to the other. I would wait until the train would Stop to take wood. no coal or water. then I would run from car to car with corn beef Sandwich hard tacks and coffee . . . no chairs, no table, a tin Spoon. a tin cup. talk about wining the war.[17]

As the train banged its way north to Murmansk, Francis scrawled a letter to Perry briefly describing the past twenty-four hours, although "the main object" of the letter, he acknowledged, was to complain about losing money on the *Republic,* a recurring theme. He suggested issuing five or six hundred thousand dollars worth of preferred stock to avoid a foreclosure, which "would hurt the reputation of the paper."[18]

When the train pulled into Murmansk, Philip Jordan wrote, "We did See one grand and glorous Sight. the harbor was full of english and French war Ships mine Sweeprs torpedo destroyers and every kind of boat that could kill people. all looked good but the grandest Sight of them all was the U.S. battle Ship Olympia with the Stars and Stripes flying in the breeze."[19]

For the first few days of August, Francis and his companions lived aboard the *Olympia,* in the comforting surroundings, as Jordan put it, of "huge guns and tons and tons of ammunition." The *Olympia* had been the flagship at Manila Bay during the Spanish American War, and Francis lived in the quarters once occupied by Admiral Dewey. "When the Ambassador wanted to go ashore I would tell the man on watch," Jordan wrote. "He would call all officers and Sailors on attention and Salute as he passed." Jordan would follow him down the gangplank as the battleship's twenty-piece band played "My Country 'Tis of Thee," which Jordan, and undoubtedly Francis as well, "found very touching."

In the meantime, the anticipated anti-Bolshevik coup had taken place at Archangel. On August 2, General Poole sailed into the port with about two thousand men, where a group calling itself "The Provisional Government of Northern Russia" welcomed them. Francis cabled Washington that he wanted to return to Archangel. He got quick approval in a cable that noted, "Department believes important you should remain in Russia."[20]

Francis, Jordan, Earl Johnston, Lindley, Noulens, and a few of the other diplomats returned to Kandalaksha by the primitive Kola Peninsula Railway. From there, they took a ship and arrived in Archangel on August 5. For eight days, the Americans lived on the ship and then moved into the newly bustling port city, where they remained for about three months. Francis and Jordan rented a three-room apartment in a very large house that already had a family of six living in it. Francis hired a Russian maid and a Chinese cook, but Jordan was in charge of the kitchen, bribing local officials to get the proper food and trading flour and corn beef from the "embassy" stores for fresh eggs and butter, fighting to restore the ambassador's health, which was again failing.

Archangel, newly crowded with soldiers, was not a healthy place. Philip Jordan wrote home that rats "crawl all over me at night" and asked Jane Francis to have someone order and send the best roach and rat powder available.[21] Within a few weeks, Francis was running a fever, constantly fatigued, and finding it painful to urinate as he grew increasingly ill from what turned out to be a severe bladder and prostate infection.

Francis's fear that Allied diplomats who stayed in Bolshevik territory would be taken hostage proved to be legitimate. At two o'clock on the morning of August 3, several dozen uniformed men carrying submachine guns stormed the clubhouse embassy in Vologda, took Norman Armour prisoner, and shipped him, the other remaining Allied diplomats, and about twenty American citizens under guard to Moscow. Armour had suspected the embassy would be raided. Before the soldiers arrived, he put a top hat Francis had left behind in the otherwise empty office safe, locked it, and wrapped it in security tape. The Bolsheviks were so eager to see what was inside they resorted to dynamite.

In Moscow and other Bolshevik-controlled cities, hundreds of Allied embassy, consul, and military staff members, as well as many Western private citizens, were arrested and imprisoned by the Soviet secret police. "The Bolsheviks have gone quite mad," Armour wrote from Moscow in mid-August. "They are on their last legs and know it, but unfortunately there seems to be no one . . . to take their place."[22]

Near the end of August, a large group of Americans and other Westerners, including the remaining representatives of the Red Cross, the YMCA, and the National City Bank, were shipped from Moscow to Petrograd, apparently on their way to Finland. They lived under guard in the Petrograd railroad yards on August 30, in a bureaucratic limbo, when the head of the Petrograd secret police—the Cheka—was shot to death in front of his headquarters by a former military cadet.

That same evening, in Moscow, Dora Kaplan, a young firebrand from the Left Socialist Revolutionaries, seriously wounded Lenin. In retaliation, a British naval attaché in Petrograd, Captain Francis N. A. Cromie, was killed in a battle with a mob on the staircase of the British Embassy. More Westerners were thrown into prison. Bruce Lockhart spent weeks locked up near the Kremlin, in the soon-infamous Lubyanka Prison, an experience that helped convince him that intervention to overthrow the Bolsheviks was a viable option. That fall, back home in England, he proclaimed the Russian people would "rally to the White Russian cause" if one hundred thousand Allied troops marched in from Siberia and the north.[23]

Hundreds of Russians were summarily executed. Thousands more would follow in the ensuing Red Terror. Consul DeWitt Poole, who had bravely chosen to stay in Moscow to help the remaining Allies, many of whom were imprisoned, wrote Chicherin on September 4, "It is impossible for me to believe that you approved of the mad career into which the Bolshevik government has now plunged. Your cause totters on the verge of complete moral bankruptcy. . . . You must stop at once the barbarous oppression of your own people."[24]

But the slaughter continued and intensified, particularly in the city the Bolsheviks detested, cosmopolitan Petrograd. Soon the great Petrograd poet Anna Akhmatova wrote:

> Westward the sun is dropping,
> And the roofs of town are shining in its light.
> Already death is chalking doors with crosses
> And calling the ravens and the ravens are in flight.[25]

Finally, in late September and early October, groups of Americans and other Allies were permitted to leave the country, in some case after they had paid large bribes at the border. By the middle of October, almost all of the Westerners, including Armour, DeWitt Poole, and Lockhart, were out of Russia. Francis remained. Increasingly sapped by fatigue and fever, he fought to deal with the chaos of northern Russian in the midst of both a civil war and invasion by Allied troops—troops who sometimes had conflicting orders: were they to protect the ports from the Germans, or were they to use Archangel as the staging ground for forays south into Russia?

After a doctor had ordered him to stay in bed, Francis wrote Perry, with his usual cheerful bluster:

> [the order] makes the impression that I am ill but the trouble is confined to my bladder. For some time before leaving Petrograd I was forced to 'pump ship' [urinate] frequently and that kept up during my five months stay at Vologda; since my arrival at Archangel about sixteen days ago those desires to make water have been attended by acute pain at the end of the penis. I finally called in a French doctor who was connected with the French Military Mission and told him I had gravel [kidney/bladder stones]; he did not give me his diagnosis of the case but told Earl Johnston that it was not gravel but an enlarged prostate gland.

In fact, it was both.

General Poole recommended a British surgeon, Dr. Fitzwilliams, in charge of the British hospital at Archangel. Francis remarked in admiration that Dr. Fitzwilliams, whom he had met in Petrograd, had married the daughter of a member of the Filley family, prominent St. Louisans. Fitzwilliams immediately emptied the suffering ambassador's bladder with a catheter, giving him "six or eight hours of relief," and confirmed that the problem was an enlarged prostate. He recommended two weeks of rest. Fitzwillams told Francis that he could continue to "transact business" from his apartment because "there was no connection whatever between the mind and the prostate gland."[26]

For two months, a doctor came to Francis's apartment twice a day and emptied his bladder. Ironically, the catherization—necessary to relive the pressure on his infected bladder—may well have had the secondary effect of spreading bacteria through seepage from his bladder into his bloodstream, leading to urinary septicemia, which produces high fever and can be fatal.[27] But for a time, Francis's condition improved.

The Americans had set up a makeshift embassy in sparsely furnished rooms six blocks from the house where Francis and Jordan lived, but the rooms were badly heated, and as fall came and the frigid Arctic winds blew in across the White Sea, Francis, Johnston, and Jordan worked out of Francis's living quarters. Francis spent much of the time in bed, although, he insisted in letters home, he was not "bedridden" and could move from room to room.

In his apartment, he held conferences and dictated cables and dispatches and actually wrote a much-promised "autograph" letter to Jane. He was sick and irritable and missed his family. He wrote to Perry, "Say to Dave and Talton and Tom and Sidney that

I have ceased to expect letters from them as they write so seldom."[28] There was little or no communication possible with Americans in Petrograd or Moscow, and he worried in particularly about the fate of Armour. Then, in early September, all his waking hours were spent trying to deal with a major crisis.

On September 4, forty-five hundred American infantrymen went ashore at Archangel, to be under the command of the British. Francis sent for their commander, Colonel Stewart, and asked him his orders. The colonel replied, "To report to General Poole, who is in command of the Allied forces in Northern Russia."

Francis said, "I interpret our policy here. If I should tell you not to obey one of General Poole's orders, what would you do?"

"I would obey you," Stewart replied.[29]

The American Government said its goals for intervention were to prevent the Germans from establishing a submarine base at Archangel and to assure that diplomats and other Allies were permitted to leave Russia as they wished. Woodrow Wilson and State Department Counselor Frank L. Polk both had stated clearly that the troops were not to be used for incursions into the interior from Archangel. However, the troops also were ordered to "protect" munitions and supplies as well as "the Czecho-Slovaks." This order presumably referred to the Czech Legion in Siberia, although it was vague, probably by intention.[30]

By late September 1918, the British, much more open in their anti-Bolshevism than the Americans, intended to fight south and east and eventually link up with the Czech Legion and other anti-Bolshevik forces, which were still winning victories in Central Russia and advancing along the Trans-Siberian Railway to within six hundred miles of Moscow. Francis confirmed this from a Czech spy who had made his way across hundreds of miles to Archangel disguised as a Bolshevik officer.[31]

British command led three thousand American soldiers nearly two hundred miles into Russia to fight beside White Russian soldiers against the Red Army. America clearly had invaded Russia, albeit in relatively small numbers. But there was no official American recognition of this fact. Woodrow Wilson insisted, "We are not at war with Russia and will in no circumstances that we can now foresee take part in military operations there against the Russians." Defending crucial ports was one thing; invasion of the interior was another, and officially forbidden. It remains unclear how much Wilson knew of American incursions into the Russian interior—he maintained what would later be called "deniability"—but it seems improbable that he was not unofficially briefed on the whole affair.[32]

Francis chose to give wide latitude to the order to protect munitions and aid the Czechs. He wrote Lansing, "I shall encourage American troops to obey the commands of General Poole in his effort to effect a junction with the Czecho-Slovaks [at Perm] and to relieve them from the menace which surrounds them; that menace is nominally Bolshevik but is virtually inspired and directed by Germans."[33]

Although cable communication with Washington had been reestablished, Francis chose to put that information into a letter, perhaps to avoid a quick "no" from

Washington. (Lansing did not receive the message until October 15; by then, the point was moot. The Czech Legion, its members having little desire to remain on Russian soil long-term and fight an increasingly competent Red Army, had begun to disintegrate.)

Francis went into more detail in a letter to Charles Crane, saying that he would approve of American troops going along "with any of the Allied forces that General Poole may send to . . . join with the Czecho-Slovaks who seem to be approaching along the Siberian Railway." In other words, if Poole wanted to use American troops to invade Moscow and rendezvous with the Czechs on the Trans-Siberian Railway, bully for him. Francis added, "I don't, however, wish to have you tell the Department or the President that I propose to construe the declaration in that way. My instructions are quite as definite as they could be made under the circumstances and I would not have them more so."[34]

"The real truth," observed Captain Hugh S. Martin, an American military attaché in northern Russia, "was we were waging war against Bolshevism. Everybody knew that. Yet no Allied government ever stated that was our policy in intervening."[35]

This policy of no policy seems to have been typical of Wilson, particularly in his later years. Francis, who found the vague and seemingly contradictory statements issuing from Washington in early August "mystifying," was once again in a situation that forced him to make up foreign policy as he went, a challenge he eagerly accepted.

Francis supported using American troops to aid the Czechs and urged that more Americans be sent to northern Russia. He wrote to Crane, "The Russian people have been in a dream or a drunk and are now beginning to awaken or to sober up. I have never despaired of their ability to organize a Government on proper lines if guided and assisted by us and I am hoping to be spared in order to do my bit toward that end."

Despite his illness, Francis met daily with other Allied diplomats and with leaders of the two opposing elements of anti-Bolshevism in Archangel—reactionary former Tsarist officers led by a Russian naval officer named Chaplin and moderate Socialist Revolutionaries led by an old populist, Nicholas Chaikovski. Chaikovski had been a prominent supporter of Kerensky's Provisional Government, and Francis knew and liked him. The White Russian Chaplin, leader of the forces that had evicted the Bolsheviks from Archangel, was so close to the British that at times he wore a British naval uniform. Francis did not trust him.[36]

Once the Bolsheviks had been ousted, Chaikovski and his moderate socialists had the political organization to take control of the municipal government, with little room for Chaplin. The two sides fought constantly. The British and the French favored the more conservative Chaplin, but they had to deal with the reality that Chaikovski had the upper hand. Francis tried to play the role of mediator between the two Russian groups and between the British and Chaikovski. The result was a chaotic political situation that increasingly frustrated the people of Archangel.

Francis, a democrat at heart still hoping that anti-Bolshevik Russians would rejoin the fight against Germany, sided with the liberal socialist Chaikovski. The overthrow of Chaikovski, which Chaplin and his cadre of former Tsarist officers tried to promote, would, he believed, "prolong civil dissention, strengthen [the] Soviet Government and Bolsheviks generally and would injure the Allied cause." The Chaikovski government, which was trying to mobilize an army to fight the Germans, "should be protected and encouraged," he urged Lansing. If the Allies appeared to be coming as conquerors, he argued, placing their own puppets in control, the people of north Russia would "recklessly resist." This seems to have been a shrewd political judgment and in line with Wilson's policy that intervention should be based "upon the sure sympathy of the Russian people."[37]

Ironically, the arrival on September 4 of the American troops helped give General Poole the confidence to encourage Chaplin and the other White Russians to take over the government. Two of the three American battalions were dispatched immediately to the south of the city, where Allied and anti-Bolshevik troops kept the Reds at bay; but the third battalion stayed in Archangel, and on September 6 General Poole paraded it through the streets, apparently as a show of force.

Francis dragged himself out of his sickbed and stood on the reviewing stand next to General Poole. As the last of the troops passed, Poole dropped his salute and turned to Francis. He said that there had been a coup during the night and that the leaders of the city's socialist government had been arrested and taken to a nearby island in the White Sea.

"The hell you say!" was Francis's astonished reaction. "Who pulled it off?"

"Chaplin," was the answer.

"There is Chaplin over there now," Francis replied. He gestured for the White Russian officer to join them. As he approached, Poole remarked that Chaplin intended to issue a proclamation of the coup at 11 A.M. Francis checked his watch. It was 10:15.

"Chaplin," Francis asked, "who pulled off this revolution here last night?"

"I did," Chaplin proudly replied. "I drove the Bolsheviks out of here, I established this government, and the ministers were in General Poole's way and were hampering Colonel Donop." Donop was the French provost marshal.

Summoning up all his flagging energy, his face reddening, Francis barked, "I think this is the most flagrant usurpation of power I ever knew, and don't you circulate that proclamation that General Poole tells me you have written until I can see it, and show it to my colleagues."

Francis was furious at Poole, particularly since the timing of the coup right after the arrival of the American battalions gave the impression that the United States approved of or even had instigated the removal of the popular Chaikovski government. He remarked, "British soldiers have been colonizers for so long that they do not know how to respect the feelings of socialists."[38] There is something particularly striking about the crusty Missouri capitalist and former adversary of unions adjusting once again to a situation in which the socialists were clearly the more honorable of the parties.

In the serious game he played, Francis had a hole card: the control over American troops he had established in his meeting two days before with Colonel Stewart. Francis called the other three Allied heads of mission in Archangel—British, French, and

Italian—to his apartment at noon. He passionately pled his case, and the diplomats ended up agreeing with him that Chaikovski and his ministers had been, in effect, kidnapped, and that they should be released and reinstated.[39] Poole's decision had been overturned with the help of his own country's chargé d'affaires, F. O. Lindley. Within little over a month, Poole would be replaced.

The coup provoked popular uprisings, including a streetcar strike. Delegations of workers and peasants in support of the deposed socialists visited Francis. Within thirty-six hours, Chaplin bowed to the will of the people and the Allied diplomats. Chaikovski and his ministers were released and restored to power, although the situation remained chaotic, with top officials coming and going and the bitter battles between the two sides continuing to disrupt the city.

For about a day and a half, until some order was restored, American soldiers ran the streetcars. Francis, who had some experience with streetcar strikes and the political consequences of strikebreaking, worried that this would be seen as an example of America laying its heavy hand on the Russian people. He warned American officers that having U.S. soldiers manning the streetcars could create "commotion" and told them that he didn't want the men caught in the middle of a civil war. At the same time, he let it be known that the soldiers, if fired upon by Russians, would fire back. Fortunately, the strike ended before serious incidents could occur.

In early October, the replacement of General Poole ended some of the friction between the British and the liberal socialists of the Archangel government. But Francis continued to mistrust the British, particularly after American Military Attaché Hugh Martin had reported from Murmansk that the British were busy negotiating exclusive commercial treaties at that crucial year-round port. The report confirmed what Francis always had maintained: the ultimate British goal was economic domination.

As his illness worsened, Francis battled to keep the Provisional Government of northern Russia viable, and at times he appeared to be as much in charge of Archangel as Chaikovski or Chaplin. Although he still insisted in letters home that he was not bedridden, in fact, he spent most of his days in bed, dictating letters to Johnston and conducting meetings.

When duty called, however, Philip Jordan helped him dress, and Francis made official appearances. One was captured by a camera of the U.S. Army Signal Corps. Francis had arranged a meeting between Allied officers and Chaikovski and other leaders of the Archangel government. After the meeting, he stands outside the hall, wearing a thick wool overcoat and a fedora, and in a momentary close-up his face looks drawn but determined. He vigorously shakes hands and bids goodbye to a couple of dozen men, giving no sign he is ill and in pain.[40]

Francis repeatedly cabled Washington to send food and other supplies for the people of Archangel. And he kept working to inspire the Russians of the north, for the moment free of Bolshevik control, to rejoin the fight against the Germans. In early October, Francis issued a fiery public statement condemning the "thousands of unjustifiable, cruel, merciless executions which the Bolsheviks, at the instigation of their German masters, are daily perpetuating on your own brothers and sisters." He asked, "How much longer will you suffer such conditions to exist? . . . The blood of your murdered brothers cries to you from their unmarked graves to put an end to this senseless slaughter." He ended with the questionable promise, "Your Allies are willing and ready to come to your aid if you will request them to do so." The liberal *Nation* magazine reprinted the statement, calling it "an extraordinary document," not necessarily a compliment.[41]

He met secretly twice with Mikhail Tereshchenko. The former foreign minister in the Provisional Government was in the north under an assumed name, hoping to slip through the lines and join up with Alexander Kolchak, leader of the White Russian forces fighting the Bolsheviks along the Trans-Siberian Railway.[42]

Francis offered what help he could and proposed forming an "American-Slavic legion" to fight the Germans and, if necessary, the Reds. He cabled Washington about the proposal, asking for more troops. But in early October, with the Germans now clearly losing the war, Woodrow Wilson told the secretary of state, "I think that Francis ought to be definitely apprised of the fact that we can supply no more [troops]. . . . We cannot maintain an army, our own or another, in Northern Russia, much as we would wish to do so, and while I would wish Francis to know how much we admire the spirit and success with which he had guided matters at Archangel, I think we ought to apprise him very definitely of the limiting facts." Lansing, in a cable to Francis, passed on Wilson's praise as well as his refusal to commit more soldiers.[43]

As the cold winds whipped in off the frigid White Sea, and the freezing autumnal rains swept across the low-lying city, Francis grew sicker and weaker. In early October, three doctors—two British, one American—examined Francis and concurred that his swollen prostate gland needed to be removed before his kidneys incurred serious damage. Given the news, Francis said, "Fine, take it out." But the doctors insisted that the operation be performed in a modern hospital, recommending he be taken either to London or New York. In an October 7 cable to Lansing, he complained of the threat of being forced to leave when he was "otherwise perfectly well [and] strong."

He wrote, "Words fail to express my impatience almost exasperation at whole situation as think my presence here of the greatest importance. . . . In any event desire to return to Russia and after shortest possible absence. If you decide I should return here from London please advise Perry Francis come to London by the twenty-second and bring my wife if possible."[44]

Lansing received the cable on October 9, and immediately replied: "The Department regards your devotion to duty as an example of the highest traditions of the service. In order to be able to continue your valuable service, I believe you should proceed at once to London for consultation as to whether surgical assistance can be rendered there. . . . You will leave [DeWitt] Poole in charge. Please accept my cordial good wishes for your speedy restoration to active work."[45]

Lansing, fearing Francis would resist leaving Russia, asked Perry for his advice and help. Perry replied that he was "strongly of the opinion the operation should be performed and only in London." Perry said he intended to meet his father there, and if Francis didn't show up, he would go to Archangel and get him.[46] And the State Department wired Consul DeWitt Poole, who had barely escaped from Russia on September 20 and was enroute from Stockholm to England, to return immediately and take over at Archangel. It was expected to take him until at least October 20.[47]

Pressed by Lansing to leave Archangel immediately, Francis proposed that he place Earl Johnston in charge of the embassy and leave October 14 on the British ship that was taking his adversary General Poole home.[48] Then, Francis proceeded to stall, missing his ocean voyage with General Poole, announcing that he wanted to wait until DeWitt Poole arrived. On October 25, with DeWitt Poole still en route, Francis remarked that he could not consider leaving until his replacement arrived; otherwise, his departure might create "great uneasiness among the Russian population and . . . result in a panic and in strengthening the Bolsheviks by driving the socialist Russians over to Bolshevism."

Even if he would go to London for the operation, he said, he wanted to return as soon as possible, "as I feel my services are needed here and that I can do more than any other American toward helping the Russian people." And, as usual, he fretted about business, saying that he wanted Perry in London "for as short a time as possible," since he did not see "how my interests can be as well looked after by any of the other boys during his absence."[49]

By then, he had received word that Perry and his wife, Mimi, were heading toward London. He tried, without success, to get the State Department to stop them from crossing the Atlantic until he had determined when, and if, he would leave.

There is no telling how long Francis would have tried to stall his departure—perhaps until Perry arrived in Archangel and dragged him onto a ship—if his illness had not severely worsened. On the evening of October 30, Francis had what he described as "a chill." Philip Jordan used stronger words, writing that "he was a very sick man, he did not improve but was growing worse so the doctors decided that the best thing was to get the Ambassador to London just as soon as possible." Francis tried to no avail to get the Allied doctors in Archangel to perform the operation, telling them that he was "a Presbyterian," and would rather lose his right arm than leave Russia.[50]

Johnston cabled Washington that Francis had caught the flu, which may have been the case. The Spanish Influenza epidemic, probably spread by Allied troops, was engulfing northern Russia. The *Olympia*, the U.S. cruiser that had been his home in Kandalaksha, was sent to Archangel for Francis. DeWitt Poole finally arrived, and Francis agreed to sail on the afternoon of November 6. Weak as he was, he insisted on leaving his apartment under his own power, and left his Russian maid weeping. He was still beset by disputes. The Red Cross representatives in Archangel, led by an officious major named Williams, insisted on leading the way, trying to stick the three consular officers—Felix Cole, Shelby F. Strother, and a man named Pierce—at the rear of the line.

Hot-tempered Cole, who had fought vehemently with Francis over intervention—Cole was against it, not without reason—wanted to stay out of the small procession entirely.

Strother, a fellow native of Kentucky, recalled years later that "the Governor," whom he admired greatly, "was always a pacificator, and he asked us to stay in the show." The comic-opera exodus proceeded, with Philip Jordan, as Strother later remarked, "flitting about, always near the Ambassador," with a box of cigars under his arm. He also told Jordan he thought "Governor Francis was one of the great diplomats of the war. . . . I think he takes his place with [U.S. Ambassador Walter] Page of London and [U.S. Ambassador James] Gerard at Berlin. He had more to do than either of these two, more trouble, more upsets, and a harder road. . . . [He was] one of the biggest men of the Great War."[51]

Francis tried to walk to the ship, but his strength soon gave out and he was carried on a stretcher by eight sailors to the *Olympia,* up the gangplank, and to the admiral's cabin. Jordan and Earl Johnston followed him on board. Ice already had formed in the harbor, and within a few weeks the port would be locked in for five or six months. It was time to leave. Major Williams of the Red Cross and Captain Newton A. McCully, the naval attaché who supervised the carrying of Francis onto the ship, both said later that Francis was so ill that they never expected to see him again alive.[52]

Before leaving, Francis issued an address to the American troops, among whom he had become a familiar and popular figure. He stated:

> I trust you do not underestimate the importance of the service you are per-
> forming as American soldiers in Russia. The Bolsheviks are completely under
> the domination of Germany and consequently in resisting them you are not
> only performing a humanitarian service but you are preventing Germany from
> establishing a much stronger foothold in Russia than she has up to this time
> been able to establish. . . . I have no doubt that you would prefer to be in
> France or in Italy, but like soldiers you are performing the duty to which you
> are assigned and are entitled to all the more credit therefor.[53]

DeWitt Poole cabled Lansing:

> Although the Ambassador has been anxious that you should not know of 'his
> incapacity' it has seemed to be my duty to obtain from the surgeon of the
> Olympia a statement of his condition for your confidential information. The
> statement follows: 'Senile hypertrophy of the prostate gland, with an infection
> of the gland of about one week duration. He has lost considerable weight and
> strength and the removal of the gland will be necessary and several weeks will
> elapse before he is able to be about again.'[54]

On the morning of November 8, after waiting a day and a half for the right tide to carry the ship over the shallow bar at the edge of the harbor, the *Olympia* left Archangel.

The White Sea was choppy and the winds gusting. Hugging the coast of the Kola Peninsula, the ship reached Murmansk late on November 10 or very early on November

11 and spent two days taking on coal for the upcoming voyage: through the Barents Sea, an arm of the Arctic Ocean, around the northern tip of Norway, and south along the coast through the Norwegian Sea to the British Isles.

The ship left Murmansk well before dawn on November 13. In the admiral's cabin, Francis ran an alarmingly high fever and was so ill that not until the voyage of almost six days through perilous seas ended would he realize how dangerous it had been.

The *Olympia,* according to Jordan, "slipped out of the harbor as though she was stealing away from the other ships. I am not at all superstitious, but I shall never forget that morning of the 13th of November. In about three hours we steamed into the Arctic Ocean and then our troubles began. We struck the worst gale that any ship ever went through without being wrecked. For five days we fought that gale."

The Central Powers and the Allies had signed an armistice in Paris on November 11. But the *Olympia*'s captain, Bion Bierer, did not trust the Germans not to attack, and the ship ran under wartime conditions, with a blackout after dark. By mid-November in the Arctic, it was dark twenty hours a day.

Jordan wrote, "All this time the Ambassador is in Admiral's cabin and is a very sick man. Out of a crew of four hundred almost all was deathly seasick, old timers that was never seasick before were all down and out. The captain told me that the wind was blowing 90 miles an hour." The ship was pitching so badly that veteran sailors in the boiler room were being tossed around like landlubbers and, Jordan said, more than one was knocked unconscious. The ship kept steaming ahead.[55]

As they rounded the tip of Norway, at two in the morning Francis weakly called for Jordan, who was seldom far away. "Phil," he said, "I am burning up. Can't you get me a cold drink of some kind?" The ship's doctor took his temperature and it had risen to 104. Jordan himself reeled from seasickness.

"How are you feeling, Phil?" the doctor asked.

"Oh, doctor, I am so sick," Jordan replied.

"You'll be all right when you get on land," the doctor replied.

"I'm afraid I'll die before I see land," Jordan said.

"Well," the doctor said, "you know, people are dying every day."

"Such encouragement," Jordan remarked to himself as he fought his way through the rolling, pitching ship to the pantry, where he whipped up a malted milk with an egg in it for Francis. Francis choked it down and pronounced it "a great relief."

Jordan tried to return to sleep on his "bucking cot"—he had lashed it to a six-inch gun to keep it from sliding across the heaving deck—but in twenty minutes Francis called again and said, half delirious, that he could not sleep. Jordan decided to give him a rubdown. The ship's doctor had run out of medicinal alcohol, but he had some bourbon. For once in his life, Francis was too sick to drink it, but the bourbon rubdown seemed to soothe him. Finally, about seven in the morning, he went to sleep as the storm raged on.

On the afternoon of November 18, after being escorted through the North Sea mine fields by two British destroyers, the *Olympia* docked at Invergordon on the northeast coast of Scotland. Francis was carried off the boat on a stretcher, onto the soil of his ancestors. He was put into an ambulance and driven eighteen miles into the highlands to the American naval base at Strathpeffer, a vacation spa in a spectacular location near Inverness. Strathpeffer had an excellent naval hospital. The chief surgeon was head of surgery at the Stanford medical school.

On November 20, J. D. Perry Francis and his wife, Mimi, who had docked in London two days before, arrived to be at David Francis's bedside. They were shocked at his pale, gaunt appearance. Francis was overjoyed at seeing them. To Basil Miles at the State Department, he wrote a letter full of cheer, noting, "I cannot tell you how much comfort my Son and his Wife are to me here. . . . Did you ever meet Mrs. Perry Francis? She is not only a charming woman beautiful in my eyes, but has a keen sense of humor and is a most entertaining talker." Typically, he added, "She is a direct descendent of Pierre LaClede who founded St. Louis in 1763 and consequently does not love the Bolshies—in which she is congenial with her Husband and her Husband father."[56]

Francis's navy doctors decided he needed to rest and recover some strength before he was strong enough to go to London for the operation. He soon reported to Lansing that he was "regaining strength rapidly" and was itching to return to Russia. The day after Perry and Mimi arrived, Francis dispatched Johnston to London to get a "green code" from the American Embassy that would permit him to send diplomatic communications. Johnston was sent back without the code, and a cable from Francis to Lansing reiterating the request went unanswered. Baffled and angry, Francis wrote Lansing, "I cannot account for this. It must be that you did not receive my cable. I am still American Ambassador to Russia. . . . I am endeavoring to keep in touch with the Department and with occurrences in Russia and with international developments."[57] However, as he privately acknowledged, the State Department wanted him to forget about diplomatic matters and get well.[58]

After a few days in the hospital, Francis felt strong enough to go for a walk every day. He, Johnston, Perry, and Mimi played bridge, and occasionally they went for dinner at the nearby hotel where Perry and Mimi stayed. Ever a superior scrounger, Philip Jordan managed to find a turkey for Thanksgiving dinner.

As his strength returned, Francis wrote the State Department recommending that he be sent back to Petrograd as soon as he recovered from the operation. His plan was to "occupy" the embassy and "enable the Russian people to hold a free election. . . . I would require not more than 50,000 American soldiers. As soon as the English, the French and the Italians learned I was returning to Petrograd they would send their Ambassadors [and soldiers] to join me."[59]

He wrote his sister Mollie to thank her for sending him a biography of Joel Chandler Harris but noted, "My attention however is devoted to more serious subjects. We are entering a new world—new in thought—new in duties and new in all the relations between individual members of society. I would give all my earthly possessions to be able to turn the clock back even twenty years."

Brother to sister, he remarked, "You said in your last letter to me or insinuated that I sometimes frittered my time away on women. Your sex has been an interesting study always [and] an attraction to me, but if I ever wasted any time upon them I did not know it and have arrived at that age where I am too appreciative of my time to waste it on anything."[60]

About this time, he received a letter from an American diplomat in Norway. It referred to a telegram Francis had sent from Archangel asking for information about the embassy in Petrograd and the welfare of some of the city's residents, including Madame de Cramm. The diplomat had made inquiries, presumably through the Norweigans, and had received a letter from Karin Sante, the bright, efficient young Finnish woman who had stayed at the embassy when the Americans had gone to Vologda.

Miss Sante passed on a brief note from Matilda de Cramm for Francis: "Thanks for remembrance. Glad to see America on the head of universal conditions. Myself without money. Impossible to find any employment. . . . Without news from the doctor. Curiosity enquiry may be satisfied herewith. Another sentiment would dictate a kind of help. Body weak. Spirit still strong. Sons alive."[61]

The best place for the prostate operation, Francis's doctors agreed, was the large U.S. naval hospital in London. On December 4, Francis, his son and daughter-in-law, Jordan, and Johnston sailed for England. They moved into the Hyde Park Hotel and went for walks in the park just across the street, when it was not raining. It rained a great deal, and was cold—"Russia is a summer resort compared to London," Philip Jordan complained.[62]

Secretary Lansing sent Dr. Hugh H. Young of Johns Hopkins from France, where he was serving as an army colonel, to perform the operation. He arrived on December 22, ready to begin cutting. However, after learning that Woodrow Wilson, who was in Europe for the upcoming peace conference, was scheduled to visit London for a few days around Christmas, Francis pleaded with the doctor to postpone the operation so that he might attend the official receptions and dinners for the president. Francis hoped very much to meet with Wilson before the peace conference.

The doctor reluctantly agreed.

The day after Christmas, Francis attended a dinner given for Wilson by King George V at Buckingham Palace. Philip Jordan went as his valet and always remembered that he was "face to face with the King and Queen."[63] Francis, in his memoirs, recalled, "At the dinner, the President remarked to me that he had hoped to have some opportunity there to talk with me about Russia. But we were not thrown together. While he was talking to the King and the Premier, Lloyd George . . . I was talking to the ladies."

At the end of the dinner, Francis met King George, who had Mrs. Wilson on his arm. The king asked Francis what he thought the Allies ought to do about Russia. Francis replied that the Allies should overthrow the Bolsheviks. The king said he felt the same way but that President Wilson disagreed.[64]

On December 27, Earl Johnston hand-delivered to Buckingham Palace a note from Francis to Wilson. It read, in part: "Am keeping in touch with Russian developments by cable communication with my Embassy at Archangel and also with the State Department Washington. If it is possible I should like to have an audience on Russian affairs and hope you can grant it to me. I can come any place you designate at any hour. . . ." Wilson replied the same day:

My dear Mr. Ambassador:
My inclination jumps with yours. I should be very glad indeed to have a conference with you, but it is already painfully evident that it is going to be all that I can do to carry out the programme already set for me, without additions, and I know of no time which will really be my own. . . . I hope that you will not consider it a hardship if I should a little later ask you to come over to Paris for a conversation.[65]

Francis tried unsuccessfully a few more times to talk with Wilson at official events, and he even offered through intermediaries to ride with him on his two-hour train trip to Dover for the channel boat, but he was rebuffed politely.

On Friday, January 3, with Wilson gone to Paris, Francis went into the U.S. Naval Hospital at 26 Park Lane (also on Hyde Park). The next day, just before noon, with Perry and Earl Johnston hovering over him (Mimi was in bed with a bad cold) and Philip Jordan holding his hand, he went under the ether in his hospital room. It took twenty minutes and several doses to knock him out, with Francis repeatedly chanting, "I am going, I am going, I am going," until finally he murmured, "I am gone."

Francis was carried on a stretcher into the operating room. Jordan tried to go with him, telling Dr. Young that he had "gone through a great deal of trouble with the Ambassador and . . . if he didn't have any objections I would like very much to go through this one with him." But the doctor refused. The operation took twenty minutes, and Young quickly removed the prostate gland and a stone from the bladder about a half inch in diameter.

Francis was carried back to his room, and when he opened his eyes, he saw Jordan. "Phil," he asked, "have they finished with the operation?" Jordan assured him they had. Dr. Young said, "Governor, you went through it all like a brick. Your nerve was stronger than mine."

"That was because I did not have the same responsibility," Francis replied.[66]

After the operation, Jordan tried to leave long enough to go for a walk and get some fresh air, telling Francis that the nurses would take care of him. "Nurses, hell," growled Francis. "I want you here." Jordan later explained, with mixture of pride and exasperation, that he couldn't leave Francis alone for "ten minutes without getting a scolding." After Francis told Dr. Young that he and Jordan had been together for many years, the doctor reluctantly agreed to have a cot for Jordan brought into Francis's room. Jordan also had dug a portrait of Jane out of Francis's trunks and placed it on the mantel of Francis's hospital room.

Francis spent the next four weeks in the hospital. Johnston and Jordan moved into a room down the hall. Perry and Mimi visited daily.

Laura Perry sent word from St. Louis of Jane. Her sister, Laura wrote, was "not well, not seriously I think a kind of let down after the nervous strain she was under while you [were] sick and undergoing the operation. I think now it is over and the news about you continues to be good she will soon feel all right again."[67] Laura also sent news of Francis's grandchildren, now six in number—Alice, Anne, David III, Jane, Miriam, and the baby, Sidney, Jr., "a very beautiful and precocious youngster."

Francis continued to fret about his business interests at home, mentioning in a letter to his sister Mollie that he was "incurring immense losses, both in the M & N. A. R. R. and in the *Republic*. I really should return to America to look after such interests as they demand my individual time, but am unwilling to quit an unfinished task. . . . I am loath to return to America as long as conditions are what they are in Russia." Francis had lost about a half-million dollars on the failing Missouri and North Arkansas Railroad. He lost at least one hundred thousand dollars a year on the *Republic*.[68]

In the hospital, he received a bittersweet letter from Rolla Wells, who was taking the waters at the spa in French Lick, Indiana:

> We look forward to the hearing of the story [of Russia] from your own lips. I am also anticipating the renewal of our weekly pilgrimage to the 'Log Cabin Club,' there you will find the same old links, the same old beer, the same old high ball, the same old *smeercase* and *some* of the same old friends.
>
> Dave, you have devoted many years in public service, do you not feel that you have done your part? Do you realize in our long association we have had our share of dear and intimate companions and they are passing away one by one until there is but few of us left. Then why longer the separation [the more] we want you to return where a glorious welcome is awaiting.[69]

On January 18, 1919, the peace conference began at Versailles, just outside Paris. Led by the heads of the four great powers—President Wilson, British Prime Minister David Lloyd George, French Premier Georges Clemenceau, and Italian Prime Minister Vittorio Orlando—twenty-seven Allied and associated nations took four months to cobble together an unwieldy treaty. It would take another month to get the Germans to sign it.

From his hospital bed in London, David Francis sent several lengthy dispatches to American officials in Paris, outlining his recommendations for massive Allied intervention in Russia. By then, there were strong forces in Britain supporting his view, including Bruce Lockhart, former Ambassador Buchanan, and Lloyd George's secretary of state for war and the air, Winston Churchill. Like Francis, Churchill argued that a large force of volunteers could be found without great difficulty to free the Russian people from their new oppressors.[70]

On February 1, Francis was judged well enough to leave for Paris. Perry, Mimi, Earl Johnston, and, of course, Phil Jordan accompanied him. They stayed at the Ritz. Francis was eager to be heard in person about Russia. He tried his best to see Woodrow Wilson, but Wilson, who so often preferred to keep his own council, always found himself too busy.

Francis was able to speak to Secretary Lansing, to Colonel House, and to General Pershing. After he had made his case, each of these men, according to Francis, said, "You tell that to the president." The president's physician, Dr. Cary Travers Grayson, a rear admiral, said he would try and set up a meeting. Francis had been in Paris for more than a week without word from Grayson when he ran into him at a dinner at the Ritz Hotel. Francis told Grayson that he was "awaiting the President's pleasure," but if he did not hear from him in a week, he would leave for America.

Wilson, Grayson replied, planned to return to the states during a break in negotiations to promote the proposed League of Nations, currently under heavy attack in Congress from the Republicans. The admiral said he and the president would leave Paris on February 14 and sail the next day from Brest on the steamer *George Washington*. "Come and go with us," he said.[71]

Francis replied that the secretary of state had "ordered" him to stay in Paris until further instructed. (He probably overstated or misinterpreted what Lansing had told him.) Francis saw Lansing the next day, February 12, probably at a dinner at the Ritz hosted by young John Foster Dulles, a future secretary of state.[72] Lansing urged him to grab the opportunity to accompany Wilson to the United States, because that might be his only chance to speak with him.

Francis agreed. Before he left Paris, he met with Edgar Sisson at the Ritz. They had a long chat, "sitting companionably in his rooms," Sisson recalled. Sisson admitted he had made a mistake in sending the cable calling for Francis's recall, but added, "We all make mistakes, Governor, as you know." Francis accepted the apology, and said he only wanted two things: "to see the President and to go home." Fortunately, Sisson noted, "Both desires could be met together."[73]

On the morning of February 14, 1919, the Wilsons, Admiral Grayson, David R. Francis, Perry and Mimi Francis, Philip Jordan, and Earl Johnston left Paris on a special train. Philip Jordan wrote, "All along the track for miles you could see thousands of American soldiers on each side standing at attention." At Brest, they boarded the *George Washington*, which was full of American troops going home and was escorted by a battleship and four destroyers.[74]

As soon as he was settled into his stateroom, Francis sent a note to Wilson, saying he "awaited his pleasure" for a meeting. Two or three days later, Wilson came to Francis's cabin and the two men had a long talk.

Francis, who had had months to work out his plans in detail, proposed that the Allied diplomatic missions—including Ambassador David Rowland Francis—return to Petrograd accompanied by one hundred thousand Allied troops: American, British, French, and Italian volunteers. The Allied missions, he said, should disclaim any intention of interfering in the internal affairs of Russia, make it clear that the Russians still were considered Allies, and announce that their only purpose was to restore order and provide for free elections.

Wilson replied that sending more American troops to Russia after the signing of the armistice would be very unpopular in America. Francis disagreed, stating that many of the two million American soldiers in Europe were "disappointed that the armistice was signed before they could engage in battle." Apparently, neither man thought to poll the thousands of American doughboys accompanying them on the boat ride home.

The president said he had mentioned to Clemenceau and Lloyd George that Francis had recommended that the Allies send large numbers of troops into Russia. Lloyd George had told him the British troops would "refuse to go," and Clemenceau said the French troops would mutiny. Wilson suggested "permitting the Russians to settle their own differences." Francis replied, "That would entail great human slaughter."

No one abhorred bloodshed more than he, Wilson said wearily, but he feared, if Francis was right, "it must needs come." He told Francis he would keep his recommendations in mind and ended the meeting. They never discussed official matters in any detail again.[75]

Francis later decided that Wilson's negative reaction to his recommendations may have been "influenced by my emaciated condition and apparent weakness, or he may have thought the League of Nations would be formed and America would join the League and that would serve the same purpose"—in other words, a large League of Nations force could occupy Russia and guarantee free elections. The concept of a multi-national force defending democracy would not materialize until the world had fought another devastating war.[76]

The two men, who agreed on most issues and had known each other since the World's Fair, had several friendly visits on the ship as it steamed westward. Sisson, who met Francis later in New York, said the "Ambassador . . . told me how courteously the President had received him and chatted with him." On the deck of the *George Washington,* "the two tired men talked at ease."[77] Both men were not just tired, but exhausted. How exhausted Wilson had been would be clear by the fall of the year.

Wilson invited Francis for lunch on Washington's Birthday, February 22. Francis told the president he thought the American people would support the League, and Wilson said it would be a "great pity" if they did not. "The failure of the United States to back it," he said, "would break the heart of the world, for the world considers the United States as the only nation represented in this great conference whose motives are entirely unselfish."[78]

Among the guests were Assistant Secretary of the Navy Franklin Delano Roosevelt and his wife (and cousin), Eleanor. Roosevelt took the occasion to inform Francis that he had ordered that the first contingent of American troops to arrive in Archangel—two hundred marines—were to be under his command.[79]

The next day, Sunday, February 23, the last full day aboard ship, Wilson invited Perry and Mimi Francis to lunch with a small group and spoke at length of his visit with King George, who had been vehement in discussing his hatred of his German relatives, including his cousin, the Kaiser. That evening, the ship lost its bearings in a thick fog bank and, after nearly crashing into a destroyer sent out as an escort, anchored off Boston Harbor.[80]

The next morning the fog cleared somewhat, and at about 10:30 the Americans boarded a shallow draft destroyer for the trip to Boston. At the dock, President and Mrs. Wilson went down the gangplank first, followed by David Francis, and "then on down the line." Jordan wrote: "As an escort we had hundreds of different types of ships. They fired twenty salutes and then we were off for Boston. Just as we arrived I believe every bell and whistle in the city were ringing and blowing."[81]

The presidential party was driven through the city, its streets lined with "millions of people," according to Jordan. After lunch at the Copley Plaza Hotel, Francis, Jordan and Johnston boarded the special presidential train for Washington where they checked into the new Willard Hotel. (Presumably, Perry and Mimi headed for St. Louis.)

Francis went to the State Department to tell his story and present his case. And Philip Jordan dined at the White House, something he was very proud of for the rest of his life. As he remarked to someone later that year, "I was born in Hog Alley, and I think you know that a kangaroo can jump further than any other animal, but I don't believe he could jump from Hog Alley to the White House—which was some jump."[82]

In his letter to Talton and Betsey, Jordan recounted his triumph:

I want to tell you that this traveling with the President of the United States is the life. I never had the pleasure of being with any one that was so pleasant as both the President and Mrs. Wilson. Every one on board both boat and train were in love with them. They had a pleasant word and smile for every one.

The President had his negro valet and Mrs. Wilson had her negro maid. We had a delightful time coming over. For forty years, it has been my heart's desire to see the White House. I have been in Washington several times but I could never get in the White House.

So on Sunday March 2, Arthur Brooks, the President's valet, phoned for me to come to the White House and have lunch with him, which I was very glad to do. Now I am satisfied. I think I have seen my share of the world and its great men.

I think I told you that during the great World's Fair at St. Louis I had in my charge Presidents Roosevelt; Cleveland; Taft; Vice-President Fairbanks, Speaker Cannon, and William J. Bryan. They were all guests of Ambassador Francis.

In Petrograd Russia, I was lucky enough to get to see the Czar of Russia, and on December 26, when President Wilson paid London a visit, I was at Buckingham Palace and was face to face with the King and Queen. On February 14, 1919, I had the great honor of being one to help bring President Wilson back from the United States. On the way over the President and Mrs. Wilson both put their signatures on a picture of the ship George Washington for me, so that I would always remember them. The smile which both the President and Mrs. Wilson has is not a sham. It is always on their faces.

The Ambassador and I left Washington on March 3rd, for White Sulphur Springs, West Virginia. We will be here for a month then return to St. Louis for a few days and if the Ambassador is well enough we will return to Russia.

Goodbye. I hope to see you before going to Russia.

Sincerely yours,

Philip Jordan.[83]

CHAPTER 22

Who Lost Russia?

D AVID FRANCIS AND PHILIP JORDAN NEVER RETURNED TO RUSSIA.
After a few days at White Sulphur Springs, about 250 miles from Washington,
Francis was summoned back to the capital to testify at a Senate Judiciary
Subcommittee hearing on Bolshevik propaganda, a symptom of what became a full-
blown Red Scare. Francis and Jordan had returned home to a notably ugly period of
political rancor, as a nation united by war lurched uncertainly into peace, and the
Progressive Era drew to a close.

Progressives in both parties, led first by Teddy Roosevelt and then by Woodrow
Wilson, had smoothed over the more superficial societal fissures in Gilded Age America
with such liberal policies as trust busting, federal control of banking, and the introduction, in 1913, of an income tax. But deep class divisions and resentments remained. As
America became more industrialized, the labor movement grew stronger and more militant. The shock of the Bolshevik Revolution galvanized both sides of the class struggle,
inspiring the left while it frightened the right. Hundreds of thousands of Americans
embraced socialism. The forces of conservatism and reaction fought back.

Ambitious men promoted and seized upon the Red Scare, just as would happen in
the McCarthy era after World War II, as if the vacuum of hatred left by the end of the
slaughter needed to be filled. The Espionage and Sedition Acts, passed during the war,
continued to deal severely with those suspected of being unpatriotic, including socialist
leader Eugene Debs, who had been jailed during the war for his pacifist pronouncements
and would still be in prison in 1920, when he received 920,000 votes for president of the
United States.

Having spent almost two years watching Lenin and Trotsky at work in Russia,
Francis was astonished at the fervent following the Bolsheviks enjoyed in the United
States. He was equally astounded at the fury of the political reaction in America against
anyone on the left who shared goals with the Reds. Francis knew the difference between
democratically inclined labor organizers and true Bolsheviks. He wrote home from his
hospital bed in London, "Bolshevism is a war against civilization, society and Christianity.

The I.W.W.s in our country, who are imprisoned and suppressed when they make demonstrations, do not commit murders in cold blood [as do] the Bolsheviks in Russia."[1]

By 1919, Francis, who had made his peace with labor unions many years before, had become even clearer on the difference between what he called "labor unrest," an ordinary occurrence in the context of a free, democratic society, and Bolshevism. Indeed, the suppression of labor unions became another reason for Francis's hatred of the Bolsheviks.[2]

For Francis, a foreshadowing of the bitter winds that would blow across America in 1919 and 1920 had come while he was still in his hospital bed in London, recuperating from his operation. On January 22, 1919, during a debate in the House of Representatives on an appropriations bill for U.S. embassies and consulates, two congressmen launched attacks on Francis. It is perhaps emblematic of those heatedly confused times that he almost simultaneously was attacked for being too close to the Bolsheviks and for not being close enough. The search for scapegoats to blame for "losing Russia" had begun, as a similarly divisive debate over who lost China would come at a comparable historical juncture some thirty years later.

The more ferocious attack came from Republican Fiorello La Guardia, later to achieve secular sainthood as the three-time mayor of New York. Though a Progressive who would later run for Congress on the Socialist ticket, La Guardia at this early stage in his career was sucked into the hysteria of the Red Scare, driven in part by his intense patriotism and his concern about the growing appeal of Bolshevism to his poor immigrant constituents.[3]

Stripped of considerable rhetoric, and a sly allusion to Francis's "friends of Teutonic tendencies," the core of La Guardia's criticism of Francis was that he had failed to support General Lavr Kornilov in his attempted coup against Alexander Kerensky. (See chapter 16.) The New York congressman proclaimed, "France and England backed Kornilov, because Kornilov would have kept the army on the Eastern front, but, I am informed, on Mr. Francis's report to the Department of State we backed Kerensky and backed the wrong horse. Not only did we do that . . . but we brought pressure to bear upon our allies, and they were guided by our judgment."

In a memoir of his early years, La Guardia described the roots of his animus toward Francis. While La Guardia was commander of the U.S. Air Forces in Europe in the summer of 1918, he met former Petrograd Naval Attaché Walter Crosley (whom he repeatedly refers to as "Crowley") and former Petrograd Consul North Winship, both of whom, La Guardia maintained, were highly critical of their former boss. Winship, La Guardia recounted, "had been recalled from Russia at the request of our Ambassador, David R. Francis, because he was critical of the counter-revolutionary activities the Allies were carrying on there."[4]

On the floor of the house, La Guardia made specific reference to conversations with Crosley and Winship and described Francis's performance in Petrograd as "absolutely hopelessly incompetent." He insisted that Francis "was not in sympathy" with the

March Revolution "in the beginning" and had never really understood it. He charged that Francis had not kept his government informed of what went on in Russia.

Even a cursory reading of official cables and letters from 1917 shows that Francis was almost giddily enthusiastic about the March Revolution early on and that he did keep the State Department up to date on the political chaos in Petrograd. He may have stuck with Kerensky too long, but it's difficult to envision a man of Francis's deeply democratic principles supporting a right-wing military coup against a moderate socialist who had the support of a nation's parliament.

At the same debate, Republican Congressman Clarence Miller of Minnesota criticized Francis more hesitantly for being so close to the aristocracy that he failed to back the beleaguered Kerensky with sufficient vigor. Miller also contended Francis should have recommended recognition of the Bolsheviks after they took over. He proclaimed, "Proper work of America and the allies, I feel sure, would have saved Russia from the awful state into which she has fallen."

At one point, Champ Clark of Missouri, the Kentucky-born Democratic Speaker of the House, added to the bombast by inaccurately accusing Miller of having "intimated that maybe Francis was afraid."

"Let me tell you something," Clark declaimed. "A man born in Kentucky and raised in Missouri is not afraid of the devil himself." Cheers went up from Southern and Border State Democrats.

Democratic Representative Henry D. Flood of Virginia, chairman of the House Committee on Foreign Affairs, took the floor to defend Francis on more substantive grounds, noting that he had discussed Francis's performance with the State Department and had been assured that "Francis was one of the most efficient diplomatic representatives we had in the service." Flood praised Francis as "the one man whom all the other representatives of the allied powers [looked to] for advice and strength," even after he became ill and bedridden. Flood said:

> The only criticism that he ever heard made against Mr. Francis that was supported by investigation made by the State Department was that when he first went to Russia he did not live in the magnificent style that the Russian people and the nobility desired him to live in; that he traveled around Petrograd in a Ford car instead of a Pierce-Arrow, and lived in moderate quarters, quarters that did not appeal to the wealthy people of Russia. . . . I wanted to say this in defense of a man who has made great sacrifices for his country and for civilization.

There was sustained applause, and the debate moved back to its original intent, the funding of foreign embassies.[5]

Francis was in Paris in early February when he received American newspaper reports of the debate. On February 13, 1919, Francis cabled the secretary of state, wondering what Winship and Crosley had told La Guardia. Lansing passed on to Francis a letter from Winship saying he was "at a loss" to know where La Guardia "obtained his information."

Winship recalled:

One day he asked me about the Russian situation but, as I remember, he did
most of the talking. . . . His statements are at variance with what I know. For
instance, Mr. Francis was in sympathy with the [March] revolution and the
first temporary government from the first day. Further, I was not recalled from
Russia because of differences with Ambassador Francis. . . . Mr. Francis often
called me to confer with him and we were on the best of terms. When my
transfer came, he . . . said he did not want me to leave and that, if I wished to
stay, he would cable the Department urging that I be left in Petrograd.[6]

A few months later, Crosley wrote Francis that he had spent about fifteen minutes
with La Guardia and had said nothing that "which could be, by any reasonable person,
construed as a criticism of you. On the contrary, I have uniformly said the kindest things
of you. . . . My memory of you leads me to believe that you are a very powerful man and
I can't reconcile you with lack of strength."[7]

O N MARCH 8, after hurrying back to Washington from West Virginia, Francis testified
at the Bolshevik Propaganda hearings, held before a five-man subcommittee of the
Senate Judiciary Committee and presided over by North Carolina Democrat Lee S.
Overman. The stated purpose was to investigate "efforts being made to propagate in this
country the principles of any party claiming to exercise authority in Russia" and "to
inquire into any effort to incite overthrow of the Government of this country or all government by force."

Among the two dozen or so witnesses who had preceded Francis in the month-long
hearings were Samuel Harper; John Reed and his firebrand wife, Louise Bryant;
Catherine Breshkovskaya, the socialist "grandmother of the revolution" who spoke
strongly against the Bolshevik reign of terror in her country; and Raymond Robins, who
said of David Francis, "The ambassador worked harder, stayed longer, met the situation
with more steadiness, in my judgement, than any other ambassador there."

The Reverend George A. Simons, superintendent of the Methodist Episcopal Church
in Petrograd until October 1918, was asked about Robins and said, "I had always thought
highly of him until he came over to Russia and embarrassed our embassy in many ways.
. . . We thought that our ambassador, who was doing such magnificent work over there,
ought to have the support of every last American."

He noted that Francis was not popular with the Bolsheviks, who thought of him as
a "typical capitalist," while Robins was considered to be more of a "working man."
Louise Bryant made the same point, although she identified the Bolsheviks with the
Russian people as a whole: "all the Russian people felt that Colonel Robins was a true
representative of America. . . . They considered Mr. Francis to be an old man, entirely out
of sympathy with the revolutionary movement."

Robins, in his testimony, denied reports that he had supported the Bolsheviks.

"I rather got the impression that you did," noted Republican Senator Knute Nelson of Minnesota.

"That's one of the difficulties that I have been in since I came back from Russia," he said. "If I told the truth, as I have tried to do in this presence under the pains and penalties of an oath, and did not lie and slander folks, and did not say they are German agents and thieves and murderers, criminals utterly, then I am a Bolshevist. . . . I refuse to libel either side of this controversy."

Robins referred to an editorial cartoon by J. N. Darling in the *New York Herald Tribune* that showed a man being carried roughly down the street by a group of men. When a bystander demanded an explanation, one of the men replied, 'This fellow is incurably insane. . . . He thinks he knows all about the Russian situation.'"

Typically, Robins didn't stop at that succinct explanation but went on to say, "If I don't know more about it than any other Allied representative—even though that may seem arrogant—I wasted my time."

Raymond Robins would return to Room 226 of the Senate Office Building. But first, Francis testified.

He appeared late in the morning on Saturday, March 8, and testified for several hours. Four members of the five-man subcommittee were present, and all of them treated Francis with the respect they must have felt was due a dignified, white-haired sixty-eight-year-old man in an old-fashioned high dress collar, still weak and drawn from the serious illness that had nearly killed him while he served his country overseas. He and Senator Nelson even chatted briefly about working together when Francis was Cleveland's secretary of the interior.

He briefly described his tenure in Russia and characterized the major figures of the time, noting that Kerensky was a lawyer who knew nothing about the military and made a crucial mistake by abolishing the death penalty for army deserters, adding to the breakdown of discipline. But his main mistake, Francis said, was not imprisoning Lenin and Trotsky after the July uprisings and trying them for treason.

Francis said:

Lenin is the brains of this whole movement. He has a great intellect. He is a fanatic and I think has sincere convictions. I could not say the same about Trotsky. I think Trotsky is an adventurer. He has great ability. He has more executive ability than Lenin, but when they have differed, Lenin has always been able to dominate Trotsky. . . .

I wish to say here that I think that Lenin was a German agent from the beginning. They would never have permitted him to come through Germany if they had not thought or known they could use him. He disbursed [German] money very liberally. Lenin, however, was not so much [working for] Germany as he was in favor of promoting a world-wide social revolution. . . . He would have taken British money, American money, and French money and used it to promote this objective of his.

Later, Francis said, when Lenin's "power was tottering and could not be maintained in any other way, he encouraged or permitted the reign of terror that is now prevailing in Russia." Francis said he had "been told of blood flowing from the place of execution in Moscow. . . . It is impossible to tell the story in all its horrors."*

Francis was quizzed in detail about Robins. He pointed out that he had gone against orders from the State Department by encouraging Robins to maintain relations with the Bolshevik Government and had told him, "I will stand between you and the fire." At one point, in answer to a question about Robins's feelings towards the Bolsheviks, Francis said Robins had stated shortly after the November Revolution that he "approved of their principles, but he did not approve of their excesses."

Francis was quick to say, "The relations between Colonel Robins and myself were always pleasant. We did not agree about the Bolshevik government at all."

Senator Nelson pressed the issue: "He was rather inclined to favor them, was he not?"

Francis replied cautiously. "Well, he was importuning me, I think, all the time to demand recognition of their government."[8]

The next morning, Raymond Robins, who was in Chicago, picked up a Sunday paper and read about Francis's testimony. The story quoted Francis as saying that Robins, after his initial visit to Soviet headquarters in November 1917, had "told me that they had told him their principles and said he approved of them."

Francis, indeed, had said something very close to that, but he had added that Robins had not approved of the Bolsheviks' "excesses."

In sane times, little would have been made of the statement, which was an accurate reflection of what Robins had said, and what would become the conventional wisdom for millions of American liberals in coming decades—Lenin and Trotsky's intentions were good, but their methods were cruel. These were not, however, sane times, and Robins was understandably paranoiac about being tied too closely to the Reds. He immediately contacted Senator Overman, hopped on a fast train and, on Monday, March 10, at his insistence, appeared again before the subcommittee. He read the "principles" reference in the news story aloud and protested, "On the contrary, Mr. Chairman and gentlemen of the committee, at all times, in this country and in Russia during my stay there, and since my return, I have been opposed to the principles of the Bolshevik program." He pointed out, accurately, that even before his assignment to Russia, he vocally had been opposed to international socialism.

Robins presented copies of the two documents referred to in Chapter 18 in which Francis gave the Red Cross colonel limited authority to deal with the Bolsheviks. The documents were complete, including the handwritten cautionary notes from Francis that were later omitted in *Raymond Robins' Own Story*. Robins went into considerable detail to make it clear that he had worked with the approval of Francis, something

---

*Under the six-year regime of Lenin and Trotsky, terror became a policy of the state. In a process that was well underway by 1919, the Russian secret police employed more than 250,000 people, from local informants to concentration camp guards, and torture became routine. Hundreds of thousands were killed—before Stalin took power, and eventually killed millions.

Francis, too, had made clear. Finally, as Robins rambled on, Senator Overman impatiently broke in to tell Robins he was beating a dead horse: "I understood Mr. Francis to say that you were transacting business for him with his permission, and were of service to him."

That, said Robins, was not the impression he had gotten from newspaper reports of the testimony, which indicated "friction between Mr. Robins and the ambassador, and other things indicate a lack of confidence."

Senator William King, a Utah Democrat, said, "I got just the other impression from his testimony, Colonel Robins, that you were acting for him unofficially, and he recommended that you continue to act so that he would have a conduit—I think he used that word—to receive information from the Bolshevik government."

"I'm very glad if that was the result of the testimony," said Robins.

"There is no doubt about that," said Senator Overman, who assured Robins that Francis had said that "Colonel Robins was of great value to him, and that you were friendly and that there was no criticism."

Still, Robins continued to defend himself at great length, and finally three senators broke in, one after another, all to assure Robins that Francis had spoken well of him. Senator Nelson again insisted that he "did not see any real conflict between you and Ambassador Francis."

Robins said he was glad if that was true, but from that point on he clearly held a grudge against Francis.[9]

Shortly after the hearings had concluded, the *New York Times* editorialized against recognition of the Bolsheviks in the Versailles peace settlement, invoking the testimony of Francis and calling him "the best-informed witness of conditions in Russia."[10] And the *Christian Science Monitor* wrote that Francis would "go down in history as one of the great ambassadors of the world. He constitutes a compelling force of honesty, directed by a clear and vigorous understanding, and utterly untrammeled by fear. . . . Reading his straightforward and unvarnished story of the Russian revolution, as given to the Senate Committee . . . one is filled with hope that the public will grasp more intelligently the meaning of that portentous event, in its innumerable ramifications, and will be prepared to grapple with and master the specter of Bolshevism."[11]

Edgar Sisson wrote Earl Johnston that "the whole country honored" David Francis for his testimony.[12] If Robins attacked Francis, Sisson said, he would "take his heart out." Francis later remarked that he took that threat as a figure of speech, not "a surgical operation."[13]

Francis and Jordan headed back to White Sulphur Springs for a two-month stay at the posh Greenbriar resort. At first, typically, Francis exhausted himself by trying to play a full course of golf. After nearly collapsing, he cut back for a few weeks, but by the middle of April he again played eighteen holes almost every day. Friends, including railroad tycoon S. M. Felton and Frank Polk, who was acting secretary of state while Lansing was at Versailles, joined him for a few days, and he relaxed as much as he ever did in the fragrant spring breezes of the Appalachians.

At Greenbriar, Francis had time to think long thoughts about his life and his children. He wrote his sister Mollie:

> I think my absence has been beneficial for the boys. Perry has had great
> responsibilities but they have broadened and matured him; from everyone I
> hear that he has taken a stand in St. Louis that has commanded universal
> respect. Dave and Talton and Tom and Sidney have also been thrown on their
> own resources to a greater extent than they would have been in I had been at
> home and I think it has been helpful to them. None of the boys have reprehen-
> sible habits, at least not to my knowledge, and those who have married [all
> but Charles] have good wives. Charlie seems to have been the least fortunate
> of the boys and has been afflicted by impaired health many years of his life; he
> is extremely nervous and undecisive and procrastinating but when he reaches
> the limit of endurance everyone who knows him gets out of his way. I am
> pleased that Charlie and Tom have gone into the hog feeding enterprise [at
> Uplands Farm]. It seems to me it should be profitable.[14]

On April 18, 1919, Raymond Robins, who was on tour giving speeches about the sit-uation in Russia, appeared in St. Louis and spoke for several hours in two appearances. He was critical of the Allied ambassadors in general and the British and French ambas-sadors in particular: "Silk hats and broadcloth could not understand the Russian peo-ple," he exclaimed. He barely mentioned David Francis, although at one point he said that Francis was not so good a friend these days as he had been in Russia.

Robins insisted that Lenin and Trotsky were sincere but misguided, and he said that it was "stupidly and brutally false" to say they were in the pay of Germany. He described reports of massacres as "boulevard chatter," noting that he knew Soviet Russia well, hav-ing traveling six thousand miles through the country with documents bearing Lenin's frank. He compared provincial Soviets to New England town meetings and suggested they could be the basis for a democratic movement that would displace the dictatorial Lenin and Trotsky. He caused sustained laughter when he said of Allied ambassadors, "What a representative of a democratic government likes is a palace, what he likes bet-ter is a Prince, and what he likes best is a Princess."[15]

Francis's paid leave from the State Department ended about May 1, and he offered to resign as ambassador. Acting Secretary of State Frank Polk asked him to stay, saying it would be embarrassing to replace him because it would require recognizing the Soviet Government. So Francis remained in the post on unpaid leave.[16]

Used to lifelong robust health, he was frustrated at how long it took to recover fully from his illness and operation. Doctors warned him it could take a year. To make mat-ters worse, Philip Jordan, a bedrock of strength and support through all the horrible times in Russia, began feeling pain in his abdomen. Francis sent him to a doctor, who decided nothing was seriously wrong with him but that he had been under a consider-able amount of strain and suffered from a nervous stomach. Despite the relaxing condi-tions of the resort, however, the pain persisted. Several other doctors were consulted.

None of them could find anything physically wrong with Jordan. As the spring wore on, the pain grew worse.[17]

About May 11, Francis and Jordan left Greenbriar and headed northeast. They stopped in Washington and New York, visiting with friends in both places. By May 15, the two men and Jane Francis had all arrived at Rye Beach, about an hour and a half north of Boston by rail.[18] David had not seen Jane for more than three years, and their happy reunion was tinged with worry. Not well himself, Francis was disturbed that his wife seemed neither well nor strong.[19]

In early June, Francis received, through the State Department, a letter dated April 1 from Matilda de Cramm. She said nothing about how she got along in Petrograd but asked if he had any information on her husband. Francis wrote Polk, inquiring about Edgar de Cramm and seeking advice on how to respond to the letter. Polk replied, "The last we heard of Mr. De Cramm he had left the country and we have no knowledge of his present address. I appreciate the motives which prompt your desire to answer the inquiry of his wife, but I would question the advisability of your doing so, particularly in view of your own interests."[20]

If Francis ever replied to Matilda's letter, no record of it exists. As far as we know, her letter was the last communication between the two. In his Russia memoir, published in 1921, Francis refers to her once, in connection with a visit to Kerensky, as "Mme. D. C., a Russian lady" and adds "I would give her name but as she is still in Petrograd it might cause her trouble."[21]

Francis also heard from Hugh Moran, Robert Breck's grandson, who had spent three years in Siberia doing relief work with the YMCA and had survived the influenza and returned home. Moran reported, remarkably, that his aunt, Belle Breck, had returned to Siberia amid the influenza epidemic and civil war and now ran a canteen in Vladivostok.[22] Moran asked for help in entering the diplomatic service. Francis wrote a glowing letter of recommendation to Woodrow Wilson, saying he had known Moran since his infancy and reminding Wilson that Moran's grandfather, the Reverend R. L. Breck, had been a close friend of Wilson's Presbyterian minister father.[23]

A serialized version of *Raymond Robins' Own Story* began appearing in the July issue of *Metropolitan* magazine. Colonel (Ret.) William Judson, after seeing the first installment, mentioned it unfavorably in the cover letter to his long-delayed report to the War Department on "the troubled days of 1917–18." (Robins's memoir and Judson's report are referred to in chapters 16 through 19.) The former military attaché, who remarked that he wanted to offer "a truthful contribution to the history of those days, which seems in some danger of becoming but 'a pack of lies agreed upon,'" said he regretted to see Robins's version of the story published: "He is not entirely accurate in what he says about me, although I have no doubt he intends to be." Of David Francis, Judson reported that he was "fond of the old Ambassador, which may be hard to believe, and I am confident that it cannot hurt him greatly to have the truth reported thus confidentially."[24]

THAT SUMMER, most of the Francis family visited Rye Beach. Perry, Dave Jr., and Talton, who took a few weeks off from managing the Francis businesses, all were shocked by the condition of Philip Jordan. He had grown hard of hearing and complained of a buzzing in the ear as well as of the constant stomach ache.

Francis took the fifty-year-old valet to the hospital at the nearby Portsmouth Naval Base. A doctor cleaned a dense accumulation of wax out of one ear, and the ringing stopped. But the pain in his stomach grew more intense. Francis telephoned a prominent doctor he knew in Boston and made an appointment for Jordan. On June 18, Jordan had X-rays in Boston, and he was diagnosed with chronic appendicitis. He was admitted to Bay State Hospital on June 21 for an operation the next day, and Francis hurried to Boston. The two men talked for a long time about their lives together before Jordan was taken into the operating room to remove his appendix. Francis was in the room for the operation and didn't leave the hospital until he was assured Jordan would recover. He called Jordan almost every day from Rye Beach.

Jordan later spoke with pride of Francis having been present at the operation.[25] Francis described the illness and the operation in a letter to Ellen Green, the woman he knew as Jordan's mother (See chapter 8). He remarked that "Phil . . . was very faithful to me and exceedingly useful during my sojourn in Russia and throughout my subsequent illness. . . . You should be proud of such a son."[26]

Jordan returned to Rye Beach in time for the July 4 weekend. His stomach still bothered him, and a doctor described his condition, in Francis's words, "as nervous trouble." It seems quite possible that Francis, unhappy with the quality of cooking at Rye Beach, could not stop pestering Jordan with problems.

Around the end of July, on a doctor's recommendation, Francis reluctantly gave Jordan a two-week leave and sent him to Asheville, N.C., to rest. In a letter to a friend, Francis noted, "It's a nervous trouble with him as it was with Mrs. Francis," and recalled, with a mixture of pride and chagrin, that socialite Billie Orthwein had said that whoever associated with David Francis became "afflicted with nervous prostration."[27]

Although not fully recovered from the January operation, and what he called "my wound" continued to seep and cause him pain, Francis made trips to Boston, New York, and Washington that summer. On July 8, he went to New York to be in a parade for Woodrow Wilson, back again from Paris.

Francis rode in a car with top Democrats of New York City and state, including Norman Mack, a friend and the owner of the *Buffalo Times*. They discussed the *Republic*, whose circulation was plunging now that the war no longer screamed from the front page. Mack said that if he owned the *St. Louis Globe-Democrat*, he would pay $1 million for the competing *Republic*. That confirmed Francis's notion of its value, and it became the asking price in informal discussions with potential buyers, although Francis admitted to Perry that he would take less. Francis, Bro. & Co. held notes worth more than seven hundred thousand dollars, and Francis wanted at least to get that money back. He finally started to give up on keeping the *Republic* afloat, and it was a bitter pill to swallow. After seeing the Sunday *Post-Dispatch* for June 29, he wrote Perry, "Its advertising makes me sick when compared with the *Republic*'s of the same date."[28]

Francis's mood about selling the paper seemed to go up and down with his health. On July 10, he wrote Perry, "The wound has not flowed for several days, and I begin to feel that I should like to undertake some work that will require energy, application and initiative." He just might "sever my connection with all the companies of which I am a director and devote my time and thought and energies to the *Republic*," putting three hundred thousand dollars more of his own money into the paper and taking charge himself. Even he must have known this was quite unrealistic, in part because his health remained uncertain. Although his weight was back up to two hundred pounds, only ten pounds short of his pre-operation normal, the incision continued to bother him: "It closes for four or five days and then if the water does not find an exit pains me so that I cannot concentrate my mind on any subject."[29]

At the parade in New York, Francis met for the last time with Woodrow Wilson. The president then headed into the heartland on his futile, grueling, and ultimately debilitating mission to sell the American people on the Versailles Treaty and the League of Nations, under brutal attack by isolationist Republicans let by Henry Cabot Lodge, chairman of the Senate Foreign Relations Committee. But opposition to the League of Nations was not limited to Republicans, and the leading "America First" Democrat was Francis's old opponent, Senator James Reed of Missouri.

Late that summer, with Francis still at Rye Beach, the president spoke in St. Louis. Wilson said passionately that if the League of Nations failed he would feel that the country had betrayed the American boys he sent overseas to fight "a war against wars." And inevitably, he said, there would come "in the vengeful Providence of God, another struggle in which, not a few hundred thousand fine men from America will have to die, but as many millions as are necessary to accomplish the final freedom of the peoples of the world."[30]

Walter Stevens visited Rye Beach for several weeks in July and early August and urged Francis to write his memoirs.[31] Stevens was still around on Saturday, August 2, when reporter Charles A. Merrill of the *Boston Globe* came up for an interview. A servant at the main house told him that the governor was at the "bungalow," and Merrill crossed a small stretch of grass and came to what he described as "a quaint little stone structure nestling in the corner of a grove of pines." Earl Johnston opened the door and ushered the reporter inside, where Francis and Stevens chatted.

Francis looked up over his round eyeglasses, rose, and extended his hand. Merrill noted that Francis's hair and mustache were now snow white. "Little wonder," he remarked.

"The ladies were all up at 'the big house,'" Merrill wrote. "For the bungalow has always been a sort of 'stag retreat.' Mr. Francis built it some years ago with the idea of entertaining his men friends there." It was cool and dark in the two-story-high main room, whose dominant feature was an enormous stone fireplace with its chimney rising through the roof.

Francis talked frankly and vigorously about the situation in Russia and said the most urgent matter facing the world was the need to ratify the peace treaty and establish the League of Nations, which he hoped would extend a protectorate over Russia to ensure an honest election and the seating of a truly representative constituent assembly. Francis contended that Lenin did not represent more than one-tenth of the population of Russia. "We owe it to humanity to put a quietus on Bolshevism in Russia," Francis proclaimed. "Bolshevism, in my opinion, means a return to anarchy. It is neither democracy nor Socialism."

The reporter noted that Francis carefully pointed out several times that he was "not quarrelling with Socialism," stressing that he had been very close to such anti-Bolshevik socialists as Kerensky and Chaikovski and saying that "sane Russian socialists" would have nothing to do with Bolshevism. "Socialism has so many degrees, it means so many things," he said, that he was not prepared to pass judgment on its possible success in the United States. "But eminent Socialists think that Socialism has sufficient difficulties to overcome, without being charged with Bolshevism."

Asked if Lenin was "sincere," Francis replied yes, that he was a sincere fanatic: "An honest fanatic is more dangerous than an intellectual knave." The long interview was ended by a man bringing Francis his golf clubs. It was time for his daily round of golf at the nearby Abenaqui private golf course.[32]

Francis kept busy that summer. He had many visitors, among them E. Lansing Ray, publisher of the *Republic*'s rival for morning readers, the *St. Louis Globe-Democrat,* who spent four weeks in August at a Rye Beach hotel. Two weeks into Ray's visit, Francis fretted that they still had not discussed the failing *Republic*. In light of subsequent events, it is reasonable to assume they eventually did.[33]

He remained ambassador to Russia, and in the fall of 1919, Francis accepted an invitation from Princess Cantacuzene to become president of a relief committee for Russian refugees. State Department officials kept him apprised of the situation in Russia. In early September, reports seeped through from Petrograd that the American and other embassies had been sacked and looted in July and now housed the families of high-ranking Bolsheviks. Karin Sante, who had been in charge of the embassy for the Americans, was arrested and sent to Moscow. By then, virtually all representatives of Allied and neutral nations had been imprisoned or expelled by the Bolsheviks.[34]

Thousands of British and American troops had been withdrawn from the north. On September 14, Felix Cole and the remaining American Embassy personnel left Archangel. Five months later, it fell to the Bolsheviks.[35] By the end of 1920, the civil war ended and the Bolsheviks, barely three years earlier a powerless splinter party of angry radicals, held sway over a vast empire that was to endure for more than seventy years.

On SEPTEMBER 9 AND 10, Francis took the train down to New York for the annual directors' meetings of New York Life. Two weeks later, the Francises returned to St. Louis. They moved into the large apartment Jane had rented in the St. Regis at 4931

Lindell, overlooking Forest Park. The apartment stood about three blocks from the mansion at Maryland and Newstead.

The day they returned, September 25, Woodrow Wilson collapsed from exhaustion after a speech in Pueblo, Colorado. In less than two months, he had traveled eight thousand miles and delivered about forty speeches. The president was put on a special train and sent back to Washington. The following evening, a telegram from Wilson was read at a welcome-home banquet in downtown St. Louis for David Francis:

> I wish with all my heart that I might be present at the reception and banquet to be given Ambassador Francis. Inasmuch as it is impossible for me to be there, will you not convey my sincerest congratulations to the Ambassador. He has merited the admiration and gratitude of the country. No one could have been more steadfast, more courageous, or more consistently guided by principles than he was in all his dealings with a situation which was difficult to the point of impossibility.

Francis brought most of the large crowd to its feet by saying he did not see how any patriotic American could fail to support the League of Nations, and he hoped it would be established soon. He called again for intervention into Russia to displace the Bolsheviks, not just by the Allies but by an army with the backing of the League of Nations.

Francis praised conservative labor leaders like Samuel Gompers, founder of the American Federation of Labor, for resisting Bolshevism and said, "I don't see how any workman can be misled or influenced in the slightest degree by the Bolshevik spirit, which is broadcast in this land. It all emanated from Russia."

Holding forth for almost two hours, he described his experiences in Russia and condemned the "beastly cruelties" of the Bolsheviks, whom he accused of "murders by the thousands." He brought the crowd to its feet again with the exclamation, "I hold myself ready to go back to Russia at the call of my Government; I may even return without that call."[36]

On October 2, in Washington, Woodrow Wilson suffered a severe stroke and partial paralysis, sealing the doom of America's participation in the League of Nations. Wilson never recovered fully from the stroke and died an invalid in 1924.

With Wilson effectively out of the way, ambitious Attorney General A. Mitchell Palmer launched a series of raids on homes and labor headquarters, arresting and threatening with deportation thousands of Americans, many of them not even associated with radical groups. Across the country, outspoken liberals, foreigners, Jews, and blacks were scapegoated. Race riots, almost entirely instigated by whites, broke out across the country, including, in July 1919, in Washington, D.C., itself. The Ku Klux Klan underwent a revival; "The Protocols of the Elders of Zion," ironically thought to have been created by the Tsar's secret police to justify pogroms, resurfaced in a paper owned by the increasingly anti-Semitic Henry Ford; and crazed talk of Zionist plots against the nation poisoned the air. With the European enemy now defeated, the nation split into battling factions.

THAT FALL, PHILIP JORDAN wrote a remarkable letter to a woman we know only from the salutation, "My dear Friend Mrs. Green." (The first two sentences of the letter, among other things, suggest Mrs. Green is not Ellen Green of Kansas City, whom Francis knew as Jordan's mother and who is listed as his mother in Jordan's death certificate.) The letter included a small photograph of Jordan. It read:

> I am sure you will be much surprised to receive this letter and contents from me. I am writing you this to show you after all these years how much I appreciated what you did for me up in Jefferson City. After you have finished reading all that I have sent you and if you think I have had any success in life, I want you to know and feel that I give you more credit than anyone I know for that success.
>
> Do you remember, about twenty years ago, when I was trying to drink all the whiskey there was in Jefferson City and was all in, down and out, do you remember one August morning while I was standing on the corner of High and Madison Streets and you were passing on the south side of the street, you crossed over to where I was standing and I was oh, so drunk, and you with all your kindness, pinned a little white ribbon on the lapel of my coat, and told me whenever I wanted a drink of beer or whiskey to look at the ribbon?
>
> Well, Mrs. Green, from that day I made up my mind I was going to do all in my power to stop drinking. It was an awful battle, but the little white ribbon did the work. It has been nineteen years since I have touched a drop of anything and if I should live to be a thousand years old I shall never drink again; thanks to you and the little white ribbon.
>
> Since I left Jefferson City I have had the great pleasure of meeting personally the brain[i]est and the leading men of this country and also Europe. I have passed through something that a few men go through and live to tell the details. I passed through the great World War, and in Petrograd, Russia, I went through two Revolutions, and in Archangel, Russia, I went through another. I only tell you this to show what part you played in them.
>
> While under fire I thought of you and when battling the submarines and dodging floating mines on the high seas I thought of you also. You will find a small picture of me which was taken in Petrograd, Russia. This picture has quite a little history; it also went through the two (or the three) revolutions, has traveled sixteen thousand miles and crossed six different oceans.
>
> Enclosed you will find my card showing that I am President and owner of the Colored Waiter's Club. I also owned the saloon on the corner of 23rd and Market Street. All caused from the pinning on of a little white ribbon. . . .
>
> Goodbye. Please don't think I am writing a history of my life, but just to tell you how much I appreciate what a little piece of white ribbon did for me.[37]

On December 4, after three weeks of intense negotiations, the *Republic* was sold to the *Globe-Democrat* for $733,812.74. "Old 1808"—the nickname referred to the year of its founding—was dead. The *Globe-Democrat* became St. Louis's only morning newspaper.

(There were three in the afternoon—the magisterial *Post-Dispatch* and the tabloid-style *Star* and *Times*.)[38]

The era when major urban newspapers were unapologetic organs of major political parties drew to a close. The Republican *Globe-Democrat*, with the absorption of the Democratic *Republic*, became less overtly partisan. Publisher E. Lansing Ray—whose son, ironically, later would marry David Francis's granddaughter Miriam, bringing the paper back into the family—announced that the *Globe* would be "an independent Republican newspaper . . . printing the news accurately and fairly without fear or favor." Soon, at Ray's command, the word "Republican" dropped from its statement of editorial independence.

The *Republic* was done in by a number of factors, some of which David Francis could have done something about. In the late nineteenth century, management had failed to see that the business and commercial center of St. Louis was moving to the west, responding to the decline in river traffic and the general tendency of American cities to abandon their oldest sections. The *Globe* became the voice of expanding, westward-moving St. Louis business, while the *Republic* clung to its Third Street headquarters and its Third Street mind set. The *Globe* was not just further west—on Sixth Street—but was better written and edited, with crisper stories and editorials. It contained more news, with effusive use of illustrations on page one; inoffensively gossipy society news; judicious muckraking; and splashy page-one headlines.

By the turn of the century, the *Republic* was caught in an unbreakable spiral: as its circulation declined, its advertising followed, and fewer pages meant a smaller news hole. Ironically, the *Globe-Democrat* could devote more than twice as many pages to the World's Fair as the paper partly owned by David Francis, the president of the Fair.[39]

Even in early 1919, when it was clear that the *Republic* either must change drastically or close up shop, Francis still fought the notion that great twentieth century newspapers must maintain a certain distance from close allegiances and strive to print the news "without fear or favor," as Joseph Pulitzer put it. Francis wrote disapprovingly from his London hospital bed, "Perry has been associated so much with newspaper men since I left home that I tell him he has become iconoclastic, but he denies it. He says he can see faults even in people he admires and thinks that a newspaper should have no friends whom he favors nor enemies to punish."[40]

Not long after that, the Francises hired a new editor, Sam Hellman of the *Post-Dispatch*, in a last-ditch effort to save the *Republic*. In May 1919, Hellman wrote Francis:

> In the past the *Republic* has devoted too much of its space and energies to the so-called society people. We have defended big business at every turn, fought labor unions, derided social reformers and otherwise distinguished ourselves as a class organ—a paper of the property interests of the city.
>
> And what has the *Republic* gained by its championship of the vested interests? Nothing. The rich advertiser whom we defended at every turn gave his advertising to the *Post-Dispatch*—a newspaper that has always fought for the masses, or pretended to. The wealthy class have praised us for our

editorial attitude, cussed out the *P-D,* and then given all their business to the *P-D.* The reason is simple. The *Post* reached the masses and the advertiser wanted to reach the masses.[41]

Francis, who had gained new respect for the common man in Russia, gave Hellman carte blanche to change the direction of the paper to make "the masses" feel that "we have taken up the cudgel on its behalf." But it was too late, and Francis, personally having lost about one hundred thousand dollars a year for the four preceding years, found himself looking at a loss of three hundred thousand dollars for 1919 alone.[42] So he sold out to the *Globe-Democrat,* the paper that the *Republic,* undoubtedly under Francis's influence, had described as "heathen" for its longstanding opposition to Woodrow Wilson's internationalism.[43]

The sale adds poignancy to a note in the will that Francis made before he left for Russia. Francis expressed his wish that the *Republic* "should be retained by my sons . . . the control of a great metropolitan daily affords an unequalled opportunity to benefit the community . . . and gives its owners potentialities to promote the good of society to an incalculable degree."[44]

David Francis's dream of a newspaper that reflected his ideals and kindled the flame of civic duty in the breasts of his sons was over. But he was not through dreaming.

CHAPTER 23

The Final Years

"A man told me the other day that Emerson had written that a man only counts years who has nothing else to count. I have read much of Emerson but never came across that chunk of wisdom."
—David Rowland Francis[1]

FROM THE HIGH WEST WINDOWS OF THE APARTMENT at the St. Regis, David Francis could look out on Forest Park and see the Palace of Fine Arts, now the St. Louis Art Museum, perched on top of Art Hill, with children running and sledding down the slope where the Cascades once spilled. The apartment was large—some twenty-eight hundred square feet—but, with the mansion on Maryland Avenue closed, family gatherings were held at the even roomier white-frame house at Uplands Farm, the spread in north St. Louis County that Francis had bought for his parents. Fifth son Thomas and his wife, Leila, lived there with their seven-year-old son David R. Francis, III, and five-year-old daughter Anne.

On Christmas Day 1919, nineteen members of the Francis family gathered for dinner at the Uplands Farm, and they posed on the front steps and porch for a photograph.

Spread out along the top step and the front of the porch are the six sons—Perry, forty-three; David, Jr., forty; Charles, thirty-nine; Talton, thirty-seven; Thomas, thirty-five; and Sidney, thirty-one. All the men have slight, serious smiles above their rolled, cleft Francis chins. Mixed in with their husbands are the five wives. Particularly striking is oval-faced, dark-complected Betsey Coste Francis, who was partly of Basque ancestry. Perched jauntily on the porch railing next to her husband, Talton, she is wearing a color-dappled fur coat and has a brightly patterned gypsy scarf wrapped around her head.

On the lower steps are five of the grandchildren—Jane, Miriam, Sidney, Jr., Anne, and David, III. They range in age from eight (Jane) to three (Sidney, Jr.). Halfway up the steps, between the neat little row of grandchildren and the straggling line of tall sons and their wives, is a sixth grandchild, Alice Francis, David, Jr.'s fifteen-year-old daughter by his first wife. Mimi, the seventh Francis grandchild as of Christmas 1919, is probably inside the house being watched over by a nanny—Mimi was only four months old.

Mr. and Mrs. David Rowland Francis, Sr., stand in the middle of the family gaggle. Jane Francis, in her sixty-fifth year, looks tired, her face lined and weary. She also looks cold. She is bundled up, with a fur collar pulled up around her cheeks, and frowning, as if she would much rather be in Palm Beach—as she soon would be. Next to her, David Francis stands erect, in a heavy wool coat with a fur collar, holding a cane, his neck rod-straight in a high stiff collar a decade or more out of fashion. His eyes are bright behind his round gold-rimmed glasses, and he is looking straight ahead with confidence, as if proud of what he has done in his sixty-nine years on earth; and sees no earthly reason to doubt that more successes await him.

ANNE FRANCIS CURRIER, who was five when the picture was taken, was born at the Uplands Farm and lived there until she was twelve. She recalled in a 1997 interview with the author that her grandfather had wanted to have all his sons living nearby in the West End, but her father "didn't like to be all that close, so we lived on the farm." Thomas's main business was real estate, but he dabbled in farming.

"My father had a pigpen to the west of the house, and when the west wind blew, it was horrible," she recalled. Since the winds in St. Louis generally blow from the west, it must have been horrible a lot, at least in summer. Thomas, who seems to have inherited at least some of his father's frugality, had arranged for restaurants from the city to truck garbage out to the farm for the pigs.[2]

All his sons were, in one way or another, disappointments to David Rowland Francis, if only because none of them went into politics—or "public service," as Francis called it with a sincerity that only sounded hollow in later, more cynical times. David Francis, like many self-made men, was very demanding of his sons and very critical of them about small matters and over relatively tiny sums of money. Well into David, Jr.'s adulthood, his father continued to bring up something the son had said when he was ten years old (and must have regretted saying ever since). Francis had asked the boy why he had not done something, and David replied "because I did not have to." That "rule of conduct," Francis wrote from Russia in 1917, "always reaps a harvest and that harvest is one of regret if not remorse." David, Jr., was then thirty-eight years old.[3]

Considering the fate of so many of the children of the rich and illustrious, David Francis in reality seems to have been fortunate with how his sons turned out. Three of the six—Perry, David, and Talton—worked for most of their adult lives in the family brokerage firm after graduating from Yale. Perry seems to have assumed quite capably the oldest son's role of head of the family. Francis, Bro. & Co., which grew to deal in real estate as well as stocks, bonds and commodities, continued to prosper under his leadership until his retirement in 1942, when it was sold.

Perry, David, and Talton were all heavy drinkers, according to Talton's daughter, Jane Francis Williams. Their father, on the other hand, she described as "a social drinker only."[4] The young men's drinking may have bothered their father, but in those days a functional alcoholism was common among men in business and professions.

David, Jr., probably disappointed his father in another way—he had been divorced, and he is shown in the Christmas photo with his petite second wife, Nina. David Francis, Sr., abhorred divorce; indeed, the ease with which married couples could break their contract was one of the reasons he often gave for his strong opposition to Bolshevism. Perry later would divorce amid scandal after he ran off with Mimi's best friend, but that came many years after his father had died. David Francis would have been crushed; he adored Mimi.

Independent-minded Tom, who attended Yale but did not graduate, was not much of a success as a gentleman farmer, but by 1919 he had subdivided and sold some of the 125 acres in the original Upland's Farm as suburban St. Louis advanced in that direction. Tom used the profits to fund a soon-prosperous downtown real-estate firm. Francis, Bro. and Co. lent Tom money to build up the business at 6 percent interest.[5]

Only Charles and Sidney were in any sense failures, and only playboy Sidney really could be blamed for his faults. Charles was bright but probably mentally handicapped; at the least, he never seems to have matured emotionally. He was very intelligent—he, too, was a graduate of Yale—but highly impractical. Charles was a lost soul. For most of his life, while his parents were alive, he lived with them, or with his mother when his father was in Russia. He spent some of his life in private sanatoriums in Asheville, N.C., and elsewhere. After the death of his parents, he moved to a small house in the West End, where Mary Comer, his mother's longtime personal maid, cared for him.

David Francis came to accept that Charles would have to be taken care of. In 1916, when he updated his will before leaving for Russia, he set up a trust fund for Charles that would pay him a yearly income in case of Francis's death, noting that Charles "has expressed an unwillingness to engage in mercantile pursuits."[6]

"Uncle Charley was well taken care of by his father," recalled Francis's grandson, Sidney Francis, Jr. "He had an excellent mind. I remember talking with the guy. I used to admire him as a boy because he could tie his shoelaces in about five seconds. He would come up with very sophisticated ideas. But he couldn't get off the dime. They have a name for it today. He never married. I think he was terrified of women."[7]

Sidney, the youngest, was also a Yale dropout: "He got a football injury in his freshman year and didn't stick around" recalled Sidney Francis, Jr. Embracing the Roaring Twenties with Fitzgeraldian passion, Sidney spent money with abandon and astonishing speed, committed flagrant adultery with flappers and showgirls, and fairly quickly abandoned his wife and two children to become the kind of man the St. Louis newspapers referred to as "the globe-trotting son of former Governor David Rowland Francis." For a while, in the late teens and early twenties, Sidney was nominally a salesman in St. Louis and Southern California for the New York Life Insurance Co., of which his father was still a director, but he seems not to have sold many policies. Sidney was a gambler, a luckless oil wildcatter, and an unsuccessful entrepreneur, a man described by his son, embittered for life by his father's desertion of wife and family for the Texas oilfields and another woman, as "a born loser."

His daughter, Emilie (Mimi) Francis Cushman, has kinder memories but said that her father was "never successful, and was always asking his father for money. . . . We were the poorest of the grandchildren."[8]

Within a few weeks of the Christmas picture at Uplands Farm, Jane Francis was on the train for Florida. In January, her husband and Philip Jordan joined her for a few weeks at the Breakers in Palm Beach. By then, she spent most of her winters away from the damp, windy cold of St. Louis and the social requirements of being the wife of a man known variously as "The Governor," "The President," "The Ambassador," and "Our Dave." Jane Francis had no desire to be "Our Jane."

"They had to entertain a lot, being in public life, and my grandmother hated it," recalled granddaughter Mimi Cushman. "She was good at it, but she hated it. She wanted to be left alone with her friends."

Anne Francis Currier remembered her grandmother as "formal and Victorian. . . . She wore big hats. She had a very feminine figure, and she had been a beautiful young woman. . . . She was a strong woman. I think you would have to be with six sons and the father gone all the time." Mrs. Currier said the old people she called Grandma and Grandpa seemed close. They frequently would come out together to the farm for Sunday dinner with her parents. "I always saw her when I saw him," she recalled.[9]

Jane Francis Williams, three years older than Mrs. Currier, recalled that her grandparents fought frequently, and that Jane Francis once got so mad at her husband she kicked him out of bed. Her grandmother was "preoccupied with herself," Mrs. Williams said. "She had little interest in the substance of her husband's work."[10] This latter judgment seems accurate, yet Francis trusted his wife's political acumen and often asked for her opinion on political matters, and she sacrificed much of her own cherished privacy for his career.

IN MAY 1920, Francis gave a free, ten-year lease on the Maryland Avenue mansion to the Boy Scouts and the Junior Chamber of Commerce. Most of the furniture, including many huge Victorian pieces, stayed there. The Francises never again lived in the house they had built and loved, although they occasionally borrowed it back for a large family dinner or party.

As a girl in the 1920s, Theoline Bostwick Francis, the widow of David Francis, III, lived on Taylor Avenue, a block from the mansion. "I remember all the lights being on in that outdoor dance floor they had. My mother would tell me the Francises were having a party."[11] At parties and special Sunday dinners at the mansion, Philip Jordan would preside over the service, although he was clearly more than just a servant. "Philip was very close to both of them," Anne Francis Currier recalled.

Jordan continued to live in his quarters at the mansion, and a city directory of the period lists him as "valet for the Junior Chamber of Commerce."[12] Presumably, Francis had arranged that designation so Jordan could live at the mansion and keep an eye on it. He continued to work for the Francises and to go on trips with his boss, and, thankfully, to write letters home.

In the winter of 1920, as the hoopla built up to the summer's political conventions and fall elections, Missouri Democrats began plumping David Francis for the vice presidency. In response, Francis said, according to the *New York Times,* "I am in no sense a candidate, but if the Democratic Party should nominate me for any office my interest in Democratic success and my sense of party duty would impel me to accept." He also was talked about running for an open Senate seat but said he would not consider that nomination unless he could receive it without opposition, noting that his old friend Breckinridge Long, the eventual nominee, already had announced.[13]

At the state Democratic convention, the party unanimously instructed its delegation to the national convention to vote as a unit for David Francis for vice president. The resolution described Francis as "Missouri's first citizen" and "one of the greatest of Americans, a man who had made a splendid record in every position he has filled."[14] By the time of the national convention, David Francis was one of a half-dozen men mentioned by the *New York Times* and the *Globe-Democrat* as having a shot at second place on the ticket. The favorite for the top of the ticket, and Francis's candidate, was former Secretary of the Treasury William Gibbs McAdoo, Wilson's son-in-law.[15]

On June 21, Francis and Philip Jordan took a train to Kansas City, where they joined two hundred other convention delegates and supporters headed by Governor Fred Gardner, who placed Francis's name in nomination for vice president. In a letter to Talton and Betsey Francis, Philip Jordan vividly described the trip to San Francisco on the Democratic Special with "the most democratic crowd I ever traveled with. . . . They did everything to make it pleasant, no airs or frills of any kind. Just a good old Democratic hound dog crowd . . . who will help to nominate and elect the next Democratic President of this great and free Republic."[16]

In San Francisco, after more than a week of bitter, exhausting intraparty battles that sometimes broke into fistfights, the Democrats nominated, on the forty-fourth ballot, neither McAdoo nor his main opponent, red-chasing Attorney General A. Mitchell Palmer, but a compromise candidate, little-known Wilsonian James M. Cox, the governor of Ohio. By the afternoon of Tuesday, July 6, when the convention reassembled to nominate a vice president, many of the delegates simply wanted to get the business over quickly and go home. David Francis was one of the names placed in nomination; another was Francis Delano Roosevelt, the young assistant secretary of the navy whom Francis had befriended on the trip from France.

Cox let it be known that he preferred running with Roosevelt, and after Governor Al Smith of New York seconded the nomination, indicating support of the Tammany machine, the Roosevelt groundswell grew quickly. The climax came when Francis stood, withdrew his name, and called for the suspension of the rules and the nomination of Roosevelt by acclamation. The result was a shout of "Aye!" that, according to the *Post-Dispatch,* "shook the roof" of the convention hall. Weary, grateful delegates began filing out even before the convention was officially adjourned.[17]

In the subsequent campaign, the Democratic candidates argued forcefully for the League of Nations but lost in a near-landslide to the Republican nominee Warren G. Harding, who ushered in an era of isolationism and unbridled public plundering. Wilsonian liberalism, which David Francis had come to embrace, had died. And the League of Nations, without American participation, was fatally crippled, despite Wilson's prophetic warning that without a strong international assembly that included the United States another world war would occur in only a generation.

WHEN TIME PERMITTED, Francis and Walter Stevens continued working on Francis's Russia memoir, which was published by Scribner's in August of 1921 as *Russia from the American Embassy: April, 1916–November, 1918.*

The book was well reviewed, receiving a full-page encomium in the Sunday *New York Times* book section. The anonymous reviewer described Francis's book as "authoritative" and "as interesting a story as has been written about the revolution" and noted that "Mr. Francis adds considerably to the infamy of the name of John Reed, who in book after book is beginning to emerge as the conspirator who did the most to set Russia against the United States."[18]

The book, which quotes extensively from Francis's letters, is loosely assembled, with many minor errors involving dates or names. It is at times revealing, and even self-deprecating, while at other times repetitious and self-justifying. The memoir is best when it sticks to specifics, such as Francis's haunting description of troops parading outside the foreign office the morning before the November Revolution. It doesn't approach in descriptive power and immediacy John Reed's *Ten Days that Shook the World,* published in 1919, or, for that matter, the letters from Russia of Philip Jordan.

Francis never fully recovered from his illness in Russia and the subsequent operation, and the years began to catch up with him. In early February 1921, as the seventy-year-old ex-governor was getting ready to go to Jefferson City to testify on an appropriations bill for the state university, he slipped in the bathtub and fell and broke two ribs.

That, it turned out, was his last year as a curator of the university he was credited with saving. (He had been named to the board of curators by his sometime foe Governor Joe Folk in 1905.) He began cutting back on the few public activities that remained to him and began thinking about the end of his life. In May 1921, he made a codicil to his will that named his six sons as co-executors of his estate, replacing friends and business associates, and made some detailed provisions involving them in case he should die before Jane. Still, Mimi Cushman recalled, "My grandfather said he was going to live forever. . . . And then he had a stroke."

The first stroke, early in 1922, was relatively minor and left him ambulatory but unable to form some words. This eloquent man found it maddening not to be able to speak clearly, and after St. Louis doctors failed to help him, he and Philip Jordan that summer took the so-called "road to Wellville"; they went to Dr. J. H. Kellogg's famous

Battle Creek Sanitarium in Battle Creek, Michigan, where the regimen was whole grains, cathartic fruits, and frequent enemas. Philip Jordan wrote a half-serious, half-jocular letter to Perry Francis headed, "Two weeks in a Sanitarium or is Cereal a Food?":

> I have been waiting to see if I could see some change in his talking, but I am sorry to tell you that I do not. At times he talks and acts as though he was improving, but then he drops back into the same old rut. . . . I will say this much, if these doctors here at the Sanitarium cannot cure him, no one can. . . .
>
> The other morning when I entered the Governor's room, he looked up at me with a sad look in his eye and said; 'Phil, do they give you meat at your hotel? . . . The Governor has eaten so much cereal that he can spit sawdust. . . . Every morning at seven o'clock all the sick and well are up and out in front. The piano is playing and a physical instructor takes you through different kinds of exercises for thirty minutes. All are supposed to be up at seven, but I guess you have a picture of the Governor doing stunts of this kind at that hour in the morning—in other words, you can drive a horse to water, but you can't make him drink.[19]

There was a golf course nearby, and Francis found some golf cronies, men his age or older. They included retired General Nelson Miles, a renowned Indian fighter in his eighties whom Francis had met at the World's Fair. "No Smoking" signs were posted throughout the sanitarium, and one day, Jordan noted, "The Governor was all dressed for golf and one of his friends said, 'Well, Governor, are you going for a game of golf?' The Governor whispered to him—'No, I am going for a smoke.'"

After Battle Creek, which did nothing to alleviate Francis's speech impediment, Jordan and the Francises spent most of the rest of the summer at Rye Beach. When Jane and David Francis returned to St. Louis in the fall, they lived in a new apartment, across Lindell Boulevard from the old one, in the brand new Chase Apartments, 4931 Lindell. But the couple, particularly Jane Francis, whose respiratory problems grew worse and who also suffered from high blood pressure, spent less and less time in miasmic St. Louis, heading south for the winter, and to the seashore or the dry Southwest for the summer. In the winter of 1923, the Francises went to San Antonio, where they stayed for almost three months.

During the previous year's visit to Battle Creek, Francis had befriended fellow stroke victim Robert Kleberg, who had married into the family that owned the King Ranch—at about eight hundred thousand acres, the largest in the world. Kleberg had run the ranch for many years before his stroke; now his son ran it. At the invitation of the elder Kleberg, Francis and Jordan took the train from San Antonio south to Kingsville, where they were met and driven to the ranch house, or "the villa" as it was called. They stayed in two of the twenty-five guest rooms and spent two days being driven around the place by a skillful if lead-footed Mexican chauffeur, trailing thick clouds of South Texas dust as Kleberg pointed out antelope, white-tailed deer, coveys of quail, herds of cattle—the ranch held one hundred thousand—and vast fields of cotton.

At one point, Kleberg grabbed his rifle and shot a rattlesnake in the middle of the road, knocking it two feet in the air. Kleberg said rattlesnakes, which attacked cattle, had gotten so thick on the ranch one year that he had armed all two hundred of his ranch hands and in eight months they had killed ten thousand of them.

"Think of it!" Jordan wryly remarked later. "And these are prohibition times."

All in all, Jordan decided, the ranch was "the most wonderful sight I ever saw."

Jane and David Francis and Philip Jordan returned to St. Louis at the end of April, planning on staying for a few weeks and then heading for what Jordan described as "one of the most delightful places on the face of the earth"—Rye Beach.[20]

However, for Jordan and Francis, there was a brief and bizarre detour. No sooner had they arrived home than Francis, whose difficulties with speech increased, decided to head right back to Texas and try a sanitarium he had heard about. It was operated by a Dr. Snyder in Glen Rose, about eighty miles from Waco.

After an overnight trip from Missouri deep into Texas on a Pullman car, Bart Moore, an old friend of Francis, met Jordan and Francis at the railroad station and drove them to the Raleigh Hotel. Francis registered and told the clerk he also wanted a room for his "colored valet."

The clerk replied, "I'm very sorry but you know this is Texas, and the South. We do not allow colored people to stop at this hotel, but I will see that your man is well taken care of. Aunt Mary who had a house up the road will fix him up."

"Aunt Mary" said her bedrooms were full, but she could put a cot in a front room for him. It was Saturday night, and a party got started about 11 P.M. and lasted until five in the morning. The landlady charged Jordan $2.50 for, he wrote, "keeping me awake all night."

In Waco, Jordan discovered, the locals "had just finished burning a colored man alive on the public square. . . . I don't know whether this was put on for my special benefit or not. . . . They seemed to take great pride in it, because twice while riding around the city with white men the spot was pointed out to me as this 'Place where we burned the nigger.'"[21]

The next morning, Moore drove Francis and Jordan to Glen Rose, a town of 250, and to the sanitarium, which was packed with patients. On his own, curious as usual, Jordan wandered around the grounds, talking to patients. At about 9 P.M., he rejoined Francis and Moore. At 9:30, Francis said, "Phil, Mr. Moore and I are going to bed. Where are you going to sleep?"

Jordan was astonished. He said, "Governor, do you mean to tell me that you have brought me out here in this God's forsaken country and made no provisions for me to sleep?"

Dr. Snyder, the superintendent, walked by, and Francis said, "Doctor, have you a place where my man can sleep?"

All the rooms were taken, the doctor said, but Jordan could sleep in his office. "Tomorrow, I'll find a place for him."

The next morning, after a restless night, Jordan was again "out mingling with the people. . . . We talked about different things. They all seemed to think I was a human being. No one seemed to be afraid of me. We talked and talked for hours. I discovered to my great sorrow that the Governor was also doing some talking. He told them that I started to work for him 34 years ago. He also told them that I had traveled all over the world with him. He also told them that he had spent three years in Russia. Some one asked him what was my nationality. He said, 'He is a colored man.'"

Jordan wrote:

> Well, that was the same as putting a bomb in a furnace, it took only a short time to circulate through the crowd. The ones I had been talking with began to pull away as though I had smallpox. . . .
> Mr. Moore . . . told me some awful things about that part of the world that we up [St. Louis] way never heard about. He said, 'Phil, I don't want to frighten you, but I shall never forget the evening I passed this road. I saw four colored men hanging from that large tree.' This was no ghost story because I found out later that it was the gospel truth.

Such furor erupted over a black man being on the premises that Dr. Snyder told Jordan he had better sleep in his office again. At about 11 P.M., Jordan was outside the office smoking a cigar when the doctor passed. Jordan said, "Doctor, I have made up my mind that I am going to leave here in the morning."

Dr. Snyder agreed with alacrity. He said, "Phil, the Governor has made a big mistake in saying anything about you being a colored man. I have been here for over twenty years and I know these people as well as any one. If they get started all Hell cannot stop them."

Jordan lay awake all night. "I thought a million things a minute. I began to think, what if the mob should come to the sanitarium to get me . . . all at once it occurred to me if they should come I would get up dress join them and help them look for the 'nigger.'"

The next morning, Jordan went to Francis and told him he was leaving on the first train. Francis's friend Moore said, "Phil, you are using good judgment." But Francis said he wanted Jordan to stay. "Don't be afraid," he said. "No one is going to hurt you."

"I'm sure they won't if I can get away before they do it," replied Jordan.

Francis kept insisting, and finally Jordan said, "Governor, I will put it to you like this. What would you rather say? 'There he goes or there he hangs?'"

"If you feel that way about it," Francis said with a sigh, still not completely getting it, "you better go."

Moore drove Jordan to the nearest train station and put him on the train for Waco and St. Louis. "I came out of Glen Rose like a bat out of the lower regions," he remarked.

Back home, he reflected on the incident and remarked, "I have traveled in all the principal cities of the south, but always find it hard to do what is right." To many white people, Jordan did not appear to be African American, and that made "doing right" even more difficult. He recalled being in Jacksonville, Florida, and taking a ride on a street-car. A sign labeled the rear seats "For Niggers." He walked to the rear and sat next to a black lady. The conductor tapped him on the shoulder and told him he would have to move because "those seats are for niggers."

Jordan said, "That's all right, I would just as soon ride with a negro as a white person," but the conductor insisted that he move. In conclusion, he wrote, "If I was given from Palm Beach, Florida, to San Antonio, Texas, I would not live in the south."

The Glen Rose sanitarium failed to help Francis's speech, which continued to deteriorate, and he was deeply embarrassed by his inability to articulate clearly. At one point, he sought the help of Emile Coue, the French psychologist whose theories of "auto suggestion" were popular in the United States in the 1920s. Coue famously contended that all sorts of benefits could come if a person frequently repeated the phrase "Day by day, in every way, I am getting better and better." He could do nothing to improve the halting speech of David Francis.[22]

In early February 1924, David and Jane Francis, Charles Francis, and Philip Jordan again fled the St. Louis cold and damp for San Antonio. They planned on staying for three months at an apartment they had rented at 122 East French Place. On the evening of Thursday, March 20, Jane had a heart attack and died. She was sixty-nine years old.

David and Charles Francis and Philip Jordan left San Antonio the next night on the train that carried Mrs. Francis back to St. Louis. The house at 4421 Maryland Avenue was opened for the funeral, which was held March 22 and presided over by an Episcopal priest. Mrs. Francis then was taken to Bellefontaine Cemetery, where many prominent St. Louisans were buried. She was the first person buried in the large family plot. With the temperature near freezing, the gravediggers had to break through snow and icy earth. Eight inches of snow had fallen in St. Louis the day Jane Francis died in San Antonio.

Jane Francis passed on to her sons an income-yielding trust fund from her father containing stocks and bonds worth roughly two hundred thousand dollars. Each also received through her will between ten and fifteen thousand dollars. And she left fifteen hundred dollars to her maid, Mary Comer, and one hundred dollars each to Philip Jordan and caretaker James Riney.[23]

Francis commissioned a memorial statue of his wife from World's Fair sculptor George Julian Zolnay, who had done a bust of Francis for the Missouri Historical Society and an ornamental drinking fountain for Francis Field, as well as the Kentucky pioneer piece that Francis had presented to his hometown of Richmond, Kentucky, in 1906.

Probably at Francis's suggestion, Zolnay created a life-sized, shrouded dark bronze figure of a woman, bending forward on her stone seat, hands clasped in her lap, as if in mourning. The piece was completed in 1925 and installed in a high granite niche, embossed with a Celtic cross, at the rear of the family plot. Stone benches curve out from either side of the figure.

The sculptor, who now lived in Washington, D.C., clearly had been influenced by the famous Augustus Saint Gaudens statue of a cloaked woman in Rock Creek Cemetery in Washington. Writer-scholar Henry Adams had commissioned that piece for his late wife after she committed suicide. Completed in 1891, it touched a chord in many people and quickly became well known. After his death in 1918, Adams was buried next to his wife under the statue's sad and brooding gaze.

Francis greatly admired the autobiographical *The Education of Henry Adams,* with its perceptive and sometimes biting commentary on the St. Louis World's Fair, and had recommended it to Jane after he read it in 1919. Over the years, he would have had many opportunities to see and contemplate the statue of which Mark Twain once said, "All human grief is shown in this sad figure."[24]

After Jane Francis died, her husband and son Charles moved into a large two-story brick house at 6464 Ellenwood Avenue, a few blocks west of Forest Park. The house, built in 1912, was in Clayton, the seat of St. Louis County. It was remodeled to provide for a man who was becoming frail with age. Mrs. Francis's maid, Mary Comer, moved in. Philip Jordan was there every day, although there is no record of him living there. The house was a block south of Washington University, on the site of forestry exhibits and just east of a former Indian encampment at the World's Fair.[25]

In May 1924, for the first time, Francis missed the semi-annual meeting of the directors of the DRF Realty and Investment Co. Perry, the vice president, presided. That summer, although Francis was "in very poor physical condition" according to a political friend, he went to New York to watch the Democratic National Convention, which seesawed between wet and dry candidates for 104 ballots before choosing a compromise, corporation lawyer John W. Davis, who would lose badly to Vice President Calvin Coolidge in the general election.[26]

In October, Francis felt well enough to go East again and visit the new headquarters of the New York Stock Exchange on Wall Street.[27] But he was increasingly an invalid and seems to have suffered more small strokes. The family hired a male nurse. By 1926, according to his granddaughter Anne Currier, "He had nurses around him 24 hours a day." Francis essentially was bedridden for the last year of his life.

By early January 1927, he clearly was slipping away. Five of his sons and Philip Jordan were at the bedside at 6:10 P.M., Saturday, January 15, a bitterly cold day, when the seventy-six-year-old patriarch took his last breath. Sidney was in California but made it back to St. Louis in time for the funeral on the morning of Tuesday, January 18. Telegrams of condolence came in from across the country, from senators and congressmen and ambassadors and the heads of major national corporations, and from the widow of Woodrow Wilson.

In a long eulogy, the *Globe-Democrat* reached all the way back to the 1888 Democratic National Convention, when forty thousand men marched through the downtown streets in a torchlight parade:

Near its head, welcomed with roaring local cheers as it passed, was an open carriage arched over with rockets above and framed with other blazing fireworks below. From hotel doorways and windows and sidewalks, crowded with thousands of strangers, there was an eager craning of necks for a glimpse of the face and figure of the 'Boy Mayor of St. Louis' . . . about whom much had even then been heard.

In the city he loved and which he saw gather to itself mighty forces from a time of small beginnings, this 'Boy Mayor'—how queer the title must seem to those of this generation—has come, full of years, to the end of a life spanning some of the most interesting and satisfying experiences that can come to a member of the human family. The figures in our national affairs then who . . . saw him for the first time were destined to see much more of him later. . . . Political wise men said that . . . he inevitably would some day be President . . . it is hard to visualize to this generation of St. Louisans the prepossessing, intensely popular and even dashing and gallant figure Governor Francis was to a multitude of his contemporaries . . . the city which seemed to many the poorer because of the infirmities that fell upon his declining years will seem still the poorer because of his death.[28]

The old Francis mansion was opened for the service. The *Post-Dispatch* wrote:

The body of Governor Francis was taken to the house at 7:30 from his recent home at 6464 Ellenwood avenue. . . . An hour later, automobiles began to enter the gate on Newstead Avenue, and to leave their passengers at the doorway where presidents and foreign potentates were received in bygone days. . . . Within, the pillared hallway was hung with wreath upon wreath of roses and floral coverings hid the railings of the central staircase. To the left, in the long south parlor, the roses were mingled with lilies, and at the west end of the room stood the [open] casket.[29]

Two Presbyterian ministers conducted the funeral service. The six sons were pallbearers. More than one hundred honorary pallbearers included dozens of business and political leaders, five former and current mayors and governors, former and current presidents and directors of the Merchants' Exchange, ten surviving directors of the World's Fair, representatives of Washington University, Missouri University, and the Missouri Historical Society, the Catholic archbishop and Episcopal bishop of St. Louis, and a prominent rabbi.

After the service, a procession of thirty-five automobiles drove north three miles on Kingshighway to Bellefontaine Cemetery, where David Francis was buried next to his wife, beneath the hovering bronze figure of a shrouded woman bent over with the heavy pain of mourning.

Three and a half months later, on the twenty-third anniversary of the opening of the World's Fair, the annual meeting of the Missouri Historical Society was held at the

Jefferson Memorial in Forest Park. The meeting was devoted mainly to honoring David Rowland Francis.

The main address was delivered by U.S. Senator Harry B. Hawes, an old friend and political ally of Francis who had also come to Missouri from the hardscrabble hills of Kentucky. Hawes, an elegant, eloquent man, recalled in a flowery speech:

> Governor Francis enjoyed a cigar, a horse, a drink; delighted in a bright eye, a pretty face; responded to a good song, a good story, and a good friend. . . . He knew by first name more men than any other man in the city and more men knew him and called him 'Dave.' . . . When the ball game was opened, he was there; when a school was dedicated he spoke; when a park was opened he presided; when a new Union Station was needed, he led the way; when a bridge was required, he made the plan. He built the very hall in which we are assembled tonight. . . .
>
> Francis attended the wedding; he kissed and danced with the bride; he sent the silver spoon or cup to the baby; he acted as pallbearer and followed the friend's body to the grave. . . . Rarely did he go out alone. He loved companionship. When he moved or visited, he was usually in company with two or three companions. He drew attention and held it; he made other people do things under his inspiration who were unaware of the fact that he had caused them to act. . . . As one of our papers editorially expressed it, he was 'our most distinguished St. Louisan.' . . .

Hawes made much of Francis's Scotch-Irish toughness and pride, the legacy of "men who fought for liberty, for tolerance, for local government in the crags and mountains of Scotland." But Francis, Hawes said, also had a gentler, more cultured side: "He, like Jefferson, was fond of music, of the dance, of literature, fine paintings, fine horses, courageous men and amiable women. He liked children, and the children all loved him. . . ."

Francis, Hawes said, "a big man who had big conceptions, surrounded himself with big men and did big things." He briefly but effusively praised Francis for creating the World's Fair, "an awakening of the spirit of the city to do better things." Hawes said, "I will not detain you with an extended discussion of that event. Suffice it to say he invited the nation and the nation came; he invited the world, and the world came."[30]

Epilogue

D AVID FRANCIS ONCE TOLD HIS WIFE, "I have never had the ambition to leave a large fortune to my sons as I have grave doubts as to whether it would prove beneficial to them. A man reared in luxury or accustomed to rich environments does not feel the spirit of necessity of effort, and this is particularly so if he is not saturated with the desire or ambition to succeed."[1]

As it turned out, Francis did leave his sons a sizable estate—about half a million dollars apiece, the equivalent of almost $5 million in the year 2001. Despite his pessimism, most of them accepted the responsibility of preserving their legacy, at least the monetary one. Four of the six worked hard most of their lives and did well financially. Charles's share of the estate was left in trust, and he received a monthly stipend. Only Sidney could be considered a wastrel.[2]

Shortly before he died, Francis told his sons that he wanted Philip Jordan to have a two-family flat owned by the Francis realty and investment company. The brick duplex, at 4251/4253 West Belle Place in a pleasant lower-middle-class neighborhood many African Americans had moved into after the war, was valued at about eight thousand dollars, and after the sons deeded it to Jordan he rented it out for income. The sons also followed through on Francis's request that they make sure that two other longtime family employees, caretaker James Riney and maid Mary Comer, had enough money to live on.

Sidney Francis, his wife, and two small children lived at the Ellenwood house for about a year—"We were looking for a roof," Sidney, Jr., said—and then, after the funds were distributed, they moved back to California. Sidney soon headed off for the Texas oil fields.

Tom and his family moved to 6464 Ellenwood and lived there for many years. The other four sons also stayed in St. Louis for most of their lives, although Perry and Talton left for warmer climes upon retirement.

By the end of the twentieth century only three direct descendents of David R. Francis still lived in St. Louis: Tom's daughter, Anne Francis Currier; her son, Thomas Currier; and Diana Francis, Tom's granddaughter. But his name is spread across the city, on the names of streets, at Francis Park, and on the campus of Washington University at Francis Field and Francis Gymnasium. The fundraising arm of St. Louis 2004, formed to promote civic activities on the one hundredth anniversary of the Fair (St. Louisans take their century-old World's Fair very seriously) is called the David R. Francis Society. And his presence is ubiquitous in the buildings of the Missouri Historical Society, which recently underwent a $30 million renovation and expansion. The building he dedicated to the memory of Thomas Jefferson now serves as the city's History Museum. It sits just to the east of the now-grassy site of the old Plaza of St. Louis, where in the spring of 1904 one hundred thousand people stood and cheered as David Francis pressed a golden key.

AFTER HIS FATHER DIED, Perry Francis bought a magnificent mansion at 20 Portland Place, in an elegant conclave of private streets west of Kingshighway and north of Forest Park. Jordan soon moved to the mansion. Anne Francis Currier recalled, "Philip took care of uncle Perry Francis after the Governor died. He took care of everybody."[3]

Over the years, including the period in Russia, Jordan regularly had put money into a savings account. Francis also appears to have left a small trust fund for his servant and friend.[4] So Jordan had a good steady income in addition to free room and board in the carriage house of one of the city's most elegant mansions. In later years he had his own stationery, with "Philip Jordan 20 Portland Place Saint Louis Missouri" across the top.

Jordan turned sixty in 1929, and he undoubtedly could have retired and lived quite well. But the bonds between Jordan and the Francis family were unbreakable, and he continued to work for Perry Francis for the rest of his life—he "took care of Perry" until he was too ill to work, and then Perry took care of him.

In the fall of 1930 Jordan chauffeured some family members on a long trip through the West. On the way home, Jordan took a short detour to Jefferson City so he could visit his aunt Emily. Jordan took time to make a lone pilgrimage to his old haunts and to reflect on his early years. Afterward, he wrote to his aunt:

> After leaving your house I walked to High and Madison streets and I found John standing on the same old corner where I left him standing thirty years ago. That was the old stomping grounds of all the gang. We all would stand on that corner for hours waiting for Duek [Duke] Diggs to come by and load us in his moving van and take us some place to move a piano so that we could have enough money to rush the can [get drunk]. I guess this does not sound so good to you, especially during these prohibition times, but Aunt Emily, those were the happy days. . . . I thought to myself after all it is best to have been born in Hog Alley, than not to have been born at all. . . . I drank for fifteen years from one end of Hog Alley to the other, and I also fought from one end to the other.
>
> I fought Herman Smith from the Center [of town] up to Madison Street, but I was successful in whipping him with the assistance of a brick. I also fought Grip, a gambler, who I caught trying to get away with a card in a game of poker. After the fight we shook hands and he told me that I gave him the

best fight he ever had. No he did not whip me, but he tied me. Sheep Head and I fought Gus Morelock and about twenty others in Nick Grisehammers saloon but I gave him the best whipping he ever had. And Aunt Emily it must be fresh in the minds of all that memorial [sic] battle that was fought by me down at the base ball park, where I whipped the bully of the town, Less Miller. Yes Aunt Emily, those were the happy days. Thirty years ago no man or woman ever walked the streets or the mud of Hog Alley that had anything on me when it came to drinking or fighting.

I do not know anything that the City of Jefferson could do that would be more fitting than to erect a monument to me, standing at the head of Hog Alley with outstretched arms with a can of beer in one hand and a bottle of Old Crow in the other, at the base reading something like this: This monument was erected to the memory of Philip Jordan, a pretty good fighter and the best drinker in Jefferson. . . . I am proud of my record—I never lost a fight in Hog Alley, and thirty years ago we did some fighting in Hog Alley.[5]

In late 1940 or early 1941, Jordan moved to Santa Barbara with Perry Francis, who had divorced Mimi and married her former best friend. By then, Jordan had been suffering from cancer for several years, and two years earlier his cancer-ridden right kidney had been removed. On May 20, 1941, at the age of seventy-three, he died. A long obituary in the *Post-Dispatch* noted that he had served four presidents at the Maryland Avenue mansion, had accompanied Francis to Russia, and after Francis "suffered a breakdown from which he never recovered," had nursed him on the "midwinter journey home . . . into the Arctic Circle—farther North, Jordan used to say, than any other member of his race had gone, except the man who had accompanied Rear Admiral Peary to the North Pole."

The Francis family, the obituary noted, "still has a plaster cast of Governor Francis on the golf links, made by George Julian Zolnay, in which the carefully executed figure of Philip Jordan appears, the valet kneeling to tee up the ball."[6]

IN HIS 1927 EULOGY, Senator Harry Hawes said, "David Francis's contribution to American history will be written later, but even now we know it will be a chapter of American courage."[7] Indeed, Francis emerged from World War I much more a hero than a goat.

But in the 1930s, perhaps in part because of the leftward movement of American thought during the Great Depression, Francis's reputation plummeted. The first major blow was struck in 1932 by R. H. Bruce Lockhart in his *Memoirs of a British Agent,* which was very popular in this country as a book and in the 1934 movie version. Lubyanka prison had helped Lockhart come around to Francis's point of view on the Bolsheviks. But, as we have seen, he described Francis as "a charming old gentleman of nearly 80" who understood little about the Russian political situation.

In 1935, William Thompson's biographer, Herman Hagedorn, dismissed Francis as "not-too-wide awake," an "aging and amiable Missourian" with a "childlike trust" in the "discretion" of "his French teacher." Francis, Hagedorn opined, was "filled with good intentions, but no one looked to him for vision or initiative."[8]

David Loth, in *Woodrow Wilson: The Fifteenth Point,* published in 1941, described Francis as "one of the accidents of Missouri politics, chiefly remarkable for an impervious shell of complacency, [who] went through the greatest upheaval in more than a century without a single mark on the shining blankness of his mind."[9]

In 1954, Robert Warth, in *The Allies and the Russian Revolution,"* called Francis "Babbitry personified." Warth made references to poker and spittoons and Francis's "philistine nature" that suggest he, like other historians of America's presence in revolutionary Russia, depended upon Bruce Lockhart for much of his information.[10]

In 1956, George Kennan weighed in with a balanced view that was informed by a careful examination of the record, including thousands of pages of documents in the Francis collection at the Missouri Historical Society. In *Russia Leaves the War,* the Pulitzer Prize–winning first volume of his two-volume *Soviet-American Relations, 1917–1920,* Kennan wrote that it had been an "injustice" to Francis to send him to Russia considering his age and lack of diplomatic experience and added:

> One could wish for Francis's own sake that he had been withdrawn betimes to the quiet old age he deserved, and that the post had either been given to a younger man of superior education and foreign experience or left in the hands of a career charge d'affaires. But once there, he had to 'make do' with the qualities he possessed; and this, it must be acknowledged, he did—with courage and enthusiasm. It is difficult to retrace the old gentleman's adventures and activities in the first months of Soviet power—to note his stormy reactions, his vigorous opinions, his maneuverings among his impetuous associates, and even his frequent vacillations—without being moved to sympathy for him in his unexpected and unprecedented position, and to respect for the fidelity he showed to the standards and obligations he knew and for his courageous persistence in the face of much frustration and adversity.

Kennan, a professional diplomat, had his own fights with political appointees in diplomatic posts, yet he, a generous man in most of his assessments, seemed willing to give Francis the benefit of the doubt. Kennan was also generous in his assessment of the de Cramm affair, suggesting that those around Francis should have been more sympathetic to the understandable loneliness that caused an elderly man far from home and family to seek the friendship of a cultured and attractive woman.[11]

The de Cramm relationship has been a focus of many historians, who generally portray Francis as a foolish old man acting unprofessionally because of his crush on a bright, attractive younger woman. And there is no question, no matter what his relationship with Madame de Cramm really was, and no matter what relationship, if any, she had with the German government, that he was foolish and unprofessional with respect to her.

In 1962, Christopher Lasch published *The American Liberals and the Russian Revolution,* a detailed account of the ways wishful thinking led many American intellectuals, journalists, and even internationalist business leaders like Thompson to trust the Bolsheviks and see them as heroes in the war against Tsarist tyranny, failing to perceive that Bolshevism itself was "a form of tyranny."

"The Bolsheviks," Lasch wrote, "were constantly characterized in America as idealistic to the point of fanaticism; as doctrinaire, impractical, irresponsible, naive," not, "as we would speak of them, forceful, ruthless and imperious, fanatical only in their willingness to apply on a grand scale the philosophy that the end justifies the means."[12] But Lasch's seminal book is about the wrongness of Francis's critics and enemies, not Francis's rightness.

Harsh criticism of Francis continued through the Vietnam era, when one historian described Francis as a "wealthy hack dating from Cleveland's time [who] remained hopelessly befuddled" throughout the revolutionary period.[13]

The image of Francis as a naive and boorish bumbler, a man seriously out of his depth and too old and confused to notice that he was drowning, persisted through the 1980s. A striking demonstration of the pervasiveness of anti-Francis sentiment comes from Robert Chadwell Williams in his introduction to a 1985 collection of Francis's diplomatic papers. Williams wrote, "David R. Francis was a man too large for his times and too small for his job" and called Francis "an overfed American who much preferred golf, cigars, whiskey, cards and his portable cuspidor to the responsibilities of diplomatic office."[14]

In 1991, in a biography of Raymond Robins, Neil V. Salzman dug up a particularly scathing, previously unpublished quote from decades earlier. A Red Cross official in Russia with Robins had called Francis "a stuffed shirt, a dumb head who never found out what the whole thing was all about. He leaned on everybody, keenly enjoying his authority, while spies slipped in and out under his nose and diplomats made a monkey of him."[15]

By the time of Salzman's book, however, a reassessment was already underway, one that took on momentum as the Soviet Union came apart. The end of the Cold War took the bitter edge off the doctrinaire disputes of the past three-quarters of a century and made it easier for liberal, as well as neo-conservative historians, to take a more realistic look at the Bolshevik era. It quickly became clear to all but the most resolute left-leaning historians that many of the excesses of the Bolsheviks had their roots in the rule of Lenin. And documents released in the early 1990s showed the truth of what Francis long had contended: Lenin received millions of rubles and other aid from the Germans even as he was acting principally in pursuit of his own dream of world revolution.[16]

In *Alternative Paths: Soviets and Americans, 1917–1920,* published in 1993, David W. McFadden wrote at length, generally favorably, about Francis in relationship to Raymond Robins. McFadden rebutted, on the basis of the "voluminous" correspondence between Francis and Washington, the "common belief about Francis is that he was cut off from information and knowledge about Soviet society and the process of revolutionary change around him, thus somehow trapped in an unhealthy reliance on Robins and his access." McFadden noted, "The materials in the Francis papers also dispute that contention. The papers are full of information from all manner of sources concerning Bolshevik government and Russian life and society, including translations of all key articles from *Pravda*, the *Bulletin of the Bolshevik Central Executive Committee*, the Council of Workers' and Soldiers' Deputies, and non-Bolshevik newspapers. . . . The Francis papers . . . show Francis trying to maintain a dual policy of contact (Robins) and hostility (Summers)."[17]

Historian David S. Foglesong thoroughly reassessed Francis's Russia years in his writings of the early to mid-1990s. Foglesong wrote in a 1992 article on Francis in Russia:

> A careful review of the available evidence suggests the need to revise the common image of Ambassador Francis as a doddering, diplomatic dilettante. From the abdication of the tsar to Kornilov's abortive revolt against Kerensky, Francis performed creditably in Petrograd. His vigorous, dedicated efforts to support the Provisional Government in its first months earned him the respect of many Russian liberals and the admiration of most American diplomats in Russia. Although he never opened communication with leaders in the Soviet of Workers' and Soldiers' Deputies, he showed considerable flexibility in adapting to the repeated changes in the composition of the Provisional Government, and he worked effectively with the moderate socialist Kerensky.
>
> While some United States representatives were influenced by their connections to Russian aristocrats, Francis had only a few acquaintances in Russian high society, and he did not blindly adopt their views. Like most American and Allied officials in Russia, Francis believed that strong measures were needed to suppress anti-war agitation, yet he did not succumb to the extreme pessimism and reactionary sentiment displayed by many of his colleagues.
>
> On balance, then, it seems doubtful that American interests would have been represented much more effectively by other United States diplomats in Russia or by any of the other men whom Wilson considered for the post of Ambassador.[18]

Foglesong expanded on this theme in his 1995 book *America's Secret War Against Bolshevism*. Although Foglesong noted that Francis was not always "as bold and devious as he liked to make out," he portrayed him as a wily politician, not afraid to make crucial decisions in the Wilsonian vacuum. He showed Francis secretly but busily running spies in both the south and the north of Russia, wielding his limited power skillfully to prevent a right-wing takeover of Archangel, and in general shrewdly playing a complicated, subtle, serious, and at times dangerous game whose rules constantly shifted.[19]

To Alexander Vladimirovich Bykov of Vologda, Russia, David Rowland Francis is a hero. Bykov is among a group of relatively young Russian historians in Vologda, St. Petersburg, and Moscow who view with favor the attempts of Francis and other American and Allied diplomats and agents to subvert the Bolsheviks. These scholars' main regret, if not criticism, is that the Allies would not go further. "The only way to stop the Bolsheviks was to kill Lenin and Trotsky," says Bykov. "And Francis was too much of a democrat to do that."[20]

In 1993, as opportunities for entrepreneurs opened up in Russia, and as government paychecks began to arrive later and later, if at all, Bykov quit his job as a history professor at a Vologda teacher's college and opened a small business to print academic papers and books.

Growing up in Vologda, he also had grown up with the legend of the days at the end of the First World War when Vologda was the diplomatic capital of Russia, and he had become the local authority on the period. With sadness, he had watched the old embassy building, on a wide, busy thoroughfare in this bustling little city, deteriorate over the years.

Bykov worked out a deal with the regional government, which owned the dilapidated wooden building and had designated it a historic landmark, to move his printing business into several of the rooms and renovate all of it. His dream was a museum devoted to David Francis and the other Allied diplomats, a museum that would form the basis for a center devoted to Russian-American friendship.

Along with Vologda's deserved reputation as a center of lace-making and the several dozen striking onion-domed churches that had survived the Stalin era, the museum and center, he believed, would make the city of three hundred thousand attractive to tourists, academics, and conference planners. It was a heady dream, similar, he realized, to one David Francis had dreamed a century earlier to promote another city in danger of becoming a forgotten backwater.

Bykov, his five employees, and some outside workers began restoring the building room by room. By the summer of 1997, when I visited Vologda, Bykov had twenty-eight employees, and about two-thirds of the building had been restored. On the second floor in the rear, overlooking the courtyard guarded by a shepherd dog named Francis, Bykov had created a replica of the ambassador's office, with a heavy wooden desk, a green-shaded desk lamp, and a photograph of Francis on the wall.

Downstairs was the printing business and a handsome little museum that featured framed documents, including telegrams to and from Francis and a monthly expense report in the hand of Philip Jordan, photographs of Francis and the Allied diplomats, and other memorabilia. Bykov collected much of the material the year before on a visit to St. Louis, where I had first met him.

Bykov and local and regional officials had hoped that the American ambassador, Thomas R. Pickering, would be able to attend the opening, but Secretary of State Madeleine Albright had chosen that day to visit Moscow. The ambassador sent his regrets. (A year later, new U.S. Ambassador James F. Collins made amends by coming to Vologda for a conference on the Allied diplomatic period.)

On July 16, 1997, at 6 P.M., six hours before sunset, a writer from St. Louis and his wife were the closest things to official American representatives on the premises when a few dozen people gathered at the old clubhouse for the official opening of the Museum of the Diplomatic Corps. Speeches were made extolling Vologda and the Herculean efforts of Alexander Bykov, and champagne toasts were exchanged among Russian officials and historians and prominent citizens of Vologda. At Bykov's request, I spoke, quite briefly, partly in Russian, noting that only after meeting Bykov had I come to fully understand how important Vologda had been in the life of David Francis and in the warm if sometimes troubled friendship between the American and Russian peoples.

The main speaker, of course, was Alexander Bykov, who described David Francis in terms that would have been considered treasonous a few years before: "He was a friend of the Russian people, but an enemy of the Bolsheviks."

Bykov and I spoke for many hours over the next few days, often with translation from his assistant, Marina Barandina. After I returned to St. Louis from my Russian research excursion, we stayed in touch by e-mail. Bykov's admiration for David Francis was almost unbounded; he described him at one point as "a person of great vitality, high morality and decency" and added that "these personal peculiarities" in a diplomat may have baffled many of his contemporaries. In light of present knowledge, he said, historians have every reason to see Francis as "a fair politician and a sincere friend of common Russian people, whose interests he always tried to take into account."

Some of the documents Bykov and his colleagues, Vologda historians Leonid Panov and Alexander Bulanov, are researching come from the massive files of the local security police, the FSB. That's the new name of the KGB, although most Russians tend to use the old acronym. Indeed, a sign of the times was the presence at the opening ceremonies of a friendly young man who was introduced, with a grin, as "the public relations man from the KGB."

Bykov, who continues to assemble his portrait of Vologda in 1918, remains convinced that Francis, the embassy, and the National City Bank of New York were even more active in funding and otherwise supporting anti-Bolshevik activities than even the revisionist post–Cold War historians of the mid- and late 1990s realized. "Francis was involved in counter-revolutionary activities," Bykov said, in a typically romantic statement, "because he loved the Russian people and wanted to help them get rid of the Bolsheviks."

I asked him if his research had led him to any conclusion about whether or not Madame de Cramm had been a German spy. "I don't think she was," he said, and then the deep, sad smile that would emerge from time to time crept over his round face. "But it was a lovely story. I think he loved her. I think he cared about her personal problems." He sighed. "But his relationship with Matilda broke his reputation with the State Department." Francis, Bykov added, "was a decent person who, when his close friends needed help, did not think of his career."

And what about remarks by Bruce Lockhart and others that Francis knew very little about the Russian political situation?

"Francis knew about our political parties equal with other diplomats," Bykov said. "Nobody in 1917 or 1918 knew the specifics of the political situations in Russia. Changes came so quickly. In July of 1917, Kerensky is a national hero. In December, he is a zero."

"Today we can suppose what we want," he said, "but at the time David Francis was searching for a gray cat in a dark room."

Acknowledgments

Thanks to:

Lee Sandweiss, Matthew Heidenry, Duane Sneddeker, and the staff of the Library and Research Center of the Missouri Historical Society, repository of the papers of David R. Francis.

Charles C. Hays, III, and his colleagues at the Special Collections and Archives at Eastern Kentucky University.

Staff of the National Archives in Washington, D.C., and at College Park.

The Library of Congress, in particular the staff of Manuscripts, Prints and Photographs; Newspapers and Current Periodicals; and the reference librarians in the Reading Room.

The St. Louis Public Library, particularly the staff of the History and Genealogy section.

Pius XII Memorial Library at Saint Louis University.

Staff of the archives and special collections at the university libraries of Chicago, Columbia (Rare Book and Manuscript Library and Oral History Research Office), Georgetown, Missouri (Western Historical Manuscript Collection), Princeton (Seeley G. Mudd Manuscript Library), Saint Louis University, Yale, University of California at Berkeley, and Washington University.

Archivists at New York Life Insurance and Citibank.

Alexander Bykov and his colleagues, with special thanks to Marina Barandina, for their help and hospitality in Vologda; former First Lady, now Senator Jean Carnahan and Missouri State Archivist Ken Winn for their help and hospitality in Jefferson City.

Anne Francis Currier, Theoline B. Francis, Diana Francis, Sidney R. Francis, Jr., Mrs. Robert L. Cushman, David L. Ray, and Lawrence Rouse and the Rouse family.

And finally, deep and abiding thanks to Talton Francis Ray, who initiated the project and did much of the basic research, from sifting through Francis family records to doing extensive digging in libraries and historical archives in St. Louis, Kentucky, Washington, and elsewhere.

Endnotes

PROLOGUE

1. Philip Jordan to Annie Pulliam, November 30, 1917, MHS.
2. Draft of cable, March 1917, MHS.
3. Winston S. Churchill, *The World Crisis* (New York: Scribner's, 1931), 63.
4. David Francis, *Russia from the American Embassy* (New York: Scribner's, 1921), 102.
5. Bruce Lockhart, *Memoirs of a British Agent* (New York: G.P. Putnam's Sons, 1933), 249, 282–83.
6. Bolshevik Propaganda Hearings, February 11 to March 10, 1919 (Washington, D.C.: Government Printing Office, 1919), 797.

CHAPTER 1

1. Rep., December 13, 1898.
2. Bil Gilbert, *Westering Man: The Life of Joseph Walker* (New York: Atheneum, 1983), 13–25. On July 26, 1998, historians interviewed by the *New York Times* blamed America's high murder rate in part on Southern people "referred to today as Scotch Irish," people whose inheritance included "a penchant for family feuds, a love of whisky and a warrior ethic that demanded vengeance."
3. Sophia Fox Sea, "The Irvines of Madison County, Kentucky," *Register of Kentucky State Historical Society* (May 1905): 88.
4. William Ellis, E. H. E. Everman, and Richard Sears, *Madison County* (Richmond, Ky.: Madison County Historical Society, 1985), 7–56; *Biographical Cyclopedia of the Commonwealth of Kentucky*, 503–6.
5. Ellis et al., *Madison County*, xvi.
6. Ellis et al., *Madison County*, 85, 230.
7. *Biographical Cyclopedia*, 506.
8. Ellis et al., *Madison County*, 88–89; Robert M. Ireland, *The County Courts in Antebellum Kentucky* (Lexington: University Press of Kentucky, 1972), 79–90.
9. David Francis to Jane Francis, June 23, 1918, MHS.
10. Tax records, 1856 and 1859 Madison County, Kentucky.
11. David Herbert Donald, *Lincoln* (New York: Simon & Schuster, 1995), 147.
12. Census records, 1860, Madison County, Kentucky.
13. Thomas Brown, *Politics and Statesmanship: Essays on the American Whig Party* (New York: Columbia University Press, 1985), 91–93; Samuel Eliot Morison, *The Oxford History of the American People* (New York: Meridan, 1994), 456, 459; Walter Stevens, "David R. Francis: His Recollections and Letters." An edited version of Stevens's unpublished biography of David Francis appeared in installments in seven consecutive Sunday issues of the *St. Louis Globe-Democrat*, from July 17 to August 28, 1927. Hereafter designated Stevens, GD, I–VII.
14. Ellis et al., *Madison County*, 85–86, 100–2.
15. Ellis et al., *Madison County*, 76–78.
16. Ellis et al., *Madison County*, 80–81.
17. Robert L. Breck file, Special Collection and Archives, Eastern Kentucky University, Richmond.
18. 1906 Homecoming Speech, MHS; Stevens, GD, I.
19. Ellis et al., *Madison County*, 105–44, 154–60.
20. Ellis et al., *Madison County*, 177.
21. Kentucky State Archives, www.kdla.state.ky.us/arch/civil.
22. D. Warren Lambert, *When the Ripe Pears Fell* (Richmond, Ky.: Madison County Historical Society, 1996), 13–21.
23. Lambert, *When the Ripe Pears Fell*, 67.
24. Lucia Burnam, "What I Remember" (Eastern Kentucky University, unpublished manuscript, 1933), 11.
25. Lambert, *When the Ripe Pears Fell*, 162.
26. Burnam, "What I Saw," 8, 13.
27. Ellis et al., *Madison County*, 178–79.
28. Ellis et al., *Madison County*, 243–45.
29. Stevens, GD, I.
30. 1906 Homecoming Speech, MHS.
31. Mark Twain and Charles Dudley Warner, *The Gilded Age*, 2 vols. (New York: Harper & Brothers, 1915), 1:13.

CHAPTER 2

1. James Neal Primm, *Lion of the Valley: St. Louis, Missouri*, 3d ed. (St. Louis: Missouri Historical Society Press, 1998), 294–95.
2. James Parton, "The City of St. Louis," *Atlantic Monthly* (June 1867): 655–56.
3. L. U. Reavis, *St. Louis: The Future Great City of the World* (St. Louis: C.R. Barns, 1876), 688–92.
4. Primm, *Lion of the Valley*, 88, 117, 137.
5. Missouri Writers' Project, *Missouri: The WPA Guide to the "Show Me" State* (St. Louis: Missouri Historical Society Press, 1998), 53.
6. 1905 Commencement Speech, MHS.
7. William E. Parrish, *A History of Missouri*, 5 vols. (Columbia: University of Missouri Press, 1971–2000), 3:203.
8. Stevens, GD, I.
9. Mary Bartley, *St. Louis Lost* (St. Louis: Virginia Publishing, 1998), 97–101.
10. Camille N. Dry and Richard J. Compton, *Pictorial St. Louis* (St. Louis, 1876), 81, 102.
11. Stevens, GD, I.
12. Washington University Archives, catalogs and class enrollments.
13. Stevens, GD, I.
14. Irving Union Program, MHS.
15. Ralph Morrow, *Washington University* (St. Louis: Missouri Historical Society Press, 1996), 119–21; Orrick Johns, *Time of Our Lives* (New York: Stackpole Sons, 1937), 57–58; Primm, *Lion of the Valley*, 335–44.
16. Stevens, GD, I; Howard Miller and Quinta Scott, *The Eads Bridge* (St. Louis: Missouri Historical Society Press, 1999), 94–101.
17. Morrow, *Washington University*, 111.
18. Stevens, GD, I.
19. Mike Fanning to David Francis, February 28, 1889, MHS.
20. Cosmo Joseph Pusateri, *A Businessman in Politics: David R. Francis, Missouri Democrat* (Ph.D. diss., Saint Louis University, 1965), 19.
21. *Missouri Republican*, June 17, 1870.
22. Commencement Program, June 16, 1870, Washington University Archives.
23. *Missouri Republican*, June 17, 1870.
24. Stevens, GD, I.
25. Stevens, GD, I.
26. St. Louis City Directory, 1871; Jean Carnahan, *If Walls Could Talk: The Story of Missouri's First Families* (Jefferson City, Mo.: MMPI, 1998), 75.
27. Stevens, GD, I.
28. Stevens, GD, I.

CHAPTER 3

1. Primm, *Lion of the Valley*, 287–90.
2. Reavis, *St. Louis: The Future Great City of the World*, 11–13.

3. Wyatt W. Belcher, *The Economic Rivalry Between St. Louis and Chicago, 1850–1880* (New York: Columbia University Press, 1947), 16–17.
4. Parrish, *A History of Missouri*, 3:205–15.
5. Belcher, *The Economic Rivalry Between St. Louis and Chicago*, 13–19. For further analysis of the early roots of St. Louis fiscal conservatism and entrepreneurial caution and support of the notion that St. Louis had effectively lost the race with Chicago before the Civil War, see also Jeffrey S. Adler, *Yankee Merchants and the Making of the Urban West: The Rise and Fall of Antebellum St. Louis* (Cambridge: Cambridge University Press, 1991).
6. Primm, *Lion of the Valley*, 234–38.
7. Parton, "The City of St. Louis," 655–58.
8. William Henry Bishop, *St. Louis in 1884*, 9.
9. Julian Rammelkamp, *Pulitzer's Post–Dispatch, 1878–1883* (Princeton, N.J.: Princeton University Press, 1967), 228.
10. PD, October 19, 1998.
11. See Belcher, *The Economic Rivalry Between St. Louis and Chicago*, and Adler, *Yankee Merchants and the Making of the Urban West*.
12. Stevens, GD, I.
13. Parton, "The City of St. Louis," 667.
14. Stevens, GD, I.
15. Johns, *Time of Our Lives*, 57.
16. Stevens, GD, I.
17. Miller and Scott, *The Eads Bridge*, 122–24; Primm, *Lion of the Valley*, 305–7.
18. GD, December 22, 1875.
19. William Hyde and Howard Conard, *Encyclopedia of the History of St. Louis* (New York: The Southern History Company, 1899), 1719–21.
20. Eleanor Park and Kate S. Morrow, *Women of the Mansion: Missouri, 1821–1936* (Jefferson City, Mo.: Midland Printing Company, 1936), 235.
21. GD, obituary, March 22, 1924.
22. Park and Morrow, *Women of the Mansion*, 238–40.
23. Isabella Bird, *A Lady's Life in the Rocky Mountains* (Norman: University of Oklahoma Press, 1960), 169–71.
24. Ardis Webb, *The Perry Park Story* (Denver, 1974), 20–21.
25. Marilyn McCarthy, *Stones of Remembrance: A History of Central Presbyterian Church, 1844–1994* (St. Louis: Central Presbyterian Church, 1994), 27.
26. Stevens, GD, I.
27. Primm, *Lion of the Valley*, 328–32.
28. Thomas M. Spencer, *The St. Louis Veiled Prophet Celebration: Power On a Parade,*

1877–1995 (Columbia: University of Missouri Press, 2000), 9–20.

29. Rep., October 6, 1878.

30. Spencer, *The St. Louis Veiled Prophet Celebration*, 9–12.

31. Harry B. Hawes, *Memorial Address, David Rowland Francis* (Washington, D.C.: Government Printing Office, 1929), 4.

32. Charles C. Savage, *Architecture of the Private Streets of St. Louis: The Architects and the Houses They Designed* (Columbia: University of Missouri Press, 1987), 22–28.

33. Harry M. Hagen, *This Is Our St. Louis* (St. Louis: Knight Publishing Co., 1970), 340.

34. James Cox, *Old and New St. Louis* (St. Louis: Central Biographical Publishing Co., 1894), 176; Pusateri, *A Businessman in Politics*, 109.

35. David Francis to Perry Francis, May 15, 1917, MHS.

36. Stevens, GD, I.

37. Robert Sahr, Oregon State University inflation calculator at http://www.orst.edu/Dept/pol_sci/fac/sahr/sahr.htm.

38. Johns, *Time of Our Lives*, 70.

39. Hagen, *This Is Our St. Louis*, 363.

CHAPTER 4

1. Mark Twain, *Life on the Mississippi* (New York: Bantam, 1990), 113–14.

2. W. A. Swanberg, *Pulitzer* (New York: Scribner, 1967), 66.

3. Johns, *Time of Our Lives*, 57.

4. Katharine T. Corbett and Howard S. Miller, *St. Louis in the Gilded Age* (St. Louis: Missouri Historical Society Press, 1993), 10.

5. Twain, *Life on the Mississippi*, 114–15.

6. GD, January 10, 1884.

7. Pusateri, *A Businessman in Politics*, 33–34.

8. GD, July 8, 1884.

9. PD, July 9, 1884.

10. Pusateri, *A Businessman in Politics*, 34.

11. GD, July 7, 1884.

12. Edward C. Rafferty, "The Boss Who Never Was," *Gateway Heritage* 12, no. 3 (winter 1992): 55.

13. Theodore Dreiser, *Newspaper Days* (Philadelphia: University of Pennsylvania Press, 1991), 133.

14. PD, March 26, 1885.

15. GD, March 27, 1885.

16. Stevens, GD, I.

CHAPTER 5

1. Rep., March 27–28, 1885.

2. PD, March 26, 1885.

3. GD, March 27, 1885.

4. Stevens, GD, II.

5. PD, April 8, 1885; Pusateri, *A Businessman in Politics*, 12.

6. Author interview with William Barnaby Faherty, S.J., historian, Midwest Jesuit Archives, St. Louis, July 20, 1998; Primm, *Lion of the Valley*, 332.

7. GD, April 12, 1885.

8. GD, April 22, 1885.

9. David Francis to J. A. Hockaday, March 10, 1888, MHS.

10. Stevens, GD, II.

11. PD, June 1, 1885; Rep., June 19, 1885.

12. Stevens, GD, II.

13. NYT, October 9–10, 1885.

14. Primm, *Lion of the Valley*, 247.

15. Pusateri, *A Businessman in Politics*, 43.

16. GD, December 16, 1885.

17. PD, December 16, 1885; GD, December 17, 1885.

18. Myra Himelhoch, "St. Louis Opposition to David R. Francis in the Gubernatorial Election of 1888," *Missouri Historical Review* 68, no. 3 (April 1974): 338–39.

19. Rafferty, "The Boss Who Never Was," 54–73.

20. PD, March 30, 1886; Pusateri, *A Businessman in Politics*, 55–57.

21. House Select Committee on Existing Labor Troubles, "Investigation on Labor Troubles in Missouri, Arkansas, Kansas, Texas, and Illinois," *Congressional Record* (April–May 1886): 101–5.

22. PD, October 6, 1910.

23. PD, July 9, 1886.

24. Rep., July 10, 1886.

25. PD, May 17, 1887; Pusateri, *A Businessman in Politics*, 68.

26. Pusateri, *A Businessman in Politics*, 71.

27. Pusateri, *A Businessman in Politics*, 73–74.

28. Allan Nevins, *Grover Cleveland: A Study in Courage* (New York: Dodd, Mead & Company, 1932), 333.

29. Pusateri, *A Businessman in Politics*, 79.

30. Nevins, *Grover Cleveland*, 333–38; Walter Stevens, "When Cleveland Came to St. Louis," *Missouri Historical Review* 21, no. 2 (January 1927): 145–55.

31. Pusateri, *A Businessman in Politics*, 86–87.

32. David Francis to Grover Cleveland, September 12, 1887, MHS.

33. Stevens, "When Cleveland Came to St. Louis," 151; Hagen, *This Is Our St. Louis*, 340.

34. GD, October 5, 1887.

35. David Francis to His Majesty the Veiled Prophet, September 9, 1887, MHS; Stevens, "When Cleveland Came to St. Louis," 153.

36. Pusateri, *A Businessman in Politics*, 94.

37. David Francis to E. W. Best, April 11, 1888, MHS.

38. David Francis to W. W. Sherman of the National Bank of Commerce in New York, December 2, 1887, MHS.
39. GD, January 12, 1893.
40. Stevens, GD, II.
41. GD, February 24, 1888.
42. Pusateri, *A Businessman in Politics*, 110.
43. Stevens, GD, II.
44. Pusateri, *A Businessman in Politics*, 105.
45. Pusateri, *A Businessman in Politics*, 106.
46. David Francis to A. S. Hardy, American ambassador to Spain, accompanying a gift case of Old Crow, April 10, 1903, MHS.
47. David Francis to J. D. Crisp, October 11, 1888, MHS.
48. David Francis to G. L. Turton, October 11, 1888, MHS.
49. David Francis to Dr. Howard, April 7, 1888, MHS.
50. Pusateri, *A Businessman in Politics*, 107–8.
51. Stevens, GD, II.
52. Pusateri, *A Businessman in Politics*, 110.
53. David Francis to J. Clayton, June 19, 1888, MHS.
54. Stevens, GD, II.
55. Charles Dudley Warner, *Studies in the South and West* (London: T. Fisher Unwin, 1890), 318–19, 329–30, 346–47.
56. *The Critic*, July 15, 1888, David R. Francis Collection, MHS.
57. PD, August 23, 1888.
58. PD, January 4, 1889.
59. Quoted by Walter Stevens in his introduction to *The Messages and Proclamations of the Governors of the State of Missouri*, vol. VII, edited by Sarah Guitar and Floyd C. Shoemaker (Columbia: The State Historical Society of Missouri, 1922–), 210–11.
60. Stevens, GD, II.
61. Stevens, GD, II.
62. See, for instance, David Francis to J. E. Smith, May 3, 1918, MHS.
63. Stevens, GD, II.
64. Stevens, GD, III.
65. Stevens, GD, II and III.
66. Himelhoch, "St. Louis Opposition to David R. Francis," 340.
67. F. C. Shoemaker, *A History of Missouri and Missourians* (Columbia, Mo.: Lucas Brothers, 1927), 127–28; Pusateri, *A Businessman in Politics*, 117–18.
68. Pusateri, *A Businessman in Politics*, 126; Himelhoch, "St. Louis Opposition to David R. Francis," 340–42.
69. The author is indebted to former St. Louis Alderman Daniel McGuire, an avid local historian, for calling his attention to this distinction.
70. David Francis to James Gibson, November 12, 1888, MHS.
71. David Francis to Ben M. Anderson, November 12, 1888, MHS.
72. David Francis to C. E. Perkins, December 8, 1888, MHS.
73. David Francis to Breedlove Smith, December 25, 1888, MHS.

CHAPTER 6

1. NYT, December 11, 1895.
2. Rep., January 15, 1889; Park and Morrow, *Women of the Mansion*, 236.
3. David Francis to Jane Francis, May 21, 1917, MHS.
4. Francis, *Messages and Proclamations*, 218–22.
5. Nettie Beauregard, notes for the Jane Perry Francis chapter of *Women of the Mansion*, MHS.
6. Park and Morrow, *Women of the Mansion*, 237.
7. GD, January 14, 1889.
8. PD, May 22, 1941.
9. Philip Jordan to Auntie Emily and America, October 24, 1930, Talton F. Ray Collection.
10. Park and Morrow, *Women of the Mansion*, 245–47.
11. Nettie Beauregard, notes for the Francis section of *Women of the Mansion*, MHS.
12. Carnahan, *If Walls Could Talk*, 78–80.
13. Park and Morrow, *Women of the Mansion*, 235, 238–39.
14. Park and Morrow, *Women of the Mansion*, 238–40.
15. Augustus Thomas, *The Print of My Remembrance* (New York: Scribner's, 1922), 257.
16. David Francis to Breedlove Smith, December 25, 1888, MHS.
17. Pusateri, *A Businessman in Politics*, 145–47.
18. Stevens, GD, III.
19. David Francis to C. H. Jones, March 27, 1889, MHS.
20. David Thelen, *Paths of Resistance: Tradition and Democracy in Industrializing Missouri* (Columbia: University of Missouri Press, 1991), 87–92.
21. *Nevada Democrat*, January 14, 1889.
22. Mary Hartman and Elmo Ingenthron, *Bald Knobbers: Vigilantes on the Ozarks Frontier* (Gretna, La.: Pelican Publishing Co., 1988), 230–32.
23. Thelen, *Paths of Resistance*, 87–92; David Francis to Charles H. Jones, May 10, 1889, MHS.
24. Stevens, GD, III.
25. Stevens, GD, III; Pusateri, *A Businessman in Politics*, 155–58.

26. Stevens, GD, III.
27. David Francis to J. E. Smith, May 3, 1918, MHS.
28. James Olson and Vera Olson, *The University of Missouri: An Illustrated History* (Columbia: University of Missouri Press, 1988), 23–24.
29. Henry Severance, *Richard Henry Jesse: President of the University of Missouri, 1891–1908* (Columbia, Mo., 1937), 21–23.
30. Pusateri, *A Businessman in Politics*, 163–65.
31. Francis, *Messages and Proclamations*, 226–27; Stevens, GD, III.
32. Pusateri, *A Businessman in Politics*, 172–73; two-page summary of Francis's statement, apparently pages 54 and 55 of a larger document, dated March 1889 and filed by date in the David R. Francis Collection, MHS.
33. Francis, *Messages and Proclamations*, 223–64, 275.
34. Severance, *Richard Henry Jesse*, 21–41.
35. Park and Morrow, *Women of the Mansion*, 238.
36. Carnahan, *If Walls Could Talk*, 79.
37. Francis, *Messages and Proclamations*, 304–17; David Francis to S. H. H. Clark, April 22, 1889, MHS.
38. Stevens, GD, III.
39. Olson and Olson, *The University of Missouri*, 29–33; Francis, *Messages and Proclamations*, 267, 285.
40. Stevens, GD, III.
41. Park and Morrow, *Women of the Mansion*, 242–43.
42. David Francis to Thomas H. West, April 19, 1918, MHS.
43. Stevens, GD, IV.
44. GD, August 25, 1896.
45. PD, January 8, 1893.
46. Francis, *Messages and Proclamations*, 333–34.
47. GD, January 7, 1893.
48. Stevens, GD, IV.
49. GD, August 25, 1896.
50. Beauregard notes, MHS.
51. Philip Jordan to Mrs. Green, November 7, 1919, Talton F. Ray Collection.

CHAPTER 7

1. Bartley, *St. Louis Lost*, 149; PD, August 2, 1935.
2. St. Paul School records.
3. Rep., December 13, 1898; GD, November 28, 1894.
4. Rolla Wells, *Episodes in My Life* (St. Louis: W.J. McCarthy, 1933), 74–76.
5. GD, May 19, 1893.
6. Walter Stevens, "The New Journalism in Missouri," *Missouri Historical Review* 19, no. 4 (July 1925): 680–81.
7. Dreiser, *Newspaper Days*, 253–55.
8. Walter Stevens, "The Tragedy of the St. Louis Republic," *Missouri Historical Review* 22, no. 2 (January 1928): 139.
9. Stevens, GD, IV.
10. Harold Faulkner, *Politics, Reform and Expansion, 1890–1900* (New York: Harper, 1959), 141–43.
11. GD, January 18, 1927.
12. William E. Parrish, Charles T. Jones, Jr., and Lawrence O. Christensen, *Missouri: The Heart of the Nation* (Arlington Heights, Ill.: H. Davidson, 1992), 242.
13. Cox, *Old and New St. Louis*, 26.
14. Rep., January 23, 1889; Alexander Scot McConachie, *The "Big Cinch": A Business Elite in the Life of a City, Saint Louis, 1895–1915* (Ph.D. diss. Washington University, 1976).
15. PD, October 6, 1910; McConachie, "The Big Cinch," 110; Ernest Kirschten, *Catfish and Crystal* (Garden City, N.Y.: Doubleday, 1960), 332.
16. Primm, *Lion of the Valley*, 375.
17. Dreiser, *Newspaper Days*, 106, 120–21.
18. Bartley, *St. Louis Lost*, 149–51. The Benoist memoir, quoted by Bartley, appeared in the *West End Word*, a neighborhood paper, in 1979.
19. PD, August 2, 1935.
20. David Francis to Jane Francis, May 6, 1918, MHS.
21. Rexford Tugwell, *Grover Cleveland* (New York: Macmillan, 1968), 202–5.
22. Ron Chernow, *The House of Morgan: An American Banking Dynasty and the Rise of Modern Finance* (New York: Atlantic Monthly Press, 1990), 70–75.
23. Nevins, *Grover Cleveland*, 600–3.
24. Shelby Strother to Philip Jordan, July 19, 1933, Talton F. Ray Collection.
25. Stevens, GD, IV and VI; Rep., May 18, 1894; GD and Rep., August 6–7, 1894.
26. Nevins, *Grover Cleveland*, 604–5.
27. GD, August 6–7, 1895; Pusateri, *A Businessman in Politics*, 255–66, 275.
28. Pusateri, *A Businessman in Politics*, 270.
29. William Vincent Byars, ed., *An American Commoner: The Life and Times of Richard Parks Bland* (Columbia, Mo.: E.W. Stephens, 1900), 130–32.
30. Swanberg, *Pulitzer*, 212–51; PD, July 6–11, 1896.
31. NYT, December 7, 1895.
32. William Jennings Bryan and Mary Baird Bryan, *The Memoirs of William Jennings Bryan* (Philadelphia: United Publishers of America, 1925), 108.
33. Nevins, *Grover Cleveland*, 700–1.
34. GD, July 5–6, 9–10, 1896.

35. Stevens, GD, VI.
36. Clarence Darrow, *The Story of My Life* (New York: Scribner's, 1932), 89–92.
37. GD, July 11, 1896.
38. PD, July 5, 1896.
39. Rep., August 25, 1896; Nevins, *Grover Cleveland*, 710–11.
40. GD, August 25, 1896.
41. Rep., August 26, 1896.
42. *Washington Post*, August 27, 1886.
43. NYT, August 25, 1896.
44. NYT, September 11, 1896.
45. NYT, December 5, 1896.
46. St. Paul's archives.
47. Rep., October 24, 1896.
48. Chernow, *The House of Morgan*, 76–77.
49. NYT, November 27, 1896.
50. Rep., August 26, 1896.
51. GD, January 5, 1897.
52. NYT, January 19, 1897; GD, January 21, 1897.
53. Rep., August 26, 1896.
54. Pusateri, *A Businessman in Politics*, 299–300.
55. Angie Debo, *A History of the Indians of the United States* (Norman: University of Oklahoma Press, 1970), 117–18.
56. NYT, December 20, 1896.
57. Angie Debo, *The Rise and Fall of the Choctaw Republic* (Norman: University of Oklahoma Press, 1961), 259–69.
58. Gifford Pinchot, *Breaking New Ground* (New York: Harcourt, Brace, 1947), 93–95.
59. Pinchot, *Breaking New Ground*, 107.
60. Pinchot, *Breaking New Ground*, 105–12.
61. David Francis to William Gorham Rice, May 6, 1919, MHS.
62. Ibid.
63. Ibid.
64. Ibid.
65. Debo, *Rise and Fall*, 260; Brian W. Dippie, *The Vanishing American: White Attitudes and U.S. Indian Policy* (Middletown, Conn.: Wesleyan University Press, 1982), 308.
66. *Philadelphia Ledger*, February 23, 1916.

CHAPTER 8

1. Stevens, GD, VI.
2. Mary Kimbrough, *St. Louis Country Club* (St. Louis: St. Louis Country Club, 1992).
3. William Sidney Porter, "Seats of the Haughty," in *Heart of the West*, edited by O. Henry (Garden City, N.Y.: Doubleday, 1919), 82.
4. PD, March 29, 1908.
5. McConachie, *The "Big Cinch,"* 141–42. Reedy is identified as the pseudonymous author by McConachie. James Neal Primm questions that judgment in *Lion of the Valley* (p. 378), noting that Reedy would be unlikely to include

Campbell in this list, since Campbell was one of the financial patrons of *Reedy's Mirror*. But like any good, honest interpretative journalist in an insular, provincial city—contemporary Washington, D.C., for example—Reedy was quite able to criticize his friends, although he might have been judicious enough to use a pseudonym when doing so.
6. McConachie, *The "Big Cinch,"* 82–83.
7. McConachie, *The "Big Cinch,"* 91–93; Mary Kimbrough, *St. Louis Country Club*
8. Walter Ehrlich, *Zion in the Valley: The Jewish Community of St. Louis* (Columbia: University of Missouri Press, 1997), 339–41.
9. David Francis, *The Universal Exposition of 1904* (St. Louis: Louisiana Purchase Exposition Company, 1913), 21. In this official history of the exposition, the labor organization that endorsed the Fair is mis-identified as the "St. Louis Building Trades and Labor *Union.*" The Building Trades Union was a militant socialist organization that did endorse labor action against the Fair; Francis's agreement was with the more conservative Building Trades Council. See Martha R. Clevenger, *"Indescribably Grand": Diaries and Letters from the 1904 World's Fair* (St. Louis: Missouri Historical Society Press, 1996), 7, 35.
10. Swanberg, *Pulitzer*, 251.
11. PD, January 22, 1900.
12. Stevens, GD, IV.
13. Francis, *Universal Exposition*, 29.
14. GD, February 1, 1900.
15. St. Louis City Directory, 1901–1904; John W. Leonard, ed., *The Book of St. Louisans: A Biographical Dictionary of Leading Living Men of the City of St. Louis and Vicinity* (St. Louis: The *St. Louis Republic*, 1906), 201.
16. GD, April 26, 1903.
17. Ibid.
18. Ibid.
19. Francis, *Universal Exposition*, 23–26.
20. PD, October 6, 1900.
21. PD, October 7, 1910.
22. PD, June 10–12, 1900.
23. *Reedy's Mirror*, June 14, 1900.
24. Dina M. Young, "The St. Louis Streetcar Strike of 1900: Pivotal Politics at the Century's Dawn," *Gateway Heritage* 7, no. 1 (summer 1986): 4–17; Steven L. Piott, *Holy Joe: Joseph W. Folk and the Missouri Idea* (Columbia: University of Missouri Press, 1997), 20–22.
25. Piott, *Holy Joe*, 24–29.
26. Francis, *Universal Exposition*, 98.
27. Robert Rydell, *All the World's a Fair: Visions of Empire at American International Expositions, 1876–1916* (Chicago: University of Chicago

Press, 1984), 58–62.

28. Francis, *Universal Exposition*, 50–51.

29. Primm, *Lion of the Valley*, 398.

30. For a fuller discussion of this controversial transaction, see Morrow, *Washington University*, 164–67.

31. Francis, *Universal Exposition*, 41–47.

32. Wells, *Episodes in My Life*, 99–100, 114–17.

33. Johns, *Time of Our Lives*, 140.

34. *Reedy's Mirror*, April 4, 1901.

35. Lincoln Steffens, *The Autobiography of Lincoln Steffens* (New York: Harcourt, Brace and Company, 1931), 24, 70–73.

36. Stephen Raiche, "The World's Fair and the New St. Louis," *Missouri Historical Review* 67, no. 1 (October 1972): 105–8.

37. Dreiser, *Newspaper Days*.

38. Karen M. Keefer, MD, "Dirty Water and Clean Toilets: Medical Aspects of the 1904 Lousiana Purchase Exposition," *Gateway Heritage* 9, no. 1 (summer 1988): 34.

39. *Birthday Anniversary Dinner Given by Joseph Pulitzer, April 10, 1907*, St. Louis: Woodward & Tiernan, 1907, pamphlet, 14–15.

40. Don Seitz, *Joseph Pulitzer: His Life and Letters* (New York: Simon & Schuster, 1924), 234–35; Stevens, "Tragedy of the Republic," 141.

41. Stevens, GD, IV.

42. Stevens, GD, V.

43. Stevens, GD, IV.

44. Stevens, GD, IV.

45. Francis, *Universal Exposition*, title page.

46. Rydell, *All the World's a Fair*, 152–53.

47. Caroline Loughlin and Catherine Anderson, *Forest Park* (Columbia: University of Missouri Press, 1986), 68–80.

48. Robert C. Williams, "The Russians Are Coming!" *Louisiana Purchase Exposition: The St. Louis World's Fair of 1904* (St. Louis: Missouri Historical Society, 1979), 70–93; Jean Strouse, *Morgan: American Financier* (New York: Random House, 1999), 409–11, 546.

49. Raiche, "The World's Fair and the New St. Louis," 120; PD, March 13, 1903.

50. Lincoln Steffens, *The Shame of the Cities* (New York: McClure, Phillips & Co., 1904), 24.

51. William Reddig, *Tom's Town: Kansas City and the Pendergast Legend* (Columbia: University of Missouri Press, 1986), 60.

52. Piott, *Holy Joe*, 55–58; Primm, *Lion of the Valley*, 391–92.

53. PD, October 11, 1910.

54. Ibid.

55. Ibid.

56. PD, October 6–7, 1910; Stevens, GD, V.

57. PD, October 11, 1910.

58. David Francis to Perry Francis, April 21, 1918.

59. Francis, *Universal Exposition*, 103.

60. Francis, *Universal Exposition*, 100–2.

61. Edmund S. Hoch, "The Olympic Games," *World's Fair Bulletin* (March 1903): 10.

62. Hoch, "The Olympic Games," 14–15.

63. Bill Henry, *An Approved History of the Olympic Games* (New York: G.P. Putnam's Sons, 1976), 52; Peter Andrews, "The First American Olympics," *American Heritage* (May/June 1988): 41.

64. Francis, *Universal Exposition*, 538. See also Mark Dyreson, "The Playing Fields of Progress: American Nationalism and the 1904 St. Louis Olympics," *Gateway Heritage* 14, no. 2 (fall 1993): 5–8.

65. Loughlin and Anderson, *Forest Park*, 66–74.

66. George R. Leighton, "The Year St. Louis Enchanted the World," *Harper's* (August 1960): 40.

67. Adolphus Busch to David Francis, July 22, 1902, MHS.

68. Francis, *Universal Exposition*, 117–18.

69. David Francis to Executive Committee, February 14, 1903, MHS.

70. David Francis to Isaac Taylor, February 19, 1903, MHS.

71. David Francis to Executive Committee, February 14, 1903, MHS.

72. David Francis, *A Tour of Europe in Nineteen Days: Report to the Board of Directors of the Louisiana Purchase Exposition* (St. Louis, 1903), 63–70.

73. Stevens, GD, VI.

74. Katharine T. Corbett, *In Her Place: A Guide to St. Louis Women's History* (St. Louis: Missouri Historical Society Press, 1998), 179. In the book, Corbett presents an incisive, critical overview of women's roles at the Fair.

75. Quoted in PD, May 19, 1904.

76. Francis, *A Tour of Europe*, 78–80.

77. Francis, *A Tour of Europe*, 28–31.

78. PD, May 19, 1904.

79. NYT, March 10, 1903.

80. Francis, *A Tour of Europe*, 46–50.

81. GD, March 8, 1903.

82. NYT, March 18, 1903.

83. Rep., March 19, 1903; Stevens, GD, IV.

84. GD, March 21, 1903.

85. GD, March 23, 1903.

86. Ibid.

87. Ibid.

88. GD, April 13, 1903.

89. GD, March 21, 23; April 13, 1903.

CHAPTER 9

1. GD, April 27, 1903.

2. GD, March 2, 1903.

3. Stevens, GD, V.
4. The first figure is the lowest estimate of the GD, the second that of the official Fair history. GD, May 1, 1903; Francis, *Universal Exposition*, 134.
5. Jean Jules Jusserand, *What Me Befell* (New York: Houghton Mifflin Company, 1934), 230–33.
6. Francis, *Universal Exposition*, 140–52.
7. David Francis to Wm. Gorham Rice, May 6, 1919, MHS.
8. Francis, *Universal Exposition*, 152–54; GD, May 1–2, 1903.
9. Francis, *Universal Exposition*, 153.
10. NYT, May 2, 1903.
11. Leighton, "The Year St. Louis Enchanted the World," 43.
12. David Francis to Henry King, June 15, 1903, MHS.
13. NYT, May 3, 1903.
14. Rep., May 12, 1903.
15. NYT, May 1, 1903.
16. GD, April 26, 1903.
17. Ibid.
18. Philip Jordan to Mr. and Mrs. T. T. Francis, June 25, 1920, Talton F. Ray Collection; Webb, *Perry Park*, 43.
19. Rep., August 9, 1903.
20. Leighton, "The Year St. Louis Enchanted the World," 42.
21. William Marion Reedy, *Literary Digest* (June 13, 1903).
22. Rydell, *All the World's a Fair*, 162; Francis, *Universal Exposition*, 60.
23. Timothy J. Fox and Duane R. Sneddeker, *From the Palaces to the Pike: Visions of the 1904 World's Fair* (St. Louis: Missouri Historical Society Press, 1997), 26.
24. Williams, "The Russians Are Coming!" 73.
25. GD, February 17, 1904; David Francis to Frank L. Polk, November 28, 1916, MHS.
26. St. Louis birth records, St. Louis Public Library.
27. GD, February 12 and April 24, 1904; the seven previous U.S. fairs were at Philadelphia, Chicago, Buffalo, Omaha, San Francisco, Nashville, and New Orleans.
28. Stevens, GD, V.
29. Stevens, GD, V, original source unattributed.
30. PD, May 19, 1904.
31. Wells, *Episodes in My Life*, 166–67; GD, March 19, 1904.
32. Raiche, "The World's Fair and the New St. Louis," 113.
33. Primm, *Lion of the Valley*, 401.
34. GD, April 20, 1904.
35. Primm, *Lion of the Valley*, 404.
36. Williams, "The Russians are Coming!" 75–77.

37. Francis, *Universal Exposition*, 564–65.
38. GD, April 8, 1904.
39. GD, April 19, 1904.
40. Mark Twain to David Francis, May 26, 1904, Mark Twain Papers, Bancroft Library, University of California, Berkeley.
41. Alexander Alland, *Jessie Tarbox Beals: First Woman News Photographer* (New York: Camera/Graphic Press, 1978), 46–50. Many of Beals's photographs are reproduced in Fox and Sneddeker, *From the Palaces to the Pike*.
42. GD March 27, 1904.
43. GD, October 3, 1904.
44. GD, January 21, 1904.
45. PD, March 14, 1904; GD, January 16, 1927.
46. Fox and Sneddeker, *From the Palaces to the Pike*, 28.
47. GD, April 21 and 24, 1904.
48. GD, April 29, 1904.
49. GD, April 30, 1904.
50. GD, May 1, 1904.
51. Nathan Miller, *Theodore Roosevelt*, 367–68.
52. PD, April 30, 1904; GD, May 1, 1904; NYT, May 1, 1904.
53. Sally Benson, *Meet Me in St. Louis* (New York: Bantam, 1963), 149–50.
54. Benson, *Meet Me in St. Louis*, 138–39.
55. NYT, May 1, 1904.
56. PD, May 1, 1904.
57. Stevens, GD, VII.
58. GD, May 3, 1904.
59. Francis, *Universal Exposition*, 178; GD, May 13, 1904.

CHAPTER 10

1. Henry Adams, *The Education of Henry Adams* (Boston: Houghton Mifflin Company, 1946), 465–68.
2. GD, May 30, 1904; Francis, *Universal Exposition*, 615–17.
3. GD, May 27, 1904.
4. GD, May 28, 1904.
5. PD, May 28, 1904.
6. GD, June 6, 1904.
7. Rydell, *All the World's a Fair*, 160–63. Also see Francis, *Universal Exposition*, 522–34.
8. Francis, *Universal Exposition*, 230, 528–29; Rep., December 4, 1904. A true census of the tribal peoples at the Fair was never made, but McGee and Francis both said it exceeded two thousand. However, that figure included several hundred men and women employed by the Boer War reenactment and at Pike attractions. Also, many of the tribal people arrived late, left early, or came and went unnoted, so roughly fifteen hundred at any given time in the Anthropology Department's villages seems like a reasonable average.

9. Rep., December 4, 1904.
10. Rydell, *All the World's a Fair*, 181.
11. Francis, *Universal Exposition*, 522–24.
12. GD, May 14, 1904.
13. PD, August 18, 1904.
14. Phillips Verner Bradford and Harvey Blume, *Ota Benga: The Pygmy in the Zoo* (New York: St. Martin's Press, 1992), 137–38.
15. Susan Curtis, *Dancing to a Black Man's Tune: A Life of Scott Joplin* (Columbia: University of Missouri Press, 1994), 138.
16. Curtis, *Dancing to a Black Man's Tune*, 140–42; *St. Louis Palladium*, July 16, 1904; "Many Blacks Cherished Memories of Fair," PD, April 11, 1998.
17. PD, May 1, 1904.
18. Curtis, *Dancing to a Black Man's Tune*, 136–38.
19. Stevens, GD, V.
20. Jordan obituary, PD, May 22, 1941.
21. PD, July 6, 1904.
22. GD, July 25, 29–30, 1904; Rep., August 30, 1904.
23. GD, July 30, 1904.
24. GD, July 30, August 12, 1904.
25. Williams, "Russians Are Coming!" 78–79.
26. GD, August 13, 1904.
27. GD, May 20, 1904.
28. Bradford and Blume, *Ota Benga*, 114; Clevenger, *"Indescribably Grand,"* 113.
29. Francis, *Universal Exposition*, 619; GD, August 17 and 22, 1904.
30. GD and PD, August 31, 1904; Fox and Sneddeker, *From the Palaces to the Pike*, 208–15.
31. Rep., August 30; GD, August 22, 1904.
32. GD, September 16, 1904.
33. GD, October 4–5, 1904.
34. GD, October 17, 1904.
35. GD, October 19, 1904.
36. GD, October 25, 1904. A vendor named Charles E. Menches is often credited with inventing the ice-cream cone at the Fair on July 23, 1904. See PD, July 23, 1999.
37. GD, October 25 and 31, 1904.
38. GD, November 27, 1904.
39. Alice Roosevelt Longworth, *Crowded Hours* (New York: Scribner's, 1933), 65.
40. Alland, *Jessie Tarbox Beals*, 46ff.
41. GD, November 27, 1904.
42. GD, November 28, 1904.
43. GD, December 1, 1904.
44. GD, December 2, 1904.
45. Fox and Sneddeker, *From the Palaces to the Pike*, 29.
46. GD, December 2, 1904.
47. Francis, *Universal Exposition*, 306–7.

CHAPTER 11

1. Benson, *Meet Me in St. Louis*, 150.
2. PD, December 4, 1904; Loughlin and Anderson, *Forest Park*, 88–90; PD, May 3, 1999.
3. William Everdell, *The First Moderns: Profiles in the Origins of Twentieth-Century Thought* (Chicago: University of Chicago Press, 1997), 219–26.
4. Thomas Wolfe, *Look Homeward Angel* (New York: The Modern Library, 1934), 56–57.
5. Thomas Wolfe, "The Lost Boy" in *The Hills Beyond* (New York: Pyramid Books, 1958), 30–39.
6. Francis, *Universal Exposition*, 657.
7. Francis, *Universal Exposition*, 613, 619; Hubert Howe Bancroft, *The Book of the Fair* (Chicago: The Bancroft Co., 1893), 957.
8. *Chicago Tribune*, September 9, 1904.
9. PD, February 20, 1999.
10. Francis, *Universal Exposition*, 690.
11. *Reedy's Mirror*, December 1, 1904.
12. Loughlin and Anderson, *Forest Park*, 82–105.
13. GD, January 5, 1905.
14. Francis, *Universal Exposition*, 690.
15. Williams, "The Russians Are Coming!" 79–99; Conversation in October 1997 between Talton F. Ray and former Missouri Congressman James Symington, who helped facilitate the return of "Forest Fire" from Busch to the Russians.
16. All letters and memoirs by Jordan are in the collections of the Missouri Historical Society unless otherwise noted. They are quoted as they have come down to us. In some cases, we have handwritten notes in pencil, highly expressive but with many mistakes in grammar and spelling and the old-fashioned use of capital letters for important nouns; in others, we have typewritten copies of the originals, sometimes, it appears, with some diction and spelling mistakes corrected; finally, we have what seem to be typewritten originals by Jordan himself, with few mistakes and in graceful, evocative colloquial language. These last documents come after 1919, when Jordan had truly mastered the English language. The two-page memoir, headed "OUR WESTERN TRIP; OR, SEEING THE GOLDEN WEST, St. Louis, June 13, 1905" and quoted here, seems to be in that category, which suggests that it was written at least fifteen years after the trip it describes.
17. Remarks of Governor Francis in Presenting Loving Cup to Governor E. O. Standard, Merchants' Exchange, January 5, 1906, MHS.
18. Pusateri, *A Businessman in Politics*, 309–10.

19. Jonathan Truman Dorris and Maud Weaver Dorris, *Glimpses of Historic Madison County, Kentucky* (Nashville: Williams Printing Company, 1955), 264–69; Homecoming Speech, Richmond, Kentucky, June 18, 1906, MHS.

20. PD, September 18, 1906.

21. PD, September 20, 1906.

22. PD, September 25; GD, September 27, 1906; Stevens, GD, VI.

23. Annual reports, New York Life Insurance Co.; Chernow, *The House of Morgan*, 152.

24. Official Proceedings of Trans-Mississippi Commercial Congress, 1906.

25. Proceedings of the Eighteenth Session of the Trans-Mississippi Commercial Congress, November 19–22, 1907.

26. Walter B. Stevens, *A Trip to Panama* (St. Louis: Commercial Club of St. Louis, 1907); Remarks of David R. Francis of St. Louis at dinner given by Havana Post, Miramar, March 9 [1907]; Wells, *Episodes in My Life*, 430–33.

27. Chernow, *The House of Morgan*, 126–29.

28. David R. Francis, Remarks at Millers' National Federation, Planter's Hotel, May 30, 1907.

29. David Francis to Robert Lansing, April 10, 1916, MHS.

30. Yale University records; interview with Sidney Francis, Jr., May 16, 1997.

31. Collins Thompson to B. W. Stone, August 15, 1907.

32. Address of Hon. David R. Francis at Carnegie Hall, Business Men's National Bryan and Kern Mass Meeting, October 20, 1908, MHS.

33. Stevens, GD, V.

34. See, for example, Editorial Page, PD, October 9, 1910.

35. See particularly PD, October 11, 1910.

36. Johns, *Time of Our Lives*, 189–91.

37. Johns, *Time of Our Lives*, 192–93.

38. David Francis to Festus Wade, August 29, 1918.

39. Louise Tallman to Talton Ray, October 14, 1997; Records at the Recorder of Deeds, Rockingham County, New Hampshire; interviews 1997 and 1998 by the author with Anne Francis Currier.

40. Proceedings, Third Annual Convention, Southern Commercial Congress, Atlanta, Georgia, March 1911.

41. Loughlin and Anderson, *Forest Park*, 90ff.

42. Stevens, "The Tragedy of the *St. Louis Republic*," 139–49.

43. David Francis to Champ Clark, January 29, 1914, Western Historical Manuscript Collection, University of Missouri–Columbia.

44. Stevens, GD, VII.

45. NYT, March 9, 1913.

46. James Neal Primm, *A Foregone Conclusion: The Founding of the Federal Reserve Bank of St. Louis* (St. Louis: Federal Reserve Bank of St. Louis, 1989), 41–50.

47. Rep., February 21 and March 25, 1914.

48. GD and Rep., August 26, 1914.

CHAPTER 12

1. Robert W. Tucker, "An Inner Circle of One: Woodrow Wilson and His Advisors," *The National Interest* (spring 1998), 3ff.

2. Note, William Phillips to Woodrow Wilson, February 11, 1916. State Department files, NA.

3. Charles Crane to Josephine Crane Bradley, March 19, 1916, Charles R. Crane Papers, Columbia University.

4. David Francis to Breckinridge Long, August 7, 1917, MHS; also Woodrow Wilson to Charles Crane, February 21, 1916, Charles R. Crane Papers, Columbia University.

5. Samuel Harper, *The Russia I Believe In: The Memoirs of Samuel N. Harper, 1902–1941* (Chicago: University of Chicago Press, 1945), 91.

6. Gilbert C. Kohlenberg, "David Rowland Francis: American Businessman in Russia," *Mid-America* (October 1958): 197.

7. David Francis to Clifton R. Breckenridge, May 5, 1916, MHS; David Francis to Frank L. Polk, August 26, 1916, MHS.

8. PD, February 23, 1916.

9. Kohlenberg, "David Rowland Francis," 199–200.

10. Oscar Straus to David Francis, May 15, 1916, MHS.

11. NYT, February 24, 1916.

12. *Reedy's Mirror*, February 25, 1916.

13. Will of David Rowland Francis, Document 7643, Microfiche files, probate court, St. Louis County Courthouse, Clayton, Mo.

14. Chernow, *The House of Morgan*, 195–96.

15. Author interview, Professor Henry Berger, history department, Washington University, July 30, 1997.

16. David Francis to Woodrow Wilson, April 8, 1916, MHS.

17. Harper, *The Russia I Believe In*, 91–93.

18. W. V. Judson, report to General Payton C. March, June 18, 1919, War Department file, NA.

19. David Francis to Robert Lansing, December 4, 1917, MHS.

20. David Francis to Robert Lansing, April 10, 1916, MHS.

21. David Francis to Robert Lansing, April 10, 1916, MHS.

22. David Francis to Woodrow Wilson, April 8, 1916, MHS.
23. Chernow, *The House of Morgan,* 153, 180–81; Harold van. B. Cleveland and Thomas F. Huertas, *Citibank, 1812–1970* (Cambridge, Mass.: Harvard University Press, 1985), 99–100.
24. David S. Foglesong, *America's Secret War Against Bolshevism: U.S. Intervention in the Russian Civil War, 1917–1920* (Chapel Hill: University of North Carolina Press, 1995), 59–61, 86–92.
25. David Francis to Woodrow Wilson, April 8, 1916, MHS.
26. David Francis to John Scullin, April 16, 1916, MHS.
27. David Francis to Paul Brown, April 16, 1916, MHS.
28. David Francis to Oscar Straus, April 16, 1916, MHS.
29. Harper, *The Russia I Believe In,* 92–93.
30. Edgar de Cramm, War Department report, February 11, 1918; David Francis to Herman Bernstein, January 8, 1918, MHS.
31. Fyodor Dostoevsky, "White Nights" in *Uncle's Dream and Other Stories* (London: Penguin Books, 1989), 75.
32. Orlando Figes, *A People's Tragedy: The Russian Revolution, 1891–1924* (London: Jonathan Cape, 1996), 108–11.
33. Figes, *People's Tragedy,* 129, 148–50, 384.
34. Datebooks are in the David R. Francis Collection, MHS.
35. State Department translation of *Russkoe Slovo* article, filed May 3, 1916, NA.
36. David Francis, *Russia from the American Embassy* (New York: Scribner's, 1921), 8–9.
37. David Francis to Robert Lansing, May 2, 1916, MHS.
38. Francis, *Russia from the American Embassy,* 9–10.
39. David Francis to Perry Francis, May 1, 1916, MHS.
40. Francis, *Russia from the American Embassy,* 4.
41. Edgar Sisson, *One Hundred Red Days: A Personal Chronicle of the Bolshevik Revolution* (New Haven: Yale University Press, 1931), 31.
42. David Francis to Perry Francis, May 1, 1916, MHS.
43. David Francis to Frank L. Polk, May 9, 1916, MHS.
44. Francis, *Russia from the American Embassy,* 13–18.
45. David Francis to Frank L. Polk, May 9, 1916, MHS.
46. Francis, *Russia from the American Embassy,* 17–18.

CHAPTER 13

1. Francis, *Russia from the American Embassy,* 11.
2. DeWitt Poole, *Oral History of Years in Russia,* 87, Columbia University.
3. David Francis to Jane Francis, May 9, 1916, MHS.
4. David Francis to Perry and Dave Francis, August 7, 1916, MHS; Kohlenberg, "David Rowland Francis," 214; David Francis to Senator William J. Stone, February 13/26, 1917, MHS.
5. David Francis to Jane Francis, May 9, 1916, MHS.
6. Natalie Townsend to David Francis, March 12, 1916, MHS.
7. David Francis to Perry Francis, May 15, 1916, MHS.
8. David Francis to Herman Bernstein, January 18, 1918.
9. David Francis to Perry Francis, July 5, 1916, MHS.
10. David Francis to John C. Atwood, June 25, 1916, MHS.
11. Datebooks, May, September, and December 1916, January 1917, MHS.
12. David Francis to Perry Francis, July 5, 1916, MHS.
13. Oscar Straus to David Francis, May 15, 1916, MHS.
14. David Francis to Frank L. Polk, August 30, 1916, MHS.
15. David Francis to Darwin Kingsley, July 10, 1916, MHS.
16. David Francis to Frank L. Polk, August 30, 1916, MHS.
17. Francis, *Russia from the American Embassy,* 20–23.
18. Francis, *Russia from the American Embassy,* 22–23.
19. Francis, *Russia from the American Embassy,* 23.
20. Figes, *A People's Tragedy,* 283.
21. Hugh Moran to David Francis, June 20, 1916, MHS.
22. David Francis to Charles Crane, July 25, 1916.
23. Harper, *The Russia I Believe In,* 94–95.
24. Frank L. Polk to David Francis, August 18, 1916, Polk Papers, Yale University.
25. David Francis to Perry Francis, May 15, 1916, MHS.
26. David Francis to Darwin Kingsley, July 10, 1916.
27. Oscar Straus to David Francis, January 6, 1917, NA.
28. David Francis to Robert Lansing, March 7, 1917, NA.

29. Francis, *Russia from the American Embassy,* 24–25.
30. David Francis to Perry Francis, July 31, 1916, MHS.
31. David Francis to Perry and Dave Francis, August 7, 1916, MHS.
32. "Who's Who in Petrograd," notes by Francis, September 15, 1916, MHS.
33. David Francis to Jane Francis, August 29, 1916, MHS. This letter informs us that Jordan was already writing letters to Jane Francis, the woman who taught him to write. Unfortunately, these early letters are lost, and the letters we have, with Jordan's unique, richly detailed descriptions of what was going on in the streets of Petrograd, don't begin until September 1917.
34. David Francis to Jane Francis, September 26, 1916.
35. David Francis to Jane Francis, October 14, 1916, MHS. Datebook for June 23 and July 6, MHS.
36. Frank L. Polk to David Francis, July 24, 1916, MHS.
37. David Francis to Frank L. Polk, August 30, 1916, MHS.
38. David Francis to Frank L. Polk, November 6, 1916, Polk Papers, Yale University.
39. Inventory filed with October–November 1916, MHS.
40. David Francis to Breckinridge Long, November 21/December 4, 1917, MHS.
41. War Department intelligence report, February 28, 1918, NA.
42. David Francis to Perry and Dave Francis, March 15/28, 1917, MHS.
43. David Francis to Perry Francis, October 24, 1916, MHS.
44. David Francis to Nina Francis, November 20, 1916, MHS; "The National City Bank of New York in Petrograd," *The City Bank Club,* February 1917, archives of National City Bank.
45. Entries for November 23 and November 28, 1916, and January 20, 1917, diaries of Joshua Butler Wright, Princeton University.
46. David Francis to Perry Francis, November 22/December 5, 1916, MHS.
47. David Francis to Frank L. Polk, August 26, 1916, MHS.
48. David Francis to Perry and Dave Francis, March 28, 1917, MHS.
49. David Francis to Frank L. Polk, November 7, 1916, Polk Papers, Yale University.
50. Francis, *Russia from the American Embassy,* 35–39.
51. Francis, *Russia from the American Embassy,* 40.
52. Francis, *Russia from the American Embassy,* 40–42.
53. Samuel Hoare Templewood, *The Fourth Seal: The End of a Russian Chapter* (London: W. Heinemann, Ltd., 1930), 67–68.
54. David Francis to Perry Francis, November 22/December 5, 1916, MHS.
55. Tim Fox, unpublished 1998 article on Francis Park.
56. Figes, *A People's Tragedy,* 289–91.
57. David Francis to Frank L. Polk, March 10, 1917, MHS.
58. Francis, *Russia from the American Embassy,* 46–47.
59. Francis, *Russia from the American Embassy,* 50–51.

CHAPTER 14

1. Figes, *A People's Tragedy,* 307ff.
2. *Baedecker Guide to St. Petersburg,* 1996 edition, 186.
3. Francis, *Russia from the American Embassy,* 55; David Francis to Robert Lansing, March 9, 1917, NA; David Francis to Robert Lansing, February 22/March 7, 1917, NA.
4. Lloyd Gardner, *Safe for Democracy: Anglo-American Response to Revolution, 1913–1923* (New York: Oxford University Press, 1984), 124–25.
5. David Francis to Robert Lansing, February 22/March 7, 1917, MHS; Francis, *Russia from the American Embassy,* 55–56.
6. Francis, *Russia from the American Embassy,* 58.
7. Figes, *A People's Tragedy,* 323.
8. Solomon Volkov, *St. Petersburg: A Cultural History* (New York: Free Press, 1995), 199–202.
9. Figes, *A People's Tragedy,* 309.
10. Francis, *Russia from the American Embassy,* 57.
11. Figes, *A People's Tragedy,* 315–21.
12. Figes, *A People's Tragedy,* 153–54; 210–11; 294–95; 387.
13. Figes, *A People's Tragedy,* 323–24.
14. David Francis to Senator Stone, February 13/26, 1917, MHS.
15. Francis, *Russia from the American Embassy,* 59–63.
16. Francis, *Russia from the American Embassy,* 62–63.
17. Francis, *Russia from the American Embassy,* 63–64.
18. Francis, *Russia from the American Embassy,* 65.
19. Francis, *Russia from the American Embassy,* 66–67.
20. Francis, *Russia from the American Embassy,* 66–67.

21. Francis, *Russia from the American Embassy*, 67–68.
22. Francis, *Russia from the American Embassy*, 68–69.
23. Francis, *Russia from the American Embassy*, 70–71.
24. Francis, *Russia from the American Embassy*, 72.
25. David Francis to Robert Lansing, March 17, 1917, *Papers Relating to the Foreign Relations of the United States* (FRUS), 1917, Russia section, 1205.
26. David Francis to Perry and Dave Francis, March 15/28, 1917, MHS.
27. Francis, *Russia from the American Embassy*, 62–63.
28. Francis, *Russia from the American Embassy*, 88.
29. Francis, *Russia from the American Embassy*, 89–90.
30. David Francis to Perry and Dave Francis, March 15/28, 1917, MHS.
31. David Francis to Robert Lansing, March 18, 1917, FRUS, 1917, 1207.
32. David Francis to Perry and Dave Francis, March 15/28, 1917, MHS.
33. Ibid.
34. J. Butler Wright diary, March 19, 1917.
35. Robert Lansing to David Francis, March 20, 1917, FRUS, 1917, 1208.
36. David Francis to Robert Lansing, March 22, 1917, FRUS, 1917, 1211.
37. David Francis to Perry and Dave Francis, March 15/28, 1917, MHS.
38. March 23 and March 29, 1917, J. Butler Wright diary.
39. Walter Page to David Francis, June 11, 1917, MHS.
40. Francis, *Russia from the American Embassy*, 95.

CHAPTER 15

1. Princess Cantacuzene to David Francis, May 3, 1917, MHS.
2. David Francis to Robert Lansing, March 1917, MHS.
3. Princess Julia Cantacuzene, *Revolutionary Days* (New York: Arno Press, 1970), 221–23, 261–64.
4. Col. W. V. Judson report to General Peyton C. March, June 18, 1919, NA.
5. J. Butler Wright diary, March 29–April 1.
6. Robert Lansing, *War Memoirs of Robert Lansing, Secretary of State* (Indianapolis: Bobbs-Merrill, 1935), 330–31.
7. Charles Crane to Richard Crane, May 4, 1917, Richard Crane Papers, Georgetown University.
8. Consul Winship to Robert Lansing, March 20, 1917, FRUS, 1208–10.

9. David S. Foglesong, "A Missouri Democrat in Revolutionary Russia," *Gateway Heritage* 12, no. 3 (winter 1992): 29–33; J. Butler Wright diary entries for late March.
10. George Kennan, *Russia Leaves the War* (Princeton, N. J.: Princeton University Press, 1958), 18.
11. David Francis to Jane Francis, May 8/21, 1917, MHS.
12. David Francis to Robert Lansing, March 1917, MHS.
13. Figes, *A People's Tragedy*, 369.
14. Figes, *A People's Tragedy*, 352–53, 651.
15. Figes, *A People's Tragedy*, 388.
16. J. Butler Wright diary, April 29, 1917.
17. J. Butler Wright diary, May 19, 1916.
18. Francis, *Russia from the American Embassy*, 101–2.
19. Philip Jordan obituary, PD, May 22, 1941.
20. Foglesong, *America's Secret War Against Bolshevism*, 89.
21. Francis, *Russia from the American Embassy*, 102.
22. Francis, *Russia from the American Embassy*, 102.
23. Author interview with Talton F. Ray, 1997.
24. Francis, *Russia from the American Embassy*, 102.
25. Francis, *Russia from the American Embassy*, 105–6.
26. David Francis to Alexander Kerensky, April 19/May 2, 1917, MHS.
27. David Francis to Matilda de Cramm, October 30, 1917.
28. David Francis to Jane Francis, April 4/17, 1917.
29. Francis, *Russia from the American Embassy*, 113.
30. David Francis to Robert Lansing, April 25/May 8, 1917, MHS.
31. David Francis to Robert Lansing, April 25/May 8, 1917, MHS.
32. J. Butler Wright diary, April 27/June 3, 1917.
33. J. Butler Wright diary, May 2/15, 1917, MHS.
34. Foglesong, "A Missouri Democrat in Revolutionary Russia," 34.
35. David Francis to Julia Francis, May 3/16, 1917, MHS.
36. J. Butler Wright diary, May 18, 1917.
37. David Francis to Jane Francis, May 8/21, 1917, MHS.
38. Bernard Pares, *My Russian Memoirs* (London: Jonathan Cape, 1931), 442–43.
39. NYT, June 30, 1917.
40. Foglesong, "A Missouri Democrat in Revolutionary Russia," 33.
41. David Francis to Jane Francis, May 31/June 13, 1917, MHS.

42. J. Butler Wright diary, June 22, 1917.
43. Elihu Root to David Francis, August 29, 1917, MHS.
44. Figes, *A People's Tragedy,* 401, 404.
45. Philip Jordan to Jane Francis, September 19, 1917, MHS. The Jordan letters from Russia, mostly written in cheap ink or pencil in a scrawling hand, are now in the collection of the Missouri Historical Society. Most of them were printed in the society's *Bulletin* of January 1958, pages 139–166, with a preface and some explanatory material by Mrs. Clinton Bliss. The article is a valuable resource. In most cases, the letters are quoted here as Jordan wrote them. A few originals have been lost and we are left with typed transcriptions that may have been edited by someone else.
46. Cantacuzene, *Revolutionary Days,* 221–22; Figes, *A People's Tragedy,* 433.
47. Francis, *Russia from the American Embassy,* 141.
48. David Francis to Frank L. Polk, July 13, 1917, MHS.
49. David Francis to Jane Francis, July 10/23, 1917, MHS.
50. David Francis to Jane Francis, May 31/June 13, 1917.
51. Earl Johnston to J. D. Francis, July 27/August 9, 1917, MHS.
52. William V. Judson, *Russia in War and Revolution: General William V. Judson's Accounts from Petrograd, 1917–1918,* edited by Neil V. Salzman (Kent, Ohio: Kent State University Press, 1998), 48.
53. Philip Jordan to Annie Pulliam, November 30, 1917, MHS.

CHAPTER 16

1. Kennan, *Russia Leaves the War,* 55–56.
2. Herman Hagedorn, *The Magnate: William Boyce Thompson and His Times* (New York: Reynel and Hitchcock, 1935), 180–200.
3. Earl Johnston to J. D. Francis, July 27/August 9, 1917, MHS.
4. Kennan, *Russia Leaves the War,* 56–57.
5. Hagedorn, *The Magnate,* 206.
6. David Francis to Perry Francis, August 14, 17–18, 1917, MHS.
7. David Francis to Perry Francis, August 14, 17–18, 1917, MHS. This appears to be the first time Francis mentioned Madame de Cramm by name in a letter to his family. In his Russia memoir, Francis summarizes the tale of Mrs. Pankhurst, Madame de Cramm, and Kerensky, but downplays the role of "Mme. D. C., a Russian lady."
8. Francis, *Russia from the American Embassy,* 143–44.
9. David Francis to Perry Francis, August 14, 17–18, 1917, MHS.
10. Philip Jordan to Jane Francis, September 19, 1917, MHS.
11. Francis, *Russia from the American Embassy,* 157.
12. Francis, *Russia from the American Embassy,* 162.
13. Foglesong, "A Missouri Democrat," 38; David Francis to Robert Lansing, October 4, 1917, FRUS, vol. 1, 198.
14. Robert Lansing, *War Memoirs,* 339.
15. Francis, *Russia from the American Embassy,* 158–61.
16. Col. W. V. Judson report to Gen. Peyton C. March, June 18, 1919, NA.
17. David Francis to Perry Francis, September 12/25 1917, MHS.
18. J. Butler Wright diary, September 25, 1917.
19. David Francis to Madame Breshkovskaya, August 3/16, 1917, MHS.
20. See, for example, Maddin Summers cable to Robert Lansing, March 28, 1918, NA.
21. David Francis to Frank L. Polk, July 13, 1917, MHS.
22. Ted Morgan, *Maugham* (New York: Simon and Schuster, 1980), 226.
23. Somerset Maugham, *Ashenden; or, The British Agent* (London: W. Heinemann, 1928), preface, 199ff.
24. Datebook, September 17/30, September 19/October 2, MHS.
25. Meriel Buchanan, *The Dissolution of an Empire* (New York: Arno Press, 1971), 211.
26. Francis, *Russia from the American Embassy,* 162.
27. Philip Jordan to Jane Francis, September 19, 1917.
28. Francis, *Russia from the American Embassy,* 167; Francis datebook, August 31/September 13, 1917.
29. Robert Rosenstone, *Romantic Revolutionary* (New York: Knopf, 1975), 289.
30. Alexander Kerensky, *Russia and History's Turning Point* (New York: Duell, Sloan and Pearce, 1965), 387–88; George Buchanan, *My Mission to Russia* (New York: Arno Press, 1970), 192–93.
31. *Washington Post,* October 8, 1917.
32. David Francis to Herman Bernstein, January 8, 1918, MHS.
33. L. S. Perkins Military Intelligence report in Re: Edward Kramm, August 28, 1917, NA.
34. Marion Lyon statement to Military Intelligence, February 14, 1918, NA.
35. Military Intelligence Files, Edgar de Cramm, October–November, 1917, NA.

36. Col. W. V. Judson report to Gen. Peyton C. March, June 18, 1919, NA.
37. David Francis to Breckinridge Long, July 25/August 7, 1917, MHS.
38. Breckinridge Long to David Francis, October 19, 1917, MHS.
39. Morgan, *Maugham*, 230–31.
40. Figes, *A People's Tragedy*, 470–72.
41. Francis, *Russia from the American Embassy*, 170–74.
42. John Reed, *Ten Days that Shook the World* (New York: Boni and Liveright, 1919), 8ff.
43. Cantacuzene, *Revolutionary Days*, 270.
44. Francis, *Russia from the American Embassy*, 178–79.
45. Foglesong, *America's Secret War Against Bolshevism*, 191.
46. Francis, *Russia from the American Embassy*, 177.
47. Francis, *Russia from the American Embassy*, 179ff; David Francis to Robert Lansing, November 7–8, 1917, FRUS, 1918, vol. 1, 224; and PWW, 532; Kennan, *Russia Leaves the War*, 72–73.
48. Philip Jordan to Annie Pulliam, November 30, 1917, MHS.
49. Figes, *A People's Tragedy*, 502.
50. David Francis to Robert Lansing, November 7, 1917, FRUS 1918, vol. 1, 224–25.

CHAPTER 17

1. Kennan, *Russia Leaves the War*, 75–76.
2. Philip Jordan to Annie Pulliam, November 30, 1917, MHS.
3. Figes, *A People's Tragedy*, 494–95.
4. Francis, *Russia from the American Embassy*, 186.
5. David Francis to Robert Lansing, November 8, 1917, FRUS, 1918, vol. 1, 226.
6. David Francis to Maddin Summers, November 8, 1917, MHS.
7. Arthur Bullard to George Creel, November 17, 1917, Bullard Papers.
8. David Francis to Robert Lansing, November 7–8, 1917, marked as received on November 10, FRUS, 1918, vol. 1, 224–26.
9. Francis, *Russia from the American Embassy*, 188.
10. Philip Jordan to Annie Pulliam, November 30, 1917, MHS.
11. Francis, *Russia from the American Embassy*, 180.
12. Philip Jordan to Jane Francis, November 18, 1917, MHS.
13. Judson, *Russia in War and Revolution*, 136.
14. Francis, *Russia from the American Embassy*, 173–77.

15. Figes, *A People's Tragedy*, 433; Francis, *Russia from the American Embassy*, 112–13.
16. David Francis to Robert Lansing, November 20, 1917, MHS.
17. Robert Lansing to David Francis, November 14, 1917, NA; Col. W. V. Judson report to Gen. Peyton C. March, June 18, 1919, NA; Kennan, *Russia Leaves the War*, 114.
18. David Francis to Robert Lansing, November 13/26, 1917, MHS.
19. J. Butler Wright diary, November 27, 1917.
20. David Francis to Madame de Cramm, November 17/30, 1917, MHS.
21. Robert Lansing to David Francis, November 30, 1917, NA.
22. David Francis to Breckinridge Long, December 4, 1917, MHS.
23. David Francis to Robert Lansing, November 21/December 4, 1917, MHS; David Francis to Madame de Cramm, March 22, 1918, MHS.
24. Col. W. V. Judson report to Gen. Peyton C. March, June 18, 1919.
25. Edgar Sisson, *One Hundred Red Days: A Personal Chronicle of the Bolshevik Revolution* (New Haven: Yale University Press, 1931), 94.
26. David W. McFadden, *Alternative Paths: Soviets and Americans, 1917–1920* (New York: Oxford University Press, 1993), 90.
27. David Francis to Robert Lansing, March 20, 1918, MHS.
28. Arthur Bullard to George Creel, November 17, 1917, Creel Papers.
29. Albert Rhys Williams, *Journey Into Revolution: Petrograd, 1917–1918* (Chicago: Quadrangle Books, 1969), 199.
30. Sisson, *One Hundred Red Days*, 29ff.
31. Francis, *Russia from the American Embassy*, 188–89.
32. Lansing, *Memoirs*, 339–42.
33. William Hard, *Raymond Robins' Own Story* (New York: Harper & Brothers, 1920), 72.
34. Sisson, *One Hundred Red Days*, 38.
35. Judson, *Russia in War and Revolution*, 193–94.
36. David Francis to Robert Lansing, March 20, 1918, MHS. Judson, *Russia in War and Revolution*, 154–56; Sisson cable to State Department, December 4, 1917, PWW, vol. 45, 216–218; J. Butler Wright diary, December 1–2, 1917; Kennan, *Russia Leaves the War*, 119.
37. Judson, *Russia in War and Revolution*, 156, 193.
38. David Francis to Robert Lansing, December 1, 1917, FRUS, 1918, vol. 1, 279.
39. David Francis to Robert Lansing, March 20, 1918, MHS.
40. David Francis to Robert Lansing, December 2, 1917, FRUS, 1918, vol. 1, 282.
41. Judson, *Russia in War and Revolution*, 165.

42. Robert Lansing to David Francis, December 6, 1917, FRUS, 1918, vol. 1, 289.
43. Kennan, *Russia Leaves the War*, 124.
44. David Francis to Robert Lansing, December 9, 1917, FRUS, 1918, vol. 1, 295.
45. Kennan, *Russia Leaves the War*, 58–60.
46. Poole, *Oral History*, 89, 122–24.
47. Philip Jordan to Annie Pulliam, November 30, 1917, MHS.
48. See, for example, David Francis to Jane Francis, April 4/17, 1917, MHS.
49. Unidentified notes, July 1918, probably after a conversation with William Judson, in the Arthur Burleson Collection, LOC.
50. David Francis to Robert Lansing, March 20, 1918, MHS.
51. J. Butler Wright diary, November 30 and December 3, 1917.
52. Sisson cable to State Department, December 4, 1917, PWW, vol. 45, 216–218.
53. Note from W. W. to Secretary of State, December 8, 1917, PWW, vol. 45, 243.
54. Sisson, *One Hundred Red Days*, 90–91.
55. David Francis to Robert Lansing, December 12, 1917, FRUS, 1918, vol. 1, 301.
56. Hard, *Raymond Robins' Own Story*, 111–12.
57. Sisson, *One Hundred Red Days*, 152–55; Hard, *Raymond Robins' Own Story*, 118–19; Kennan, *Russia Leaves the War*, 208–10.
58. Robert Lansing to David Francis, December 20, 1917, FRUS, 1918, vol. 1, 319.
59. Hard, *Raymond Robins' Own Story*, 119ff. Francis's version was similar. He recalled telling Robins, "I think it unwise for you to sever your relations abruptly and absolutely. . . . I want to know what you are doing, and I will stand between you and the fire." See chapter 22.
60. David Francis to Robert Lansing, December 24, 1917, MHS.
61. Philip Jordan to Jane Francis, December 20, 1917, MHS.
62. Arthur Ransome, *The Autobiography of Arthur Ransome* (London: J. Cape, 1976), 227.
63. Sisson, *One Hundred Red Days*, 170; Kennan, *Russia Leaves the War*, 229.
64. Frederick Corse to Darwin Kingsley, December 29, 1917, archives of New York Life.
65. Judson, *Russia in War and Revolution*, 191–92.
66. Kennan, *Russia Leaves the War*, 231–32.
67. Ibid.
68. McFadden, *Alternative Paths*, 66.
69. Judson, *Russia in War and Revolution*, 202–3; Kennan, *Russia Leaves the War*, 234.
70. David S. Foglesong develops this notion at length in "A Missouri Democrat in Revolutionary Russia," 28–40.
71. J. Butler Wright diary, December 4, 1917.
72. Lansing, *War Memoirs*, 340–41.
73. Z. A. B. Zeman, *Germany and the Revolution in Russia, 1915–1918* (New York: Oxford University Press, 1958), 51, 116–17.
74. Bertrand Russell, *Bolshevism: Practice and Theory* (New York: Harcourt, Brace and Howe, 1920), 40; Richard Pipes, *The Russian Revolution* (London: Collins Harvill, 1990), 617.
75. Kennan, *Russia Leaves the War*, 385.

CHAPTER 18

1. Arthur Bullard, *The Russian Pendulum: Autocracy-Democracy-Bolshivism* (New York: Macmillan, 1919), 111.
2. Sisson, *One Hundred Red Days*, 190–91.
3. Judson, *Russia in War and Revolution*, 201–4, 301; Jane Gilmer Weyant, "The Life and Career of General William V. Judson" (Ph.D. diss., Georgia State University, 1981), 213–15.
4. Kennan, *Russia Leaves the War*, 238.
5. Hard, *Raymond Robins' Own Story*, 121ff.
6. Bolshevik Propaganda hearings, Senate Judiciary Subcommittee, February 11–March 10, 1919, 1009.
7. Kennan, *Russia Leaves the War*, 240–41.
8. Buchanan, *My Mission to Russia*, 256.
9. R. H. Bruce Lockhart, *Memoirs of a British Agent* (New York: Putnam's, 1933), 222–32.
10. Judson, *Russia in War and Revolution*, 205.
11. Arthur Bullard to Maddin Summers, January 11/24 1918, Bullard Papers.
12. Sisson, *One Hundred Red Days*, 207–9.
13. McFadden, *Alternative Paths*, 102; Kennan, *Russia Leaves the War*, 258–63.
14. Lockhart, *Memoirs of a British Agent*, 222.
15. Sisson, *One Hundred Red Days*, 213–14; Kennan, *Russia Leaves the War*, 412–13.
16. Basil Miles to Robert Lansing, January 8, 1918, PWW, vol. 45, 543–44.
17. David Francis to Robert Lansing, January 2, 1918, NA.
18. See, for example, the entry about the November 26 bridge game in Notes for the Ambassador's Diary, October 26–December 3, 1917, MHS.
19. David Francis to Herman Bernstein, January 8, 1918, MHS.
20. David Francis to Col. Edward House, January 8, 1918, MHS.
21. Frank L. Polk to David Francis, January 26, 1918, NA.
22. Military Intelligence report, March 1, 1918, NA. On the report, the year is mistakenly given as 1917.
23. Philip Jordan to Jane Francis, January 10, 1918.
24. Sisson, *One Hundred Red Days*, 221.

25. Sisson, *One Hundred Red Days,* 222.
26. Sisson, *One Hundred Red Days,* 222–23.
27. Note from Lenin, January 1, 1918 (old Russian calendar), MHS.
28. Sisson, *One Hundred Red Days,* 223.
29. Quoted in Kennan, *Russia Leaves the War,* 334–35. Translation checked against the original by the author.
30. Francis, *Russia from the American Embassy,* 216ff.
31. According to the official Soviet record of the meeting, as reported by Kennan, *Russia Leaves the War,* 335.
32. Francis note to State Department and enclosed Phelps meeting memo, January 9/22, 1918, NA; Francis, *Russia from the American Embassy,* 217–18.
33. Sisson, *One Hundred Red Days,* 223.
34. Francis, *Russia from the American Embassy,* 219.
35. Robert Lansing to David Francis, January 18, 1918, NA.
36. Philip Jordan to Jane Francis, dated January 17, 1918, but mostly written on January 18.
37. Figes, *A People's Tragedy,* 516.
38. Jordan to W. H. Lee, January 18, 1918. This letter was apparently typed by a secretary who cleaned up the spelling, orthography, and syntax.
39. Francis, *Russia from the American Embassy,* 208.
40. Francis, *Russia from the American Embassy,* 208ff.
41. Poole, *Oral History,* 123.
42. David Francis to Perry Francis, January 18/31, 1918, MHS.
43. Judson War Department report, June 18, 1919. Note: the basic report was written in 1918 and only slightly revised the following year.
44. J. Butler Wright diary, January 30, 1918.
45. Robert Lansing to Woodrow Wilson, February 9, 1918; Robert Lansing to David Francis, February 14, 1918, PWW, vol. 45, 300–1.
46. Sisson, *One Hundred Red Days,* 290ff, 484ff.
47. Kennan, *Russia Leaves the War,* 413ff.
48. Bolshevik Propaganda hearings, 802–3.
49. David Francis to Robert Lansing, February 8, 1918, FRUS, 1918, vol. 1, 370.
50. David Francis to Robert Lansing, March 20, 1918, MHS.
51. George Kennan, "The Sisson Documents," *Journal of Modern History* 28 (June 1956): 130–54.
52. Zeman, *Germany and the Revolution in Russia,* 51, 117, 123–25, 133.
53. Vladimir Ilich Lenin, *The Unknown Lenin: From the Secret Archive,* edited by Richard Pipes (New Haven: Yale University Press, 1996), 12, 53.
54. David Francis to Robert Lansing, February 9, 13, FRUS, 1918, vol. 1, 371ff.
55. David Francis to Robert Lansing, March 20, 1918, MHS.
56. J. Butler Wright diary, January 30, 1918.
57. Volkov, *St. Petersburg,* 206.
58. Sisson, *One Hundred Red Days,* 299–300.
59. Sisson, *One Hundred Red Days,* 332.
60. Francis report to Robert Lansing, March 17, 1918, NA.
61. David Francis to Robert Lansing, February 21, 1918, MHS.
62. Kennan, *Russia Leaves the War,* 434.
63. Francis, *Russia from the American Embassy,* 235.
64. Francis, *Russia from the American Embassy,* 234–35.
65. Bolshevik Propaganda hearings, 799.
66. J. Butler Wright diary, February 22.
67. Note in the margin of Francis report to Robert Lansing, March 17, 1918, NA.
68. David Francis to Robert Lansing, February 22, 1918, MHS.
69. Francis, *Russia from the American Embassy,* 236.
70. Kennan, *Russia Leaves the War,* 438.
71. Philip Jordan to Jane Francis, March 9, 1918.
72. Francis report to Robert Lansing, March 17, 1918, NA; Kennan, *Russia Leaves the War,* 439–40.
73. Bolshevik Propaganda hearings, 799–800.
74. Kennan, *Russia Leaves the War,* 440.
75. Ransome, *The Autobiography of Arthur Ransome,* 238–39.

CHAPTER 19

1. Philip Jordan to Jane Francis, March 9, 1918, MHS.
2. First Vologda interview, March 4, 1918, MHS.
3. Paraphrase of Special Cipher Message, David Francis to Robert Lansing, March 9, 1918, MHS.
4. Philip Jordan to Jane Francis, March 9, 1918, MHS.
5. Ransome, *The Autobiography of Arthur Ransome,* 241.
6. Norman Armour to Sheldon Whitehouse, August 19, 1918, Armour Papers; Vologda historian Alexander Bykov has reviewed some secret police files from the diplomatic era, which are held in the Vologda headquarters of the FSB, successor to the KGB, and says that there is considerable evidence that City Bank funded counterrevolutionaries from Vologda. Author interviews in person and by e-mail, 1997–98.

7. Philip Jordan to Jane Francis, March 15, 1918, MHS.

8. Paraphrase of Special Cipher Message, David Francis to Robert Lansing, March 9, 1918, MHS.

9. Kennan, *Russia Leaves the War,* 500–3.

10. Christopher Lasch, *The American Liberals and the Russian Revolution* (New York: Columbia University Press, 1962), 89.

11. Col. James Ruggles to Warcolstaf, March 12, 1918, NA.

12. Francis, *Russia from the American Embassy,* 132–33; George Kennan, *The Decision to Intervene* (Princeton, N. J.: Princeton University Press, 1958), 112–17.

13. Kennan, *Russia Leaves the War,* 510–16.

14. Francis, *Russia from the American Embassy,* 231–32.

15. David Francis to Robert Lansing, March 17, 1918, NA.

16. David Francis to Perry Francis, March 17, 1918, MHS.

17. Francis, *Russia from the American Embassy,* 237–38.

18. Sisson, *One Hundred Red Days,* 95–96.

19. Kennan, *Russia Leaves the War,* 126.

20. David Francis to Robert Lansing, March 20, 1918, MHS.

21. David Francis to Jerome Landfield, August 28, 1919, MHS.

22. Arthur Bullard to George Creel, March 14, 1918, Bullard Papers.

23. David Francis to Robert Lansing, March 18, 1918, NA.

24. Robert Lansing to David Francis, March 22, 1918, NA.

25. David Francis to Robert Lansing, March 20, 1918, MHS.

26. See David Francis to Karin Sante, March 16, 1918, MHS.

27. David Francis to Madame de Cramm, March 22, 1918, MHS.

28. David Francis to Madame de Cramm, March 25, 1918, MHS.

29. Note to Madame de Cramm, March 27, 1918, MHS.

30. David Francis to Madame de Cramm, April 18, 1918, MHS.

31. War Department Intelligence reports on Edgar de Cramm, February 7–April 19, 1918, NA.

32. David Francis to Robert Lansing, March 26, 1918, MHS; Kennan, *The Decision to Intervene,* 117–21, 174.

33. Kennan, *The Decision to Intervene,* 99–102.

34. Kennan, *The Decision to Intervene,* 101–4.

35. Maddin Summers to David Francis, March 25, 1918, MHS.

36. Kennan, *The Decision to Intervene,* 171–72.

37. Maddin Summers to David Francis, April 11, 1918, MHS.

38. David Francis to Maddin Summers, April 14, 1918, MHS.

39. Note to Am. Consul & Col. Raymond Robins, April 15, 1918, MHS.

40. David Francis to Maddin Summers, April 19, 1918, MHS.

41. David Francis to Perry Francis, April 23, 1918, MHS.

42. Frederick Gardner to Robert Lansing, April 20, 1918, NA.

43. Robert Lansing to Frederick Gardner, April 22, 1918, NA.

44. David Francis to Perry Francis, April 21, 23, 1918, MHS.

45. Philip Jordan to Jane Francis, April 28, 1918, MHS.

46. Philip Jordan to Jane Francis, April 28, 1918, MHS.

47. David Francis to W. H. Lee, April 23, 1918.

48. Kennan, *The Decision to Intervene,* 182.

49. Sisson, *One Hundred Red Days,* 425–26.

50. Kennan, *The Decision to Intervene,* 182.

51. Pipes, *The Russian Revolution,* 589–90.

52. Raymond Robins to David Francis, April 26, 1918, MHS.

53. Francis statement, April 28, 1918, MHS.

54. Philip Jordan to Jane Francis, April 28, 1918, MHS.

55. David Francis to Robert Lansing, May 2, 1918, MHS.

56. David Remnick, "Time 100: Vladimir Ilyich Lenin," *Time* magazine South Pacific edition, April 13, 1998.

CHAPTER 20

1. Maddin Summers to David Francis, May 1, 1918, MHS.

2. Kennan, *The Decision to Intervene,* 186.

3. David Francis to Maddin Summers, May 3, 1918, MHS.

4. NYT, May 6, 1918.

5. Norman Armour to W. A. Williams, June 16, 1959, Armour Correspondence; Kennan, *The Decision to Intervene,* 187.

6. Kennan, *The Decision to Intervene,* 201.

7. Francis, *Russia from the American Embassy,* 238–39.

8. Kennan, *The Decision to Intervene,* 187–89.

9. Poole, *Oral History,* 133, 188–89.

10. Entries in Francis's datebook for May 8–9. There are no datebook entries after the move to Vologda except for these two days.

11. David Francis to Robert Lansing, May 11, 1918, PWW, vol. 47, 112–14.

12. David Francis to Perry Francis, June 4, 1918, MHS.

13. Lockhart, *Memoirs of a British Agent*, 249, 275.
14. David Francis to Robert Lansing, May 11, 1918, PWW, vol. 47, 112–14.
15. David Francis to Prof. Jerome Landfield, September 3, 1919, MHS.
16. David Francis to Robert Lansing, May 11, 1918, PWW, vol. 47, 112–14.
17. Lockhart, *Memoirs of a British Agent*, 276.
18. Arthur Bullard to George Creel, May 9, 1918, Bullard Papers. I am grateful to Russian historian Alexander Bykov for first pointing out this discrepancy during my 1997 visit to Vologda.
19. David Francis to Jerome Landfield, September 3, 1919, MHS.
20. In a 1919 letter to Francis, writer/scholar Jerome Landfield said he had heard from "two sources" in whom he had "the fullest confidence" that Robins had named Judson, Wright, and Summers as being instrumental in drafting, encoding, and sending the Sisson recall cable. (Of course, they may have only been repeating what Francis had told them.) Landfield asked for details, and Francis provided the only direct account of the meeting we have. Jerome Landfield to David Francis, August 19, 1919; Francis replies to Landfield, August 28 and September 3, 1919, MHS.
21. Neil V. Salzman, *Reform and Revolution: The Life and Times of Raymond Robins* (Kent, Ohio: Kent State University Press, 1991), 274.
22. Kennan, *The Decision to Intervene*, 217–25.
23. David Francis to Robert Lansing (passed on to Wilson), May 16, 1918, PWW, vol. 47, 141–43.
24. David Francis to "Madam," May 18, 1918, MHS.
25. David Francis to Imbrie, May 25, 1918, MHS.
26. Kennan, *The Decision to Intervene*, 303; Foglesong, *America's Secret War Against Bolshevism*, 113.
27. Lockhart, *Memoirs of a British Agent*, 246, 280–83.
28. Earl Johnston to Sarah, June 1, 1918, MHS.
29. Earl Johnston to Sarah, June 1, 1918, MHS.
30. David Francis to Perry Francis, June 4, 1918, MHS.
31. David Francis to Perry Francis, June 4, 1918, MHS.
32. David Francis to Frank L. Polk, June 3, 1918, PWW, vol. 47, 277–78.
33. Francis, *Russia from the American Embassy*, 302; Earl Johnston to Sarah, June 1, 1918, MHS.
34. David Francis to Perry Francis, June 4, 1918, MHS.
35. David Francis to Perry Francis, June 4, 1918, MHS.
36. Francis, *Russia from the American Embassy*, 303.
37. David Francis to Felix Cole, June 13, 1918, MHS; Foglesong, *America's Secret War Against Bolshevism*, 112–13.
38. David Francis to Robert Lansing, June 20, 1918, MHS.
39. David Francis to Madame de Cramm, June 23, 1918, MHS.
40. David Francis to Mrs. Livingston Phelps, June 1, 1918, MHS.
41. Francis, *Russia from the American Embassy*, 303–4; McFadden, *Alternative Paths*, 141–43.
42. Kennan, *The Decision to Intervene*, 50–51.
43. Foglesong, *America's Secret War against Bolshevism*, 100–3.
44. David Francis to William G. Sharp, June 17, 1918, MHS; David Francis to DeWitt C. Poole, June 15, 1918; Foglesong, *America's Secret War Against Bolshevism*, 85–90, 111–14, 120–22.
45. Foglesong, *America's Secret War Against Bolshevism*, 123–28; Alexander Bykov, information gathered from secret police files in Vologda passed on to the author in 1997 and 1998.
46. Russell, *Bolshevism*, 40; Zeman, *Germany and the Revolution in Russia*, 123, 130–31.
47. Kennan, *The Decision to Intervene*, 441.
48. Francis, *Russia from the American Embassy*, 239–43.
49. McFadden, *Alternative Paths*, 142.
50. Francis, *Russia from the American Embassy*, 243–45.
51. Kennan, *The Decision to Intervene*, 50–51, 443.
52. Francis, *Russia from the American Embassy*, 245–46; Kennan, *The Decision to Intervene*, 443–44.
53. Lockhart, *Memoirs of a British Agent*, 304–5.
54. Francis, *Russia from the American Embassy*, 246.
55. David Francis to Imbrie, July 8, 1918, MHS.
56. Ransome, *The Autobiography of Arthur Ransome*, 247.
57. Figes, *A People's Tragedy*, 699; Kennan, *The Decision to Intervene*, 445; Ransome, *The Autobiography of Arthur Ransome*, 254–58.
58. Ransome, *The Autobiography of Arthur Ransome*, 255–57; Francis, *Russia from the American Embassy*, 246–50.
59. Francis, *Russia from the American Embassy*, 246–50.
60. Ransome, *The Autobiography of Arthur Ransome*, 257.
61. Lockhart, *Memoirs of a British Agent*, 304–5.
62. Kennan, *The Decision to Intervene*, 446.
63. Francis, *Russia from the American Embassy*, 250–51.
64. Foglesong, *America's Secret War against Bolshevism*, 159–68.
65. Foglesong, *The American War Against Bolshevism*, 188, 204–5.
66. Francis, *Russia from the American Embassy*, 253ff.

67. Francis, *Russia from the American Embassy,* 256–59.
68. David Francis to Robert Lansing, July 27, 1918, NA.
69. Kennan, *The Decision to Intervene,* photo caption opposite 468.
70. Francis, *Russia from the American Embassy,* 260.

CHAPTER 21

1. Military Intelligence report from Biddle on de Cramm, June 21, 1918, NA.
2. San Francisco Military Intelligence report on Edward [sic] de Cramm, June 29, 1918, NA.
3. See, for example, Col. Van Deman's memo of April 19, 1918, NA.
4. Col. Churchill memo, July 25, 1918, NA.
5. Dr. De Cramm statement on relations with John Maher, July 17, 1918, NA.
6. Telegram from Col. Churchill to Intelligence Officer, San Francisco, July 24, 1918, NA.
7. Cable from MI Tokyo to MI D.C., September 10, 1918.
8. See David Francis to Breckinridge Long, December 4, 1917, MHS.
9. Kennan, *The Decision to Intervene,* 451.
10. Francis, *Russia from the American Embassy,* 262ff.
11. Kennan, *The Decision to Intervene,* 15–25.
12. David Francis to Robert Lansing, July 27, 1918, NA.
13. Francis, *Russia from the American Embassy,* 262ff.
14. David Francis to Robert Lansing, July 27, 1918, NA.
15. Francis, *Russia from the American Embassy,* 260.
16. David Francis to Perry Francis, July 31, 1918, MHS.
17. Philip Jordan to Jane Francis, September 8, 1918, MHS.
18. David Francis to Perry Francis, July 31, 1918, MHS.
19. Philip Jordan to Jane Francis, September 8, 1918, MHS.
20. Frank L. Polk to David Francis, August 3, 1918, FRUS, 1918, Russia, vol. 1, 625.
21. Philip Jordan to Jane Francis, September 8, 1918. MHS.
22. Norman Armour to Sheldon Whitehouse, August 19, 1918, Armour letters; Kennan, *The Decision to Intervene,* 458–59.
23. Michael Kettle, *Churchill and the Archangel Fiasco, November 1918–July 1919* (New York: Routledge, 1992), 1.
24. Kennan, *The Decision to Intervene,* 464.
25. Anna Akhmatova, *Selected Poems of Anna Akhmatova,* translated by D. M. Thomas (London: Penguin, 1988), 49.
26. David Francis to Perry Francis, August 26, 1918.
27. Author interview, March 1, 1998, Dr. Linda Fischer, director of health for St. Louis County.
28. David Francis to Perry Francis, August 26, 1918, MHS.
29. Francis, *Russia from the American Embassy,* 270–71.
30. Francis, *Russia from the American Embassy,* 313.
31. David Francis to Perry Francis, August 26, 1918, MHS.
32. Foglesong, *America's Secret War Against Bolshevism,* 168–69, 188–89; Kennan, *The Decision to Intervene,* 426–29.
33. Foglesong, *America's Secret War Against Bolshevism,* 210–12.
34. David Francis to Charles Crane, August 29, 1918, MHS.
35. Foglesong, *America's Secret War Against Bolshevism,* 188.
36. Francis, *Russia from the American Embassy,* 270.
37. David Francis to Robert Lansing, September 3, 1918, FRUS, 1918, Russia, vol. 2, 516–18; Foglesong, *America's Secret War Against Bolshevism,* 212–13.
38. Francis, *Russia from the American Embassy,* 269–72.
39. Francis, *Russia from the American Embassy,* 265, 270–75.
40. "339th Infantry AEF in Northern Russia (1918–1919)," control number NNSM (m)-111-H-1227, National Archives Film Division. Seventy-eight-minute black and white film from the US Army Signal Corps.
41. *The Nation,* January 11, 1919.
42. Francis, *Russia from the American Embassy,* 292.
43. Notes from Woodrow Wilson to Robert Lansing, September 18 and October 2, 1918, and footnotes, PWW, 49, 50–51, 178.
44. David Francis to Robert Lansing, October 7, 1918.
45. Robert Lansing to David Francis, October 9, 1918, NA.
46. J. D. Francis to Robert Lansing, October 19, 1918, NA.
47. Kennan, *The Decision to Intervene,* 467–68.
48. David Francis to Robert Lansing, October 10, 1918.
49. David Francis to Jane Francis, October 25, 1918, MHS.
50. Philip Jordan from Strathpeffer, November 30, 1918; PD, September 27, 1919.

51. Shelby Strother to Philip Jordan, July 19, 1933, Talton F. Ray Collection.
52. Francis, *Russia from the American Embassy,* 336–37.
53. Francis, *Russia from the American Embassy,* 296.
54. Poole/Whitehouse to Robert Lansing, November 16, 1918, NA.
55. Philip Jordan from Strathpeffer, November 30, 1918.
56. David Francis to Basil Miles, November 29, 1918, MHS.
57. David Francis to Robert Lansing, November 29, 1918, NA.
58. David Francis to Mary (Mollie), November 30, 1918, MHS.
59. Francis, *Russia from the American Embassy,* 306.
60. David Francis to Mary (Mollie), November 30, 1918, MHS.
61. Letter from Christiana with enclosure, signature of diplomat illegible, November 27, 1918, MHS.
62. Philip Jordan to Jane Francis, January 5, 1919, Talton F. Ray Collection.
63. Philip Jordan to a friend, March 5, 1919, MHS.
64. Francis, *Russia from the American Embassy,* 307.
65. Notes between Francis and Wilson, December 28, 1918, MHS.
66. Philip Jordan to Jane Francis, January 5, 1919, Talton F. Ray Collection.
67. Laura Perry to David Francis, January 16, 1919.
68. David Francis to Heimenz, January 16, 1919, MHS; David Francis to Mollie Ellerbe, January 24, 1919, MHS.
69. Rolla Wells to David Francis, January 19, 1919, MHS.
70. Kettle, *Churchill and the Archangel Fiasco,* 112–20.
71. Francis, *Russia from the American Embassy,* 308–9.
72. Dulles invitation, February 10, 1919, MHS.
73. Sisson, *One Hundred Red Days,* 96; David Francis to Prof. Jerome Landfield, August 28, 1919, MHS.
74. Philip Jordan to Mr. and Mrs. T. T. Francis, March 5, 1919, Talton F. Ray Collection. Also at MHS, addressed "Dear Friend."
75. Francis, *Russia from the American Embassy,* 309–12, 342–44; David Francis to Robert Lansing, February 23, 1919, MHS.
76. Francis, *Russia from the American Embassy,* 343–44.
77. Sisson, *One Hundred Red Days,* 96.
78. From the diary of Dr. Grayson, February 22, 1919, PWW, vol. 50, 224.
79. Francis, *Russia from the American Embassy,* 265.
80. Grayson diary, February 23, 1919, PWW, vol 50, 228–29.
81. Philip Jordan to Mr. And Mrs. T. T. Francis, March 5, 1919, Talton F. Ray Collection.
82. Philip Jordan to Mrs. Green, November 7, 1919, Talton F. Ray Collection.
83. Philip Jordan to Mr. And Mrs. T. T. Francis, March 5, 1919, Talton F. Ray Collection.

CHAPTER 22

1. Stevens, GD, VII.
2. David Francis to Mrs. Charles Clark, August 5, 1919, MHS; *Boston Globe* interview, August 3, 1919.
3. Ronald H. Bayor, *Fiorella La Guardia: Ethnicity and Reform* (Arlington Heights, Ill.: Harlan Davidson, 1993), 42–43; Lawrence Elliott, *Little Flower: The Life and Times of Fiorello La Guardia* (New York: Morrow, 1983), 98–101.
4. Fiorello La Guardia, *The Making of an Insurgent: An Autobiography, 1882–1919* (Philadelphia: Lippincott Co., 1948), 193–94.
5. Congressional Record, January 22, 1919, 1876–1882; NYT, January 23, 1919.
6. North Winship to Robert Lansing, February 12, 1919, MHS.
7. Walter Crosley to David Francis, July 4, 1919, MHS.
8. Bolshevik Propaganda hearings, February 11 to March 10, 1919, Washington, Government Printing Office, 109–18; 465–71; 510–11; 797; 821–31; 864–88; 935–85.
9. Bolshevik Propaganda hearings, February 11 to March 10, 1919, Washington, Government Printing Office, 1007–27.
10. NYT March 30, 1919.
11. *Christian Science Monitor,* March 11, 1919.
12. Edgar Sisson to Earl Johnston, March 10, 1919, MHS.
13. David Francis to Jerome Landfield, August 28, 1919, MHS.
14. David Francis to Mollie, April 14, 1919, MHS.
15. Rep., GD, PD, April 19, 1919.
16. David Francis to Mollie, April 14, 1919, MHS.
17. David Francis to Ellen Green, June 30, 1919, MHS.
18. David Francis to William Rowland, April 30, 1919, MHS.
19. David Francis to Melville Stone, June 4, 1919, MHS.
20. Frank L. Polk to David Francis, July 8, 1919, MHS.
21. Francis, *Russia from the American Embassy,* 148.
22. High Moran to David Francis, June 21, 1919, MHS.

23. David Francis to the Woodrow Wilson, September 8, 1919.
24. Col. W. V. Judson to Gen. Peyton D. Marsh, June 18, 1919, NA.
25. Note headed "Philip Jordan," June 29, 1919, MHS.
26. David Francis to Ellen Green, June 30, 1919, Talton F. Ray Collection.
27. David Francis to Mrs. Clark, August 5, 1919, MHS.
28. David Francis to Perry Francis, July 1 and July 10, 1919, MHS.
29. David Francis to Perry Francis, July 10, 1919, MHS.
30. William Reddig, *Tom's Town: Kansas City and the Pendergast Legend* (Columbia: University of Missouri Press, 1986), 209–12.
31. David Francis to Princess Julia Cantacuzene, August 6, 1919, MHS.
32. *Boston Globe,* Sunday, August 3, 1919.
33. David Francis to Norman Mack, August 21, 1919, MHS.
34. *New York World,* September 1, 1919; NYT, September 10, 1919.
35. William Allison, "Into the Cauldron: David R. Francis, Felix Cole, and American Intervention in North Russia, 1918–1919," *Gateway Heritage* 14, no. 3 (winter 1993–94): 28.
36. PD September 27, 1919.
37. Philip Jordan to Mrs. Green, November 7, 1919, Talton F. Ray Collection.
38. Jim Allee Hart, *History of the St. Louis Globe-Democrat* (Columbia: University of Missouri Press, 1961), 198–205, 229.
39. Hart, *History of the St. Louis Globe-Democrat,* 184–84, 198.
40. David Francis to Fred G. Allen, January 14, 1919, MHS.
41. Walter Stevens, "The Tragedy of the *St. Louis Republic,*" Missouri Historical Review 22, no. 2 (January 1928): 147.
42. Stevens, "The Tragedy of the *St. Louis Republic,*" Missouri Historical Review 22, no. 2 (January 1928): 147–48.
43. Hart, *History of the St. Louis Globe-Democrat,* 193.
44. Will of David Rowland Francis, probated in August, 1927, File number 7643, St. Louis County Probate Court, Clayton, Missouri.

CHAPTER 23

1. David Francis to Jane Francis, June 23, 1918, MHS.
2. Author interview with Anne Francis Currier, May 8, 1997.
3. David Francis to Perry Francis, November 26, 1917, MHS.
4. Talton Francis Ray interview with Jane Francis Williams, May 26, 1996.
5. Will of David Rowland Francis, probated in August 1927, file number 7643, St. Louis County Probate Court, Clayton, Missouri.
6. Will of David Rowland Francis, probated in August 1927, file number 7643, St. Louis County Probate Court, Clayton, Missouri.
7. Author telephone interview with Sidney Francis, Jr., May 16, 1997.
8. Author telephone interview with Emilie Francis Cushman, May 16, 1997.
9. Author interview with Anne Francis Currier, May 8, 1997.
10. Talton F. Ray interview with Jane Francis Williams, May 26, 1996.
11. Author interview with Theoline Bostwick Francis, May 8, 1997.
12. Gould St. Louis directory, 1920.
13. NYT, February 22, 1920; David Francis to Ovid M. Bell, February 12, 1920, Western Historical Manuscript Collection, Columbia, Missouri.
14. GD January 16, 1927.
15. GD July 5, 1920.
16. Philip Jordan to Mr. and Mrs. T. T. Francis, June 25, 1920, Talton F. Ray Collection.
17. James M. Cox, *Journey Through My Years* (New York: Simon and Schuster, 1946), 232–33; PD, GD, July 7, 1920.
18. NYT, book section August 21, 1921.
19. Philip Jordan to Mr. J. D. Francis, July 22, 1922, Talton F. Ray Collection.
20. Philip Jordan to Mrs. J. D. Francis, April 14, 1923, Talton F. Ray Collection.
21. Philip Jordan, "My experiences in Glenrose, Texas, or Eighty Miles from Civilization," undated memoir, probably May 1923, MHS.
22. GD, January 16, 1927.
23. Report of Directors of DRF Realty and Investment Co., May 12, 1924, MHS; Jane Francis will and disposition documents, File No. 59574, probated 1924, St. Louis Probate Court.
24. Burke Wilkinson, *Uncommon Clay: The Life and Works of Augustus Saint Gaudens* (San Diego: Harcourt Brace Jovanovich, 1985), Chapter 26; also helpful was Kathleen M. Bourgeois's "Bellefontaine Cemetery: David R. Francis Memorial," a paper for a 1988 class in "America's Art" at the University of Missouri–St. Louis, Bellefontaine Cemetery Collection.
25. Margaret Johnson Witherspoon, *Remembering the St. Louis World's Fair* (St. Louis: Folkestone Press, 1973), 88–89. The book contains a map of the Fair and a to-scale tissue overlay of modern streets.

26. Harry B. Hawes speech on David Rowland
    Francis, April 30, 1927, MHS.
27. NYT, October 2, 1924.
28. GD, January 17, 1927.
29. PD, January 18, 1927.
30. "David Rowland Francis," by Hon. Harry B.
    Hawes, Missouri Historical Society Reprint,
    vol. 5, no. 1, 1927.

EPILOGUE

1. David Francis to Jane, June 23, 1919, MHS.
2. Will of David Rowland Francis, probated in
   August 1927, File number 7643, St. Louis
   County Probate Court, Clayton, Missouri.
   Francis also left $10,000 to the University of
   Missouri; $5,000 to the Missouri Historical
   Society; and $5,000 to the charity he had head-
   ed for many years, the Hospital Saturday and
   Sunday Association. The original pre-Russia
   will gave $10,000 to Washington University, but
   a later codicil cancelled that bequest, noting
   that Francis had already given the university
   that amount in four annual gifts of $2,500
   apiece beginning in 1921.
3. Author interview with Anne Francis Currier,
   May 8, 1997.
4. David Francis to Perry Francis, April 23, 1918,
   MHS.
5. Philip Jordan to Aunt Emily and America, Oct.
   24, 1930, Talton F. Ray collection.
6. PD May 22, 1941.

7. Harry B. Hawes, "David Rowland Francis,"
   Missouri Historical Society Reprint, vol. 5 no. 1,
   1927.
8. Hagedorn, The Magnate, 183, 206.
9. Loth, Woodrow Wilson, 185.
10. Warth, The Allies and the Russia Revolution,
    30.
11. Kennan, Russia Leaves the War, 40–41.
12. Lasch, The American Liberals and the Russian
    Revolution, 127ff.
13. Wiebe, The Search for Order 1877–1920, 275.
14. Robert C. Williams introduction to David
    Francis, Russia in Transition, vii–x.
15. Salzman, Reform and Revolution, 228 and foot-
    note 11, 420.
16. See, for example, Pipes, ed., The Unknown
    Lenin, 12ff., and Zeman, Germany and the
    Revolution in Russia, 51, 124–25.
17. McFadden, Alternative Paths, 98–99.
18. Foglesong, "A Missouri Democrat in
    Revolutionary Russia," 39–41.
19. Foglesong, America's Secret War Against
    Bolshevism, in particular 110–26, 211–17.
20. Quotations from Bykov come from discussions
    between this writer and Bykov and his
    colleagues in Vologda, July 15–18, 1997, and
    subsequent letters and e-mails from Bykov in
    the author's collection. Also useful were the
    two works by Bykov and Leonid Panov on
    Vologda's diplomatic period that are listed in
    the bibliography.

Bibliography

Manuscripts and Other Unpublished Documents

"Decimal File 123 (1910–1929)." Department of State Central Files, National Archives at College Park.

"Edgar E. DeCramm, Dr. File." Military Intelligence Archives, National Archives, Washington D.C.

Armour, Norman. "Norman Armour Papers." Library of Princeton University.

Bullard, Arthur. "Arthur Bullard Papers." Library of Princeton University.

Burleson, Albert S. "Albert S. Burleson Papers." Library of Congress.

Burnam, Lucia. "What I Remember." Unpublished Manuscript, 1933. Eastern Kentucky University.

Clark, Champ. "Champ Clark Papers." Western Historical Manuscript Collection, University of Missouri.

Crane, Charles R. "Charles R. Crane Papers." Bakhmeteff Archive, Columbia University.

Crane, Richard. "Richard Crane Papers, Part II." Georgetown University.

Francis, David R. "David R. Francis Papers." Missouri Historical Society.

Harper, Samuel N. "Samuel N. Harper Papers." Library of the University of Chicago.

Johnston, Earl M. "Earl M. Johnston Papers." Missouri Historical Society.

Lansing, Robert. "Personal and Confidential Letters From Secretary of State Lansing to President Wilson, 1915–1918." National Archives at College Park.

McConachie, Alexander Scot. "The 'Big Cinch': A Business Elite in the Life of a City, Saint Louis, 1895–1915." Ph.D. dissertation, Washington University, 1976.

Polk, Frank L. "Frank Polk Papers." Library of Yale University.

Poole, DeWitt C. "Oral History." Butler Library, Columbia University.

Pusateri, Cosmo J. "A Businessman in Politics: David R. Francis, Missouri Democrat." Ph.D. dissertation, Saint Louis University, 1965.

Robins, Raymond. "Raymond Robins Papers." State Historical Society of Wisconsin.

Sea, Sophia Fox. "The Irvines of Madison County, Kentucky." *Register of Kentucky State Historical Society* (May 1905).

Stevens, Walter B. "Draft and Notes of Unpublished Biography of DRF." David R. Francis Papers, Missouri Historical Society.

Weyant, Jane Gilmer. "The Life and Career of General William V. Judson, 1865–1923." Ph.D. dissertation, Georgia State University, 1981.

Wright, J. Butler. "Joshua Butler Wright Papers." Library of Princeton University.

Books

Book of St. Louisans: A Biographical Dictionary. St. Louis: St. Louis Republic, 1906.

Papers Relating to the Foreign Relations of the United States: 1918, Russia, vols. 1–3. Washington, D.C.: U.S. Government Printing Office, 1932.

World Almanac and Book of Facts for 1925. New York: World Publishing Co., 1925.

Adams, Henry. *The Education of Henry Adams.* Boston: Houghton Mifflin Company, 1946 (c. 1918).

Adler, Jeffrey S. *Yankee Merchants and the Making of the Urban West: The Rise and Fall of Antebellum St. Louis.* New York: Cambridge University Press, 1991.

Akhmatova, Anna. *The Complete Poems of Anna Akhmatova.* Translated by Judith Hemschemeyer, vols. 1 and 2. Somerville, Mass.: Zephyr Press, 1990.

—————. *Selected Poems of Anna Akhmatova.* Translated by D. M. Thomas. London: Penguin, 1988.

Alland, Alexander. *Jessie Tarbox Beals: First Woman News Photographer.* New York: Camera/Graphic Press, 1978.

Allison, William. *American Diplomats in Russia: Case Studies in Orphan Diplomacy, 1916–1919.* Westport, Conn.: Praeger, 1997.

Andrew, Christopher. *Her Majesty's Secret Service: The Making of the British Intelligence Community*. London: Viking, 1986.

Bailey, Thomas A. *America Faces Russia*. Gloucester, Mass.: Peter Smith, 1964.

Bancroft, Hubert Howe. *The Book of the Fair*. Chicago: The Bancroft Co., 1893.

Bartley, Mary. *St. Louis Lost*. St. Louis: Virginia Publishing, 1994.

Bayor, Ronald H. *Fiorella La Guardia: Ethnicity and Reform*. American Biographical History Series. Arlington Heights, Ill.: Harlan Davidson, 1993.

Belcher, Wyatt Winton. *The Economic Rivalry Between St. Louis and Chicago, 1850–1880*. New York: Columbia University Press, 1947.

Bell, William A. *New Tracks in North America: A Journal of Travel and Adventure . . . During 1867–8*. Albuquerque: Horn and Wallace, 1965.

Benson, Sally. *Meet Me in St. Louis*. Pathfinder ed. New York: Bantam, 1963 (c. 1942).

Bird, Isabella L. *A Lady's Life in the Rocky Mountains*. New York: G.P. Putnam's Sons, 1879.

Birmingham, Stephen. *The Right People: A Portrait of the American Social Establishment*. Boston: Little, Brown and Company, 1968.

Bradford, Phillips Verner and Harvey Blume. *Ota Benga: The Pygmy in the Zoo*. New York: St. Martin's Press, 1992.

Browder, Robert Paul. *The Origins of Soviet-American Diplomacy*. Westport, Conn.: Greenwood Press, 1953.

Brown, Thomas. *Politics and Statesmanship: Essays on the American Whig Party*. New York: Columbia University Press, 1985.

Bryan, William Jennings and Mary Baird Bryan. *The Memoirs of William Jennings Bryan*. Philadelphia: John C. Winston Co., 1925.

Buchanan, Meriel J. *The Dissolution of an Empire*. London: Murray, 1932.

Buchanan, Sir George. *My Mission to Russia*. London: Cassell and Company, Ltd., 1923.

Bullard, Arthur. *The Russian Pendulum: Autocracy–Democracy–Bolshivism*. New York: The Macmillan Company, 1919.

Byars, William Vincent, ed. *An American Commoner: The Life and Times of Richard Parks Bland*. Columbia, Mo.: E.W. Stephens, 1900.

Bykov, Alexander and Leonid Panov. *Diplomaticheskaya Stolitsa Rossii* (The Diplomatic Capital of Russia). Vologda, Russia: Ardvisura Publishing House, 1998.

Cantacuzene, Princess Julia Grant. *Revolutionary Days: Recollections of Romanoffs and Bolsheviki, 1914–1917*. Boston: Small, Maynard and Company, 1919.

Carnahan, Jean. *If Walls Could Talk: The Story of Missouri's First Families*. Jefferson City, Mo.: MMPI, 1998.

Chenault, John Cabell. *Old Cane Springs: A Story of the War Between the States in Madison County, Kentucky*. Louisville, Ky.: Standard Printing Company, 1937.

Chernow, Ron. *The House of Morgan*. New York: Atlantic Monthly Press, 1990.

Churchill, Sir Winston S. *The World Crisis,* vol. 5. New York: Charles Scribner's Sons, 1957.

Churchill, Winston. *The Crisis*. New York: MacMillan, 1921.

Cleveland, Harold van. B. and Thomas F. Huertas. *Citibank 1812–1970*. Cambridge, Mass.: Harvard University Press, 1985.

Clevenger, Martha R. *"Indescribably Grand": Diaries and Letters from the 1904 World's Fair*. St. Louis: Missouri Historical Society Press, 1996.

Cockfield, James H. ed. *Dollars and Diplomacy: Ambassador David Rowland Francis and the Fall of Tsarism, 1916–17*. Durham, N.C.: Duke University Press, 1981.

Corbett, Katharine T. *In Her Place: A Guide to St. Louis Women's History*. St. Louis: Missouri Historical Society Press, 1999.

Cox, James. *Old and New St. Louis*. St. Louis: Central Biographical Publishing Company, 1894.

Curtis, Susan. *Dancing to a Black Man's Tune: A Life of Scott Joplin*. Columbia: University of Missouri Press, 1994.

Darrow, Clarence. *The Story of My Life*. New York: Scribner's, 1932.

Debo, Angie. *Geronimo: The Man, His Time, His Place*. Norman: University of Oklahoma Press, 1976.

—————. *A History of the Indians of the United States*. Norman: University of Oklahoma Press, 1970.

Debo, Richard K. *Revolution and Survival: The Foreign Policy of Soviet Russia, 1917–18*. Toronto: University of Toronto Press, 1979.

Dippie, Brian W. *The Vanishing American: White Attitudes and U.S. Indian Policy*. Middletown, Conn.: Wesleyan University Press, 1982.

Donald, David Herbert. *Lincoln*. New York: Simon & Schuster, 1995.

Dorris, Jonathan Truman and Dorris Maud Weaver. *Glimpses of Historic Madison County, Kentucky*. Nashville, Tenn.: Williams Printing Company, 1955.

Dosch-Fleurot, Arno. *Through War to Revolution*. London: John Lane, 1931.

Dostoyevsky, Fyodor. "White Nights" in *Uncle's Dream and Other Stories*. London: Penguin Books, 1989.

Dreiser, Theodore. *Newspaper Days*. Philadelphia: University of Pennsylvania Press, 1991 (c. 1922).

Dry, Camille J. and Richard Compton. *Pictorial St. Louis: The Great Metropolis of the Mississippi Valley*. St. Louis: Compton & Co., 1875.

Ehrlich, Walter. *Zion in the Valley: The Jewish Community of St. Louis, Vol. 1*. Columbia: University of Missouri Press, 1997

Elliott, Lawrence. *Little Flower: The Life and Times of Fiorello La Guardia*. New York: Morrow, 1983.

Ellis, William E., H. E. Everman and Richard D. Sears. *Madison County: 200 Years in Retrospect*. Richmond, Ky.: The Madison County Historical Society, 1985.

Everdell, William. *The First Moderns*. Chicago: University of Chicago Press, 1997.

Faulkner, Harold U. *Politics, Reform and Expansion, 1890–1900*. New York: Harper & Brothers, 1959.

Figes, Orlando. *A People's Tragedy: A History of the Russian Revolution*. New York: Viking, 1996.

Filene, Peter G. *Americans and the Soviet Experiment, 1917–1933*. Cambridge, Mass.: Harvard University Press, 1967.

Fischer, Louis. *The Life of Lenin*. New York: Harper & Row, 1964.

————. *Men and Politics: An Autobiography*. New York: Duell, Sloan and Pearce, 1941.

————. *The Soviets in World Affairs, Vol. 1*. New York: Jonathan Cape and Harrison Smith, 1930.

Foglesong, David S. *America's Secret War Against Bolshevism*. Chapel Hill: University of North Carolina Press, 1995.

Ford, James E. *A History of Jefferson City*. Jefferson City, Mo.: The New Day Press, 1938.

Fox, Timothy J. and Duane R. Sneddeker. *From the Palaces to the Pike: Visions of the 1904 World's Fair*. St. Louis: Missouri Historical Society Press, 1997.

Francis, David R. *The Messages and Proclamations of the Governors of the State of Missouri, Vol. VII*. Columbia: The State Historical Society of Missouri, 1926.

————. *Russia from the American Embassy, April 1916–November 1918*. New York: Charles Scribner's Sons, *1921*.

————. *Russia in Transition: The Diplomatic Papers of David R. Francis, Ambassador to Russia, 1916–1918*. edited by Robert Lester. Frederick, M.D.: University Publications of America, 1985. advisory editor: Robert Chadwell Williams.

————. *The Universal Exposition of 1904, Vol. 1*. St. Louis: Louisiana Purchase Exposition Company, 1913.

Gaddis, John Lewis. *Russia, the Soviet Union, and the United States: An Interpretive History*. New York: McGraw-Hill, Inc., 1990 (c. 1978).

Gardner, Lloyd C. *Safe for Democracy: The Anglo-American Response to Revolution, 1913–1923*. New York: Oxford University Press, 1984.

Geiger, Louis G. *Joseph W. Folk of Missouri*. Columbia: University of Missouri Press, 1953.

Hagedorn, Herman. *The Magnate: William Boyce Thompson and His Times (1869–1930)*. New York: Reynal & Hitchcock, 1935.

Hagen, Harry M. *This Is Our St. Louis*. St. Louis: Knight Publishing Co., 1970.

Hale, William Harlan. "When the Red Storm Broke" in *America and Russia: A Century and a Half of Dramatic Encounters*. New York: Simon & Schuster, 1962.

Hard, William. *Raymond Robins' Own Story*. New York: Harper & Brothers Publishers, 1920.

Harper, Samuel N. *The Russia I Believe In*. Chicago: University of Chicago Press, 1945.

Hart, Jim Allee. *A History of the St. Louis Globe-Democrat*. Columbia: University of Missouri Press, 1961.

Hartman, Mary and Elmo Ingenthron. *Bald Knobbers: Vigilantes on the Ozarks Frontier*. Gretna, La.: Pelican Publishing Co., 1988.

Hendrick, Burton J. *The Life and Letters of Walter H. Page, Vol. 1*. Garden City, N.Y.: Doubleday, Page & Company, 1925.

Henry, Bill. *An Approved History of the Olympic Games*. New York: G.P. Putnam's Sons, 1976.

Henry, O. *Heart of the West*. Garden City, N.Y.: Doubleday, Page & Co., 1919.

Hinsley, Curtis M. "Fin-de-Siecle: The Rise and Fall of William John McGee, 1893–1903" in *Savages and Scientists: The Smithsonian Institution and the Development of American Anthropology, 1846–1910*. Washington, D.C.: Smithsonian Institution Press, 1981.

Hoare, Sir Samuel. *The Fourth Seal: The End of a Russian Chapter*. London: William Heinemann Ltd., 1930.

Hyde, William and Howard L. Conard, eds. *Encyclopedia of the History of St. Louis*. New York: The Southern History Co., 1899.

Ireland, Robert M. *The County Courts in Antebellum Kentucky*. Louisville: University Press of Kentucky, 1972.

Jensen, Billie Snell. "St. Louis Celebrates" in *Louisiana Purchase Exposition: The St. Louis World's Fair of 1904*. St. Louis: Missouri Historical Society, 1979.

Johns, Orrick. *Time of Our Lives: The Story of My Father and Myself*. New York: Stackpole and Sons, 1937.

Judson, William V. *Russia in War and Revolution: General William V. Judson's Accounts from Petrograd, 1917–1918*. edited by Neil Salzman. Kent, Ohio: Kent State University Press, 1998.

Jusserland, Jean Jules. *What Me Befell: The Reminiscences of Jean Jules Jusserland*. Boston: Houghton Mifflin Company, 1934.

Kennan, George F. *Memoirs, 1925–1950*. Boston: Little, Brown and Company, 1967.

————. *Russia and the West Under Lenin and Stalin*. Boston: Little, Brown and Company, 1960.

————. *Soviet-American Relations, 1917–1920: Russia Leaves the War*. Princeton, N.J.: Princeton University Press, 1956.

————. *Soviet-American Relations, 1917–1920: The Decision to Intervene*. Princeton, N.J.: Princeton University Press, 1958.

Kerensky, Alexander. *Russia and History's Turning Point*. New York: Duell, Sloan and Pearce, 1965.

Kettle, Michael. *Churchill and the Archangel Fiasco: November 1918–July 1919*. London: Routledge, 1992.

Kimbrough, Mary. *St. Louis Country Club: The First 100 Years*. St. Louis: St. Louis Country Club, 1992.

Kirschten, Ernest. *Catfish and Crystal*. Garden City, N.Y.: Doubleday, 1965.

Klebaner, Benjamin J. *American Commercial Banking*. Boston: Twayne Publishers, 1990.

Klein, Maury. *The Life and Legend of Jay Gould*. Baltimore, M.D.: Johns Hopkins University Press, 1986.

Kohler, Foy D. and Mose L. Harvey, eds. *The Soviet Union: Yesterday, Today, Tomorrow*. Miami: International Affairs Center for Advanced Studies, University of Miami, 1975.

Kubiak, Lavinia H. *Madison County Rediscovered: Selected Historic Architecture*. Richmond: Madison County Historical Society and The Kentucky Heritage Council, 1988.

La Guardia, Fiorello H. *The Making of an Insurgent, An Autobiography, 1882–1919*. New York: J.B. Lippincott Co., 1948.

Lambert, D. Warren. *When the Ripe Pears Fell: The Battle of Richmond, Kentucky*. Richmond, Ky.: Madison County Historical Society, 1996.

Lansing, Robert. *War Memoirs of Robert Lansing*. Westport, Conn.: Greenwood Press, 1970 (c. 1935).

Lasch, Christopher. *The American Liberals and the Russian Revolution*. New York: McGraw-Hill, 1962.

Laserson, Max M. *The American Impact on Russia: Diplomatic and Ideological, 1784–1917*. New York: The Macmillan Company, 1950.

Libbey, James K. *Alexander Gumberg and Soviet-American Relations, 1917–1933*. Lexington: The University of Kentucky Press, 1977.

Lincoln, W. Bruce. *Red Victory: A History of the Russian Civil War*. New York: Simon & Schuster, 1989.

Lindsay, Vachel. "Bryan, Bryan, Bryan, Bryan" in *Chief Modern Poets of England and America*. 2 volumes. New York: The Macmillan Co., 1962.

Lockhart, R. H. Bruce. *Memoirs of a British Agent*. London: MacMillan, 1974 (c. 1932).

————. *Ace of Spies*. London: Hodder and Stoughton, 1967.

Longworth, Alice Roosevelt. *Crowded Hours: Reminiscences of Alice Roosevelt Longworth*. New York: Charles Scribner's Sons, 1933.

Loth, David G. *Woodrow Wilson: The Fifteenth Point*. Philadelphia: J.P. Lippincott, 1941.

Loughlin, Caroline and Catherine Anderson. *Forest Park*. St. Louis: Junior League, 1986.

Maugham, W. Somerset. *Ashenden; or, The British Agent*. New York: Arno Press, 1977 (c. 1927).

Mayer, Martin. *The Diplomats*. Garden City, N.Y.: Doubleday & Company, Inc., 1983.

Mayers, David. *The Ambassadors and America's Soviet Policy*. New York: Oxford University Press, 1995.

McAdoo, William G. *Crowded Years*. Port Washington, N.Y.: Kennikat Press, 1931.

McCarthy, Marilyn. *Stones of Remembrance: A History of Central Presbyterian Church 1844–1994*. St. Louis: Central Presbyterian Church, 1994.

McFadden, David W. *Alternative Paths: Soviets and Americans, 1917–1920*. New York/Oxford: Oxford University Press, 1993.

Miller, Howard S. and Quinta Scott. *The Eads Bridge*. St. Louis: Missouri Historical Society Press, 1999.

Miller, Nathan. *Theodore Roosevelt: A Life*. New York: William Morrow & Co., 1992.

Missouri Writers' Project. *Missouri: A Guide to the "Show Me" State*. WPA American Guide Series. New York: Duell, Sloan and Pearce, 1941.

Moorehead, Alan. *The Russian Revolution*. New York: Harper & Brothers, 1958.

Morgan, Ted. *Maugham*. New York: Simon & Schuster, 1980.

Morison, Samuel Eliot. *The Oxford History of the American People*. New York: Oxford University Press, 1965.

Nevins, Allan. *Grover Cleveland: A Study in Courage*. New York: Dodd, Mead & Co., 1932.

Nicolson, Harold. *Diplomacy*. London: Thornton Butterworth Ltd., 1939.

Norris, Frank. *The Pit: A Story of Chicago*. New York: Doubleday, 1903.

Nostitz, Countess Lilie de Ferdandez-Azabel. *The Countess From Iowa*. New York: G.P. Putnam's Sons, 1936.

Noulens, Joseph. *Mon Ambassade En Russie Sovietique, 1917–1919* (My Ambassadorship to Soviet Russia). Paris: Librarie Plon, 1933.

Olson, James and Vera. *The University of Missouri: An Illustrated History.* Columbia: University of Missouri Press, 1988.

Pares, Bernard. *My Russian Memoirs.* London: Jonathan Cape, 1931.

Park, Eleanora and Kate C. Morrow. *Women of the Mansion.* Jefferson City, Mo.: Midland Printing Co., 1936.

Parrish, William E. *A History of Missouri, Vol. III, 1860–1875.* Columbia: University of Missouri Press, 1971.

Parrish, William E., Charles T. Jones, Jr., and Lawrence O. Christensen. *Missouri: The Heart of the Nation.* Arlington Heights, Ill.: Harlan Davidson, Inc., 1992.

Pershing, John J. *My Experiences in the World War.* New York: Frederick A. Stokes Company, 1931.

Pinchot, Gifford. *Breaking New Ground.* Seattle: University of Washington Press, 1972 (c. 1947).

Piott, Steven L. *Holy Joe: Joseph W. Folk and the Missouri Idea.* Columbia: University of Missouri Press, 1997.

Pipes, Richard. *The Russian Revolution.* New York: Alfred A. Knopf, 1990.

————, ed. *The Unknown Lenin.* New Haven, Conn.: Yale University Press, 1996.

Primm, James Neal. *A Foregone Conclusion: The Founding of the Federal Reserve Bank of St. Louis, Vol. 1.* St. Louis: Federal Reserve Bank, 1989.

————. *Lion of the Valley: St. Louis, Missouri.* Boulder, Colo.: Pruett Publishing Co., 1990.

Prucha, Francis Paul. *The Great Father.* Lincoln: University of Nebraska Press, 1984.

Putzel, Max. *The Man in the Mirror: William Marion Reedy and His Magazine.* Westport, Conn.: Greenwood Press, 1963.

Ransome, Arthur. *The Autobiography of Arthur Ransome.* London: Jonathan Cape, 1976.

Reavis, L. U. *St. Louis: The Future Great City of the World.* St. Louis: The County Court of St. Louis, 1870.

————. *St. Louis: The Future Great City of the World.* St. Louis: C.R. Barns, 1876. Includes biographical appendix.

Reddig, William. *Tom's Town: Kansas City and the Pendergast Legend.* Philadelphia: J.B. Lippincott Co., 1947.

Reed, John. *Ten Days That Shook the World.* New York: Bantam Classics, 1987 (c. 1919).

Reps, John W. *St. Louis Illustrated: Nineteenth-Century Engravings and Lithographs of a Mississippi River Metropolis.* Columbia: University of Missouri Press, 1989.

Richardson, Elmo R. *The Politics of Conservation.* Berkeley: University of California Press, 1962.

Rosenstone, Robert A. *Romantic Revolutionary: A Biography of John Reed.* New York: Knopf, 1975.

Rummelkamp, Julian S. *Pulitzer's Post-Dispatch, 1878–1883.* Princeton, N.J.: Princeton University Press, 1967.

Russell, Bertrand. *Bolshevism: Practice and Theory.* New York: Harcourt, Brace and Howe, 1920.

Rydell, Robert W. *All the World's a Fair.* Chicago: University of Chicago Press, 1984.

Salzman, Neil V. *Reform and Revolution: The Life and Times of Raymond Robins.* Kent, Ohio: Kent State University Press, 1991.

————. *Russia in War and Revolution: General William V. Judson's Accounts from Petrograd, 1917–1918.* Kent, Ohio: Kent State University Press, 1998.

Saul, Norman. *Concord and Conflict: The United States and Russia, 1867–1914.* Lawrence: University Press of Kansas, 1996.

Savage, Charles. *Architecture of the Private Streets of St. Louis: The Architects and the Houses They Designed.* Columbia: University of Missouri Press, 1987.

Schuman, Frederick Lewis. *American Policy Toward Russia Since 1917.* New York: International Publishers, 1928.

Seitz, Don C. *Joseph Pulitzer: His Life and Letters.* New York: Simon & Schuster, 1924.

Severance, Henry O. *Richard Henry Jesse, President of the University of Missouri, 1891–1908.* Columbia, Mo.: Self-published, 1937.

Shavit, David. *United States Relations With Russia and the Soviet Union.* Westport, Conn.: Greenwood Press, 1993.

Shoemaker, Floyd. *A History of Missouri and Missourians.* Columbia, Mo.: Lucas Brothers, 1927.

Sisson, Edgar. *One Hundred Red Days: A Personal Chronicle of the Bolshevik Revolution.* Westport, Conn.: Hyperion Press, 1931.

Spencer, Thomas M. *The St. Louis Veiled Prophet Celebration: Power on Parade, 1877–1995.* Columbia: University of Missouri Press, 2000.

Steffens, Lincoln. *The Autobiography of Lincoln Steffens.* New York: Harcourt, Brace and World, Inc., 1931.

————. *The Shame of the Cities.* New York: Hill and Wang, 1957 (c. 1904).

Stevens, Walter B. *A Trip to Panama.* St. Louis: Commercial Club of St. Louis, 1907.

Strakhovsky, Leonid I. *The Origins of American Intervention in North Russia (1918).* Princeton, N.J.: Princeton University Press, 1937.

Strouse, Jean. *Morgan: An American Financier.* New York: Random House, 1999.

Swanberg, W. A. *Pulitzer.* New York: Scribner's, 1967.

Teichman, Howard. *Alice: The Life and Times of Alice Roosevelt Longworth.* Englewood Cliffs, N.J.: Prentice-Hall, 1979.

Thelen, David. *Paths of Resistance: Tradition and Democracy in Industrializing Missouri.* Columbia: University of Missouri Press, 1991.

Thomas, Augustus. *The Print of My Remembrance.* New York: Charles Scribner's Sons, 1922.

Travis, Frederick F. *George Kennan and the American-Russian Relationship, 1865–1924.* Athens: Ohio University Press, 1990.

Tugwell, Rexford G. *Grover Cleveland.* New York: The Macmillan Company, 1968.

Twain, Mark. *Life on the Mississippi.* New York: Bantam, 1990 (c. 1883).

Twain, Mark and Charles Dudley Warner. *The Gilded Age: A Tale Today.* 2 volumes. New York: Harper & Brothers, 1915.

U.S. Department of State. *Register of the Department of State as of December 19, 1917.* Washington, D.C.: Government Printing Office, 1917.

Volkov, Solomon. *St. Petersburg: A Cultural History.* New York: Free Press, 1995.

Warner, Charles Dudley. *Studies in the South and West.* New York: Harper & Brothers, 1889.

Warth, Robert D. *The Allies and the Russian Revolution.* Durham, N.C.: Duke University Press, 1954.

Webb, Ardis. *The Perry Park Story.* Denver: Self-published, 1974.

Weeks, Charles. *An American Naval Diplomat in Revolutionary Russia.* Annapolis, Md.: Naval Institute Press, 1993.

Wells, Rolla. *Episodes in My Life.* St. Louis: Self-published, 1933.

Wiebe, Robert H. *The Search for Order, 1877–1920.* New York: Hill and Wang, 1967.

Williams, Albert Rhys. *Journey into Revolution: Petrograd, 1917–1918.* Chicago: Quadrangle Books, 1969.

Williams, Robert Chadwell. "The Russians Are Coming!: Art and Politics at the Louisiana Purchase Exposition" in *Louisiana Purchase Exposition: The St. Louis World's Fair of 1904.* St. Louis: Missouri Historical Society, 1979.

Williams, William Appleman. *American Russian Relations, 1781–1947.* New York: Octagon Books, 1971.

Wilson, Woodrow. *Papers of Woodrow Wilson.* ed. Arthur Link, vols. 45–47. Princeton, N.J.: Princeton University Press, 1984.

Witherspoon, Margaret Johnson. *Remembering the St. Louis World's Fair.* St. Louis: Comfort Printing Co., 1973.

Wolfe, Thomas. *Look Homeward Angel.* New York: The Modern Library, 1934.

————. "The Lost Boy" in *The Hills Beyond.* New York: Pyramid Books, 1958.

Zeman, Z. A. B. ed. *Germany and the Revolution in Russia, 1915–1918.* London: Oxford University Press, 1958.

Zincke, F. Barham. *Last Winter in the United States.* Freeport, N.Y.: Books for Libraries Press, 1970 (c. 1868).

ARTICLES, PAMPHLETS, FILMS, AND MISCELLANEOUS OTHER SOURCES

Birthday Anniversary Dinner Given by Joseph Pulitzer, April 10, 1907. St. Louis: Woodward & Tiernan, 1907. pamphlet.

Bolshevik Propaganda Hearings Before a Subcommittee of the Committee on the Judiciary, United States Senate, 65th Congress, Third Session. Washington, D.C.: Government Printing Office, 1919.

Allison, William. "Into the Cauldron: David R. Francis, Felix Cole, and American Intervention in North Russia, 1918–1919." *Gateway Heritage* 14, no. 3 (winter 1994).

Andrews, Peter. "The First American Olympics." *American Heritage* (May/June 1988).

Bishop, William Henry. "St. Louis in 1884." *Harper's New Monthly Magazine,* 1977. pamphlet.

Bliss, Mrs. Clinton A. ed., "Philip Jordan's Letters From Russia, 1917–1919." *Bulletin of the Missouri Historical Society* 14, no. 2 (January 1958).

Brietbart, Eric. *A World on Display: The St. Louis World's Fair of 1904.* Corrales, N.M.: New Deal Films, 1994. 53–minute videotape.

Ghost Dance. Ken Burns. episode 8 of *The West.* Washington, D.C.: Insignia Films and WETA-TV, 1996. 59–minute videotape.

Diplomatic Corps in Vologda, 1918, Alexander and Leonid Panov Bykov. Translated by Marina Barandina. Vologda, Russia: Ardvisura Publishing House, 1997. pamphlet.

Dyreson, Mark. "The Playing Fields of Progress: American Athletic Nationalism and the 1904 St. Louis Olympics." *Gateway Heritage* 14, no. 2 (fall 1993).

Foglesong, David S. "A Missouri Democrat in Revolutionary Russia." *Gateway Heritage* 12, no. 3 (winter 1992).

Francis, David R. *Report to the Board of Directors of the Louisiana Purchase Exposition on European Tour.* St. Louis: Louisiana Purchase Exposition Company, 1903.

Hawes, Harry B. "Memorial Address: David Rowland Francis" in *Louisiana Purchase Day at the Annual Meeting of Missouri Historical Society.* St. Louis: Missouri Historical Society Collections 5, no. 1, 1927. reprint.

Himelloch, Myra. "St. Louis Opposition to David R. Francis in the Gubernatorial Election of 1888." *Missouri Historical Review* 68, no. 3 (April 1974).

Hoch, Edmund S. "The Olympic Games." *World's Fair Bulletin* (March 1903).

Keefer, Karen M., MD. "Dirty Water and Clean Toilets: Medical Aspects of the 1904 Lousiana Purchase Exposition." *Gateway Heritage* 9, no. 1 (summer 1988).

Kennan, George. "The Sisson Documents." *Journal of Modern History* 27 (June 1956): 130–54.

Kohlenberg, Gilbert C. "David Rowland Francis: American Businessman in Russia." *Mid-America* (October 1958).

Leighton, George R. "The Year St. Louis Enchanted the World." *Harper's Magazine* (August 1969).

Parton, James. "The City of St. Louis." *Atlantic Monthly* (June 1867): 655–70.

Powers, Joseph. "A Missouri Democrat's Observations of the Election of 1896." *Missouri Historical Review* 68, no. 2 (January 1974).

Pusateri, C. Joseph. "The Road to Jefferson City: David R. Francis' Campaign for the Governorship, 1888." *Bulletin of the Missouri Historical Society* 24, no. 3 (April 1968).

Rafferty, Edward C. "The Boss Who Never Was." *Gateway Heritage* 12, no. 3 (winter 1992).

Raiche, Stephen J. "The World's Fair and the New St. Louis: 1896–1904." *Missouri Historical Review* 67, no. 1 (October 1972): 98–121.

Sahr, Robert. *Consumer Price Index Conversion.* Available on the World Wide Web: http://www.orst.edu/Deptpol-Sci/fac/sahr/sahr.htrn. Based on a collation of two U.S. government publications: *Historical Statistics of the United States* and *A Statistical Abstract of the United States.*

Schwartz, E. A. *Native American Documents Project.* Available on the World Wide Web: http://ww2.csusm.edu nadp.

Sea, Sophia Fox. "The Irvines of Madison County." *Register: Kentucky State Historical Society* 3, no. 8 (May 1905).

Stevens, Walter B. "Missourian Abroad: David R. Francis." *Missouri Historical Review* 13, no. 3 (April 1919): 195–225.

———. "The New Journalism in Missouri." *Missouri Historical Review* 19, no. 4 (July 1925).

———. "The Tragedy of the *St. Louis Republic*." *Missouri Historical Review* 22, no. 2 (January 1928).

———. "When Cleveland Came to St. Louis." *Missouri Historical Review* 21, no. 2 (January 1927): 145–55.

Tucker, Robert W. "An Inner Circle of One: Woodrow Wilson and His Advisors." *The National Interest* (spring 1998): 3–26.

U.S. Army Signal Corps. *339th Infantry AEF in Northern Russia (1918–1919).* videotape. Film Division, National Archives at College Park.

Young, Dina M. "The St. Louis Streetcar Strike of 1900." *Gateway Heritage* 12, no. 1 (summer 1991).

Abbreviations

DRF	David Rowland Francis
FRUS	Papers relating to the Foreign Relations of the United States: 1918 Russia, vols. 1–3
GD	*St. Louis Globe-Democrat*
LOC	Library of Congress
LPE	Louisiana Purchase Exposition
MHS	Missouri Historical Society (Unless otherwise noted, all letters to and from David R. Francis are from the Francis archives at the Missouri Historical Society.)
NA	National Archives
NYT	*New York Times*
PD	*St. Louis Post-Dispatch*
PWW	Papers of Woodrow Wilson, vols. 45–47
Rep.	*Missouri Republican/St. Louis Republic*

Index